Ecology and Coal Resource Development

Pergamon Titles of Related Interest

Ecology and Coal Resource Development

Based on the International Congress for
Energy and the Ecosystem held at the
University of North Dakota
Grand Forks, North Dakota
12-16 June 1978

Edited by
Mohan K. Wali

Volume One

Pergamon Press
NEW YORK • OXFORD • TORONTO • SYDNEY • FRANKFURT • PARIS

Pergamon Press Offices:

U.S.A.	Pergamon Press Inc., Maxwell House, Fairview Park, Elmsford, New York 10523, U.S.A.
U.K.	Pergamon Press Ltd., Headington Hill Hall, Oxford OX3 0BW, England
CANADA	Pergamon of Canada, Ltd., 150 Consumers Road, Willowdale, Ontario M2J, 1P9, Canada
AUSTRALIA	Pergamon Press (Aust) Pty. Ltd., P O Box 544, Potts Point, NSW 2011, Australia
FRANCE	Pergamon Press SARL, 24 rue des Ecoles, 75240 Paris, Cedex 05, France
FEDERAL REPUBLIC OF GERMANY	Pergamon Press GmbH, 6242 Kronberg/Taunus, Pferdstrasse 1, Federal Republic of Germany

Cover design by Morris McKnight

Library of Congress Cataloging in Publication Data

International Congress for Energy and the Ecosystem,
  University of North Dakota, 1978.
  Coal resource development.

  Includes bibliographical references and indexes.
  1. Coal—Congresses.   2. Coal mines and mining—
Congresses.   3. Energy policy—Congresses.   4. Environ-
mental protection—Congresses.   I. Wali, Mohan K.
II. Title.
TN799.9.I63   1978   333.8'2   78-26238
ISBN 0-08-023863-7

Printed in the United States of America

CONTENTS

VOLUME II

xi

PREFACE

We live in a period unique in human contradictions. At no previous time in history have we had the technological capabilities of the present magnitude to manipulate and utilize earth's resources, nor so heightened a sense of awareness of and the need for environmental protection for future survival. The decisions that we make now may significantly affect the course of human civilization in the decades ahead. Lessons learned in the very immediate past from widespread tampering with the environment and from the global fuel energy shortage may well prove to be historic. The importance and power of the industrial-technological-arms complex notwithstanding, fuel energy and food production have surfaced as two of the most potent commodities upon which the nations in the future may bargain the hardest. Their distribution may even determine many of the future alliances and some of the political boundaries of the world's nations. "The world is not united by a common past," noted Zbigniew Brzezinski, "but increasingly it has a common future." It is essential, therefore, that we pool wisdom internationally to achieve rational development of resources.

Coal, not too long ago, was the only *major* source of energy. For some time, however, it has been overshadowed in its overall energy contribution by oil, gas and the over-estimated promise of nuclear power. It has, however, become apparent in the past few years that coal resources may be developed more worldwide than ever before; in the United States alone two to three times its current production is stipulated. But such expansion cannot be achieved without regard to the proper pre-mining planning, economic considerations and the post-mining land use strategies. It was with these considerations in mind that this International Congress was born. It was planned to provide a forum for discussion for managers in government and industry, researchers and environmentalists on the current state of our knowledge pertaining to these issues with the overall aim of facilitating a harmonious "technology transfer". Tendencies toward making the deliberations of this Congress simplistic, "utopian or apocalyptic", were discouraged. The planning effort for the Congress took nearly two years; its success must be judged both by those attending the Congress and the readers of these volumes. This book has been organized into different parts and sections each with a common theme in the subject matter. The chapters within the parts and sections have been arranged to facilitate some continuity and the flow of information; at times this attempt may not have been completely successful. All but a few papers in this book deal with coal; those which do not, provide useful information on related subjects. The opinions expressed in the papers are the authors' own and do not necessarily reflect the opinions of their employers, the sponsors of this Congress or the editor.

The planning for and the execution of conferences can be very time consuming and must therefore depend upon the unselfish motivation and generous logistic help of numerous people. This Congress was no exception. My friend and Co-Chairman of the Congress, Professor John L. Thames of the University of Arizona, was both appreciative and supportive of my efforts. I am most grateful to the members of the International Congress Planning Committee, to the invited speakers and session chairpersons, to field trip leaders and the staff of coal companies in western North Dakota, to the keynote speaker the Honorable Joan M. Davenport, Assistant Secretary for Minerals and Energy, U.S. Department of the Interior, and to the Honorable Arthur A. Link, Governor and the Honorable Wayne G. Sanstead, Lieutenant Governor, State of North Dakota, for spending many hours with the Congress participants despite a heavy call on their time. This Congress would not have been possible without the financial support provided by the Bureau of Mines, U.S. Department of the Interior. This support is gratefully acknowledged, and so is the interest and excellent cooperation extended by Mr. Donald G. Rogich, Chief, Division of Mine Systems - Engineering, and his staff. Special thanks are due Dr. Joseph J. Yancik, Vice President - Research, National Coal Association and Chairman, Bituminous Coal Research Inc. for helping in many ways.

The University of North Dakota was most gracious with its help and I would like to express my personal indebtedness to each and every person who gave so much of his/her time and suggestions willingly. I should in particular acknowledge the constant encouragement and support of President Thomas J. Clifford; the unhesitating hard work of the Local Planning Committee Chairman, Dr. L. Elliot Shubert; the Congress Coordinators, Ms. Rita C. Monson and Ms. Linda M. Gabbert; and the timely help with abstracts by Dr. Nirander M. Safaya, besides his duties as General Chairman of the Poster Sessions. I am grateful to Ms. Ginny Ballintine and Mr. Alden L. Kollman for help in preparing the author and subject indices. Without the able supervision, hard work and assistance of my secretary, Ms. Leonie M. Orchard, the task of producing these volumes would have been impossible. I extend to her many more thanks than she may realize.

Despite the diverse backgrounds and vocations that each of the Congress participants represented, there appeared to be more substance that united us than differences that divided us. I hope the papers presented in these volumes will bring us a few steps closer to scientifically sound and environmentally acceptable solutions.

Grand Forks, ND
June 11, 1979

Mohan K. Wali

PART I: COAL DEVELOPMENT AND THE ENVIRONMENT

In this part, the broad environmental issues pertaining to coal resource development in the United States, Australia, Great Britain and other countries, are discussed with perception and first hand experience of the authors. The urgent need for furthering the wise development and utilization of coal with careful controls, alternative strategies, governmental, public and private responsibilities are highlighted. So is the basic need for expanding the scope and dimensions of environmental research. Included also is the highly useful information on environmental pollution caused by coal burning.

U.S. COAL DEVELOPMENT POLICY: RESOLVING THE ENERGY–ENVIRONMENT CONFLICT

Joan M. Davenport *

Ever since man reached the moon, we have had a profoundly different view of our world. That first glimpse of Earth from space showed our true boundaries. We could see with our own eyes the real limits to our resources, and any lingering visions of new territories to conquer are quickly vanishing. This view of the whole earth, it seems to me, has also put an end to our traditional notions of international borders. We have moved into a new era, a time in which nations must begin to recognize their interdependence and shape their policies accordingly.

Perhaps nowhere is this more apparent than in energy. The United States uses more energy per capita than any other nation in the world, much of it in the form of imported oil. We have only recently come to recognize that our consumption of foreign oil must be reduced—not only in our own interests, but in the interests of our allies and trading partners as well. President Carter has emphasized this point many times.

One way to do so is to cut down or eliminate energy waste; in fact, we consider energy conservation the cornerstone of our National Energy Plan. But we also know that we are going to have to make a large-scale transition to other energy sources as well. Coal, the most abundant fossil fuel in this country, is our hope for the immediate future.

The need to expand development first became apparent to us, as you might imagine, as a result of the oil embargo. While we once relied extensively on coal, the availability of inexpensive oil and gas after World War II led to a sharp decline in production. So in a sense we are planning to revive an industry in some parts of the country and to introduce it in others.

But as the Government began to press for accelerated development, it ran headlong into the opposition of those who were all too familiar with the permanent scars of past practices. Mining had ruined the lands and often the lives of many in the Appalachian coal belt. Farmers, ranchers, loggers and others feared the consequences of devoting large amounts of land to coal mining.

It is important to keep in mind that in this country, as in others, the 1960's had culminated in a heightened sensitivity to the environmental consequences of our actions. The Congress had passed a National Environmental Policy Act and major air and water pollution control laws. By the early 1970's, the public was concerned about belching smoke-stacks and vanishing wildlife, and many were loath to see newly-established principles of environmental protection suddenly set aside in order to meet other goals.

*U.S. Department of the Interior, Washington, D.C. 20240.

For several years, then, despite a policy called "Project Independence," despite ambitious targets for coal production, we lacked the means to reconcile our energy goals with others of equal importance to our people.

While Americans recognize that we must increasingly turn to coal to meet energy needs, it is clear that they are not prepared to see those needs met at the cost of environmental degradation. A recent nationwide poll finds public opinion strongly against slowing down environmental clean-up to ease energy shortages. Americans are instead saying that we can and must do both. When questioned about strip mining in particular, only one-third of those polled would support an increase; but when environmental protection was added, support for strip mining rose to 80 percent.

It is this belief—that environmental goals should not be sacrificed—that underlies this Administration's policy toward coal development and use. In an Environmental Message delivered a year ago, President Carter told the Congress and the nation that his goals for coal use must be met in an environmentally sound manner. He directed the responsible Federal agencies to expand their efforts to develop adequate pollution control technology and standards for the direct combustion of coal. Recognizing the dearth of information, the President called for expanded research to identify the health and environmental effects of coal-using technologies now under development. He also called for the development of procedures to establish environmental standards for these new technologies.

At the same time, the President recognized, and emphasized, that the mining of coal in this country must follow similar principles.

The United States, of course, has been a major coal producer for many years. Most of that coal—nearly 90 percent on an annual basis—has come from privately-owned reserves in the eastern part of the country. In order to expand production to meet current goals, we will undoubtedly have to turn to the West, where most coal reserves lie.

The vast majority of these are owned by the Federal Government. Until recently, however, western coal has been of little interest to users outside the western states; western coal is subbituminous and lower in energy value than that found in the East and Midwest. Consequently, the Government's role in managing coal production has been a relatively small one, and it has only been of late that we have begun to take a fresh look at it.

What we found, simply stated, is that we were awarding Federal coal leases indiscriminately. In most cases, there was little or no competition for these leases, and publicly-owned resources were transferred for private development with little or no return to the Treasury. Until a moratorium was declared in 1971, the Federal Government had transferred more than 17 billion tons of coal to private ownership and had claims on another 9 billion tons, without ever taking into account how, or even whether, the lessees planned to produce the coal. Moreover, coal is only one of many resources that can be developed on the public lands. Other minerals, water, timber, wildlife, recreation—none of these had been considered in issuing leases, yet all of these are values which the Government has an equal responsibility to protect and foster.

In 1976, the Department of the Interior finally adopted a new coal leasing system. It drew sharp criticism from industry and concerned citizens alike. Both charged that the program was poorly described and its leasing objectives and plans ill-defined. The environmental impact statement prepared for the program was, in fact, successfully challenged in court by several environmental and agricultural groups who believed that the Interior Department had failed to consider proper alternatives to its program, including an appraisal of the need to resume Federal coal leasing.

These concerns were shared by many. In late 1976, legislation was enacted which finally gave the Interior Department the necessary authority to plan comprehensively for the public lands.

The first task for the new team at the Interior Department was, therefore, a re-evaluation of the entire coal leasing system. The Interior Department has had a coal policy review underway since last July. In addition, in response to the court order issued last September, a supplement to the coal program environmental impact statement will be prepared as a part of the review. Careful planning is what is required, and that process should include an examination of whether we need additional leasing at all.

The Department is looking at the more than 500 existing leases. Covering nearly 800,000 acres, these lands may contain about 18 billion tons of recoverable coal. Not all of it is mineable, however. Some of the leased lands are small, isolated tracts; some contain recoverable beds which are nonetheless uneconomic because of new reclamation require-ments. Still other leased reserves may be environmentally unsatisfactory. So a major function of the review is to evaluate existing leases in terms of their production potential, their environmental suitability, and their ability to meet projected coal demand. We have been instructed by the President to deal with nonproducing and environmentally unsatis-factory leases, and we will be looking into regulatory means to exchange leases for environ-mentally acceptable coal lands of equal value. We may also seek new legislation, if it proves necessary, authorizing us to condemn outstanding rights upon payment of reasonable compensation.

Following the timetable laid out for the coal review, we expect to have a comprehen-sive coal program in place by mid-1980. The programmatic environmental impact statement will provide the basis for public review and comment on the proposed program. We should then be able to determine where, when, and how much leasing is required to meet the production goals set by the Department of Energy.

Coal produced on Federal lands will no doubt play a large part in meeting our needs, and we intend that our leasing program will satisfy those needs in an environmentally acceptable manner. Nonetheless, for the time being, privately-held lands still yield almost all our coal—nearly 95 percent in 1977.

Controlling the adverse effects of mining on both public and private lands, particularly the surface effects, holds the key to the sound development of our coal resources. Over the past 20 years, we have witnessed a major change in the way coal is mined in this country. Although underground mines were once predominant, more than half our coal is now mined by surface methods. This shift has been particularly rapid in recent years, as it has become less expensive to strip mine, and as demand has risen for the low-sulfur western coal deposited in thick beds near the surface.

This nation discussed strip mining for years, and intensely debated legislative proposals to control it. The Congress finally agreed on a bill, but it was twice rejected by former President Ford. It was not until August, 1977 that the landmark Surface Mining Control and Reclamation Act was signed into law, with President Carter's wholehearted endorse-ment. Indeed, the President recognized that passage of strong national strip mine legislation was essential to the environmentally sound use of coal.

In many ways, the Surface Mining Act is representative of the American political process at its best, for it offers a peaceable solution to the conflict in which we were entangled for several years. As the results of the poll I cited earlier reveal, Americans are simply not prepared to increase mining without adequate protection for the environment. The Government's approach to coal policy in the past was just not working, beset by conflict, bitterness, and despair. In the Surface Mining Act, the Congress said, in essence: coal is important, we have to expand our production, and we know that surface mining can cause tremendous harm. But we also recognize that techniques exist for mining and reclamation so that these adverse effects can be minimized. In short, the Congress found that we can and must balance our need for coal with the equally pressing need to protect other resources vital to our well-being.

I began my remarks by discussing the view of the earth from the moon. Those of you who have seen unreclaimed surface-mined land know that it is not necessary to leave the earth to see a moonscape. Beyond the loss of scenic beauty, surface mining without adequate reclamation can cause severe erosion and flooding, it can pollute waters and destroy fish and wildlife habitats, and it can leave the land unusable for other purposes. Whole communities have perished in its aftermath. By 1974, surface coal mining had left nearly a million acres in need of reclamation.

Thus one of the important features of the new law is a program to reclaim and restore lands and waters seriously harmed by past mining activities. A special fund is established for this purpose, to which mine operators are required to contribute on the basis of tonnage produced. The fund now contains about $54 million, but we expect it to expand to about $200 million a year as coal production goes up.

The law recognizes that states, as well as the Federal Government, have a part to play in reclaiming abandoned mine lands. Half the fees collected in each state are therefore set aside for a state reclamation program; and states are also eligible for matching funds for up to 90 percent of the cost of land acquisition.

We have a lot of work ahead of us, and we have started by identifying what we expect to be the first seven major projects under the Interior Department's program. In all these cases, abandoned mines have for some time posed serious threats to the health and safety of local residents. Cleaning up a severely polluted water supply, putting out an underground fire whose noxious fumes are already a substantial health hazard, filling in collapsed shafts and entryways--these are typical of the needs of many communities. The first seven projects represent a broad spectrum of problems in a wide range of geographical areas, and we hope to gain experience quickly in these types of reclamation efforts.

The way coal mining is practiced from now on will have a far greater impact. And here lies the heart of the Surface Mining Act: Mining can proceed only with careful planning--only in areas suitable for mining, only with environmental safeguards during mining, and only with adequate reclamation afterwards.

As part of the application for a permit to mine, operators must submit a detailed reclamation plan whose contents are spelled out quite clearly in the law. The reclamation plan must identify all the lands subject to surface mining over the life of the operation, it must describe what the land has been used for and its productive capacity, and it must indicate the use to be made of the land after reclamation and how that use is to be achieved.

The plan is also to include detailed statements of engineering techniques and equipment and timetables required to meet the environmental protection performance standards set forth in the Act. And these are extensive: They require restoration of the land to original of "higher or better" uses, and restoration of original land contours. Standards are set for topsoil management, preservation of the hydrologic balance on and around the mine site, waste management, mountain top removal, and revegetation. Special provisions must be followed for mining on prime farmlands and in the fragile alluvial valley floors of the West. Operators must use the best technology available to protect fish and wildlife and related environmental values, and they must carry out their operations in a way that avoids the necessity of returning to strip the same area a second time.

Having a say in *how* mining is to be conducted is one-half of the planning process; having a say in *whether* it will be is the other half. The Surface Mining Act sets an important precedent in this regard because it requires the Federal Government and the states to identify those areas that may be unsuitable for all or certain types of surface coal mining. The law says that an area may be designated as unsuitable if mining is incompatible with existing land use plan programs, if it would significantly damage fragile or historic lands or the long-range productivity of farm or forest land or water supply, or if it would take place in unstable geologic areas or areas subject to frequent flooding. However, the process for designating an area unsuitable for coal mining requires analysis of economic and energy factors—as well as environmental considerations. New mining is prohibited in lands within the National Park, Wildlife Refuge, Wilderness, Recreation, Trails, and Wild and Scenic Rivers systems. Mining in National Forests and in National Historic Sites is permitted only under certain limited conditions, and it is banned entirely from the immediate vicinity of an occupied dwelling, public building or park, or roadway.

Enforcement of the law is the responsibility of the Office of Surface Mining, established in fall, 1977 within the Department of the Interior. As you might imagine, a law that so exactly stipulates standards contains stringent deadlines. In December, 1977 we issued interim program regulations, and we will be issuing regulations for the permanent program in early 1979. As of May 3, 1978, all new and existing mines must be in compliance with a minimum set of standards; the permanent program will add others and may refine and amplify many of those now in force.

We are thus a very young regulatory agency, but by no means a naive one. We have now had nearly a decade of environmental legislation, and I think we have all learned a great deal from both the successes and failures of the past.

Certainly one of the lessons we have learned is that the most carefully wrought standards are of little value without the knowledge needed to implement those standards. So while we are committed to firm and fair enforcement of the regulations, we are equally committed to support the research needed to make sure those standards can be met. The Surface Mining Act itself authorizes funds for state mining and mineral resources and research institutes, as well as for university coal research laboratories and graduate training programs. Separate funds are also authorized for research and demonstrations of alternative coal mining technologies.

The Bureau of Mines, as many of you know, has for some years conducted R&D in mined land reclamation. and we will continue to emphasize the Bureau's environmental research program. We hope to see emerge from it better tools for mine planning and better methods for eliminating or minimizing mining-related environmental problems.

Experience has also shown us that many good intentions can sometimes result in an administrative morass because of the lack of coordination among different regulatory programs. And perhaps the most unfortunate victims of this bureaucratic thicket are the environmental goals themselves, obscured in a battle over procedure. We aim to keep the process as simple as the law permits in order never to lose sight of what we are after in the first place.

Our goal, after all, is complex enough: to maintain a delicate balance between energy development and environmental protection. And we have made great strides in the last couple of years toward ensuring that both these values can be sustained.

If our voyage to the moon graphically demonstrated the need for cooperation among nations, it also revealed to us a new responsibility, one which we are acutely aware of in this country. Two hundred years ago, we were a nation of 2.5 million people living in nearly a million square miles of land. By the 19th century, our Government was giving away as much land as it could, believing land to be inexhaustible and there for our convenience. Today, the United States has a population of over 200 million in 3½ million square miles, and we have come to recognize that our resources—all of the earth's resources—

are not inexhaustible, nor does their exploitation and use come without heavy costs.

Progress today must be measured not by how *much* we use, but by how *well* we use. Our policy for developing and using our coal resources is based on this view, one which we believe will best serve the interests of this country—and this planet—for years to come.

UNWINDING THE PARADOX
UNWRAPPING THE PROMISE

Robert H. Quenon*

The impressive number of scientific papers presented at this Congress on subjects of great importance to the coal industry, have made a valuable contribution to the state-of-the-art. I am also impressed by the presence of the international visitors, because it emphasizes the worldwide significance of protecting the environment as we learn how to make the transition from oil and gas back to coal. Especially noteworthy, our international visitors remind us of the interest that other countries have in the United States reducing its reliance on foreign oil. The other nations of the world are urging us, as a country, to conserve oil and develop our indigenous resources. And they are doing this in the interest of international economic stability and the equitable sharing of available supplies of oil.

The American coal industry has been offered a promise that coal will be the cornerstone of our nation's energy future. My industry has been handed a torch, and uniquely challenged to light the way to a secure energy and economic future for our nation.

The promise, however, is wrapped in a paradox. We firmly believe we can meet the needs of our country, that we can mine the coal required in the years and decades ahead. But reaching that promised land, that future time when coal will regain its rightful place in the energy mix of this nation, will require the best efforts of people in the coal industry. It will require the best efforts of many of you scientists gathered here. And most of all, it also will require the best efforts of the thousands of people who make up federal, state and local governments.

It has been our national expectation that coal will fill our energy needs simply because of its natural abundance. In fact, an underlying assumption in President Carter's National Energy Plan (NEP) is that we do not really need a coal development policy. The NEP does not really address coal development. What the policy effectively says is that there is plenty of coal, and we can always get to it. We will have it when we need it, where we need it and at a reasonable price.

To some extent, this is quite true. There is plenty of coal, and we have the know-how to bring it out of ground to the market. But whether or not we can bring it out of the ground in a timely fashion and whether or not it will be at a reasonable price will, in large part, depend upon more than the policies expressed in President Carter's NEP.

It will depend mainly on how prudently the Administration implements the package of laws which Congress has passed in recent years to improve environmental quality, protect the health and safety of our miners, and preserve land values after mining. These laws have

*National Coal Association, and Peabody Coal Company, 301 North Memorial Drive, St. Louis, MO 63102.

been shaped to achieve laudable goals, and we subscribe to them. But this package of legislation will have a far more significant impact on coal supply, coal demand and coal economics, than the widely publicized NEP will ever have.

At present, there appears to be little or no coordination between the National Energy Plan and this shadow NEP. But it is in this area that the nation's energy future will be determined. For all of these laws and regulations affect energy production, and specifically coal production. Together they constitute, at least for the present, the nation's energy policy. Herein lies the paradox for coal: Many features of this package of legislation are going to restrain rather than encourage coal production. And it is already having or is anticipated to have an alarming effect on cost and efficiency in our coal mines.

In the short run, the supply of coal will probably be adversely affected by the imposition of new regulations under the Surface Mining Control and Reclamation Act. In particular, provisions which limit mining on prime farmlands or preclude mining in alluvial valley floors will restrain mining opportunities. The requirement to maintain "hydrologic integrity" is a subjective requirement which, if used unwisely, can severely restrict coal mining.

Some other aspects of the new surface mining law add significantly to the costs of mining and reduce productivity with little or no environmental benefit. As an example, we have many areas of this country where mining can be conducted without separating topsoil, as the law requires, and the land can be recontoured, revegetated and brought back to equal or better than its native condition. But we are granted no exceptions. So we are in the process at all surface mines in this country of picking up topsoil, storing it, and then replacing it after the mined land has been restored. This is very costly, at some of Peabody's mines it is even equal to the cost effect of the recent wage agreement with our miners.

New requirements of the Mine Health and Safety Act of 1977 will also have a negative effect on mine productivity and costs and will affect coal supply. In some cases, the new safety rules will render mines uneconomic, which could disrupt coal supplies for specific customers or in specific areas.

Perhaps the most significant new regulatory authority affecting coal is the Clean Air Act Amendments of 1977. While it is generally understood that this law would have a constraining effect on coal demand, the designation of areas of the country into either non-degradation or non-attainment areas may prove to have as great an effect on coal mining as it does on coal burning. There has been a trend to designate areas in and adjacent to national parks and other scenic areas into the highest air quality classification. But in these cases, such a designation precludes any significant development activities in the vicinity, including surface mining of coal.

There are many other requirements, such as permitting, licensing and preparation of Environmental Impact Statements, where regulations or policies increase costs, delay coal mine development or even prevent mining. But it is a fact that we are a nation of great environmental concern. We spend billions in public and private resources both to prevent environmental degradation and to restore areas already degraded.

We in the coal industry are only too conscious of our environmental responsibility. We have come to face an indisputable fact: That if coal is to thrive as an industry and a major source of energy, we are going to have to compete successfully with other fuels, compete not just in price, but in environmental considerations as well. If coal is to once again assume the role as our basic energy fuel, we are going to have to learn to mine, ship, and burn it in a manner that is both economically and environmentally acceptable, both to the present and future generations of Americans.

Hence, we are in an awkward position, knowing what we have to do, accepting the challenge of making coal environmentally safe, and yet having to resist government actions which appear to be pushing us in the direction we profess to want to go. Some of the appearances are deceiving. What we resist are not those regulatory actions which are cost-effective and which help attain the goals that industry and the public jointly seek. We are resisting only those actions whose benefits are not commensurate with costs and which also exceed the authorities granted by Congress. We feel it is a question of responsibility, both to ourselves and to the public which ultimately pays, to resist regulatory requirements which are neither cost-effective nor based in law. Unfortunately, it is this resistance which catches the attention. Very little is said about the resources we expend, and have expended, to make our activities as compatible as we can with nature. This is not to say that we have always been environmentalists in the modern sense of the word. Mining is, by definition and deed, a disruptive business. It is full of scientific and engineering problems and obstacles which must be overcome--you are aware of this.

And we in industry see the challenge now. We must strive to make coal acceptable to the public. We must make coal clean, efficient, safe, and competitively priced. Those are our goals. And, we will take exception when attainment of one or another of these objectives is frustrated by inefficient or unnecessary regulation. Because the nation must rely on coal to a much greater extent in the future, it is increasingly important that the coal industry remain efficient and responsive to demand. Both our efficiency and our ability to respond are suffering, and we have been urging the federal government to reexamine the dozens of subjects where its actions affect our ability to meet the nation's energy needs. And there are hopeful signs. Several encouraging actions have been taken in recent weeks that may indicate a realization within government of the crucial need for coordination of our national goals of energy and environment.

I am encouraged by the creation of the Presidential Commission on Coal headed by Governor Rockefeller of West Virginia. This action brings attention at the highest national levels to some of the industry's most pressing problems. The President has charged the commission with studying productivity and capital investment in the coal industry; labor relations; and health, safety and living conditions in the coalfields. The commission was also directed to look into new technology for mining and using coal and the impact of federal regulations on the coal industry.

In addition to this action, the President's Office of Management and Budget has established three federal interagency task forces to study policy, planning and regulatory problems affecting the siting and operation of new coal-burning plants and the coal mines needed to supply them. Other areas to be studied include industrial use of coal and federal regulations and policies, such as coal leasing, that may constrain coal supply.

This Congress has offered a promising sign that we can learn the ways to unwind the paradox of coal. Forums such as this offer an excellent opportunity to share our knowledge on the complex environmental aspects of coal mining. It is your knowledge, research and judgments which will allow us to find the ways to mine coal efficiently, safely and in the best interests of the nation as a whole. The coal industry welcomes and whole-heartedly endorses your efforts here.

As a nation, we must begin to bring into better focus the uncertain area between our national energy objectives and other legitimate interests. It must be our national goal that our mines will be the safest and most environmentally acceptable mines possible, but we must also include in that goal that these mines will be the most efficient and most productive mines possible.

If we do not begin to think in these terms, the results will be that productivity will continue to be lackluster, expansion of capacity will be slow and costly, and we, as a nation, will fail to realize the true potential of our coal resource. Coal can be our domestic, low cost, abundant, politically secure, and socially and environmentally acceptable source of energy. We must make this potential a reality.

I believe that we can unwind the paradox and release the promise. I believe we can do it with your help and the help of our government leaders. But we must get on with it.

COAL'S RESPONSE TO THE CHALLENGE IN THE NATIONAL ENERGY PLAN: DEMAND AND SUPPLY PROJECTION THROUGH 1985

*Joseph J. Yancik**

When reading the announcement of this meeting, I couldn't help but note that the International Congress for Energy and the Ecosystem is an appropriate title for an assemblage of international experts who accept the growing recognition that coal will become an important part of their energy fuel supply. It is also worth noting that this Congress convenes at a time when our industry, elected, and government officials are at the crossroads of decision paths. Which paths are chosen will determine to what extent and where our most abundant energy resource will be exploited and how wisely it will be used. It may be fortuitous, but more likely by design by the organizers of this Congress, that it takes place in a state that contains vast quantities of lignite reserves and in a state which also recognizes their value to the future quality of life of its citizens. And finally, but most importantly, the convening of this Congress by the Universities of Arizona and North Dakota and the Bureau of Mines symbolizes, in my mind, the commitment of the scientific and engineering community to take an active part in seeing that coal remains a viable fuel choice for our country.

The crux of this commitment must be the wise use of the knowledge we collectively possess. It seems to me that the theme of this International Congress -- broadly described as planning, production, economics, and the social and ecological consequences of mining -- is, in reality, the heart of the matter around which the issues must be debated. The basic issue is -- can coal be mined and used in quantities that will reduce our dependence upon imported energy while, at the same time, not damaging the environment we live in and enjoy?

Our debate here of this issue will not produce the final answers, but certainly we can expect this Congress to make an important contribution toward an intelligent resolution of the issues involved. How well we, as scientists and engineers, work together will determine the degree of success we achieve in striking a balance between our national objectives of securing an ample and economic supply of coal while the environment is protected from undue change. Whether we represent public interests, the industrial community or the government, we have an obligation to use the knowledge we have and to promote and use wisely the new and improved technology as it becomes available. A commitment to this obligation is what this Congress is all about and I'm thankful I was invited to take part in its deliberations.

*National Coal Association and Bituminous Coal Research, Inc., Washington, D.C. 20036.

The purpose of this paper is to look at the future demand and supply projections for coal and to examine those counter prevailing forces which could affect the anticipated energy supply role for coal. Through this examination, I believe, it is possible to gain an insight into the difficult problems and delicate balancing act our government leaders face in making decisions which will determine how we reach our national energy plan goals.

Although this Congress is focusing on the technological considerations of the supply side or production of coal, it is useful to establish demand since coal production tradition- ally has been demand-limited. All available evidence indicates that production will continue to be limited by market consumption.

The demand projections in this paper will extend to 1985, which is the time frame of most intense interest since it coincides with President Carter's time period goals in the National Energy Plan (NEP). These projections are based on extensive studies and analyses by the National Coal Association (NCA 1977). Our estimates are then compared against those contained in the President's April 1977 energy plan that forecasted domestic consumption and exports at about 1.2 billion tons by 1985, about double the use in 1976.

The coal demand figures in this paper for 1977 are based on the revised numbers published by the Department of Energy on March 3, 1978 (Energy Information Administration, Department of Energy). The National Coal Association projections for 1978 consumption were made in November 1977, prior to the United Mine Workers strike. At this writing, the 110 day-old strike has just been settled and there was insufficient time to revise these earlier estimates to reflect the 85 days of production lost in 1978 from most UMW mines. It is expected that the pre-strike 1978 consumption projections will have to be revised downward to reflect fuel switches by utilities and conservation measures practiced by the consumers. However, we believe the earlier estimates are useful as a base reference and, for the long-term, probably represent the normal rate of growth through the 1985 time period.

In the National Coal Association analysis of the outlook for demand in the year 1985, the markets are divided into six areas (NCA 1977). Five consuming areas represent the domestic market and the sixth covers the export market.

Electric Utilities

Steam coal for power generating accounts for the largest share of the domestic market -- in 1977, utilities consumed about 475 million tons or 77% of the total. The initial projections for 1978 are 508 million tons or close to 70% of the total coal used domestically. This projection is in close agreement with the utility industry's projection of an annual average increase of about 6% over the next ten years. As of April 1977, the utility industry reported to the Federal Power Commission that they would bring on line 250 new coal-fired power plants by 1985. These new units would consume an aggregated total of 390 million tons of coal. Adding this total to the present amount of coal used, the utilities could require up to 850 million tons. The National Coal Association has projected a lower-range, conservative figure of 820 million tons, since it appears reasonable that delays will occur in the construction schedules of these new plants.

Industrial Coal Use

General industrial use of coal in 1977 was about the same as in 1976 or about 60.5

million tons. The pre-strike projection was very optimistic as a 75 million ton market was predicted in 1978. This figure now appears too high, but the industrial use of coal will show a major long-term increase as coal-fired boilers ordered in the last two years go into service.

The information available right now about the anticipated general industry demand in 1985 is not sufficient for accurate forecasting. However, the American Boiler Manufacturers Association is projecting that coal-fired boilers will account for 33% of the boilers going on line in 1985. This percentage is about three times the historical and present rate of 10%. Based on the American Boiler Manufacturers Association's views, we have conservatively estimated the demand to range from 130 to 160 million tons in 1985. These figures could be low, particularly if the price advantage and security of supply over oil and gas become sufficient to act as powerful incentives to choose coal as the energy fuel.

Coking Coal

The use of coking coal, which declined 8% to 77 million tons in 1977 because of a slackening demand for steel, is expected to recover in 1978 to 84 million tons, about the same as consumed in 1976. The future competitive position of the U.S. steel plants will have the greatest effect on the accuracy of any forecast -- and that competitiveness is an uncertainty at this time. A pessimistic view would keep coking coal needs close to the present 84 million tons; an optimistic view would predict demand to rise annually at about 4% which would produce a market of about 110 million tons in 1985.

Household and Commerical Uses

The retail sales of coal are not expected to expand much beyond the present demand of about 7 million tons. Pending a major breakthrough in the development of "minimum attention" home heating units, the market will not show much movement either way.

Conversion to Synthetic Fuels

There are few positive signs of any appreciable coal market developing in synthetic fuel plants by 1985. However, the National Coal Association continues to be optimistic that federal and state governments will establish incentive programs that will encourage the beginning of a commercial industry, especially for the synthetic pipeline gas industry. Assuming these incentives are established in the next year or two, and several liquid fuel plants are built, we see a market of from 5 to 10 million tons by 1985.

Export Market

Coal exports were sluggish in 1977, due in part to a depressed worldwide market for steel, and are not expected to improve much in 1978. Shipments to Canada dropped 3% in 1977 to 16 million tons and are expected to rise slightly to 17 million tons in 1978. Shipments overseas fell 11.4% this past year to 38 million tons, down from 42.9 million in 1976; for 1978 they are expected to rise only slightly to 39 million tons.

The future export market will continue to be essentially metallurgical grade coal and the demand will be tied to the world economy. There are many reasons for a pessimistic view of the future -- the U.S. producers are becoming less competitive due to higher labor costs and increased governmental regulations, and the entrance of China and third world countries into the international coking coal market.

Recapitulation – Total Demand

The projections for coal demand in 1985, as summarized in Table 1, show a total of 1,040 million to 1,140 million tons for domestic needs and 1,120 to 1,250 million tons with coal exports included. These figures agree in total with the National Energy Plan, but the individual market uses differ somewhat from the NEP projections. This comparison is shown in Table 2.

Table 1. 1985 Estimated Demand for U.S. Bituminous Coal.

	1977* Million Tons	Share of Domestic or Export Market	1985 Projected Million Tons
DOMESTIC			
. Electric Utilities	475.0	77%	820 - 850
. Coking Coal for Steel	77.3	12%	80 - 110
. General Industry	60.3	10%	130 - 160
. Retail Dealers	7.0	1%	7
. Synthetic Fuels	**	**	5 - 10
Total Domestic	619.6	100%	1040 - 1140
EXPORTS			
. Canada	17.2	32%	
. Overseas	36.5	68%	
Total Exports	53.7	100%	80 - 110
TOTAL DEMAND	673.3		1120 - 1250

 * U.S. Bureau of Mines data, estimated consumption.
** Negligible.

Table 2. NCA - Versus - NEP Demand Projections for 1985.

	Millions of Tons		
Markets	NEP Estimates	NCA Estimates	
Utility	779	820 -	850
Industrial	278	130 -	160
Metallurgical	105	80 -	110
Other	13	12 -	17
Export	90	80 -	110
Total	1265	1120 -	1250

NCA developed their projections for coal demand in 1985 with an acute awareness of the constraints placed on the use of coal today. Further, we believe that we made a realistic impact assessment of the potential and future constraints anticipated from pending government actions. However, we recognize that these projections could be distorted through the imposition of even more restrictive controls on coal's use. In particular, we note the uncertainty of impact of the Clean Air Act Amendments of 1977 and, specifically, the regulations for application of the "best available control technology" and "prevention of significant deterioration" concepts. Under these rules and their interpretations, and other rules now under development by the Environmental Protection Agency, the demand for coal could be reduced.

In addition to the environmental controls, other federal and state actions could result in altering the anticipated demand for coal. Among the many possibilities, there are a few that can have a direct influence. These are the treatment given to pollution control capital investments by public utility commissions, land use zoning or plant siting requirements, price controls on competing fuels, import taxes and controls on energy fuels, and transportation incentives/disincentives.

Nevertheless, the National Coal Association and the coal producers continue to be optimistic and we anticipate an annual sustained growth in coal demand to 1985 and beyond with continuing yearly increases into the next century.

THE SUPPLY OR PRODUCTION OF COAL

Beginning with the basics, the United States has vast resources of coal and its demonstrated reserves are over 400 billion tons. The reserve base by area, rank of coal and potential method of mining, as published by the Bureau of Mines (Special Publication, August 1977) and shown in Table 3, is widely distributed in the United States, with 46% east of the Mississippi River and 54% west of the river and in Alaska. We have sufficient coal to last hundreds of years.

Table 3. Demonstrated Reserve Base [1] of Coals in the United States on January 1, 1976, by Area, Rank and Potential Method of Mining [2].

(Million Tons)

	Anthracite	Bituminous	Subbituminous	Lignite	Total
East of the Mississippi River:					
Underground Minable	7,104.3	155,233.8	—	—	162,338.0
Surface Minable	142.7	39,362.1	—	1,083.0	40,587.8
Total	7,246.9	194,595.9	—	1,083.0	202,925.8
West of the Mississippi River					
Underground Minable	116.4	26,785.8	107,736.1	—	134,638.3
Surface Minable	7.8	7,542.9	60,688.9	32,533.6	100,773.2
Total	124.2	34,328.7	168,425.0	32,533.6	235,411.5
Total East and West of the Mississippi River	7,371.1	228,924.6	168,425.0	33,616.6	438,337.3
Underground Minable:					
East of the Mississippi River	7,104.3	155,233.8	—	—	162,388.0
West of the Mississippi River	116.4	26,785.8	107,736.1	—	134,638.3
Total	7,220.7	182,019.6	107,736.1	—	296,976.3
Surface Minable:					
East of the Mississippi River	142.7	39,362.1	—	1,083.0	40,587.8
West of the Mississippi River	7.8	7,542.9	60,688.9	32,533.6	100,773.2
Total	150.5	46,905.0	60,688.9	33,616.6	141,361.0
Total Underground and Surface Minable	7,371.1	228,924.6	168,425.0	33,616.6	438,337.3

[1] Includes measured and indicated resource categories as defined by the USBM and USGS and represents 100% of the coal in place.
[2] Data may not add to totals shown due to rounding.

Current Productive Capacity

In 1977, coal production was an estimated 685 million tons. An analysis in mid-1977 by the National Coal Association suggested that the industry's annual production capacity is from 780 to 800 million tons and broken down between the east and west as follows:

East	630 million tons
West	150 million tons
Total	780 million tons

Last fall, when consumers were building up their stockpiles in anticipation of the strike, coal producers had one of their rare opportunities to run wide open. The coal producers then mined and shipped over 16 million tons a week. On an annualized basis, the total production at that rate would be over 800 million tons.

This National Coal Association assessment was corroborated by Secretary of Energy James Schlesinger in a speech he made last December 1977 at the AFL-CIO convention. Basing his comments on the same 16 million tons a week production figure, Mr. Schlesinger said the coal industry "already has the capacity" to produce in excess of 800 million tons annually. He noted that to meet President Carter's goal of 1.2 billion tons by 1985, "we have to expand our capacity between now and (then) by little better than 4 percent annually (Schlesinger)."

For comparison purposes, figures for 1977 and projections for 1978 are shown in Table 4. As mentioned earlier, the NCA projections for 1978 were made in mid-1977. These original estimates did not include the effects of a prolonged UMW strike. Revised figures were not available at this writing.

Table 4. Production Breakdown - Bituminous Coal.

	Estimated 1977*	Projected 1978**
East	526	539
West	159	191
Total	685	730

* NCA Estimate.
** Estimate made prior to the UMWA strike; revisions downward were required.

Future Coal Production

The National Coal Association makes an annual study of the industry's plans for new mines and expanded production from existing operations. In the latest study released in November 1977, the findings were:

Nationally

. 594 million tons annual production would be brought on line 1977-1985. This
594 million tons would come from:
- 142 mines operating at the end of 1976, which plan to add additional annual
  production of 170 million tons through 1985.
- 190 new mines which would be opened 1977-1985 with an expected annual
  production of 424 million tons.

In the East

. Expansion of 95 mines and the opening of 111 new mines would bring on line
199 million tons of new and replacement production in the 1977-1985 period.
. Just over 155 million tons, 78.0 percent, would be mined underground; 44.5
million tons, or 22 percent would be mined on the surface.
- 123 million tons, or 61.6 percent, of the new production will be for steam
  coal; 76.6 million tons, 38.4 percent, will be for metallurgical use.
- Almost all -- 92.6 percent or 76.6 million tons -- of the total planned new or
  replacement metallurgical production 1977-1985 would be in the East. Two
  eastern states, West Virginia and Alabama, account for 60 percent, 48 million
  tons, of the planned metallurgical coal production.

In the West

. Expansion of 47 mines and the opening of 79 new mines would add 394 million
tons new production in 1977 through 1985. (This is new production as replacement is not a factor in the relatively new western coal industry.)
- Over 90 percent of the new production in the West, some 358.8 million tons,
  will be surface mines; 98.5 percent (388.2 million tons) will be for steam use,
  in utility boilers and industrial use.
- The 388.2 million tons planned new steam production in the West represents
  over 75 percent of all reported steam coal production additions in the United
  States; 40 percent of the national steam coal total is scheduled to come from
  one state -- Wyoming.

The following, Table 5, summarizes the new and replacement production which the
National Coal Association study shows coming on line 1977-1985.

Table 5. New Production [1] at Mines Covered by This Summary, 1977-1985.

	East	West	Total
		(Million Tons)	
Use:			
Steam	123.0	388.2	511.2
Metallurgical	76.0	6.2	82.8
Type of Mining:			
Surface	44.5	358.8	403.3
Underground	155.1	35.6	190.7
Total	199.6	394.4	594.0

[1] Includes both new and replacement production.

A more detailed summary of the future production by states, by use and type of mining is presented in Table 6.

A word of caution must be given on the use of these study results. First, the results do not represent the expansion plans of the entire coal industry. This study represents plans of coal producers which accounted for 65.6 percent of output in 1976 as well as most companies that are expected to become major coal producers by 1985. Second, the plans reported by companies are, in many instances, far from complete. Some firms did not consider their plans for the 1982-1985 period sufficiently firm to warrant specific identification. Additionally, it is believed that plans reported herein for western mines are more complete than are the plans for eastern mines.

The net effect of these caveats is that actual production additions, and thus the actual capability of the industry to produce coal, will be higher than the data reported would indicate.

Assuming the future production plans of the reporting companies can be carried out as indicated -- and not prevented or distorted by government imposed constraints -- all evidence indicates that the 1.2 billion tons of coal called for by the President could be produced by 1985. More specifically:

                                                        Million Tons

. Production capability of the industry as
  currently demonstrated   780 - 800

. Expected depletion 1977 through 1985   108

. Current plans as reported by major firms
  that will be producing coal in 1985   594

. Expected production for producers not
  covered by survey   ***

. Planned mine expansions and additions
  not reported by producers covered
  (mostly in the 1981-1985 period)   ***

                                                          1,266*** - 1,286***

*No valid way of estimating.

CONSTRAINTS ON COAL PRODUCTION

In the preceding section, the optimism of the coal producers was demonstrated by their planning for new capacity to meet the expected substantial increase in demand. While their optimism at the drawing board is real, there exists a sobering realization in the corporate offices where investment decisions are made that their future plans may be delayed or even thwarted by governmental actions. Extensive delays in expanding or opening new mines are being encountered today and the future looks bleaker with the almost daily requirements added to environmental assessments, application requirements, and the review and hearing processes required by laws and regulations.

Heading the list of potentially constraining laws is the Surface Mining Control and Reclamation Act of 1977, because of its many unnecessary and costly impediments to mining. Even the partial list that follows of constraints imposed by the surface mining regulations -- constraints which are not easily surmounted with today's mining technology -- is ample evidence that this conference, if it can focus on these problems and point the way to solutions, can make a significant contribution to the U.S. mining industry. Today's technology is inadequate to meet all or some of the requirements for efficient operation to meet the regulations imposed on:

. blasting -- air noise and ground vibration level restrictions.
. hydrology -- aquifer reconstruction, water quality requirements, and runoff and
  groundwater control measures
. waste management -- temporary and permanent construction designs for dams,
  fills and roads to exacting specifications without regard to native construction
  materials.
. reclamation -- topography reconstruction, soil placement and revegetation
  productivity requirements.

Although each of these areas justifies a thorough examination of their problem, they will not be discussed in this paper. An analysis of these problems will be left to the many excellent papers which will be presented here at this Congress.

The federal coal leasing program, or lack of one, is another serious concern to western coal producers. The decision by Judge John H. Pratt last September 1977, in the case of NRDC vs. Hughes, set into motion another round of long-term uncertainties relating to the availability of federal lands for coal mining. In his decision, Judge Pratt enjoined the Department of the Interior from issuing coal leases except under very limited leasing to alleviate short-term hardships such as in the case of bypassing of federal coal uneconomic to mine, to avert mine closings if contracted tonnages cannot be shipped, and to meet hardship cases not explicitly defined in the above. Judge Pratt's order also required the Interior Department to prepare a new environmental impact statement (EIS) on a revised coal leasing program and, according to the Department, the EIS will be completed in May

TABLE 6　New Coal Mines and Expansions of Existing Mines

State Summary, by Use and Type of Mining
(Millions of Tons)

Expected Incremental Production at Mines Listed, 1977-1985

State	Total Production At Mines Listed 1976	Use		Type of Mining		Total Incremental Production 1/	Total Expected Production 2/ at Full Operation
		Steam	Metal-lurgical	Under-ground	Surface		
East							
Alabama	2.525	7.901	13.324	17.725	3.500	21.225	23.750
Illinois	5.752	29.948	1.250	23.224	7.974	31.198	36.950
Indiana	6.387	11.413	--	--	11.413	11.413	17.800
Kentucky, Eastern	2.348	16.612	7.490	15.702	8.400	24.102	26.450
Kentucky, Western	1.623	17.877	--	12.581	5.296	17.877	19.500
Kentucky, Total	3.971	34.489	7.490	28.283	13.696	41.979	45.950
Maryland	--		2.000	2.000	--	2.000	2.000
Ohio	3.586	11.214 3/	--	8.714	2.500	11.214	14.800
Pennsylvania	3.806	12.449	11.795	23.047	1.197	24.244	28.050
Tennessee	0.490	0.800	0.810	1.610	--	1.610	2.100
Virginia	--	0.750	5.200	5.950	--	5.950	5.950
West Virginia	5.918	14.039	34.683	44.491	4.231	48.722	54.640
Total East	32.435	123.003 3/	76.552	155.044	44.511	199.555	231.990
West							
Arizona	4.667	3.333	--	--	3.333	3.333	8.000
Arkansas	--	--	0.200	0.200	--	0.200	0.200
Colorado	3.908	16.430	3.962	11.680	8.712	20.392	24.300
Iowa	0.100	0.100	--	0.100	--	0.100	0.100
Kansas	--	0.250	--	--	0.250	0.250	0.250
Montana	23.556	65.144	--	--	65.144	65.144	88.700
New Mexico	9.331	11.169	0.500	--	11.669	11.669	21.000
North Dakota	9.714	25.136	--	--	25.136	25.136	34.850
Oklahoma	--	0.650	1.500	1.500	0.650	2.150	2.150
Texas	8.400	35.700	--	--	35.700	35.700	44.100
Utah	4.265	23.235	--	17.735	5.500	23.235	27.500
Washington	4.023	2.977	--	1.000	1.977	2.977	7.000
Wyoming	19.878	204.122	--	3.400	200.722	204.122	244.000
Total West	87.842	388.246	6.162	35.615	358.793	394.408	482.250
Total United States	120.277	511.249 3/	82.714	190.659	403.304	593.963	714.240

1/ Excludes 1976 production from mines operating in 1976. This total includes only expected incremental production from expansion of existing mines and production from new mines 1977-1985.

2/ This figure includes 1976 production levels and represents total expected annual production at full operation.

3/ Includes 2.5 million tons for gasification.

Note:　All totals include some data which has not been verified by NCA.

1979. The Secretary of the Interior, in a letter to the President of the National Coal Association, said that "if new leasing is warranted, we would proceed with site specific coal leases EIS's, with the first lease sales occurring in mid-1980 (Andrus)." Needless to say, there are too many "ifs" and uncertainties still present to say at this time that the federal government's coal leasing program is back on the track.

There are other constraints to coal production, such as the rigid application of the coal mine health and safety laws and regulations, labor-management relations, unauthorized work stoppages, productivity declines and transportation bottlenecks. All of these constraints can and are being managed, but more consistent policies from and cooperation between the federal and state governments would do much to reduce these problems to a minimum.

CONCLUSION

It has become increasingly clear to the U.S. coal industry that President Carter must undertake a thorough review of the conflicts between energy production and other national objectives. Present and future laws and regulations need to be examined to determine their impact on coal-related projects. If government imposed constraints will prevent or delay the opening of any of the 332 new or expanded mines or the construction of the 250 power plants identified in the Federal Power Commission report, then our government should identify these plants and the specific constraining factors. With these facts in hand, our government should then institute corrective actions.

The National Coal Association, on January 12, 1978, submitted a proposal, as outlined above, to President Carter. We have provided copies of the proposal to over 100 executives in the Executive Branch, every governor, member of Congress, head of state utility commissions, labor unions, state legislators, and to the heads of the nation's electric utilities. The proposal has received support from a number of these people. Senator Jackson wrote to the President on February 9, 1978, asking that he focus attention on the problem of conflicts among energy and environmental objectives (Jackson).

We believe that a study based on our proposal would bring the facts to light about the nature and extent of conflicts between energy and environmental goals. We are hopeful that the Administration will make these facts known and then proceed with programs to deal with the tough decisions that are ahead. Coal can and will meet the challenge of the National Energy Plan. All the coal industry needs is reasonable and balanced rules and regulations under which it can operate.

ABSTRACT

This paper discusses the National Coal Association's projections for the demand and supply of coal in 1985. The primary constraints to increased use of coal in the principal domestic and export markets are identified. Adequate supplies or production of coal are forecasted through 1985, as the present surplus production capacity condition will continue to exist in 1985. However, production capacity is very sensitive to government actions and a number of identified constraints could, if not properly managed by the state and federal governments, result in a distortion of coal supply estimates. The paper concludes that coal can meet the challenges of the National Energy Plan if it is given a reasonable economic and regulatory climate in which to operate.

REFERENCES

Andrus, C.D. 1978. Private Communication to President of the National Coal Association, March 3, 1978.

Bureau of Mines, Department of the Interior. 1977. Special Publication: The Demonstrated Reserve Base of Coals in the United States on June 1, 1976 (Corrected). August 1977.

Department of Energy, Energy Information Administration. 1978. Energy Data Report -- Weekly Coal Rpt. No. 22, March 3, 1978.

Jackson, H. 1978. Private Communication to President of the United States, February 9, 1978.

National Coal Association. 1977. Study of New Mine Additions and Major Expansion Plans of the Coal Industry and the Potential for Future Coal Production. November 1977, Washington, D C.

Schleede, G.R. 1977. The Outlook for Coal Demand and Supply. October 12, 1977, National Coal Association, Washington, D C.

Schlesinger, J.R. 1977. Before the AFL-CIO Convention, Los Angeles, California, December 9, 1977, Department of Energy, Office of Public Affairs, Washington, D C.

COAL UTILIZATION AND SUPPLY

*Robert L. Davies**

The Department of Energy was formed in October, 1977, by aggregating the energy functions of a number of federal agencies. This paper describes the work of this Department in general and coal utilization and supply in particular.

One of the lessons we have learned in recent years, and which was put into use in forming the Department of Energy, is that inventing a better mouse trap is not enough. Once invented, it cannot become useful unless adopted in the marketplace. The Department, therefore, organized its energy development activities around functional areas of responsibilities. This is how it works.

Basic research is supervised by an office of energy research. When basic ideas look promising, they are turned over to the Assistant Secretary for Energy Technology whose job it is to resolve technical questions relating to them. Once this has occurred, and the technologies in question appear ready for commerical deployment, they are turned over to two other Assistant Secretaries: one for conservation and solar applications; and one for all other programs, called resource applications. It then becomes the job of these latter two Assistant Secretaries to assure introduction of the new technology in the marketplace.

This organization, which is managed by the Department's Under Secretary, reflects the concept that, while technology development is a continuum, different kinds of management skills are required along the way. This organization plan avoids entrusting all stages of a project to a single manager or organization. In this way, we can concentrate specialized areas of expertise on the problems which are unique to a technology at various stages of development. Staff members from each office serve on the project teams of the others, but the center of gravity shifts from the scientific to engineering and marketing as a technology is developed. Thus we now have one office which deals with coal technologies in their later stages of development and initial commercialization.

It seems clear that if the energy demand is to continue to grow as it has grown in the past, the world will, for all practical purposes, run out of oil and natural gas during our lifetime. If recent projections prove accurate, world demand for petroleum will exceed world supply in something like ten years. It is also clear that the technologies which must ultimately be developed to provide a real solution to the planet's energy supply problem -- solar, nuclear fusion, wind, tidal, and so forth -- are not going to contribute much in the very near future. Instead, we must make a go of it with what we already have.

*Office of Resource Applications, U.S. Department of Energy, 12th & Pennsylvania Avenue, N.W., Room 3310, Washington, D.C. 20461.

These technologies are fairly easy to summarize:

- . nuclear fission;
- . new and enhanced oil and gas recovery;
- . shale oil; and
- . coal

Others, of course, are also available. Solar energy systems, geothermal, and wind are fairly well developed. But they aren't likely to achieve any market penetration in the next ten years which can significantly replace the use of oil and natural gas. This is because they are not readily adaptable to our big energy consumers: Industry, electric utilities, and most of all, the transporation sector.

My own area of responsibility within the Department is coal. Fourteen months ago, President Carter sent to Congress the proposed National Energy Plan. The major thrust of the National Energy Plan is to reduce our reliance on foreign sources of energy. One provision of the plan calls for doubling the output of coal, our most abundant energy resource. Doubling the nation's annual output of coal is no mean feat. And it certainly is not going to happen unless we change the methods by which we use coal. In most parts of the country, we cannot burn coal directly because the price of doing so, in damage to our environment, is simply too high. We are not likely to do it by using such devices as stack gas scrubbers, either. They cost too much. No, we're going to have to find clean ways to use coal, and that means using the new technologies.

I would like to discuss what some of these technologies are, and how they will collectively reduce, if not end, our need for foreign oil. The technologies are coal lique-faction, coal gasification, combined cycle electrical generation, and atmospheric fluidized bed combustion.

COAL GASIFICATION

I will elaborate on three types of coal gasification. They are low-btu, medium-btu, and high-btu, as well as *in situ* coal gasification. The technical sophistication, size of the plants, cost of the plants and the cost of the product fuel gas increases, as one progresses from low-btu gas to high-btu gas. Thus the uses and customers are different for each.

Low-btu Gasification

By adding steam to coal in the presence of air, we can produce a gas with a heating value of 100-300 btu/cubic feet. This gas, mostly hydrogen and carbon monoxide, is suitable for use as a utility and industrial fuel. For many years, it was this gas, called coal-gas or town gas, which was used for lighting and cooking, both in Europe and in this country. However, because its heat content is so low, it cannot be used as a direct substitute for natural gas. This would require changes in existing gas systems so extensive as to make it, in most cases, quite uneconomical. There are two notable exceptions, however, the first is where a large energy consumer, such as a medium sized factory, cannot obtain supplies of higher quality gas. For such a consumer, a low-btu coal gasifier is an especially attractive alternative to oil. The second situation where low-btu gas will be very attractive, is with electric utilities adding new base-load generating facilities. Although most turbine generators are not terribly energy-efficient, by adding a heat recovery cycle, called a bottoming cycle, to a low-btu gas powered turbine, a very efficient system results. However, we are still a couple of years away from this application because of uncertainties about the endurance ability of high temperature turbine generators powered by low-btu gas. The Department of Energy, Office of Energy Research, has an ongoing program to find the solution to this problem.

At the present time, there are very few small commerical-size low-btu plants in operation. However, the required equipment is available on the commerical market, and since the technology is so well developed for industrial applications, low-btu gasification presents very few technical risks to the potential user.

Medium-btu gasification

The manufacture of medium-btu gas is a somewhat more sophisticated process using oxygen instead of air. It creates a gas with a heating capacity of 300-600 btu/cubic feet. This is more than adequate for most industrial applications, and the gas can be transported economically by pipeline for reasonable distances. It does, however, require a greater outlay of capital to construct a medium-btu facility than a smaller, less sophisticated low-btu plant and the product is more costly on a btu basis.

Some of the likely potential users of medium-btu gas are large single users or concentrations of multiple users which can be supplied from a centralized plant. One of the financial advantages of medium-btu gas to these industries is the fact that since there is a similarity between medium-btu gas and natural gas, retrofit problems will be minimal.

High-btu Gasification

High-btu gasification is a more sophisticated process, requiring the injection of hydrogen to product the main constituent, methane. The synthesis produces a fuel with a heating value of 950 to 1000 btu/cubic feet and which is essentially identical to natural gas.

The development of high-btu gas will have to be accelerated to help offset the intensification of the natural gas shortage. In recognition of this fact, the Department recently announced its intention to intervene before the Federal Energy Regulatory Commission to support the application of a consortium of companies to construct a high-btu facility in Mercer County in North Dakota.

In Situ Coal Gasification (Underground Coal Conversion)

Since 85 percent of our coal deposits are not economically recoverable by conventional mining methods, in situ coal gasification, a process of converting coal to gas on-site underground may prove an attractive method of making use of this resource. Although the technology is still in the experimental stage, it is one we are watching closely.

COAL LIQUEFACTION

Coal liquefaction processes being developed in the U.S. produce a clean-burning synthetic crude oil. This syncrude is extremely valuable, especially in environmental terms because it is a low-ash, low-sulphur product which can be used directly as a boiler fuel. It has the potential to fire not only powerplants but industrial boilers as well. Most important, with further refining, syncrude can be upgraded to motor and heating fuels.

Other liquefaction processes are available, as well. Methyl alcohol, or methanol, is easily produced from coal and can be used directly as a fuel to power utility gas turbines or can be blended with gasoline. Methanol can also be converted into gasoline.

In all, there are some half-dozen different coal liquefaction technologies in various states of development. You may remember much of Germany's battle equipment was powered by coal-based liquids during World War II and South Africa has been producing coal-based motor fuels for over thirty years. Some of the newer technologies hold great promise for reducing the economic and environmental costs of producing coal-based liquid fuels.

It is hard to overstate the importance of coal liquefaction. Motor fuels alone represent almost half of all the petroleum consumed in the U.S. We import about one-half of the petroleum. The conclusion is obvious: replacing motor fuels means replacing imports. In the near term, there are only three methods of doing this which have prospects of success on a large scale. The first is increased domestic oil production from new fields or by means of tertiary recovery techniques from old fields. Shale oil is an important domestic resource, but its environmental implications, particularly the availability of water resources, are troublesome. Coal liquefaction, is close at hand. It has been used successfully in the past and is in use in other countries today. Its major stumbling block is cost. But, with rising oil prices and more sophisticated technology, the situation has improved dramatically.

FLUIDIZED BED COMBUSTION TECHNOLOGY (AFB)

Fluidized bed combustors burn a mixture of pulverized coal and limestone and they have shown great potential for directly burning coal while considerably lowering emissions of sulphur and nitrogen oxides without scrubbers. It is due to this, that AFB's are quite a technological advance over the conventional combustors with stack gas scrubbers. The capital cost of AFB's is expected to be less than that of conventional systems with scrubbers. AFB's have demonstrated their proficiency for burning coal, coal-oil slurries, char and coal waste, all in an environmentally acceptable manner.

Other factors which make AFB's attractive are that over 90% of the nation's fuel utilization process is done through direct combustion. As of now, only 20% of our fuel utilization is coal. The increase in the prices of oil and natural gas make coal all the more attractive, thereby, pushing the AFB's into the spotlight as clean and energy efficient combustion systems.

SUPPLY

So far, I've confined my comments to the utilization of coal. This is because, for the next couple of years, we view coal as being a demand-restricted commodity. This does not mean, however, that we are unmindful of the supply implications of encouraging coal demand.

There has been considerable interest in the nation's ability to transport this increased coal production. This work continues to go forward. We are also working with the

Department of the Interior to improve leasing and production procedures on federal lands. We have established offices to find uses for our anthracite coal resources and to broaden the industrial base of coal production. The Coal Loan Guarantee Program is taking applications from small mine operators who wish to open new underground mines or to reopen or expand old ones. We are looking hard at ways and means of improving the productivity of coal mines through training of miners and introduction of improved equipment. We currently do not perceive coal supply as our major problem. However, if we are successful in the coal utilization field, we must be ready in the area of coal supply, too.

In summary, for the remainder of this century coal must play the dominant role in solving our energy problem. The new coal technologies, that are on the verge of becoming commerical, offer the prospect that coal can be used or converted into clean, nonpolluting energy at a cost that is less than the projected price of imported oil. For an engineer, which I am, coal technologies have a particular attraction. They offer an unusually rare opportunity for a truly elegant solution of huge engineering problems on a grand scale.

Consider the fundamental chemistry of the process. What we want to do is remove carbon and hydrogen from the ground and combine it with oxygen. This will give us energy. Along the way, with some of the technologies, we also have to borrow water. But this is returned to the biosphere in the combustion processes, as well. The carbon dioxide produced is photosynthesized by plants into its constituent elements; oxygen is returned to the atmosphere and carbon is returned to the soil. A perfectly contained and balanced system, powered by the sun. An engineer's dream -- on a planetary scale.

Of course, there are some weak links in this process when practically applied, not the least of which is mother nature herself. Her coal process takes millions of years, and photosynthesis is not very efficient. Someday, renewable energy sources will be dominant energy sources but in the meantime we must use coal effectively and cleanly.

OFFICE OF SURFACE MINING:
COMBINING ENERGY AND THE ENVIRONMENT

*Walter N. Heine**

Like this International Congress, the Office of Surface Mining (OSM) is concerned with the economics, ecology and planning of coal resource development. We are the "new kid on the block" as far as Federal environmental agencies are concerned. OSM truly is an agency where the national concern for energy is combined with the national need for environmental protection. We were created because coal has become an important energy source in the United States. I would like to tell you why we were created and what we are doing, and relate this to the interests of the delegates here at the International Congress.

Last year, 688.6 million tons of coal were mined in the United States. Of this total, 416.9 million tons were obtained from surface operations. A goal of the Carter Administration is to increase U. S. Coal production to 1 Billion tons a year by 1985. This means that thousands of acres of additional lands will be mined for coal each year in the 1980's. It also means that without accompanying environmental protection, much of our country would be left with barren lands, denuded forests, and polluted streams.

To prevent this, OSM was established within the Department of the Interior, created by the Surface Mining Control and Reclamation Act signed by President Carter on August 3, 1977. Although the legislation took many years in coming, and final passage reflected the inevitable compromises of Capitol Hill, the final product still was a strong bill. It affords protection from the ravages of coal mining before, during, and after these operations. And the law has "teeth" in it.

Let me give you some examples. Under the Act, citizens can petition the State regulatory authority to designate certain areas unsuitable for mining of coal. In response to a petition, the State regulatory authority must "designate an area unsuitable for all or certain types of surface mining"; if it determines that reclamation is not technologically and economically feasible under the standards of the law. Further, a State regulatory authority may, in response to a petition, designate certain fragile, historic, renewable resources, or natural hazard lands unsuitable for all or certain types of surface mining.

The law requires that OSM "assist the States in developing objective scientific criteria and appropriate procedures and institutions for determining those areas of a State to be designated unsuitable for all or certain types of surface coal mining." All of these environmental actions may be taken, of course, before mining begins, and it is important to note that they come about as a result of citizen initiative. Congress intended that individuals who might be adversely affected by coal mining should have a significant role in the

*Office of Surface Mining, Reclamation and Enforcement, U.S. Department of the Interior, Washington, D.C.

programs under the Act.

After mining has begun, coal operators must adhere to certain performance standards promulgated by OSM when it issued interim regulations in December, 1977. For instance, they must restore mined land to its approximate original contour, and remove topsoil, saving it for later replacement. In addition, operators must design, maintain, or remove mine waste embankments in accordance with regulations established with the concurrence of the U. S. Corps of Engineers, and provide permanent vegetative cover on affected areas after mining is completed.

The performance standards are also designed to control the placement of spoil outside the actual mining area, minimize damage to the hydrologic balance both on and off the mine site during mining and reclamation operations, control the use of explosives in surface mining operations, and restore mined land so that it can support its original use or an approved higher or better use. Special performance standards are included for mining on steep slopes, mountaintop removal operations, mining of prime farmlands, and surface effects of underground coal mining.

To insure that the performance standards are complied with, OSM has an inspection force currently visiting coal mining sites across the country. The initial force, now 28 inspectors, recently graduated from a two-week training session held in Madisonville, Kentucky. More inspectors will be in training by the end of 1978 and eventually 150 inspectors will be employed by OSM. These inspectors are empowered to shut down mining operations completely when violations that endanger the public health and safety are discovered. Already OSM inspectors have served several violation notices and issued a few partial cessation orders, demonstrating the effectiveness of the law when operators do not comply.

The law also addresses the *past* abuses of coal mining. Title IV of the Act provides for the reclamation of abandoned mine areas. Some of these abandoned mines have been reclaimed "naturally" with time. Millions of acres in the United States have been surface mined, but at least half of them can be considered non-reclaimed. In addition, a large and costly job involves the correcting of adverse effects of underground coal mining, such as, subsidence, mine fires, open shafts.

To tackle these problems, the Act established an Abandoned Mine Reclamation Fund financed primarily by fees assessed from coal mine operators. Maximum fees are 35 cents per ton of coal produced by surface mining, 15 cents per ton for underground mining, and 10 cents per ton for lignite. OSM recently announced its first seven major projects, one of them in North Dakota, supported by the fund. All of the projects are intended to eliminate extreme hazards to health and safety, and all were targeted by the States involved as their top priority.

The North Dakota project involves a school in Scranton. Subsidence from old coal mine excavations in a 50-acre area bordering a schoolground and on a nearby 20-acre area have created caverns that are readily accessible to (and frequently explored by) the youngsters, many of them of elementary age. The mined area also contains a large strip pit. Reclamation work will consist of filling the subsided areas and revegetating the land as work progresses. The project should take 15 to 18 months. It furnishes a good example of the value of the fund. This fiscal year, about $12 million is expected to be committed by OSM directly for reclamation projects. OSM cannot spend any money collected from operators until it is subsequently appropriated by Congress.

The law will have an effect on past, present, and future mining for coal in the United States. Yet, the law does not exist, OSM does not exist, to drive the coal industry out of business. In fact, the requirements of the law should add only incremental costs to mining activities. Furthermore, the implementation of minimum Federal standards will ensure to responsible coal operators that the environmental exploiters will no longer enjoy an unfair competitive advantage. In the past, some operators have been able to sell coal for less, because they cut corners, and displayed insensitivity to area citizens, including future generations who must live with an inheritance of despoiled lands and waters.

Another point bears mentioning. The economic aspects of mining control and reclamation under the new Act, that is, not all of the advantages can be calculated in dollars and cents. There are social costs, reflected in the broken spirits of persons and communities as they see their mountains, forests, streams, and homes despoiled by bad mining practices.

But you know as well as I that we can have both....coal and environmental amenities.... if we are thoughtful and careful. The federal legislation, therefore, sets forth a level of stewardship to our land with respect to coal mining, a fundamental moral obligation to ourselves.

While the Federal standards may set the moral tone, regulatory activity will be carried out primarily by the States. In effect, the surface mine Act says to the States: "Here are some minimum standards....you enforce them and adapt them to your own particular administrative process." A full Federal program will be implemented in a State only after that State has failed to submit an acceptable program of its own. Of course, OSM will be available to help along the way, with technical assistance when needed and with Federal Grants. As I mentioned, North Dakota received the first grant under the Act, $200,700 on April 13, 1978 in a ceremony in my office. This money will help the State cover additional costs incurred in administering and enforcing the initial regulatory program of the new Federal law. North Dakota is right on the mark in its surface mining reclamation efforts. It already has one of the strongest laws in the country.

In the research area, OSM this fiscal year will be making grants totaling almost $5 1/2 million to 20 colleges in 20 States to support programs at their mineral institutes. This money will be available for research, for general administration, and for fellowships.

We must not lose the opportunity which the new Act affords us. We are not going to correct all problems overnight, but I do think we are going to see significant progress quickly. And in the process, we are going to demonstrate that we can make energy progress and environmental progress "hand-in-hand". Our country cannot survive without both together.

MINING ENVIRONMENTAL RESEARCH IN THE BUREAU OF MINES

Donald G. Rogich*

BACKGROUND AND INTRODUCTION

The Bureau of Mines was established by Congress in 1910 with the passage of the Organic Act (P.L. 61-179). Since 1910 the Bureau's mission has been shaped and modified by many items of legislation, several of which have extended and enhanced the Bureau's role in addressing the Nation's changing mineral and materials needs. For example, the Strategic and Critical Materials Stockpiling Act of 1946 (P.L. 79-520) authorized and directed the Bureau to make scientific, technologic, and economic investigations of mineral substances essential to the common defense or the industrial needs of the Nation. Later, the Wilderness Act of 1964 (P.L. 88-577) directed the Bureau, in cooperation with the Geological Survey, to determine mineral values of lands proposed for protection and preservation within the wilderness system. And recently, the Federal Mine Health and Safety Amendments Act of 1977 (P.L. 95-164) reemphasized the important role of Bureau research in providing technological solutions to health and safety hazards in mining operations. Thus, the mission of the Bureau of Mines has been a dynamic, evolving mandate, adjusted and refined to meet the needs of the day.

Today the Bureau seeks "to assure the continued viability of the domestic mineral and materials economy and the maintenance of an adequate minerals base so that the nations' economic, social, strategic and environmental needs can be better served." This mission is carried out through the Bureau's programs of supply/demand analysis and research and development. To pursue this mission in Fiscal Year 1978 the Bureau of Mines had available the funding and personnel shown below:

	1978 appropriation (Dollars in thousands)	Permanent positions
Metallurgy Research	$ 26,665	817
Mining Research	88,474	878
Assessments, Data Collection and Analysis	20,131	566
	$135,270	2,261

*Division of Mine Systems Engineering, Bureau of Mines, U.S. Department of the Interior, 2401 "E" Street N.W., Washington, D.C. 20241.

Research on, and correction of, environmental problems associated with mining and metallurgy has been an integral part of the Bureau's work for many years. This work has covered a wide range of subjects, including:

. stability of waste and tailings
. subsidence
. acid mine water
. corrective reclamation projects
. blasting ground vibrations and air shock
. pollution abatement
. recycling of waste products

The work was carried on as parts of many programs that were concerned with the total spectrum of minerals extraction, including health and safety, processing, use, and recyling. With the creation of the Department of Energy (DOE) an opportunity presented itself to consolidate and highlight within the Bureau certain portions of the Bureau's work concerned with environmental problems. The Bureau transferred to DOE a number of functions dealing with fuels data, coal preparation, and coal extraction research aimed at improving production efficiency. Research on the environmental aspects of extracting all minerals was retained by the Bureau. Since that research had been part of several other programs, consolidation was a logical step. The consolidated and expanded work on the environmental aspects of minerals extraction is the nucleus of the Mining Environmental Research Program.

The Mining Environmental Research Program has as its goal the minimization of environmental impacts arising from the mining of all solid minerals. The program considers environmental problems associated with all aspects of minerals extraction from preliminary discovery to ultimate return of the land to productive use. A common approach to all of these problems is an examination of existing technology and a consideration of the potential technologic improvements that might accrue from an aggressive research, development, and demonstration program. The program is divided into three parts: Environmental Engineering Systems, Environmental Control Technology, and Mined Land Reclamation Technology. The following sections of this paper describe the types of research projects conducted in each of these three subprograms and the funding for this work.

ENVIRONMENTAL ENGINEERING SYSTEMS

Research funded under the Environmental Engineering Systems subactivity seeks to develop baseline data and the environmental assessments technology for use in determining the potential environmental impacts of minerals development. Assessments are made of environmental changes arising from minerals extraction, and engineering techniques are developed which incorporate state-of-the-art mining environmental technology into the design and planning of minerals extraction operations. Finally conceptual and innovative mining systems are investigated which can reduce or eliminate the adverse environmental impacts of minerals extraction.

Fiscal Year 1978 funding for this portion of the program is as shown below:

Environmental Engineering Systems FY 1978 Funding

(Dollars amounts in thousands)

Baseline Studies	$4,104
Innovative Mining Systems	1,274
Technical Assistance	615
Total	$5,993

Baseline Studies

These are systematic investigations to measure important environmental factors (air quality, water quality, soil structure, flora, fauna, etc.) before mining takes place. Subsequent measurements of these parameters during mining and after reclamation are compared with pre-mining baseline data to assess the type and magnitude of changes to the environment resulting from mining operations. In some mining districts, little is understood about the effects of mining on the environment and hence little can be done at present to minimize the effects. As an example, baseline support for evaluation will be provided by geotechnical data pertinent to the design of environmentally safe mining systems for the thick deposits of oil shale, nahcolite, and dawsonite in deep underground workings, including the effect of possible subsidence and possible groundwater disturbance.

Rapid and cost effective environmental assessments require the proper tools and technologies. Bureau research examines the entire spectrum of data gathering measurements and records that are necessary for environmental evaluations associated with all phases of the minerals extraction process. The identification of instrumentation and measurement deficiencies and the development of improved and new capability is then undertaken.

Innovative Mining Systems

Research is undertaken to develop and evaluate environmentally engineered mining systems and techniques that minimize land disturbance and either maintain or improve existing ecology, hydrology, and surface soil quality. Innovative mining systems are sought that can aid compliance with environmental standards while maintaining safe and healthful working conditions for the individual miner and assuring his continued productivity. Innovative mine plans using unique equipment combinations are developed and feasibility studies are conducted prior to demonstration.

Technical Assistance

This element embraces all activities associated with the conduct of the contractual portion of the entire Mining Environmental Research Program. The functions covered by this element include planning, problem prioritization, preparation of statements of work, proposal evaluations, clarification and negotiation sessions, and contract monitoring. The technical monitoring of contractual work is an extremely important function to insure that useful research products are developed which complement developments in the in-house research portion of the program.

Some recent accomplishments under the Environmental Engineering Systems subprogram include:

- An eight foot diameter research shaft, the first to reach the deep oil shale beds of the Piceance Basin in Colorado, was drilled by the Bureau in 1977. This pioneer shaft, which is 2,371 feet deep, will provide the Bureau and other Federal agencies with geologic, hydrologic, and environmental information for use in forecasting the environmental effects of future deep-shale mines.
- A monitoring network has been established at a site in the Powder River Basin to permit study of the direction and rate of flow, water quality, and aquifer characteristics of shallow groundwater systems in that area. Data currently collected are being used to develop a regional and local computer model of the effects of surface mining.
- A report on environmentally acceptable water management methods for oil shale development, entitled "Water Management in Oil Shale Mining," has been published. The results of this study will provide government planners and the mining community with reliable guidelines for managing water resources associated with oil shale mining.
- A recent Bureau study has addressed the problems of surface mining on the North Slope of Alaska. The effort considered the quantity and quality of the North Slope deposits and the economic, technical, and environmental constraints of the mining systems suggested. The effect of mining operations on the delicate permafrost environment received particular consideration.

ENVIRONMENTAL CONTROL TECHNOLOGY

Research under the Environmental Control Technology subactivity seeks to analyze and define the full spectrum of environmental problems that arise during the active mining process and to develop methods, equipment, and associated technologies to minimize these impacts. Principal environmental impacts which receive primary attention are the disposal of waste, interim handling of overburden, subsidence, hydrologic disturbance, and noise, vibration, and dust associated with the mining process.

Major products are developed to facilitate meeting environmental goals at reduced costs through improved technology, and the technological base for more rigorous standards and more economical compliance is developed.

Fiscal year 1978 funding for this portion of the program is as shown below:

Environmental Control Technology FY 1978 Funding

	(Dollar amounts in thousands)
Mine Waste Handling	$1,309
Surface and Subsidence Effects	1,757
Noise, Vibration, Water and other Mine Source Impacts	506
Total	$3,572

Mine Waste Handling

Technology is being examined for effective, economical seepage control for tailings dams, and a methodology will be developed for evaluating consequences of liquefaction type failures. Underground waste disposal systems and methods are being studied to aid in preventing subsidence in coal and oil shale areas, reduce land requirements for surface disposal, and increase the percentage of recoverable resources. The physical-property data base for decision-making on environmental problems of oil shale mining is being completed and design work is beginning on a cost effective underground waste disposal system and a method of backfilling for the modified *in-situ* oil shale process.

Surface and Subsidence Effects

Four major subsidence program elements are being carried out: prediction, control, prevention, and subsidence damage abatement. The Bureau develops and tests methods of predicting the effects of changes in the mining operations on the overburden deformations and the associated environmental damage. A data base will be established containing subsidence-related data collected from a broad spectrum of mining operations. Empirical formulas are being developed to provide a short-range predictive capability that is applicable to mining operations where conditions are relatively constant and subsidence models will be developed that are applicable over a wide range of geologic and mining conditions to provide a more general predictive capability.

Guidelines will be developed, based on state-of-the-art technology, for mining practices that control subsidence within prescribed levels. Finally, new mining techniques--such as the use of variable air pressure supports--are being evaluated for possible use in controlling subsidence without unduly affecting resources recovery or productivity.

Noise, Vibrations, Water and Other Mine Source Impacts

Work is being conducted to minimize the pollution of surface and groundwaters while mining and to introduce new mining and processing methods that optimize conservation of water resources. Improved techniques are being studied and will be demonstrated for control of pollution caused by sediment from coal mine haulage roads. Investigations are being conducted to define more clearly the mechanisms contributing to mining-induced surface and groundwater pollution and to gain a better understanding of the interrelationships among different pollutant factors and their relative severity.

Air quality research is planned to characterize the source emissions for a range of mining conditions and to ascertain the size distribution, concentration, and composition of emitted dusts. Problem areas will then be ranked and research priorities assigned. As part of its current research, the Bureau will establish maximum criteria for air blast and ground vibration due to mine blasting. Knowledge of these levels helps minimize or prevent structural damage associated with blasting operations.

Some recent work of significance includes:

. A Bureau investigation has provided state and local planners with improved information on locations where subsidence has occurred or has a high potential to occur in the future. This information may help minimize subsidence-induced damage to existing buildings and prevent damage that might occur to future structures envisioned for the area.

. The physical and chemical properties of spent shale from the Paraho Oil Shale Project were analyzed in laboratory and field tests and described in a recently published report entitled "Disposal of Retorted Oil Shale from the Paraho Oil Shale Project."

. Ground vibration and airblast response and damage measurements were made in several metropolitan areas throughout the country. Current measurement methods have been evaluated and new measurement techniques are being developed. Results from these and other studies will be utilized in determination of new criteria for blasting.

MINED LAND RECLAMATION TECHNOLOGY

The Mined Land Reclamation Technology research activity seeks to improve the technology associated with reclamation so that the highest possible benefits may be obtained from post-mining land use. Involved are the development of methods for determining best ultimate uses, methods to achieve these conditions, and technologies to prevent environmental impacts in the post-mining phase. These projects are aimed at producing results that can be applied by mine operators for more cost effective compliance with regulations and for obtaining the best ultimate land use.

Fiscal Year 1978 funding for this portion of the program is as shown below:

Mined Land Reclamation Technology FY 1978 Funding

(Dollars amounts in thousands)

Surface Stabilization	$2,273
Land Use	1,643
Total	$3,916

Surface Stabilization

Problems associated with the stability of materials disturbed by past mining are studied to improve existing stabilization techniques or devise new techniques so that stability can be predicted, if not assured. In the shorter term, the problems associated with stabilization of new surface spoil materials are examined and methods are sought to reduce erosional processes and their related adverse impact on air and water quality.

Land Use

Both the societal and environmental aspects of post-mining use are encompassed in the Bureau's research. Detailed examination provides the mechanism for finding the most beneficial post-mining land use consistent with the capabilities and productivity potential of the land and the needs of surrounding areas. Possible residual adverse effects of mining activities such as toxic drainage or physical safety of the area are examined and techniques are devised to minimize or eliminate these problems.

Typical recent outputs from this research subprogram include:

. A contract study to the Colorado School of Mines under which field investigations have been conducted to determine topsoil requirements for revegetation of mined lands in the Northern Great Plains states. These studies indicate that topsoil and spoil variability between mine sites in this area make optimum topsoil depths for revegetation site specific.

. A Bureau study being done by the University of Arizona has determined that water harvesting methods, which collect rainwater for subsequent use can be applied to reduce erosion and return mined land to valuable condition. The project is now developing a computer model for use in developing optimal treatments that can minimize surface runoff in reclaimed areas, and for predicting the probable effect of mining and reclamation on the hydrology of an area.

An ongoing study with Project Reclamation at the University of North Dakota, to provide ecologically comprehensive information on the interrelationships of a number of environmental variables with the growth of native and introduced species. Their field, growth chamber and laboratory studies concentrate on the effects of topsoil and spoil physico-chemical properties on the establishment, productivity and succession of seeded and naturally revegetated plant communities.

PROGRAM IMPLEMENTATION

The Mining Environmental Research program, as with all the Bureau mining research activities, is a coordinated in-house and contracted research effort. The Bureau's internal research capability resides in four research centers located in Pittsburgh, Denver, Minneapolis and Spokane. Each center has some participation in the entire spectrum of research activities, i.e. health and safety, mining technology, and the environment. This encourages the development of a broad based capability and a sensitivity to regional variations.

For the Mining Environmental Research Program about 25% of the available funds are used for support of in-house work, with the remainder being spent on contracts, grants, and cost sharing agreements. This is believed to be a manageable ratio which permits the utilization of expert capability in all sectors while at the same time retaining a sizable in-house research program which provides for the development and maintenance of technical competence. Without this internal technical expertise, the quality of work from the contracted portion of the program would suffer considerably.

The Mining Environmental Research program is best characterized as applied research. It recognizes that minerals extraction must occur with a minimum impact on the environment but also that extraction must occur at reasonable cost. The creation of technologies which are evolutionary and can be applied today, and innovative for tomorrow's needs, is designed to satisfy both of these requirements. The users of the program results are - mining companies, regulatory agencies, and environmental groups, all of which the Bureau has worked cooperatively with for many years. It is expected that the continuing interaction between the Bureau's health and safety research program and the Mining Safety and Health Administration (MSHA) will typify the roles that will evolve between the Bureau and the Office of Surface Mining (OSM). We expect that OSM will provide input to our program in terms of needs definition and that the Bureau will provide a technologic basis for OSM's regulatory action.

Since its inception, the Bureau has worked closely with the mining industry. We currently have numerous cooperative agreements, cost sharing arrangements, and in-mine demonstrations, covering a wide spectrum of technology and mining situations.

Interaction between the Bureau and other agencies engaged in environmental research recognizes that extensive and valuable work is being done elsewhere that complements the projects we are engaged in. The Bureau's strength is in mining and its allied technologies. In order to be effective in the realm of correcting and preventing environmental problems it is necessary to understand and interface with a number of technical areas not normally considered as part of mining. The Bureau acknowledges that it does not possess all of the skills necessary for total problem solution and therefore has not oriented its program towards generic environmental research. The program does, however encompass the full range of mining induced environmental problems and, through proper interfacing with all other resource groups, these problems will be solved.

ASSESSING THE EFFECTS OF ALTERNATIVE
PUBLIC POLICIES ON WESTERN COAL DEVELOPMENT

Joseph R. Barse and John W. Green*

INTRODUCTION

The future of U.S. coal development is still very uncertain, despite many reappraisals of our energy situation in the years since the 1973 Middle East oil embargo. Western coal resources could be developed in a number of different patterns, depending partly on future economic demand for coal, and partly on how public policies are shaped today and in the next few years.

Alternative futures for the extraction and use of Western coal are being investigated systematically by the Economics, Statistics, and Cooperatives Service (ESCS) under the project "Economic Consequences of Coal and Oil Shale Development" (Schaub et al., 1976, Barse and Green 1977). This multi-year project is proceeding in cooperation with the U.S. Environmental Protection Agency (EPA), as part of EPA's Interagency Energy/Environment R and D Program. To assess effects of alternative policies, an interregional analytical system (linear program) is being constructed in ESCS. This system will be completed by 1980 and will cover all coal regions of the U.S. Economic tradeoffs, attributable to alternative policies among these regions can then be evaluated. As of Spring 1978, geographical coverage of coal supply origins is limited to areas within North Dakota, South Dakota, Montana, and Wyoming [the Northern Great Plains (NGP) coal supply region] and within Colorado, Utah, New Mexico and Arizona [the Rocky Mountain (RM) coal supply region]. These NGP and RM regions together are defined as the Western coal supply region.

Limiting coverage to Western coal supply is an interim arrangement only until coal supply regions of other parts of the nation can be added to help achieve nationwide supply-demand coverage. The analytical system for the NGP and RM coal supply regions is a proto-type for the nationwide system, which will also include coal supply regions of Midwestern, Appalachian, Gulf, and Pacific States. However, the analysis of demand for Western coal which is built into the spring 1978 version of the linear program is not limited to the West, but includes demand for this coal from other parts of the country also. Both the Western and non-Western demand for Western coal--some of which is very low in sulfur content--derives from a mixture of economic and public policy factors such as regulations to help abate air pollution.

Projecting where and to what extent coal activity takes place under alternative demand patterns and alternative policy assumptions is a prerequisite to analyzing impacts on rural

*Natural Resource Economics Division, Economics, Statistics, and Cooperatives Service, USDA, Washington, D.C. 20250.

people and communities, regional economies, agriculture, land, water, or air. For example, given any projected configuration of coal activity, other methodologies being developed in ESCS under this project (Bender and Temple 1977) can be applied to estimate community impacts and flows of State revenues from taxation of mining.

INTERREGIONAL COAL ANALYSIS

Supply Regions and Areas

The coal supply region of the NGP States is defined, for this analysis, as all those NGP counties containing strippable coal reserves of at least 10 million tons each. NGP deep mineable reserves were not considered in order to simplify the analysis; almost no deep mining now takes place in these States. As a result, 47 NGP counties are included, together comprising 31 percent of the total land area of the four NGP States. However, only 3 percent of the surface area of this 47-county coal supply region actually overlies strippable coal reserves. Therefore, the concept of "coal supply region" should be thought of as a combined natural resource-agricultural-economic-demographic-governmental region which may be affected by coal development. Such a regional concept can only be delineated in some arbitrary fashion; using county boundaries has seemed the best compromise, since much data is organized by county.

Of course, various impacts of coal development will be felt outside as well as inside a coal supply region. The broader impacts will have to be analyzed separately. However, this analytical system can help identify many of the subregional geographical impacts because the 47-county coal supply region is subdivided into 13 Coal Production Areas (CPA's). Each CPA consists of a contiguous group of some of these 47 counties; each county is assigned to some CPA, usually based on physical similarities in coal reserves among counties. Although it is not practical in general to disaggregate geographical coverage to the mine site or individual county level, by using the CPA concept of county groupings within a coal supply region the linear program can show relationships between national or regional coal development patterns and relatively local effects upon a certain CPA.

The coal supply region of the RM States encompasses all the counties each containing at least 10 million tons of either deep mineable or strippable reserves. Meeting this definition are 40 RM counties, which thus comprise the RM coal supply region. These counties cover 34 percent of the land area of the four RM States, although only 2 percent of the area of the 40-county region actually overlies deep or strippable reserves. The RM coal supply region is subdivided into 15 CPA's on the same basis as for the NGP.

Mathematical Programming Approach

To analyze total source to end use coal energy systems, a mathematical programming problem has been set up as a linear program. Although a linear program calculates optimal or least-cost solutions to resource allocation problems, we are not attempting to find "the" optimum pattern of coal development. Rather, as remarked above, we seek to compare many alternative future patterns. The comparisons should be done under consistent ground rules that the solution is always least-cost. In effect, the optimizing model specifies that the economy is as efficient as possible in carrying out whatever set of policies is being analyzed.

Mathematical programming deals with conditions under which a set of resources in limited supply, such as materials, labor, and machines, is to be utilized to produce a given quantity or variety of products. In the coal system problem, mathematical formulations can efficiently assess how varied assumptions about the above factors can affect mining location. Local, state, and federal policies designed to regulate the provision of coal energy can be evaluated to assess their impact on the spatial location of mining and conversion facilities. Mathematical formulation allows for additional restrictions to be placed on the problem. These additional conditions may be specific or follow broad categories such as the total amount of each input available or the minimum quantity of each product desired. From all the possible allocations of scarce resources, mathematical programming allows identification of those combinations which maximize or minimize a quantifiable function such as cost or profit.

Linear programming deals with problems in which all relationships between the variables may be cast as linear functions. Specifically, a number of constraints in the form of linear inequalities are to be solved while maximizing or minimizing a linear combination of these variables. The objective of our problem is to minimize the cost of meeting coal energy demand while insuring that all constraints are satisfied. The objective function will reflect the relationship between the production levels of different coal regions and their respective prices. To solve the problem, a combination of production levels must be found in the feasible solution set that results in the smallest value of the objective function.

Analytical Concepts

The coal energy systems of the United States may be described by a number of variables, each of which may be linked to the others through a set of linear inequalities. For the model described below, the objective function is to minimize the cost of meeting electricity demands. All other equations that are required to define the structure of the energy system constitute the linear constraint equations.

The linear constraint equations are extremely important. These equations reflect externalities such as social issues, water policies, and reclamation. Given the assumptions of certain scenarios, the constraint equations may be of far greater importance than the objective function. Each variable or activity in the system is assigned a unit cost. The product of the activity level and its unit cost is the total cost for that activity. The sum of total costs for all activities is the objective function to be minimized. The constraint equations are based on mass and energy balances, economic costs, thermal efficiencies, etc. The linear programming energy model is demand driven; that is, electricity demands are met in a manner leading to lowest total cost. If the specified electrical demands cannot be met, the associated scenario is not technically feasible.

Model activities deal with the following general areas:

- production and availability of coal fuels
- transportation of coal by various transportation modes
- conversion of coal from one form into another including synthetic liquids, gas, and electric power

Two types of constraints are present in the model--column constraints and row constraints. Column constraints are activity bounds that force the level of a particular activity to be greater than, less than, or equal to a given value. Row constraints force the sum of a set of activities to be greater than, less than or equal to a defined value. For example, the total amount of coal that can be mined in a region must be less than or equal to the mining capacity of the region. The row constraints in our model may include:

- coal reserve rows. These limit the production of coal in a region to be less than or equal to the reserves of coal in that region.
- coal transhipment capacity rows. These insure that the flow of each coal type between regions is less than or equal to the capacity of the particular transhipment mode.
- SO_2 emission rows. These limit the amount of SO_2 per million btu's that may be released in each region.
- generation capacity rows. These limit the total generation of power from plants to the total capacity of each plant.
- advanced coal conversion process capacity rows. These limit the total generation of electric power by advance processes and the production of coal liquids or gases to the total capacity of such facilities.
- regional water availability rows. These limit the total quantity of water consumed by all coal conversion processes in each region to the amount of water available in each region.
- coal derived electric energy demand rows. These insure that the quantity of electrical energy available in each region is at least equal to the demand for electrical energy in that region.
- nonelectric coal energy demand rows. These insure that the quantity of coal energy available from synthetic sources is at least equal to the demand for that energy in each region.
- accounting rows. These are nonbinding rows that eliminate arithmetic calculations within the report writing programs and provide summaries of variables for a quick overview of model results. For the purposes of our model these accounting rows may include land, labor, accumulative production and transportation, water, pollutants, and reclamation. In addition to the above constraint rows, all conversion facility activities are potentially capacity limited; that is, the levels of these variables may be upperbounded.

Limitations

Model limitations derive from the input data, the systems structure, and the appropriateness of the modeling methodology used. Specific problems arising from the data are of two kinds: (1) the uncertain nature of future "data", particularly that dealing with new energy systems not yet commercially available, and (2) the problems of projecting historic data, however good, to future years. An important aspect of projecting data on future costs is the choice of appropriate rates of inflation. There are several model structure limitations. These include the ability of various electric utilities to switch from gas and oil to coal use, the blending of various coal types, and the mixing of transportation modes to supply coal to various end users.

The most important advantage of the mathematical programming structure is that it allows the model user to formulate rational economic choices based on the best available technical and cost information. Nevertheless, the methodology has at least two important drawbacks. The first is the simplifying assumption that all relationships between the variables are linear. The second is that a linear programming model is never a strictly accurate representation of the economic system with which it deals. It is merely a method of conceptualization that allows the analyst to formalize the basic strategic relationships controlling the phenomena it describes, thereby permitting manipulation of the situation. The purpose of this linear programming model will be to sort through a large number of possible activities to determine the optimal set while insuring that all system constraints are met. If key constraints on the system are omitted, the model is no longer valid.

DATA FOR THE WESTERN STATES ANALYSIS

Data on Electric Power Plants

Since this model is being designed to measure the impact of coal development, and since the major market for coal is the electric utility industry, a reasonable beginning point for assessing the demand for Western coal is to inventory all electric utility power plants which burn coal to generate electricity. There are 413 power plants in the United States which burn coal to generate some or all of their electricity (Table 1). These coal-burning plants contributed 38 percent of the total generation capacity in the United States in 1975. Because of the difficulty in obtaining information for individual power plants, we are analyzing only those coal-fired plants with a nameplate capacity[1] of 100 megawatts (MW) or greater. As can be seen from Table 1, this eliminates 103 small plants, but only two percent of the total coal-fired nameplate generating capacity in the United States.

Table 1. U.S. Power Plant Statistics, 1975[a].

Total number of power plants	2,709
Total MW capacity	528,647
Total number of power plants using coal	413
MW capacity of power plants using coal	201,383
Percent of MW capacity from coal fired plants	38
Percent of power plants using coal	15
Coal fired power plants < 100 MW	103
MW capacity of power plants < 100 MW	4,010
Percent MW capacity from coal fired plants < 100 MW	1.99
Percent of coal fired power plants < 100 MW	25

[a]Includes 50 States and Puerto Rico

Source: Trends in Power Plant Capacity and Utilization Inventory of the Power Plants in the U.S. Federal Energy Administration, 1976.

[1]Nameplate capacity is the generation capacity which each power plant is designed and built to produce. Operating conditions may prevent a plant from producing at nameplate capacity. For example, the retrofitting of SO_2 scrubbers lowers the operating efficiency of a power plant, thus decreasing its ability to attain its nameplate production capacity.

The smaller plants are usually the older, less efficient ones which are likely to be retired as soon as larger, more efficient plants can be built. Recent trends in new generating capacity have been towards larger plants. There are 291 power plants which will be included in the interregional coal analysis model, all greater than or equal to 100 megawatts in name-plate generating capacity. These include all plants supplied by Western coal as well as all other coal-fired power plants in the U.S.

Data on Electricity Demand and Derived Demand for Coal

Demand for electric power is described or estimated in terms of individual utility service areas. Descriptions or estimates of the relative weight of coal-fired vs. nuclear, oil-or-gas-fired power are also being made. These estimates are the basis for an additional calculation of the coal demanded to meet the observed or projected electricity output of the coal-using plants in the service area.

About 90 percent of all the coal-fired plants being studied tend to produce mainly for one service area, although there are, of course, many interties in the electricity transmission grid. However, about 10 percent of the coal-fired plants are owned jointly by more than one electric utility and may be presumed to supply some power to each utility. As a simplifying and admittedly arbitrary assumption, the analytical system allocates the power output of jointly-owned coal-fired plants to each of the owning utilities according to the ownership share of each utility in the plant. Data on plant ownership has been collected in order to make the allocation of power output.

Data Linking Power Plants and Western Coal

Data showing which power plants received Western coal in 1975, how much coal, its physical properties, CPA origin, and transportation links are in computer file. Thus, we can identify those Coal Producing Areas which mined coal for use by each power plant. Therefore, for the interregional linear programming model, we have the Coal Producing Area which supplies the coal, a transportation link from the CPA to the individual power plant, and the individual power plant identification. For example, we can code the Coal Producing Area (MNGSAZ01), the transportation link (AZ019014), and the power plant (CEG9014). In addition, we can calculate the proportion of each plant's output supplied by each transportation link. This number is in the form of a coal input to electricity output ratio, (million btu's per million kilowatt-hours).

ENERGY CONVERSION AND TRANSPORTATION RELATIONSHIPS

These relationships are expressed as coefficients for (1) Western mining activities, (2) coal transportation, and (3) electrical generation activities. Coefficients describing conversion values for coal produced were obtained from the Bureau of Mines estimates of NGP and RM coal reserves (Hamilton 1975). Since strip mining in the West recovers approximately 90 percent of the coal in mined seams, the coefficient describing depletion from reserves becomes 1.1111. Since underground mining in the Western states recovers approximately 50 percent of the coal, the coefficient describing depletion of resources for underground mining becomes 2.000. Production is described in both thousands of tons and in millions of btu's.

The coefficient describing the entry into the mining transportation activity is also described in btu's. This is done because costs for transporting coal are expressed in dollars per million btu's for shipment from CPA to power plant. Each transportation activity has a cost, an input from the mining transfer row, an output to the power plant transfer row, and a coefficient to account for the capacity of the movement in thousands of tons. Therefore, the basic function of these transportation activities is to transport one million btu's of coal at a cost.

The movement volume of the transportation activity is accumulated because of future limitations which may be imposed on specific transportation links. The transfer of coal through these transportation activities is assumed to be 99 percent efficient. Therefore, the input coefficient is 1.000 while the output coefficient is 0.9900. Transportation costs for certain mine mouth power plants are zero.

Each electrical generation activity receives coal from each of its CPA suppliers and converts those btu's of coal input to kilowatt hours of electricity output. This is accomplished at a cost expressed in dollars per million kilowatt hours of electrical production. The amount of electricity produced is accumulated and the capacity of the electrical generation plant is constrained. Each generation plant produces electricity which meets a specific demand, as explained above.

In reality, coal-fired generating plants are used almost entirely to meet base and intermediate load electricity demand. Therefore, the electrical demand requirement which drives the interim linear programming model does not yet fully reflect the demand designed to be met by coal-fired plants. This total electrical demand will be reduced in the future to reflect the portion of it intended to be met by coal-fired plants. This will be done by analyzing the utilization factors for coal-fired power plants. These portions for each power plant will be modified over time depending upon the age of the power plant and the decline in the utilization factor assumed for each utility system.

DEVELOPMENT SCENARIOS

Data Needs

Planned additions to coal-fired electrical generation capacity are reported publicly in several sources. (For example, FPC 1977). If we are interested in a 1985 scenario, we could incorporate into the model all or some of the proposed additions to electrical generation capacity from 1976 through 1985 to reflect one kind of demand projection. Econometric electricity demand projections will also be employed. In those cases where captive reserves[2] will supply a power plant or where supply contracts have been signed, we will place those linkages into the solution by a program constraint. In the cases where new power plants have not determined their supplier, we will allow several suppliers to be eligible based on characteristics of the coal needed. Other pertinent utility information

---

[2]The term "captive reserves" describes the vertically integrated situation where the utility system controlling the power plant also owns or controls the coal supply source (the mine). The utility may also own the rolling stock (usually railroad cars) in which the coal is transported.

which may be needed for scenario development deals with power plants which may be ordered to burn coal.

Another future market for coal may be synthetic fuel plants. Proposed additions to coal derived synthetic fuel capacity have been compiled. In most cases the coal source is not known. Based on the situation existing at the time of scenario development, these proposed plants may or may not be included in each specific scenario analyzed by the model. Yet another future market for coal is in industry. Some plants which presently exist may be induced or ordered to switch to coal. Or new industrial plants may be built with coal-fired capability. A list of industries which apparently will be prohibited from burning fuels other than coal as of May 1977 has been compiled also.

Key Scenarios

We shall probably be using at least the following scenarios:

(1) Examine the effects of Federal, State and local energy development policies on the location of coal mining and the resulting impacts on rural resource use. Policies may include Federal air pollution control regulations such as sulfur dioxide emissions standards, Federal incentives toward coal development, State mining and tax policies, and State and Federal mining and land reclamation laws. Some of these may be expressed in coal demand patterns and constraints, others in mining activity constraints.

(2) Examine the effects of Federal, State and local resource use policies on the location of coal mining and the resulting impacts on rural resource use. Policies may include State water resource regulations, mine siting requirements of States, and Federal land use programs. These can be expressed as mining activity constraints in certain CPA's.

(3) Examine the effects of alternative locations of coal processing facilities on the location of coal mining.

(4) Examine shifts in regional coal development and resource use resulting from changes in consumer demand. These changes in demand may be the result of coal and other fuel price changes, consumer preferences, and industrial production levels.

STATUS OF ANALYSIS AND REPORTING OF RESULTS

During 1977 and early 1978, we have completed the data base for specific mines and CPA's in the West and for power plants nationwide, existing and planned through 1985. As of early Spring 1978, the initial run of the Western States model has been completed. The model is now operational and is being used to analyze Western coal development. Results of the initial analysis will soon be available and will be reported separately.

REFERENCES

Barse, J.R. and J.W. Green. 1977. Status of an integrated assessment of coal development. pp. 263-266, In Energy/Environment II. Proc. Second National Conf. on the

Interagency R and D Program. Rpt. No. EPA 600/9-77-012, U.S. EPA, Washington, D C, 563 p.

Bender, L.D. and G.S. Temple. 1977. Integrated systems simulation of local community impacts in the Northern Great Plains. pp. 267-273, In Energy/Environment II. Proc. Second National Conf. on the Interagency R and D Program. Rpt. No. EPA 600/9-77-012, U.S. EPA, Washington. D C, 563 p.

Federal Power Commission (FPC). 1977. Bureau of Power. Status of Coal Supply Contracts for New Electric Generating Units 1976-1985. Washington, D.C. (The FPC has been renamed the Federal Energy Regulatory Commission and is now part of the Department of Energy.)

Hamilton, P.A., D.H. White, Jr. and T.K. Matson. 1975. The Reserve Base of U.S. Coals by Sulfur Content (In Two Parts), 2. The Western States. U.S.D.I., Bureau of Mines, Info. Circ. 8693, Washington, D C. 322 p.

Schaub, J.R., J.R. Barse and L.D. Bender. 1976. Research program on the economic and social consequences of coal and oil shale development. pp. 334-336, In Health, Environmental Effects, and Control Technology of Energy Use. Proc. of the First National Conf. on the Interagency R and D Program. U.S. Environmental Protection Agency, Washington, D C, 340 p.

ENVIRONMENTAL MEDIATION: BRIDGING
THE GAP BETWEEN ENERGY NEEDS AND ECOSYSTEM

John Busterud*

As one who has recently concluded nearly five years of service in the Council on Environmental Quality (CEQ) I am pleased to see the emphasis on environmental issues in preparing the agenda for this Conference. Perhaps our country would have mined much more coal by this time had we always shown a similar sensitivity to such problems.

Many of the participants here have addressed substantive issues of coal development, and indeed it was such substantive issues that were of particular concern to CEQ. At the same time, in our emphasis upon substance we have tended to overlook the importance of working out more effective methods of resolving the inevitable environmental disputes that have arisen--and will continue to attract our attention.

It was this imbalance between procedure and substance in dealing with environmental issues that caused me to shift my interest from substantive environmental needs to the problem of developing more effective processes for resolving such issues and to organize RESOLVE, a new national Center for Environmental Conflict Resolution. In this paper I will dwell principally upon environmental mediation and related forms of what lawyers call consensual dispute resolution, and the relationship between this subject and the other issues that concern this conference. Mediation can be a tool in many different kinds of environmental conflict, but here I will discuss principally its use in coal and other energy-related disputes.

As industry continues its search for adequate reserves of energy to meet our country's needs, one might safely predict that environmentalists will likewise continue their fight against such efforts when it appears to them that the development of those resources would impose damage upon ecosystems or have other adverse impacts on the human environment. This process of "protracted warfare" has become nearly as predictable as the rising and the setting of the sun--just as have the endless legislative, regulatory and legal battles which have accompanied the enactment of new energy and environmental laws and the promulgation of their regulations.

But while the wars continue to be fought, there is a growing desire on both sides to minimize the "bloodshed," and by that I mean the costs, the delays, the personal and public acrimony which persist far beyond the battle of the moment. Unfortunately, prolonged court suits often increase polarization, making it more difficult to resolve the next conflict. The most damaging result is that the fundamental, longer-term issues of energy development and environmental protection are seldom addressed, and it is these that continue to fester

*RESOLVE: Center for Environmental Conflict Resolution, 525 University Avenue, Suite 1205, Palo Alto, CA 94301.

until the next skirmish breaks out.

Environmental mediation, and other related techniques, offer an alternative to protracted litigation and its many repercussions. By mediation, I refer to a process of consensual dispute settlement in which the parties seek to resolve their differences with the aid of a neutral mediator. The process is wholly voluntary and the mediator is unable to impose settlements on the parties. Yet his role is a critical one, and adds a third dimension to the negotiations. A good mediator can focus discussions, prevent acrimony and often suggest imaginative proposals that none of the parties to the controversy thought of or would be willing to suggest.

Other conflict resolution techniques include: joint planning and conciliation at the early stages of a project, task force problem-solving and policy formulation, mutual fact-finding and conflict assessment, and combinations of the above. Techniques which anticipate and avoid conflict are equally as important, if not more so, than those which resolve conflict that already exists.

There are several impressive examples of how environmental conflict resolution has been put to practice, but thus far they represent isolated experiments with little national focus. RESOLVE, the organization I now head, was founded in recognition of the urgent need to develop better procedures and new institutions for resolving critically important national and regional issues involving energy, land use, the environment and socio-economic progress. We plan to serve as a clearing house for emerging consensual dispute settlement techniques and to develop both cadres of skilled mediators and facilitators and a list of conflicts which the parties are willing to submit to new conflict resolution processes.

RESOLVE's Board of Directors consists not of theoretical academicians but of national leaders who have "been there and back" in the environment-land use-energy confrontation. Russell Train, former Administrator of the U.S. Environmental Protection Agency (EPA) and now President of the World Wildlife Fund, is our Chairman. Other directors include people like Michael McCloskey, Executive Director of the Sierra Club; William Ruckelshaus, former E.P.A. Administrator and Deputy Attorney General; Elvis Stahr, head of the National Audubon Society; Louis Austin, Chairman of Texas Utilities; and Lloyd McBride, President of the United Steelworkers Union. All of us want to make an important contribution toward better dialogue in environmental disputes.

The most intense environmental disputes arise as a result of energy development issues. Yet energy is a necessary ingredient in our society and in no other circumstance is there greater need for effective conflict resolution, dealing both with site-specific controversies and more generic issues. While coal development has been accepted by environmentalists as a substitute for nuclear power, many environmental issues need to be dealt with in mining, processing, transporting and burning coal. The new surface mining legislation provides a charter for protecting the environment in the first stage of this process, while the Clean Air Act limits emissions in the use of the product. There will be many opportunities, both in the development of regulations and their subsequent application, to apply newly emerging consensual dispute settlement techniques to the resolution of issues.

There are few examples where environmental conflict resolution has been used successfully in energy-related disputes--particularly in non-site-specific ones--but one in particular deserves mention: the National Coal Policy Project. This ambitious effort involved nearly 100 people and 10,000 man-days over a two-year period. It represented an attempt to get environmentalists and industry to agree on coal production issues removed from the usual battleground of the legislatures and the courts.

The Project was initiated by Gerald Decker, Corporate Energy Manager for Dow Chemical, and subsequently chaired by Decker and Larry Moss, former President of the

Sierra Club. Mutual fact-finding and policy formulation was conducted by five task forces under the "rule of reason," defined in a book of that name by Milton Wessel, corporate attorney and Professor of Law at New York University. Wessel argues, as do those of us in the business of environmental conflict resolution, that normal litigation procedures, with their inherent delays and win-lose tactics, are often inappropriate in environmental cases dominated by complex cost/benefit and impact assessment issues. The "rule of reason" forbids opponents from withholding data, employing deceitful tactics, expounding dogmatism, impugning others' motives, and so on.

There appear to be two significant sets of outcomes from the Coal Policy Project. The first includes the substantive agreements themselves, especially important to those operating in the energy field. Other papers will most certainly discuss their content. The second significant outcome represents the processes used to reach the agreements, and these are of particular interest to those of us in the environmental conflict resolution field. It is hoped that these processes will be applicable to other, non-site-specific, energy issues needing resolution. The Coal Project was characterized by methods including: mutual planning sessions; joint fact-finding and data collection efforts; the use of topical task forces where joint study and negotiations took place; extensive field trips to investigate key coal production issues; and plenary sessions to oversee the total Project and to approve task force agreements. The Project functioned with two "caucuses," one industry-oriented and the other consisting of environmentalists.

The philosophy behind this total process was a simple one: "Let the other guy walk around in my shoes a little, while I walk around in his, and maybe we can agree on some things after all." This may not sound particularly profound, but it is revolutionary. The idea that environmental and energy industry representatives can work together within a consensual framework is a bold concept. Michael McCloskey, Executive Director of the Sierra Club and a Coal Project participant, has made several comments on such a possibility. First, he points out that a crucial value of mutual negotiations is mutual education:

> We're able to massage details until we've worked them out. We may still disagree on a few big points, but at least we're not doing violence to each other simply by the accident of not understanding each other's point.

Finally, he thinks that the type of process used by the Coal Policy Project should be extended to other similar disputes:

> I am now persuaded that in many cases the possibilities for resolving policy issues are better in this kind of setting than they are in public legislative bodies. There's not the same overlay of extraneous issues, the opportunities for public advancement, the competition for attention. When a topic gets that extra political twist on it, it often gets simplified and horribly mangled. Confrontation politics leads to sweeping generalizations rather than fine distinctions and both sides conceal their ultimate aims.

I have dwelt a good deal on the National Coal Policy Project because I think there is much to learn from it for other environmental conflict resolution efforts. Numerous disputes concerning "energy v. the ecosystem" loom on the horizon, and many, like the Coal Policy Project, relate to broad policy issues rather than to site-specific conflicts. Let me mention three or four other examples.

The first two involve oil and gas production in the arctic regions. Just recently an extremely thorough inquiry was conducted in Canada to investigate the issues and possible impact of building a northern natural gas pipeline through the MacKenzie Valley to markets in southern Canada and the U.S. The inquiry itself, while not aimed at mutual fact-finding or at mutual conflict resolution, did employ some processes which might be adaptable to a dispute settlement framework. The use of preliminary and overview hearings prior to the official inquiry; the coupling of formal, technical hearings with community hearings; the requirement for free information exchange and disclosure of sources; the availability of funding to citizen groups to enable their meaningful participation; the coverage of hearings by radio and television--some or all of these procedures might be adapted for use in a conflict resolution arena. Or, perhaps of greater importance is the fact that inquiry-type proceedings may establish a proper foundation for a follow-up dispute settlement project. At the same time, policymakers would have to exercise care that an inquiry of this type not actually increase polarization to the point where forward-looking dispute settlement proceedings would become impossible.

The second arctic energy issue to which I alluded concerns the total effect of oil and gas development in the circumpolar region of Alaska, Canada and Greenland and on the native Inuit, or Eskimo, populations. When oil was discovered in the North Slope of Alaska, the Inuit peoples began challenging the state and federal government over ownership of their land and its resources. Shortly thereafter the North Slope Borough home-rule government was formed to control energy development in the Eskimos' backyard and to protect the traditional way of life. The Borough has since become the prime mover in constructively challenging all major oil and gas operations in the circumpolar region. It initiated an Arctic Coastal Zone Management Program and in June 1977 convened the first Inuit Circumpolar Conference.

Within the last year or so, the Borough has proposed a dialogue between the circumpolar peoples and the five U.S.-based transnational corporations holding the largest amount of land under lease or permit above the Arctic Circle in Alaska, Greenland and Canada. The goal of the dialogue is to define and agree upon the terms of partnership between private enterprise and the people in the development of public land in the circumpolar region. It would work toward more expeditious and less costly energy resource development while minimizing disruption of the lives of the people and their environment.

Here again is a unique opportunity for environmental conflict resolution. Like the National Coal Policy Project, it would require techniques appropriate to resolving complex policy issues. In fact, could not many of the Coal Project procedures be applied here? Joint task forces with native and industry representation could be set up to collect information and formulate policy recommendations, for example, in the areas of land claims; current technology and environmental security; local economic development; community relations and cultural preservation; and so forth. On-site field trips would also be extremely useful. Plenary sessions could formalize recommendations and develop legislative proposals. Mediation might be used as a follow-up process in the cases where preliminary agreement could not be reached.

Other energy policy issues, although quite different from the ones described above, might profit from consensual dispute settlement processes. The Department of Energy and, ultimately, the Nuclear Regulatory Commission have the responsibility for developing appropriate criteria for locating nuclear waste disposal sites and then actually approving one or more specific sites. The development of location criteria is yet another example of a policy issue certain to arouse lively debate and disagreement. A dialogue among government experts, the environmentalists, industry and other identified groups over the question of nuclear waste management could be organized as a consensual fact-finding, problem-solving effort leading to joint recommendations where feasible.

A similar approach could be employed in the case of disputes between electrical power agencies, environmental leaders and other consumers over such factors as energy allocation formulas, load determination, rates and conservation policies.

Up to this point I have been alluding to conflict resolution techniques most appropriate to non-site-specific energy disputes. More often than not, however, energy disputes are "site-specific." Finding sites for conventional and nonconventional energy plants, converting individual plants from oil to coal, locating nuclear waste disposal sites, leasing lands on the Outer Continental Shelf, restoring areas developed for strip mining, all of these are potential subjects for conflict resolution methods appropriate to site-specific disputes. O.C.S. legislation, for example, involves dozens of new sets of regulations which provide nearly an unlimited number of opportunities for litigation. Responsible government might well give consideration to building alternative conflict resolution processes into tract selection procedures and other aspects of the offshore development program.

Mediation, for example, could be particularly appropriate in these cases, since the issues are normally clear, and opposing viewpoints well defined, if not solidified. For mediation to be employed, there should be some relative balance of power among the parties and they should share both a commitment to negotiate and a willingness to compromise. The environmental situation should be one where mitigation or implementation measures are both available and feasible.

One might think from my remarks thus far that environmental conflict resolution processes will work only in the context of newly created institutions. That is not necessarily the case. There is much that can be done within existing institutions and processes to improve dispute resolution techniques. Much of the current emphasis on the National Environmental Policy Act and citizen participation in decision-making reflect this possibility. Legislatures, regulatory agencies and courts should all engage in an intensive self-examination in an effort to incorporate alternate conflict resolution systems into their decision-making processes. RESOLVE will be looking at this question and studying the feasibility of new approaches.

Agencies already appear to be moving in this direction. E.P.A., encouraged by the provisions of the Administrative Procedure Act, is planning to rely on "panels of decision-makers" in analyzing issues in initial licensing cases. Other agencies looking at such possibilities include C.E.Q. and the Geological Survey; the Department of Energy and the Nuclear Regulatory Commission; and the Forest Service, within the Department of Agriculture. The usefulness of these newly emerging dispute settlement techniques goes well beyond public institutions, however. Often the principal actors in environmental conflicts are in the private sector. Take, for instance, issues arising between competing issues of coal-rich lands, the forests or the coastal zone.

Much remains to be learned before environmental mediation will play a major role in resolving disputes. We at RESOLVE hope to speed up that learning curve and to assist in providing new remedies for environmentalists, industry, labor and government alike as they wrestle with increasingly complex environmental problems in the years ahead. We hope you will ask yourselves as you face such issues: Could mediation help us here? Or some other new method of dispute resolution? If you think they could, then we at RESOLVE, and a growing number of other mediation centers, stand ready to assist you.

OPENCAST COAL MINING
AND THE ENVIRONMENT IN THE UNITED KINGDOM

G.F. Lindley*

INTRODUCTION

Although coal is known to have been recovered from surface workings in Roman times, opencast coal mining as we practice it today only began in earnest in the early days of the last war in 1941 to meet the urgent need for fuel. Over the intervening years, output fluctuated between a peak production of 13.815 million tons saleable in 1958 and the lowest production of 6.213 million tons saleable in 1970.

In 1973, the era of cheap oil came to an end. The result was an agreement between the government, the National Coal Board, and the mining unions which was published as Plan for Coal in 1974. Plan for Coal committed the government and the Board to expanding the size of the coal industry. At that time, opencast coal was being produced at a rate of 10 million tons saleable per annum. During the year ending 25th March, 1978, the Opencast Executive produced 13.315 million tons saleable. Production has been rising steadily every year since 1974 towards a target set by Plan for Coal of 15 million tons per annum. We plan to achieve that target by the mid-1980's.

This increased production not only helps the Board to maximize output but also provides additional supplies of special coals which cannot be supplied from deep-mine sources at present. The Executive produces half of all the anthracite used in the country and substantial tonnages of coking coals. In addition, particular coals from opencast sites assist in making certain deep-mine outputs acceptable to the market and in this way ensure the continuing viability of deep-mine sources of supply.

Opencast profits have also made an important contribution to the Board's finances. In 1976/77, the Opencast Executive share of the Board's overall operating profit on mining operations was £65.4 million out of a total of £84.4 million.

For these reasons - tonnage, coal quality and financial contribution - opencast coal has an essential role to play in the continuing importance and prosperity of the National Coal Board and the support now being given to the Executive is in sharp contrast to the fluctuating pattern of demand and output experienced over the last 20 years. The Executive consists of a Chairman who is also a member of the National Board, a Managing Director, and two other Directors, who are responsible for the day-to-day running of the industry. Five separate Regions, each under a Regional Director, manage operations in the coalfields. At the present time the Executive operates 70 sites.

*National Coal Board, Opencast Executive, Lichfield Lane, Berry Hill, Mansfield, Notts., England NG18 4RG.

PLANNING

Nationalization of opencast coal mining took place in 1952, five years later than deep-mines, and until 1958 opencast operations were still carried out under the wartime Defense (General) Regulations 1939 which covered prospecting, land requisition and coal working. Compensation for land used was paid under the Compensation (Defense) Act, 1939.

The Opencast Coal Act of 1958 placed opencast operations on a statutory basis and provided new terms of compensation together with a closer control of the planning of working operations and the restoration of land. By Section 1 of the 1958 Act, authorization of opencast workings and the imposition of conditions governing opencast operations is reserved to the Minister - at present the Secretary of State for Energy. Because of the extreme importance of coal to the national economy, applications for opencast sites are made direct to the Minister and not to local planning authorities so that decisions can be made in the national interest. Self-contained disposal points and stocking grounds, however, are subject to normal local planning permissions.

Of course, in practice, owners and tenants, local planning authorities, district councils, statutory undertakers and others had always been consulted about the Board's proposals prior to working and these procedures were formalized by the 1958 Act. The Executive is required to consult more than 20 statutory interests before a formal application for working can be made to the Minister. The original mandatory list consisted of 20 parties with a secondary list of 10 parties to be consulted if necessary; our experience and changes over the years have somewhat reduced the total number of parties consulted but it still remains a considerable task for our planners.

On the other hand, this process of consultation in depth often results in applications being made to the Minister in which most, if not all, working proposals have been mutually agreed so that objections to the proposals are few. Up to the 31st March, 1978, out of 304 applications for site working, only 39 applications were referred to a Public Inquiry and of those the objections made by interested parties were upheld in the case of 9 applications and permission to work was refused by the Minister. This is a success rate of 97 out of every 100 applications.

Looking at the figures, however, we find that from 1958 until 1969, only 8 Public Inquiries took place; there have been 32 Public Inquiries within the past 9 years. Of these 32, 19 took place in the last three years. This fact crystallizes the changing situation we face in the United Kingdom which is similar to the way in which changes in attitudes are developing in a number of other countries including the United States. The United Kingdom is a densely-populated and highly-developed country and there is mounting concern about the effects of new industrial installations on local communities. Local planning authorities and others now seek to regulate our activities in ways which were not even suggested some years ago. We are increasingly subjected to pressures based on environmentalist arguments; the two main problem areas are (1) objections to working operations, and (2) land being taken for opencast operations in the first place.

APPLICATION AND AUTHORIZATION

The application consists of a statutory letter of application to the Minister supported by three schedules and an application map, and a statement of case by the Board justifying working of the site. The first schedule describes the land and names the various interests affected; the second deals with the proposed working operations; and the third deals with the restoration of the land after working. In the statement of case, the Board outlines the need for the coal, the state of the coal market, the extent of agreements reached with interested parties and other points not dealt with in the schedules.

The authorization consists of a covering letter, a formal notice, a schedule of the land involved, a schedule of conditions governing working operations and restoration which number 40 or more, and an authorization map showing the limits of the land authorized to be worked.

Working operations are strictly controlled in accordance with the authorization to preserve local amenities as far as is possible and to prevent nuisance to local residents. Opencast coal production contracts have the authorization conditions written into them; their implementation is always a condition of the authorizations to work granted by the Minister. Out of 65 standard specification clauses in the production contracts, 28 are specifically directed at the preservation of amenities and the prevention of nuisance. Among other things, they detail measures to be taken to control noise, dust, blasting and water pollution during working operations. The Board's site engineers who are engaged full-time on our production sites have, as a vital part of their responsibilities, the duty of exercising this control over the environmental impact of opencast mining.

COAL PRODUCTION CONTRACTS

Apart from National Coal Board staff engaged in overall supervision and direction of operations, all aerial survey work, drilling, coal production and coal preparation is carried out by contractors working for the Opencast Executive. When 'contractual' site restoration has been completed by the production contractor, another contractor takes over to complete 'agricultural' restoration over a period of a further 5 years.

The Executive currently have 27 production contractors on their tender list. Tenders are usually invited on a selected tender list of up to about 6 contractors depending on the size of the job, its location and the commitments of contractors at the time of tender.

Production contracts require the contractor to nominate a 'Manager' under section 98 of the Mines & Quarries Act, 1954 to be statutorily responsible to Her Majesty's Inspectorate of Quarries for all operations on the site including matters relating to health and safety. In addition, the contractor is required to nominate to the Executive an official to be responsible for dealing with and taking any necessary action on any complaint about working operations made by local authorities, residents, or members of the public.

OVERBURDEN EXCAVATION

Power-line diversions are usually dealt with in advance of site working. Diversions of main services and/or roads are included in production or dealt with separately depending on the stage reached in site programming. As soon as the contractor is given possession of the site, he must complete preliminary measures intended for the prevention of nuisance before main excavation is permitted to commence.

Main muckshifting begins with topsoil stripping followed by subsoil stripping. The soils are stocked in mounds so as to be available for eventual site restoration. Topsoil mounds act as baffle embankments where necessary on the site perimeter and help considerably to reduce noise outside the site. They are seeded to grass and act as a screen for the working operations. All available topsoil is recovered and 600 mm of subsoil, except in one of the Executive's Regions where 900 mm of subsoil is recovered. If there is likely to be a deficiency in soil thicknesses, the soil mounds are supplemented by soil-making material recovered from the overburden at lower depths during excavation. This soil-making material is identified during prospecting against the eventuality of a shortage of topsoil and/or subsoil. Nowadays, soil stripping is usually done using motorized scrapers.

The choice of main excavating plant is related to the geology of the site. Dragline working is favored wherever possible because it is the cheapest method of moving overburden in the United Kingdom. Larger draglines over 11 cu. m capacity are electric walking draglines. There are 10 walking draglines now employed on opencast sites and 3 more are currently on order by the Executive alone. The largest machine being used is a Bucyrus Erie 1550W 49 cu. m dragline. Where the economic depth for the dragline is exceeded, large mining shovels up to 10.5 cu. m capacity are used for advance overburden reduction. They are also used on sites with steeply-dipping seams where draglines cannot be employed.

Large hydraulic shovels and backhoes have been introduced into opencast sites for overburden excavation in recent years. These machines are diesel-engined and the largest hydraulic shovel employed so far has a 7.5 cu. m dipper, although one backhoe has been fitted with a 10 cu. m bucket. Servicing the shovels and hauling overburden within the site are dumptrucks of various capacities up to the largest, the Lectra Haul Unitrig M100 which has a payload of 100 short tons. The most common class of dumptruck is the 50-short-ton dumptruck.

Production contracts define the 'provisional ratio' as the ratio of the volume of overburden vertically above the coal to the volume of the coal itself, all *in situ*. Average provisional ratios are about 15:1 at present and the maximum provisional ratio 35:1, but working ratios for our contractors must take account of safe batters around the excavations and are substantially higher. Average depth of working is 50 m and the maximum depth will be 214 m in Phase III of our Westfield site in Scotland.

ENVIRONMENTAL CONTROLS

Public Highways

To ensure that no mud or coal is deposited on public highways, washing installations must be installed and operational before coaling is commenced. Loading is controlled so that there is a generous freeboard between the top of the coal and the top of the coal-lorry body sides and tailboard to avoid spillage. If necessary, particularly in disposal points, road brushes are used.

Blasting

Blasting is controlled by a blasting schedule based on an initial test blast and vibration investigation carried out by explosives experts who are independent of the Board. Currently, the criterion used for control is the peak particle velocity (p.p.v.) of the ground motion and Executive blasting procedures and blasting schedules are deliberately designed to govern p.p.v. values to below a maximum limit of 12 mm/sec for property generally. This limiting value is very much below the p.p.v. of 50 mm/sec generally regarded as a safe level of vibration below which structural damage is unlikely in well-founded and well-constructed buildings - in fact, it applies a factor of safety of 4 to 1. At this level of blasting, there is no possibility of structural damage, but people are still conscious of blasting vibration. So for occupied properties p.p.v. values are reduced still further as far as possible dictated by what is practicable and desirable; if explosive charges are reduced to too great an extent, the rock is merely shaken instead of being broken and one does more harm than good.

The times of blasting are strictly controlled and a complete record is kept of every shot fired. Electric detonation is required on the surface of excavation benches to reduce noise but detonating fuse can be used down the blasthole.

Dust

The main sources of dust on opencast sites are the dirt haul roads within the excavation areas. Access roads outside the excavation are constructed of tarmacadam or concrete. Water bowsers are provided to keep haul roads damp at all times during dry weather. The contractor is required to have a minimum of 2 bowsers available for the first 1.6 ha of internal haul road and 1 more bowser for every additional 1.2 ha. Purpose-built bowsers are often used and bowser capacities of over 36,000 liters are not uncommon.

Plant and vehicles must have engine exhausts which point in an upward direction and blasthole drills are required to be fitted with dust-collection equipment. Special arrangements are often made for dumptruck tipping on overburden tips, or for dragline casting, when high winds blowing across the site pose problems of dust control.

Water Pollution

Proper drainage and anti-pollution facilities must be provided as necessary before soil stripping is commenced. Oil traps are constructed wherever oil is stored or vehicles are serviced.

Clean water entering the site is diverted around the excavation areas to avoid contamination. Site effluents are subject to consent by Water Authorities who stipulate consent conditions for a number of parameters, the most important of which are pH value, usually required to be within a range of values from 6 to 8, phenol content, usually limited to a maximum value of 5 mg l^{-1}, and suspended solids. Standards set for suspended solids have varied widely and have been set as low as 30 mg l^{-1} which is regarded as unnecessarily stringent by the Executive; in our view, a practicable limiting value should be no lower than 100 mg l^{-1}, except in special circumstances. We have not always been able to comply with consent conditions for suspended solids by using settlement lagoons alone. Various flocculants, including polyelectrolytes, have been used.

Flooding has sometimes occurred in the past during the summer months, immediately following contractual restoration, when the surface has been restored but vegetation has not been reestablished and sudden thunderstorms with rainfall of high intensities have passed over the site. We now design ditches and culverts for worst possible conditions during the contractual restoration phase. Watercourses downstream are assessed and any necessary stream improvements carried out. Ditch erosion is overcome by stone pitching, forming cascades or weirs, or, if required, placing stone-filled gabions or using concrete channels.

Noise

The control of noise and the reduction of noise to a minimum is one of the most important aspects of site control. All plant and vehicles must be adequately silenced before they are put into service and our measurements show that, after silencing, most items of excavating plant and dumptrucks are within a maximum sound level of 90 dB(A) at 7 m.

However, for an extended area with mobile plant moving over it and, moving from the deep belowground level to considerable heights above on overburden tips, the main criterion is not the noise generated by any item of plant in its near vicinity but what the combined effect of all items of plant is on neighborhood noise - that is, the effect outside the site. Baffle embankments have already been mentioned; in addition, over part of the haulage cycle, the excavations themselves act as baffles and effect a considerable attenuation of noise levels. The Executive have been accumulating noise records around the boundaries of opencast sites for some 6 years. We have found that only very infrequently are noise levels greater than 70 dB(A) observed on site boundaries and, generally, noise levels are much lower than this during general site working.

Now, however, noise control is required in terms of the equivalent continuous sound level, Leq. We have a more limited experience of Leq, but on what has been done so far we can say that general site noise can be limited at site boundaries, or at the nearest noise-sensitive property depending on site topography, to a maximum level of 65 dB(A) Leq during daytime hours, although throughout the life of the site, noise levels at any one particular location are very much lower than that for most of the overall period. Leq levels are measured over a shift period of 8 hours. Exceptions to the limiting level of 65 dB(A) Leq must be made for motorized scrapers working close to the site boundary on soil stripping and the construction and removal of soil mounds. For night work, the Executive restricts noise levels at site boundaries or at noise-sensitive properties to a maximum level of 55 dB(A) Leq.

Visual Amenity

Overburden tips and soil mounds are shaped and graded to make them as unobtrusive as possible. Vegetation is left undisturbed for as long as possible and land clearance and soil stripping kept only as far in advance of main excavation as is necessary to maintain the site working program. As far as is practicable, restoration is progressive so that the land can be reinstated and grass cover reestablished as soon as possible after coaling. Plant yards and service areas are screened from the public view and the standards of site offices and buildings have been improved in recent years.

CONTRACTUAL RESTORATION

The philosophy of the Opencast Executive on restoration is well-known; we regard land used for opencast mining as land which has been borrowed temporarily for that purpose. It does not matter what condition the land is in when we acquire it - it may be arable farmland, rough grazing or moorland, or derelict areas left over from the industry of an earlier age - we work it and restore and rehabilitate it in an integrated process in which the restoration of the land is an essential part of the whole enterprise.

When coaling has been completed, the production contractor backfills the final void with overburden, grades it out and respreads separately the subsoil and topsoil layers which were stripped initially from the excavation areas. Before any soil respreading is undertaken or permitted, the overburden surface is shaped to grades and levels to effect the best possible drainage of the restored site to conform with an agreed contractural restoration plan. The final surface profile is agreed with all those parties having an interest in the land, owners, tenants, local authorities, etc., at a meeting held on the site before soil respreading is commenced. Watercourses are reestablished on their original lines, diversions and lagoons filled in, access roads broken up, and office and plant yard areas cleared.

Before the subsoil goes back, the surface of the overburden is rooted in two directions at right angles. This operation is intended to break up surface 'panning' and to assist in drainage; it is carried out to varying depths depending on the area of the country and the nature of the land involved. Three of the Executive's Regions require a rooting depth of 300 mm, one a depth of 500 mm, and the remaining Region requires rooting to the full depth of the rooting tyne. Any large boulders and other extraneous material brought up during this operation are collected and disposed of. A similar rooting process is carried out in each layer of subsoil and topsoil in its turn and any large stones or other extraneous material collected and disposed of during each operation. A rooter with 3 tynes is often used for subsoil which is always rooted to its full depth. A light rooter is used on topsoil.

Topsoil rooting is much more varied than for overburden or subsoil depending again on the area of the country and the nature of the restoration required. It is most often left to be specified for the individual site so that the final restored surface achieved is matched to local conditions as far as it is possible to do so. Where rooting is carred out, it is normally done to the full depth of the topsoil, but in one Region it is carried into the subsoil as well up to 230 mm. In this case, tynes are set at 600 mm centers for the greater depth, but for normal full-depth topsoil rooting, they are usually set at 300 mm centers. Depending on circumstances, rooting may be dispensed with and the final surface merely harrowed with short tynes spaced at no more than 75 mm centers. All these decisions about final treatment are taken in the field by my staff working in conjunction with officials of the Ministry of Agriculture who are consulted at all stages of soil stripping and respreading. When the production contractor has completed soiling and the restored surface has been accepted, he has then finished his contract and leaves the site.

AGRICULTURAL RESTORATION

During the 5-year period of agricultural restoration, two parallel programs of work are undertaken by the agricultural contractor under the supervision of the Land Commissioner of the Ministry of Agriculture acting for the Opencast Executive. Firstly, the land is rehabilitated by a process of fertilizing and cultivation. Secondly, the reinstatement of fixed farm equipment, among them farm roads, internal hedging, fencing and ditching, gates, water supplies, under-drainage systems, and shelter belts of trees, is undertaken. The culmination of this process is land ready to be handed over for normal agricultural use as fertile and productive farmland. It will already have been used in part during the five years for grazing during the summer months.

The most intensive agricultural restoration is done in the Midlands and Northern England. Restoration in South Wales and Scotland varies considerably depending on the land, which is often of poorer quality, and includes afforestation where moorland or woodland may be involved. If restoration is for forest, the work is done by the Forestry Commission acting for the Opencast Executive, again over a 5-year period. At the end of that 5-year afforestation period, the area is handed over to the Forestry Commission for them to manage on a permanent basis.

Since 1942 to the present time, some 68,000 ha have been used for opencast working by the Executive of which some 55,000 ha have been or are being restored.

RECLAMATION

Over the past 13 years there has been widespread cooperation with local authorities on the reclamation of derelict areas, including old collieries and their spoil heaps, in association with adjacent opencast sites. By March, 1976 over 142 schemes of varying size had been undertaken involving 1,732 ha. These are only the major schemes; in almost every opencast application the opportunity is taken to eliminate minor dereliction and disused shafts and adits within the site boundaries. We have received more than one award under The Countryside Award Scheme for such reclamations.

Local authorities have also appreciated the opportunities given to them to cooperate with the Executive in providing facilities for leisure activities on restored opencast sites. The Shipley Lake Country Park opened in May, 1976 is only one example of this type of development; in the past, we have provided a number of golf courses, cricket pitches, tennis courts, and children's play areas, among other things.

The restoration and reclamation carried out by the Executive has received worldwide recognition and continued efforts will be made in the future to maintain the high standard achieved and, if possible, to improve upon it.

CONCLUSION

Reserves of coal are in the ground in the United Kingdom which can only be excavated by opencast methods, and proved reserves of more coal continue to be found. That coal is a national asset which must be recovered and used in the national interest. The main challenge for the Opencast Executive of the National Coal Board in the days ahead must be to find ways and means of coming to terms with the many and varied pressures exerted upon us so that we can continue to provide the coal our country needs and be accepted by local communities as we do so.

MINING ECOLOGY AND ENVIRONMENTAL PROBLEMS OF COAL MINING IN AUSTRALIA

J.E. Coaldrake*

INTRODUCTION

This review deals with mining and shipment of coal, but not with power generation from coal. It will concentrate on those environmental, ecological and social problems that require distinctive treatment based on local experience in Australia; this applies especially to rehabilitation (Coaldrake 1973). Mining of coal outcrops started near Sydney in 1799, 11 years after europeans arrived. Sustained open cut mining started in 1895 with brown coal in Victoria and expanded early in the 1920's to modern large scale operations. But it is not until about 1965 that we find governments beginning to require attention to environmental problems, including rehabilitation. In an annotated bibliography completed in 1973 (Coaldrake et al. 1973, Coaldrake and Beattie 1974), only two papers by Blandford (1965a, 1965b) seem to mark the start of literature on rehabilitation after coal mining in Australia, and there have been few Australian papers since. This timing, relates, of course, to the worldwide surge of concern for environmental matters among the developed nations which began in about 1960.

In Australia the ownership of all minerals (irrespective of land title) rests with state governments, or the federal government in the case of federal territories. State governments control all aspects of mining, including rehabilitation. The federal government can refuse to permit import of finance for mining or refuse permission to export minerals, including coal. Access to coal resources in Australia has generally worked effectively through the mutual desires of government and industry to achieve the necessary workable arrangements. In response to the recent upsurge of community interest in environmental matters, governments now include such concerns when deciding conditions of access. One of the more difficult concepts still to be established clearly is the value to be placed on land after open cut mining in relation to costs imposed on the miner for rehabilitation. The multiple ownership and control leads to so many variations in policy and enforcement that one cannot hope to encompass them completely in this review.

Three of the terms used here involve the personal attitudes of the author. It is accepted that others may have a different understanding, but the use of these terms is described (rather than defined) at this early point in the review so that the reader may be on common ground.

Mining Ecology is the study and practice of the manipulation of ecosystems that is necessary before, during and after mining. It necessarily involves a concern with many things

*A.A. Heath & Partners Pty. Ltd., Leichhardt Street, P.O. Box 156, Brisbane, Australia.

besides soils, plants and animals. Mining ecology is an area where conventional ecology derived from the earth, plant and animal sciences needs modification to interact closely with many aspects of agricultural science, forestry, engineering, economics and what can only be described broadly as "sociology".

Environment is taken in this review as anything that affects the functioning of ecosystems either in the absence or presence of man. As Tansley (1935) realized, *Ecosystem* is a concept that still defies a short yet satisfying definition. Within the context of this review it includes man as a component of those ecosystems where he has effects through his works or his needs for living.

Rehabilitation is the conversion of disturbed land to a desired form and function. In mining this commonly requires the preparation of land for other use after mining. This sequential use may be for other forms of production, for urban use, or for open space. Rehabilitation does not necessarily lead to "restoration" in the absolute sense; in some situations after mining, restoration is not possible on a time scale that has any meaning in human terms, especially with some types of natural landscape.

The major known coal-bearing regions of Australia are shown in Fig. 1. Although accurate and recent figures are hard to establish, the reserves are large for a country with small population. Noakes (1974) stated that recoverable reserves of black coal in 1971 were 12,600 million tons of which 7,600 were coking coal. Noakes also pointed out that these figures did not include coal at depths beyond 1,000 to 2,000 feet, and that there are "enormous reserves" at these depths if price ever supports mining there. The major deposits of black coal are restricted to Queensland and New South Wales, i.e. north of latitude 35°S on or near the east coast. The major deposits of brown coal are in Victoria chiefly in the Latrobe Valley and total about 97,000 million tons. Using a different standard of measure, CSIRO (1977) quotes the total of "well established" reserves of coal in Australia as 480×10^{18}J, and estimates that by the year 2000 only 2% of our available black coal and 16% of available brown coal will have been used. A threatening shortage of internal supplies of oil points to increasing demand for coal as a source of energy in Australia; some suitable deposits may be used through conversion to oil (CSIRO 1977).

THE AUSTRALIAN ENVIRONMENT

As a preamble, it is necessary to describe very briefly some features of the Australian environment which affect coal mining in Australia, or which are likely to affect it in the future. Australian readers will have their own favored sources of detailed literature from which to expand beyond the brief summaries below. Readers outside Australia will find such publications as those of Leeper (1970), Moore (1970), and the "Atlas of Australian Resources" (Anon. 1970), which provides an authoritative summary in text to accompany each of the resource maps, very useful.

Geology

While the Australian continent has an area of about 7.7 million sq. km (3 million sq. miles), the known distribution of coal is limited almost entirely to the fringes of this land-mass (Fig. 1). This distribution relates to major geological structures in which about one half of the area consists of Pre-Cambrian granites, gneisses and metamorphics forming the stable western and central core of the continent. While this "Western Platform" contains

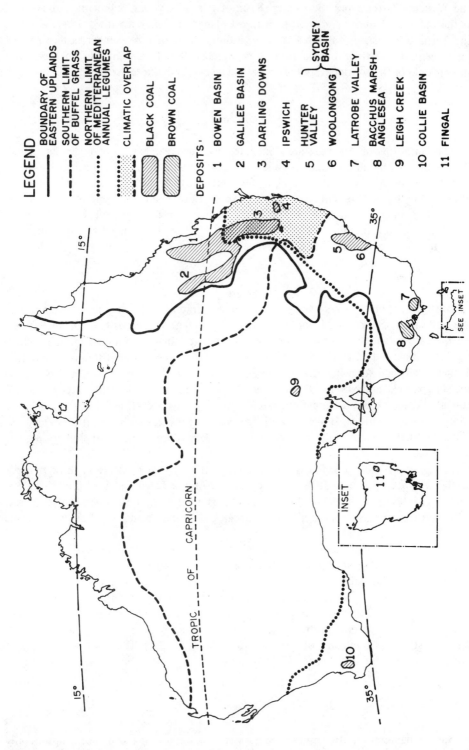

LEGEND

——————	BOUNDARY OF EASTERN UPLANDS
— — —	SOUTHERN LIMIT OF BUFFEL GRASS
··········	NORTHERN LIMIT OF MEDITERRANEAN ANNUAL LEGUMES
	CLIMATIC OVERLAP
	BLACK COAL
	BROWN COAL

DEPOSITS:

1 BOWEN BASIN
2 GALILEE BASIN
3 DARLING DOWNS
4 IPSWICH
5 HUNTER VALLEY ⎫
6 WOOLONGONG ⎭ SYDNEY BASIN
7 LATROBE VALLEY
8 BACCHUS MARSH– ANGLESEA
9 LEIGH CREEK
10 COLLIE BASIN
11 FINGAL

Fig. 1. Major coal bearing regions of Australia in relation to some major factors of natural environment.

some sedimentary basins, these are not known to contain significant deposits of coal. East of the Western Platform lies the Central Basin of relatively young sedimentary rocks, and then the older orogenic region of the Eastern Uplands rejuvenated with differential uplift in the Tertiary and later. Tasmania is, geologically, a part of this younger eastern part of the continent. Formations of coal-bearing type occur as only a thin strip on the south-western margin of the continent, but are more extensive along the eastern side.

Landform

The landforms of Australia are dominated by the great extent of plains and table-lands lacking high mountain ranges. While Australia has winter snowfields in the southeast corner that cover an area roughly that of Switzerland, these are only a small part of the total area. Only limited areas of the continent exceed 1,000 m and only one summit exceeds 2,000 m. The main belt of high land is in the Eastern Uplands and this places the main drainage divide close to the eastern coast. Only a little of Australia's river flow does not go direct to the coast via relatively short rivers.

Climate

Australian climate offers plenty of incoming energy but relatively little precipitation. In the mid-summer month of January, average daily radiation exceeds 600 cal cm^{-2} except along the eastern and far northern coasts where the cloudiness of summer rainfall reduces up to 150 cal cm^{-2} day. In the mid-winter month of July there is a latitudinal orientation with mean daily radiation increasing from 200 cal cm^{-2} in the south to 400 to 450 in the north (Fitzpatrick and Nix 1970). Summer temperatures are warm to hot over the whole continent. Frosts are mild, temperatures seldom drop below -10°C even on the highlands, and only for short periods. However, both frosts and heatwaves are of great significance in relation to establishment and maintenance of vegetal cover during rehabilitation after mining.

Precipitation from snowfall is not an important source of moisture in those parts of Australia where coal is mined. With the exception of the Leigh Creek coalfield most of the other coal-bearing areas (Fig. 1) receive what is good rainfall by Australian standards. This is significant because one-third of the total area is desert and a further one-third is semi-arid.

There are three main patterns of annual rainfall in such areas. The first is the regular winter-dominant rainfall within a mediterranean-type of climate across southern Australia giving the zone indicated suitable for "mediterranean annual legumes" (Donald and Bryan 1970) (Fig. 1). The second is a transition zone in the eastern sub-tropics where annual rainfall is a mixture of summer and winter dominant rainfall with high variability within and between years (Coaldrake 1964). This zone lies broadly between latitudes 22° and 33° east of the boundary of the Eastern Uplands (Fig. 1). The third zone is that of summer dominant rainfall across northern Australia.

Soils

Since rehabilitation after mining involves at best the use of re-emplaced topsoil, only a few general attributes of Australian soils may be summarized. Prescott (1931) was the first to point out that the majority of soils in Australia are deficient in nitrogen and phosphorus by normal agricultural standards. Deficiencies of potassium, sulphur and minor elements needed for plant growth such as copper and zinc (and molybdenum for legumes) are widespread, as is salinity (Williams and Andrew 1970). These characteristics relate largely to the regional geology that provides the sub-surface earth material that becomes the new surface "soil" of spoil heaps on which rehabilitation has to commence. The same range of deficiencies has to be expected.

There is a second attribute of the essential infertility of most Australian soils that combines with the aridity of so much of the continent to pose a latent problem that may confront the mining industry. When open-cut mining expands into some new areas, it will involve loss of crop land that is highly fertile and well watered. This type of land represents a combination found in only relatively small areas of the continent; the Darling Downs region is one such area. A conflict in resource allocation seems likely.

Population

A feature of the Australian environment, now clearly established, is the extreme concentration of population close to portions of the eastern and southern coasts. Coaldrake (1973) using census figures for 1970 calculated that 77% of the total population of the country lived within 40 km of the sea. In this narrow coastal belt between Woolongong and the Tropic of Capricon (Fig. 1), one-third of the total population lives against one-twelfth of the coastline on 4 percent of the total area of the continent.

Most of the coal bearing regions are within or close to this 40 km strip. The notable exceptions are the extensive deposits of the Bowen and Gallilee Basins and the Darling Downs. While this means that much of Australia's coal is close to the home market, it also means that the coal industry will have to live increasingly with the inevitable pressures that come from the proximity to population centers and hence attention to "environmental" matters.

Water

Australia is the driest of the populated continents of the world with a mean annual rainfall of 419 mm compared with a mean of 660 mm for all land areas of the world. Aridity is emphasized by comparing the mean annual runoff of 33 mm for Australia with 249 mm for all land areas of the world (Williams 1975). The major coal bearing regions of Australia are (with the exception of Leigh Creek) in regions of major river discharge as follows (Australian Water Resources Council 1973):

Regions	River Discharge (m^3 x 10^7)
Eastern and Southern Coast	11.90
Southwest (Collie)	0.72
Total for Australia	35

Other areas of major discharge are across the northern coast and Tasmania (13.7 and 4.7 m^3 x 10^7 respectively). The present concentrations of population combine with geography, climate and resource distribution to suggest that population growth in these two regions will be slow to increase beyond the present population of about 150,000 in the northern coast region and 400,000 in the Tasmanian region.

COMMUNITY ATTITUDES

Broad geological control places most of Australia's currently known coal deposits (working or prospective) in a relatively narrow band   close to the eastern and southern coasts. The interactions between climate, landform and soil fertility have made these same coastal bands the regions where about 90% of the country's total population is concentrated. This concentration of population is finally a response to availability of surface water from rainfall, and this basic control on population pattern seems likely to persist within the foreseeable future.

Much of Australia's coal will continue to be excavated within easy traveling time of major urban communities, and thus under the notice of many who are not directly reliant on mining for their income. This creates possibilities for the pressures that finally lead governments to place additional constraints on mining, or to deny access to part of the coal resource. Such pressures have already led to denial of access to coal for one major project proposed for the southern end of the Sydney basin in the early 1970's.

There is still a marked ambivalence of attitude among much of the Australian community towards disturbance of landscape for different forms of production. The Hunter Valley (at the northern end of the Sydney Basin) provides an interesting example of this for which Holmes and Loughran (1976) have provided a summary of damage caused by agricultural and pastoral production. The Hunter Valley involves a total catchment of 20,460 km^2 and includes extensive resources of coal worked for about 170 years, with open cut mining becoming extensive in recent years.

Holmes and Loughran describe the Hunter Valley as "the valley with the second longest history of settlement in Australia, and one in which deterioration has been very marked". They also comment that "the clearance of the protective cover of vegetation, stock management techniques and (introduced) rabbits have all presented accelerated soil erosion in the Hunter Valley". In one section in the lower reaches, the river distance was reduced from 27 km in 1877 to 9.7 km in 1952; this followed clearing of the banks and aggradation of the stream bed due to increased sediment after european settlement. Holmes and Loughran refer to "bank erosion of disastrous proportions during the flood of February 1955". This history, and the attendant expenditure of large sums of public money on corrective works, are set before 1955 when open-cut mining had scarcely commenced in the Hunter Valley. Pit mining may have contributed in some measure through accelerated clearing of forests for pit-props but Holmes and Loughran clearly blame agricultural and pastoral practice.

This one example could be repeated in varying forms in many of those regions of Australia where coal is mined or sought. The history of social attitudes in Australia is such that rural production of crops and animals generally escapes public and financial responsibility for the damage to landscape. Until recently, much of this rural production could only be described as agricultural mining. By contrast, mineral mining, and more recently forestry, are being held responsible to answer for analogous types of damage when these industries cause it. A reviewer can only draw attention to this facet of human behavior; to devise ways of inducing consistency of attitude to all land-based industries is a problem for sociologists and political scientists.

Another aspect of community attitudes to coal mining in Australia relates to conflict in allocation of land as a basic resource open to various uses. McMichael (1974) in discussing federal government attitudes of the time, spoke of the conflict between mining and other "higher uses" for land such as national park and watershed.

The argument over allocation, as between mining and national park, is the subject of lively and continuing debate in Australia in which it is still too early to see any clear developing trend in attitude. The problem is exacerbated by the increased size of national park that is a part of the wilderness concept now being advocated freely by some sections of the conservation movement in Australia. The ultimate difficulty in the conflict with allocation as between national park and any form of mining is the establishment of values for the two forms of use that allows a more factual basis for decision-making. Economic and financial values can be placed on the opportunity lost if mining is denied. Potential values can be assigned to expenditure on recreation if land goes to use as national park, but this leaves other nonquantifiable values which are important to some people. At present these are bracketed under such (?) descriptive terms as that of "higher uses" referred to by McMichael. One present outcome of this particular conflict over resource allocation is a challenge to the mining industry to harmonize engineering with ecology so that disruption of landscape is minimized within the financial constraints operating.

Conflicts between coal mining and watershed use are not yet prominent in Australia. They should be amenable to resolution through due care in design and operation of mines, especially with proper handling of wastes, and to rehabilitation after mining.

Mining Ecology

Hall (1957) was probably the first to link ecology with the effects of mining on landscape. There have been others since but, in general, ecologists have been slow to accept the challenge of understanding ecological pattern and process in the disturbed landscape that results from mining. The reasons would be too complex to speculate on, but they would certainly include the problem of what is/is not fashionable in research. Whatever the reasons, ecologists have generally been content to stand aside and leave much of the early work in mining ecology to other professions such as agricultural science, forestry and engineering. And yet, the effects of mining offer some special opportunities to ecologists in relation to both "technik" and "wissenschaft".

The problems confronting the mining ecologist go far beyond the obvious ones of toxicity and deficiency of nutrients, rooting substrates that are often a poor substitute for a proper soil profile, and the extreme exposures of a bare surface. They include some very real problems of management since the mining ecologist commonly has to coordinate his work with the availability of equipment that is decided by the priorities of production. But it is my experience over 12 years, and a variety of forms of mining, that these problems can be overcome by suitable modification of standard research techniques for the design, conduct and analysis of experiments. Similarly adjustments can be made when converting experimental results into management prescriptions for broad scale application.

The basic approach with both glasshouse and field experiments is to simplify designs and increase replication to overcome the variability on site that has always to be coped with. For example, Russell (1979), found from experimental work at four mine sites spread over a distance of 240 km that "variation is greater in adjacent areas on the small scale than it is between mines and on the large scale". Again problems of plant establishment related to the harshness of sites on spoil heaps can often be overcome by increasing seeding rate by a factor of up to 10 times that of normal rates for the species concerned; some caution is needed however, to avoid the effects of competition from excessive numbers of seedlings.

These and other "luxury" practices should not normally be accepted as subject to constraints of cost when seeking a first permanent ground cover. In rehabilitation of spoil piles it is common that 80 to 90% of the total cost is absorbed by the use of machinery in reshaping, so that increases in costs for ecological measures are only a small part of the total.

The problems that confront the mining ecologist need to be balanced against the opportunities and challenges available to him. Not the least of these relates to the very large areas of disturbed landscape that now require treatment in the wake of open cut mining, and the increased volume of waste from underground mining. In the United States, Atwood (1976) refers to a 10-fold increase in wastes from underground coal mines in the 30 year period from 1940. A similarly comprehensive figure for the increased creation of disturbed land in the United States is not available, but Wali and Kollman (1977) give an estimate of 5,300 km^2 of mineable land in the Northern Great Plains region alone. Presumably much, if not all, of this land will be rehabilitated at some time in the future. Coaldrake (1973) referred to the Bowen Basin (Fig. 1) as containing coal over a north-south distance of 500 km and quoted a figure of 90 ha of disturbed land per open-cut mine per year. Later figures for increased production per mine and an increased number of mines (Collins 1976), combine with the existence or commissioning of other mines to indicate that in the Bowen Basin alone disturbed land will soon be resulting from mining at a rate of 1,000 ha per year. The total area liable to such disturbance (but at an unpredictable rate) from the Bowen, Gallilee and Darling Downs Basin could equal the 5,300 km^2 of Wali and Kollman. These are extensive areas for treatment through the methods of mining ecology; the scope of the problem enlarges when allowance is made for the variation within and between individual mine sites (Russell 1979).

There are two aspects of basic ecological interest where mining ecology ought to offer scope for research into some of the fundamental processes that operate in the functioning of ecosystems. When a spoil pile is reformed, or dressed with topsoil or other mulching layer in readiness for fertilizing and seeding, it can be regarded as a new ecosystem at day 1. All inputs to the ecosystem from there on can be measured and recorded e.g. energy from both radiation and fertilizers, seed, water; losses may be more difficult to quantify completely. It is not possible here to spell out the opportunities for studying the development of an ecosystem through the increasing complexity that must develop with time in such a situation. The restricted range of propagules and organisms available leads to an initially simple biological component of the ecosystem that should be amenable to studies of functioning. Such studies in "newfield succession" ought to be as rewarding as earlier studies on oldfield succession by H.J. Oosting and those who followed him.

The mining ecologist involved with initial measures of rehabilitation will need to be wary of having his thinking constrained by the ideas fashionable in recent years that have developed from the concept that diversity begets stability. Whatever its validity with regard to animal communities in mature complex ecosystems, this concept is of no special relevance in the early years of rehabilitation after mining. This concept has already been misapplied as one of the major grounds for refusing access to mining on Fraser Island in Australia. The report of the Public Inquiry includes the statement that "ecosystem stability depends to a considerable extent upon the development of diverse community types at macro and micro-scales". As Coaldrake et al. (1977) pointed out this statement in the Fraser Island report, and the lengthy argument developed from it, were strongly opposed to earlier comments by Margalef, May and others in van Dobben and Lowe-McConnell (1975). The lengthy conference discussions involved in the latter reference led to a comment from the editors that "this phenomenon has led to the naive if well-intentioned view that complexity begets stability, and its accompanying moral that we should preserve or even create complex systems as buffers against man's importunities (May 1975, p. 164). However, May argues that the reverse is more plausible...".

Another misleading concept for the mining ecologist is the idea that the natural climax community, or one whose ecological requirements most closely resemble it is the one likely to be best adapted to the environment of a given area (Coaldrake et al. 1976). The American range scientists' concepts of "condition" and "trend" are of much more use in the management of areas rehabilitated after mining.

One of the problems that may confront mining ecologists in some of the major coal basins of Australia is that of mobilization of significant quantities of salt by erosion or leaching from spoil heaps. The existing sub-soils over large parts of the Bowen Basin are well known for their salinity, and Coaldrake and Russell (1978) discuss the high total soluble salts measured in some of the overburden at mines in the Bowen Basin. The quantities of salt being mobilized from such saline overburden may finally become significant in regional drainage systems. The magnitude of quantities involved can be judged from an analogous situation in Western Australia (Dimmock et al. 1974). They found that the pallid (deeply weathered) zone of lateritic soils contained from 0.2 to 9.5 x 10^5 kg/ha of total salts. Parts of the overburden in the Collie Basin may be involved at the lower end of this range of content.

This brief discussion of mining ecology as seen from Australian experience is intended to suggest that mining ecology is a challenging and satisfying field for work of high professional standard. If ecologists are to exert the influence that many of them would like to claim, then they must accept the responsibility of being directly involved with the problems of the mining industry. They must also accept the reality that desires for ecological perfection will normally be constrained by the practical realities of management that is under pressure to maintain production. Some of the mining ecologist's other problems will relate to interaction with other professions, especially that of engineering as discussed elsewhere in this review.

Rehabilitation - Comments on Theory and Practice

Quilty (1975) commented recently that the "field of rehabilitation is in its infancy in New South Wales" when discussing mining other than for mineral sands and coal. The paper by Hannon (1976) and discussion elsewhere in this review indicate that the same is true for coal. In Queensland a serious experimental approach to rehabilitation after coal mining only dates back to the work of Coaldrake and Russell (1978) which started in 1971. Tacey et al. (1977) describe a complete operational program for rehabilitation after open-cut mining of brown coal in Victoria, including storage and replacement of topsoil.

While rehabilitation to productive sown pasture is now proceeding successfully in some mining areas (Coaldrake and Russell 1978, Hannon 1976), I am not aware of any examples in the coal mining industry in Australia where land passes from cropping through open-cut mining and back to cropping on a cycle of only a few years. We have nothing to compare in this direction with some of the operations of Rheinbrau in Germany or of essentially similar operations in parts of the eastern United States. There is, however, an Australian precedent from a gold dredging operation on alluvial farmland in the Loddon Valley of Victoria in 1938. Here the operator had to store and replace topsoil to a depth of up to 2 m and establish a sown pasture before handing the land back to the owners for normal use under crop-pasture rotation (McGeorge 1943). Costs were quoted (in 1938 values) of A$355 per ha with 88% of this spent on reshaping the land and spreading topsoil.

From the limited work completed in Australia some clear general guidelines have emerged. There is a need for close cooperation from the outset between the mining engineer, management, and the rehabilitation specialist so that experimental work is sited and completed in a manner that allows sensible extrapolation to a prescription for broad scale work. A policy decision has to be made at the outset as to whether or not irrigation is to be used to achieve initial establishment for the broad scale works in rehabilitation; this affects both the range of species available for use and scheduling of operations within the year where rainfall is seasonal or variable. It has to be accepted that each new mine site is likely to require some separate investigation to determine if it is within the range of agronomic variability for which an earlier prescription has been established. Standard chemical analyses for soil fertility parameters will normally indicate if this is so, and they should be regarded as a necessary first step at any new site.

The Australian experience indicates that it is best to start rehabilitation with a first plant cover of crop or pasture species known to be adapted to the conditions of prevailing soil and climate. The species used in experiments on plant nutrition, mulching or other forms of treatment, should be selected from the range of species that will later be used on the broad scale. At this first stage of rehabilitation the work should generally be regarded as an agronomic exercise in which adjustments are made for the physical and chemical peculiarities of mining sites. It is worth noting here that in Australia all species used for sown crops and pastures are imported from other parts of the world; thus Australians have long been conditioned to the idea of working with introduced species anywhere outside the arid zone. The geographic limits indicated on Fig. 1 for buffel grass and for Mediterranean annual legumes are all involved with introduced species; in both cases these limits embrace large areas of semiarid land.

The agronomic component of rehabilitation (i.e. up to the establishment of a first complete plant cover) is normally a small component of the total cost structure for rehabilitation after mining. This means that the cost-consciousness normally applied to work with fertilizers and seeding rates in the conventional farm situation does not have to be applied with the same rigorousness.

The question of sequential use intended for rehabilitated land is a policy matter that is best settled before a rehabilitation program commences. If the land is to continue in rural production through crop, pasture or forest, then the problem is one for the basic approach of the agronomist, or forester, rather than the ecologist. If the land is to be used as open space for some form of recreation, or for watershed then the ecologist has the major role once the first plant cover is established. But in general the ecologist needs to be wary of trying to proceed straight to a plant cover of native species, rather than through the intermediary of a first cover crop or grass cover.

The practice of storage and replacement of topsoil is one that needs to be assessed most critically in each case (e.g. Tacey et al. 1977). It is the Australian experience that storage of topsoil for more than about four months results in severe loss of viable seed. This still leaves the topsoil with many other useful physical and chemical characteristics; but if topsoil is being used as an important source of seed of native species that are desired on the rehabilitated land, then the program for handling and re-spreading it has to be carefully planned. Because of the expense of removing topsoil to separate storage, and of respreading it, there needs to be a deliberate decision in each situation as to whether the use of topsoil is warranted.

Rehabilitation - Policy and Administration

There is enough experience now in Australia to indicate that decision-making regarding rehabilitation involves complications that extend beyond the quantification possible through economic and financial analyses. While cost-benefit analyses have their uses both to governments and to operating companies, it is beyond the scope of this review to discuss these techniques in any detail in relation to decisions as to whether rehabilitation shall be required by government and undertaken by operators. It is, however, instructive to consider situations in which policies have been devised and applied by both government and miners in Australia.

The first branch of the Australian mining industry to have firm provisions for rehabilitation applied on a wide scale was heavy mineral sand mining on coastal dunes on the central east coast. Most of the land involved is covered with natural vegetation and a policy has evolved since 1960 of requiring such land to be rehabilitated to a cover of native plant species. The costs for such rehabilitation are now known, and the penalty for failure to rehabilitate is based on such costs without reference to the value of the land before or after mining. These requirements are written into the mining leases issued under the relevant State Mining Act.

By contrast, when the operations of Utah Development Company over large areas of the Bowen Basin were authorized by a franchise under a separate Act of Parliament (Anon. 1968), the Act included a penalty for failure to rehabilitate that was related to value of the land. The Act requires a deposit of $123 per ha against failure to rehabilitate. The size of the penalty was determined at the time by standard techniques of discounting the then market value of the land when used as sown pasture for beef cattle. The market value of such (unmined) land is currently much less than it was at the time the penalty was calculated. Russell (1978) and Collins (1976) describe the elaborate program of experiments and broad scale work now being carried out by Utah Development Company in its rehabilitation of spoil piles. The cost of this work is given by Utah Development Company (1977) as averaging $8,500 per ha, of which 90% is for machinery costs in reshaping the spoil piles to the new land form illustrated by Russell (1978).

There is a striking disparity between the size of the penalty for failure to rehabilitate ($123) and the cost of rehabilitation ($8,500). In an analogous case where an earlier franchise established a smaller penalty the mining company concerned has elected (so far) not to attempt a regular program of rehabilitation, thus risking forfeiture of the penalty (The company now has a regular program). Both policies are legal, both are set by multinational companies subject to the particular forms of criticism often leveled at such companies. Australian owned companies exhibit a similar variety of policies.

As indicated by the 1976 Annual Report of the Joint Coal Board of N.S.W., the situation regarding policies for rehabilitation after open-cut mining is one of recent change and continuing evolution. The report quotes a total area stripped up-to-date in New South Wales of 696 ha with rehabilitation "final" on 63 ha and proceeding on 160 ha. The two largest open-cuts in the State are owned by the government and operated by private contractors. The contracts for these two open-cuts were issued in 1968 and contained no provisions for rehabilitation. This report refers to recent experiments on a test area of 40 ha to establish techniques and costs for recontouring and establishment of plant cover. The report also refers to small scale experiments on rehabilitation at another old open-cut. The report does not specify but, presumably, the costs are being met by the government in both of these cases.

Hannon (1976) indicates that work has also begun on rehabilitation of wastes around old underground mines in New South Wales. He describes a case history from a mine in the Hunter Valley that operated for about 80 years until closure in 1972, with a few small open-cuts being worked in its last years. For the whole program of work over 32 ha Hannan quotes an average cost of $7,800 ha. The paper does not state clearly how the costs were borne but some of the comments appear to indicate that they were shared between the mining company and the government.

In rehabilitation after the large-scale open-cut mining for brown coal in Victoria, references to rehabilitation are limited except that of Tacey et al. (1977) for the operations of Alcoa of Australia Limited; it is interesting that the operation concerned is by a company and not by government. Costs are not quoted. Personal enquiries revealed that this dearth of literature is largely a reflection of the slow consumption of surface area in these operations; it is common to have less than 20 m of overburden overlying up to 200 m thickness of coal. A recent environment impact statement for a combined open-cut mine and power station at Loy Yang in the Latrobe Valley (State Electricity Commission 1975) emphasizes that the chief environmental problems in these Victorian operations relate to the lake that must eventuate. Emphasis is placed on controlling effects of acid water on regional aquifers, on disposal to sea of saline concentrates from water treatment, on treatment of batters from above water level (including fire control), and on cosmetic treatment of the spoil pile that has to be placed outside the open-cut during the early years.

The Leigh Creek Coalfield in South Australia is in remote semi-arid land of low pastoral productivity. So far as I am aware no rehabilitation has been undertaken. Open-cut mining in the Collie Basin of Western Australia has only started to become extensive in recent years. Enquiries with the State Department of Mines revealed that the government is still developing a policy regarding rehabilitation. It seems likely with the Collie Basin that rehabilitation procedures will eventually have to recognize problems of altered salinity levels within a watershed from which urban water supply may eventually be needed.

This brief survey shows that Queensland was apparently the first State to start developing regulatory action regarding rehabilitation after open-cut mining for coal. While these procedures have been developing since the early 1960's, there are still inconsistencies. There still does not seem to be a deliberate sequence of decision-making in any State. This could well involve the determination of:

(a) The type and standard of rehabilitation to be used in relation to sequential land use and environmental values sought. Some of these decisions are commonly implicit in the original decision to permit mining.
(b) The method and apportionment of funding for rehabilitation.
(c) The basis of mechanisms to ensure performance e.g. penalty provisions. In both (b) and (c) escalation of costs is a factor.

Within this framework of evolution of government policy, the example of Utah Development Company indicates that some mining companies are apparently responding to the pressures of changing public attitudes in advance of government response. The elaborate program of rehabilitation by Alcoa of Australia at its Victorian brown coal operation may represent a similar response.

Other Environmental Problems

As indicated by Campbell (1978) in his discussion of the scope of work required for an Australian EIS on coal mining matters there is a common list of environmental matters which has to be encompassed. Many of these relate to environmental engineering for handling of wastes, dust, storm-water drainage and water borne effluent from washeries; these are handled by standard procedures for treatment that do not need discussion here.

A research program by CSIRO (1977), now in pilot plant stage, offers scope for reducing the problem of washery and other carbonaceous wastes by special techniques of firing to produce heat for generation of electricity. The resultant ash has possibilities for use as a construction material. These new processes may well be very useful in areas of shaft mining but no comment is available yet on their application (in terms of cost-effectiveness) at the large open-cut mines now becoming increasingly common at remote sites such as those in the Bowen Basin.

The types of high sulphur coals that cause acute problems of acid mine drainage (AMD) are not widespread in Australia; acute problems of AMD are known so far to be associated with only one area in the Hunter Valley and one in the Bowen Basin. The limited information available indicates that AMD in these areas can be handled along the same general lines as followed in other parts of the world.

Much of the black coal now being mined from the Bowen Basin is being exported through two ports nearby. In the case of Gladstone, a small port handling beef and grain on a seasonal basis, developed by about 1970 into a major port handling coal year round. In the second case further north at Hay Point, a complete new port facility solely for coal has been operating for some years; at least one other such new port is a possibility. These new ports serving the northern end of the Bowen Basin have to be located within the area of the Great Barrier Reef where the extensive coral reef system is sensitive to pollution. The terms of reference for an EIS for a new port in these areas require particular effort on pollution control for dust and drainage from stock piles, and spillage of coal during loading. Studies on the effectiveness of pollution control at these sites are not available. But the lack of public criticism of any such effects in an area where many people have a close concern suggests that no such problems have developed yet. The routes for new railway lines that serve such new ports are also subject to scrutiny for environmental effects.

The development of large scale coal mining in the Bowen Basin has resulted in the development since 1968 of three new towns specifically for housing the work-forces. One of these resulted from enlargement of a rural village of about 50 people to a town of about 5,000 people; the other two were established in virgin bushland. Similar new towns have been established rapidly to service other forms of mining elsewhere in Australia in the last 15 years. From all of these new towns there is a common history of problems while a new population achieves some degree of social stability. These social problems of new mining towns have been studied extensively but so far there is a confusion between the results from different studies. Whether these differences in results are due to differences in methodology or to differences between towns remains to be proven.

A recent study of the source of social problems in three such new mining towns in Western Australia by Stockbridge et al. (1976) emphasizes the importance of moving on as quickly as possible from the situation of a planned town governed by company management or government department. This needs to be replaced as soon as possible by some form of local government where residents do most of their own decision-making.

Stockbridge et al. also comment:

> "At the risk of giving grave offense to many people ..... it must be asserted that the plight of women in the Pilbara (region) seems to have been greatly exaggerated" (p. 197).

"…. it may be that homogeneity of living conditions is an ideal of community planners for which the cost is too high" (p. 206).

THE E.I.S. AND DECISION MAKING

Campbell (1978) discusses the Environmental Impact Study in relation to coal mining in the State of New South Wales which is a State where mining is extensively diversified between government and private industry. His study reflects a steady evolution of the EIS towards rational and satisfying standards in which the extremes of biological detail are no longer allowed to dominate in every EIS. However, there is one aspect of procedures with the EIS on which Campbell did not have space for extended comment; this is the problem of dealing with an EIS for a major project that requires some form of public inquiry.

Australians, both at state and federal level, have yet to find a mechanism that is satisfying to all of the parties concerned when an industrial project poses problems that lead to widespread public concern.

Since the Cooloola conflict of 1969 over mineral sand mining, there have been various attempts to devise procedures for public hearings that meet the following criteria:

(1) That all of the relevant factual material both for and against a proposal should be entered for consideration.

(2) That "evidence" in the scientific sense should be clearly distinguished from "evidence" in the legal sense, and that scientific matter should be clearly classified along the lines of "evidence", "inference", "opinion" or "speculation" as suggested by Coaldrake et al. (1977).

(3) That all parties wishing to be heard on either side of a dispute should be allowed to participate without prejudice to legal rights elsewhere.

(4) That necessary legal precision should be achieved without the need for this being allowed to dominate the entire proceedings.

(5) That opinion should be allowed in areas where factual or quantitative assessment is not possible e.g. on social attitudes.

(6) That proceedings and subsequent decision-making should not lead to unbearable escalation of costs for participation in a hearing, or for long delays in subsequent decision-making.

Dempsey (1976) argued that formal court procedure was the best for determining the outcome where an EIS was involved. This may be true in the United States due to aspects of its legal system. The Australian experience suggests otherwise in relation to attempts to win areas for various types of mining. The Australian experience in the last ten years also shows that procedures for public hearings have not yet matured to the point of satisfying all of the six criteria listed above. Bryan (1971) reviewed existing procedures in Britain for deciding through a public inquiry whether planning permission is granted for access to land for mining. His account of formal proceedings heard by an Inspector (equals Commissioner) plus two expert assessors, with legal counsel permitted to appear but not to dominate, seems to satisfy all six of the criteria listed earlier.

There is not the space here to detail the variety of procedural devices adopted by the six state governments for dealing with an EIS for a major project; Campbell (1978) summarizes them for New South Wales and Queensland. They have ranged from strict adversary procedure in a lower court sitting under the authority of a State Act (such as a Mining Act or a Local Government Act) to semi-formal procedures under a Commissioner(s) not drawn from the legal profession. They have extended from 2 or 3 days with 10 to 15 witnesses to longer hearings such as the Moreton Island Inquiry (1977), which lasted 43 days and heard 74 witnesses and addresses from six counsel; the resulting transcript was of 2,686 pages. This Inquiry was based on examination of an EIS that totaled the equivalent of 800 pages of typescript.

At present there is a general tendency amongst the state governments to turn away from forms of public inquiry where standing and access is granted freely to everybody who wishes to appear. This tendency has probably been accelerated by two Inquiries held by the federal government; neither of these concerned coal but the reactions in terms of alterations to procedures may affect coal mining equally as any other industry. While state governments control both the access to minerals and the operation of mining, the federal government controls access to finance from overseas and also controls export of raw or processed minerals. These powers enable it to intervene in decisions on many mining projects.

In 1974, the Australian Federal Government passed the Environment Protection (Impact of Proposals) Act 1974 (Anon. 1974). This Act basically enabled the requirement for an EIS to be imposed by the responsible Minister with regard to actions proposed either by departments of the federal government or by private interests. The Act and its regulations set out in detail the matters to be covered in an EIS, and elaborate in some detail the procedures to be followed if a public inquiry is held. Special Commissioners are appointed for these hearings who have the "same protection and immunity as a Justice of the High Court". They may or may not be judges. Two public inquiries have been held under this Act. The first (The Fraser Island Inquiry) had to be reconstituted after about ten sitting days to meet a legal challenge. The Inquiry deliberated for a further 31 days and finally received a total of 3,496 pages of transcript and 658 exhibits from 102 witnesses. A notable feature of this Inquiry was the absence (on legal grounds) after the first hour of the sittings of the reconstituted Inquiry of the mining company that had most at stake in the Inquiry. In the event this led to a negation of the first three of the six criteria listed earlier in this section.

The second Inquiry was the Ranger Uranium Environmental Inquiry which had to deal, of course, with an environmental issue of great importance and widespread public concern. Its deliberations were also complicated by the placement of major uranium ore bodies involved within an area keenly sought for a wilderness type of National Park, and where there are acute problems of aboriginal land rights. In the event the Ranger Inquiry lasted 121 days to hear 303 witnesses compile a transcript of 13,525 pages; from the commencement of hearings until delivery of the final report required a time span of 20 months (Ranger Inquiry 1977). The Commissioners recorded the cost to the government as $828,000 until just before delivery of the final report. The direct cost to the mining company concerned probably equaled this, apart from costs due to delayed commencement of mining. The cost to other parties to the hearing remains undetermined.

The financial costs for the Ranger Inquiry may be justified on a national basis for the determination of such an important issue. But there has been a tendency among some sections of the Australian community to demand equally exhaustive procedures for lesser and more localized issues. Australian governments now seem to be accepting the reality that the EIS and its attendant procedures have to be used with discernment, and that many minor environmental problems can be handled through other administrative channels. This should increase the prospects of retaining the EIS as an effective tool for resolving major environmental problems. Had the indiscriminate use of the EIS continued, there was a danger that it would be "blacklashed" out of use. Governments do finally have to govern and the experience now shows that in many situations the EIS will not save government from its ultimate responsibility in decision-making. One of the realities here is that public decision-making can seldom wait for scientific perfection.

These problems have been discussed previously (Coaldrake 1976, Coaldrake et al. 1977) partly on the basis of personal experience as a professional witness in many types of jurisdiction for appearances of up to 4 consecutive days. Such appearances mostly leave the professional witness with a clear feeling that criteria 1, 2, and 4 listed above are seldom satisfied. This is a problem that should be as much of concern to the scientist as to the lawyer if environmental problems are ever to be resolved in public hearings to the satisfaction of all the professions involved, as well as management and government. Adversary procedure can be stultifying if practiced fully on these problems; inquisitorial procedure can be inordinately time-consuming and place too much emphasis on the individual. A blending of the two would seem desirable, and ought to be possible. Some of the difficulties involved in these matters are discussed at greater length by Hammond and Adelman (1976); they comment *inter alia* that "the adversary system suffers from an ascientific commitment to victory rather than truth; the person-oriented approach suffers from an ascientific focus on persons and their motives rather than on the adequacy of methods".

Bryan (1971) in discussing the problems of planning appeals for mining access in Britain commented that "the *general public* need to be convinced that those whose business is to develop mineral resources are not reckless profiteers .... More and more the community will demand that its total needs are taken into account". This need to inform and convince the general public is the ultimate reason for preparing an EIS and subjecting it to the scrutiny of a public hearing. It will not necessarily be done better by subjecting the EIS and associated procedures to the total scientific constraints advocated by Schindler (1976). Public decision-making can seldom wait on scientific perfection. One has to ask, is Schindler sure that a study framed within his "bona fide scientific framework" will provide all the answers sought within the time-span requested by the scientists assigned to a given EIS? Or will they tread the path of all good biological scientists by completing a report that poses new questions in place of those it set out to answer?

The emergence of the EIS over recent years has uncovered some deep-seated problems in relation to a basic difference in training between scientists and engineers. The scientist is trained to uncover questions (sometimes as hypotheses to be tested by others), whereas the engineer is trained to provide solutions that will work. He may use safety factors of appropriate type and scale, and these may put a project beyond financial acceptability. But he will provide a solution even if an apparently precise design does in fact incorporate sources of uncertainty that have been overcome by safety factors. The EIS and its attendant procedures may be producing the type of professional biologist who can responsibly equilibrate to the performance of the engineer. If such people do not evolve, then the engineer will continue to outstrip the biologist in his influence on public decision-making, because the majority of the general public will not wait indefinitely for the decisions they require of government.

CONCLUSION

After 170 years of coal mining dominated by shaft mining, Australia is now in a period of rapid expansion of use of its coal resources chiefly through open-cut mining. Many of the environmental problems arising from coal mining in Australia can be handled by methods common around the world. It is in rehabilitation of spoil heaps, especially after open-cut mining, that Australians are having to develop their own modifications of methods due to differences in such factors as climate, soil fertility, and natural vegetation. There is now enough experience to indicate the need for mining ecology to be recognized and encouraged as a distinctive form of ecological thought and work. Mining ecology is a branch of ecology where ecologists must expect to interact closely with other professions, notably engineering. It is to be expected that some of the traditional concepts and methods of ecology will need changing to adapt to the different circumstances of newfield succession and the processes involved.

Due partly to division of control between state and federal governments, the use of the EIS has brought difficulties in Australia, especially in the testing of the EIS through public inquiries. The whole system for use of the EIS is still evolving towards selective use on major aspects of major projects. Industry, government and the public have yet to resolve this.

REFERENCES

Anon. 1968. Central Queensland Coal Associates Agreement Act, 1968. Queensland Govt. Printer, Brisbane.

Anon. 1970. Atlas of Australian Resources.   Dept. of Natl. Development, Canberra.

Anon. 1974. Environment Protection (Impact of Proposals) Act 1974-75. Govt. Printer, Canberra.

Anon. 1976. Joint Coal Board of N.S.W., Annual Report. N.S.W. Govt. Printer, Sydney.

Atwood, G. 1976. Surface and underground disposal of coal mine wastes. Underground Space 1:111-121.

Australian Water Resources Council. 1973. Groundwater Resources of Australia. Canberra.

Bryan, A. 1971. Planning permission and the place of the Public Inquiry in the development of mineral resources in Britain: problems of potash extraction in Yorkshire. Trans. Inst. Min. Met. 80:63-71.

Blandford, C.M. 1965a. Erosion Control in the restoration of open-cut coal mining areas. Part 1. J. Soil. Conserv. Serv. N.S.W. 21:70-79.

Blandford, C.M. 1965b. Erosion Control in the restoration of open-cut coal mining areas. Part 2. J. Soil Conserv. Serv. N.S.W. 21:127-145.

Campbell, A.P. 1978. Environmental Impact Statements for the Australian Coal Mining Industry. In M.K. Wali (ed.), Ecology and Coal Resource Development (this volume), Pergamon Press, N Y.

Coaldrake, J.E. 1964. The sub-tropical environment of eastern Australia (a) climate. In Some Concepts & Methods in Sub-tropical Pasture Research, Commw. Bur. Past. Fld. Crops Bull. 47.

Coaldrake, J.E. 1973. Conservation problems of coastal sand and open-cast mining. In Nature Conservation in the Pacific. pp. 299-314, Aust. National Univ. Press, Canberra.

Coaldrake, J.E. 1976. Environmental Public Inquiries. Australian Mining Industry Council - Environmental Workshop, Adelaide, A.M.I.C., Canberra.

Coaldrake, J.E. and K.J. Beattie. 1974. Supplement No. 1 to Coaldrake, McKay and Roe (1973).

Coaldrake, J.E. and M.J. Russell. 1978. Rehabilitation with pasture after open-cut coal mining at three sites in the Bowen Coal Basin of Queensland. Reclamation Review, 1:1-7.

Coaldrake, J.E., M. McKay and P.A. Roe. 1973. Annotated bibliography on the ecology and stabilization of coastal sand dunes, mining spoils, and other disturbed areas. CSIRO, Div. Plant Ind., Canberra, 157 p.

Coaldrake, J.E., P.A. Roe and T.L. Turner. 1977. Fraser Island environmental inquiry - a critque of ecological aspects of the report. Queensland Govt. Mining J. 78:274-291.

Coaldrake, J.E., J.C. Tothill and P. Gillard. 1976. Natural vegetation and pasture research. In N.H. Shaw and W.W. Bryan (eds.), Tropical Pasture Research, Hurley, Commw. Bur. Past. & Field Crops. Bull. 51.

Collins, A.G. 1976. Reclamation of open-cut spoil piles. Australian Mining, July 1976: 17-19.

CSIRO. 1977. Husbanding our coal resources. Ecos. (No. 13):1-9, CSIRO, Melbourne.

Dempsey, S. 1976. Environmental Impact Procedures - The USA Experience. Australian Mining Industry Council-Environmental Workshop, Adelaide, A.M.I.C., Canberra.

Dimmock, G.M., E. Bettenay and M.J. Mulchay. 1974. Salt content of lateritic profiles in the 'Darling Range', western Australia. Aust. J. Soil. Res. 12:63-69.

Dobben van, W.H. and R.H. Lowe-McConnell. 1975. Unifying Concepts in Ecology. Dr. W. Junk, The Hague.

Donald, C.M. and W.W. Bryan 1970. Map of Australia showing postulated inland climatic limits of various sown pasture plants. pp. 74-75, In G.W. Leeper (ed.), The Australian Environment. C.S.R.I.O., Melbourne.

Fitzpatrick, E.A. and H.A. Nix. 1970. The climatic factor in Australian grassland ecology. In R.M. Moore (ed.), Australian Grasslands. Aust. National Univ. Press, Canberra, 3-26.

Hall, I.G. 1957. The ecology of disused pit heaps in England. J. Ecol. 45:689-720.

Hammond, K.R. and L. Adelman 1976. Science, values and human judgement. Science 194:389-396.

Hannon, J.C. 1976. Conservation and the coalfields. Quarry Mine & Pit 15(7):4-5.

Holmes, J.H. and R. Loughran. 1976. Man's impact on a river system: the Hunter Valley. pp. 96-114, In Man and the Environment: Regional Perspectives. Longman, Melbourne.

Leeper, G.W. (ed.) 1970. The Australian Environment. C.S.I.R.O., Melbourne, 163 p.

May, R.H. 1975. Stability in ecosystems: some comments. pp. 161-168, In W.H. van Dobben and R.H. Lowe-McConnell (eds.), Unifying Concepts in Ecosystems. W.Junk, The Hague.

McGeorge J.H.W. 1943. Notes on resoiling with special reference to the dredging and reclaiming of auriferous farmlands at Newstead, Victoria. Trans. Ins. Min. Met. 52:347.

McMichael, D.F. 1974. Mining and the environment—a government viewpoint. pp. 35-39, In R.L. Whitmore (ed.), Minerals—the Future of Australia's Mineral Industry. Searchlight Ser. No. 2 A.N.Z.A.A.S. Sydney.

Moore, R.M. (ed.). 1970. Australian Grasslands. Aust. National Univ. Press, Canberra, 443 p.

Moreton Island Inquiry. 1977. Report of the Committee of Inquiry-Future Land Use-Moreton Island, Queensland Govt. Printer, Brisbane, 87 p.

Noakes, L.C. 1974. Mineral Resources of Australia. pp. 5-10, In R.L. Whitmore (ed.), Minerals-the future of Australia's Mineral Industry. Searchlight Series No. 2, A.N.Z.A.A.S., Sydney.

Prescott, J.A. 1931. The soils of Australia in relation to vegetation and climate. CSIRO, Bull. 52.

Quilty, J.A. 1975. Guidelines for rehabilitation of tailings dumps and open-cuts. J. Soil Cons. Serv., N.S.W. 31:95-107.

Ranger Inquiry. 1977. Ranger Uranium Environmental Inquiry-Second Report. Aust. Govt. Publishing Service, Canberra, 415 p.

Russell, M.J. 1979. Spoil heap revegetation at open-cut coal mines in the Bowen Basin of Queensland. In M.K. Wali (ed.), Ecology and Coal Resource Development (this volume), Pergamon Press, N Y.

Schindler, D.W. 1976. The impact statement boondoggle. Science 192:Editorial.

State Electricity Commission. 1975. Loy Yang Project. Statement on Environmental Effects, S.E.C. of Victoria, Melbourne.

Stockbridge, M.E., B. Gordon, R. Nowicki and N. Paterson. 1976. Dominance of Giants. Report, Dept. Social Work, Univ. of West. Aust., 243 p.

Tacey, W.H., D.J. Olsen and G.M.H. Watson. 1977. Rehabilitation of mine wastes in a temperate environment. Australian Mining Industry Council-Environmental Workshop, Sydney, A.M.I.C., Canberra.

Tansley, A.G. 1935. The use and abuse of vegetational concepts and terms. Ecology 16: 284-307.

Utah Development Company. 1977. The Environment, Brisbane, Utah Dev. Co., 6 p.

Wali, M.K. and A.L. Kollman. 1977. Ecology and mining or mining ecology. pp. 108-115, In J.L. Thames (ed.), Reclamation and Use of Disturbed Land in the Southwest. Univ. of Arizona Press, Tucson.

Williams, C.H. and C.S. Andrew. 1970. Mineral Nutrition of Pastures. pp. 321-338, In R.M. Moore (ed.), Australian Grasslands, Aust. National Univ. Press, Canberra.

Williams, W.D. 1975. Inland Water. In Managing Aquatic Ecosystems. Proc. Ecol. Soc. Aust., 8:19-40.

MINING, DEWATERING AND
ENVIRONMENTAL EFFECTS: A MULTIOBJECTIVE APPROACH

Istvan Bogardi*, Ferenc Szidarovszky** and Lucien Duckstein***

INTRODUCTION

Mining of natural resources may have an environmental impact not only at the location of mining but also over a large surrounding region (Down and Stocks 1977). This impact often has adverse consequences, such as sinking groundwater levels, deterioration of groundwater quality, land subsidence. Mining development takes place so that the "best" trade-off is found between mining production, water supply and environmental impact.

This problem is important for two reasons: (a) mineral resource utilization has become one of the most important national objectives, whether in large countries such as the USA, or small ones such as Hungary (Kapolyi 1977); (b) regional development models should attempt to integrate mineral resource extraction, water management and environmental issues.

This paper investigates a specific area of the general problem mentioned above: regional mining under water hazards, with due consideration to water supply and recharge for thermal baths in the region. This is one of the key problems of mineral resource development in Hungary; further, it offers a good possibility to apply a multiobjective optimization method, called compromise programming, and thus to provide a solution methodology for other conflicts between mineral resource management and environment (Bower 1975).

PROBLEM DESCRIPTION

Generalities

In Hungary, large-scale mining development of coal and bauxite is being planned in the Transdanubian Mountain region over the next 50 years. Mineral resources are located under the underground (karstic) water level; thus, mining activity is necessarily to include water control. At the same time, the main water resource of the region is the karstic water, which is to supply rapidly growing municipal and industrial water demands. And then, a sinking karstic water level has adverse environmental effects; namely, the world-famous

* Mining Research Institute, 1037 Budapest III, Mikoviny u. 2-4, Hungary.

** University of Agriculture, Department of Computer Sciences, Menesi ut. 44, 1118 Budapest, Hungary.

*** Department of Systems and Industrial Engineering, and Department of Hydrology and Water Resources, University of Arizona, Tucson, Arizona 85721.

82

thermal waters of Budapest receive their natural recharge from this karstic aquifer. These three points are described below in detail.

Mine Water Control

Every planned mine in the region exhibits water hazard (Schmieder et al. 1975). The principal water problem is caused by the karstic aquifer which has a depth of several hundred meters. To control this mine water, one can use a combination of several methods, the efficiency of which depends upon costs and volumes withdrawn. By increasing control costs, the amount of withdrawal can be diminished (Schmieder et al. 1975). Also, to a highly efficient water control system, there corresponds a low mining production cost. This cost reduction stems from two factors: less expensive mining methods can be used, and losses due to water inrushes can be averted.

Production schedule of the mines is determined by national energy demand, considered as given in the present investigation. However, the production costs of mining--even in view of growing demand--cannot exceed a certain limit, because energy demand will then be satisfied from other sources.

Regional Water Supply

The karstic aquifer is considered to be the most important source of water supply in the region. The aquifer is being pumped at certain existing mines to supply regional drinking water works. As a result of industrialization, both municipal and industrial water demands are growing. It is predicted that a high percentage of the safe yield of karstic water will be necessary to meet water demands.

Environmental Aspects

This region provides the natural recharge of the world-famous Budapest thermal waters. According to numerous studies (Szilagyi 1976), an average natural recharge of $30 \text{ m}^3 \text{ min}^{-1}$ is used by the Budapest spas and thermal baths through various springs and wells. This natural recharge originates from rainfall over the karstic region; namely, some proportion of rainfall infiltrates and, through deep percolation, leaves the system. Then it appears again outside of the system, in the Budapest region, as thermal water. A necessary constraint for any kind of mining development consists in maintaining the existing discharge and quality of thermal waters. If the natural recharge of $30 \text{ m}^3 \text{ min}^{-1}$ is provided at adequate locations, the above goal of not disturbing thermal waters will be satisfied. In addition to the Budapest thermal water problem, the mine water control may cause local damages, such as drying up of wells or land subsidence, which must be compensated.

In summary, planned mining development in the region should satisfy three conflicting goals: (1) mining must be an efficient enterprise, (2) in spite of mining development, regional water demands should be met by using the available karstic water resources, (3) environmental losses should be either averted (Budapest thermal baths) or fully compensated (local problems).

A multiobjective model is formulated in order to find a trade-off among the three goals, that is, a "satisfactum".

MULTIOBJECTIVE MODEL

Multiobjective Programming Formulation

Multiobjective decision-making may formally be described as an optimization procedure OP, (Duckstein and Opricovic 1978):

$$OP: (S,Q,G), \to d*$$

i.e., OP maps the triplet (S,Q,G) into an optimal point in the decision space, in which S = system description; Q = optimization criterion; G = constraints and $d*$ = "the best" solution or decision.

In the present case, system description S refers to a mathematical model which enables us to calculate karstic water levels and system outflows at any point in the system as a function of time, withdrawals (mining, water supply) and natural recharge (rainfall). This mathematical model is described elsewhere (Heinemann and Szilagyi 1976, Bogardi et al. 1977).

The optimization criterion Q enables us to compare and evaluate the feasible alternatives or admissible controls, designated by D. Formally, $Q: D \to R^n$ where R^n is a finite, n-dimensional space whose typical element r is the n-tuple $(r_1, ..., r_n)$ of real numbers; thus r_i may denote the value of the ith real-valued objective function. A one-dimensional objective function corresponds to the mapping $Q: D \to R^1$ which reduces the optimization problem to choosing the maximum element in a given set of real numbers.

If n > 1 then the mapping $Q: D \to R^n$ results in a set of n-tuples, but the optimization procedure is not considered to be finished because there is not a unique mathematical algorithm to determine "the best" n-tuple, especially when elements of r are not in the same units. In this case, an algorithm must be developed to determine "the best" n-tuple. In the general case, the optimization criterion is a multiple-criterion function with a preference structure: $Q = [F(x),P]$. In other words, Q is a two-tuple whose first element is a vector-valued criterion function, $F(x) = [f_1(x), ..., f_n(x)]$, and second element is a preference structure P which defines a preference relation over the set of objectives. The structure P is used to indicate which elements of the criteria space are preferred to others. The optimization procedure will thus result in an optimal solution, sometimes called a "preference optimal" solution (Stadler 1976).

A sequential optimization procedure is used in this paper. In a first optimization stage, the vector-valued criterion function, F(x) is evaluated; in the second stage, the preference structure P is introduced to find a set of noninferior or Pareto-optimal solutions (Szidarovszky 1977). Compromise programming is then applied to find a trade-off among the three goals considered. In the next section, the optimization criterion is shown for each of the goals.

Optimization Criterion

a. Mining Objective

Let x_i = decision variable, the annual withdrawal from mine i;

v_{ik} = decision variable, the annual amount of water conveyed from mine i to recharge point k;

$n = n_1 + n_2$ = number of mines n_1 and other intakes n_2;

$$r = \text{number of artificial recharge spots: } i = 1, ..., n, k = 1, ..., r;$$
$$b_i(x_i) = \text{annual capital cost for withdrawal } x_i \text{ from mine } i;$$
$$\theta_i(x_i) = \text{annual operation cost for withdrawal } x_i \text{ from mine } i;$$
$$A_i = \text{annual amount of total inrushes into the mine } i;$$
$$L_i(A_i\text{-}x_i) = \text{annual economic losses due to presence of mine water volume } (A_i\text{-}x_i);$$
$$B_{ik}(v_{ik}) = \text{annual costs of conveying } v_{ik}.$$

With this notation, the cost function of a mine is:

$$f_{li} = b_i(x_i) + \theta_i(x_i) + L_i(A_i - x_i) + \sum_{i,k} B_{ik}(v_{ik}) \tag{1}$$

The regional mining objective is thus: $\min f_1 = \Sigma f_{li}$, which is a usual objective in the mining industry (Lucas and Adler 1973). Constraints are:

(i)   withdrawal x_i cannot be greater than the total amount of mine water A_i: $x_i \leq A_i, i = 1, ..., n;$

(ii) similarly, for transport: $\sum_k v_{ik} < x_i$

b. Water Supply Objective

The goal of regional water management is to satisfy water demands at minimum cost. Possible groundwater intake points (including mines) and water demand points are considered to be located on a grid, so that the water supply objective can be expressed as (Bishop and Hendricks 1974):

$$\min f_2 = \sum_{i,j} s_{ij}(y_{ij}) \tag{2}$$

in which $j = 1,2,...m$, the number of water demand grid points;

y_{ij} = decision variable, the annual amount of water supplied from mine or other intake i to water demand grid point j;

s_{ij} = the annual costs of supply including investment, operation, treatment and conveyance.

The following constraints must be observed:

(i)   the demands must be satisfied: $\sum_i y_{ij} = d_j$; for every j

(ii) $\sum_j y_{ij} + \sum_k v_{ik} \leq x_i$ for every mine $i = 1,...,n$

c. Environmental Objective

The environmental objective is fully satisfied for those decisions $[x_i]$, $[y_{ij}]$, $[v_{ik}]$ which maintain the recharge of thermal baths. Thus, the environmental objective can be formulated as:

$$f_3 = b\text{-}h([x_i], [y_{ij}], [v_{ik}]) \tag{3}$$

The function h calculates underground outflow at given locations as a function of the decision variables. If this environmental objective were the only one considered, the decision variables would simply be chosen so that h = b. There are three possible ways to estimate function h:

(i) For each combination of decision alternatives, system description S calculates a value of h. This method would be straightforward except that its use in conjunction with the multiobjective optimization model poses difficulties as yet unresolved.

(ii) Using system description S, a multivariate regression model based on phenomenological considerations is constructed to estimate h; the optimization proceeds with this regression equation entered into Equation 3. In our practical example, this is the procedure used.

(iii) The value of h is again calculated by means of a regression equation, but this equation is estimated from past observation data. This approach can be used only in an existing system for which a better operation is sought.

Compromise Programming

Compromise solutions are those which are the closest, by some distance measure, to the ideal one (Zeleny 1973, Starr and Zeleny 1977). Among all achievable scores for the ith criterion, there is at least one value that is preferred to all remaining ones; for example, $f_i^* = \min f_i$, $i = 1,...,n$. The vector f^* whose elements are all such minima is called the ideal vector: $f^* = (f_1^*,...,f_n^*)$; it is generally not a feasible solution of OP. One of the most frequently used measures of "closeness" is a family of L_p- metrics, defined as follows:

$$L_p = \left[\sum_{i=1}^{n} \alpha_i^P (f_i^* - f_i)^P \right]^{1/p} \tag{4}$$

or

$$L_p = \sum_{i=1}^{n} \alpha_i^P (f_i^* - f_i)^P \tag{5}$$

where weights α_i are either assessed subjectively by the decision maker (DM) or derived from the preference structure p. The objective of the optimization is:

$$\min_{x} \sum_{i=1}^{n} \alpha_i^P D_i^P \tag{6}$$

in which D_i is a deviation from the ideal value. Since D_i can be positive or negative, let D_i be defined as:

$$D_i = \left| f_i^* - f_i \right| \tag{7}$$

If objective functions f_i are not expressed in commensurable units, then a scaling function $S_i (D_i)$ is defined to ensure the same range for every objective function; usually, this dimensionless range is the interval (0,1). Let the scaling function be linear:

$$S_i(D_i) = \frac{|f_i{}^* - f_i|}{|M_i - m_i|} \tag{8}$$

in which M_i and m_i are, respectively, the maximum and minimum value of f_i. The objective of compromise programming is then to minimize the following L_p norm:

$$L_p = \sum_{i=1}^{n} a_i^p \frac{|f_i{}^* - f_i|}{|M_i - m_i|} \tag{9}$$

If the weights $[a_i]$ and parameter p are given, then the minimization in Equation 9 yields an optimal or compromise solution. It is, however, useful to the DM to be provided with compromise solutions with different values of p. For $p = 1$ and $a_i = 1$, $i = 1,...,n$, compromise programming is reduced to goal programming; for $p = 1$ and $\Sigma a_i = 1$, to a linear weighting approach, and for $p = \infty$, $a_i = 1$, $i = 1,...,n$, to a minimax problem. In the next section, the methodology is used to solve a practical problem.

NUMERICAL EXAMPLE

Simplifying Assumptions

The numerical example shown in this section reflects the problem, the region and the underlying conditions as described formerly; however, in order to make the example tractable by hand calculations of the reader if he so wishes, the following simplifications have been introduced:

(a) a reduced number of intake and demand points is used;
(b) costs and losses are taken as linear functions of the decision variables;
(c) f_3 is defined by a multivariate regression on the decision variables.

Objective Functions

a. Mining Cost Objective

There are three mines planned ($n_1 = 3$) and two possible recharge points ($r = 2$) in the region, so that:

$$f_1 = f_{11} + f_{12} + f_{13} \tag{10}$$

in Forints (Ft)/year (1 Ft equals about 5 cents), with

$$f_{11} = b_1 x_1 + e_1 x_1 + L_1(A_1 - x_1) + a_{11} v_{11} + a_{12} v_{12}$$

$$f_{12} = b_2 x_2 + e_2 x_2 + L_2(A_2 - x_1) + a_{21} v_{21} + a_{22} v_{22}$$

$$f_{13} = b_3 x_3 + e_3 x_3 + L_3(A_3 - x_1) + a_{31} v_{31} + a_{32} v_{32}$$

Data for f_1 are given in Table 1.

TABLE 1. Coefficients of objective functions f_{1i}

mine	A_i m^3/min	b_i	e_i	L_i Ft/m^3	a_{11}	a_{12}
1	150	2.8	1.5	5.5	9	9
2	100	2.5	1.6	5.5	8	8
3	60	3.2	1.7	5.5	7	11

The constraints for f_1 are:

$$x_1 \leq 150, \quad x_2 \leq 100, \quad x_3 \leq 60$$

$$v_{11} + v_{12} \leq x_1$$

$$v_{21} + v_{22} \leq x_2$$

$$v_{31} + v_{32} \leq x_3$$

and

b. Water Supply Objective

There are $n = 6$ possible intake sites including $n_1 = 3$ mines and $n_2 = 3$ other sites, and $m = 7$ demand points

$$f_2 = \sum_{i=1}^{6} \sum_{j=1}^{7} s_{ij} y_{ij} \qquad Ft/year \qquad (11)$$

The values of s_{ij} (Ft/m^3) are given in Table 2.

TABLE 2. Values of s_{ij} in Ft/m^3 for objective function f_2

i \ j	1	2	3	4	5	6	7
1	10.5	6.4	5.7	7.7	12.3	12.3	14.7
2	8.9	5.4	8.2	10.0	12.3	13.5	16.5
3	5.8	11.8	12.5	15.3	18.2	20.0	22.4
4	10.0	7.0	3.2	6.0	12.0	12.3	13.3
5	13.0	8.5	6.0	3.2	11.5	10.0	11.0
6	17.5	11.5	12.0	10.0	7.0	3.2	8.0

The constraints for f_2 are:

$$\sum_{i=1}^{6} y_{ij} = d_j \quad \text{for every j with:}$$

Demand point j	1	2	3	4	5	6	7
Demand d_j in $10^6 m^3$/year	9.6	4.	24.5	4.	4.	24.5	12.4

and

$$\sum_{j=i}^{7} y_{ij} + \sum_{k=1}^{2} v_{ik} \leq x_i \quad \text{for all three mines.}$$

c. Environmental Objective

$$f_3 = b - h(\{x_i\}, \{y_{ij}\}, \{v_{ik}\}) \qquad \text{(Szilagyi 1976).}$$

$$b = 30 m^3/\text{min}$$

The following linear multiple regression equation was found (in m^3/min):

$$E(h) = c_0 - c_1 x_1 - c_2 x_2 - c_3 x_3 - c_4 \sum_{j=1}^{7} y_{4j} - \tag{12}$$

$$c_5 \sum_{j=1}^{7} y_{5j} - c_6 \sum_{j=1}^{7} y_{6j} + c_7 \sum_{i=1}^{3} v_{i1} + c_8 \sum_{i=1}^{3} v_{i2}$$

in which the regression parameters are:

k	0	1	2	3	4	5	6	7	8
C_k	45.0	0.19	0.22	0.22	0.15	0.10	0.08	0.55	0.50

Multiobjective Analysis

The objective functions $f_i(x)$ are not expressed in the same units; thus, a scaling function (Equation 8) is used. The objective function of compromise programming is taken as Equation 9 with $p = 1$ and $\Sigma a_i = 1$; that is, a linear weighting approach is used, to yield the L_p norm:

$$L_p = \sum_{i=1}^{3} \alpha_i \frac{|f_i* - f_i|}{|M_i - m_i|} \tag{13}$$

which is evaluated by means of data given in Table 3.

TABLE 3. Elements of L_p-norm

	f_1	f_2	f_3	$m_i = f_i^*$	M_i	α_i
$f_1, 10^6$ Ft	-	246	70	135	416	0.5
$f_2, 10^6$ Ft	392	-	72	118	397	0.2
$f_3, m^3/min$	392	237	-	-101	88	0.3

In Table 3 each row refers to an objective function treated independently of the other two. The numbers in the rows correspond to the objective function values; M_i is the maximum, that is, the worst value of f_i, a_i is the weight of f_i in the L_p norm (Equation 13). To illustrate the conflicts among objectives, let mining cost objective f_1 be minimized: then both water supply objective f_2 and environmental objective f_3 are close to their worst values. Next, let either f_2 or f_3 be minimized: then the mining cost objective comes in turn close to its worst value. Thus the necessity of finding a compromise is evident. In Table 4, objective function values f_i calculated by minimizing L_p in Equation 13, and corresponding values of x_i, v_{i1}, v_{i2}, are given. Note that: f_2 is equal to its ideal value $f_2 = f_2^*$, a relatively small loss occurs for f_1 (23%), but a large loss is found for f_3 (110%). If the DM is not satisfied with this compromise, new weights can be selected--probably with greater emphasis on the environmental objective--and a new compromise solution is calculated. It is assumed in this example that the numerical solution is satisfactory and thus Table 4 contains compromise decisions. Note that artificial recharges v_{i1} and v_{i2} are not necessary and mining withdrawals are also either zero (for x_1) or relatively small. If the environmental objective were given greater weight, some artificial recharge would become necessary and, consequently, mine water withdrawals would also be larger. As a result of the assumption of linear cost functions, water demands are satisfied gradually from the cheaper sources to the more expensive ones, as shown in Table 5.

TABLE 4. Values of f_i, x_i, v_{i1} and v_{i2} in the compromise solution

i	f_i	x_i	
1	167	0	
2	118	12	and $v_{i1} = v_{i2} = 0$
3	18	30	

TABLE 5. Values of y_{ij} in the compromise solution

i \ j	1	2	3	4	5	6	7
1							
2		12					
3	30						
4			79				
5				11			
6					13	78	39

CONCLUSION

This paper illustrates how multiobjective programming can be used efficiently to find a compromise among conflicting objectives in regional natural resource development. As a specific problem, mining under water hazard, water supply and thermal spas recharge has been selected to illustrate the methodology. However, the level of analysis reached in this paper represents only the first step toward a more comprehensive investigation, which should address itself to the following areas:

a. Numerical calculation which covers only the first phase of the compromise programming algorithm, i.e., the determination of a trial compromise solution (Duckstein and Opricovic 1978), should be carried into a second phase, in which the algorithm is run one or more times with new weights provided by the DM. This second phase can also be considered as a sensitivity analysis.

b. The selection of the type of L_p-metrics may strongly affect the compromise solution: in fact, there is no available technique to find the "best" value of p. Again, sensitivity analysis can be used to reveal the effect of the type of metric on the solution.

c. In reality, cost and loss functions are rarely linear. For a better approximation to actual functions, piecewise linearization may be used; then linear programming can be applied using, for example, separable convex programming technique (Hillier and Lieberman 1974). Note that nonlinear and nonconvex functions are difficult to handle, especially in a multiobjective analysis (Goicoechea et al. 1978).

d. Different objectives usually have different measures of effectiveness (i.e., average annual cost, recharge volume, percentage of demand satisfaction), the choice of which affects the compromise solution.

e. In such a regional problem as described herein, a number of stochastic elements exist, namely: the amount of minewater A; water demands d_j; and the error term in the linear regression defining f_3 (Equation 12). In fact, in a single objective analysis of either mine-water control or water-supply, these state variables are considered as random variables (Duckstein et al. 1978, Bogardi et al. 1978). However, the introduction of stochastic elements into multiobjective models usually results in numerical difficulties. Also, the values of the A_i's may not be independent, since high inrush volume in a mine could cause lower inrushes in a neighboring mine.

f. Decision analysis in this paper refers to a single year. To be realistic, the DM would need design data for the complete horizon and dynamic multiobjective decision models would have to be developed.

g. As far as the environmental objective is concerned, a methodology should be developed so that the system description model can be used interactively with the decision model. Also, measures of effectiveness other than recharge volume may be required to characterize thermal baths, such as water temperature or chemical composition. The introduction of these additional measures are not expected to cause major difficulties, because of the existence of adequate system description models (heat conductivity, diffusion).

ACKNOWLEDGMENT

Research leading to this paper was performed in part within the framework of a cooperative research project between the Hungarian Mining Research Institute and the University of Arizona, under a grant from the United States National Science Foundation, titled: "Decision Making Under Uncertainty in Natural Resources Management," and matching grants from the Hungarian Institute for Cultural Relations and the Ministry of Heavy Industry.

ABSTRACT

A multiobjective decision-making model is applied for trading-off mining operations under water hazards, demands for water supply and environmental protection. Under natural conditions often found in underground coal extraction, mining operations require a proper water-control system. Depending on the mode of economic control, variable and possibly random amounts of mine water (resulting for example from underground floods) must be withdrawn. On the other hand, this dewatering may exert various adverse effects on the environment, such as sinking groundwater levels, drying up of springs, and decreased recharge for thermal waters. The decision-maker seeks a solution called "satisfactum" which corresponds to the "best" compromise among conflicting interests. A specific multiobjective programming algorithm, called compromise programming, is used to formulate goal functions for the case of planning regional mining development and find such a satisfactum. A numerical example is presented to provide a step-by-step illustration.

REFERENCES

Bishop, A.B. and D.W. Hendricks. 1974. Analysis of water reuse alternatives in an integrated urban and agricultural area. pp. 324-363, In R. de Neufville and D. Marks (eds.), Systems Planning and Design, Prentice-Hall, N J.

Bogardi, I., Zs. Kesseru, A. Schmieder and F. Szidarovszky. 1977. Multiobjective approach for trading-off the mining of natural resources with environmental considerations. pp. 151-163, In Proc. IIAS-TEKHA Conf. on Complex Utilization of Natural Resources, Sopron, Hungary.

Bogardi, I., F. Szidarovszky and L. Duckstein. 1978. Optimal sequencing of a multipurpose water supply system. Advances in Water Resources 1:275-284.

Bower, B.T. 1975. Residuals management in the use of coal to generate electrical energy. pp. 305-319, In Proc. Intl. Seminar on Regional Planning and Environmental Pollution Control, Katowice, Poland.

Down, C.G. and I. Stocks. 1977. Environmental Impact of Mining. Applied Sci. London, 371 p.

Duckstein, L., I. Bogardi and J. Casti. 1978. Control model of underground flooding. Paper presented at the Session of Systems Design, Spring Natl. Meeting of ORSA, NY.

Duckstein, L. and S. Opricovic. 1978. Multiobjective optimization and environmental decision-making: A study in river basin development. Working paper No. 77-41, Dept. of Systems and Industrial Engineering, Univ. Arizona, Tucson.

Goicoechea, A., L. Duckstein and M.M. Fogel. 1978. Multiple objectives under uncertanty: An illustrative application of PROTRADE. Water Resources Research (in press).

Heinemann, Z. and G. Szilagyi. 1976. Simulation of the karstic water system of the Transdanubian Mountain. pp. 68-81, In Proc. Conf. on Minewater Protection, Budapest, Hungary.

Hillier, F.S. and G.J. Lieberman. 1974. Operations Research, 2nd Ed. Holden-Day, 632 p.

Kapolyi, L. 1977. Role of natural resources in the structure of Hungarian economics. pp. 10-22, In Proc. IIASA-TEKHA Conference on Complex Utilization of Natural Resources, Sopron, Hungary.

Lucas J.R. and L. Adler (eds.) 1973. Groundwater and groundwater control. Section 26 in SME Mining Engineering Handb, NY, 55 p.

Monarchi, D., C. Kisiel and L. Duckstein. 1973. Interactive multiobjective programming in water resources: A case study. Water Resources Res. 9:837-850.

Schmieder, A., Zs. Kesseru, J. Juhasz, T. Willems and F. Martos. 1975. Water Hazard and Water Management in Mining (in Hungarian). Muszaki Konyvkiado, Budapest, Hungary, 446 p.

Stadler, W. 1976. Sufficient conditions for preference optimality. pp. 129-148, In G. Leitmann (ed.), Multi-Criteria Decision-Making and Differential Games. Plenum Press, NY.

Starr, M.K. and M. Zeleny. 1977. MCDM - State and future of the arts. pp. 5-30, In M.K. Starr and M. Zeleny (eds.), Multiple Criteria Decision-Making. North-Holland Pub. Co., NY.

Szidarovszky, F. 1977. Game Theory (in Hungarian). Tankonyvkiado, 389 p.

Szilagyi, G. (ed.) 1976. Investigation into the effect of mining activity on the karstic waters in the Transdanubian Mountain (in Hungarian). Res. Rpt. No. 13-9/75, Hungarian Mining Research Institute (MRI), Budapest, Hungary.

Yu, P.L. and M. Zeleny. 1975. The set of all nondominated solutions in the linear cases and a multicriteria simplex method. J. Math. Anal. and App. 49:91-101.

Zeleny, M. 1973. Compromise programming. pp. 262-301, In J.L. Cochrane and M. Zeleny (eds.), Multiple Criteria Decision-Making. Univ. South Carolina Press, Columbia.

TRACE ELEMENTS IN THE ENVIRONMENT – EFFECTS AND POTENTIAL TOXICITY OF THOSE ASSOCIATED WITH COAL

*Arthur Wallace and Wade L. Berry**

INTRODUCTION

Definition and Examples of Toxicity

Of 90 naturally occurring elements, eight elements compose 98% of the lithosphere. The rest of the elements, or 91% of the naturally occurring elements make up the remaining 1.5% of the lithosphere (Epstein 1972). Due to the low concentration of these latter elements in nature, most of them were historically recognized as being present in trace amounts only. Thus many of these elements were grouped together under a common heading of trace elements although chemically they were quite divergent.

At least six of the trace elements, iron, boron, manganese, zinc, copper, and molybdenum are essential in the metabolism of higher plants (Epstein 1972). At least an additional 10 are essential to animals or other organisms (cobalt, iodine, selenium, chromium, flourine, arsenic, tin, vanadium, nickel, and silicon). Although these essential trace elements are normally found only in very small amounts in organisms, they are co-factors in metabolism. The levels, or better, ranges of trace metals in organisms which are optimum for life processes are relatively narrow and it is as easy to have an excess as a deficiency. Complexity enters because there are interactions among many of the trace metals (Olsen 1972) and the interactions can even involve synergistic effects (Wallace and Romney 1977).

At the high end of the concentration spectrum, all elements can be potentially, but differentially, toxic to biological systems if present and available in the environment in large excess over their normal concentrations. This means that these essential trace elements must be maintained in the environment in a relatively narrow concentration range between deficiency and toxicity in order to maintain viable and productive biological systems. However, in terms of absolute amounts, the essential trace elements are generally less toxic to animal systems than the less abundant ones such as cadmium, lead, beryllium and mercury (Schroeder 1973).

Most of the trace elements naturally occurring in the undisturbed biosphere were originally derived from the soil via the parent material, the rock from which the soil was formed. The natural pathways by which additional trace elements can enter the terrestrial ecosystem are relatively few and of very low magnitude. These pathways include rain and

*Laboratory of Nuclear Medicine and Radiation Biology, 900 Veteran Avenue, University of California, Los Angeles, CA 90024.

95

dust arising from adjacent terrestrial systems, sea spray, volcanic activity and small additions from meteroric material. Therefore, it does not require a substantial amount of trace element pollution to significantly alter the present equilibrium because of these very limited natural inputs (Bertine and Goldberg 1971). Our industrial society mines and concentrates several of these trace elements many-fold for use in industry and eventually disposes of them in environments that normally contain relatively low concentrations of them. Therefore, biosystems or organisms in these environments which usually have had to conserve these essential trace elements and even concentrate them find themselves in the situation where a relatively small amount of biological enrichment (magnification or concentration) can lead to concentrations of trace elements which are potentially toxic.

Perhaps even more insidious are the trace elements that are not essential and are commonly found in nature in very low concentrations. Mammals do not generally seem to have homeostatic mechanisms to exclude or to excrete them and such elements accumulate in the mammalian tissues with age and exposure.

Examples of trace element toxicities are numerous and varied. Numerous examples have occurred where annual applications of pesticides and/or fertilizers and/or soil amendments (e.g., sludges or flyash) containing trace elements have resulted in toxic effects. Benson (1968) recorded the toxicity of arsenic in old apple orchards. The arsenic was applied routinely for a number of years as an insecticide. When it was time to replant the orchard, arsenic had accumulated to such an extent in the upper horizons of the soil that young trees could not be established without removing the arsenic-contaminated soil. Another example is the occurrence of zinc toxicity from sprays used for pesticide control on peaches (Lee and Craddock 1969). Trace element deficiency was common in Florida citrus soils; however, with repeated micronutrient applications it was quickly overcome and shortly overcorrected in many cases. When this happened, yields were reduced due to copper toxicity (Westgate 1952, Reuther and Smith 1954). The addition of sludges to soils for sludge disposal and/or soil improvement can result in trace element toxicity when added in excessive amounts or over prolonged periods (Lunt 1959).

Toxicities as the result of pollution from the activities of man are not the only examples of trace element toxicity. Antonovics et al. (1971) have reported many populations of plants that are restricted in distribution because of mineralized areas. The whole field of geobotanical prospecting is based upon the fact that certain plants are either restricted to or from certain mineralized areas and that certain plants accumulate high concentrations of trace elements in their tissues (Cannon 1960). There are extensive areas in the Western United States where the concentration of selenium is high. The occurrence of selenium toxicity to animals from food crops produced in certain of these areas was sufficiently high to cause the United States Government to remove some of these lands from crop production (Anderson et al. 1961). The addition of more selenium to such land is undesirable.

A very urgent conclusion from these facts is that man can little afford not to control the amounts of many of the trace metals that enter his food chain or his environment. Some states are moving to do just that. The control then will have to be at many different sources of trace metals. Farmers sometimes use trace metals in pesticides. Sometimes they attempt to overcome trace-metal deficiencies by trace metal application or they even add fertilizers containing trace metals to assure that no deficiencies are present. Automobile gasoline is a source of lead at least which settles out on land, crops and elsewhere. Cadmium and other trace metals escape from rubber as tires on vehicles wear out. Galvanized pipes are sources of zinc and cadmium in water. Industrial fumes and wastes contain various trace metals. Coal contains a number of trace metals mostly, but not entirely, because of its biological origin. Some of these trace metals are volatilized when coal is burned and they escape to the atmosphere. Others escape in the form of coal flyash although much of the flyash is trapped to eventually find other uses. Some of these other uses of flyash are in agriculture and quite frequently in land reclamation projects such as those following strip mining. This source is being evaluated (Heit 1977), Gough and Shacklette 1976). Metal mining industries are sources of trace metals in the environment.

Sulfur is not a trace metal. It is a macroelement so far as the growth of plants is concerned. Even so, sulfur can be one of the environmental problems of an industrial society. It is a matter of extreme importance in the bioavailability of trace metals to plants. Sulfur whether reduced (as H_2S) or oxidized (as H_2SO_4) forms acids and soil acidification greatly increases the bioavailability of most trace metals, not only of those added to the environment by activities of man, but also of those naturally present in soil (Hutchinson 1977). Trace metal control then also involves sulfur control. Coals contain various amounts of sulfur (Babu 1975). In general, western coals tend to have lower sulfur concentrations than eastern coals.

Man has to be concerned not only about what and how much of the trace metals enter into his food chain, but he also has to be concerned about what excess levels of trace metals do to the yields of his crops. The two problems are related to some degree, but not entirely. For example, leaf surfaces can become contaminated externally with trace metals such as in flyash. Animals grazing on such crops can pass the metals on to man or, if leafy vegetables are involved, they can be passed directly to man. Such leaf contamination would have, in all likelihood, no bearing on the yields of the crops, but could add trace metals to the food chain of man. Some foliar deposited trace metals can enter leaves of plants, however (Wallace et al. 1978). Herbivores can ingest soil directly and pass the trace metals to man.

In addition to these two environmental concerns, there are three other environmental concerns with trace metals: (1) volatilized metals or those present in respirable aerosols can become deposited in lungs; (2) the deposition of trace metals in drinking water; (3) destruction or disruption of natural ecosystems on both land and water.

The Ecology of Trace Elements

This paper will emphasize those trace elements present in coal which appear to be present in concentrations that could potentially be toxic given the appropriate circumstances. In assessing the potential hazard of trace elements, it should be remembered that in passing through the food chain even seemingly harmless concentrations of trace elements may be increased to injurious levels ("biological magnification"). In addition different classes of organisms and in some cases different cultivars of the same species respond differently to different concentrations of a trace metal (Wright 1976).

Biological enrichment or magnification is the life process whereby organisms such as plants accumulate mineral elements against a concentration gradient. The magnification is often increased as the trace elements move from one trophic level to a higher one. Under natural conditions this concentration is often necessary for the survival of the organisms. Normally the required mineral nutrients are in smaller concentrations in the environment than they are required by organisms for metabolism. When the environmental concentrations of the minerals are increased, the organism will still accumulate these elements. The trace elements, therefore, can be concentrated to the extent that they become toxic to the plant itself, to the animals that eat the plants, or to subsequent vegetation growing on the same lands. When both the physical and biological mechanisms are operating, it is easy to see that even low rates of trace element pollution occurring over a long period of time can cause substantial enrichment. Enrichment ratios of 30 for moss and 44 for humus were given by Tyler (1972) for cadmium in a spruce forest.

The trace elements barium, cadmium, chromium, cobalt, copper, lead, lithium, manganese, nickel, strontium, tin, and zinc exist in the soil solution predominately as cations although complex ions and ion pairs are known to occur. These trace elements usually occur in the soil solution of neutral soils (pH = 7) at concentrations less than 0.05 ug ml^{-1} (Bradford et al. 1971). In acid soils (pH 5-6) their concentration in the soil solution increases and it usually decreases in calcareous or alkaline soils (pH 7.5-8.5). Taking this into consideration as well as the limited solubilities of their phosphates, carbonates and hydroxides and their strong absorption by the cation exchange sites of the soil, their resultant mobility in the soil is very low. These trace elements are mostly retained in the surface layers of the soil and are very resistant to leaching to lower depths except in sandy or very acid soils or in the presence or organic chelators. Thus, in most cases they are not a problem to the underground water supply, but they could become a problem when transported along with runoff and dust. These same characteristics, however, are the factors which make low-level, long-term pollution dangerous. These trace element cations are not distributed throughout the soil, but are concentrated in the surface layers and will reach toxic levels with time.

Mercury in the soil may exist in a number of forms. Mercury can be lost from the soil as the volatile elemental mercury or be retained in the organic fraction of the soil. Boron at pH values below 8.5 occurs in the soil solution as the undissociated boric acid and therefore is very mobile in the soil and can be leached quite readily into the groundwater supply.

The trace elements arsenic, molybdenum, and selenium exist in the soil solution as divalent anion complexes. These anions react in the soil somewhat analogous to phosphate. The solubility of these elements is limited in the presence of active iron, aluminum, and calcium. These trace anions are more soluble under neutral or calcareous conditions because the calcium forms are more soluble than either the iron or aluminum form. In the soil these anions are relatively more soluble than the cations but less so than boron.

The essential trace elements are accumulated by all plants and all elements are accumulated by some plants (Peterson 1977). However, the affinity of different plant species for different elements varies widely. For example, selenium is not readily absorbed by some plants while other plants such as some *Astragalus* spp. accumulate vast amounts (Ganje 1966). This is true even when the plants are grown side by side on the same soil. Some *Astragalus* spp. will accumulate so much selenium that the plant will be toxic to any animal eating it while the other plants growing next to it will be completely innocuous.

The distribution of trace elements within the plant after absorption is not necessarily uniform. This is especially so when high concentrations of trace elements are involved. For most of the trace element cations the major portion of the absorbed fraction remains in the root system of the plant and very little is translocated to the tops of the plant and even less is transferred to the fruit or grain.

Although there is a vast amount of information in the agronomic literature on the availability, absorption, and metabolization of trace elements, almost none existed until very recently on excess or toxicity of the trace elements with the possible exception of boron. The older information has been collected by Chapman (1966) and Allaway (1968); but the information is very spotty and consists mostly of isolated analyses of plants and soils from locations where plant growth was reduced due to toxicities. Four recent symposia (Drucker and Wildung 1977, Hutchinson 1975, Howell et al. 1975, Adriano and Brisbin 1978) have added to knowledge of trace elements, particularly in ecosystems.

Some Elements of Concern with Coal Technology

Arsenic (As)

Arsenic is unbiquitously present throughout the entire natural environment in trace amounts at an average of 5 µg g^{-1} in the upper lithosphere (Goldschmidt 1954). The soil chemistry of As is such that it resembles phosphorus and is fixed in the soil as is phosphate in the iron, aluminum, and calcium fractions. In aerated soils the pentavalent form is the most common (Schroeder and Balassa 1966). Arsenic can be lost slowly from the soil system by leaching, plant extraction or by the volatilization of arsine produced by fungi.

Plants or processed foods prepared from plants rarely contain more than 1 µg g^{-1} or ml of As according to Allaway (1968). Hodgson (1970) gave the concentration ratio of As in plants to that in soil as 0.12. The roots of plants are severely affected by As before As is accumulated in the tops to any extent. Some plants are able to tolerate a higher concentration of As than others. Liebig (1966) listed the relative tolerance as follows: Very tolerant - asparagus, potato, tomato, carrot, tobacco, dewberry, grape, and red raspberry; Fairly tolerant - strawberry, sweet corn (on fine and medium soils), beet and squash; Low or no tolerance - snap bean, lima bean, onion, peas, cucumber, alfalfa, and other legumes, sweet corn and strawberry (on coarse-textured sandy soils). Although most plants have low tissue concentrations of As, some plants under extreme conditions contain up to 10 µg g^{-1} (Robinson and Edgington 1945). Concentrations as low as 3.4 µg g^{-1} can be toxic to sheep. The recommended maximum concentration for irrigation water applied to coarse-textured soils is 0.1 µg ml^{-1} of arsenic (NAS 1973).

The toxicity of As is a function of its chemical state. The free element is not considered very poisonous while many of its compounds are extremely toxic as denoted by their use as pesticides. The pentavalent oxidation state usually found in biological systems is not as toxic as the trivalent form. Vallee et al. (1960) have suggested that As is carcinogenic; however, this is disputed by Frost (1967) and Schroeder and Balassa (1966). Certain organic As compounds are added to the diet of poultry and livestock for the control of parasites and for antibiotic purposes. Arsenic has been reported to counteract some of the toxic effects of selenium.

Arsenic is released into the environment mainly from its use as a pesticide, metal smelting, and the combustion of fossil fuel. The old orchard soils of eastern Washington were reported by Benson (1968) to be so highly contaminated with As from pesticide sprays that they were toxic to many plants. The As concentrations of coal ranges from 2 to 25 µg g^{-1} (Lisk 1972). Goldschmidt (1954) reported that the concentration of As in coal ashes ranged upward to 8,000 µg g^{-1} and that concentrations of 500 to 1,000 µg g^{-1} were quite common. During the combustion of coal, As compounds are released by volatilization and can be passed directly into the atmosphere. As noted earlier, plants seem to be selective against As during the process of absorption by their roots from the soil. Thus, the greatest danger to animals, and through them to man, would be the ingestion of dust and dirt adhering to plant foliage grown in contaminated areas and also of surface waters from these areas.

Coals in the U.S.A. contain from 1 to 93 µg g^{-1} As and are very variable. Average values may be around 15 µg g^{-1}. Its range in soil is from 0.2 to 6 µg g^{-1} (Liebig 1966).

From 3 to 9 $\mu g\ g^{-1}$ soluble As has led to crop damage. Crops contain from 2 to 7 $\mu g\ g^{-1}$ As per g dry weight when it is available, but much more As than that enters food chains from soil contamination because of dietary habits, especially of cattle. This is pronounced with cows with resulting entry of As into milk although the transfer coefficient is low (Underwood 1962).

Burning of coal with very high (500 to 1,000 $\mu g\ g^{-1}$) As at one site in Europe resulted in hot spots accumulating about 50 $\mu g\ g^{-1}$ in 15 cm soil equivalent (Hluchan et al. 1968). Milk from the area contained 7.7 mg As per 100 g dried milk. It is the rare conditions such as this that must be avoided. It is expected that As levels in most conditions will be at least 100-fold lower than these.

Arsenic from flyash added to agricultural land has led to crop toxicities (Chrenekova and Holobrady 1970). Industrial smoke causes As toxicity in crops (Engmann et al. 1969). Only 2 $\mu g\ g^{-1}$ As in peach leaves is sufficient to be toxic (Lindner 1943).

Arsenic in coals has a potential for being toxic to crops and hazardous to man in areas near plants burning large amounts of coal. However, the toxicity of As to man depends greatly on the form in which it is acquired. Elemental As is relatively nontoxic, but many combined forms are toxic.

Barium (Ba)

Barium has not been shown to be essential for either plants or animals. Barium is relatively common in the lithosphere and found at surprisingly high concentrations in some plants. It may be toxic to plants at very high levels (Chaudhry et al. 1977). The average soil concentration range of Ba is 100 to 3,000 $\mu g\ g^{-1}$ soil (Vanselow 1966). Its concentration in some coals is up to 1%. Soluble forms of Ba are highly toxic to man. However, many forms of Ba are so insoluble that they can be ingested without danger such as sulfate which is used as a radioopaque aid to x-ray diagnosis.

Beryllium (Be)

Goldschmidt (1954) listed 2 $\mu g\ g^{-1}$ Be as the average concentration in the upper lithosphere; however, he reported concentrations of Be in coal ashes of up to 8,000 $\mu g\ g^{-1}$ with 4 $\mu g\ g^{-1}$ being a more common concentration. Lisk (1972) gave the range of 0.1 to 1,000 $\mu g\ g^{-1}$ as the concentration of Be found in coal. The ashes of some coals contain up to 2% Be (Schubert 1958). Beryl, $Be_3Al_2Si_6O_{18}$ is the common source of Be and when crystalline and green is the rare gem emerald. Beryl and many other compounds have extremely low solubility under natural conditions. However, the halogens of Be do have a significant vapor pressure.

Romney and Childress (1965) studied the effect of soluble Be compounds and found them toxic to plants at 2 $\mu g\ g^{-1}$ in culture solution or when they comprised more than 4% of the cation exchange capacity of the soil. Most of the absorbed Be remained in the roots and very little of it was translocated to the shoots.

Beryllium as a metal is very toxic to man. Small amounts of dust or fumes inhaled can result in berylliosis, with a mortality rate of about 30%. The average aerial concentration of Be should not exceed 0.1 $\mu g\ m^{-3}$ of air in nonworking areas (Schubert 1958). In 1947 about 40 people in a community surrounding a Be processing plant received a dose of sufficient size to cause berylliosis. The exposure was due to traces of Be being emitted with the plant's stack gases. The amount of Be found in some coals could be sufficient to cause problems if Be did not remain as very insoluble compounds of low vapor pressure during combustion. The exact fate of Be under different conditions of coal combustion should be verified.

Boron (B)

Boron is high in sea water: 4.8 µg ml^{-1} as given by Goldschmidt (1954). He contends that the geochemistry of B distribution is dominated by its concentration in sea water and marine sediments. In a review, Bradford (1966) concluded that B excess in soils would most likely be found in the following situations: soils derived from marine sediments; arid soils; soils derived from young deposits; and soils from parent material rich in B minerals. In the soil, B occurs as the undissociated boric acid except in highly alkaline soils (pH 8.5), and relatively is very mobile. Mineral soils do not retain B in their upper horizons as they do most other trace elements. Therefore, B can be leached to lower depths in the soil profile and can constitute a potential pollution problem in the groundwater. Boron interaction with soil organic matter is not well defined and soils high in organic matter may not react the same as mineral soils.

Boron is an essential element for the growth of higher plants, but it has not been shown to be essential for growth of animals. In plant nutrition, the tolerance range between deficiency and toxicity of B for plants is very narrow. Although the tolerance range of an individual plant may be narrow, the amount of B required by different species varies so much that the concentration of B which one species may find as inadequate, another may find toxic.

Toxicity occurs either due to high B soils or due to irrigation waters containing high concentrations of B. For irrigation waters the National Academy of Sciences (1973) recommended that B should not exceed 0.75 µg ml^{-1}. However, it is well known that plants differ in their sensitivity to B toxicity and 0.75 µg ml^{-1} is too high for some plant species. Hewitt (1966) reports that the general requirement of cereals is less than dicots and that some plants do not reach optimum levels until the B concentration is 15 µg ml^{-1} in solution culture, but that sub-clover shows toxicity at 0.5 µg g^{-1} of B. Bradford (1966) lists the relative B sensitivity of many plants. Because of B's high solubility in soil the concentration of B in the saturation extract can be used to evaluate its toxicity to plants. If the saturation extract is below 0.5 µg ml^{-1}, there will be no toxicity to higher plants. If the concentration is between 0.5 and 1 µg ml^{-1}, sensitive plants may show visible injury, between 1 and 5 µg ml^{-1} semitolerant crops may show visible injury; and between 5 and 10 µg ml^{-1} tolerant crops may show visible injury. Holliday et al. (1958) used flyash containing 19 to 51 µg g^{-1} of B as a soil amendment. This is sufficient to cause B toxicity on the plants growing on the flyash-amended soils. At this concentration of boron, even B-tolerant crops showed injury.

Cadmium (Cd)

Cadmium is toxic to both plants and animals and is not known to be essential for either one. Schroeder and Balassa (1961) have related tissue Cd to hypertension and reduced longevity in laboratory animals. The studies of Carroll (1966) showed a close correlation between the atmospheric Cd level of 28 cities and the incidence of death from hypertension and arteriosclerotic heart disease in these cities.

Bolton et al. (1973) cited studies which showed that 70% of the Cd in flue gas was in particles smaller than 5 u in diameter. It appears usually in a ratio with zinc of about 1 to 200, but as great as 1 to 50. If Zn concentrations of soil range from 10 to 300 $\mu g \, g^{-1}$, Cd would range from less than 0.1 to about 6 $\mu g \, g^{-1}$. Its content in plants is generally around 0.3 $\mu g \, g^{-1}$ (Huffman and Hodgson 1973).

A survey of institutional diets by Murthy et al. (1971) showed that Cd was a common constituent of these diets with concentrations ranging from 0.027 to 0.062 $\mu g \, g^{-1}$. Sea foods and meats are normally higher in Cd than are food grains and vegetables. Not only does Cd enter the food chain from natural sources such as soil where the average Cd concentration is 0.6 $\mu g \, g^{-1}$ with a range of 0.01 to 7 $\mu g \, g^{-1}$ (Allaway 1968), there are also many sources of Cd pollution. Coal contains 0.2 to 0.5 $\mu g \, g^{-1}$ Cd (Lisk 1972) and coal ashes up to 50 $\mu g \, g^{-1}$ (Goldschmidt 1954). The smelting of Zn and Pb produces large amounts of Cd; however, most of it is recovered and is the commerical source of Cd. Cadmium is used in many industries such as electroplating, pigments, alloys, batteries, tires, and as a stabilizer in the plastic industry all of which can and do contribute to Cd pollution.

Japanese studies (Yamagata and Shigmatsu 1970) have demonstrated that Cd from polluted soils and waters can be incorporated into the food chain in sufficient quantities to be toxic to humans. Mammals have a low tolerance for Cd which may be the result of the absence of a homeostatic mechanism to expel or excrete Cd; the body continues to absorb Cd regardless of the concentration within the body. A number of crop plants have been shown to be capable of accumulating Cd. John (1973) found in Cd-treated soils that the edible portions of radishes and lettuce averaged 387 and 138 $\mu g \, g^{-1}$ Cd, respectively. In solution culture, Page et al. (1972) found values up to 1,122 $\mu g \, g^{-1}$ in tomato leaves. Lagerwerff (1971) showed that aerial contamination accounted for more than 40% of the Cd content of radishes grown 200 m from a busy highway.

The factors presented above suggest that Cd toxicity from pollution is indeed a real danger in many cases. Animal systems have an extremely low tolerance for Cd. The mammalian body burden of Cd increases with each exposure. In the case of Cd, plants do not constitute an effective barrier in the pathway from soil to plant to man and animals as plants do with many other trace elements. Therefore, considering Carroll's (1966) report that present levels of Cd pollution in 28 U.S.A. cities are correlated with the incidence of death from certain heart problems, any additional sources of Cd pollution no matter how small should be considered serious.

Chromium (Cr)

Chromium is one of the trace elements essential to man and animals (Mertz 1967), but has not been demonstrated to be essential to higher plants. It is required for the proper metabolism of glucose and, therefore, the action of insulin in preventing diabetes. Chromium has also been indicated as being a factor in preventing arteriosclerosis and is antagonistic to lead toxicity (Lisk 1972). However, Cr is toxic to animals at somewhat higher levels, especially when in the hexavalent form, but the concentration range between essentiality and toxicity is large (Mertz 1967). There is a possibility that an increase in the Cr status of man might result in a decreased incidence of diabetes (Allaway 1968).

There is a broad range of Cr found in soils of 5 to 3,000 $\mu g \, g^{-1}$ with 6 $\mu g \, g^{-1}$ Cr being a representative value (Allaway 1968). Serpentine soils are often especially high in Cr (Cannon 1970) to the extent that Cr can become toxic to plants. The concentration of Cr in coal has been reported to be 5-60 µg g^{-1}, considerably more than the 0.0015-0.018 µg g^{-1} reported for petroleum (Lisk 1972). The soil chemistry of Cr is largely unknown. Oxides of Cr in the soil are very insoluble and unavailable to plants. However, it has been reported that absorption of Cr is increased after sewage waste application and that absorption occurs upon foliar application of river water (Lisk 1972). The ratio of Cr in plants to that in soil is 0.02 as reported by Hodgson (1970). In culture solution, small amounts of Cr (0.5 µg g^{-1}) have been reported to stimulate seedling growth, but it became toxic at 5 µg g^{-1} (Pratt 1966). He also reported that toxicity symptoms are stunting and a type of iron chlorosis and that the main toxic effect was exerted on the roots where the greatest accumulation of Cr occurred. The concentration of Cr found in food plants ranged from 0.03 to 1 µg g^{-1} (Allaway 1968) not much greater than the 0.15 to 20 µg g^{-1} Cr in the diets, Murthy et al. (1971) found a range of 0.36-0.89 mg of Cr consumption per day.

Cobalt (Co)

The concentration of Co and the lithosphere is relatively low, 0.004%. In soils its usual range of concentration is 1 to 40 µg g^{-1}, but it can range widely from concentrations in plants and soil derived from serpentine to concentrations so low that animals become deficient when fed forage (0.03-0.07 µg g^{-1} tissue) grown on these soils. Cobalt is an essential element for animals being part of the vitamin B$_{12}$ molecule. In the case of higher plants it has only been shown to be utilized by legumes when fixing nitrogen in association with *Rhizobium*. Plant species vary widely in their tolerance of Co; some accumulate very high concentrations, up to 10,000 µg g^{-1}, while tissue concentration of 1 µg g^{-1} is more common. In solution culture soluble concentration of Co in the range of 0.1 to 1 are toxic to many common agricultural plants.

In man the total body burden has been estimated at 1.1 mg. Epidemologic studies suggest that the incidence of goiter is greater where there is higher concentrations of Co in water and soil.

Copper (Cu)

The average Cu concentration of U.S. soils is 20 µg g^{-1} with a normal range of 1-50 µg g^{-1} (NAS 1977). As a rule, subsoils contain somewhat less Cu than the topsoil (Reuther and Labanauskas 1966). There is a very wide difference in tolerance to Cu between organisms. For aquatic organisms Cu is the most toxic of the common heavy metals and is accumulated by marine organisms with a concentration factor of 30,000 reported for phytoplankton. An example of different sensitivities is that diatoms, dinoflagellates and blue-green algae are more sensitive than green algae. A wide range of tolerance is also found in higher plants where common horticultural plants have tissue concentrations from 5-30 µg g^{-1}, however, a hyper accumulator *Aeolanthus biformeolius* has been reported to contain up to 13,000 µg g^{-1} (McLaisse et al 1978).

There is also a wide range in tolerance between oxide in that animal and mammalian tolerance is 100 to 1,000 times greater than that of more primitive animals. Ruminants are more sensitive to Cu by a factor of 10 than are nonruminants and man is apparently not susceptible to chronic Cu toxicity because of a well-developed homeostatic mechanism.

In fish it is reported that Cu, Zn, and Cd are synergistic in their toxic effects.

Fluorine (F)

Fluorine as fluoride is widely distributed in the earth's crust occurring chiefly as fluoropatite, fluorspar, and cryolite. Soil fluoride is mainly derived from these minerals and ranges in concentration from 20-500 µg g^{-1} (Robinson and Edgington 1945). Total soil fluoride is a poor indication of plant available fluoride which is controlled by soil type, Ca and P content of the soil and pH (Brewer 1966). Coal was found to contain 100-480 µg g^{-1} and the fluoride content increased going from coal to shale. Marine sediments were found to contain more fluoride than those of terrestrial origin. Fluorine is present in all natural plants and animal tissues and has been shown to be required by animals (Schwarz 1974, Wolf 1978), but has not been shown to be essential to plants. The usual F content of plant tissue is 2 to 20 µg g^{-1} (Brewer 1966), but the variability in the degree of tolerance which plants have for F is wide. Some plants such as citrus, apricot, cherry, plum, grape, and certain ornamentals are very susceptible to fluoride as an air pollutant and some are injured by exposure to concentrations less than 0.6 µg m^{-3} (Compton and Remmert 1960). Some plants such as tea are tolerant of F and even accumulate it to a high degree, 8,000 µg g^{-1}. Flourine is readily absorbed by the plant either through the roots or leaves and is redistributed within the plant on a soils to source basis (Romney et al. 1969). Atmospheric and gaseous forms are readily accumulated in or on the foliage and therefore is readily incorporated into the food chain. Chronic fluoride poisoning (fluorosis) of livestock occurs when the fluoride content of forage exceeds 40 µg g^{-1}. The order of sensitivity of farm animals is dairy cows>beef cows>sheep>swine>chickens>turkeys (NAS 1971). Fluorosis also occurs if the drinking water exceeds 1-2 µg F ml^{-1}.

Lead (Pb)

The potential health hazards of Pb to animals and humans is of concern. The role of Pb in air pollution has been well documented with the major increases being engine exhausts, smelting operations, pesticides, paints, and fossil fuels (National Research Council 1972). It has been estimated that over half of the normal body burden of Pb in the U.S.A. comes from food (Goldsmith and Hexter 1967). However, it is not clear how much of the Pb in the food supply comes from airborne deposits and how much arises from plant absorption and translocation of soil Pb. It has been found that near highways the Pb concentration of foliage is proportional to the concentration of Pb in the air; however, on protected plant parts this was not the case (Ganje and Page 1972). The availability of soil Pb to plants is poorly understood, but soil type and pH strongly affect Pb uptake (John 1972). Lead is more available in low pH soils. Lead is poorly translocated to the tops of plants even when the Pb is soluble and available in the soil. Soil pH and chelators regulate Pb transport in plants (Patel et al. 1977).

The soil in rural areas of the U.S.A. has a background concentration of Pb very similar to the average Pb concentration of the earth's crust, 10-15 µg g^{-1}. The soil Pb concentration of many urban areas is much higher suggesting substantial, but localized, pollution. Much of this comes from the burning of gasoline. In 1968 when coal production in the U.S.A. was 504 million tons with an average of 7 µg g^{-1}, 3,528 tons of Pb were released. The clinkers and flyash contained 74% of the Pb leaving 915 tons of Pb released as other forms.

Lithium (Li)

Lithium is found in small amounts in most soils. Swaine (1955) gave the range as 8-500 $\mu g\ g^{-1}$. The average Li concentration in plants is low, 0.85 $\mu g\ g^{-1}$ for monocotyledons and 1.3 $\mu g\ g^{-1}$ for dicotyledons (Bradford 1966). Some accumulators have over 1,000 $\mu g\ g^{-1}$ leaves without harm (Cannon 1960). The Li concentration of coal is given by Lisk (1972) as 0.5 to 25 $\mu g\ g^{-1}$; however, there is some evidence that Li concentrations of some coal can be much higher.

Naturally-occurring Li toxicity is known only in the case of citrus (Aldrich et al 1951). Bradford (1966) reported that 16 $\mu g\ g^{-1}$ of Li in soil will cause toxicity symptoms. Wallace et al. (1977) found 60 μg Li g^{-1} Yolo loam soil to be toxic with 600 to 1,000 μg Li g^{-1} leaves.

Mercury (Hg)

The average Hg concentration of coal is only 0.23 $\mu g\ g^{-1}$ in the survey of Ruch et al. (1973) (top value was 0.50 $\mu g\ g^{-1}$ in one set of samples), but Hg is a very dangerous element. Hazard is usually greater for elements found in the smallest supply. Some workers (Billings and Matson 1972) have reported some coals with 38 $\mu g\ g^{-1}$ Hg. In 1972 they found that flue gas emitted up to 82 μg Hg m^{-3}. Some 90% of that of the mercury found in coal is volatilized upon combustion (Bolton et al. 1973). If coal burned at the Moapa plant in Nevada contained 0.5 $\mu g\ g^{-1}$ Hg, over 900 pounds would be volatilized per year. The fate and consequences of airborne Hg are largely unknown. If the 900 pounds of Hg were discharged and spread out into 1,000 cubic miles of air, each m^3 air would contain 0.1 μg Hg. This is probably a safe level (Foote 1972). If it all settled and on the vegetation, the level would approach the tolerance limit, but no one seems to know what happens to the Hg vapor. Mercury is converted to organic forms and much can yet be learned of the process and of its chemistry in soil. Bolton et al. (1973) found three times elevation of Hg in a moss relative to soil near a coal-fired steam plant in Tennessee. The effects of low levels of Hg in soils must be determined even if we suscept that they cannot be injurious. Mercury vapors are toxic to plants, but plant species differ greatly in sensitivity (Zimmerman and Crocker 1934).

Molybdenum (Mo)

Soils generally contain less than 5 $\mu g\ g^{-1}$ Mo with 2.5 as a reasonable average. In soil Mo is generally found as the MoO_4^{2-} anion (+6 valence) and its solubility is controlled by its adsorption on Fe_2O_3. The availability of Mo to plants is high in alkaline soils, soils rich in organic matter and soils derived from volcanic rock. The availability of Mo is increased in poorly drained soils. The concentration of Mo in coal varies from west to east with about 6 $\mu g\ g^{-1}$ in western coal and only 0.5 ppm in eastern coal. Molybdenum concentration in flyash is increased by a factor of 10 to 600 from that present in coal.

Molybdenum is an essential element for bacteria, plants and animals. It is required for nitrogen fixation by *Azotobacter* and nitrate utilization in higher plants. Molybdenum excess or toxicity in plants is rarely, if ever, observed in the field. Plants appear to tolerate relatively high tissue concentrations (>375) without apparent toxicity symptoms. Wallace et al. (1977) found severe toxicity at 710 μg Mo g^{-1} leaves of bush beans. In contrast there are major land areas which show deficiency symptoms with tissue concentrations of 0.1 µg Mo g^{-1}. The critical level for Mo deficiency (0.5 µg g^{-1} or lower) is about one or more magnitudes lower than than the critical level of the other trace elements.

Large bioaccumulation of Mo in forage plants, especially legumes which normally contain more Mo than grasses, results in molybdenosis (a Mo-induced Cu deficiency) when eaten by ruminants. If the forage of ruminants contains greater than 10 µg g^{-1} Mo or if the Cu/Mo ratio is less than 5, the possibility of molybdenosis is high. Nonruminants and man do not seem to be susceptible to molybdenosis.

Nickel (Ni)

Nickel, despite its relatively high abundance in the lithosphere (0.01%) is among those trace elements about which little is known of either soil chemistry or biological activity. Swaine (1955) reported soil concentration of 5-100 µg g^{-1} with an average of about 100 µg g^{-1}. Nickel in nature normally occurs in the +2 valance state. Coal contains 10-50 µg g^{-1} and petroleum is high with 49-345 µg g^{-1} (Lisk 1972). The Ni concentration of coal varies as a function of location of origin; in North America eastern (19.4 µg g^{-1}) and midwestern (27.5 µg g^{-1}) coal contains more than western coal (5.3 µg g^{-1}) (NAS 1973). Plants are relatively sensitive to Ni in that in some cases a concentration of 0.5 µg m^{-1} in nutrient solutions will produce toxicity symptoms. The tissue concentration of Ni on natural vegetation is generally 0.05-5 µg g^{-1} and concentrations greater than 50 µg g^{-1} generally are toxic to plants (Wallace et al. 1977). However, there are some plants very tolerant to Ni and tissue concentrations up to 25% have been reported (Jaffre et al. 1976). Natural-occurring Ni toxicity has been observed in plants growing on serpentine-derived soils (Proctor and Woodell 1975).

Selenium (Se)

Selenium is an essential element for animals as shown by Schwarz and Foltz (1957). Selenium deficiency has been related to liver necrosis, white muscle disease and many others. Selenium is required in the diet of animals in the range of 0.04-0.2 µg g^{-1} to prevent deficiency (Allaway 1968). Selenium also is protective against the toxic effects of Cd or Hg (Lisk 1972). At slightly higher levels of Se in animal diets, 4-5 µg g^{-1}, toxicity results. Thus, for animals there is a very narrow range between deficiency and toxicity. This is not the case with plants. Selenium has not been shown to be essential to plant growth. Plants vary considerably in their ability to absorb Se. Common vegetables may accumulate 5 µg g^{-1}. Needless to say, Se is not a direct problem in plant growth, but could be a significant factor when considering the entire soil-plant-animal system.

Selenium is found in the lithosphere at an average concentration of 0.09 µg g^{-1}. However, the distribution in the U.S.A. is far from uniform. The distribution of Se has been studied by many people (Anderson et al. 1961) and areas of potential toxicity delineated. Some extremely toxic areas in the Western U.S.A. have been purchased by the U.S. Government and removed from crop production. There are other areas in the U.S.A. such as the northeast which are deficient in Se for good animal growth. The soil chemistry of Se is not well understood and it is not presently possible to predict plant uptake for Se from its concentration in soil. The Se concentration of plants varies by a factor of 100,000-fold, the most of any element (Robinson and Edgington 1945). Plants with high

Se have a garlicky odor which is quite specific and can be used as a diagnostic criterion. Certain plants that accumulate Se thrive on high seleniferous areas and can be used in mapping such areas and are listed by Ganje (1966).

Fossil fuels contain a fair amount of Se, 5 and 1.5 μg g^{-1} for coal and petroleum, respectively. Whether or not Se pollution will present a problem will depend on local conditions. If it occurs in the Western States where the soil is already high in Se, an increase could cause toxicity problems. In the northeast some additional Se could, in fact, be desirable. Selenium is the only trace element with West-East relationship which would give more toxicity in the west than in the east of the U.S.A.

Vanadium (V)

Vanadium is a trace element found in low concentrations in most soil and plant material. The V concentration of soil usually ranges from 20-500 μg g^{-1} as reported by Swaine (1955). The concentration in coal is 10-50 μg g^{-1} as reported by Lisk (1972). The ash of some oils contain more than 70% V oxide (Goldschmidt 1954). It has not been shown that V is essential for higher plants, but Arnon and Wessel (1953) have shown it to be essential for a green alga. In human nutrition, V seems to be useful in controlling levels of cholestrol in the blood and it may have a role in the prevention of dental carries (Allaway 1968). Although V may be required, it is also toxic to man and animals in higher levels. Vanadium is toxic to chickens at dietary concentrations of 25 μg g^{-1} and concentrations of 0.5 μg g^{-1} or greater are toxic to plants in culture solutions (Pratt 1966).

As with many other trace elements when present at toxic concentrations, V is retained by the roots of plants and very little is translocated to the shoots. The shoots of plants seldom contain more than 1 μg g^{-1} of vanadium.

Zinc (Zn)

The lithosphere has an average Zn content of 80 μg g^{-1} according to Goldschmidt (1954). On the basis of extensive surveys, Swaine (1955) reported that the Zn content is generally in the range of 10-300 μg g^{-1}. Zinc is usually uniformly distributed throughout the soil profile. It is believed that organic matter in the surface horizons keeps Zn available to plants (Lindsay 1972). Viets et al. (1954) reported that plants vary a great deal in their ability to utilize the native Zn found in the soil. It has been reported by Robinson et al. (1947) that a good indication of Zn material outcrop is the presence of luxuriantly growing ragweed when other vegetation is stunted. The tissue of plants inadequately supplied with Zn generally contains less than 15-20 μg g^{-1} Zn. Plant tissues containing Zn in excess of 400 μg g^{-1} generally show toxicity symptoms (Chapman 1966).

The toxic effects of Zn as a trace element were recognized before it was shown to be an essential plant nutrient (Brenchley 1927). It has been used extensively as a fungicide. In some cases protracted use has resulted in Zn toxicity to agronomic plants (Lee and Craddock 1969). Zinc toxicity occurs naturally on some acid peats and on soils developed on mineralized zones and outcroppings. It also has been known to occur upon acidification of some soils.

According to Lindsay (1972), Zn deficiency in agricultural crops is one of the most common micronutrient deficiencies. Zinc is not only low in plants, but also has low availability to animals because of the formation of insoluble complexes of calcium and phytic acid (Allaway 1968). Prasad (1967) has reported cases of Zn deficiencies in man.

Additional Aspects of Trace Metals Related to Coal Technology

The energy crisis facing the U.S.A., and for that matter the entire world, does pose potential problems to the environment including some relating to trace elements.

It can be anticipated that the use of coal in electrical generation will be greatly increased in the U.S.A. within the next few decades perhaps by a factor of 2 or 3. Even high sulfur-containing coals may be used in order to meet demands. About 40% of the world's known coal reserves are within the U.S.A. and they amount to somewhere around a trillion tons. As use of coal becomes more necessary, annual consumption could be in the order of well over a billion tons or more per year. About 500 million tons currently are used (Bond et al. 1972). Waste products would amount, roughly, to 200 million tons of ash (that collected plus that escaping as flyash), 20 million tons of particulates depending upon type of incineration (Bond et al. 1972) (trace elements can become concentrated in the particulates), 150 thousand tons of volatile trace metals, and 20 to 40 million tons of sulfur.

Disposition of hundreds of million tons of waste products from use of coal will present some environmental problems (Berry and Wallace 1974, Babu 1975, Lee and Craddock 1969. Bradford et al. 1978). Fortunately many uses are being developed for flyash. An interesting use is as a medium for plant growth, especially in the revegetation process (Townsend and Gillham 1975). Some mine spoils are extremely acid and mixing of the alkaline ash with such spoil will not only permit plant growth, but will also allow both to be used together as agricultural amendment if it is undesirable to increase soil pH. One use of flyash is to overcome boron deficiency (Plank and Martens 1974). Care must be taken in such use of flyash because of plant uptake of trace metals. The amount of ash applied must be below levels which would exceed the tolerance of metals in question. Furr et al. (1976) with 10% added flyash to soil, observed increased plant concentrations of metals in several vegetables. The trace elements included arsenic, boron, copper, iron, mercury, iodine, nickel, antimony, selenium and increases were usually observed in edible portions.

Not all mine spoil is acid. Some are alkaline and saline (Wali and Freeman 1973, Yamamoto 1976). These types of spoil result in different problems than acid nonsaline spoils. Phosphorus deficiency is common in the alkaline spoils and revegetation attempts have been hindered as a result. But also trace element deficiencies are common and some like zinc are a result of phosphorus fertilization. Autoallelopathy involving P-Mn and P-Zn relationships can be involved (Wali and Iverson 1978). Part of the sulfur disposition can be on calcareous lands without too much change in trace metal status (Wallace et al. 1976/1977).

ABSTRACT

The trace element composition of fossil fuels, particularly of coal, is extremely variable, and this results in considerable uncertainty in generalizing potential toxicity problems. Studies should assume worst possible conditions, and serious consideration should be given to regulation of upper limits in the trace element composition of fuels that are burned.

The fate of the volatile trace elements released from fossil fuels upon combustion is largely unknown, but there are indications that they are condensed and concentrated on particulates in the respirable size range. The volatile group includes antimony, arsenic, beryllium, bromine, cadmium, fluorine, gallium, mercury, and selenium, all of which save antimony, bromine, and gallium pose serious health hazards to man. The nonvolatile trace elements of significant abundance in fossil fuels include boron, chromium, cobalt, copper, iodine, lead, lithium, manganese, nickel, vanadium and zinc. They afford a lesser, but still significant, direct hazard and also an indirect hazard via the food chain. One of the latter group, boron, is certain to present soil-plant problems whenever considerable coal ash is applied to soil and will pollute groundwaters if any leaching occurs. Other trace elements in the ash could also pose problems if they occur in abnormally high concentrations. Some trace element problems are involved in land restoration following strip coal mining.

REFERENCES

Aldrich, D.G., A.P. Vanselow and G.R. Bradford. 1951. Lithium toxicity in citrus. Soil Sci. 71:291-295.

Allaway, W.H. 1968. Agronomic controls over the environmental cycling of trace elements. Adv. Agron. 20:235-274.

Anderson, M.W., H.W. Lakin, K.C. Beeson, F.F. Smith and E. Thacker. 1961. Selenium in agriculture. U.S. Dept. Agr., Agr. Handb. 200:53-55.

Antonovics, J., A.D. Bradshaw and R.G. Turner. 1971. Heavy metal tolerance in plants. Adv. Ecol. Res. 7:1-85.

Arnon, D.I. and G. Wessel. 1953. Vanadium as an essential element for green plants. Nature 172:1039-1040.

Adriano, D.C. and I.L. Brisbin, Jr. (eds.) 1978. Proc. Mineral Cycling Symposium, U.S. Energy Research and Develop. Admin., Washington, D C.

Babu, S.P. (ed.) 1975. Trace Elements in Fuel. Advances in Chemistry Ser. 141, Amer. Chem. Soc., Washington, D C.

Benson, N.R. 1968. Can profitable orchards be grown on old orchard soils: Proc. Wash. State Hort. Assoc. 64:109-114.

Berry, W.L. and A. Wallace. 1974. Trace elements in the environment. Rpt. No. 12-946, Univ. California, Los Angeles.

Bertine, K.K. and E.D. Goldberg. 1971. Fossil fuel combustion and the major sedimentary cycle. Science 173:233-235.

Billings, C.E. and W.R. Matson. 1972. Mercury emissions from coal combustion. Science 176:1232-1233.

Bolton, N.E., W.S. Lyon, R.I. Van Hook, A.W. Andren, W. Fulkerson, J.A. Carter and J.F. Emery. 1973. Trace element measurements at the coal-fired Allen Steam Plant. Prog. Rpt. June 1971-Jan. 1973, Oak Ridge Natl. Lab., ORNL-NSF-EP-43.

Bolton, N.E., J.A. Carter, J.F. Emery, C. Feldman, W. Fulkerson, L.D. Hulett and W.S. Lyon. 1975. Trace element mass balance around a coal-fired steam plant. pp. 175-187, In S.P. Babu (ed.), Trace Elements in Fuel, Advances in Chemistry Ser. 141, Amer. Chem. Soc., Washington, D C.

Bond R.G., C.P. Straub, and R. Prober (eds.) 1972. Handbook of Environmental Control, I. Air Pollution. C.R.C. Press, Cleveland, OH.

Bradford, G.R. 1966. Boron, pp. 33-61, Lithium, pp. 318-224, In H.D. Chapman (ed.), Diagnostic Criteria for Plants and Soil, Div. of Agr. Sci., Univ. Calif., Los Angeles.

Bradford, G.R., F.L. Bair and V. Hunsaker. 1971. Trace and major element contents of soil saturation extracts. Soil Sci. 112:225-230.

Bradford, G.R., A.L. Page, I.R. Straughan and H.T. Phung. 1978. A study of the deposition of fly ash on desert soils and vegetation adjacent to a coal-fired generating station. pp. 383-393, In D.C. Adriano and I.L. Brisbin (eds.), Proc. 2nd Mineral Cycling Symp. Environmental Chemistry and Cycling Processes, Augusta, GA, April 1976.

Brenchley, W.E. 1927. Inorganic Plant Poisons and Stimulants, 2nd Ed. Cambridge Univ. Press, London, 134 p.

Brewer, R.F. 1966. Fluorine. pp. 180-196, In H.D. Chapman (ed.), Diagnostic Criteria for Plants and Soils, Div. of Agr. Sci., Univ. California, Los Angeles.

Cannon, H.L. 1960. Botanical prospecting for ore deposits. Science 13:591-598.

Cannon, H.L. 1970. Trace element excesses and deficiencies in some geochemical provinces in the U.S. pp. 21-43, In D.P. Hemphill (ed.), Trace Substances in Environmental Health, Vol. III, Proc. MO. 4th Ann. Conf., Univ. Missouri Press, Columbia.

Carroll, R.E. 1966. The relationship of cadmium in the air to cardiovascular diseases death rate. J. Amer. Med. Assoc. 198:267-269.

Chapman, H.D. 1966. Zinc. pp. 484-499, In H.D. Chapman (ed.), Diagnostic Criteria for Plants and Soils, Div. of Agr. Sci., Univ. California, Los Angeles.

Chaudhry, F.M., A. Wallace and R.T. Mueller. 1977. Barium toxicity in plants. Comm. Soil Sci. Plant Anal. 8:795-797.

Chrenekova, E. and K. Holobrady. 1970. Flyash in connection with content of arsenic in the soil-plant system. Pol'nohhospodarstvo 16:34-44.

Compton, O.C. and L.F. Remmert. 1960. Effect of airborne fluorine on injury and fluorine content of gladiolus leaves. Proc. Amer. Soc. Hort. Sci. 75:663-675.

Drucker, H. and R.E. Wildung (eds.) 1977. Proc. 15th Ann. Hanford Life Science Symp. Biological Implications of Metals in the Environment. Richland, Washington, 1975. Tech. Info. Center ERDA.

Engmann, F., H.G. Dassler and S. Bortitz. 1969. Investigations on smoke injuries to agricultural plants by means of pot experiments. Arch. PfluSchutz 5:223-232.

Epstein, E. 1972. Mineral Nutrition of Plants - Principles and Perspectives. John Wiley, N Y., 412 p.

Foote, R.S. 1972. Mercury vapor concentrations inside buildings. Science 177:513-514.

Frost, D.V. 1967. Arsenicals in biology - retrospect and prospect. Fed. Proc. 26:194-208.

Furr, A.K., W.C. Kelly, C.A. Bache, W.H. Gutenmann and D.J. Lisk. 1976. Multielement uptake by vegetables and millet grown in pots on flyash amended soil. J. Agric. Food Chem. 24:885-888.

Ganje, T.J. 1966. Selenium pp. 394-404, In H.D. Chapman (ed.), Diagnostic Criteria for Plants and Soils, Div. of Agr. Sci., Univ. California, Los Angeles.

Ganje, T.J. and A.L. Page. 1972. Lead concentration of plants, soil and air near highways. Calif. Agr. 26:7-9.

Goldschmidt, V.M. 1954. Geochemistry. A. Muir (ed.), Oxford Univ. Press, 912 p.

Goldsmith, J.R. and A.C. Hexter. 1967. Respiratory exposure to lead - epidemiological and experimental dose - response relationships. Science 158:132-134.

Gough, L.P. and H.T. Shacklette. 1976. Toxicity of selected elements to plants, animals, and man--an outline. U.S.D.I. Geol. Surv., Open-file Rpt. No. 76-746.

Heit, M. 1977. A review of current information on some ecological and health related aspects of the release of trace metals into the environment associated with the combustion of coal. Health and Safety Lab., ERDA, HASL-320, UC-41.

Hewitt, E.J. 1966. Sand and water culture methods used in the study of plant nutrition. Commonw. Bur. Hort. and Plantation Crops. Tech. Bull. No. 22, 2nd Ed.

Hluchan, E., M. Jenik and M. Sedlak. 1968. Arsenic (soil) content in the vicinity of an aluminum plant. Cslka Hyg. 13:591-595.

Hodgson, J.F. 1970. Chemistry of trace elements in soils with reference to trace element concentration in plants. pp. 45-58, In D.D. Hemphill (ed.), Proc. Univ. Missouri 3rd Ann. Conf. Trace Substances in Environmental Health, Vol. III. Univ. Missouri Press, Columbia.

Holliday, R., D. Hodgson and W.N. Townsend. 1958. Plant growth on flyash. Nature 181:1079-1080.

Howell, F.G., J.B. Gentry and M.H. Smith (eds.) 1975. Proc. Symp. Mineral Cycling in Southeastern Ecosystems, Augusta, GA, May 1974, Tech. Info. Center, Office Public Affairs, US-ERDA.

Huffman, E.D.W., Jr. and J.F. Hodgson. 1973. Distribution of cadmium and zinc/cadmium ratios in crops from 19 states east of the Rocky Mountains. J. Environ. Qual. 2:289-291.

Hutchinson, T.C. 1977. The effects of acid rainfall and heavy metal particulates on a boral forest ecosystem near the Sudbury smelting region of Canada. Water, Air and Soil Pollution 7:421-438.

Hutchinson, T.C., (Program Coordinator). 1975. Intl. Conf. on Heavy Metals in the Environment. October 1975, Toronto, Ontario, Canada.

Jaffre, T., R.R. Brooks, T. Lee and R.D. Reeves. 1976, *Sebertia acuminata*: a hyper-accumulator of nickel from New Caledonia. Science 193:579-580.

John, M.K. 1972. Lead availability related to soil properties and extractable lead. J. Environ. Qual. 1:295-298.

John, M.K. 1973. Cadmium uptake by eight food crops as influenced by various soil levels of cadmium. Environ. Pollut. 4:7-15.

Lagerwerff, J.V. 1971. Uptake of cadmium, lead, and zinc by radish from soil and air. Soil Sci. 111:129-133.

Lee, C.R. and G.R. Craddock. 1969. Factors affecting plant growth on high zinc medium. Agron. J. 61:565-567.

Liebig, G.F., Jr. 1966. Arsenic. pp. 13-23, In H.D. Chapman (ed.), Diagnostic Criteria for Plants and Soils, Div. of Agr. Sci., Univ. California, Los Angeles.

Lindner, R.C. 1943. Arsenic injury of peach trees. Proc. Amer. Soc. Hort. Sci. 42:275-279.

Lindsay, W.L. 1972. Zinc in soils and plant retention. Adv. Agron. 24:147-186.

Lisk, D.J. 1972. Trace metals in soils, plants, and animals. Adv. Agron. 24:267-325.

Lunt, H.A. 1959. Digested sewage sludge for soil improvement. Connecticut Agr. Expt. Sta., New Haven, Bull. 622:1-30.

McLaisse, F., J. Gregoire, R.R. Brooks, R.S. Morrison and R.D. Reeves. 1978. *Aeolanthus biformifolius* DeWild: a hyperaccumulator of copper from Zaire. Science 199:887-888.

Mertz, W. 1967. Biological role of chromium. Fed. Proc. 26:186-193.

Murthy, G.K., V. Rhea and J.T. Peeler. 1971. Levels of antimony, cadmium, chromium, cobalt, manganese and zinc in institutional diets. Environ. Sci. Tech. 5:436-442.

National Academy of Sciences. 1971. Fluorine. Government Printing Off., Washington, D C.

National Academy of Sciences, National Academy of Engineering. 1973. Water quality criteria. 1972. U.S. Government Printing Off., Washington, D C.

National Academy of Sciences. 1975. Nickel. Government Printing Off., Washington, D C.

National Academy of Sciences. 1977. Copper. Government Printing Off., Washington, D C.

National Research Council. 1972. Biologic Effects of Atmospheric Pollutants, Lead-Airborne Lead in Perspective, Natl. Acad. Sci., Washington, D C., 330 p.

Olsen, S.R. 1972. Micronutrient interactions. pp. 244-251, In J.J. Mortvedt, P.M. Giordano and W.L. Lindsay (eds.), Micronutrients in Agriculture. Soil Sci. Soc. Amer., Madison, WI.

Page, A.L., F.T. Bingham and C. Nelson. 1972. Cadmium absorption and growth of various plant species as influenced by solution cadmium concentration. J. Environ. Qual. 1:288-291.

Peterson, P.J. 1977. Element accumulation by plants and their tolerance of toxic mineral soils. In Intl. Conf. on Heavy Metals in the Environ. Proc., Vol. 2, Toronto, Canada, 1975.

Patel, P.M., A. Wallace and E.M. Romney. 1977. Effect of chelating agents on phytotoxicity of lead and lead transport. Comm. Soil Sci. Plant Anal. 8:733-740.

Plank, C.O. and D.C. Martens. 1974. Boron availability as influenced by application of fly-ash to soil. Soil Sci. Soc. Amer. Proc. 38:974-975.

Prasad, A. 1967. Nutritional metabolic role of zinc. Federation Proc. 26:172-185.

Pratt, P.F. 1966. Chromium. pp. 136-141, In H.D. Chapman (ed.), Diagnostic Criteria for Plants and Soils, Agr. Sci., Univ. California, Los Angeles.

Proctor, J. and S.R.J. Woodell. 1975. The ecology of serpentine soils. Adv. Ecol. Res. 9:255-366.

Reuther, W. and C.K. Labanauskas. 1966. Copper. pp. 157-179, In H.D. Chapman (ed.), Diagnostic Criteria for Plants and Soils, Div. of Agri. Sci., Univ. California, Los Angeles.

Reuther, W. and P.F. Smith. 1954. Toxic effects of accumulated copper in Florida soils. Soil Sci. Fla. Proc. 14:17-23.

Robertson, D.E., J.S. Fruchter, E.A. Crecelius and J.D. Ludwick. 1975. Heavy metal mobilization from geothermal areas. pp. C-71, In T.C. Hutchinson (ed.), Intl. Conf. on Heavy Metals in the Environ., Toronto, Ontario, Canada 1975.

Robinson, W.O. and G. Edgington. 1945. Minor elements in plants and some accumulator plants. Soil Sci. 60:15-28.

Robinson, W.O., H.W. Lakin and L.E. Reichen. 1947. The zinc content of plants on Fridensville zinc slime ponds in relation to geochemical prospecting. Econ. Geol. 42:572-582.

Romney, E.M., R.A. Wood and P.A.T. Wieland. 1969. Radioactive fluorine 18 in soil and in plants. Soil Sci. 108:419-423.

Romney, E.M. and J.D. Childress. 1965. Effects of beryllium in plants and soil. Soil Sci. 100:210-217.

Ruch, R.R., H.J. Gluskoter and N.F. Shimp. 1973. Occurrence and distribution of potentially volatile trace elements in coal: An interim report. Environ. Geol. Notes No. 61, Illinois State Geol. Surv.

Schroeder, H.A. 1965. Diebetic-like serum glucose levels in chromium deficient rats. Life Sci. 4:2017-2062.

Schroeder, H.A. 1973. Recondite toxicity of trace elements. Essays in Toxicology 4:107-199.

Schroeder, H.A. and J.J. Balassa. 1966. Abnormal trace metals in man: Arsenic. J. Chron. Diseases 19:85-106.

Schroeder, H.A. and J.J. Balassa. 1961. Abnormal trace metals in man: cadmium. J. Chron. Diseases 14:236-258.

Schubert, J. 1958. Beryllium and berylliosis. Sci. Amer. 199:27-33.

Schwarz, K. 1974. Recent dietary trace element research exemplified by tin, fluorine and silicon. Federation Proc. 33:1748-1775.

Schwarz, K. and C.M. Foltz. 1957. Selenium as an integral part of factor 3 against dietary necrotic liver degeneration. J. Amer. Chem. Soc. 79:3292-3293.

Swaine, D.J. 1955. The trace-element content of soils. Commonwealth Bur. of Soil Sci., Harpenden, Eng., Tech. Comm. 48, Herald Printing Works, York, England.

Townsend, W.N. and E.W.F. Gillham. 1975. Pulverized fuel ash as a medium for plant growth. In M.J. Chadwick and G.T. Goodman (eds.), The Ecology of Resource Degradation and Renewal, 15th Symp. Brit. Ecol. Soc.

Tyler, G. 1972. Heavy metals pollute nature - nature may reduce productivity. Ambris 1:52-59.

Underwood, E.J. 1962. Trace elements in Human and Animal Nutrition. Academic Press, N Y.

Vallee, B.L., D.D. Ulmer and W.E.C. Wacker. 1960. Arsenic toxicology and biochemistry. AMA Arch. Ind. Health 21:132-150.

Vanselow, A.P. 1966. Barium. pp. 24-32, In H.D. Chapman (ed.), Diagnostic Criteria for Plants and Soils, Div. of Agr. Sci., Univ. California, Los Angeles.

Viets, F.G., Jr., L.C. Boawn and C.L. Crawford. 1954. Zinc contents and deficiency symptoms of twenty-six crops grown on a zinc-deficient soil. Soil Sci. 78:305-316.

Wali, M.K. and P.G. Freeman. 1973. Ecology of some mined areas in North Dakota. pp. 25-47, In M.K. Wali (ed.), Some Environmental Aspects of Strip Mining in North Dakota, Educ. Ser. 5, North Dakota Geol. Surv., Grand Forks.

Wali, M.K. and L.R. Iverson. 1978. Revegetation of coal mine spoils and autoallelopathy in *Kochia scoparia*. Abstr. AAAS Ann. Meeting, Feb. 1978, pp. 121-122, Washington, D C.,

Wallace, A. and E.M. Romney. 1977. Synergistic trace metal effects in plants. Comm. Soil Sci. Plant Anal. 8:699-707.

Wallace, A., J. Procopiou, E.M. Romney and S.M. Soufi. 1976/77. Massive sulfur applications to highly calcareous agricultural soil as a sink for waste sulfur. Resource Recovery and Conservation 2:263-267.

Wallace, A., E.M. Romney, G.V. Alexander and J. Kinnear. 1977a. Phytotoxicity and some interactons of the essential trace metals iron, manganese, molybdenum, zinc, copper, and boron. Commun. Soil Sci. and Plant Anal. 8:741-750.

Wallace, A., E.M. Romney, J.W. Cha, S.M. Soufi and F.M. Chaudhry. 1977b. Nickel phytotoxicity in relationship to soil pH manipulation and chelating agents. Commun. Soil Sci and Plant Anal. 8:757-764.

Wallace, A., E.M. Romney, J.W. Cha and F.M. Chaudhry. 1977c. Lithium toxicity in plants. Commun. Soil Sci. and Plant Anal. 8:772-780.

Wolf, W.R. 1978. Nutrient trace element composition of foods: analytical needs and problems. Anal. Chem. 50:190A-194A.

Westgate, P.J. 1952. Preliminary report on copper toxicity and iron chlorosis in old vegetable fields. Proc. Fla. State Hort. Soc. 65:143-146.

Williams, K.T. and R.R. Whetstone. 1940. Arsenic distribution in soils and its presence in certain plants. Tech. Bull. USDA 732.

Wright, M.J. (ed.) 1976. Plant Adaptation to Mineral Stress in Problem Soils, Office of Agric. Tech. Assistance Bur., Agency for Intl. Develop., Washington, D.C.

Yamagata, N. and I. Shigmatsu. 1970. Cadmium pollution in perspective. Inst. Public Health, Tokyo.

Yamamoto, T. 1975. Coal mine spoil as a growing medium: AMAX Belle Ayr South Mine, Gillette, WY., Pup. Symp. Surf., Min. Reclam., 3rd 1:49-61, Natl. Coal Assoc., Washington, D C.

Zimmerman, P.W. and W. Crocker. 1934. Plant injury caused by vapors of mercury and compounds of mercury. Contr. Boyce Thompson Inst. 6:167-187.

COMBATING POLLUTION CREATED BY COAL-BURNING GENERATING PLANTS IN YUGOSLAVIA

Dragoljub Draskovic*

INTRODUCTION

The development of the economy in Yugoslavia rests, among others, on provision and use of energy and a growing control over that provision and use in order to protect the environment. Adequate energy production and environmental protection are vital to the economy and society of Yugoslavia. The contemporary demand for environmental protection has been rapid and widespread. Interest in protecting ecology now and for the future is an officially stated goal in which the government and public have been awakened to the realization that there should be effective scientific measures for protection.

In Yugoslavia, public interest in environmental protection has been stimulated by environmental protection groups and associations, young people, activists, scientists and academics. In a number of cases, most notably in the siting of energy facilities, the proponents of environmental protection have been in conflict with the proponents of energy development. But, society has got to make a choice between plentiful energy or saving the environment if appropriate and relatively low cost environmental protection and energy conservation measures are taken. The demands for appropriate energy production and for environmental protection are therefore not incompatible.

The environmental effects of coal-burning generating plants involve problems. Much of the coal comes from strip mines. This mining process not only disrupts the soil above the coal seam, but if done carelessly can cause siltation and acid runoff to the streams.

Public intention has been to press for the enactment of strong state laws requiring care and planning in the mining operation and reclamation of strip mined areas. These activities have been buttressed with research and demonstration in improved methods of mining and reclamation. In addition, instructions to many coal burning plants contain strict reclamation of the land stripped. But, in spite of these steps, strip mining still requires careful attention and additional measures. Large coal burning power generating plants in the Kolubara River Basin have proposed, for example, a large scale financial effort to reclaim lands which were drastically disturbed by coal mining.

Water Pollution from Surface Mining

The chemical pollution of water from surface mining has appeared in many forms.

---

*Tanaska Rajica 38, 36000 Kraljevo, Yugoslavia.

Polluted water can be too acid, too alkaline, or contain excessive concentrations of dissolved substances such as iron, manganese and copper. Minerals containing sulphur are usually found in the proximity of coal, i.e. they are in rocks which are near seams of coal or sometimes together with coal, and as such are the main causes of water pollution. When exposed to air and water, they are oxidized and form sulphuric acid which can enter water courses in two ways. The soluble acid salts formed at the surface of coal detritus enter solution in periods of intensive surface runoffs, or groundwater, which has previously undergone a chemical change by percolation through masses of waste material from coal mines. However, there are other adverse chemical effects caused by surface mining. Even in insignificant concentrations, the salts of metals such as zinc, lead, arsenic, copper and aluminium are toxic to aquatic flora and fauna.

Indirectly linked with the drainage of acids are ferro-hydrates which are deposited in river as a reddish brown sediment or as light yellow deposits on rocks in the watercourse. Discoloration of the water has also been noted, most often in association with mining of coal, clay, sand and gravel, iron and phosphate ores. It should be mentioned that rivers are often polluted with acids from pit mines or from water flowing over still uncovered deposits of coal of other strata containing pyrite. Although the conditions for the formation of acids are linked with coal mining, the problem can be considerably mitigated if the relief and topography are not extreme and in certain cases limestone formations act as neutralizing factor. In the latter, the concentration of certain soluble substances may still be high, and water must be treated before it can be used.

The physical pollution of water is a very serious problem in areas with erosion because of the steepness of terrain and intense precipitation in the form of hard showers and cloud-bursts, particularly in areas of coal mining. Studies have shown that the quantity of sediment from mining basins in Yugoslavia is some 3,000 tons km^{-2}, whereas erosion of wooded areas is barely 25 tons km^{-2}. The obvious conclusion is that main cause of the problem of sedimentation and pollution of rivers is a lack of adequate control of surface runoff and erosion in coal mining basins, both in arid and in humid regions.

Investigations into soil pollution in coal mining basins have shown that waste materials with pH 4 or less are fatal for the majority of plant life. The filtering out of free acids may take place over a period of three to five years, so that replanting can be done, but this process will not improve soil conditions if erosion is allowed to uncover minerals with a high sulphur content. Although certain plants can grow successfully when the pH value is below 5, most plants require a lower acid content in the soil. Investigations have further shown that almost 50% of the waste materials from surface coal mines tested had a pH value between 3 and 5.

Harmful Effects and Justification for Action

To sum up, the harmful effects of water pollution from surface mining of coal involve:

(1) The complete disappearance of fish, water flora and insects. The only form of life in a polluted river is the only long, ribbon-like acidophilic algae;

(2) Rapid corrosion of the pillars of bridges, conduits, industrial equipment, pipes, navigational equipment, and structures in the water since acid attacks even concrete as well as steel and iron;

(3) The contamination of water supply for communities and industrial needs. Control of pollution from toxic materials from coal mining which are thrown onto the

surface, other earth materials exposed to the effect of erosion in periods of long rains, rapid melting of snow or occasional showers, is a difficult and expensive undertaking.

From the standpoint of social and economic interests, it is obvious that in Yugoslavia there is an urgent need for stabilization of devastated land in order to reduce its contribution to pollution of rivers.

REGULATORY MEASURES

Restoration of land damages by strip mining results in satisfactory reclamation if it is conducted by professional people. There is a tendency for operators to reclaim the land so as to just meet the minimum requirements of the regulations.

The reclamation requirements should be flexible enough to take into account differences in precipitation, soil quality, methods of mining and the nature of terrain. At the same time the land should be returned to a condition at least as satisfactory as original or better, if it can be done at reasonable costs.

Trees have always been the objective in the reclamation and improvement of surface mined areas. Their propagation still stands as one of the best methods of attaining an improved economic benefit by restoring the natural beauty of an area very extensively disturbed.

The Institute for scientific investigation in forestry started a research study of the problem. The technical personnel located, classified, and mapped all areas disturbed by surface mining in the Kolubara river watershed. Revegetation research was undertaken under controlled conditions upon mine spoil to determine growth, survival rate and suitability for cover and screening. Results of the study have provided information for tree planting upon spoil banks in the region and also have indicated areas where additional studies are required. It also was found that certain species are suited to certain spoil types. Species selection is important on good sites to produce commerical timber and is essential on poor spoils for obtaining the best cover. One of the best solutions to the problem of recapturing the beauty of the coal mined areas is the planting of trees which will turn unattractive spoil areas into esthetically pleasing wooded areas. Evergreens, which provide year-round cover, are most suitable for this purpose. Our knowledge and progress in the reclamation and revegetation of mined areas has improved. Much research in this field needs to be done before the problem of revegetation mine spoils is solved.

We need a greater knowledge of the physical and chemical characteristics of spoil materials. Our knowledge of the species of trees, shrubs, herbs, grasses, and methods for their establishment on highly acid spoils must be enlarged. Active research in this direction is being continued by foresters and soil scientists.

Satisfactory reclamation regulations should include the following elements:

(a) Permit applications before the mining operation commences that include a detailed examination of the mining site, an explanation of the reasons for selecting the mining method chosen, and practices that will be followed to restore the land to a satisfactory condition;

(b) Permit an opportunity for participation through consultation in the approval process by local authorities and interest groups and Commission for Water Protection;

(c) The reclamation plan must include information on the grading of the land, methods for restoring topsoil, of fertilization, for reseeding, replanting or refore-station, and a timetable for these reclamation activities to be completed;

(d) Provisions should be made for economic sanctions for violations of the permit terms and conditions;

(e) An organization of sufficient size to administer and effectively enforce the regulations should be established.

Costs of Strip Mine Reclamation

Cost of restoring strip mine lands depend on the original condition of the land, the meteorological and soil conditions that prevail and the degree of reclamation that is practiced. Reclamation can restore lands and prevent silting of streams of acid mine-waters and flowing into the streams or it can treat lands to a degree so that its usefulness may be greater than before mining, e.g. farm, grassland, pasture, meadow, orchard, forest, land for industrial development, wildlife preserves, recreation areas, and forage crops. The costs of reclamation will vary widely for each type of use but these must be balanced against the benefits that result. It is possible, in spite of the great variability, to generalize on the range of costs that may be involved.

The complete restoration conducted in the German Rhineland brown coal region is estimated at $3,000 to $4,500 per acre, and at about $4,000 per acre for the U.K. reclamation; costs estimated for the U.S. varied between $100 and $4,000 per acre depending on the degree of reclamation to be achieved.

All the above reclamation costs were estimated in 1972 or earlier, so that 1978 costs would be perhaps as much as 25 to 50 percent higher. Actual costs per ton of coal mined will depend on the thickness of the overburden. With the reclamation costs at $1,000 per acre for the thick western coal of the U.S. reclamation costs would be less than 5 cents per ton of coal or about 1% of the selling price. Using the higher costs of reclamation of $4,000 per acre and the thinner Eastern Appalachian coals, the costs, under the most difficult conditions, could approach $1 per ton or about 8% of the selling price. This compares with the reported National Coal Board figure of about 4% of production costs required for reclamation of their coal lands. In Yugoslavia, costs of converting drastically disturbed areas in forests are estimated between $2,800 and $3,000 ha^{-1}.

For best final results with minimum cost to all concerned, a joint mining and reclamation plan is a most useful tool. In most areas much information is available to guide the mining engineer, the soil scientist, and the foresters in deciding how best to move and to use the waste material.

It is still necessary to find remedies that are more satisfactory and more efficient for the use of the mined areas. Research by Institutes has opened the way for swifter return benefits and beauty to mined areas and to the return of clear, clean streams. Mining minerals, restoring the mined areas to the best use for the greatest number of our people will be a continuing challenge.

Recommendations

Strip mining can be carried out in an environmentally acceptable manner in many areas of Yugoslavia. Large reserves of strippable coal in Yugoslavia are available which can be extracted without permanent damage to the environment.

It is recommended that:

(a) In extraction of coal by strip mining the best available mining methods which enable the adequate restoration of the land and hydrological systems should be applied;

(b) Extraction of coal by strip mining methods is not undertaken in those areas where the land cannot be restored until acceptable mining methods for the particular terrain are developed, or reclamation methods are devised that will restore the land and hydrological systems to an environmentally satisfactory condition.

(c) The necessary research and development programs be undertaken to develop mining methods for those strippable seams for which no satisfactory methods now exist, and to initiate a large scale program to develop the technology necessary for the reclamation of land for a wide variety of soil types, including arid areas.

It is recommended that strip mining legislation provide high standards for reclamation that are economically justified and provide flexibility, for imposing even more rigid standards as new technology is developed.

RECLAMATION OF MINED AREAS AS INTEGRAL PARTS OF BASIN PROGRAMS

Reclamation of drastically disturbed mined areas and pollution control are included in comprehensive river basins programs with clear recognition of their interrelationship with surface and groundwater resources. Water, land and minerals have been studied fully and integrally to see how they might efficiently contribute both production and income of regional economy and population.

There need be little doubt as to the far reaching effects of the completed programs of developing water and land resources of the large river basins in Yugoslavia. With the completion of these programs, the regions with floods, erosion and torrents, and dominated by destructive exploitation of natural resources, will be transformed into major centers of energy production. In brief, these programs involve: a system of main-stem and tributary dams, the treatment of tributary lands, so as to minimize erosion, sediment flow, and runoff from mined areas and badly eroded lands; the treatment of industrial and municipal wastes, and the measures for environmental protection. Multiple purpose reservoirs are planned so as not to aggravate but contribute to the control of pollution. This will include regulation of releases of water to make fullest use of the stream's potential self-purification capacity.

Increasing low flow in polluted streams is an important contribution to the solution of water pollution problems. However, this is only a partial solution, as at least primary sedimentation is needed to remove sludge deposits, floating sewage solids and scum. Additional benefits also accrue from reduction of hardness and temperature when stream is used for cooling water.

General Situation

Yugoslavia covers an area of 256,000 sq km. Rivers take waters to other countries.

They empty into three seas, the Adriatic, the Black, and the Aegean Sea. To the Black Sea catchment area belongs 178,000 sq km. The rainfall here is normally 900 mm per year. Under these conditions the outlet coefficient varies between 0.28 to 0.65, and the specific outlet is between 7-1 (sec) sq km. The Black Sea catchment area covers more than 177,000 sq km.

To the Adriatic Sea catchment area belongs over 54,000 sq km. The rainfall here averages more than 1,300 mm yearly, the outlet coefficient 0.51, the specific outlet 25-1 (sec) sq km.

The Aegean Sea catchment area has 24,000 sq km. The rainfall averages 700 mm yearly, the runoff coefficient 0.30, and the specific runoff 6.80 lit (sec) sq km.

The per capita use of water distributed by waterworks is quickly increasing. Growing industrial activities and agricultural uses, and generally higher standards of living explain, in large part, the increase in use.

The largest consumptive use of drinking water is projected to reach 2,300 million m^3/year (in 1980) with an average consumption of almost 300 liters per capita per day. The demand for industrial water supply is projected to reach 40,000 million m^3/year.

The growing urbanization and industralization have led to heavy pollution of streams and some lakes in Yugoslavia. Only mountainous rivers are still in class I, and the largest among them is the Tara river (average discharge-77.1 cu. m/sec.). About one-third of Yugoslav rivers are ranked into class II, while the Sava, the Velika Morava, the Vardar and other belong to class III. Due to unregulated torrential river flows, particularly the ever increasing quantities of water used and the unpurified waters entering river-courses, pollution of water increases every day, so that practically there are not sufficient quantities of pure water in the SR of Serbia.

At the present, SR of Serbia consumes over 45 cu. m/sec. In 1980, the consumption level will be about 83 cu. m/sec. Around the year 2,000, Serbia will require 290 cu. m/sec.

The Hydrological Service in Yugoslavia for the last ten years has been engaged in a systematic water quality control. Tests of the self-purification capacity of watercourses and sections of watercourses were also performed. The torrential regions cover almost two-thirds of the territory of Yugoslavia.

The Basic Law on Waters and other codes have created regulative principles for a sound water preservation policy. General economic and financial principle in water preservation is the established rule that cost of water quality improvement shall be allocated to and borne by those who are polluting water resources.

In most river basins of Yugoslavia, 70 percent or more of the land is in agricultural use, including timber production. With much of the land used for agricultural purposes, agriculture has a significant influence on watershed management. It is reported that about 70% percent of the total damages (from erosion and torrents) occurring in Yugoslavia is in upstream areas. These damages are closely related to land and water problems that originate on agricultural lands, and denuded slopes. Sedimentation is one of the major problems associated with water and related land resources. Protective measures for cropland, pastureland, woodlands, and strip mining areas are known soil and water conservation measures, which where properly applied, go beyond their erosion control function to greatly enhance the environment. Mining and associated dredging operations contribute large quantities of sediment to streams and large reservoirs. Although most of the sediment comes from land, a relatively small amount is contributed from the spoil banks of mining operations and smelters. Inorganic salts and minerals in the effluent from certain metallurgical and chemical industries, and the acidic drainage from many operating and abandoned mines, can seriously impair the quality of water. Such water is generally unsuitable for domestic, industrial and agricultural needs.

Future Trends

Over ten years have passed since a comprehensive plan has been developed for the Morava region of 37,000 km^2, the plan was limited primarily to the flood control and irrigation. In the interim period, both the SR of Serbia and communities have recognized the value and importance of including municipal and industrial water supply, water quality, recreation, fishery, and preservation values in the planning process. It expects to complete a comprehensive joint plan in desired detail within a 10-year period and will concurrently establish a planning process that will continually update the plan to meet changing technology and social desires.

In the SR Hrvatska, the principal element of the hydrographic unit is the Sava river. The planning process recognizes interregional and even interrepublican aspects in dealing with such functions as power, navigation and pollution control. Other functions relate directly to economic or population centers, such as provision for industrial and municipal water supply, water quality treatment and enhancement.

The Sava river basin is the largest in Yugoslavia comprising 37% of her territory and 35% of total national population. Its complex water development scheme with multi-purpose structures and water utilization has both interrepublic and regional economic significance. Its key objectives and measures, and the funds for its implementation are determined. In brief this study involves:

- The construction of 33 big reservoirs, resulting in the total reservoir capacity to 8,000 x 10^6 m^3.
- The construction of 51 hydro-power plants with total capacity of 2,583 MW, will generate 10,590 GHW.
- On present estimates, about 520,000 ha are expected to be irrigated annually.
- In planning for the multiple use of water in Sava river basin, adequate consideration is given to the importance of domestic and industrial water supply.
- The protection of agricultural lands before floods.
- The construction of more than 1,000 wastewater treatment plants, resulting in a substantial improvement of the surface water quality.
- Multiple-purpose dams and reservoirs will provide commerical navigation from Beograd to Zagreb. An increasing number of inhabitants using public sewerage and distribution systems may be expected.
- The Sava river watershed will be transformed into one region with a healthy balance between agriculture, forestry and industry.

The primary aims of watershed management in upstream areas of these large river basins are:

(1) To control soil erosion and reduce sediment pollution from badly eroded areas and strip mining.
(2) To reduce floodwater and sediment damage to agricultural crops, pasture, live-stock, and farm improvements, to roads and bridges; and to urban, residential and industrial water supplies in downstream floodplains;
(3) To provide water supply for rural communities in upstream areas; for municipal and industrial uses, irrigation, water-based recreation, fish enhancement, and

water quality management;

(4) To guide local communities in water resource developments that will contribute to community development and stimulate economic growth;

(5) To build small earth dams which can be used to store water for domestic, agricultural and industrial uses. The assurance of steady supplies of good quality water will greatly stimulate the local economy in many cases. Water storage reservoirs can also have recreational uses and be managed for fish. Reservoirs are used to store water for irrigation and for water quality management to boost streamflow in drought or heavy waste disposal.

Control of Air Pollution

The bulk of emissions arise from large installation, such as electric power generation. But, domestic and commerical heating and small industry usually make the largest contribution to the average ground level concentrations in urban regions.

A number of technical means are available for reducing emissions of sulphur oxides namely use of various abatement techniques, substitution of high sulphur fuels by lower sulphur containing fuels, and reduction in fuel consumption. The large installations, on the other hand, have the choice of using low sulphur fuels, removing sulphur from the combustion gases where this is considered practicable, and rejecting residual emissions through tall stacks.

Where high sulphur coals are used for energy policy reasons, Organization for Economic Cooperation and Development suggests two possible means for using them in an environmentally acceptable way. First, a portion of the sulphur, 40-60% depending on the coals, can be removed by physical separation techniques at a cost of $2.50 to $3.25 per ton at 1975 prices. The current U.S. price of coal is $20-25 per ton and in Western Europe it is about $60 per ton, in Yugoslavia it is about $40 per ton. Secondly, experience is being gained with four different types of stack gas scrubbing processes and present indications are that costs range from $9.50 to $11.50 per ton, at 1975 prices for new installations. The control of air pollution from steam plants has been an evolving process. In Yugoslavia, all new plants are installing electrostatic precipitators which will remove over 95% of the flyash.

The problem of sulphur dioxide emissions, in the absence of a technology for sulphur removal, has been handled by building chimneys sufficiently high to dilute and disperse the gases over a very wide area. It is recognized, however, that the safest solution in an environmental sense would be the removal of sulphur dioxide before it goes up the chimney.

Heat

Tremendous quantities of hot water flow from the cooling of great thermal power plants. These waters are usually returned to the streams or lakes from which they were withdrawn. Large quantities of heat are thus transferred to these water bodies. The waste heat causes the so-called thermal pollution which can be observed as negative influences upon ecology and downstream uses.

Regarding ecology one can distinguish:

(a) Influences upon the physical-chemical characteristic of water (sluggishness and diminished density and the reduction of oxygen content);

(b) Influences upon the growth, reproduction and structure of the water fauna and flora.

Adverse effects on downstream uses are that:

(a) The qualitity of drinking water is reduced (temperature, taste, smell, color, salts);

(b) The losses for the industries which need cooling water of a low temperature and high quality, leading to the decrease of energy production or to the need for cooling towers.

The increasingly bad effects of the thermal pollution lead to the necessity of finding efficient solutions for the diminishing of these effects. The struggle against thermal pollution includes measures within the thermal power plants on the river upstream of the discharge in the discharge area and upstream the outlet.

Since much is yet to be learned about the process of heated waters and their effects upon our rivers, extensive monitoring of the river and its life is being conducted. Research will be conducted to determine precisely the heat tolerances of the many forms of life which exist in the river.

Flyash

Flyash is a waste product from burning coal at electric power generating plants. It is the lightweight ash that is electrically precipitated and mechanically removed to disposal dumps. A number of properties of flyash make it attractive as an additive and conditioner for reclaiming agricultural and drastically disturbed mined areas. These are: abundance of quantity, a high pH to neutralize acid soils, a higher content of some macro and micro plant nutrients than many soils, better moisture retention than many soils, and a loosening effect when mixed with heavy textured soils.

Revegetation of flyash is effected by applying fertilizer at higher than normal rates and by planting tolerant species. Institute for Agricultural Research is considering revegetation of flyash in the context of land restoration for agriculture. Investigations for flyash include its use as a cement additive, and for making building bricks and lightweight building blocks.

CONCLUSION

Water, land and coal are key resources in our efforts to achieve economic progress. We must be sure that water and land are not diminished in usefulness by the operation of our power plants. Therefore, pollution caused by coal burning generating plants can never be viewed in isolation. Planning for coal resources and energy production cannot be dissociated from planning for all resources, particularly water and related land resources. This leads to the further conclusion that environmental protection and pollution abatement should be planned as integral parts of basin programs.

We must take into consideration the interrelationship of resources and environment, and in the same time the interrelationship of environment to man, his health and his economy.

ABSTRACT

Yugoslavia, with one of the largest remaining reserves of coal, has already indicated that it intends to put greater reliance on coal as an energy resource in the future. This paper will consider only the most important potential environmental effects of increased coal production-pollution caused by strip mining, and extensive generation from coal burning steam plants. These pollution problems with the thought in mind that accelerated economic development in a continuing process in Yugoslavia, had to be examined and were approached with the same fundamental policy of considering all the resources in there complex interrelationship.

In Yugoslavia surface mining of coal is practiced on a large scale. Surface mining costs are generally lower than for underground production, so that if strippable reserves are available, it can be expected that much of the increased demands for coal would be met by increased strip mining.

Reclamation of strip mine areas is treated as integral parts of basin programs. Some useful references are listed below.

Downing, M.F. 1972. Drainage and erosion control. Landscape Reclamation 2:36-44.

Draskovic, D. 1969. Reclamation methods to prevent water pollution in the Morava River Watershed. pp. 36-44, In R.J. Hutnik and G. Davis (eds.), Ecology and Reclamation of Devastated Lands, Vol. 2, Gordon and Breach, NY.

Hadgson, D.R. and W.N. Tounsend. 1969. The amelioration and revegetation of pulverized fuel ash. pp. 361-379, In R.J. Hutnik and G. Davis (eds.), Ecology and Reclamation of Devastated Lands, Vol. 2, Gordon and Breach, NY.

Petch, G. 1974. Die Halden des Ruhrgebietes, ihre Begrunung und landshaftliche Eingliederung als Massnahmen zur Verbesserung der Umweltverhaltnisse im Verdichtungsraum. Internationale Fachtagung Halden im Ruhrgebiet und ihre Integrirung in die Landshaft. SVR 22:201-223.

Sisesti, D.J. 1976. Special works on rivers in the discharge area of hot wastewater from thermal and nuclear power plants for the reduction of their pollution effect. Congress sur la Protection des Eaux de Mer, Lacs et Riviers 12:163-175.

U.S. Department of the Interior. 1967. Surface Mining and Our Environment. U.S. Government Printing Off., Washington, DC.

Tuszko, A. 1971. Upsets in the biological equilibrium in the water environment and the loss of its capacity for self-purification. Proc. of the Fourth Intl. Conf. on Science and Society, Herceg-Novi, Yugoslavia 4:202-206.

PART II: PLANNING CRITERIA, POLICY, AND LEGAL COMPLIANCE

A discussion on the existing and envisioned criteria for planning, policy, and legal compliance, which form the foundation of any decision making process in relation to coal resource development, is the theme of this part. Apparent from the papers herein is the quest for making coal mining an economically feasible and environmentally sound endeavor. The facts and fallacies of some existing criteria of evaluation have been explored. Some innovative schemes based on simulation models as well as the current capabilities of compromising economics with environment are presented.

POLICY DEVELOPMENT TO MINIMIZE MINING IMPACT: REPORT OF THE U.S. NATIONAL COAL POLICY PROJECT

Robert R. Curry *

INTRODUCTION AND BACKGROUND

In March of 1978, final reports were completed for the National Coal Policy Project. This study attempts to develop a policy to minimize environmental impacts of coal development in a manner that is thorough yet realistic and acceptable to coal industry and environmental organizations. Energy policy studies by government agencies and appointed bodies are numerous. Many contradictory and ineffectual reports clutter book-shelves of energy agencies, congressional committees, and universities. This project attempts to be different. Although it is published in a three-volume report[1], such publication is not the primary goal of this study.

A principal difference between this and previous energy policy studies and pronouncements derives from the participants. The project was conceived by Gerald Decker, Corporate Energy Manager of the Dow Chemical Company. Funded with government and foundation grants as well as contributions from a wide range of coal mining and coal consuming industries, the membership comprises nearly of 100 specialists from universities, environmental citizen-interest organizations, industries, utilities, and consulting organizations.

Under the direction of Decker and his co-chairman, Laurence Moss, representing environmental interests, approximately 10,000 man-days in 13 months were spent developing coal policy to minimize ecosystem impact to acceptable limits to all participants. Rather than resulting in a *"least-common-denominator"* sort of policy where antagonistic factions can agree only on non-substantive issues, very creative organization and a prior agreement to abide by an experimental *"Rule of Reason"* approach[2] provided an

---

[1] A summary volume is published by the sponsoring institution, The Center for Strategic and International Studies at Georgetown University, 1800 K Street NW, Washington, D.C., 20006. The body of the report is published as *"Where We Agree, Report of the National Coal Policy Project"* by Westview Press in two volumes. This paper is taken from Volume II, the report of the Mining Task Force.

[2] Developed for use instead of traditional litigation by New York University law professor Milton Wessel and detailed in his 1976 book: *The Rule of Reason: A New Approach to*

*Department of Geology, University of Montana, Missoula, MT 59812.

opportunity to develop over 200 specific coal-energy policy recommendations. Many were considerably more forceful and "stronger" in the sense of providing greater environmental control than were similar statements on the same subject made by the U.S. Congress in the 1977 Surface Mining and Reclamation Act. Yet in many cases, some of the participants in the debates and the factual data bases were identical.

The Policy Project was subdivided into five task force groups concentrating on Coal Mining, Coal and Energy Pricing, Air Pollution, Fuel Utilization and Conservation, and Coal Transportation. This brief report will cover only the conclusions of the Mining Task Force.

MINING AND RECLAMATION

Introduction to the Mining Task Force Report

For the most part, environmental disputes have been settled without the principal parties ever discussing their differences based on facts. Instead others have settled the disputes: Congress, administrators, and the courts. What would happen if the parties did get together to address issues of this sort systematically and carefully, with a commitment to support each stance on a reasoned basis?

The National Coal Policy project provides an answer to this question, and the work of the Mining Task Force offers a case illustration. After a year of work, the members of the Task Force, drawn equally from the ranks of industry and environmentalists, came to agreement on more than 150 recommendations dealing with the future of coal production in the United States. The Task Force failed to come to agreement on only two major issues: that of a future national policy on the leasing of federally owned coal, and the question of concentration of mining in the Northern Plains. While these issues are pivotal, agreement was reached on many other difficult and controversial issues, for instance, restrictions on mining on prime farmlands.

In the first meetings of the Task Force, it did not appear that agreement would be reached easily. The members began by debating the severity of various impacts of mining on the environment. Because of the variations in local conditions, however, few generalizations seemed to offer much promise of agreement.

The participants could all agree that it was likely that more coal was going to be produced in the next decade or so and that it was desirable to find a way of doing it involving the least environmental cost. They decided, however, that it would not be productive to try to address either the question of exactly how much coal would be needed or exactly how much it was worth to spend for environmental protection. They assumed that the answer to both questions would be "more" than at present, but that any attempt at further quantification would really only dignify guesswork.

In posing the threshold question in this manner, the Task Force realized that there is no standard answer for the whole country. Since the impact of coal mining varies in different regions of the country, the Task Force decided to look at the question in the context of the principal coal provinces. All participants realized that there would be both

---

Corporate Litigation, Addison-Wesley. This technique requires essentially that all participants operate by a code of "fair-play" that demands sharing of all facts and separation of disagreement based upon perceptions or interpretations of fact from those based on absence of fact or emotional and other bases.

environmental and economic advantages and disadvantages connected with surface mining, deep mining, and coal preparation in each province. A matrix was developed to examine these questions and a series of field visits were made to five of the major coal provinces: the Gulf Coast, the Northern Great Plains, the Illinois Basin, Northern Appalachia, and Southern Appalachia. Additional background reports were prepared for the Central Rockies, Southwest, West Coast, and Alaska. The staff members studied all the published literature they could find on these provinces and their problems, and were briefed in the field by experts from operating companies, state regulatory bodies, and environmental groups.

Quite remarkably, differences began to dissolve as particpants moved away from discussing generalities and focused on specific issues. Over and again, distinctions were drawn between differing conditions between regions in order to gain consensus. Each side had to find experts or reputable reports to support its suppositions. Views would often moderate, and sometimes the sides would be blurred as individuals spoke solely for themselves in response to the data. Gradually a sense of unity began to develop, and eventually even an *espirit de corps*, as participants felt that the secret of breaking through hardened mind-sets had been found. The approach was that of working from the ground up to derive policy--first getting the physical facts on a regional basis, then looking at their implications for national policy--while refusing to try to homogenize those facts on a national basis through the whole process. Regional distinctions are important, for a valid approach used in one region may not work well in another where conditions are different.

Regional patterns emerged to provide answers to the question: "How can we produce more coal with the least environmental cost?" The group found that more than 70% of the remaining coal in the United States, in terms of its energy value, lies east of the Mississippi River and that, on a comparable basis of heat value, western coals are not particularly low in sulfur content. Moreover, most of the remaining coal east of the Mississippi can only be reached through deep mining. Therefore, the Task Force does not look for nationally significant increases in production from the Northern Great Plains region or the Southwest because changes in federal air pollution laws will create a better market for local coal in the midwest and because of the severity of environmental problems associated with surface mining in the arid west. More novel and unsolved problems affecting the environment were found to exist on the Northern Plains and other arid sites than in any other region. In the immediate future, the coal production in the Northern Great Plains will tend to concentrate around Gillette, Wyoming and Decker, Montana where the seams are thickest and the rangelands least productive. This concentration will tend to prevent social dislocations caused by production increases from spreading into many small ranching communities. Generally, the midwest and Appalachia can handle increased coal production without marked social stress since support communities oriented to coal production are already established in those regions.

Patterns emerged in discussions of other regions as well. In the midwest, surface mining should be restricted generally to the southern half of the Illinois Basin where soils tend to be less productive. In Appalachia, deep mining will tend to risk less acid drainage south of the "hinge-line" in West Virginia because less acid bearing strata are present. Lignite in Texas will become more important locally in coming years in replacing natural gas in utility boilers, but reclamation may be difficult in the southerly reach of the beds there because of increasing aridity. Generally, native hardwood forests should be restored on reclaimed areas in Appalachia, while farmland in the midwest should be restored to its original productivity. On the Northern Plains, the goal should be to restore native grasslands to a viable condition, as self-regenerating ecosystems which are able to withstand future droughts (this should be done without reliance on added water or continuing fertilization).

In sum, the Policy Project believes the country must look primarily to the Illinois Basin and Appalachia for the bulk of its future coal, with a return to reliance on deep mining (with fewer acid drainage problems to the extent production can be focused in Southern Appalachia).

The members of the Task Force did not reach these conclusions by compromising their convictions. Rather, they reached them by conscientiously examining the facts and drawing needed distinctions. This was done without much political posturing and in a mood of deepening mutual respect. In a time when it should be obvious that more of the divergent interests of the country have to learn to live together with less friction, the work of this Task Force may stand as an example of a new approach in attaining reconciliation.

Location and Pattern of Mine Development

For various climatic, geologic and hydrologic reasons, it is easier to mine in an environmentally acceptable manner in some areas than others; therefore, mining should be encouraged in areas that pose the least problems. Examples of such areas include the lignite deposits in central and east Texas, and the non-acid forming areas of the southern Illinois Basin (parts of southern Illinois, southwestern Indiana and western Kentucky). Mining should be allowed only on a carefully controlled experimental basis where it is not certain that coal can be mined in an environmentally acceptable manner. Moreover, experimental permits should only be issued when there appears to be a reasonably good chance that techniques can be developed to mine in an acceptable manner. Such areas include highly productive prime agricultural land in the central Midwest and the sub-irrigated alluvial valley floors and Ponderosa pine forests in the Northern Plains.

Mining should not be allowed in areas where specific problems cannot be addressed through reclamation. Such areas include:

(1) Areas where there is not sufficient material to bury acid forming or toxic overburden.
(2) Areas with special wildlife, botanical, cultural, uniquely scenic and/or special recreational values.
(3) Areas where a locally important aquifer cannot be replaced by a reliable alternative source of suitable water at no additional expense to the users.
(4) Areas of the Northern Plains with abundant springs.

The two caucuses agree that the following principles should be used as part of the criteria to determine where it is most desirable to locate mining in the Northern Plains:

(1) Mining thick seams is desirable because less land is disturbed per ton of coal mined, thus reducing the environmental and reclamation problems associated with mining.
(2) Mining where rangeland is least productive is desirable because reclamation practices are still largely in an experimental stage. If there are failures, the loss of productivity will be less, and if successful, subsequent mining in more easily reclaimable areas will be assured a higher probability of success.

The Environmental Caucus feels that if mining must continue in the West, it should be concentrated in areas that meet the above criteria. The Gillette area in Wyoming and the Decker area in Montana meet these criteria and the caucus feels that mining should be concentrated in these areas to the extent other recommendations in the Task Force report can be met. Furthermore, the Environmental Caucus feels that mining in other areas of the West is acceptable only on a controlled experimental permit basis to develop reclamation technologies.

The Industrial Caucus agreed that economics will generally favor concentration of mining where seams are the thickest, but did not feel that a geographic limitation was necessary if an operator is able to comply with all environmental requirements.

The mix of federal and non-federal coal is such that little non-federal coal in the West (with the exception of Indian coal) can be economically mined without including federal coal in mine tracts. Consequently, it is essential that the federal government develop its coal leasing policy and implement the regulations necessary to carry out that policy without further delay. The Task Force did not have sufficient time to reach a consensus on specific recommendations for a federal coal leasing policy. The Environmental Caucus feels strongly that there is no need for additional leasing of federal coal outside of areas that are already under lease. The caucus has recommended procedures, detailed in the Task Force report that should result in a decrease in the total amount of federal coal under lease, to the extent that tonnages of federal coal currently committed by lease and suitable preference right lease applications exceed the need for federal coal in the near and intermediate future.

Mine-mouth coal conversion facilities should not be encouraged in the Northern Plains and Rocky Mountain coal regions, or in prime agricultural areas of the Midwest. Also, large-scale mine-mouth coal conversion facilities in the arid West are likely to cause a number of major problems including:

(1) Consumptive use of scarce water resources.
(2) Adverse impacts on ecosystems which are more susceptible to damage from air pollutants than in humid areas.
(3) Large population increases in small communities where the social impacts of growth related to energy development are most severe.

The Task Force does not intend to imply that there are no serious environmental problems associated with the siting of energy facilities in the humid areas of the U.S., but that in general they are less severe than in the arid West. One exception to this may be in prime agricultural areas of the Midwest where energy facilities may remove large acreages of land from agricultural use permanently.

With the environmental constraints contained in the recommendations in this report, national production should be able to expand steadily if the market is strong enough, but major production increases must come from deep mining east of the Mississippi River. Although locally significant, from a national perspective, only modest increases in surface mined tonnage production in the Northern Plains are likely to occur, primarily due to the impact of the Clean Air Act Amendments of 1977, with more notable increases possible in parts of the Illinois Basin and in Appalachia. This pattern of development generally coincides with areas where there are less severe environmental problems associated with mining.

Coal Reserves and Quality

Current coal reserve estimates prepared by the U.S. Bureau of Mines are deficient, primarily because the criteria used to define coal reserves are not sensitive to the economic context which determined the feasibility of coal mining. Coal reserve criteria used by the federal government tend to overestimate reserves in the Western United States while under-estimating reserves in the East. An analysis of reserve data made by the Task Force indicates that approximately 65%, based on tonnage, and 71%, based on energy, of the coal in the United States is located east of the Mississippi River. Most recent federal estimates place only 46% of the coal reserves in the East.

Information on sulfur, ash and trace elements in coal needs to be published and evaluated on a uniform btu-adjusted basis. Federal reserve estimates of low sulfur coal, which are classified on a percentage by weight basis, overstate the amount of low sulfur coal in the West because these coals generally have a lower heat content than Midwestern and Eastern coals. When this factor is taken into account, significant amounts of low sulfur Western coals contain levels of sulfur equivalent to medium and high sulfur Midwestern and Eastern coal. The two coal areas with low sulfur reserves large enough for export to other regions in large amounts are the Northern Plains and Central Appalachia. A new classification system that compares sulfur in coal on a uniform btu-adjusted basis needs to be instituted.

Reclamation

Specific goals for reclamation differ between coal provinces because land use, soils, geology, and climate vary widely. The ultimate goal of reclamation in the Northern Plains and all other areas where precipitation is less than potential evapotranspiration should be to establish a viable progressive, self-regenerating ecosystem. Techniques for reclaiming land in the Northern Plains are still in an experimental stage because not enough time has passed to determine whether reestablished native ecosystems and/or the long-term agricultural productivity of mined land can be sustained through a severe drought cycle.

In the Midwest the basic goal of surface mine reclamation should be to return mined land to its previous or a higher level of productivity. This has not yet been demonstrated in the highly productive prime agricultural lands in central Illinois and Indiana, but the potential productivity of some of the less fertile soils in the southern Illinois basin may be improved if soils are properly reconstructed. This may also be the case in the lignite areas of central and eastern Texas.

In Appalachia, reclamation should achieve the short-term goal of rapidly establising vegetative cover to stabilized spoils and prevent erosion, and the long-term goal of establishing a successional native forest ecosystem. Current reclamation practices are accomplishing the short-term goal, but are generally not oriented toward establishing forest ecosystems.

Reclamation of land for uses other than the basic goals mentioned above may be desirable under certain circumstances. It is possible to reclaim mined land to a more intensive agricultural use in some regions. In this situation proper land management must be assured following the completion of mining operations. Mine land can also be used for more intensive socio-cultural uses such as housing, industry, or commerce. This is especially true in Appalachia where land naturally suitable for such use is limited. A relatively small percentage of land in mined areas is needed or suitable for more intensive agricultural or socio-cultural uses, so the restoration of land as nearly as possible to pre-mining conditions should be the general practice. The determination of post-mining land use should occur during the permit review process with input from all parties that have an interest in the post-mining land use.

Impact on Water Resources

Proper application of state-of-the-art techniques for acid drainage control and sediment control, rapid revegetation of mined land, and restoration of the approximate original topography in steeply sloping areas are able to control the most serious water quality problem associated with surface mining. There is still a need for improvement in techniques to control impacts of mining on water quality and more widespread application of currently available techniques. Mine operators should monitor water quality after reclamation bonds are released in order to determine longer term impacts of current mining practices on water quality.

Adverse impacts of mining on water resources have been most widespread in Appalachia. In order to better control impacts of surface mining on water resources in Appalachia, mine permits should be issued on a watershed basis and phased so as to minimize the amount of land disturbance and watershed impact caused by mining at any given time. More detailed site-specific studies are needed to evaluate the effect of current mining practices in this area on the hydrologic system and the long-term effectiveness of current reclamation practices in areas with acid overburden. Abandoned deep mines remain the major source of acid mine drainage in Appalachia, and publicly funded programs to abate acid mine drainage problems associated with these mines should continue.

Mountaintop removal mining and the accompanying use of head of hollow fill in southern Appalachia create a substantial alteration of the hydrologic system and the effects are not yet fully understood. Future mountaintop removal mining should proceed in conjunction with the use of a systems engineering approach in the design and construction of head of hollow fills which takes into account the hydrologic and geologic characteristics of the entire affected watershed. The Environmental Caucus feels that mountaintop removal mining in areas with acid overburden should be allowed only on an experimental permit basis to determine whether acid spoils can be handled without creating acid water problems.

Holders of current and future mine permits should take primary responsibility for the treatment of acid drainage after mining is completed for as long as the condition continues. Untreated discharges from abandoned deep mines and active deep mines are the major source of acid mine drainage. More careful hydrologic reviews of deep mines NPDES permit applications than are presently occurring in most states are necessary to assure that the best methods for mining and/or treating acid drainage will be used.

Surface mining, particularly in the West and parts of Appalachia may have severe impacts on local groundwater resources. Coal should be mined in a manner which insures that those who use groundwater do not suffer financial loss as a result of damage to their water supply. If this manner of mining is not possible, it should not be allowed.

Other Issues

The Mining Task Force also dealt with other issues not directly applicable to biophysical ecosystem impact. Among these are Socioeconomic Impacts of Mine Development; Regulation: Standards and Enforcement; Efficiency of Resource Extraction; Fugitive Dust; Strip Mine Blasting Effects; Subsidence; Mine Fires; and New Technologies.

RECLAMATION EXAMPLE

As an example of the kind of detail that the Policy Project was able to develop, the following exerpt from the Reclamation section on general technical recommendations is presented from a section on *Soil Reconstruction and Handling*. This is only a small section from a long list of site specific and general recommendations.

Soil Reconstruction and Handling

(a) Where future land use options are to be maximized, soil handling should be such that soil structure, water holding capacity, geochemical segregation, viable and diverse microbiota and macrobiota, and living seed and plant materials are preserved *in situ* and intact so far as is reasonably possible. This emphasis is particularly important in the arid west (precipitation less than potential evapotranspiration) where reclamation goals are directed toward reestablishment of viable progressive natural ecosystems.

(b) Soil handling should be minimized, and stockpiling that is detrimental to geochemical and biological stability should be minimized. Continuous handling, such that surface materials are stripped off and immediately reapplied to lands under reclamation, is to be encouraged.

(c) Soil mapping at scales of at least 8 inches to the mile should be a necessary prerequisite to the development of a reclamation and revegetation plan. This mapping should be used to assess prior soil status and to most efficiently plan a reclamation effort which maximizes prospects of soil function on reclaimed lands similar to those available prior to mining. Guidelines for mapping soils at mining sites should be developed for each state in which surface mining occurs. The final report from which this is exerpted provides an example of the type of guidelines needed. Specific details in mapping will of course vary depending on the soil and overburden characteristics in a particular coal area.

(d) It is recognized that natural soils evolve geochemically and biologically through long periods of geologic time and that it may not be possible under today's climatic conditions to reestablish soils over mined lands similar to those existing before mining. Where such future soil conditions are likely to be different from preexisting conditions to the extent that total site productivity or potential uses are more restricted than before mining, the loss of future options should be clearly stated within the mining application for consideration in the permit review process.

(e) Use of soil amendments and fertilizers is recognized as being necessary to the establishment of initial vegetative cover in some instances during revegetation but should not generally be required periodically for long-term reclamation. Fertilizer application should not destroy or significantly alter long-term geochemical evolution of a soil-vegetation succession.

(f) Overburden characterization (and interburden characterization where appropriate) should be a regular and necessary prerequisite to the preparation of any revegetation and reclamation plan. Such analysis should at minimum, include assessment of pre-mining soil moisture holding capacities and nutrient status at initial and ultimate rooting depths. It should also include all necessary chemical and physical analyses as necessary to assess potential toxicities of materials that may ultimately become part of a soil profile or are potentially able to migrate under expected soil moisture regimes and groundwater regimes and become a part of the rooting medium for future vegetation. Toxicity in this case is defined in the broad sense to include all chemical conditions which could lead to ultimate reduction of site capacity to support vegetation suitable for the chosen end-use. These conditions include salinity, sodium-absorption ratio, and chemical repression of growth of desired species of plants, soil animals, and species that consume the vegetation. Overburden analyses should be integrated and interpreted with a soil reconstruction and handling plan. In this way, a reclamation and revegetation plan can be developed that minimizes adverse impacts of geochemical homogenization on previously stratified overburden and interburden. Where ultimate reduced capacity of site-use is revealed through overburden analyses, estimates of such reductions should be included in mining plans and considered in the permit review process. It is recognized that at certain mining sites, such as those with highly saline surface soils or those with very old nutrient-depleted soil profiles, soil handling can be planned so as to increase potential site productivity and increase future site-use options. Such information likewise should be included in a mining plan in which overburden analyses show these increases to be possible. Maps should be prepared which present information on both the characteristics of soils and overburden. Map unit delineations that combine surface and subsurface characteristics, such as those developed by the Illinois Geological Survey might be a useful way to present such information (Bergstrom et al. 1976).

(g) Potentially toxic spoils should be handled and disposed in such a fashion that their ultimate negative effects upon future site use options are minimized. This should include burial of such materials at depths greater than the deepest expected root penetration and greater than depths of expected upward migration of toxic materials that can be expected to be mobilized through solution. This may mean that subirrigating groundwater systems or surface concentration downgradient in subsurface aquifers must be considered in the disposal of potentially toxic or deleterious spoil materials. Information on cases where negative on-site or off-site effects cannot be eliminated should be included in mining plans and considered in the review process. Where pre-mining soil and/or groundwater conditions are deleterious to proposed post-mining end land uses and where proposed spoils handling cannot rectify these conditions, special toxic spoils handling efforts may be justified such as off-site disposal or hydrologic isolation.

(h) A system should be developed for mapping and classification of reclaimed mined land, according to the land's capability. The Soil Conservation Service classification system for mine spoils developed in Kentucky is a good start in this direction (Ruffner 1973). However, this system needs to be expanded and refined in order to apply in other states and to take into account current reclamation requirements, such as thickness of replaced topsoil. Mapping procedures should be similar to those used by the Soil Conservation Service in detailed soil surveys (which are usually on a scale of 4 inches to the mile), but mapping will be required at a larger scale (probably 8 inches to the mile or more) because of the extreme variability in the characteristics of mined land. Mine operators should be required to prepare maps of mined land after reclamation is completed so that the reclamation plan and the final result can be compared. Such a mapping system would also be valuable for developing plans for reclamation of orphan spoils.

REFERENCES

Bergstrom, R.E., K. Piskin and L.R. Follmer. 1976. Geology for planning in the Springfield-Decatur region, Illinois. Ill. State Geol. Survey Circ. 497.

Murray, F.X. 1978. Where We Agree: Report of the National Coal Policy Project. Vol. I Air Pollution, Transportation, Pricing, Utilization and Conservation, 337 p.; Vol. II, Mining and Reclamation, 477 p. Westview Press, Boulder, CO.

Ruffner, J.D. 1973. Projecting the use of new plant materials for special reclamation problems. pp. 108-117, In National Coal Association. Selected Papers and Remarks from Research and Applied Technology on Mined-Land Reclamation, NCA, Washington, D C.

THE TROUBLE WITH WESTERN COAL

*Eugene Guccione**

President Carter wants domestic coal production to double to 1.1 billion tons per year by 1985. Obviously, the President is an optimist, meaning: he's not as well informed as a pessimist. It took the U.S. coal industry 58 years to increase domestic coal production by about 11.5 percent, from 568 million tons in 1920 to today's level of about 665 million tons. With such a growth record, it would take a few hundred years to boost coal production to the level envisioned by Mr. Carter.

Perhaps we could reach that level by 1985 if we did not have to worry about the lack of capital, and if we were not bothered by such trifles as the Mine Health and Safety Act, the National Environmental Policy Act, the Clean Air Act, and new Surface Mining Act, the pending bills for horizontal and/or vertical divesture, etc. But let's forget about all that. Let us pretend instead that we have lots of money for opening up new mines, that the economy is in great shape, and that the legislative and regulatory orgy of the past 10 years never took place.

Then what? There would still be one enormous obstacle to any substantial increase in coal production: no land available to mine. Most of the projected production increase will have to come from the coal-rich deposits of the western states. But the biggest landowner in the West is the federal government. And in recent years, the federal government has been behaving as a deranged landlord by pursuing a no-leasing policy. The tragedy today is that while energy problems are getting worse, the U.S. coal industry, which could solve most of these government-created problems, is being denied access to more than 99 percent of federal coal lands.

What President Carter does not know, and what virtually no one outside the mining industry knows, is that the non-issuance of competitive leases and preference-right leases for coal and other minerals has resulted in the de-facto nationalization of a large part of the country's mineral resources or, at least, in a gigantic step in that direction.

How the hell did this happen? The answer has been provided in two articles in *Coal Mining & Processing* by L.C. Lee ("Federal Leasing: The Need for a Perspective," May 1977, pp. 23-24) and by D.C. Russell ("Whatever Happened to Federal Coal Leasing," June 1977, pp. 60-63). Lee and Russell are mineral economists at the U.S. Department of the Interior. In this article, I merely give a synopsis of their findings, before outlining *my* tentative solution.

HOW TO GET INTO MINING

There are three ways of getting into mining:

*Coal Mining & Processing, 300 West Adams Street, Chicago, IL 60606.

(1) *Land ownership* - *If* you have land of your own, *if* you have both the surface and mineral ownership rights, *if* your land acreage is large enough to constitute a "logical mining unit" that will enable you to mine commerically, *if* you spend a small fortune on geological and mine feasibility studies, and *if* you invest an indecent amount of time (at least three years) to get the few dozen permits from local, state, and federal authorities, then you *might* be allowed to mine your own land.

(2) *Preference right leasing* - If you have neither your own land nor the money to buy somebody else's property, you can get into mining by first obtaining a *prospecting permit* from the U.S. Department of the Interior. The prospecting permit is nothing but a hunting license: with it, you are allowed to search for minerals in those areas where, according to the U.S. Geological Survey (an agency of Interior), there are no known or workable mineral deposits. Then, in the unlikely event that you find something valuable, you are entitled to a *preference-right lease* (sometimes also known as a "non-competitive lease") because, after all, you spent your own money in locating the deposit. The government, in effect, gives you the right of first refusal by issuing a preference-right lease; you don't get anything else, and, when you start mining and producing, you must still pay the same leasing fee, mineral royalties, severance taxes, etc., as everybody else.

(3) *Competitive leasing* - If you have money, you can get a competitive lease by bidding successfully against other miners for a piece of land where the U.S. Geological Survey has spent the taxpayers' money to find and identify a "workable mineral deposit."

ZERO LEASING FOR COAL

Though it was never administered to everybody's satisfaction, and though it suffered from the usual government-caused abuses (the most famous of which was the Teapot Dome scandal of 1921, to be discussed later), the leasing system worked fairly well from the late 1870's to the late 1960's. Since 1968, however, the entire federal leasing mechanism has virtually ceased to function. Today, for all intents and purposes, mineral deposits on federal land are no longer accessible. The situation is particularly grave where coal is concerned. Briefly, here is a rundown of the main events.

In 1968, the Interior Department began to withdraw more and more land from mining exploration to the point that, today, more than half the country (mostly in the minerals-rich western states) is no longer accessible even for prospecting. Such a massive withdrawal of land from prospecting and exploration, incidentally, is just about as rational as forbidding American physicians from conducting medical examinations on one-half of the human body.

In 1970, Interior began a moratorium on coal-prospecting permits. Since then, deprived of their "hunting license," many coal prospectors and exploration firms have gone out of business.

In 1973, Interior instituted a freeze on coal preference-right leases. Since then, hundreds of small mining companies that had spent their meager funds to locate a deposit have gone bankrupt.

Finally, in 1976, Congress killed the preference-right lease method for coal by amending the 1920 Mineral Leasing Act. From now on, unless you own land, the *only* way you can get into coal mining is through competitive bid leasing.

"In view of the energy crisis and of the federal government's control over coal land," says Lee, "the need for a rational leasing policy is more important than ever. But no such policy exists. Or if it exists, it certainly has not reflected any effective management, as shown by the record of federal leasing during the past nine years."

For instance:

(a) Coal land made available under federal lease is only 800,000 acres. This is equivalent to 0.8 percent of the 100 million acres of federally owned land prospectively valuable for coal (Table I).

(b) The acreage made available annually under competitive bidding since 1967 has fluctuated sharply downward, from a peak of 88,181 acres in 1968 to zero in 1972 and 1973, and the acreage presently leased is minimal (Table II). This condition was largely caused by interpretations of the 1969 National Environmental Policy Act.

(c) The acreage made available annually under preference-right leases, also known as "non-competitive leases," has plunged from the 1968 peak of 76,009 acres to 475 acres in 1975 (Table III).

(d) The acreage under prospecting permits has not changed appreciably since 1967 and is now 613,604 acres (Table IV). That is a sizeable number; but it is also a meaningless number in view of the fact that only 475 acres became available in 1975 through a few prospecting permits that had matured to preference-right leases.

Table I—U.S. lands valuable for coal (acres)

	Total acres	Federally owned
Prospectively valuable	350,000,000	100,000,000
Classified [2]	41,000,000	29,000,000
Withdrawn for classification	20,000,000	14,000,000
Known recoverable coal resource areas (KRCRA) [1]	14,200,000	9,900,000
Federal coal leases [3]	—	800,000
Annually disturbed by mining	—	1,157

[1] Formerly "Known Coal Leasing Acres" (KCLA's).
[2] Same ratio of federal to total as KRCRA's.
[3] Data through end of 1975, from USGS Annual Report 1975.

Table II—Coal land acreage leased competitively per year (public and acquired lands).

1967	43,885 acres
1968	88,181 acres
1969	0 acres
1970	18,493 acres
1971	28,546 acres
1972	0 acres
1973	0 acres
1974	4,069 acres
1975	362 acres

Source: *Public Land Statistics*, 1967-1975.

Table III—Coal acreage leased noncompetitively per year.

1967	54,224 acres
1968	76,009 acres
1969	26,777 acres
1970	13,525 acres
1971	25,149 acres
1972	961 acres
1973	0 acres
1974	1,563 acres
1975	475 acres

Source: *Public Land Statistics*, 1967-1975.

Table IV—Coal acreage under prospecting permits.

1967	541,591 acres	1972	753,485 acres
1968	471,387 acres	1973	641,192 acres
1969	494,988 acres	1974	614,079 acres
1970	733,576 acres	1975	613,604 acres
1971	882,098 acres		

Source: *Public Land Statistics*, 1967-1975.

FACTS AND FICTION ABOUT COAL LEASING

For several years the Department of Interior has defended its zero-leasing policy by stating that 800,000 acres of land already under lease contain a total of 25 billion tons of coal reserves. "This was, and still is, the argument most frequently ventilated in political and environmental circles," say Lee and Russell, "and if taken at face value, particularly by people who don't know much else, this reserve-under-lease argument carries the built-in conclusion: Let's put a halt on coal leasing."

According to Lee and Russell, the error in the reserve-under-lease argument, as any experienced geologist, mining engineer, or mineral economist can easily point out, is that such an argument would only be valid if the geology, economics and legality were completely known and understood. In the real world, unfortunately, the reserve-under-lease approach is limited by insufficient geological knowledge, as well as by traditionally misleading interpretations of just what reserves are and what they mean as far as providing a land position sufficient for coal production.

Moreover, recently enacted regulations will have an adverse effect on the 800,000 acres of coal land presently under federal lease. Most of this land, which exists in scattered leases acquired before 1973 by coal producers and would-be coal producers, was issued non-competitively, i.e., it was issued outside of those "high-grade" areas that are exclusively designated for competitive leasing. Obviously, some of these non-competitive leases will never become productive coal mines for economic reasons, and some will never become productive because of various environmental and regulatory reasons of fairly recent vintage.

Lee and Russell have further pointed out that reserve-under-lease figures are a potpourri of measured, indicated, inferred, economic and subeconomic reserves, and resource estimates, not all of which were economically and legally extractable even in 1973 when these figures were determined. The analysis also failed to include the fact that 30 or more tons of measured recoverable coal are needed to produce just one ton annually, all of which must be in a "logical mining unit." During the years of the coal leasing moratorium (1971-1975), many leases that had been applied for to complete logical mining units had not yet been issued.

Any operator must receive timely governmental permission to economically mine and market coal from measured, economic reserves in a logical mining unit, with a large enough reserve position to justify the initial capital expense of property, plant, and development. These factors were not considered, either, in totaling the 25 billion tons of coal supposedly in reserve under lease.

"Even if those bloated tonnage figures were realistic in describing how much coal is under lease," notes Lee, "industry would not and could not be interested in thin beds or poor quality; or in areas with high production costs; or in areas that lack a market; or in areas where federal, state, and local governments have placed so many restrictions, e.g. land withdrawals, restrictive land use stipulations, complex and time-consuming permit requirements, prohibitive access, arbitrary anti-pollution regulations--that often raise costs on leased land too high to justify the investment. A prime example of this can be found in the abandonment of the Kaiparowits leases."

The Kaiparowits Power Project, incidentally, was originally conceived 14 years ago to deliver 5,000 megawatts to users in Utah, Arizona, Colorado and New Mexico. Investment for this coal-burning power project was initially estimated at $600 million. But because of inflation and bureaucratic delays, this project was scaled down to 3,000 megawatts in 1975 while its capital requirements soared to $2.5 billion. Last year, when Southern California Edison and the other participating utilities were informed that they had to file yet another environmental impact statement, the entire project was scrapped. At that time, the delays were costing more than $6 million per month in plant construction alone.

A GOVERNMENT MONOPOLY

Every year since 1970, Department of the Interior has announced a "new leasing policy," which invariably increases the federal monopoly over mineral resources.

This year was no exception. In fact, at the 1977 meeting of the American Mining Congress Coal Convention in Pittsburgh, Interior Secretary Cecil Andrus promised to evaluate the entire federal coal leasing policy "as quickly and expeditiously as possible." That may take some time because a new bureaucracy, the recently formed Department of Energy (DoE), will have its finger into federal leasing practices. "The Department of Energy," said Andrus, "will take over some of the leasing functions we now have and will also carry out research and development of mining techniques. In general, the Department of Energy will tell us (at Interior) how much coal they think should come from the public lands and what the economic terms of the leases should be. The Interior Department will determine which federal lands should be leased and will call for the bids, oversee the leases, and monitor the lease operations." (Obviously, government planning is the answer because, after all, "We've tried free enterprise, and it has failed.")

Secretary Andrus, who identifies himself as a conservationist, then went on to spell out the new division of labor between industry and government: "You are the people who will do the mining, and we, meaning the federal government, are the people who will provide the regulations which will guide the mining practices, the environmental protection, the land reclamation standards and much of the coal." (Translation: "You are the people who will do the mining, and we, meaning the federal government, are the people who will provide the regulations which will guide the mining practices, the environmental protection, the land reclamation standards and much of the coal." (Translation: "You are the people who will do the mining, and we, meaning the technical illiterates who can't even spell anthracite, will tell you how to mine the stuff, where, when, how much, to whom to sell, at what price, and how to reclaim the land.") Oh well, if you like the postal system, you'll love nationalized coal.

As Lee and Russell point out, incidentally, the degree of control exercised by the federal government already greatly exceeds the official 100-million-acre figure. The reason? Because checkerboarding (i.e., a railroad's ownership of one-square-mile parcels of land on alternate sides of a railway) and complex ownership patterns of private land, state parks, national parks, Indian reservations, etc., are often the rule rather than the exception, many mining operations must include at least some federal property (especially in the West). In addition, the federal government owns over 700 million acres of surface and minerals, mostly in the western states and Alaska. "We estimate that the federal government owns 70 percent of the coal as well as equivalent or greater amounts of other leasable minerals in the western half of the United States," report Lee and Russell.

This federal monopoly so pronounced in the West has the full support of eastern politicians, organized labor, and western socialists (some of the latter posing as "environmentalists"). The United Mine Workers Union, which draws most of its membership from the eastern underground mining operations, is understandably opposed to surface mining in the West, particularly since, as the argument goes, "If we can prevent surface mining, more coal has to be mined underground, and that means more money and power for us." Many elected officials from eastern states also oppose the development of western coal because this "foreign" coal imported from Wyoming or Montana might cause unemployment at "home."

Thus, even though surface mining is the best, most efficient, safest, and most profitable technique to be developed in the past 50 years, I am certain that the development of western coal will not be allowed to reach its potential for at least the next 10 years.

THE WAR AGAINST WESTERN COAL

The new Surface Mining Act, which is merely a rehash of the old legislation vetoed twice by President Ford, was passed by Congress in July 1977. Allegedly drafted "to protect the environment," this bill in reality is nothing but a crude attempt at halting coal development in the West. Mining engineer John F. Havard, former president of the Society of Mining Engineers of AIME, points out that this bill is (a) unnecessary since "the 38 states producing most of the nation's minerals have already adopted stringent mining laws," and (b) dangerous because it overlooks the fact that "coal strip mining conditions vary from state to state. Western strip mining differs from Appalachian strip mining. Even North Dakota strip mining is different from Colorado strip mining."

Why must western coal development not be stopped? Here is a list of reasons:

(1) Surface mining is the only way to produce coal from many of the vast western deposits, which are near the surface and cannot be mined by underground methods.

(2) Surface mining, compared to underground mining, is much safer: it is 20 times less likely to result in the death of a miner. And there's no such thing as black lung disease in surface mines.

(3) Surface mining is more efficient; it recovers 80 percent of the coal; and in thick western seams, recovery rates can exceed 95 percent. Underground mining instead recovers about 50 percent of the coal (since the rest has to be left in underground pillars to hold the roof up).

(4) Surface mining is more productive. In the same amount of time it takes for an underground miner to produce one ton of coal, a surface miner can produce up to 20 tons of coal. In fact, surface mining averages about 35 tons per man per day; in the West, it can average up to 200 tons. Underground mining instead averages about 11 tons per man per day. It is interesting to note that in the United Kingdom, the average productivity in the nationalized coal industry is a mere 2.5 tons per man per day.

(5) Surface mining in the West yields *clean* coal, which contains from a half to one-tenth the amount of sulfur present in eastern coal.

(6) Surface mining in the western states would disturb at least 90 percent less land than surface mining in the East. For instance, to produce 30 million tons per year of coal in the Powder River Basin of Wyoming, in any given year only 300 acres of land would be temporarily disturbed. To strip mine 30 million tpy of coal in a heavily populated state like Illinois would disturb 4,500 to 7,500 acres of land.

(7) Surface mining represents only a temporary use of land. If half of the hoped-for 100 percent increase in coal production by 1985 comes from the West, it will require the surface mining of only 130,000 acres of land. The 130,000 acres that will be mined and reclaimed over the next 10 years is less than the amount of land covered by parking lots in one year.

(8) The average selling price of surface-mined coal F.O.B. mine is just about one-third to one-half the price of underground coal F.O.B. mine.

(9) The mining industry, whatever its ancient faults, has been making a real effort in reclaiming for at least four decades. Of the 1.47 million acres used for surface coal mining from 1930 to 1971, one million acres had already been reclaimed by 1970. And in 1971, coal people actually reclaimed 30 percent more land than they mined. Finally, in spite of the grim picture of wholesale devastation allegedly caused by surface mining, only 0.16 percent of the total area of the United States has ever been disturbed by *all* kinds of surface mining. Of that, almost half has been reclaimed, and the rest is in the process of reclamation.

One weapon against western coal is the zero-leasing policy. Another weapon is the blanket requirement for sulfur dioxide scrubbers on *all* coal-burning power plants, regardless of whether such power plants burn high-sulfur (i.e., eastern) coal or low-sulfur (i.e., western) coal; this weapon will remove whatever economic incentives the utilities might have in purchasing western coal. Another weapon is the "non-degradation" requirement that is being incorporated into the amendments to the 1970 Clean Air Act allegedly for the purpose of preventing "significant deterioration" in areas of pristine air quality, but in reality to prevent or delay the construction of western mine-mouth coal-burning power plants. Another weapon is the "horizontal divestiture" proposal (union-endorsed, of course) which would cut off the only source of risk capital for western coal development by forcing oil companies to sell their coal holdings. Another weapon is the new Surface Mining Act. I could go on, but you get the drift.

A TENTATIVE SOLUTION

The zero-leasing policy so relentlessly pursued by Department of the Interior is perhaps the biggest obstacle to fossil fuels and minerals development. It is also the logical result of almost a century of good intentions enforced by government edict and based upon three erroneous premises. Two of these premises are historical; one is philosophical.

Once the historical context is established, the solution (or at least, a tentative solution) will virtually suggest itself. "Throughout the 19th century, especially after the Civil War, the federal government encouraged settlers, war veterans and private developers to move westward and take up homesteads," say Lee and Russell, "and this is how our forefathers were given 'free' homestead for only a nominal filing fee....Several million acres of coal land, however, were excluded from the disposition of homestead laws....Eventually, the federal policy that evolved during that period was geared at keeping the nation's resources within federal control for at least two reasons: *to create a source of revenues, and to prevent private monopolies.*" (emphasis mine)

Well, the first reason might have made sense until 1916 because, before then, there was no such thing as an income tax. But it certainly does not make any sense in 1978 when government (local, state, and federal) takes in taxes more than 50 cents out of every dollar we earn as individuals *and* as corporate entities.

The second reason, i.e., that a leasing policy has to be established to "prevent private monopolies," is totally false. It was government itself that created most of those coercive private monopolies, for instance, by granting huge tracts of land to railroads (the famous "checkerboarding"). In fact, the biggest scandal in mining, a scandal rivaled only by

Watergate, occurred when government abuses were discovered: "In 1921, the then Secretary of the Interior, Albert Fall, using questionable authority, secretly leased without competitive bidding some military oil reserves in California and Wyoming (Teapot Dome) to E.L. Doheny and Henry Sinclair," report Lee and Russell. "Secretary Fall, who went as far as to call the Marines to evict Sinclair's rival claimants from the Teapot Dome reserves, was also found guilty of a corrupt conspiracy to secure for Doheny unleased land in the California reserves and accepting $100,000 in bribe.

Finally, the third reason for a leasing policy rests on the public-property premise, i.e., that unoccupied land is "public property" and that government must administer this land. This premise was *implied* in much of the legislation passed at the turn of the century, but it has now become *explicit* particularly in every piece of land legislation enacted in the past few years. The argument usually begins with the plea that "federal" land should not be made available to the multiple use of individuals and industries, but must be preserved as ecological and wilderness areas, except that the real purpose is neither of these. The real purpose is to cash in on the concept of "public property," which is a contradiction in terms.

The public is everybody in general and nobody in particular. "Property," on the other hand, is a concept that, on legal-moral grounds, identifies the relationship that exists between an individual and an object of value, and the law clearly spells out the method in which a person acquires title and possession of a particular value (The concept of a collective or public property has no validity in science either: there is no such thing as a collective property of the elements, or a collective viscosity, or a collective density, or a collective molecular weight of substances.) So, what should be done with the hundreds of millions of acres of public property?

As I see it, the solution would be to convert this land into private property, either through a new version of the old homesteading laws, or by a land-selling program quite similar to the periodic gold auction sales organized by the U.S. Treasury Department. The proceeds from such land auctions would then go to the ultimate owners, the U.S. public, via tax rebates. The chances of any such solution being put into effect are nil, at present.

An alternative or tentative solution, which I propose with many reservations, would entail the restoration of so-called federal land to the various states, each of which would then compete (I hope) in selling this land to the public. This tentative solution has at least one virtue, and one vice. The virtue is that it would appeal to the greed of many local and state elected officials (whom we can always impeach later); the vice is that such a solution might wind up replacing *one* master (the federal government) with at least 50 masters (the state legislatures).

Many mining people would be satisfied with a leasing policy such as the one that existed until the mid 1960's. Lee and Russell have suggested establishing a leasing policy based on what is known about coal or any other mineral resource, compared to what acreage is available for lease and to what has already been leased. While I greatly respect both gentlemen, and concede that *any* leasing policy is better than a zero-leasing policy, I just don't want government as my landlord. Whatever government gives, assuming it "gives" anything in the first place, government eventually takes away, a fact corroborated by Lee and Russell's findings.

Ultimately, then, the only real solution is to return all coal land to private hands, where it can be developed (or not) in accordance with the laws of economics, not the edicts of politicians and bureaucrats.

ENERGY POLICIES AND
THE USE OF INPUT-OUTPUT MODELS

Merlin M. Hackbart and R. Stafford Johnson*

It is generally agreed that the period from 1973 to 1977 was one in which progress toward the national goals of expanding coal output was achieved, albeit at an uneven pace. Moreover, significant U.S. coal reserves, emerging technology, and new public and private investment programs auger for continued expansion of coal production in the long-run. In fact, some experts suggest that U.S. coal output would reach 830 million tons by 1980 and over 1 billion tons by 1985 (Standard and Poor's 1977), compared to 665 million tons in 1977 (NCA 1976).

It is recognized that policies designed to encourage the rapid development of coal reserves, while perhaps desirable vis-a-vis national policy goals, may impose significant externalities on coal-producing regions. Therefore, it becomes important to develop analytical processes and techniques capable of efficient ex ante assessments of the socio-economic impact of energy development on a specific region. For economic impact assessments, regional I-0 Models have gained wide recognition (Hackbart et al. 1977). Such models have been utilized to estimate the economic impact of new energy policies and in the assessment of alternative national and regional policies (i.e., tax, regulatory, and infrastructure development).

The impact of many energy policies, particularly those relating to the expansion of coal, will not be felt immediately, but rather at a future date. Given the static nature of the Input-Output Models, it becomes difficult to measure impacts which occur over time. If the impact of long-term energy policies is to be estimated, it becomes necessary to adjust the model to reflect regional structure change and changes in the regional share of national output that can be expected to occur in the future, particularly in coal- or energy-producing states. The purpose of this paper is to specify, by use of an Input-Output Model, a simplified approach to account for such changes.

Model

An Input-Output (I-0) Table displays an array of inter-industry flows of goods and services among sectors in an economy. The flows depict industry or sector sales to all other industries or to final users (i.e., government, consumption, investment, inventories, and net exports). Consequently, all sector outputs are accounted for by the I-0 Tables. Moreover, the I-0 Tables can be converted to a model via the behavioral assumptions of production

*College of Business and Economics, University of Kentucky, Lexington, KY 40506.

function stability and constant returns to scale. More formally, an aggregate n-sector model can be defined as follows:

X_i = Total production in industry i,

T_{ij} = Dollar input used by industry j and produced by industry i,

a_{ij} = Ratio of dollar input used by industry j and produced by industry i,

D_i = Final demand in industry i.

Given that production in any industry is either sold to final consumers or bought by other industries, the relationship between final demand and production for industry i can be expressed as follows:

$$X_i = \sum_{i=1}^{n} T_{ij} + D_i,$$ (1)

or

$$X_i = \sum_{j=1}^{n} a_{ij} X_j + D_i.$$ (2)

Collecting the X_is to form a vector X_t^R, T_{ij}s to form a transaction matrix T_t^R, D_is to yield a vector D_t^R, and a_{ij}s to form a coefficient matrix A_t^R, allows (1) to be written in matrix form as:

$$X_t^R - T_t^R = D_t^R$$ (3)

$$X_t^R - A_t^R X_t^R = D_t^R$$ (4)

$$(I - A_t^R) X_t^R = D_t^R,$$ (5)

where t refers to the present (or base) period, and R signifies the particular region. The sector output levels, X_i, necessary to deliver all final demands, D_i, can then be expressed as:

$$X_t^R = (I - A_t^R)^{-1} D_t^R.$$ (6)

Equation (6) provides a useful description of a state economy. Moreover, this equation is useful in assessing the impact of various policies, including energy, on a state economy. As noted, one limitation of utilizing I-0 for impact assessment for energy scenarios is the fact that the impacts of many energy policies apply to future time periods. Therefore, the assessment of such energy policy impacts requires that the changes in A_t^R, X_t^R, and D_t^R be determined or alternatively that their future values—A_F^R, X_F^R, and D_F^R—be estimated for a future period.

Estimating the A_F^R Matrix

Changes in the technical coefficient, a_{ij}, can result either from technological or production developments, market changes, or price changes. It is difficult to estimate future technological or market conditions. For impact assessments, technological changes do not appear to significantly reduce impact assessment efficiency and, therefore, such changes do not pose significant projection problems. However, price-level adjustments, particularly in energy-related sectors, can be significant and can impose critical changes in the A Matrix. Fortunately, however, price-level adjustments can be estimated by using sector-specific price deflators that are forecasted by sectors. Such forecasts are routinely provided by econometric forecasting organizations. The impact of price-level changes on the A Matrix can be measured by premultiplying a price deflator Matrix P^F times the T_t^R Matrix to obtain an adjusted transaction Matrix T_F^R as follows:

$$P_F \cdot T_t^R = T_F^R, \tag{7}$$

where P_F is a diagonal matrix of estimated price deflators reflecting sector-specific price-level changes between the base period and the projected time period (Charlesworth et al. 1974). Moreover, from T_F^R, an adjusted coefficient Matrix A_F^R can be estimated.

Estimating the X Vector

While there are a number of approaches for estimating X_F^R—in particular, regional econometric models—one simplified approach is to utilize national econometric model forecasts to estimate national values for X_F^{US}, and then to make use of shift-share analysis to estimate X_F^R.

In general, shift-share analysis is an analytical technique used to measure regional growth differentials (see Emerson and Lamphear 1975). Conceptually, a region can grow at a faster or slower rate than the national economy either due to the fact that its structure contains sectors which are fast growing compared to the nation or because its industrial sectors are growing more rapidly than their national counterparts. The latter reason, referred to as the "competitive" component of differential growth, is particularly relevant to regions with rapidly expanding energy sectors (i.e., the coal regions of the United States). Such competitive shares of national sectoral output can be estimated by regression analysis of near-term regional/national sector growth rate differentials (see Lynch 1977). By projecting shifts of the regional share of sector output, X_t^R/X_t^{US}, to the future time period, X_F^R/X_F^{US}, by regression techniques, one can estimate the shares of future U.S. sector outputs which the region can expect to produce. Utilizing this technique provides a simplified way of quantifying the X_F^R Vector for a future year.

Once T_F^R and X_F^R have been estimated a new coefficient Matrix, A_F^R, depicting a regional economy in period F can be specified by standard I-0 techniques. D_F^R can then be estimated as the residual. Given this estimated structure, energy policy impact assessments estimated to occur in period F can be analyzed by an I-0 for period F as opposed to period t.

SUMMARY

As noted, the assessment of the long-term impact of many energy policies can benefit from the use of I-0 Models which describe the economy in the future as opposed to the present. If it is assumed that the major economic changes affecting a region are price-level adjustments and changes in regional/national output shares, then the preceding analysis provided a simplified approach for adjusting an I-0 Model to reflect future economic conditions. Moreover, with I-0 Models reflecting the future, the impact of energy policies that are not expected to be felt until the long-run can be better analyzed.

REFERENCES

Charlesworth, H.K., R. Thalheimer and J. Lidemenn. 1974. The Kentucky Input-Output Model. Off. of Business Develop. and Government Services, College of Business and Economics, Univ. Kentucky, 12 p.

Emerson, J. and F.C. Lamphear. 1975. Urban and regional economics: structure and change. pp. 143-144, Allyn and Bacon, Inc., Boston.

Hackbart, M.M., C.W. Hultman and J.R. Ramsey. 1977. On the economics of energy allocation. pp. 98-107, In Review of Regional Studies, Spring 1977.

Lynch, L.K. 1977. The structure and long-term growth of the Kentucky Economy. pp. 10-20, In Kentucky Council of Economic Advisors Policy Papers Ser. No. 2, Center for Public Affairs, Off. for Research, College of Business and Economics, Univ. Kentucky, Lexington.

National Coal Association. 1977. Coal Data 1976. Washington, D.C., National Coal Association, II-2 p.

Standard and Poor's. 1977. Industry Survey. NY Standard and Poor's Corp., NY October 1977, S58 p.

POLICY ASPECTS OF ENERGY
RESOURCE DEVELOPMENT ON INDIAN LANDS

G.R. Stairs* and T.R. Verma**

INTRODUCTION

A definition of energy resources need not include reference to ownership or political control in the strict conceptual sense. However, any management or reference to exploitation of the resource must clearly delineate the decision-making system in terms both historic and contemporary. The Indian lands of the United States present, in this regard, a uniquely complicated situation. History of relations between the Indian people, the Federal or State governments, and non-Indian people is documented in many ways. From cinema to authoritative texts, from treaty to court interpretations, from locally interpreted policy and attitude to trust authority, from Wounded Knee and prior to Wounded Knee again the record is a varigated scene with little to instill confidence among the Indian people in the entire process.

The nature of relationships between the Indian and the U.S. is based on treaties that were negotiated in history. Although not a uniformly understood or accepted premise among non-Indians, the nature of the treaties was inherently related to the exchange of extremely valuable land and resources for protection against foreign nations, hostile Indian tribes and other individuals, and life on a much reduced land base. In brief, a trust responsibility was accepted on the part of the federal government. The definition of the trust authority has been little understood, much argued and often violated by the federal government; nevertheless, it remains clear that the U.S. has not chosen to purposely disavow the generic relationships established by treaty. Further one may note that the treaties were founded upon principles of international law, and that through various treaties, statutes, and judicial doctrines, the U.S. has come to recognize tribal sovereignty and its feduciary responsibility to the various tribes and thus to the individual Indian.

Comprehension reviews of the Indian situation have been rare at the federal level. The latest is embodied in the American Indian Policy Review Commission Report (e.g. Final Report, Volumes 1 and 2, U.S. Government Printing Office 1977), an activity that follows by 50 years the previous effort (Meriam Report of 1928). Perhaps the earliest may be found in Committee Reports of the 1775 Committee on Indian Affairs; a committee including men such as Benjamin Franklin and Patrick Henry. In the recent report (1978), acknowledgement of authorship referenced a strong attempt to include the views of Indians

* Center for Resource and Environmental Policy Research, Duke University, Durham, NC 27706.

** School of Renewable Natural Resources, University of Arizona, Tucson, AZ 85721.

rather than only those of Indian experts. The Report suggests that fundamental concepts needed to guide future policy determinations for Indian people include:

(1) "That Indian tribes are sovereign political bodies, having the power to determine their own membership and power to enact laws and enforce them within the boundaries of their reservations", and;

(2) "That the relationship which exists between the tribes and the United States is premised on a special trust that must govern the conduct of the stronger toward the weaker."

In addition the report recommends:

(1) "The trust responsibility to American Indians extends from the protection and enhancement of Indian trust resources and tribal self-government to the provision of economic and social programs necessary to raise the standard of living and social well being of the Indian people to a level comparable to the non-Indian society."

(2) "The trust responsibility extends through the tribe to the Indian member, whether on or off the reservation."

(3) "The trust responsibility applies to all United States agencies and instrumentalities, not just those charged specifically with administration of Indian affairs."

In terms of economic development of Indian energy resources, the definition of jurisdictional control will be a paramount issue. Given the strong desire for Indian self-determination, it would appear that tribal jurisdictional control will prevail and that development of a given natural resource will eventually depend upon the tribal management system, the inherent economics of resource values, and the venture capital available to develop the resource. The federal presence will be seen primarily as one of trust-protection and assistance in a variety of forms, primarily fiscal.

THE RESOUCE BASE AND POLICY CONSIDERATIONS

The Indian lands are reported (U.S. General Accounting Office 1975) to include:

5.3 million acres of commercial forest land; 44 million acres of rangeland; and 2.5 million acres of cropland on a total land base of about 52 million acres located in 26 States and including over 200 reservations.

In addition, there is a substantial amount (ca. 40 million acres) of Indian land in Alaska claimed under the Alaskan Native Claims process. The nature of the land, skewed toward a rangeland categorization, illustrates the tenor of early treaties. Rather few apparently high-value lands were included in these agreements. In addition to the land base, valuable hunting, fishing, mineral and water rights were allocated by treaty.

Energy deposits in the form of coal, gas, and uranium are found on about 40 of the reservations across some 17 states. In recent years Indian lands produced only about 5 percent of the nation's total gas and oil output. The move to enlarge the use of coal deposits could increase the significance of Indian lands to the National energy budget by a considerable amount. This will be particularly true on the Navajo, Hopi, Crow and Northern Cheyenne reservations. In the development of these energy resources may be found the most major of policy confrontations related to environment and the present land use.

Jurisdictional authority and related policies for Indian natural resource represents a subset of all the larger issues of trust authority, state control over Indian lands and self-determination by the Indian people. Rights to control management and leasing, questions of taxation, environmental concerns, and cultural or ecosystem maintenance are at stake in relation to energy resource development.

Taken in the broad view, one may suggest that the Indian position on future response policies is embodied in recommendations put forth in the Report on Reservation and Resource Development and Protection, Task Force Seven of the American Indian Policy Review Commission (1976). These recommendations call for, *inter alia*, a Congressional bill to establish the American Indian Trust Protection Commission and other purposes related to Indian self-governance. Title III of that proposal suggest a short title: Indian Rights Amendment, Title IV establishes the Commission and Title V calls for: "notwithstanding any provision of law, no state or political subdivision thereof is authorized to tax, regulate or exercise jurisdiction in any manner within Indian Country without the consent of the governing body of the affected Indian Nation given after the date this Bill becomes law." In addition a second Bill is proposed as the "Indian Development Act" to establish an American Indian Development Authority. The Authority would be charged to receive all funds and resources from various Federal agencies or sources to consolidate and coordinate assistance activities for development. Thus, programs currently funded through departments such as Housing and Urban development, Agriculture, Health Education and Welfare, Transportation and Interior would flow through the newly established Authority.

The foregoing recommendations are comprehensive indeed in terms of potential impact. On the part of non-Indians certain concerns are predictable. Among these the issue of taxation would be significant. The states would, no doubt, be concerned about loss of revenue and also questions of economic competition within the State between Indian and non-Indian resources. Although analogous to interstate competition, the situation would be in conflict with several existing situations. At present none of the tribes tax resources although many states do so on Indian lands. The legality of the tax question remains, in most or all instances, for future court decisions. One advantage for the Indians to receive a tax plus royalty even at the cost of reduced royalty, lies in the possibility that a given contractor could deduct the Indian tax from his federal tax burden. In addition, collection of a severance tax could lend support to, and receive justification from, the need to maintain ecological integrity and environmental controls on Indian lands. The states in turn might well argue the need to receive revenues for maintenance and uniformity of statewide environmental controls and ecosystem protection. Their argument would be strengthened by suggestion that the State is in a stronger position to provide the needed technical and professional manpower to address such problems both on and off the reservation.

Contemporary environmental policy on Indian lands is fraught with all of the foregoing questions of conflict between jurisdictional authorities. Major pieces of legislation at the federal level have generally been silent in regard to Indian lands. One can interpret in most cases that these laws do include Indian lands, however, again the issue of sovereign rights of the tribes may be raised.

At the state level the issue is less clear, many would argue the generality that federal laws do apply, state laws do not. Public Law 280 (1953) conferred outright jurisdiction over Indian lands to five states and provided that other states so inclined could pass local legislation to allow them similar jurisdiction. This legislation continues to be challenged and has been diluted somewhat by subsequent legislation (e.g. The Indian Civil Rights Act 1968). The situation remains unclear and will require considerable, and expensive, litigation for final resolution.

The Intergovernmental Cooperation Act of 1968 led to Circular A-95 distributed by the Office of Management and Budget (OMB) to facilitate Federal Assistance Reviews at the state level. The OMB excluded Indians from the A-95 review process; subsequently Indian tribes have generally favored inclusion of their lands and activities in the process, as recognized separate political entities. The A-95 review process offers a potential means for assisting interaction between state and Indian governments, however, conflicts remain for consideration prior to implementation.

The establishment of Federal Regional Boundaries also provides a means for coordinating efforts in a given geographic area. Placed along state boundaries these Regions provide Federal Regional Councils where various agencies can come together for planning and implementation efforts. Theoretically, these councils could be of value in coordinating Indian assistance programs and policies have been so directed by OMB. Unfortunately some reservations fall in several states and regional areas, the Navajo, for example, lies within 3 EPA and 3 State boundaries.

The Environmental Protection Agency (EPA) is the single largest influence in policy and regulatory activities for environmental matters. They have generally adopted a policy of assistance to and control on Indian reservations, but the situation remains, like many others, in confusion regarding final legal authority.

ENERGY AND ENVIRONMENTAL MANAGEMENT AND ASSISTANCE

The specific issue of energy and environmental management on Indian lands may be categorized by: (1) the current state of planning and infrastructure at the tribal level; (2) the nature of assistance programs available; and (3) future goals or expectations. For those tribes with significant energy resources these issues may be fundamental to achievement of a reasonable degree of autonomy in this century. Added to the renewable natural resource base, the minerals and energy extraction programs could provide the necessary capital for future, stable development.

The current state of planning varies greatly from tribe to tribe. One may assume that all tribes have general goals and some planning to assure autonomy of decision-making and continuance of sound resource planning. The ability to implement or even conduct detailed resource planning is another matter. Historically, Indian tribes did not have the necessary expertise for comprehensive inventory, planning, or management. Nor have they received completely adequate support in this regard from the Bureau of Indian Affairs, other federal or state agencies. As a result they have often leased resources at less than market value, have engaged in leases that were too long to adequately compensate for inflation and have been unable to monitor operations on sound economic or environmental basis. The need for a rapid upgrading of both tribal and assistance programs in these areas is obvious and ongoing.

Tribal leadership is increasingly aware of the need for improving the level of management in resource development. Nevertheless, their ability to obtain in-depth technical back-up from tribal funds alone is limited. Several of the larger tribes have established administrative units; the Navajo tribe for example, has organized a Natural Resources Department and also has special concentration in the minerals/energy area with the establishment of an Energy Resources Department. In addition, they have added an Environmental Protection Commission and hold membership in the larger Council of Energy Resource Tribes (CERT) a nationwide association of Indian tribes for energy development. With estimates of 30-40 percent of the nation's coal, 5-10 percent of the natural gas resources and 40-50 percent of the uranium on the member tribal-lands, it is clear the CERT has the potential to become a significant force for future development.

The question of jurisdiction is also a concern to assistance programs. The Bureau of Indian Affairs has recently published (Dec. 1977) final Interim Regulations for Coal Surface Mining and Reclamation on Indian Lands, subsequent study on the regulation of surface mining on Indian lands is anticipated. At this writing the BIA had not dealt specifically with the question of jurisdiction over Indian mining operations. Other agencies at the federal level have shown a recent flurry of interest in Indian lands but effective coordination efforts are lacking.

At the state level assistance programs for Indians take a variety of forms, primarily through state agencies or technical assistance efforts from universities. The latter have been a source of sporadic assistance usually based upon contracts jointly negotiated with a third party such as a foundation or federal agency. An interesting example of the University/ Indian interaction potential may be seen in the University of Arizona Laboratory of Native Development, Systems Analysis and Applied Technology (NADSAT). The program concentrates upon technology transfer and technical assistance to Indian tribes of the Southwest. It is premised upon providing a response to needs defined by the tribes and provides a commitment over time to assure implementation of initial planning efforts.

At the private level, discussion in regard to whether, and on what terms the energy resources from the Indian lands can be developed rests with the Indian tribe. Language difficulties, lack of business experience and a fear of having their traditions and culture swept away by ambitious development plans, are all factors to be considered and appreciated by cooperate executives negotiating mining leases for energy development. Offers of substantial bonuses, royalties and rentals, however communicated, may not be enough. Guarantees of Indian employment are important and a vocational training program - a must on some reservations - can be supported with federal funds. Thus, an understanding of the needs of the Indians and an ability to communicate the offer to the Indian owner are important considerations for successful lease negotiations for energy resource development on Indian lands.

In summary, one can say with authority that the contemporary Indian situation is at a most active time. Overall tribal activity is providing challenge to past inequities on a scale not seen before and with legal and political ramifications unanticipated by the non-Indian community. Private business now encounters a "new Indian" management approach, one that seeks to drive a hard, but fair bargain in dealings for Indian resources. The tribes are particularly interested in a type of development that includes a partnership where profits are maximized and employment, training and on-reservation construction build for the future as well as providing for immediate royalties. Their desire for realistic autonomy, aligned with legal rights presents a new face for relations with federal agencies.

If one suggests that this is an active time, it seems also important to note that it is a dangerous time in the sense of urgency that may accompany energy resource development. Decisions must be made that have significant socioeconomic impact; in many situations, the decisions may not be easily reversed. There is a particular need at this time to match the magnitude of future development with adequate planning funds. The very nature of the trust relationship requires technical assistance on an expanded scale for the immediate future. Classic bureaucratic approaches, slow response times or competency inadequacies will not allow the level of performance that is now required. In overview it appears that tribal authorities working directly with private industry are moving ahead with well designed programs. For those who bear a direct trust responsibility, it is a time to provide assistance to this new, effective partnership and to facilitate the Indians efforts in a major step forward for energy development with all of its tribal and national significance.

PHYSICAL PROCESSES RELATED TO IMPACT
PREDICTION OF LAND DISTURBANCE ACTIVITIES

Leo S. Leonhart*

The nature of federal environmental legislation enacted within the past decade seems to be clear expression of a national priority aimed at harmonizing energy resource development with comprehensive environmental planning. Two items of legislation, in particular, underscore this goal with respect to surface mining: The National Environmental Policy Act of 1969 (NEPA, Pub. Law 91-190) and the Surface Mining Control and Reclamation Act of 1977 (Pub. Law 95-87). Specifically, NEPA requires the issuance of an environmental impact statement (EIS), detailing, among other things, an analysis of the ".... relationship between short-term uses of man's environment and the maintenance and enhancement of long-term productivity...." (Subsection 102(2) (C) (iv)). The Surface Mining Act complements this analytical provision of NEPA by requiring submission of a detailed reclamation plan to the regulatory authority, specifying how the proposed post-mining land use will be achieved, and in another Section (S.522) by providing for a secretarial review of coal resource lands as to their suitability for mining, particularly their post-operational stability.

As the designated Agency responsible for environmental review of proposed federal actions (pursuant to Section 309 of the Clean Air Act), the Environmental Protection Agency has logged several years experience in reviewing EISs related to various mineral resource extraction proposals and many proposed mining and reclamation plans. On the basis of this review experience, EPA has observed and commented on several outstanding and recurrent informational deficiencies which tend to diminish the quality of long-term impact prediction. As a consequence, a satisfactory determination by the responsible authority as to whether reclamation of the affected lands is attainable and assured is prevented.

Most noteworthy among these informational deficiencies are analyses related to the physical environment (particularly geomorphic and hydrologic processes) such as:

(1) Stability of reclaimed areas with respect to wind erosion (EPA 1975, 1976b, c);
(2) Area-wide impacts related to the groundwater flow regime which arise from such physical modifications as flow barriers, dewatering, recharge interference, and changes in aquifer characteristics (storage, transmissivity, confining beds, etc.) (EPA 1976a, c, d, 1977a);
(3) Changes in erosional rates and subsequent sedimentation within streams and other surface water bodies (EPA 1975, 1976a, b, c, 1977a);

*U.S. Environmental Protection Agency, Washington, D.C. 20460. Present Address: Rockwell Hanford Operations, P.O. Box 800, Richland, WA 99352.

(4) Soil and overburden weathering characteristics (EPA 1975);

(5) Modification of the natural surface water hydrology including drainage density patterns, stream gradients, channel cross-sectional profiles, and stability of impoundments, diversions, and channel relocations (EPA 1975, 1976a, b, 1977b, c);

(6) Downstream effects of the proposed operations on riparian communities (EPA 1976b, 1977c).

(7) Stresses imposed upon the area-wide geomorphic stability by the proposed land disturbance activities (EPA 1976b, c, 1977a, b).

It is recognized that, to a large extent, these informational shortcomings are an indicator of the fact that frequently there exist little baseline data upon which to formulate the necessary predictions with regard to post-operational stability, and also that we have had little experience with long-term environmental analyses. This is particularly true in the western U.S. where environmental baseline data are scant, where little experience with surface mine reclamation techniques is available, and where system and process are often not well understood. However, it remains an essential component of the decision-making process that trade-offs involving short-term uses and long-term productivity be formulated. To do so necessitates accurate prediction of land rehabilitation potential with respect to soil, natural biological productivity, and the natural hydrologic balance of the disturbed and adjacent areas, particularly with regard to the time frame within which these goals will be achieved. The fact that in many instances the operator's liability may expire before post-mining stability is attained further underscores the need for careful prediction.

In recent years, several efforts at the federal level have begun to provide advanced regional assessments of resource lands as to their sensitivity to surface mining (RALI, EMRIA, NAS, Western Energy Project, Alluvial Valley Classifications). It is likely that, in accordance with the provisions of Section 522 (Pub. Law 95-87), these programs will continue to provide information on the impact of surface mining as related to compatibility with adjacent land uses, potential damage to natural systems supported by the affected lands, the probability of diminution of long range productivity, and increasing damage from natural hazards.

As suggested previously, the formulation of predictions based on insufficient data bases is difficult, particularly for those inexperienced in dealing with uncertainties. I believe that the best available tool offsetting such situations is a thorough understanding of the existing physical environment prior to disturbance. A corollary to the Huttonian Theory in geomorphology which in essence suggests that "The present is the key to the past," is that in the arena of environmental impact prediction, observation of past and present process and response of the physical system can be the key to predicting future response to a proposed physical stress. Examples of such indicators of physical process include:

(1) Vegetative inferences including species differentiation, distribution, and density, and also tree ring dating, pollen analysis, and related techniques;

(2) Soil development, particularly weathering characteristics of overburden materials;

(3) Groundwater flow patterns, well records, depth to the groundwater table, groundwater quality, and related data;

(4) Geomorphic process as inferred from land forms and streams (floodplains, stream grading, headcuts, etc.);

(5) Meterological data which can be input into various watershed models.

Proper interpretation of these data serve to provide in many instances the best available indication of the stability of proposed land rehabilitation designs, of the time-frame required to achieve this stability, and can serve as the basis for designing monitoring systems. For example, if in a riparian community the dominant land form expression is primarily the result of extreme events such as the 100-year flood, it may be necessary to superimpose 100-year flow conditions upon the post-operational configuration in order to ascertain its long-term stability. Once an adequate prediction is made with regard to the stability of the physical environment, models for biological and human systems can then be superimposed.

In reviewing the recent works in geomorphology and hydrology, it is interesting to note that several studies have researched the role of human activities as a stress upon physical environmental systems. For example, Bull (1975) dealing with the allometric approach to land form analysis, describes man's activity as an independent variable affecting the dynamic conditions in many geomorphic systems. Bull also cites (1978) examples where human impact has resulted in an exceedance of the "critical power threshold" in discontinuous ephemeral streams in the Southwest. Knox (1975) in relating the graded stream concept considers climatic changes and man's activities as major factors contributing to "ungraded channels" (either erosional or depositional channels), directly impacting the functional relationship between discharge and sediment yield. Finally, in a paper dealing with the use of the 100-year flood parameter, Jones (1976) concludes that, under many circumstances, it is within man's power to reduce or amplify the magnitude of the 100-year flood.

In summary, a precise understanding of the probable response of the physical environment to surface manipulation is essential in making accurate, long-range impact predictions with regard to the viability of post-operational land uses. Proper use and adaptation of traditional sciences such as hydrology, geomorphology, and soil science can provide improved impact prediction techniques and serve as the basis for advanced land sensitivity analysis for such large scale resource management programs as surface mining, grazing, and water resource development.

Such programs can be particularly effective if:

(1) The system and its processes are properly interpreted and understood;
(2) Rates and time are quantified to the extent possible with respect to process;
(3) Trends intermediate to equilibrium conditions are recognized and properly evaluated;
(4) Sub-systems are placed in a proper context with regard to the macro-system.

Moreover, the data derived from these well-planned and well-conceived programs would greatly facilitate the job of writing and reviewing EISs.

REFERENCES

Bull, W.B. 1975. Allometric change of landforms. Geol. Soc. Am. Bull. 86:1489-98.
Bull, W.B. 1978. Threshold of Critical power. unpublished.
Jones, D. E., Jr. 1976. What is the 100-year flood?   Am. Geophys. Union, Proc. 2nd Ann. Midwestern Section Meeting, Oct. 22, 1976, Ann Arbor, MI.
Knox, J.C. 1975. Concept of the graded stream. In Theories of Landform Development. Proc. Annual Geomorphology Symposia Ser., Binghamton, NY. 6:169-198.

U.S. Environmental Protection Agency. 1975. EPA comment letter on DEIS for the Proposed Plan of Mining and Reclamation, Belle Ayr South Mine, Amax Coal Company, Coal Lease W-0317682, Campbell County, WY (May 27, 1975).

U.S. Environmental Protection Agency. 1976a. EPA comment letter on FEIS for the Proposed Plan of Mining and Reclamation, Cordero Mine, Sun Oil Company, Campbell County, WY (July 14, 1976).

U.S. Environmental Protection Agency. 1976b. EPA comment letter on DEIS for the Proposed Mining and Reclamation Plan, Eagle Butte Mine, Amax Coal Company, Campbell County, WY (November 11, 1976).

U.S. Environmental Protection Agency. 1976c. EPA comment letter on DEIS for the Proposed Plan of Mining and Reclamation for East Decker and North Extension Mines, Decker Coal Company, Big Horn County, MT (December 14, 1976).

U.S. Environmental Protection Agency. 1976d. EPA comment letter on DEIS for the Proposed 20-year Plan of Mining and Reclamation, Westmoreland Resources Tract III, Crow Ceded Area, MT (December 30, 1976).

U.S. Environmental Protection Agency. 1977a. EPA comment letter on DEIS for the Proposed Mining and Reclamation Plan, East Gillette Mine, Kerr-McGee Corp., Campbell County, WY (May 27, 1977).

U.S. Environmental Protection Agency. 1977b. EPA comment letter on FEIS for the Proposed Plan of Mining and Reclamation for the East Decker and North Extension Mines, Decker Coal Company, Big Horn County, MT (July 20, 1977).

U.S. Environmental Protection Agency. 1977c. EPA comment letter on FEIS for the Proposed Mining and Reclamation Plan, Eagle Butte Mine, Amax Coal Company, Coal Lease W-0313773, Campbell County, WY (November 11, 1977).

INTERACTIVE COMPUTERIZED
PLANNING OF SURFACE COAL MINING OPERATIONS

David F. Gibson, Thomas E. Lehman and Edward L. Mooney*

The 1973 Arab Oil Embargo emphasized the United States' dependency upon imported oil as a primary energy source. President Carter and his administration have outlined plans to lessen this dependence. A key element of these plans involves a dramatic increase in coal production, a goal of 1.2 billion tons per year by 1985 has been established (NEP 1977). This represents essentially a doubling of the 672 million tons produced in 1977. To a large extent, whether this goal can be achieved is a function of mine productivity and government policies regarding factors such as taxation, reclamation, and incentives of industry for conversion.

Figure 1 shows the projected coal production required to meet the 1985 goal. Estimates indicate that about 59% of the 1985 production will be from surface mines. This means that approximately 500 of 800 million tons (62%) of coal coming from mines opened after 1974 will come from surface mines (U.S.D.I.-Bur. Mines 1976).

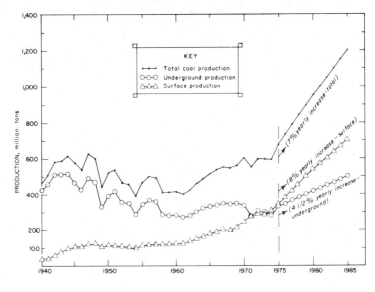

Figure 1. Projected Coal Product

*Department of Industrial Engineering and Computer Science, College of Engineering, Montana State University, Bozeman, MT 59715.

While increased surface mining activity offers the obvious benefit of increased energy supplies for our economy, one must not overlook the environmental problems that will result. If we are to enter a "second coal age", we must simultaneously develop methods to mitigate the site disturbances which accompany surface mining activity.

The renewed emphasis on coal as an energy source has spawned legislation aimed at regulating reclamation practices. In addition, funds have been allocated through many government agencies for research aimed at improving both recovery and reclamation technologies applicable to surface mines. One such research effort is the SEAM (Surface Environment and Mining) program sponsored by the U.S.D.A. Forest Service and Environmental Protection Agency (EPA). SEAM's mission relates to developing and applying technologies that would allow for increased production while preserving environmental quality. While many SEAM researchers are involved in more basic research, one project group has been developing a stand alone, minicomputer based, interactive mine planning system. By integrating research results from a variety of sources, the system enables planners to evolve mine plans to meet stated production and/or cost objectives while simultaneously considering trade-offs between productivity and environmental protection. This paper describes the basic features of the system at Montana State University (MSU).

COMPUTERIZED PLANNING SYSTEM

Data Inputs

Figure 2 illustrates the essential features of the computerized planning system under development. Basic input to the system is of three main types. First, core or drill hole data taken at the property provides a description of the physical and chemical conditions under which mining might take place. Information extracted from the drill hole data might include such things as the depth of overburden, the depth of coal, and various qualities and characteristics of each. A second type of information input to the system relates to production and capital requirements of the operation. Examples of this type of information might be required tons per year, minimum required rate of return, and projected selling price of coal. The third type of basic input is restrictions with respect to environmental protection, i.e. those specified by state and federal laws or by management objectives. Such restrictions may place constraints on things such as the basic type of mining operation, the method of spoiling overburden, and the reclamation methods employed.

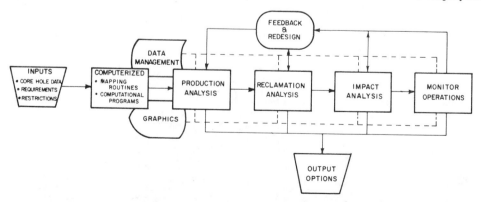

Figure 2.   Proposed Mine Planning System

Software Modules

Once the basic input is provided to the system, applications software enables the user to obtain displays of the geology, stratigraphy, and various properties of the overburden and coal. These displays include 3-dimensional views, contour plots, bar charts, and various graphical models. The necessary programs reside conceptually in the graphics block in Figure 2. Listings and computational summaries of physical and chemical characteristics of the area can also be obtained. If desired, the user can zoom in on various parts of the area under consideration and obtain information in whatever detail and form he desires. The primary purpose of this part of the system is to allow the user to be able to recall, manipulate, and display information to aid him in designing the production and reclamation operations of the mine. In addition the various computational and mapping routines greatly facilitate the process of providing the various regulatory agencies required information about the property and planned operations.

It should be noted that the data management and graphics blocks in Fig. 2 underlay or are embedded throughout the entire system. These blocks represent the techniques employed to store, manipulate, retrieve, and display in various forms the large amounts of data required for a mine planning effort. Although they are "invisible" to the user, they are a very important and integral part of the system.

After the user has obtained the various maps and computational summaries he desires, he can proceed to develop and analyze a mine plan by utilizing the production analysis module. This module provides an interactive, computer-aided design tool. The user can call on a group of models that optimize relative to various criteria, he can specify his own plan and have a series of computations made, or he can use a combination of both of these approaches.

As shown in Fig. 3, the production analysis module consists of three design levels, each level corresponding to a particular step in a macro to micro analysis hierarchy. The greatest cost component of a Western surface mining dragline operation is the removal of the overburden. Thus, the mine planning process most appropriately commences at

Design Level	Analysis, Design, Evaluation
1	Total Mine Plan
	.Transportation System
	.Equipment Balance
	.Interactions
	.Loading, Hauling
	.Production Analysis
2	Pit Design
	.Dragline Selection/Evaluation
	.Box Cut Location
	.Optimum Overburden Removal
	.Optimum Placement of Spoils
	.Optimum Move Sequence
	.Optimum Pit Geometry
	.Dragline Productivity
3	Detailed Evaluation
	.Swing by Swing Simulation
	.Overburden Removal Sequence
	.Spoil Configuration Sequence
	.Dragline Performance
	Energy Requirements
	Forces
	Operating Statistics

Figure 3.   Production Analysis Design Levels

level 2, pit design. Here the objective is to design the pit geometry and dragline operations in some optimal manner. At this level the user can evaluate a number of stripping techniques and objective functions. For example he may wish to obtain the "optimum" pit geometry for a given dragline utilizing a side benching procedure (one of a number of stripping techniques modeled) so as to minimize the amount of time required to remove the overburden. Alternately he may choose to have the module select the best boom and bucket combination to meet a certain annual production rate. A third approach may be that the user would specify his own design and have the module evaluate it in terms of feasibility and production rate. Another objective that can be optimized is the cost per ton of coal mined.

Once the pit and dragline have been designed, the user can employ either level 1 or 3. The input required at each of these levels is the output from level 2. At level 1 all the auxiliary operations in support of overburden removal are analyzed. Based on the production rate of the dragline, other operations are specified accordingly. Included are topsoil removal, drilling and blasting, coal loading and hauling, coal preparation and general support operations. Also available at this level is a series of cash flow analyses and reports.

Level 3 is available to perform a detailed evaluation of the overburden removal operation. For a given location in the mine and mining method this level can be employed to perform a swing by swing simulation. Such detail may not be required for production planning *per se* but is required in order to predict environmental responses. The techniques employed at this level will for example be able to trace a given material type from its location in the overburden to its location in the spoil pile. Various detailed dragline performance characteristics will also be available at this level.

Having specified the recovery methods and equipment, the user may analyze reclamation methods in a multilevel fashion similar to that employed during production analysis. Using outputs from the production analysis module as well as data regarding environmental limitations, the feasibility of a desired strategy will be evaluated. Next, programs to estimate reclamation costs and suggested equipment mix can be executed. Feedback shown in Figure 2 to the production analysis module includes: (i) cost information and (ii) feasibility. Hence, the planner may iterate between production and reclamation design activities until he has balanced increased recovery costs with the (hopefully) lower reclamation costs. Or, he may find that the "least cost" recovery plan unduly restricts reclamation options and will cycle back to the production analysis to respecify the mining activities until the desired reclamation goals can be achieved. The reclamation planning module, its current status and projected enhancements, is described elsewhere in more detail (Scott 1979).

Another major component of the computerized planning system is the impact analysis module. After the production and reclamation plans have been specified, this module is utilized to predict various environmental responses. Examples of such responses would include wind and water erosion, characteristics of ground and surface waters, subsidence, wildlife and vegetative recovery, etc. If some of these responses are unacceptable, the user can cycle back through the production and reclamation analysis modules as illustrated by the feedback and redesign block of the flow diagram. Identifying the causes of the adverse responses, additional constraints would be constructed for the production models and/or other reclamation approaches would be investigated. A new plan, necessarily less productive, would most likely be developed. This plan's environmental impacts would likewise be assessed. The process would continue until an acceptable balance between productivity and environmental quality goals was achieved. This procedure is perhaps the most important feature of the system. By documenting the process of cycling through modules, one can objectively evaluate the cost of trade-off between productivity and environmental protection. Once the cyclical process just described is complete, the total mine plan can be documented via a whole array of output options.

The final block of the flow diagram represents another use of the system. That is, the system is valuable for not only planning operations but also can be employed to monitor activity once mining has commenced. Features of the area may not turn out to be as they were first projected, economics of the market may change, equipment and methods may be improved, etc. Thus the original plan may have to be modified and updated. The system can be utilized to effect this. Therefore the computerized planning system is useful as a management tool in the entire spectrum from planning through actual mining operation to reclamation.

Minicomputer System Hardware

All software modules of the planning system are implemented on a dedicated stand alone minicomputer system as depicted in Fig. 4. The system centers around the CPU with 64K words of memory. Peripherals include a five megabyte cartridge disc drive and nine track tape used for secondary program and data storage. A high resolution graphics terminal (CRT) with crosshair cursors and a digitizing tablet are the means of interaction with the user. Copies of screen displays can be produced using a hard copy unit interfaced to the CRT, and high quality drawings are available on a drum plotter. The line printer is used for tabular output of computational results. In addition to serving as the system console, the teletype is used for program development and editing via a multiprogramming operating system.

The minicomputer system was chosen over the use of existing time sharing systems after a detailed analysis of the two alternatives. The selection procedure has been described in detail by Gibson et al. (1977). The stand alone system was found to be the most cost effective alternative and further offered the advantages of real time I/0 capabilities and excellent response time, both for program development and user interaction.

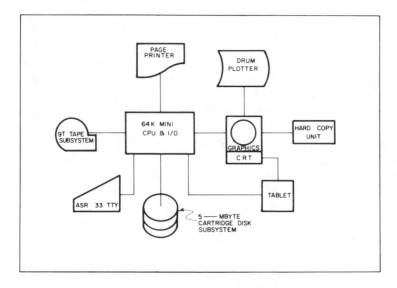

Figure 4.   Planning System Hardware Diagram

A Planning Session

The frames in Fig. 5 illustrate some of the displays and options available to the user during an interactive session with the planning system. The first frame depicts the classifications of the software modules of the system. It is essential that data be appropriately entered into the system and formated by the system via option 1 before the production analysis or impact analysis options are selected. Frame 2 shows the tasks relating to data preparation and display. Following input of drill hole or other data, option 2 allows for displays of the data such as those shown in frames 3 and 4. The "flagpole" display in frame 3 represents those elements, compounds, or other characteristics found in a core hole which exceed predefined criteria and thus may require special handling during overburden removal. Each flag on the display represents the parameter and the depth at which it is toxic. Frame 4 shows a bar graph of the concentration of a single parameter in a drill hole (in this case sodium).

Other options available to the user as indicated in frame 2 include the construction of a uniform grid of values from non-uniformly spaced input data using interpolation techniques. The cell size of a grid or subset of a grid may be modified, also through mathematical interpolation. Since these interpolation routines may introduce systematic biases in areas where data is sparse, the user is allowed to view sections of the grids and edit the Z-values if necessary. Frames 4 and 5 show this display and edit process. Each row and column of the grid data can be displayed and modified using either the digitizing tablet or the crosshair cursors. The edited section can be redrawn and further modified, if necessary.

In addition to data file output on the line printer, data may also be visualized with contour displays or three-dimensional displays. The surfaces to be displayed may be topography, isopach, stripping ratio or any other surface for which a grid has been constructed. Contour displays also allow for the editing of grid data through the use of the pen and the digitizing tablet. A three-dimensional display is shown in frame 7.

Upon termination of the data display and editing session, the user is once again presented with the options shown in frame 1. If the production analysis option is elected, the user selects options from frame 8. Macro-level analysis (level 1) is available for each, while both macro and micro analysis (level 2) has been implemented for the dragline. Having selected the desired subsystems for analysis, the user may opt for pit layout, and if he so chooses, is presented with the display in frame 9. Depending upon which data file types have been prepared, the user may choose from as many as four types of contour maps on which to interactively engage pit layout. Three modes of pit design are available to the user. A single pit may be designed based on the overburden and coal characteristics at a single point within the mine areas an "average" pit may be designed under the assumptions of uniform coal seam thickness and overburden depth based on the averages in the area, and finally individual pits may be designed using dynamic programming techniques.

As shown in frame 10, a contour map of the selected type is produced, and the user is allowed to zoom in on the desired area and modify the contour interval. Frame 11 shows the pit layout process for either the average pit or multiple pit analysis. Using the crosshair cursors, the user inputs the locations of the four corners forming the boundaries of the area to be mined. The direction of mining is established, and the routine calculates the length and width of the area to be mined. If the average pit mode was selected, the routine then determines the average overburden depth and coal seam thickness. If multiple pit design is of interest, the routine calculates the overburden depth and coal seam thickness for the point of maximum stripping ratio every fifty feet in the direction of mining. These values are used by the dynamic programming routines to determine optimal pit widths during production analysis. If the single pit mode was selected, only the overburden depth and coal seam thickness at the user-specified location is determined.

Upon completing the data preparation phase of the analysis, the user is once again presented with the general options (frame 1). During the typical planning session he would

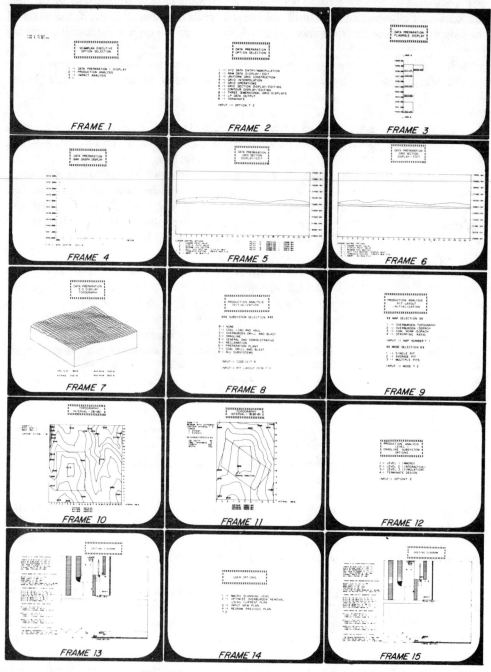

Figure 5. Typical Planning Session

be ready at this point to begin design of the mining operation. In current version of the software the first input selects from the full range of mining operations those for which analysis is desired.

While currently all operations can be analyzed within a cash flow framework, a great deal of attention has been given to the design of the dragline stripping operation itself. Hence, if the dragline design is elected in production analysis, the options shown in frame 12 will be displayed. Here the user may elect to: (1) obtain a "satisfactory" dragline using classical computer design equations, (2) interactively arrive at a design utilizing a more complex model of dragline performance, or (3) evaluate a design using a detailed simulation model. Both the 1st and 3rd options are being implemented using available computer programs.

The 2nd option, however, represents a fair amount of the modeling work done at MSU. Presently interactive design can be performed for simple side casting, fill bench, working bench and two pass mining methods. The models are restricted by the assumptions of (1) constant overburden and coal thickness, (2) a single, level coal seam, and (3) use of a single dragline. The modeling approach is described by Mooney and Gibson (1978).

Interactive design begins with specification by the user of initial dragline size and pit dimensions. Frame 13 illustrates the output generated as a result of such specifications. This casting diagram shows both plan and cross-sectional views of the design. In addition to the diagram, information regarding the design including parameter values and performance measures is displayed to the left. For this plan, estimated cost per ton of coal uncovered was 75 cents for overburden removal and annual production was 1.7 million tons. Also, as a result of evaluating mathematical constraints the user is advised regarding the feasibility of the plan.

Following output regarding the design, a list of options is once again presented. Frame 14 shows the options available. The user may: (1) elect to return to the macro (production analysis executive) level and proceed with analysis of related mining operations, (2) enter an optimization phase of the design which allows the computer to generate the "best" plan or (3) input a new design for the dragline subsystem, view the results, etc. or (4) redraw a previous plan which has been saved.

As shown in frame 14, optimization was next elected for this example. This implies that a computer search will be conducted to yield the "best" values of the design variables in the dragline model. Since a side benching method was specified here, the pit width, side bench depth, boom length and bucket size comprise the decision variables. The design criteria can be chosen as: (1) maximize annual production rate or (2) minimize cost per ton of coal uncovered.

In this case the latter was chosen, and frame 15 shows the resulting plan as generated on the computer graphics screen. Table 1 summarizes the results of the design phase. The

Table 1

Variables	Initial	Optimal
Pit Width (ft.)	159	136
Bench Depth (ft.)	30	17
Boom Length (ft.)	300	297
Bucket Size (yd^3)	63	72
Annual Production (million tons)	2.7	3.2
Cost per ton-dollars	.75	.70

optimal design while providing 1.5 million more tons per year, results in an estimated decrease of 5 cents per ton of coal (relative to overburden removal).

The process that has been briefly described is iterative. That is, following any design the user may loop back again to either change the design himself or optimize. The interactive design process is completed only when option 1 shown in frame 14 is elected. At that time, a full array of approximating models adapted from Fluor Utah [6] estimate requirements for the other operations specified. Finally, a cash flow over the life of the mine and based on production and reclamation system design can optionally be generated. No attempt has been made here to describe fully the output generated due to space limitations. However, the example given should serve to illustrate the general approach being used.

SUMMARY

As a result of the 1973 Arab oil embargo, several proposals to decrease the United States' demand for imported oil have been made. One such proposal suggests that coal production be doubled by 1985, an increase of more than 50 million tons per year over the 1977 level. Strict new reclamation requirements have also been signed into law recently and are aimed at guaranteeing that coal is recovered from surface mines with minimal long range impact on the environment. Consequently, Federal agencies such as the USDA Forest Service and EPA have funded considerable research into appropriate production and reclamation technologies and their application.

This paper has described the general scope of a portion of the work being performed within the SEAM project. A stand alone minicomputer mine planning concept was described and the functions of the various software modules under development were outlined. A planning session using the current version of the integrated software was also illustrated. The planning system, SEAMPLAN, while still being developed, has been designed in a modular fashion to facilitate expansion. Therefore, the capabilities described represent a subset of those planned for the system. Nevertheless, SEAMPLAN is presently a valuable planning tool, and represents a unique approach to balancing productivity and reclamation goals.

REFERENCES

The National Energy Plan. 1977. Executive Office of the President, Energy Policy and Planning, April 29, 1977.

U.S. Department of the Interior. 1976. Coal Equipment Forecast to 1985. Bureau of Mines, Info. Circ. No. 8710.

Scott, D.L. 1979. Computerized reclamation planning system for Northern Great Plains surface coal mines. In M.K. Wali (ed.) Ecology and Coal Resource Development, Pergamon Press, NY (this volume).

Gibson, D.F., G.A. Sattoriva and E.L. Mooney. 1977. A minicomputer system for planning surface mining operations. In Proc. AIIE Systems Eng. Conf. Nov., 1977.

Mooney, E.L. and D.F. Gibson. 1978. Optimal design of dragline stripping operations. Unpublished Working Paper, March, 1978.

Fluor Utah. 1977. Economics of large scale surface coal mining using simulation models. Vol. 10.

SIMULATION MODELS FOR SURFACE COAL MINE PLANNING

Jack M. Gillette*

SIMULATION MODEL SYSTEM

The system consists of data files for 11 equipment classes and 16 simulation models covering the major surface mining methods and the activities in each mining method. An overview of the system can be obtained by ordering report FE-1520-101 from the National Technical Information Service.

The simulation models fall into two basic categories, based on the level of operational details simulated by the model:

(1) *Micromodels*: These models simulate a mining operation using a specific equipment class. The level of detail is that normally associated with mine planning and mine layout.

(2) *Macromodels*: These models simulate all major operations in a complete mine. The level of detail is that normally associated with feasibility analysis and first-order reserve evaluation.

In addition, there is a stand-alone model for evaluation of any mining project. This is the Cash Flow Analysis (CFA) model, which makes a complete analysis of equipment, personnel, and facilities requirements; develops cash flows for the project; and determines the required sales price or return on investment using discounted cash flow (DCF) procedures.

When the micromodels are used to develop a mine plan, the engineer must prepare input for each model and analyze the results from each model. If a cash flow analysis is to be made, the user must also prepare the input based on the micromodel outputs. However, when the macromodels are used, the engineer needs to prepare only the input to the macromodel which develops all input needed for a cash flow analysis.

Thus, the engineer is involved in each step in the micromodel process and is responsible for all model interactions. In contrast, the engineer simply sets up the single macromodel input, and the computer does the rest. Obviously, the two sequences are not equivalent in terms of applying the results. The macromodels have many engineering judgments built into them, and the results fit any mining situation only as well as the judgments apply to that situation. However, the models are not rigid and engineering parameters which define the built-in judgments are model variables under user control.

The following narrative briefly reviews the various models to identify the problems they were designed to solve.

*Bonner & Moore Associates, Inc., 500 Jefferson, Cullen Center, Houston, TX 77002.

Dragline Stripping

Three models simulate the use of draglines for overburden removal; two models simulate the area stripping method using one (BSM) or two machines (EBM), while the third simulates the contour stripping method. The area models solve the pit geometry, draw a cross section of the pit, and evaluate all dragline models in the data file to show production and costs. The contour model shows how a specified dragline would operate in a pit which follows an outcrop line and digs into a hillside. It is designed to determine how deep into the hillside the operation can move before reaching operating limits. A cross-section from the BSM model is shown in Fig. 1.

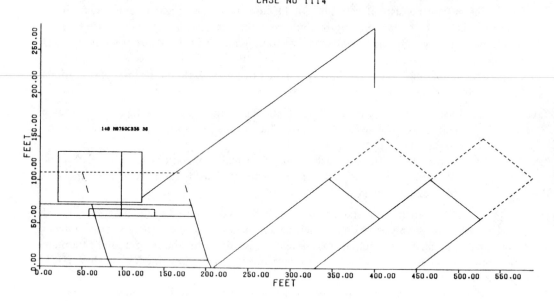

Fig. 1. Cross-section of pit - BSM model

Coal Load and Haul

There are two models for these functions: one model evaluates trucks working with a matched loader over user-specified haul roads, and develops cycle times based on the vehicle performance and braking charts; while the other model matches shovels to trucks to develop fleet requirements, production, and costs. The two models, together, are designed to evaluate shovels (or front-end loaders) and trucks in the data files and determine the loading and hauling requirements and costs.

Shovel/Truck Stripping and Hauling

Three models simulate the use of shovels (or front-end loaders) and trucks for over-burden removal and for coal loading and hauling. Individual models simulate an area stripping method, a mountaintop removal method, and multiple dipping seams mining.

All three models solve the pit geometry and divide the pit into operating benches. These models evaluate predefined sets of shovels (or front-end loaders) and trucks to determine fleet requirements and select the least-cost combination.

Drilling and Blasting

This model simulates drilling and blasting either overburden or coal. It estimates quantities and capital costs for drilling equipment and blasting materials.

Land Reclamation

This model determines fleet requirements and costs to strip and stockpile the topsoil, regrade spoil banks, respread the topsoil, and do general bulldozing. It also calculates costs for revegetation and land management.

Coal Preparation

This model factors one of three baseline coal preparation plants to fit the problem requirements, and determines capital and operating costs and personnel requirements.

General and Administrative

This model factors from a baseline solution to the problem statement to determine capital and operating costs and personnel requirements for 13 general and administrative functions.

Three macromodels, Area Dragline, Contour Dragline, and Shovel-Truck, simulate all operations in mines using these methods of overburden removal.

The CFA model was designed for economic analysis of any mining project. The input consists of information in three categories:

(1) *Personnel Data*: Includes wage and schedule classifications and wage rates and productive hours/years for each wage and schedule classification. A personnel data file, based on U.M.W. agreements, is contained in the system, but must be revised for other agreements.

(2) *Unit Operations Data*: Includes production schedules for each operation; assignments of equipment units to operations; and, for each unit-operation combination, purchase and operating costs, personnel assignments, depreciation and replacement life data, and codes for methods of purchase and depreciation and startup and shutdown.

(3) *Financial Parameters*: Includes rates for interest, taxes, investment tax credits and depletion allowances, and escalation or other regional adjustments. This category includes all the parameters needed for a complete financial analysis of a project.

If the user specifies a coal sales price, the model determines the expected return on investment; otherwise, the model determines the coal sales price that would result from a stated return on investment. The model develops production and cash expenditure schedules and a set of *pro forma* accounting schedules. The project cash flows are analyzed using DCF procedures to calculate the desired result.

Reports produced by the CFA model include parameter values, financial summary, investment list, operating and maintenance personnel lists, services and materials list, production and cash expenditures, infrastructure requirements, P&L statement, balance sheet, and sources and uses of funds.

DRAGLINE PRODUCTION SIMULATION SYSTEM

The Dragline Production Simulation System (DPS) model was designed to be used for studies aimed at improving dragline operations. It simulates the dragline operations; digging, spoiling, deadheading, walking, and maintenance. It works from a three-dimensional representation to reflect the digging and spoiling actions. The model also simulates the removal of coal from excavated panels; however, it does not simulate the actions of the equipment used to remove the coal.

While the system was designed to study operating mines, it can also be used to study proposed mines or in the dragline selection process. Typically, draglines are selected on the basis of range diagrams (see Fig. 1) which are two-dimensional representations of the proposed operation. The DPS could be used to confirm that a machine selected on the basis of range diagrams will have the expected capacity to handle three-dimensional problems.

Dragline Pit

A model run starts with the user's description of the topography of the dragline operating pit as it exists at the beginning of the operation to be simulated by the DPS model. The description is in the form of a series of x, y, z coordinates. The x, y coordinates measure horizontal distances (in feet) from a user-specified reference point. The z coordinates measure elevations of the surface (in feet) above the bottom of the coal seam which is considered to be a uniform-thickness, level layer.

It is expected that the x, y, z data will be taken from a topographic map of the pit covering the area to be included in the simulation run. The DPS model continually adjusts the z (elevation) data to reflect digging and spoiling actions.

In addition to the surface data, the DPS input includes:

(1) Dragline physical specifications: boom length, boom angle, dumping radius, bucket size, and so on;
(2) Dragline operating rates: walk, swing, hoist, lower, payout, and retrieve;
(3) Angles of the faces formed by the digging actions and for the spoil banks;
(4) Dragline maintenance schedule;
(5) For each panel to be stripped, a series of x, y coordinates which define the plan view dimensions of the top of the coal seam after the overburden has been removed;
(6) Instructions specifying the pattern of keycutting, production bailing, walking, deadheading and maintenance;
(7) Instructions for removing the uncovered coal. Coal loading is not directly

simulated; the model simply adjusts the surface elevations to account for coal removal at the end of a panel.

Each panel to be stripped in the run is defined by the user's "coal line" x, y coordinates. A coal line is the intersection of the highwall bottom with the top of the coal seam. Two coal lines define a complete panel. One line defines the bottom of the highwall being formed in the panel, and the other defines the opposite side of the exposed coal seam. Thus, the two lines define the plan-view coordinates of the top of the coal seam after the overburden has been removed.

The user controls the directions in which the dragline and the panels advance and the direction in which spoils are cast. The dragline can advance toward either increasing or decreasing x values. The panel can advance toward either increasing or decreasing y values, and spoils can be cast toward either positive or negative y values.

The panel can be defined as a box cut panel, and the faces above both coal lines will be formed by the digging routines. Alternatively, the panel may not be a boxcut, and the digging routines will form only one highwall since the opposite face was formed on the preceding panel.

Each panel is excavated in a series of "digouts". A digout is defined as the excavation made within a panel before the dragline advances a user-defined distance in the long direction of the panel. A digout may consist of a keycut excavation followed by a production bail excavation, or a production bail without preceding keycut.

The keycut digging routine forms the highwall, with the width of the cut (measured at the bottom of the drag face) as defined by the user's controls. The keycut is wedge shaped, in plan-view, conforming to the action of dragging the bucket toward the center of dragline rotation. Since the keycut is generally one or two buckets wide, the keycut removes only part of the overburden. The remaining portion must be removed by the bail routine. The bail routine is designed to form the highwall and remove all overburden when not preceded by a keycut, or to remove only the overburden remaining after a keycut has been made.

After the model has modified the surface with either of its digging routines, it uses one of its spoiling routines to form the spoil banks with one of two shapes: "conical", or "ridgeline". The conical spoil shape, if formed on a flat surface, would be an inverted cone. The ridgeline spoil, if cast on a flat surface, would be two inverted half-cones separated by a wedge. The two spoil routines simulate different dumping actions. When the dragline swing is basically stopped before the bucket is dumped, the resulting shape is conical. However, when the dumping action is started before the swing is stopped, the resulting shape is ridgeline with the ridgeline being roughly tangential to the arc enscribed by the boom point. The position of the spoils is controlled by the user.

The two digging and two spoiling routines simulate the primary actions of the dragline. There are other routines to simulate walking, deadheading, and maintenance, and to calculate cycle times, production, and costs. At the end of a panel, the model adjusts the surface elevations to account for coal removal. During this action, the model will leave coal in place if the spoils cover or encroach too much on the edge of the coal seam. The model prints appropriate messages which indicate when coal has been left in place due to spoil encroachment. After all panels are stripped, the model develops the overall production times and costs and prints a summary report. It also extends the total operating hours times the dragline hourly costs to calculate the $/cubic yard and $/ton cost of the project and the overall stripping ratio.

DPS EXAMPLES

The figures in this section demonstrate several aspects of the DPS System. The sequence of model runs which lead to these figures is as follows:

(1) The starting surface was a level area of 79 feet elevation (70 feet of overburden and 9 feet of coal). This level surface was used to simplify the projections.
(2) A run was made to develop the boxcut. In this run, the spoils were assumed to be hauled away. The surface from this run was used as the starting surface for the next run.
(3) Another run was made to strip a second panel with the dragline advancing toward the north and casting spoils toward the west. The pertinent factors for this run are:

Panel width = 150 feet
Digout length = 125 feet
Width of keycut at dragface = 25 feet
Keycut spoil angle = 65 degrees
Bail spoil angle = 61 degrees

The isometric projections in Fig. 2 show the development of a digout which consists of a keycut followed by a bail. Several things can be noticed on these projections. The long

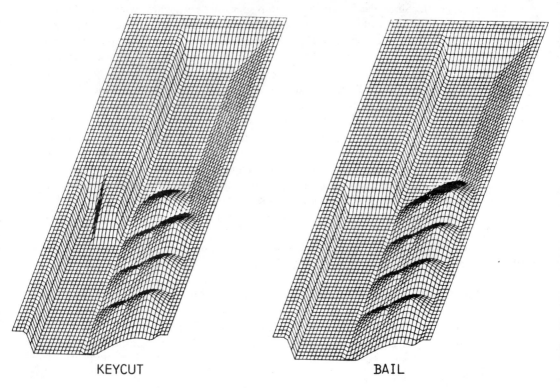

CASE EXAM SUR NO.   4208 – NORTH   CASE EXAM SUR NO.   4209 – NORTH

KEYCUT   BAIL

Fig. 2.   Surface showing development of keycut and bail

digout length causes the spoil banks to be well separated. Shorter digouts would crowd the spoils together more. The 61- and 65-degree angles caused the spoils to be cast alongside the excavation. Angles of 90 degrees cause the spoils to be cast forward alongside the dragline position. The dragline position for the keycut is over the highwall being formed so these spoils are cast rather close to the coal seam. The machine moves over to a position nearer the old highwall for the bail, so these spoils are case to the "back" side of the keycut spoils. The bail spoils nearly cover the keycut spoils.

Fig. 3 shows the completed panel after the coal has been removed. Notice the small "blips" at the bottom of the first, second, third, and seventh spoil banks. The eighth spoil bank shows a definite coal fender for the last 50 feet of the panel.

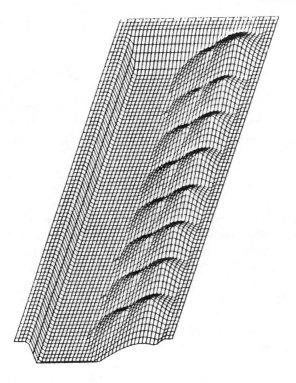

Fig. 3. Surface of final panel after coal removal

SUMMARY

The planning micromodels provide the engineer with a rapid, accurate method for evaluating mining equipment. The models "select" machines which show the lowest overall ownership and operating costs measured in $/ton of recovered coal. However, they also develop and print production and cost information for all feasible machines so the engineer can select equipment using criteria other than least cost.

The planning macromodels provide the economist and management with a fast, convenient method for evaluating a reserve or comparing mining methods.

In both types of models, all variables which define the mining situation are under user control. The macromodels also have variables by which the user can alter the predefined engineering judgments which enable these models to simulate the entire mine complex.

The Cash Flow Analysis model can be used for any mining project to examine financial alternatives such as escalation of investments, costs and/or coal price, debt vs. equity financing, equipment leasing vs. purchase, and accelerated depreciation vs. full-life depreciation.

The DPS provides the mining engineer with a method for examining the effects of alterations in dragline operating procedures. Preliminary case studies made with this system indicate considerable potential for improving dragline efficiency.

ACKNOWLEDGMENT

The author wishes to acknowledge gratefully the mining engineering knowledge and direction provided by Fluor Mining & Metals, Inc., for whom Bonner & Moore acted as subcontractor for development of both model systems. The planning model system was developed under contract to the U.S. Energy Research & Development Administration. The dragline production system was developed under contract to the U.S. Bureau of Mines.

ABSTRACT

This paper describes two sets of computer-based models for use by engineers and economic analysts in conjunction with surface coal mine planning. One set of models simulates the individual mining operations, such as overburden drilling, blasting, stripping, coal loading/hauling, etc., for use in the design of mines and the evaluation and selection of mining equipment. Another set of models depicts all mining operations for purposes of economic evaluation of coal properties and resources and to support decisions on site selection. Both sets of models can be used with an economic evaluation model which prepares a complete discounted cash flow analysis of any mining project.

The mining methods, characterized by overburden removal method, include three dragline methods and three shovel/truck or front-end loader/truck methods. A dragline operations model is also described. This model simulates the walking, digging, and spoiling actions of the dragline for use in detailed operations planning.

ND-REAP, AN INFORMATION AND ANALYSIS
SYSTEM FOR AN ENERGY EXPORTING STATE

John R. Reid, F. Larry Leistritz and Richard V. Giddings*

INTRODUCTION

Mining of lignite coal in North Dakota presumably has occurred since it was first discovered to be of value. During most of this time, use of the coal has been restricted largely to heating homes and industrial plants, but by 1927 the first lignite-fired electric generating plant in North Dakota became operational in Beulah, generating 2.5 megawatts of electricity (Montana-Dakota Utility Company records). By 1938 there were over 300 coal mines operating in North Dakota, most of them underground (State Planning Board 1938). Today, there are six major lignite power generating plants operating in North Dakota capable of producing 1,600 megawatts of electricity, most for export to other states. The need for North Dakota electricity increased only gradually until the early 1970's when it became evident that the pending energy crisis would require a significant increase in the use of coal resources. Many citizens of the state became alarmed; they feared Washington bureaucrats or eastern industrial concerns soon would be dictating the development in North Dakota. If the citizens were to have the control that they deemed to be their right, they would have to have an accurate and coordinated forecasting system so that appropriate decisions could be made by the decision-makers.

The idea for such a capability in North Dakota arose in 1974 when the North Dakota Legislative Council contracted with Battelle's Columbus Laboratories to conceptualize such a comprehensive system. Battelle prepared and presented to the Resources Development Committee of the Legislative Council a report suggesting the design and structure for a "regional environmental assessment program" (Battelle 1975). In October 1974, the concept was approved by that committee, and in November a draft bill was prepared. House Bill 1004 was adopted by the legislature and on April 10, 1975, Governor Arthur Link signed it into law establishing the North Dakota Regional Environmental Assessment Program and providing an appropriation of $2 million from a special coal severance tax trust fund.

House Bill 1004 provided two mandates for REAP: "to carry on research in regard to North Dakota's resources [and] . . . to develop the necessary data and information systems." The stated purposes were to assist "in the development of new laws, policies, and governmental actions . . . [and to provide] facts and information to the citizens of the state . . . [in order that they may know] the alternatives available to the state in any use

*North Dakota Regional Environmental Assessment Program, 316 North Fifth Street, Provident Life Building, Room 521, Bismarck, ND 58505.

and development of resources ... [and so that they will know] the results and impacts of any such use or development." The REAP staff, consisting of a director, two associate directors, and a secretary, was charged with defining what the REAP system should be, without having to rely on the experience of other states; no other state had attempted to develop such a system before. It was decided to concentrate efforts on the southwestern part of North Dakota, the area of most intensive development impact.

PROCEDURES

The first task during the summer and fall of 1975 was to identify the experts in the state, determine the existence of data relevant to environment and socioeconomics for North Dakota, and determine what types of information still were needed. Once the experts were identified, they were invited to participate in a series of task forces. As a result, 92 technical experts from state universities, state agencies, federal agencies, and local government participated in a series of 11 Technical Task Forces (TTF's). These TTF's included air quality-meteorology, geology, historic-archaeologic-paleontologic sites, land use, social impact-quality of life, socioeconomic impact and projection modeling, soils, vegetation, water, and noise-radiation-solid waste. Each identified existing data and data not presently available but needed, recommended a methodology for collecting new data, recommended the format and system by which the data should be stored and retrieved, identified organizations and persons qualified to participate in a data acquisition effort, what future monitoring was needed, and the appropriate models to be used for projecting change (REAP 1975). Perhaps the most important result of the TTF's was the recommendations for priority baseline data acquisition studies. From these, REAP issued Requests for Proposals to undertake the acquisition of the priority data for the State of North Dakota. Proposals were received from all over the United States; these were then sent to experts throughout North America for their review and recommendations. Contracts (Table 1) were eventually awarded to those investigators who demonstrated capabilities to collect and assess the data in the most cost effective manner. In every case, the contract stipulated that the investigator be required to submit a detailed bibliography for his project, undertake the acquisition of new data within a restricted time limit, and relate the results of the research to previously existing studies in North Dakota. Draft final reports were required to be received one month prior to the termination of the contract. These draft reports were reviewed by experts, and changes were required in the final report before final payment of the contract was authorized. As the final reports were received, they were published as REAP Reports.

Concurrent with the activity of the Technical Task Forces was an effort to assess the complete REAP system concept. For this purpose, International Business Machines/Federal Systems Division of Gaithersburg, Maryland (IBM), was contracted to define the system requirements and to provide the conceptual design of what the REAP system should be. This report was completed in December 1975 (IBM 1975). As part of that contract, several interim capabilities were defined. These capabilities included the development of a REAP Resource Reference System (R^3S) and an Economic-Demographic (E-D) Model, both of which will be discussed later.

Once the REAP staff was confident that IBM had adequately defined an appropriate concept for the design of the REAP system, they entered into a second contract with IBM to provide two additional reports--a high level system design, and a plan for implementation (IBM 1976a, b). The major responsibility for the first part of the system design rested with the REAP staff, with IBM support. The approach taken was to form a series of 10 REAP

User Specification Teams (RUSTEAMS) comprised of 53 technical experts drawn from expected users of REAP (31 from state agencies, 6 from federal agencies, 12 from universities, 1 from industry, and 3 from local government). The RUSTEAMS were organized by discipline (air quality-meteorology, animals, geology, historic-archaeologic-paleontologic sites, land use, social impact, socioeconomic impact, soils, vegetation, and water). Each team met for two two-day working sessions and were expected to complete additional homework assignments. To aid users with little or no computer experience in specifying system requirements, users were encouraged to visualize system output reports in any format they desired. From that point they elaborated the input data requirements, output report contents, and the processing, analysis, and modeling requirements for the support of such reports. The results of the RUSTEAM efforts were evaluated, summarized, and prioritized by the REAP staff. The conclusions of the entire effort were published in the Systems Analysis Details report (IBM 1976a). This high level of detail was required to serve as a basis for REAP system design efforts which followed.

On the basis of that report, IBM assumed the major responsibility for the second task, the design of the system architecture necessary to provide the desired capabilities and the formulation of a plan which included a time schedule and cost of implementation of a REAP system. This report, Systems Analysis and Plan report, was completed in October 1976 (IBM 1976b). This report was then evaluated by the REAP staff and, along with an alternative approach, was presented to REAP's board of directors, the Legislative Council's Resources Research Committee.

RESULTS

R^3S

The REAP Resource Reference System (R^3S) was one of the first capabilities developed by REAP. It was in response to the concern expressed by both citizens and decision-makers that researchers were literally bumping into one another in the coal impact areas, often repeating work that others had already accomplished a short time before. "If only REAP could keep track of who was doing what," they said. R^3S, REAP's attempt to address this concern, includes four separate files--Projects, People, Data Sources, and Bibliography. The initial contents were based upon data provided by the Technical Task Forces. This capability has been operational since January 1977. The *Project* File now contains 623 documents. This file contains all current studies on REAP-related areas in North Dakota. Included is the project title, sources of funding, goals, the location of the study, the expected date of completion, and the principal investigators.

The second file, *People*, is a convenient compendium of North Dakota technical experts who are doing or have accomplished REAP-related research on North Dakota. It also includes other North Dakotans who have demonstrated unusual expertise in a field relevant to REAP or who are contact persons for state or federal agencies, businesses, or industries which have the authority to sponsor or conduct REAP-related projects. This file now contains 543 documents.

The *Data Source* File contains descriptions of data collections relevant to REAP. Many of these data sources are federal repositories, such as Reston, Virginia; Ames, Iowa; Lincoln, Nebraska; and Austin, Texas. The file lists the type and availability of data and the contact person for the data. The reason for including this file was the understanding that the ultimate REAP system would not reproduce these data but merely make the data more accessible. There are currently 140 documents included in this file.

The fourth file, *Bibliography*, which at the present time contains 9,404 documents, has been the most useful. This file includes all REAP-related published and unpublished papers, reports, books, articles, and manuscripts which contain information, projections, or analyses about North Dakota. Entries include the key word abstracts and reference citation.

The uniqueness of the R^3S is that it is a computer-based on-line interactive information system with a text-search capability. This means that all words in the title or the abstract automatically become key words for an R^3S search.

E-D Model

The second capability, developed while the rest of the REAP system was being defined and planned, was the Economic-Demographic (E-D) Model. The contract for the model design was awarded to an interinstitutional social science team from North Dakota State University and the University of North Dakota, while the model implementation contract was awarded to Arthur D. Little, Inc., of Cambridge, Massachusetts. The purpose of the E-D Model was to allow predictions of the economic and demographic consequences resulting from major resource development projects. The emphasis of the model was on impacts of coal development projects. It was, therefore, restricted to 15 counties of southwestern North Dakota. The model actually consisted of four submodels: an input-output economic model capable of forecasting levels of business volume, employment, and personal income; a cohortsurvival submodel capable of forecasting population by age and sex, as well as total population; a submodel, which was a merger of the first two submodels, to provide for balancing the supply and demand for labor; and a fiscal impact model to provide the capability of projecting public sector costs and public sector revenues by type, and net fiscal balance for the state and for local governmental units (REAP 1977a, b). The model was designed to be user-interactive, providing the capability for changing many of the assumptions on which the model was based. Although this model was intended to be a test model, it proved to be so successful that a new model is being developed for the entire state, expanding on the types of developments for which projections can be made. So far, the first model has been widely used for planning, for school expenditures, for school expansions, highway planning, water system development, determining whether a TV station should be constructed, and many other uses. Subsequent to the development of the initial model, special censuses have demonstrated the accuracy of that model in projecting populations.

Land Cover Analysis

In order to measure changes in the land surface of North Dakota, REAP awarded a contract to Bendix Aerospace Systems Division of Ann Arbor, Michigan, to produce a land cover analysis of North Dakota. Using imagery collected largely by LANDSAT II, launched January 1975, but with some minor imagery from LANDSAT I, launched July 1972, Bendix processed the data by computer. Ground information was collected by a subcontracting team from the Institute for Remote Sensing at the University of North Dakota. The computer was "trained" to identify all areas having similar combinations of reflectivities from the four spectral wavelength bands on the satellite. The products of the contract included a 10-color map of each of the 53 counties of North Dakota showing the dominant land cover for every 1.1-acre cell at a scale of two miles to the inch. A mosaic of each of the counties was prepared to make a map of the entire state at a scale of about eight miles to the inch. Of greater importance, however, were some of the other products. These included the digitized tape of the dominant land cover for each 1.1-acre unit of the state, and another tape in which the detailed land cover data were merged with a digital file of the sections in the state aggregating the dominant land cover for every quarter-quarter section. Subsequently, another tape has been developed providing the dominant land cover for each of the drainage basins in the state. These land cover tapes will allow REAP to identify the dominant cover for any polygon in the state, whether it be a transmission line corridor or a planning district. Correction of urban areas, not readily discerned by satellite, and miscategorized areas, such as those few areas with cloud cover, will be accomplished in the next year.

Data Base Gathering

The efforts of the TTF's in the fall of 1975 resulted in the identification of existing baseline data for the State of North Dakota and established priorities for the collection of still needed data. On the basis of these priorities, a number of contracts were awarded (Table 1). Although most of the data gathering was restricted to the southwestern corner of the state, several contracts were for the entire state (e.g., the mapping and evaluation of known paleontologic, archaeologic, and historic sites in North Dakota). An early requirement of each contract was the submission of existing bibliography relevant to that contract for entry into the R^3S system.

The biology projects were the most numerous. Each contractor was required to identify representative sites in the southwestern part of the state, census the diversity and

TABLE 1. REAP Data Base Contracts
1976-1978

AIR QUALITY-METEOROLOGY:

Evaluation of meteorological sites in southwestern North Dakota — North Dakota State University ($57,000)

North Dakota Regional Environmental Assessment Program Air Quality Network — North Dakota Department of Health ($180,000)

BIOLOGY:
Botany:

Grasslands and wetlands of southwestern North Dakota — North Dakota State University ($77,000)

Woodlands, shrubs and algae of southwestern North Dakota — University of North Dakota ($79,700)

Zoology:

Aquatic mollusks of southwestern North Dakota — University of North Dakota ($7,400)

Arthropods of southwestern North Dakota — North Dakota State University ($40,000)

Fishes of southwestern North Dakota — University of North Dakota ($29,000)

Land mollusks of southwestern North Dakota — Minot State College ($5,500)

Soil fauna and parasites of southwestern North Dakota — University of North Dakota ($35,000)

Vertebrates of southwestern North Dakota — University of North Dakota ($85,000)

GEOLOGY:

Geology and hydrogeology of the Knife River Basin — North Dakota Geological Survey ($132,000)

LAND COVER:

Land cover of North Dakota — Bendix Aerospace Systems Division ($145,553)

SITES:

Archaeologic sites in North Dakota — University of North Dakota ($7,900)

Historic sites in North Dakota — University

of North Dakota ($16,200)

Paleontologic sites in North Dakota — University of North Dakota ($7,100)

SOCIOECONOMIC:

Longitudinal socioeconomic data in western North Dakota — University of North Dakota/North Dakota State University ($199,800)

WATER:

Water resources and model conceptualization of the Knife River Basin — North Dakota State Water Commission ($47,000) population of species, whether they be animal or plant, and integrate the results with all existing work previously accomplished for those species in North Dakota. An important part of each written report, required at the end of each contract, was recommendations for further evaluations and for the establishment of permanent monitoring sites.

REAP System

The Core of all the REAP activities is the establishment of the REAP system. Collection of data is of no value unless they are used. The goal of REAP was to build a computer system which could store data, perform integrated analyses, and make data more readily accessible to the decision-makers of North Dakota. On the basis of the recommendations presented by the IBM report (IBM 1976b), the REAP staff developed an alternative to upgrading the state computer to an IBM 370/158. A scientific timesharing computer was recommended, and eventually a Harris system 140 was purchased. Peripherals include 640 million characters of disk storage. But, the REAP system is more than just a computer; it also includes digitizers, plotters, graphics displays, highly specialized software, and analysts. Although some of the software to enter, store, and analyze the data was purchased outright, much of the software was developed by the REAP system staff. It is expected that by the fall of 1978 the REAP system will have a wide variety of data available for use. Outputs will consist of reports, maps, statistics, composite mapping, and graphs and charts. Many data bases located outside the State of North Dakota will not be directly included in the REAP system; rather, they will be accessed by computer hookup. Table 2 lists the types of data that are expected to be available to the decision-makers of North Dakota by late fall of 1978. This, however, is just a beginning.

TABLE 2. REAP Data Base Priorities
1977-79 BIENNIUM

1. STATEWIDE DATA

Distribution of prime farmland
Distribution of native range
Distribution of irrigable soils
Geological type formations and members
Coal Mines
Oil and gas wells
Mineral resources
Topographic data
Historical sites
Archaeological sites
Paleontological sites
Land cover - Landsat data
Land ownership - surface
Land ownership - minerals
Federal and state leased lands
Energy transmission facilities
Energy conversion facilities
Transportation facilities
Political and section boundaries
Drainage basin boundaries
Distribution of lakes, streams, and wetlands
Water use permits
WATSTORE
Rare, unique and fragile vegetation
Forest inventory
Rare, unique and endangered species
Grasshopper data
Parks and outdoor recreational sites
School district boundaries
Census data
Selected fiscal data

2. DATA FOR A SELECTED COUNTY(S)

Distribution of saline soils
Flood prone areas
Ground water distribution
Construction capabilities
Near surface permeability
Vegetation maps
Potential vegetation maps

3. DATA FOR SELECTED AREAS

Grassland production data
Game habitat inventory
Population of selected animal, bird and fish species

FUTURE DIRECTIONS

The future of REAP will depend upon many variables, not the least of which is being able to respond directly to changing user needs. To do this, REAP will continue to evaluate the data needs for the system. The establishment of permanent, physical, chemical, and biological monitoring stations will be of high priority during the next year. Critical data gaps missing from the baseline data will be filled as they are identified and as funds become available. The development of sophisticated models to relate the environmental factors will also be a priority for REAP over the next two years, but perhaps the most important goal is to educate the decision-makers on the proper use of the system outputs.

CONCLUSIONS

Several significant conclusions can be drawn as a result of the accomplishments of REAP so far. First, although it is clear that the development of such a system is a large and complex task, the effort to date indicates that development of such a system is feasible. In addition, the development of REAP demonstrates that it is possible to bring together research specialists and decision-makers with a wide range of interests and arrive at a design for a comprehensive, integrated, and practical system. The development of the REAP system also demonstrates that significant economies can be achieved through the development of flexible capabilities suitable for use by a number of agencies or organizations. For example, more than 40 different state and local entities have used the E-D Model. While the cost of developing such a sophisticated modeling system probably would have been prohibitive for any single user agency, this cost is quite modest when prorated over all users. In sum, REAP is developing a comprehensive and integrated system which will be adaptable to answer a variety of resource policy questions allowing the citizens of North Dakota to better understand the implications of increased development and providing decision-makers the data and analyses by which such development can be controlled. Finally, the system development process that has been described may well be applicable to other energy exporting states.

ABSTRACT

The North Dakota Regional Environmental Assessment Program (REAP) was created in 1975 in response to concerns about potential impacts of increased coal development. The mandate was to "develop the necessary data and information systems in regard to ... North Dakota's natural resources [so] the citizens of this state ... may know with a high degree of certainty the alternatives available to the state in any use or development." With the help of 92 experts, existing data were identified and priorities were set for the collection of data still needed. Approximately 20 contracts, costing $1.3 million, were then awarded to collect such data. Concurrent with this was the design of a system by which all data could be made more accessible to the decision-makers. For this task, 53 potential prime users of the system described the needed output reports. International Business Machines was contracted to work with these users to define the computer hardware and software components necessary to provide the outputs. The result was the purchase of a system based upon a Harris 140 computer. Initial capabilities included the REAP Resource Reference System, an Economic-Demographic Model, and a statewide Land Cover Analysis.

Cooperative agreements have been established with other national data sources, and selected priority data are being entered into the system. When the system is operational in late 1978, decision-makers will, for the first time, be able to perform integrated environmental analyses on existing data for North Dakota.

REFERENCES

Battelle. 1975. North Dakota Regional Environmental Assessment Program. Battelle, Columbus Laboratories, 113 p.

IBM. 1975. N.D. REAP System Requirements and Conceptual Design. International Business Machines, Federal Systems Division, Gaithersburg, MD, 175 p.

IBM. 1976a. N.D. REAP System Analysis Details Report. International Business Machines, Federal Systems Division, Gaithersburg, MD, 2,750 p.

IBM. 1976b. N.D. REAP System Analysis and Plan Report. International Business Machines, Federal Systems Division, Gaithersburg, MD, 164 p.

REAP. 1975. Technical Task Force Reports. North Dakota Regional Environmental Assessment Program, Bismarck, ND, 196 p.

REAP. 1977a. REAP E-D Model 1 User Manual. North Dakota Regional Environmental Assessment Program, Bismarck, ND, 123 p.

REAP. 1977b. REAP E-D Model Technical Description. North Dakota Regional Environmental Assessment Program, Bismarck, ND, 118 p.

State Planning Board. 1938. North Dakota Natural Resources (map). North Dakota State Planning Board, Bismarck, ND.

ENVIRONMENTAL IMPACT STATEMENTS FOR THE AUSTRALIAN COAL MINING INDUSTRY

*Allan Peter Campbell**

INTRODUCTION

Since the second half of the 1960's there have been a number of discoveries of major coal deposits in eastern Australia, stretching from central northern Queensland at about latitude 21°S to southern New South Wales (NSW) at about latitude 36°S, a distance of some 1,440 km. At the present time a few of these are actively mining and exporting coal, but the majority remain in the feasibility study phase. Consequently during the last 4 years since the energy crisis and the realization that coal was again an important mineral, there has been an intensification of activity in the planning and environmental investigation fields. This activity has taken place during the period of introduction and development of requirements for environmental investigations in Australia which began in 1971-72.

The different federal structures which exist in the United States and Australia led to differing approaches to the problem of environmental control. There is some common basis in that both federal governments require study of environmental impacts to be made in connection with any project that may involve the federal government, directly or indirectly. However, the Australian Government does not have the power to require the Australian States to either produce or enforce implementation plans. There is therefore a lack of uniformity in approach by the States and differing relationships with the federal government.

Since the major coal resources available for development lie within the States of NSW and Queensland, only the legislation of those states and the federal government is discussed. Although the federal government has no direct control over coal development projects, it gains power to intervene through the need of the project developer for import and export licenses, which are a federal prerogative.

In the past there has been considerable uncertainty relating to the overlapping needs of federal and state governments, but this has never been much of a problem with coal mining projects where Environmental Impact Statements (EIS) prepared for the state and accepted by them have also been accepted at federal level.

REQUIREMENTS UNDER SEVERAL ACTS AND THEIR REGULATIONS

Each state and the federal government operate under the Acts of Parliament and a set of regulations. The regulations may be amended from time to time without recourse

*Dames & Moore, Environmental Studies, 17 Myrtle Street, Crows Nest, Sydney, NSW 2065, Australia.

to the parliament or the parliament may amend the act and direct that changes be made to the regulations.

In each case the act lays down the general principles and intentions while the regulations are the means of effecting the act.

The Federal Act and its Regulations

A developer who wishes to export coal or to import extraction and processing machines, will require approval from

- the Department of Overseas Trade
- the Department of Natural Resources
- the Foreign Investment Review Board within the Department of Treasury

These Departments are required to consider environmental aspects when approving an export or import license for the Company, and they seek guidance from the Department of Environment, Housing & Community Development (EH & CD) which administers the "Procedure Covering the Use and Preparation of Environmental Impact Statements".

The developer may therefore be required to submit an EIS to the Department of Environment, Housing & Community Development in order for that department to assess the environmental impact and proposed safeguards so that it can advise other Australian Government departments whether approval should be given.

The Approval Process at Federal Government Level

The developer should in the first instance submit, as soon as possible, notification to the EH & CD of his intention to prospect, extract, process, and export coal. The notification should include very brief descriptions of the environment, proposed operations, possible environmental impacts, and measures to be taken to protect the environment. The Department will then determine whether an EIS is required in order that it may assess the environmental impact caused by the proposed development.

An EIS may have to be prepared if the Minister of the Department considers that implementation of the proposed action is likely to have significant environmental effects, or arouse public controversy as to its effects on the environment. In deciding whether or not the environmental effects are potentially significant, account will be taken of whether or not the proposed development will result in

- the transformation of a substantial physical area
- the establishment of a new human community
- substantial changes affecting existing human communities
- important long-term effects on the environment
- substantial impact on ecosystems of the area concerned or its environs
- diminution of scenic, recreational, scientific or conservation quality or value of the area concerned or its environs
- changes affecting areas or structures of historical or archaeological importance
- pollution
- increased demands on natural resources which are, or are likely to be, in short supply
- any irreversible or irretrievable commitments of resources.

Once a draft EIS is submitted to EH & CD, that Department should make it available to public scrutiny, which is achieved through advertising the availability of the document and seeking written comment on it. In addition, if the environmental consequences of the proposal are considered to be particularly significant, or where considerable public controversy over these consequences has arisen, a public inquiry may be held.

It is not likely that a coal development proposal would require both a state and federal public review and inquiry. It appears that the state will hold the inquiry if one is deemed necessary and recieve a submission from EH & CD concerning those issues which EH & CD feels should be covered within the Inquiry. Following the Inquiry, the draft EIS should be finalized by the developer and submitted to EH & CD who will assess it, taking into consideration comments made at the Inquiry. Assessment of the environmental consequences will be conveyed to Federal Parliamentary Cabinet at the same time as the proposal itself is put to Cabinet for consideration. Thus, there will be consideration of the economic, technological and environmental consequences of the proposal at the same time.

The New South Wales (NSW) State Act and its Regulations

The NSW Government policy has established three areas of environmental control

- The State Pollution Control Commission (SPCC) has the responsibility of ensuring that all practical measures are taken to control pollution, control waste disposal, and protect the environment, as well as the responsibility of coordinating activities of all public authorities involved with environmental aspects.
- The NSW Planning and Environment Commission (PEC) has the responsibility of ensuring that future use and development of land are planned in harmony with the environment and within environmental constraints.
- Local Government and other public 'determining authorities' are responsible for rejecting or approving planning or development proposals.

The developer is responsible for providing the determining authority (whichever it may be) with details of his proposed development which will provide sufficient evidence to show that appropriate consideration has been given to environmental factors and that necessary safeguards have been incorporated within the proposal to prevent pollution and protect the environment. The usual method whereby this information is passed from the company to the determining authorities is an EIS. The process by which environmental approval is gained is illustrated (Fig. 1).

The Queensland Act and its Regulations

The State of Queensland does not treat the need for environmental investigation and statement of impact under any single unifying act and set of regulations. Instead it has drafted a set of procedures which roughly parallel those in NSW, and relies for enforcement on existing legislation such as the Clean Air Act 1963, the Clean Waters Act 1971 and an Act to Provide for the Establishment of an Environment Control Council 1970, which latter is cited at the "State Development and Public Works Organization Act Amendment Act" 1970. The amendments to this act set out the intended functions of the Environment Control Council which are largely those of coordination. Its powers are limited to initiation of investigations and making recommendations to the Minister with respect to matters arising out of such investigations.

The procedures set out by the State Government providing for environmental approval of a development project are illustrated (Fig. 2).

APPLICATION OF THE ACTS AND REGULATIONS IN PRACTICE

The way in which the above interlocking requirements of many different authorities can be met in practice is of interest to both the coal mine developer and his consultant. The relatively simple and straight-forward federal procedures operate as laid down by the regulations. In the state system, however, this is not necessarily the case and in both NSW and Queensland close contact with just a few of the authorities listed in Figs. 1 and 2 is sufficient. Discussion and consultation is necessary only with 4 authorities in NSW and

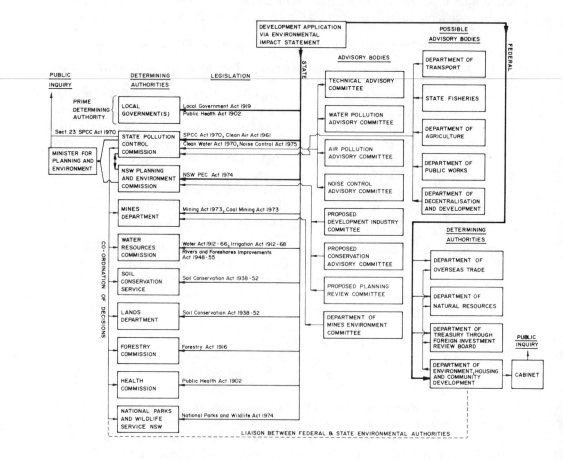

Fig. 1. Flow diagram of procedure of government assessment of environmental factors associated with major mining development applications in N.S.W.

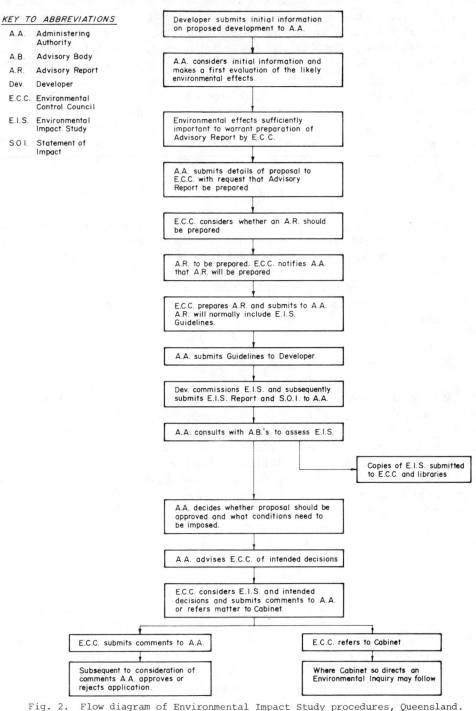

KEY TO ABBREVIATIONS

A.A. Administering Authority

A.B. Advisory Body

A.R. Advisory Report

Dev. Developer

E.C.C. Environmental Control Council

E.I.S. Environmental Impact Study

S.O.I. Statement of Impact

Developer submits initial information on proposed development to A.A.

A.A. considers initial information and makes a first evaluation of the likely environmental effects.

Environmental effects sufficiently important to warrant preparation of Advisory Report by E.C.C.

A.A. submits details of proposal to E.C.C. with request that Advisory Report be prepared

E.C.C. considers whether an A.R. should be prepared

A.R. to be prepared. E.C.C. notifies A.A. that A.R. will be prepared

E.C.C. prepares A.R. and submits to A.A. A.R. will normally include E.I.S. Guidelines.

A.A. submits Guidelines to Developer.

Dev. commissions E.I.S. and subsequently submits E.I.S. Report and S.O.I. to A.A.

A.A. consults with A.B.'s to assess E.I.S.

Copies of E.I.S. submitted to E.C.C. and libraries

A.A. decides whether proposal should be approved and what conditions need to be imposed.

A.A. advises E.C.C. of intended decisions

E.C.C. considers E.I.S. and intended decisions and submits comments to A.A. or refers matter to Cabinet.

E.C.C. submits comments to A.A.

Subsequent to consideration of comments A.A. approves or rejects application.

E.C.C. refers to Cabinet

Where Cabinet so directs an Environmental Inquiry may follow

Fig. 2.   Flow diagram of Environmental Impact Study procedures, Queensland.

SOURCE: "Procedural Manual for Environmental Impact Studies in Queensland," issued by the Environmental Control Council.

with 2 in Queensland. In NSW these are the SPCC, the Mines Department, Local Government and the National Parks and Wildlife Service of NSW. The latter assumes importance because it has responsibility for archaeological sites, rare and endangered species and conservation of habitat. Outside the parks it has no direct control over these matters, but must work through the SPCC. It is important to satisfy the Service that thorough investigations have been made into the matters concerning it in order to get ready approval of the EIS.

In NSW, the Mines Department has direct control over the manner in which a mining project is developed by way of conditions attached to the mining lease. It has developed its own set of requirements which are consistent with those of the SPCC except in special circumstances where there happens to be direct public conern and involvement. In cases such as these, the SPCC may make further requirements and will often request that the Mines Department include these within the lease agreement. Very close liaison is necessary with both the Mines Department and the SPCC to ensure that any problems which arise are dealt with at an early stage so that they do not grow out of proportion leading the authorities to gain the impression the developer is not responsive to their requests.

In Queensland the practical requirements have changed a good deal in the last 12 months. The Mines Department as the Administering Authority now has a dominant role while the Environment Control Council merely provides the vehicle for coordination with other interested government authorities. Effective control is exercised in the same way as in NSW by attaching conditions to the coal mining lease and these conditions are provided by the Mines Department.

SCOPE OF WORK REQUIRED

If the development or operation of the project requires import or export approvals, then the federal government may withhold approval until satisfied on environmental grounds. In general, however, an EIS which is acceptable to the state authorities in terms of content will also be acceptable to the federal government. The general scope and depth of work required to complete an acceptable EIS is described below.

A basic presentation requirement is for site plan drawings of sufficient detail to clearly define the extent and position of all the proposed facilities, including refuse disposal areas, loading bins and stockpiles, transport facilities and utility supplies. Vertical cross-sections are also required. These drawings need not contain engineering detail as they are used by the assessors to gain an appreciation of the relationship of one part of the development to another and how it will fit in to the surrounding landscape.

In NSW, several aspects of the proposed mine must be described in considerable detail in order to gain approval under the Clean Waters Act and the Clean Air Act. It is expected that the same degree of detail will also be provided in the EIS. Specifically, a practical and well-designed storm drainage system must be provided with provision for sediment traps and erosion control. A complete description of the water requirements of the mine and washery, recycling, water treatment plant and the character of its final effluent are also required. Figure 3 shows factors considered in a typical coal mine EIS.

In addition to these specific requirements which require design detail there are more general requirements such as presentation of sufficient baseline data to describe the environment and consideration of alternatives. The degree to which alternatives must be seriously considered depends upon individual location and public opinion at the time. It is an area in which considerable judgement is required to avoid unnecessary expenditure and yet still provide an adequate EIS. Economic factors may be considered in arriving at or discarding alternatives under the federal, NSW and Queensland requirements.

The level of detail in the assessment of likely impacts is something about which there is considerable dissatisfaction. In general this section tends to broad statement of expectation rather than conclusions based on specific knowledge and this approach has come to be accepted. Because the assessment of impact tends to be unsatisfactory there is a tendency to require very specific and detailed description of mitigation measures and to make use of similar work elsewhere on a precedent basis.

POSSIBLE ADVERSE ENVIRONMENTAL IMPACTS

POSSIBLE OPERATIONS:

Operation	Damage to surrounding buildings	Alteration of surface hydrology	Modification of existing habitat	Visual impacts	Noise & vibration effects	Erosion	Air pollution from spontaneous combustion	Air pollution from coal dust	Air pollution from earth dust	Effects from lower water table	Polluted water	Altered landforms	Preclusion of other land uses
EXPLORATION			x										
CONSTRUCTION		x	x	x	x			x			x	x	x
REMOVAL OF BORROW MATERIAL		x	x		x			x			x	x	x
DRILLING & BLASTING	x			x				x				x	
STREAM DIVERSION		x	x		x								
OVERBURDEN REMOVAL		x	x	x	x	x		x		x	x	x	x
ON-SITE DAM CONSTRUCTION		x	x		x			x				x	x
DEWATERING		x	x		x					x	x		
TUNNELLING	x											x	
COAL EXTRACTION	x			x			x				x		
COAL PROCESSING			x	x	x								x
COAL STOCKPILING		x	x	x				x			x	x	x
COARSE REJECT STOCKPILING		x	x	x			x	x			x	x	x
TAILINGS DISPOSAL		x	x	x				x			x	x	x
TRANSPORTATION	x	x	x	x	x			x			x	x	x
MAINTENANCE											x		x
ON-SITE WORKER FACILITIES											x		x
FUEL & CHEMICAL HANDLING											x		
OPERATIONAL FAILURE				x			x	x	x		x		

POSSIBLE MITIGATING PROCEDURES:

	Damage to surrounding buildings	Alteration of surface hydrology	Modification of existing habitat	Visual impacts	Noise & vibration effects	Erosion	Air pollution from spontaneous combustion	Air pollution from coal dust	Air pollution from earth dust	Effects from lower water table	Polluted water	Altered landforms	Preclusion of other land uses	Procedure
	x			x	x			x	x					REMOTENESS FROM OTHER SETTLEMENTS
			x											FERTILIZER APPLICATION
		x	x	x	x						x	x	x	EROSION CONTROL TECHNIQUES
		x	x	x								x		RECONTOURING
		x	x	x							x			SEDIMENT TRAPS
		x	x	x							x			BUNDING, DRAINS & DECANTING PONDS
						x					x			DUST SUPPRESSION EQUIPMENT
		x	x	x				x			x	x	x	SITE REHABILITATION
		x									x			PYRITES SEPARATION
						x								COMPACTION
		x									x			WATER TREATMENT FOR RE-USE
		x									x			SULLAGE & SEPTIC DISPOSAL
				x							x			INDUSTRIAL SAFETY PROCEDURES
				x	x	x	x	x			x			PROPER ENGINEERING DESIGN
		x		x							x			WATER RE-USE CIRCUIT
	x	x									x		x	COMPENSATION TO LAND OWNERS

Fig. 3. Step matrix showing possible operations, possible adverse environmental impacts and possible mitigating procedures of proposed development.

PUBLIC INQUIRIES/HEARINGS

One of the greatest differences in the environmental approval process between the United States and Australia is in the nature of the public hearing process.

Public hearings are not mandatory under any of the procedures discussed above, although public display of a draft EIS is in some cases. In addition there is no well-defined legal process by which public interest groups can force an inquiry. Instead the responsible Minister will decide to hold an Inquiry on the basis of public interest in the case. Inquiries are not legal processes, but rather are conducted under a broad set of rules which allow very wide interpretation by the presiding commissioner. In most cases legal counsel are not even present and in no cases have inquiries been conducted under court rules. This approach has been partly successful in reducing the adversary roles which seem to develop under U.S. procedures. The ruling of the commission is then made by modifications to the original proposal (including disallowance) based on the differing viewpoints and interpretations of the facts placed before it during the inquiry.

DISCUSSION

During the period 1971-1978 there has been a considerable change in the requirements for Environmental Impact Statements for coal mine development. Behind these changes lies a change in attitude of the government departments and authorities who have the responsibility for granting final approval. As they gain experience their requirements for the EIS are tending to become more standardized and their level of expectation regarding technical input to rise. It is now very unlikely that an EIS based merely on the "conceptual" planning of a project will be accepted. Some difference is evident in the attitudes taken by the two "coal states". In NSW, EIS requirements have become more rigid and specific and preparation and approval of an EIS is an essential part of gaining development approval. In Queensland the EIS has been de-emphasized in favor of conditions imposed on the mining approvals and leases granted by the administering authority. This does not mean that actual development requirements and mitigating measures are less demanding in Queensland than in NSW, but rather that the EIS process plays a smaller part in their implementation.

There has also been a change in emphasis on the content requirements for coal mine impact statements. For example biological surveys, trapping and counting of animal populations, analysis of stomach content and many other investigations have been de-emphasized in favor of detailed description of pollution control means, and the need for and degree of implementation of mitigating measures. Some biological survey, identification of threatened species and habitats is still required and soil and terrain mapping is of importance for erosion control and revegetation, but these occupy a much smaller part of the total effort than previously.

To consulting companies these changes have led to a change in staff composition and attitude. Engineers with environmental training are replacing some biologically trained staff. There is also an increased need for staff with training in economic evaluation and planning. This change in staff composition has tended to bring with it changes in attitude away from the more "preservation" minded concepts of the biologists to one which is in tune with the changes in government policy towards recognizing the need for development of resources while maintaining an environment of high quality.

OPENCAST COAL EXTRACTION IN
GREAT BRITAIN: THE SOUTH YORKSHIRE EXAMPLE

*M.J. Thompson and D. Lawton**

INTRODUCTION

Some issues involved in the opencast extraction of coal from one particular point of view are discussed here. This is not, I hope, a narrow view, but one which identifies many of the general planning problems encountered wherever coal is recovered by opencast methods, and also sets out the particular difficulties of working in one local authority area of Great Britain. I wish to concentrate on the role of a democratically elected local authority which has a major responsibility for the physical planning of its area.

South Yorkshire is one of six Metropolitan County Councils in one of the major industrialized conurbations in Great Britain. The County shares planning responsibility at local level with four smaller District Councils and is responsible in this instance for strategic planning matters, and particularly for surface mineral working. The County is small in area (156,046 ha), and by the standards of most of the world, is densely developed, with a population of about 1.3 million people living in the major City of Sheffield, together with three other settlements of Barnsley, Rotherham and Doncaster and many smaller towns and villages.

The area is located on the Yorkshire Coalfield, which contains numerous thin seams (i.e. up to 3 m in thickness) of high quality bituminous coal at depths of up to 800 m. These seams have been worked intensively by deep mined methods for well over 100 years, and where the most important seams outcrop on the surface, opencast working has also taken place extensively in the recent past, with attractive conditions for further working in the future. The Sheffield-Rotherham area is also one of the largest concentrations of steel and steel products manufacturing in Great Britain, and the coal and steel producing industries form the major part of the County's economic base.

The legacy of this long history of heavy industry has resulted in a severely damaged physical environment, with substantial areas of derelict waste tips and mineral workings, and with high levels of atmospheric pollution and water pollution in the County. To these factors are added equally large areas of land rendered derelict by neglect, and various problems of economic and social decline which are partly attributable to the unpleasant physical conditions. The County Council has identified the improvement of the physical environment as one of its major priorities, and has embarked on a massive program of land reclamation and environmental improvement at considerable public cost. This choice of priorities relates very closely to an increased public awareness of the problems of the

*Planning Department, South Yorkshire County Council, Barnsley, South Yorkshire S70 2TN, England.

area and the resulting pressures to deal with them. There is strong evidence that the tolerance levels of the population, to dereliction which historically have been very high, are now being sharply reduced, particularly in those areas where the first improvement schemes are beginning to show the changes that can occur.

It is against this background of reliance on traditional industries for employment; of physical degradation from the past, and of people's changing hopes and expectations that opencast coal extraction within the County must be judged. This background is represented strongly in the attitudes and reactions of the public in the area, and of elected members and officers of the local authorities in opencasting areas of which South Yorkshire is perhaps a typical example. The result is that the whole question of opencast coal extraction is highly emotive involving social, economic and political issues.

NATIONAL POLICY

National pressure gives rise to proposals to work coal by opencast methods, creating the need to identify and work sites, which in turn causes the conflict now unfortunately almost normal in the case of sites in Great Britain.

The first point to make is that in Great Britain, both deep mining and opencast mining occur in the same seams of the same coalfields, the only difference being the depth of occurrence of seams, which dictates the method of working. National Policy regarding the two types of extraction is therefore not one of either one method or the other, but is one of which involves varying proportions of the two at any one time. This balance has fluctuated quite drastically as opencast working has been used to accommodate variations in deep mined production over the past 15 years, with opencasting at present being about 12% of total production. Thus in 1967 when there was a surplus of coal, and concern that continued opencasting would jeopardize jobs in deep mines, the Government decided that it would give no further authorizations for opencast production except in special cases where, "because of quality or location, the coal to be produced is not in competition with coal from deep mines."[1] The flexibility of opencast production then enabled the reduced output to be concentrated on the production of particular qualities of coal, such as coking coal, anthracite and dry steam coal, with corresponding changes in the regional pressures for working. At that time the location of workings was largely on 'green field' sites, where a great deal of effort was made to ensure an extremely good record for effective restoration to full agricultural use, which has been maintained into the larger sites currently being developed. Between 1970 and 1973, there was a reversal of policy by central government largely because of the quadrupling of oil prices, making coal more competitive, and opencast production was once more increased.

The present policy is a result of recommendations included in the "Final Report of the Coal Industry Examination - 1974", following tripartite discussions between Government, the National Coal Board and the Mining Unions. This policy calls for an increase in opencast production from 10 mT in 1974, to 15 mT per annum in 1980 (now modified to 1985 as a result of difficulties in getting operational sites). Current production is running at about 13 mT per annum, which compares with deep mined production of about 104 mT, and involves about 70 sites in production at any one time. It may be of interest to note that these sites are small by international standards and are clearly defined,

[1] 1967 White Paper on Fuel Policy, Her Majesty's Stationery Office, London.

separate areas of land usually between 20 and 400 ha, which have an average coaling life of about three years, and an average production of about 600,000 mT per site)

This pattern of working results in a need for about 20 new sites to be found within Great Britain each year to maintain production targets. It is significant that where the lead time for sites to become operational 2 to 3 years ago was about 12 months, it is now nearly 3 years as a result of the increased local opposition to individual sites. This has required much greater attention to a positive approach involving prior consultation on each site, before it is required for working.

In addition to the existing problems of bringing sites on stream, a recent new factor may have an impact on the future of opencast coal extraction. I refer to a self- financing productivity agreement entered into by the mining unions and the employers in December 1977 as a means of achieving higher productivity, and of overcoming the government's current pay policy. The early indications of the increased productivity vary considerably from a few percent to 14 percent in the amount of coal raised by deep mined methods in varying parts of the country. These may prove to be sustained increases which would alter the profitability of marginal mines, but it is too early to say. This factor could, if continued, result in increased stockpiling and alter substantially the need for opencast extraction as a means of "topping up" total production, which, together with the current phase of intensive capital investment in high production deep mines, could result in yet another look at production targets.

THE ROLE OF LOCAL AUTHORITIES

In Great Britain the controlling agency for all coal extraction is the National Coal Board, which has a self-contained Opencast Executive to handle opencast production. Two types of opencast sites are allowed under existing legislation (Opencast Coal Act 1958), and these are usually based upon the size of reserves. Sites with reserves of over 25,000 mT are usually worked by the Opencast Executive themselves, under an Authorization to work which is given by the Secretary of State for Energy. In granting the authorization, the Secretary of State has to be satisfied that the National Coal Board has carried out adequate consultations with the wide range of statutory and other consultees and have taken their views fully into account. The Secretary of State can amend the Authorization and usually adds numerous conditions covering operational requirements and site restoration. The Authorization also acts as a deemed planning permission for the purposes of working operations under the relevant planning legislation (Town and Country Planning Act 1971), except where a permanent change of land use is involved.

The role of local authorities in this process is merely one of the statutory consultees, which applies to both County Councils and District Councils, and their ultimate sanction is to raise objection to an authorization, as can any consultee. The National Coal Board will usually try to meet these objections by discussion and negotiation, but if an objection by a statutory consultee, such as a local authority, is sustained, then the Secretary of State will call a public enquiry at which the relevant issues can be raised and discussed in front of an inspector.

The second type of site is one where coal reserves of less than 25,000 mT exist, and which can be worked by a private operator under the terms of a license obtained from the National Coal Board. In these cases, the operator also requires planning permission from the local planning authority, which in this case is the County Council. On these sites the local authority has full control of the operations, but usually will work very closely with the National Coal Board on matters such as restoration, as the legislation empowers the Board to retain a bond on deposit to set against the possibility of the operator's failure to restore the site.

It is in the case of National Coal Board opencast operations where the local authority can feel most strongly that it has little control or even influence over the decisions made. This is accentuated by the fact that the final decision is made by the Secretary of State for Energy, with his rather limited brief, rather than by the Secretary of State for the Environment who deals with all other mineral planning matters.

The issues involved in these decisions rest inevitably on the balance between the need to work coal, which results from National Energy Policies, and the environmental damage and land use conflicts which can result. To cover this central question therefore, let us leave the general situation and deal with particular problems using South Yorkshire as my example.

THE SOUTH YORKSHIRE EXAMPLE

Large areas of the exposed coalfield in South Yorkshire have been identified as being of interest for possible opencast coal workings, and many small sites have been worked in the past. At present, sites totaling hundreds of hectares are being actively prospected to prove reserves, or are included in the National Coal Board's five year program of working. Some of these sites involve a return to areas which have previously been worked, and the extraction of coal to greater depths and over wider areas using more modern equipment and techniques. There is a tendency for workings generally to become deeper, larger, and of longer duration which in turn adds to the environmental problems.

Several of the Local Authority Councils in Great Britain, including in South Yorkshire, have taken a hard and somewhat embittered stand against opencast coal working of any kind, anywhere in their area, and attempts are being made through regional and national channels to present a united front to central government to have the opencast program completely reviewed, if not abandoned entirely, because of the severe concern over the effect of substantial opencast extraction in an area which is already much damaged by previous industrial operations.

In the British scene, therefore, the South Yorkshire area is very much in the front line of the conflict between the arguments involved in reconciling national policy with environmental concern. In order to clarify the situation, let us balance the arguments on both sides.

Firstly, the case supporting the working of coal by opencast methods put forward by the National Coal Board consists of the following main elements.

(1) The current adopted government energy policy has considered the question of national need, and requires a continuing and increasing contribution by means of opencast coal extraction.

(2) Opencast coal extraction can respond quickly to fluctuations in demand without major capital investment, and accordingly makes a substantial contribution to the balance of payments by avoiding the need for imports, and indeed, currently produces coal for export.

(3) Opencasting produces supplies of special qualities of coal, providing for instance two-thirds of total anthracite output.

(4) Opencasting produces a clean, high quality coal which can be blended with deep mined coal to increase its salability by ensuring an acceptable ash content for power station fuel, and for coke production.

(5) Opencast coal operations are consistently profitable, and help considerably the total profitability of the Board, as can be seen from the Board's annual statement where in several areas a loss is turned into profit when the profits from opencasting are added. It is an open question whether this bonus to profits results in the continued life of marginal deep mined collieries, and in turn therefore helps retain jobs which otherwise would be lost.

(6) It is claimed, with some justification, that the problems of satisfactory restoration are solved, and that sites restored to agricultural use are as good, if not better, than before.

(7) It is also claimed that the environmental damage caused by the working operations is now overcome by a combination of screening banks, noise and dust suppression methods and agreed traffic routing.

(8) Opencasting can create opportunities for environmental improvement by reclamation of derelict land as part of the working operation, and can enable valuable changes in after-use such as industry, recreation and waste disposal, with considerable savings in public money.

(9) It is also claimed that it is best in the long-term interests to work mineral reserves from land in order to free that land for other forms of development and avoid sterilization of reserves.

The counter arguments to this have been made by local authorities, amenity organizations and the general public, in the press, in public enquiries and in response to planning consultations. The arguments against opencasting can be summarized as follows.

(1) The national production target was reached without any reference to the public or the local authorities who now have to deal with the operational and environmental repercussions of this policy.

(2) The successful restoration techniques now available notwithstanding, land is taken out of agricultural production for a period of between 3 and 10 years depending on the size of the site, and up to 5 years of management are necessary before the land is fully restored.

(3) Notwithstanding the screening and control measures taken during the working life of sites, there is still massive and unacceptable damage to the local environment as a result of noise, dust, mud on roads, traffic disturbance on adjoining roads, and the visual intrusion of massive stockpiles of overburden.

(4) Long-term damage is caused to the landscape as a result of the removal of trees, hedgerows, wildlife habitats and scenery which takes many years, if not generations to replace, and may never adequately remedy the loss involved.

(5) With appropriate techniques it is claimed that adequate coal to meet demand can be obtained by deep mined methods particularly now that a national productivity agreement has been reached and new recapitalization in deep mining is taking place, and that existing jobs would be preserved by this alternative. A widespread feeling exists in the deep mining sector of the industry that the more coal mined by opencast methods, the greater is the threat to deep mining jobs.

(6) The areas which are suitable for opencast workings are usually in areas where severe environmental damage already exists from previous industrial activity,

and where the emphasis for the future should be on improvement and not in prolonging damage to affected communities, an argument which is particularly appropriate in South Yorkshire where the land reclamation program is raising expectations of an improved quality of life.

(7) Coal suitable for opencast extraction should be left in the ground as a reserve for the future when a greater national need may exist, rather than work these areas for short-term gain.

It is obvious that many of these arguments are contradictory, and represent different interpretations of the limited available facts. Many issues are irreconcilable. For instance, the effect of opencast operations on the future of deep mines appears completely different from either the point of view of a National Coal Board accountant wishing to balance the books, or that of a miner about to lose his job in a threatened colliery. Other issues depend on subjective judgements which can vary enormously, such as the effect of noise from plant or machinery when judged on the one hand by a plant hire contractor concerned in meeting a production target, and on the other hand by a resident on the edge of an opencast site who wants to get a peaceful evening in his garden.

In the case of South Yorkshire, its tightly packed urban fabric means that accessible sites can only be found in the interstices between development and are almost always closely confined, resulting in the maximum environmental impact and public opposition. The search for acceptable sites is therefore bound to be difficult, if not impossible, and it is understandable that local authorities often find it unacceptable to participate in what is a highly charged local political situation. Basically, it can be stated that there is no credit, (or no votes) in the eyes of the local population for either an officer or an elected member in a local authority who actively supports opencast working operations. On the other hand, there are considerable advantages in opposing opencasting in all its forms, forcing the argument to public enquiry, and requiring the Secretary of State to decide the matter at national level.

This apparently tempting course of action may in fact be used increasingly by local authorities in Great Britain, and consequently could cause the increasingly long lead times mentioned earlier. It may, however, have two major disadvantages to the local population. Firstly, there is little control over the terms of the final authorization, and the remoteness of a decision by central government could result in particular local problems not being adequately appreciated and dealt with. Secondly, because of the hostile atmosphere that is usually created, it is less likely that the environmental and social benefits that can result from opencasting will be achieved. This particularly applies when, as appears to have happened in Great Britain, the case for the need to work minerals is built into national policy and it is assumed will take precedence over any local issues. The evidence for this assumption is as yet not complete, but will be assembled over the years as a result of case histories resulting from enquiry decisions by the Secretary of State. Nevertheless, several authorities are attempting to establish a method of coming to terms with the conflicting arguments.

The way ahead through this morass of imprecise and variable factors is difficult to plot, particularly as even the basic ground rules are likely to change, such as would happen if production targets were reviewed; for instance, as a result of the miners productivity agreement leading to a surplus of coal. One particular route, however, is now becoming well trodden, and many will follow it in future. This is the concept of environmental or social gain as a result of opencast operations, and to the use of opencasting as a tool, not merely to produce coal, but also to achieve a substantial improvement in appearance or land use over and above what was before, absorbing all or most of the costs of that improvement into the opencast operations.

SOUTH YORKSHIRE POLICY

The value of benefits which can result from opencasting have been identified by South Yorkshire as being worthwhile in certain circumstances, and this approach has not been incorporated as policy into the County Council's Structure Plan, which is the strategic planning policy document, now submitted to the Secretary of State for the Environment for his approval.

The particularly relevant policy is as follows:

"Opencast coal working should take place only in areas which are acceptable in relation to agriculture, the environment and transport, and where there would be an overall gain to the community in terms of after-use or improvement to the environment. Extraction should be phased to cause minimum disruption to any area."

A detailed mineral subject plan is now being prepared for the County which hopefully will set out the detailed way in which this policy can be carried out, by identifying in more detail where workings which have this benefit can be found.

In the meantime there are three active sites in the County which have been identified and made operational with the agreement of the National Coal Board and the local authorities in the area. These sites illustrate the action of the policy and are the result of very detailed discussions and negotiations over a period of years.

(1) The first site is an area of about 70 ha known as the Waverley site, near Rotherham, 90% of which was badly affected by old underground coal workings, colliery tips and other dereliction. It contains up to 150,000 mT of usable coal to a depth of 110 feet, which can be removed directly by an existing rail link. It is located in one of the most derelict areas of the County, suffering from a multiplicity of environmental problems. It is one of the highest priority areas for improvement, and is also extremely accessible in relation to the motorway network.

The opencast operations are designed to remove the derelict tips and buildings from the site, to remove the subsidence risk from old shallow mine workings, and to reinstate the land to levels and a condition suitable for industrial development for which planning permission has already been obtained.

(2) A second similar area is also near to Rotherham, and also contains major derelict spoil heaps and other degraded land. This site is 33 ha containing about 360,000 mT of coal and is only marginally economic as far as the Coal Board is concerned. As with the Waverle site, the proposed after use of the site is for industry, but designed to take advantage of its direct link with an adjoining major commercial waterway which the County Council is fighting to get improved in standard in order to carry a more efficient water-borne freight system. Special compaction may be necessary on this site to reduce the period of settlement before it is suitable for development.

(3) The final site is large by British standards, consisting of about 290 ha of poor quality agricultural land with some dereliction, containing over 1 mT of usable

coal. Opencasting is likely to take five years, and an agreed land form plan has been produced to guide the contractor towards the design of a major multi-purpose recreation area. This will include a large lake suitable for sailing, rowing, and other water sports, two smaller lakes, and generous surrounding land areas, all in a rapidly developing and highly accessible part of the conurbation.

The completed park will then be taken over and managed by a consortium of local authorities of whom South Yorkshire County Council is the major partner.

CONCLUSION FOR THE FUTURE

A number of other such sites, some of which have similar potential benefits, are under investigation by the National Coal Board throughout the Country and it is obvious that this extra bonus of social or environmental gain greatly improves the acceptability of opencast sites in a difficult local situation. Presently it is obvious that this type of site will form the easiest option for the National Coal Board to follow.

We must end on a gloomy note though, by pointing out that the stock of such sites is inevitably limited. If production is to be maintained at a rate of about 20 sites per year in the country, and particularly if it is to be raised to higher levels, then the stock will run out, and attention will once more turn to those sites which give rise to environmental and other conflicts but lack the compensating advantages of environmental or social gain. After this temporary breathing space, if that is what it is, it seems inevitable that the conflict which currently is simmering not far below the surface will erupt once again.

THE BELVOIR PROSPECT: A STUDY IN MINE SITE SELECTION

Robert McComb*

In 1974, the Government ratified the National Coal Board's "Plan For Coal" which established the goal of producing 150 mT per annum salable by 1985. This output is to be partially met and sustained into the next century by the development of approximately 20 new mines. The Selby coalfield in Yorkshire is the most recent of the new generation mines working new reserves, with a designed output of 10 mT per year. The development of the Belvoir Prospect is a continuation of the resurgence of coal as a primary energy source.

THE BELVOIR PROSPECT

The Belvoir Prospect is broadly contained within the triangle formed by the major towns of Nottingham, Melton Mowbray and Grantham in a predominantly agricultural landscape intensively developed from medieval times. The marlstone escarpment of the Vale of Belvoir is the principal landscape feature running across the coalfield from northeast to southwest bisecting the area into two distinct physiographic regions. To the north of the escarpment the Vale is a low lying, open basin of sparse tree cover with mixed farming on lias clay soils. South of the escarpment, the field is an elevated disected plateau of limestone progressively overlain by boulder clay to the southwest and is generally of better agricultural quality on more free draining soils. The escarpment itself is a recognized area of high landscape value with Belvoir Castle a prominent tourist attraction.

Small villages and hamlets are the principal settlement pattern, fairly concentrated at regular intervals on the Vale and becoming more sparse on the southeast upland. Population density is comparatively low at 1.8 persons/ha and communications remain almost exclusively "C" class roads reflecting the rural nature of the area.

Exploration has defined an area of approximately 234 sq km (90 sq miles) underlain by up to five workable seams with recoverable reserves around 510 mT. Cover rocks to the coal measures dip at about 1 in 60 to the east-southeast varying in thickness from 320 m to 650 m from west to east with several Permo-Triassic aquifers within the covering strata. The proximity of the Bunter Sandstone aquifer to the reserves defines the extractable limits of the seams to the south. Further field boundaries are determined by seam splitting and deterioration to the west, north and northeast, and by faulting in the east. Coal quality is similar to that generally worked in the Midlands and is suitable and earmarked for power station consumption.

*Owen Luder Partnership, London, England.

OVERALL MINING STRATEGY

On the basis of an optimum design life of a modern mine of between fifty and one hundred years, the annual salable output from the field would be between 5 and 10 mT/yr. Operational restraints (manpower, housing, rail capacity etc.) indicate a realistic output of about 7 mT with a field life of about 75 years. This would entail the extraction of approximately 10 mT of run of mine at a coal dirt ratio which varies from 2:1 to 4:1.

Modern mining and capital investment dictate the minimum size of any new mine working this type of coal to be at least 2 mT per year salable. Mining is ideally carried out from the center of gravity of the area of coal being worked with underground travel distances to the remote faces acceptable for productivity levels and proper ventilation. That traveling distances of 6.5 km should not be exceeded if face equipment is to operate for at least 5.5 hours per shift. The field would thus require at least three access points at centroids for men, materials and ventilation to mine the complete reserve.

Early investigation of the mining, operational and engineering parameters, concluded that three mineral outlets in conjunction with three access points within the field offered the greatest flexibility in surface location and allowed exploitation of the reserves with minimum number of shafts and surface sites. The geologic and geographic form of the field and operational requirements determined the most feasible solution to be a 3 mT mine in the central portion of the field working all five available seams with a 2 mT mine in the east and south of the field each working two seams.

SURFACE REQUIREMENTS

There are three basic elements of the mining system:

(1) The mine building complex - including at least two tower mounted winders, ventilation fan, administration building/baths, workshops/stores, stockyard, coal preparation plant, loading bunder and outstocking facilities.
(2) Communications system - including rail network for coal distribution, road access for men/materials, power and water supply.
(3) Dirt disposal facilities - the disposal of dirt from the field has been examined and planned in the context of providing for fifty years output in a phased restoration to agriculture.

A total mine building complex requires an area between 30-40 ha depending on output and site configuration. Dirt disposal averages approximately 220,000 mT/ha and the annual production rate is 2.8 mT for the whole field.

PLANNING/ENVIRONMENT STUDY SEQUENCE

Following the definition of overall mining strategy, a sieve analysis technique was employed to define zones of relative compatibility with surface mine site development and dirt disposal. Sieve maps were compiled for elements under three categories of operational factors, terrestrial factors and activity/land use factors. Each individual sieve map was compiled on a 25 ha (¼ sq km) grid square base for 600 sq km including the coalfield. The basic mapped data was as follows:

Operational Factors

(1) Road accessibility
(2) Rail accessibility
(3) Services

Terrestrial Factors

(1) Slope
(2) Vegetation and wildlife habitat
(3) High agricultural land potential
(4) Low land capability

Activity/Land Use Factors

(1) Proximity to settlement (buildings)
(2) Proximity to settlement (dirt)
(3) Landscape value
(4) Statutory designations

    Superimposition of the sieve factors allowed the identification of areas which fulfilled all or most of the criteria of basic compatibility (Fig. 1). Those large enough to accommodate mine and dirt construction were reconciled with the "ideal" mining location together with site investigation to confirm those which could realistically be considered further to achieve the overall strategy objective.

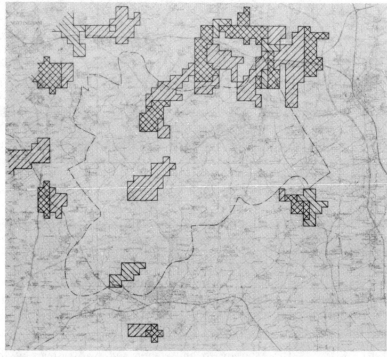

Fig. 1   SITE SUITABILITY SUMMARY - BUILDINGS

The sieve process allowed the identification of six feasible areas within or adjacent to the Belvoir coalfield. These were examined in detail to define the optimum strategy involving one site from each portion of the field - south, central and east.

Sieve Locations (Fig. 2)

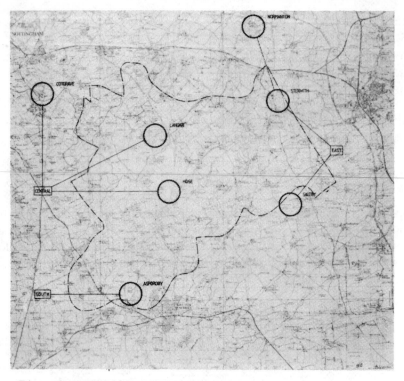

Fig. 2   SURFACE SITE LOCATIONS

South   -   Asfordby Hill, an area adjacent to the British Steel Corporation Holwell Iron Works

Central -   Hose, a wholly agricultural area at the foot of the Belvoir escarpment
         -   Langar, an abandoned World War II bomber airfield lying centrally in the Vale of Belvoir
         -   Cotgrave, an existing colliery some 3 km northwest of the edge of the field

East   -   Stenwith-Normanton, a split site with mine buildings at Stenwith and ROM conveyed to Normanton airfield
         -   Saltby, an area adjacent to an abandoned World War II airfield

Having selected a number of potential sites, the surface requirements at each site were defined, and outline design schemes prepared for each. This allowed a comparison of sites in relative capital cost terms and in relative impact. The latter was based on the four impact indicators being assessed below.

Visual   - The exposure to built fabric and road systems of the building elements up to an 8 km radius from the site

Noise   - Noise projections relative to resident population for the construction and production periods

Landscape Loss   - The perceptual reduction of landscape value as a result of mine development

Agricultural Loss - An assessment of the capital loss in agricultural production for each site

From the six potential sites, nine development options were generated, six within the central area of the field as follows:

	Option	Capital Cost Factor
South	(1) Asfordby	1.02
Central	(2) Hose total mine	1.07
	(3) Langar total mine	1.00
	(4) Langar total mine/Hose satellite mine	1.37
	(5) Langar mineral outlet/Hose service mine	1.37
	(6) Hose total mine/overland conveyor to Langar (dirt)	1.27
	(7) Cotgrave mineral outlet/Hose service	1.14
East	(8) Saltby total mine	1.00
	(9) Stenwith-Normanton	1.26

The impacts and cost factors are summarized below by expressing the relative score for each factor as Above Average (+), Average (0), Below Average (-). Summarizing the various factors in this manner, assumes they are of equal weight and importance which is clearly not the case. In the absence of an acceptable weighting scale, the table can be used as an indicator.

Factor	Option								
	1	2	3	4	5	6	7	8	9
Visual	-	+	+	0	0	0	-	+	0
Noise	-	-	0	0	0	0	+	0	+
Agricultural loss	0	-	+	+	+	+	-	+	-
Landscape loss	+	+	+	-	-	0	0	0	-
Cost	0	+	+	-	-	0	0	+	-
Summary (+)	1	3	4	1	1	1	1	3	1
(0)	2	0	1	2	2	4	2	2	1
(-)	2	2	0	2	2	0	2	0	3

Although relative impact is assessed among all nine options, the summary for individual options can only be compared with those in the same zone (i.e. South, Central, East) as they are not interchangeable in the context of an overall mining strategy.

On the basis of the assessment of site options, Saltby (8) appeared to have significant surface advantage over the Stenwith-Normanton (9) option in the east; the latter was not considered further.

COMPARISON OF ALTERNATIVE STRATEGIES

Having assessed individual sites, the objective of defining the optimum three-site strategy for the working of the field remained. The southern site option was determined by the sieve as being the only one available which fulfilled site selection criteria. The eastern option, Saltby (8), was assessed as being significantly less intrusive then Stenwith-Normanton. Therefore, strategy permutations could only be generated by the central options. No site in any part of the field was in the "ideal" mining location (Fig. 3).

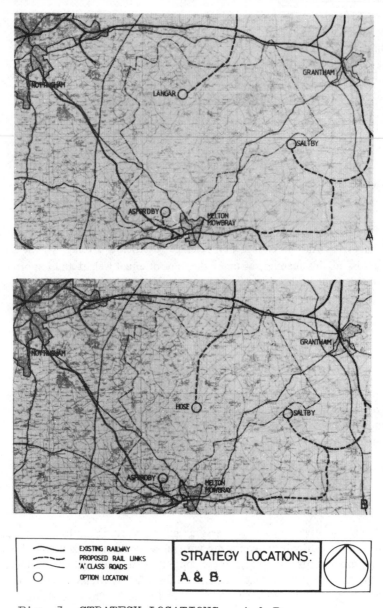

Fig. 3   STRATEGY LOCATIONS − A & B

Strategy	South Mine	Central Mine	East Mine
A	Asfordby	Langar total mine	Saltby
B	Asfordby	Hose total mine	Saltby
C	Asfordby	Hose total mine/conveyor overland to Langar	Saltby
D	Asfordby	Langar mineral outlet/Hose service	Saltby
E	Asfordby	Langar total mine/Hose satellite service	Saltby
F	Asfordby	Cotgrave mineral outlet/Hose service	Saltby

A method was adopted for arithmetically summing the individual option impacts to assess the total strategy impact. In addition, two further impact factors, road capacity/usage limitation and traffic intrusion, were introduced at this stage as they did not apply to the individual site options on their own. The impact and cost factors are summarized below:

Factor	Strategy					
	A	B	C	D	E	F
Visual	+	+	0	0	0	-
Noise	0	-	0	0	0	+
Agricultural loss	+	-	+	+	+	-
Landscape loss	+	+	0	-	-	0
Road capacity	+	0	0	0	-	-
Traffic intrusion	-	+	+	+	-	+
Cost	+	+	0	-	-	0
Summary (+)	5	4	2	2	1	2
(0)	1	1	5	3	2	2
(-)	1	2	0	2	4	3

A total mine at Asfordby-Langar-Saltby was the preferred strategy solution in surface terms, with Asfordby-Hose-Saltby the second preference. However, the underground consultants, Thyssens (Great Britain) Limited determined that Langar as a total mine could only function for approximately 10 years before an additional service mine would be necessary to extract the full five seams occurring in the richest portion of the field. Strategy A would then become similar to Strategy E, albeit with a significant time delay. On the basis of this underground factor, Strategy B became the preferred solution in both surface and underground terms and was subsequently recommended to the National Coal Board. (Fig. 4).

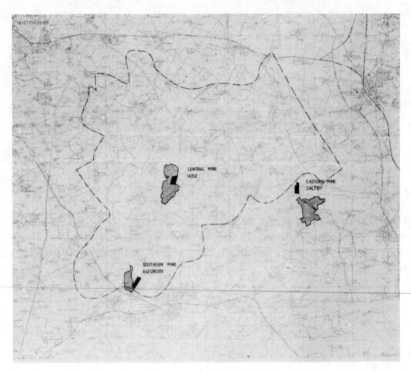

Fig. 4   SELECTED STRATEGY LOCATIONS

COAL DEVELOPMENT GUIDELINES IN BRITISH COLUMBIA

Jon O'Riordan*

INTRODUCTION

The rise in the market price of metallurgical coal has greatly increased the tempo and extent of exploration for coal resources in the Province of British Columbia. This increased activity, especially where several coal developments are being actively explored in the same geographic region, compelled the Provincial Government to review its approval process for the development of new mines to ensure orderly planning so that environmental resources could be protected at reasonable cost and public services required to support the mines could be provided when needed.

In March 1976, the Provincial Government announced this new policy for evaluating the environmental, social and economic impacts of coal developments in the Province. *The Guidelines for Coal Development* set out a systematic process which both guides coal developer in the preparation of environmental and community plans for their proposed mines and coordinate reviews of these plans by appropriate Government departments and public interest groups.

The Guidelines are administered by the Environment and Land Use Committee, a Cabinet Committee of the Provincial Government. This committee is composed of nine ministries responsible for both resource development and conservation as well as for providing major public facilities such as highways, settlements and public health services. In essence, the committee is responsible for seeking a balance, at the political level, between resource development and the preservation of environmental quality. In addition, individual Ministers on the committee are responsible for approving the several regulatory licenses and permits that must be obtained by coal developers before a mine can go into production. Thus, the Committee of Ministers is able to approve new coal developments in principle before specific permits need be approved by individual Ministers. The Guidelines therefore provide procedural direction for environmental impact assessment and management studies which lead directly to approval of all regulatory licenses required under Provincial Statutes.

The purpose of this paper is to describe this process and to assess its strengths and weaknesses. Some adjustments to the policy now being considered by the Government to improve the process are also discussed.

COAL GUIDELINES PROCESS

The four-stage assessment process is outlined on Fig. 1. The process moves system-

*Environment and Land Use Committee, Secretariat, Parliament Building, Victoria, B.C., Columbia V84 1X4, Canada.

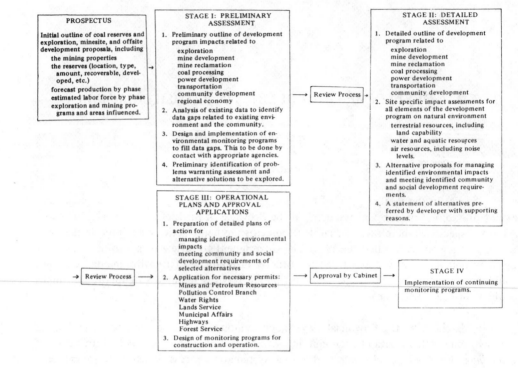

Fig. 1. Coal development assessment procedure

atically from a general overview of the project to impact assessment and finally design of specific plans to manage these impacts on both the natural and human environment. At all stages of the process, the total impacts of the mine development are considered - pit design, waste dumps, coal processing, transportation, new or expanded communities, shipping terminals, etc.

The overall process is coordinated by a Coal Guidelines Steering Committee comprised of senior government officials from a number of ministries. This committee serves as a direct contact with coal companies and their consultants regarding interpretation of procedures and provides advice for undertaking the necessary studies. It also coordinates government reviews of staged impact reports.

In addition, three technical subcommittees have been formed to advise the Coal Guidelines Steering Committee: the Minesite Advisory Committee, the Townsite and Community Development Committee, and the Economic Evaluation Committee. As many of the representatives on these subcommittees are government officials who provide technical and policy advice to senior officials responsible for approving various permits and licenses, their involvement expedites the review of major project proposals.

PROSPECTUS

The assessment process begins with a Prospectus which contains a general outline of the proposed mining and related transportation and community developments. This Prospectus is filed only after the exploration program has indicated that potential for an economic mine exists. Management of the land use, reclamation and economic impacts of exploration programs is undertaken through a separate program administered by the Provincial Ministry of Mines and Petroleum Resources. Liaison between the exploration and mine development planning is maintained through the Coal Guidelines Steering Committee.

The purpose of the Prospectus is to inform government agencies and the general public that a new mine is being considered, to notify agencies with resource inventory data to make this information available to developers and to initiate direct discussions between the developer and the Coal Guidelines Steering Committee on the scope of studies required under Stage I. The Prospectus is a relatively short document containing a description of the project, a preliminary schedule for the project planning phase, a first estimate of coal output and construction and minesite labor force. Developers are encouraged to file this document as early as possible to give government agencies maximum lead time in compiling existing data sources and identifying major data gaps.

PRELIMINARY ASSESSMENT - STAGE I

The next stage in the Guidelines process is the completion of a Stage I or Preliminary Assessment report. This report contains a more detailed description of the total project including schedules for construction, operation and termination phases. It also describes the existing natural, social and economic conditions in the zone of influence and details the monitoring program to fill major data gaps that should already be in place as a result of a review of the Prospectus. Responsibility for on-site monitoring generally lies with the coal developer, though the Government may initiate data collection programs which have regional significance.

However, the main purpose of the Stage I report is to document the environmental and social problems that are likely to result from the project and indicate design measures required for their resolution. While the solutions to these problems are not expected until Stage II (detailed assessment) is completed, it is important that a *process* for tackling these problems systematically is established in Stage I. This requires the engineering design and environmental teams employed by the developer to collaborate in minesite and transportation route design early in the planning process. Representatives of government regulatory agencies begin to participate in this problem solving process through their review of the Stage I report.

The Stage I report should not be a large document containing mounds of inventory data. Ideally, it should be a relatively small report which references existing data and information in technical appendices, but which concentrates on developing the process to be undertaken by the project design team to resolve major environmental and community impacts. Alternative approaches for managing impacts should be identified when real, practical opportunities exist. Ongoing data gathering or monitoring programs should be explicitly tailored to fill environmental baseline data gaps or to evaluate specific design alternatives for mitigating environmental impacts.

A draft of the Stage I report is reviewed initially by the Coal Guidelines Steering Committee to check for any major information gaps or misinterpretations of government policy or data which could delay its final acceptance by the government agencies. Where such problems occur, the draft is revised by the developer or an addendum is attached. This review takes about two weeks to complete, but can pay-off through saving time during the full review by government agencies and public.

Following this general review, the three subcommittees have enough information to initiate a detailed discussion with the developer on the Stage II process. As a result of this review, the developers will be able to direct their detailed analyses to resolving major environmental and community problems without expending any more energy on problems that are already basically resolved during Stage I. The developers can also proceed with some confidence that they are on the right track and there will be a more likely pay-off to further environmental design studies. Where potential environmental problems exist and no solutions are apparent at an acceptable economic cost to the developer, the Coal Guidelines Steering Committee can contact the Environment and Land Use Committees for a political decision on whether or not these problems outweigh the economic benefits of the coal development.

Thus the Stage I report acts as a traffic light to both developer and government; green, red or even amber lights (proceed with caution) are all possible, but at least the signal is understood by both parties before major investment decisions are taken to complete Stage II.

DETAILED ASSESSMENT - STAGE II

Terms of reference for Stage II studies are prepared by the developer following discussions with the three subcommittees and approved by the Steering Committee. The intent of these studies is to prepare detailed plans for all components of the project - mine-site, transportation routes, coal preparation plants, community servicing and infrastructure and any shipping facilities. Because details of plans change as new information is available from the engineering feasibility studies and economic analyses, the subcommittees meet with the developer and consultants from time to time during the preparation of Stage II to review changes and progress towards solution of design problems. To avoid expense and time delays due to report preparation, emphasis is placed on simple design drawings and typed manuscripts during these iterations. Where problems cannot be resolved at acceptable economic cost to the developer, they are brought before the Steering Committee for decision. If problems cannot be resolved at this level, their full impolications are documented in the Stage II report and passed on to the Environment and Land Use Committee for final decision.

In theory, each subcommittee should be prepared to approve the plans for each component of the project in principle before the complete plan is formally documented in the Stage II report. As noted above, any conflicts in design with resource interests are noted for higher level decisions. This plan should therefore set out the most up-to-date designs for minesite, townsite and transportation facilities plus all acceptable mitigatory measures to reduce environmental and community impacts. Responsibility for managing these impacts, both on the part of the developer and the government should be clearly documented.

To assist the government in determining its responsibilities for paying for these management measures, especially costs of transportation, community infrastructure, and services and labor training programs, the government completes an economic analysis of the project from the public viewpoint. This analysis is undertaken by the Economic Evaluation Subcommittee from data supplied by the developer. Because much of these data are highly confidential to the developer, the requests for data and level of detail in the economic analysis are tailored directly to the magnitude of anticipated public invest-ments, cost-sharing responsibilities of government and the nature of environmental impacts detailed in Stage II. For projects with relatively small impacts on public sector investment or on the environment, only basic economic data are requested; for projects which required large amounts of public financing either as a loan or as agreed in a cost-sharing formula, the entire feasibility study prepared by the developer can be requested. Regardless of the level of this economic evaluation, it is important to note that it cannot be completed until all the design, mitigation and (if appropriate) compensation plans are completed in Stage II, since these will all affect the economics of the final project plan.

As it is considered a confidential document, the economic analysis is reviewed only by the Steering Committee and the Environment and Land Use Committee. The remainder of the Stage II report is reviewed by the full array of government agencies and by public interest groups and appropriate municipal and regional government officials. Comments are again integrated by the Steering Committee and are passed on to the Environment and Land Use Committee with recommendations for approval or final decision on any unresolved design problem. Acceptance of Stage II by the E.L.U.C. represents approval in principle for the environmental, land use and community components of the project plans. However, before the project can proceed, the developer must obtain various licenses and permits as required by various Provincial Statutes.

APPROVAL OF PERMITS - STAGE III

In British Columbia, a variety of permits are necessary before a mine can go into production. These include a detailed reclamation plan for the minesite and approach roads, pollution control permits, water licenses, land use permits for use of Crown (i.e. public) lands; timber licenses, removal of lands from the Agricultural Land Reserve (if necessary) as well as detailed operating plans required for employee safety. The purpose of Stage III is to coordinate their approval so that no single permit can cause unreasonable delays in project development, yet there is additional time to prepare plans in sufficient detail to meet regulatory requirements. As all substantive issues will have been resolved in Stage II either at the technical or political level, only technical details need be completed in Stage III.

Because permit applications require some lead-time to process even with the planning studies undertaken under the Coal Guidelines, developers are encouraged to *apply* for the necessary permits after Stage I is completed. However, they are not formally *approved* until after Stage II has been accepted. In this way, not only are permit approvals coordinated, but they can all be reviewed in the broader context of the complete project, rather than as individual applications for parts of the project. Separation of permit approvals has led to poor decisions in the past. Although Stage III has not yet been completed under the Coal Development Guidelines, it is believed that final permit and license approvals will be greatly expedited as a result of the planning process that precedes such decisions.

PROJECT IMPLEMENTATION - STAGE IV

Several government agencies have specific and continuing responsibilities to ensure that design features and monitoring programs set out as conditions to various licenses are in fact carried out by the developer. Most intensive analyses are anticipated to occur during the development phase; once operational, normal regulatory functions relating to safety, reclamation, etc. will be implemented.

REVIEW OF GUIDELINES PROCESS

Although the new policy has only been underway for two years, at present some twelve different developers have submitted one or more reports according to the planning process and two developers have had their Stage II reports accepted by the Steering Committee. Thus, the Steering Committee has gained enough experience to make some preliminary comments about the strengths and weaknesses of the policy.

The main advantages lie in its flexibility and the close relationship between the planning stages and the preparation of project feasibility reports for corporate evaluation. Because each coal developer faces a different set of environmental and/or social/community conditions, the planning process must be custom-made for each developer. There is no exhaustive checklist of information that the developer must provide regardless of its relevancy to the specific project. The intent of the Guidelines and the two-stage reporting procedure is to address the major problems early and devote most resources to their solution, rather than on a broader environmental front which can lead to a misallocation of time and money. In addition, the Stage I and II reporting times should be scheduled to coincide approximately to the completion of preliminary and detailed engineering/economic feasibility studies prepared by developers for corporate purposes. The third advantage is the coordination of regulatory permit approvals though this has yet to be verified in British Columbia as no developer has completed Stage III.

There remain a number of problems, many of which are logistical. Initially, Stage I and II reports have tended to be filled with inventory data and are rather weak in defining a systematic process for identifying and resolving specific environmental, and community servicing problems. There is greater need for project engineers and their environmental consultants to work together at Stage I as well as in Stage II. In addition, due to changes in market conditions, some developments have had to make significant changes in one or more of their minesite, townsite and transportation plans between Stage I and Stage II. These changes often increase environmental or community impacts, because revised feasibility studies indicate the need to reduce expenditures on mitigation measures. Governmental reviews are still cumbersome and prolonged which can delay planning of the next stage in the process. However, some of these problems are being reduced through more explicit instructions to developers during the preparation of staged reports and better use of the three advisory subcommittees.

Two more substantial problems remain. The first is to develop a more rational approach to managing impacts on fish and wildlife resources; the second is to improve the methods for public consultation.

Most of British Columbia's reserves of metallurgical coal lie in some of the most productive big game wildlife areas not only in British Columbia but in Canada. In the Kootenay area in Southeastern British Columbia, ninety percent of the land considered to be critical winter habitat for wildlife (deer, elk, moose, caribou, mountain goats and mountain sheep) is currently held under coal licenses (permitting exploration only). In addition, several important fishery streams also drain the Province's coal bearing regions. Despite attempts to mitigate impacts on these important fish and wildlife resources, there has been a decrease in productive habitats due to the developments already under way.

Viewed as individual projects, the value of coal production will always outweigh the loss to this renewable resource at any particular site and projects are approved over the objections of government agencies responsible for managing fish and wildlife resources. Viewed in a regional context, this approach could lead to major resource management problems, for as critical habitat for supporting animal populations is decreased, the total human population and access in the area is increased due to coal development leading to an expansion in demand for recreational hunting.

Solutions to this problem require a regional rather than a site-specific approach especially when a number of different coal developments are being planned. The Coal Guidelines at present only allow project-specific assessments; these must be supplemented by regional studies. The government is now initiating such a study, with the objective of developing a strategic plan for fish and wildlife management in the S.E. Kootenays. Such a plan will assess the supply and demand for big-game species assuming various schedules for coal production, including the restoration of habitats through reclamation. With this information it will develop a management strategy for preserving the total productive capacity of the area through improvements to the carrying capacities of some habitats together with more specific hunting regulations and species management. As such a plan will likely increase costs of managing wildlife resources, cost-sharing responsibilities between industry and government will have to be determined.

While the wildlife resources could likely be maintained under a properly managed program of compensation and mitigation, the fisheries resource is more sensitive to impacts of coal development and enhancement techniques for the species found in the coal bearing regions are not well developed. At present, the only viable approach is maintenance of existing aquatic habitats and water quality which can require expensive designs of stabilization ponds and diversion channels. Once this study is complete, the government may have to make policy decisions on the level of fisheries management that is acceptable given the potential for coal development in the region.

The techniques and timing of public consultation with regard to project development proposals must also be improved in British Columbia. Release of Stage I studies to public interest groups must be undertaken with caution, as some people who want to see detailed impact management plans criticize these preliminary assessments as being inadequate. On the other hand, to delay public input until Stage II or even Stage III also creates problems, as other people desire an opportunity for input before project design is finalized. Clearly, techniques must be developed to clarify the objectives of each Stage and to identify the various levels of interest in the public early so that the public groups and individuals can provide input at appropriate stages in the planning process. These techniques can best be identified through reviewing critically experience to date both in British Columbia and elsewhere in Canada and other countries, where similar problems arise.

SUMMARY AND CONCLUSIONS

This paper has reviewed the four-stage planning process initiated by the Province of British Columbia for identifying and managing environmental, social and economic impacts associated with major coal developments in the Province. Based on a couple of years experience, the procedures appear to be sound and are accepted by most developers as a logical and rational approach to project planning. Implementation of the Guidelines policy is still cumbersome though improvements can be anticipated in preparing the planning reports and expediting government reviews, based on experience gained over the past two years. More attention will have to be given to resolving conflicts with valuable fish and wildlife resources in the major coal producing regions of the Province, and a regional approach to this problem is outlined in the paper. In addition, techniques for ensuring public consultation and response during the planning phase should also be reviewed so that this important source of information can be utilized to its best advantage.

REFERENCE

Environment and Land Use Committee. 1976. Guidelines for Coal Development, March
    1976.   Environment and Land Use Committee Secretariat, Parliament Buildings,
    Victoria, B.C., 33 p.

ENFORCEMENT OF P.L. 95-87 (THE SURFACE MINING CONTROL AND RECLAMATION ACT OF 1977) WHO DOES WHAT? AND WHEN? AND WHERE?[†]

*John W. Dwyer**

INTRODUCTION

"The bite of law is in enforcement."[1]

Many of the papers prepared for this Congress address both national and international problems associated with surface coal mining reclamation. Nobody has all the answers, but it is generally agreed that effective reclamation begins with the initial planning and applications submitted to the appropriate federal or state authority. Certain procedures and activities must then be carried out throughout the mining process if reclamation is to succeed.

It was with this in mind (reclamation begins at the initial stages and continues until bond is released) that Congress enacted the Surface Mining Control and Reclamation Act of 1977.[2] In its "purposes" section, Congress stated:

"It is the purpose of this Act to

. . . . (d) assure that surface mining operations are so conducted as to protect the environment;

. . . . (e) assure that adequate procedures are undertaken to reclaim surface areas as contemporaneously as possible with the surface coal mining operations. . . ."[3]

However, no matter how laudatory the intent of Congress may be, no matter how diligent Congress may have been in specifying reclamation procedures to be followed throughout the mining process (assuming these procedures are effective), it is unlikely that reclamation will occur nationwide if there is little or no enforcement of the federal and

---

[†]Remarks and conclusions contained herein are solely the personal opinion of the author and should not be construed in any way to represent the official views of either the North Dakota Public Service Commission or the North Dakota Attorney General's Office.

*North Dakota Public Service Commission and Atkinson and Dwyer, P.O. Box 1176, Bismarck, ND 58501.

[1] Frankfurter, J., Fisher v. United States, 328 U.S. 463, 484 (1946).

[2] Pub. L. No. 95-87 (August 3, 1977), 30 USC 1201, et. seq. See Appendix A which is an outline in flow chart form of the enforcement provisions of the federal Surface Mining Act.

[3] Sections 102(d) and (e) of Pub. L. No. 95-87, (August 3, 1977), 30 USC 1202(d) and (e).

215

state reclamation laws and regulations.[4] Of course, there may be many statutory and regulatory provisions where enforcement thereof will not result in effective reclamation, although hopefully, existing laws reflect the necessary standards to insure reclamation.

In my view, the scientific community has immense responsibilities to continually point out to both federal and state lawmakers what legislative changes are necessary to make reclamation programs more responsive to the goals of adequate reclamation. You as scientists have the knowledge, which must be communicated. I'm sure the exchange of information at this Congress will be of assistance in attaining that goal. In turn, history has demonstrated that reclamation principles developed by scientists and other technicians only have an impact if they are utilized and contained in existing law.

But just to be a part of the law is not enough either. Reclamation standards must then be *enforced* by those involved in the administration of the respective federal and state reclamation programs.

What then is enforcement?

Enforcement as defined in Black's means those actions necessary "to cause to take effect, to put into execution. . . ."[5]

For this presentation, it is my intent, in outline form[6], to first describe the important role that scientists, or technical staff, play in enforcement, and then discuss specific enforcement actions provided for under the federal Surface Mining Act. Enforcement for purposes of this discussion includes (1) inspections; (2) enforcement actions resulting from inspections such as cessation orders, notices of violation, and orders to suspend or revoke permits; (3) penalties; and (4) statutory administrative hearing procedures and judicial review thereof.

Enforcement for purposes of this discussion will *not* include (1) rulemaking process procedures; (2) procedures to be followed before the Office of Hearings and Appeals or the Board of Surface Mining and Reclamation Appeals[7]; (3) specific matters in litigation relating to the federal Act; (4) appellate judicial procedures; or (5) various state administrative and judicial procedures.

In concluding, I will make some personal predictions concerning enforcement under the federal Act.

I.   ROLE OF SCIENTISTS AND TECHNICAL STAFF IN ENFORCEMENT FROM AGENCY PERSPECTIVE.

A. INSPECTIONS AND GATHERING EVIDENCE.

B. DETERMINING WHETHER A CESSATION ORDER SHOULD ISSUE.

[4] The U.S. Soil Conservation Service indicates that there are nearly 622,000 acres of land in the United States where no reclamation is required under existing law. House Report No. 95-218, 95th Congress, 1st Session, page 76. Witness also the enactment of Title IV of the federal surface mining Act which is designed to reclaim these abandoned surface-mined lands, which is found at 30 USC 1231, et. seq.

[5] Black's Law Dictionary (Revised Fourth Edition), page 621.

[6] The complexity of the federal Act and the limitation of six pages for this paper necessitates the outline format.

[7] Proposed regulations governing procedures to be followed for notice of violations, cessation orders, and orders to suspend or revoke permits, before the Office of Hearings and Appeals (administrative law judges) or the Board of Surface Mining and Reclamation Appeals were published April 13, 1978. Final regulations have not been published as of June 1, 1978. See 43 Fed. Reg. 15441, et. seq., (April 13, 1978).

C. IMPOSING WORKABLE ALTERNATIVES TO INSURE EFFECTIVE RECLAMATION:

   1. Remedial Measures Included in Cessation Orders;
   2. Remedial Measures Included in Notices of Violation; and
   3. Remedial Measures Included in Orders to Suspend or Revoke Permits.

D. ASSISTING IN ASSESSING CIVIL PENALTIES BY UNDERSTANDING RESPONDENT'S (INDUSTRY'S) OPERATIONS, ECONOMIC SITUATION, AND COSTS ASSOCIATED WITH REMEDIAL MEASURES.

E. ANALYSIS AND EVALUATION OF EVIDENCE IN ORDER TO ASSIST NON-TECHNICAL ATTORNEY IN MAKING DETERMINATION OF STRATEGY FOR ADMINISTRATIVE AND JUDICIAL PROCEEDINGS.

F. AVOIDING LEGAL AND EVIDENTIARY PITFALLS:

   1. Improper Right of Entry;
   2. Lack of Representative Sampling; and
   3. Break in Chain of Custody.

G. PROVIDING BETTER INFORMATION FOR INFORMED AGENCY DECISION MAKING.

II. INSPECTIONS.

   A. WHO?[8]

      1. Federal—OSM; or
      2. State—State Regulatory Authority.

   B. JURISDICTION.[9]

      1. Definition of Surface Coal Mining and Reclamation Operation.
      2. Lands:

         a. Federal government—federal, state, and private;
         b. State government—state and private; federal *if* cooperative agreement in in effect;
         c. Federal role limited after approval of state programs.

   C. WHEN?

      1. *Initial Regulatory Program.*[10]

         a. Federal:

            —at least one inspection for *every* site each six months; or
            —upon receipt of two consecutive state inspections indicating violations; or
            —citizen complaint.

---

[8] 502(e), 517(c) and 701(22) of Pub. L. No. 95-87 (August 3, 1977), 30 USC 1252(e), 30 USC 1267(c), and 30 USC 1291(22) respectively.

[9] 701(27) and (28) of Pub. L. No. 95-87 (August 3, 1977), 30 USC 1291(27) and (28).

[10] Section 502(e)(1) and (2) of Pub. L. No. 95-87 (August 3, 1977), 30 USC 1252(e)(1) and (e)(2).

b.   State:

—according to state law.

2.   *Federal or State Program*[11]

a.   Federal *or* state inspections under federal and state programs respectively are to be made:

—as necessary;
—not less than one partial inspection per month;
—not less than one complete inspection per calendar quarter; and
—on an irregular basis and without notice.

b.   If state program, federal inspections to be conducted as necessary to evaluate administration of state program.

D.   WHERE?

1.   At the Mine Site.

a.   Right of entry and records.

—query, do surface mining inspections violate the Fourth Amendment?
—*Marshall, et al. v. Barlow's Inc.* (OSHA inspectors need to obtain search warrant).[12]

b.   Performance measured against reclamation plan and permit application.

2.   Non-Mine Site Inspections:

a.   Air photographs; and
b.   Monitoring and sampling data submitted by permittee.

III.   ENFORCEMENT ACTIONS RESULTING FROM INSPECTION. INITIAL ACTION TAKEN DEPENDS ON *FINDING* MADE BY INSPECTOR OR AGENCY.

A.   IF *FINDING* THAT VIOLATION CREATES AND *IMMINENT DANGER TO THE HEALTH OR SAFETY OF THE PUBLIC, OR* IS CAUSING, *OR* CAN REASONABLY BE EXPECTED TO CAUSE SIGNIFICANT IMMINENT ENVIRONMENTAL HARM TO LAND, AIR, OR WATER RESOURCES, A *CESSATION ORDER* MUST IMMEDIATELY ISSUE.[13]

1.   What is a Cessation Order?
2.   Imminent Danger Means:[14]

a.   Violation can reasonably be expected to cause substantial physical harm to persons *outside* the permit area before abatement; and
b.   Reasonable expectation a rational person would not subject himself to the condition of peril.

[11] Section 517(c) of Pub. L. No. 95-87 (August 3, 1977), 30 USC 1267(c).

[12] Civil No. 76-1143, Argued Before Supreme Court of the United States, January 9, 1978; Decided May 23, 1978. Warrantless searches under MESA were upheld in Youghiongheny & Ohio Coal Co. v. Morton, 364 F. Supp. 45 (S.D.Ohio, 1973). See also See v. City of Seattle, 387 U.S. 541 (1967); Colonnade Catering Corp. v. U.S., 397 U.S. 72 (1970); U.S. 72 (1970); U.S. v. Biswell, 406 U.S. 311 (1972); Air Pollution Variance Bd. of Colorado v. Western Alfalfa Corp., 416 U.S. 861 (1974).

[13] Section 521(a)(2) of Pub. L. No. 95-87 (August 3, 1977), 30 USC 1271(a)(2).

[14] Section 701(8) of Pub. L. No. 95-87 (August 3, 1977), 30 USC 1291(8).

3. Significant Imminent Environmental Harm is not Defined in Public Law 95-87.

    a. Federal regulations define this term as:[15]

      —significant means appreciable harm;

      —imminent means a situation which cannot be abated within a reasonable time; and

      —environmental harm means any adverse impact on the environment, including but not limited to plant and animal life.

4. Remedial Measures to Abate Violation Included in Cessation Order.

B. IF *FINDING* IS *NOT* ONE OF IMMINENT DANGER OR SIGNIFICANT ENVIRONMENTAL HARM A *NOTICE OF VIOLATION* IS TO ISSUE.[16]

1. Abatement Must be Performed within 90 Days or Less (Role of Scientists Important Here).
2. If Abatement has not Occurred within 90 Days, a *Cessation Order* must Issue with Necessary Remedial Measures.

C. IF *FINDING* IS THAT PATTERN OF VIOLATIONS EXIST, AND SUCH VIOLATIONS ARE CAUSED BY UNWARRANTED FAILURE OR WILL-FULLY BY PERMITTEE, AN *ORDER TO SHOW CAUSE* TO SUSPEND OR REVOKE THE PERMIT MUST ISSUE.[17]

1. Unwarranted Failure Means Simple Negligence.[18]
2. Violation can Involve Permit, Law, or Regulation Violation.
3. Pattern of Violations Established by Following Factors:[19]

    a. Number of violations detected by two or more federal inspections; and
    b. Extent to which violations were isolated departures from the federal Act.

4. Pattern of Violation Deemed to Exist if during any Three or More Federal Inspections within any 12 Month Period, Violations of Same or Related Requirements are Detected. Order to Show Cause Must Issue.
5. Remedial Measures are to be Included in any Order to Show Cause Issued.

D. AFTER APPROVAL OF THE STATE PROGRAM, FEDERAL ENFORCEMENT IS LIMITED TO:

1. Situations Involving Cessation Orders where there is Imminent Danger or Significant Environmental Harm; or
2. Failure of State to Enforce Its State Program.[20]

---

[15] 30 CFR 700.5 (1977).

[16] Section 521(a)(3) of Pub. L. No. 95-87 (August 3, 1977), 30 USC 1271(a)(3).

[17] Section 521(a)(4) of Pub. L. No. 95-87 (August 3, 1977), 30 USC 1271(a)(4).

[18] Section 701(29) of Pub. L. No. 95-87 (August 3, 1977), 30 USC 1291.

[19] 30 CFR 722.16(c)(2) (1977).

[20] Section 504(b); 521(a)(1); and 521(b) of Pub. L. No. 95-87 (August 3, 1977), 30 USC 1254(b), 30 USC 1271(a)(1), and 30 USC 1271(b) respectively.

IV. PENALTIES

    A. Amounts.

        1. Civil Penalties:

            a. Maximum of $5,000 for each violation, with each day of a continuing violation allowed to be a separate violation;[21]

            b. In addition to the maximum of $5,000, not less than $750 shall be assessed for failure to abate a violation within the prescribed time period for abatement;[22]

            c. Civil penalties imposed by detailed point system based on:[23]

                —permittee's history of previous violations;
                —seriousness of violation;
                —irreparable harm to environment;
                —hazard to health or safety of public;
                —whether permittee was negligent; and
                —demonstrated good faith of permittee.

        2. Criminal Penalties for Willful Violations of Permit Conditions.[24]

            a. Maximum fine of $10,000 or by imprisonment for not more than one year, or both;

            b. Director, officer, or agent of corporate permittee can also be subject to civil penalty of $5,000 and criminal penalty of $10,000; and

            c. For false statement or representation, criminal penalty is also not more than $10,000, one year's imprisonment, or both.

    B. PENALTY ASSESSMENT PROCEDURES FOR *CIVIL* PENALTIES.[25]

        1. Permittee Notified of Proposed Civil Penalty within 30 Days of Cessation Order, Notice of Violation, or Order to Suspend or Revoke Permit.

        2. If Cessation Order Issued, Agency *Must* Impose Civil Penalty; Agency has discretion to Assess Penalty *if* Notice of Violation Issued.

        3. Permittee has 30 Days from Proposed Civil Penalty Notice to Pay the Proposed Penalty Amount, *or* He Waives all Legal Rights to Contest Penalty or Violation.

        4. Opportunity for Hearing is Provided and Permittee has Right to Contest Proposed Penalty.

        5. Request for Hearing Must be Made by Permittee within 30 Days of Proposed Assessment.

        6. Burden of Proof is on Regulatory Authority.

V. STATUTORY ADMINISTRATIVE HEARING PROCEDURES AND STANDARDS OF REVIEW.

---

[21] Section 518(a) of Pub. L. No. 95-87 (August 3, 1977), 30 USC 1268(a).

[22] Section 518(h) of Pub. L. No. 95-87 (August 3, 1977), 30 USC 1268 (h).

[23] 30 CFR Part 723 (1977) and Footnote 20, supra.

[24] Section 518(e), (f), and (g) of Pub. L. No. 95-87 (August 3, 1977) 30 USC 1268(e), (f), and (g).

[25] 518(b) and (c) of Pub. L. No. 95-87 (August 3, 1977), 30 USC 1268(b) and (c).

A. CESSATION ORDERS AND NOTICES OF VIOLATION

    1. If the Administrative Hearing is not Held within 30 Days of Issuance at the Mine Site or Reasonable Proximity of Mine Site, the Cessation Order Terminates.[26]

    2. Person having an Interest which is or may be Adversely Affected shall have 30 Days from Notice of Violation or Order to Request Hearing.[27] Includes both Cessation Orders and Notices of Violation.

    3. Agency has 30 Days from Time of Hearing to make Decision if Cessation Order is Involved.[28] No Statutory Time Limit to make Decision for Notice of Violation.

    4. Must Appeal Final Agency Decision to United States District Court for District in which Surface Coal Mining Operation is Located within 30 days.[29] Includes both Notice of Violations and Cessation Orders.

B. ORDER TO SHOW CAUSE TO SUSPEND OR REVOKE PERMIT FOR PATTERN OF VIOLATIONS.

    1. Public Hearing Must be Held by Secretary, after Appropriate Notice is Given the Permittee.[30]

    2. Secretary has 60 Days (As Opposed to 30 Days for Cessation Orders and No Time Limit for Notices of Violation) to make Final Decision on Whether to Suspend or Revoke the Permit.[31]

    3. Have Right to Appeal within 30 Days Final Secretarial Decision to United States District Court in which Surface Coal Mining Operation is Located.[32]

C. TEMPORARY RELIEF.[33]

    1. Available for Notices of Violation, Cessation Orders, or Orders to Show Cause to Suspend or Revoke Permits.

    2. Applicant for Temporary Relief must Show Detailed Reasons for Granting such Relief.

    3. Temporary Relief Granted if:

        a. Hearing has been held in locality of permit area and all parties were given an opportunity to be heard;

        b. Applicant must show substantial likelihood of favorable results on merits; and

        c. Temporary relief will not be harmful to public health or safety or the environment.

[26] Section 521(a)(5) of Pub. L. No. 95-87 (August 3, 1977), 30 USC 1271(a)(5).

[27] Section 525(a)(1) of Pub. L. No. 95-87 (August 3, 1977), 30 USC 1275(a)(1).

[28] Section 525(b) of Pub. L. No. 95-87 (August 3, 1977), 30 USC 1275(b).

[29] Section 526(a)(2) of Pub. L. No. 95-87 (August 3, 1977), 30 USC 1276(a)(2).

[30] Section 525(d) of Pub. L. No. 95-87 (August 3, 1977) 30 USC 1275(d).

[31] Id.

[32] Footnote 29, supra.

[33] Section 525(c) of Pub. L. No. 95-87 (August 3, 1977) 30 USC 1257(c).

4. Secretarial Decision must be Rendered within Five Days of Receipt for Application for Temporary Relief if Cessation Order was Issued.

D. STANDARDS OF REVIEW.[34]

1. Rulemaking—Court must Affirm Secretary's Action unless Arbitrary, Capricious, or Otherwise Inconsistent with Law.
2. Adjudication (Civil Penalties)—Complaint shall be Heard Solely on the Record, the Secretary's Findings being Conclusive if Supported by Substantial Evidence.
3. Adjudication (Criminal Penalty)—Beyond a Reasonable Doubt.

E. JUDICIAL REVIEW FORUM (WHERE?)

1. Challenges to Action by Secretary to Approve or Disapprove a State Program or Promulgate a Federal Program—U.S. District Court of the Capital of the State Involved.[35]
2. Challenges to Action by Secretary to Promulgate National Rules or Regulations—U.S. District Court, D.C. Circuit.[36]
3. Any other Rulemaking Action by the Secretary—only the U.S. District Court where the Mining Operation is Located.[37]
4. Challenges to Cessation Orders, Notices of Violations, and Orders to Suspend or Revoke Permits—U.S. District Court where the Mining Operation is Located.[38]

F. CITIZEN SUITS.[39]

1. Any Person Adversely Affected may Sue to Compel Compliance.
2. Must Sue in Federal District Court where Mining Operation is Located.
3. May Sue Operator for Damages Resulting from Violations of any Regulation, Order, or Permit.
4. Court may Award Costs of Litigation to Any Party.

CONCLUSIONS

Public Law 95-87 gives the federal government and the state governments (when conforming legislation for an acceptable state program is adopted) the necessary tools to enforce the appropriate reclamation performance standards of the federal Act. The degree to which successful reclamation is attained will depend in large part on the degree of effective enforcement of reasonable reclamation laws, and on the ability of Congress and the states to incorporate or change existing laws to make them responsive to particular reclamation problems of the various regions of the United States. In addition, new develop-

[34] Section 526 of Pub. L. No. 95-87 (August 3, 1977), 30 USC 1276.

[35] Section 526(a)(1) of Pub. L. No. 95-87 (August 3, 1977), 30 USC 1276(a)(1).

[36] Id.

[37] Id.

[38] Section 526(a)(2) of Pub. L. No. 95-87 (August 3, 1977), 30 USC 1276(a)(2).

[39] Section 520 of Pub. L. No. 95-87 (August 3, 1977), 30 USC 1270.

ments and updated reclamation practices necessitate that federal and state laws have the flexibility to incorporate and apply new concepts as they become known, and are proven effective.

Besides the need for flexibility in the application of reclamation performance standards, it is important that there be flexibility in the utilization of various enforcement procedures. Congress mandated in the federal Act that the states adopt the ". . . . same or similar procedural requirements relating thereto. . . ."[40] for enforcement actions. The Office of Surface Mining can either interpret this phrase strictly or liberally. I submit that a liberal interpretation would far better serve the goals of vigorous enforcement and successful reclamation.

For example, a complicated penalty point system[41] may have application for the numerous operators of Appalachia, but it has little utility for the large surface mining operations found in the western states.

Although this author has no problem with the minimum penalty requirements of the federal Act[42], the states should not be bound by the "who, when, and how much" federal enforcement provisions. Imposition of penalties for the sake of imposition does not solve the problems of reclamation, particularly since many of the violations will be technical in nature under this federal Act.

Instead, there should be strong emphasis placed on the performance of remedial measures in the field, with severe sanctions for failure to perform. In other words, actions taken by operators to abate a violation, and to correct an adverse environmental harm to land or water resources, do more for attaining successful reclamation than imposition of a multitude of civil penalties. In many surface coal mines, the cost associated with effective remedial measures greatly exceeds the maximum civil penalty that would be imposed. Scientists and technical agency staff should also be given substantial input into the selection and accomplishment of specific remedial measures.

As Justice Holmes said in an early New England case:

"The aim of the law is not to punish sins, but is to prevent certain external results."[43]

Inspectors too must be given easy access to the premises of the surface coal mining operation. This is necessary if environmental harms are to be detected at an early stage. It is an unresolved question as of this date whether government inspectors will be required to obtain search warrants prior to inspecting a surface coal mining operation. Valid arguments can be advanced as to why the recent U.S. Supreme Court OSHA decision, *Marshall, et al. v. Barlow's Inc., supra,* should be distinguished from application to surface mining situations.[44]

The likelihood of dual federal and state enforcement under the initial regulatory program is also another problem that will have to be resolved. Dual enforcement could result in the following:

(1) Inconsistent interpretations of the applicable laws and regulations;
(2) Lack of state agency credibility with the operators due to federal officials over-

---

[40] 521(d) of Pub. L. No. 95-87 (August 3, 1977), 30 USC 1271(d).

[41] 30 CFR Part 723 (1977).

[42] Footnotes 21 through 24, supra.

[43] Holmes J., Commonwealth v. Kennedy, 170 Mass., 18, 20 (1897).

[44] No doubt this issue will be litigated in future administration of "right of entry" provisions of federal and state law. See footnote 12, supra.

ruling actions of the state personnel; and

(3) Resulting confusion for the operators, who would no doubt go "shopping" for interpretations most favorable to their interests.

Although the Director of the federal Office of Surface Mining has indicated that state personnel will be invited to accompany OSM officials on the "first inspection",[45] the state personnel should be given this opportunity in every instance. An "administrative night-mare" will result if this interface between federal and state entities is not accomplished.

Dual enforcement at the state level among various state agencies is also likely to occur in many states as a result of this federal legislation. Many states do not have the umbrella "Department of Natural Resources" which has jurisdiction over all environmental issues, whether they be reclamation, water pollution, blasting, or whatever. Although the federal Act seems to contemplate that there be one "state regulatory authority" for administering and enforcing the federal provisions[46], bureaucratic and legislative politics and special interests will probably prevent this consolidation of all reclamation functions into one state agency.[47] Thus, there will be dual state-agency enforcement in many cases.

This dual state-agency enforcement could have the following effects:

(1) Unnecessary delays and extra expenses associated with multiple hearings;

(2) Ineffective assessment and imposition of remedial measures, particularly since the operators could play the lesser reclamation standards of one agency against the stricter reclamation standards of another agency; and

(3) Operators being subject to multiple enforcement actions.

Again, close coordination and communication between the various state agencies is necessary to avoid the potential disadvantages of dual state agency enforcement.

Finally, provision shall be made at all levels of enforcement for the informal conference concept.[48] In a nutshell, an informal conference is an administrative proceeding wherein both an agency and the person adversely affected can resolve problems without the necessity of going to a "full-blown" administrative hearing. Informal conferences could be quite instrumental in preventing litigation, since it would provide an opportunity early in the process for communication among interested parties. Hopefully, proper use of the informal conferences would facilitate agreements acceptable to all before the respective participants have become too committed to one single course of action.

The potential for litigation under this Act is great, as the stakes are high. One small reclamation requirement may cost an operator thousands of dollars.

An old quotation from the famous Lord Hewart applies to the federal Surface Mining Act. He said:

"It might be possible, but I doubt it would be easy, to compress in the same number of lines, more fertile opportunities for doubt and error."[49]

[45] Speech by Walter N. Heine, Director of Office of Surface Mining, U.S. Department of the Interior before the 1978 Coal Convention of the American Mining Congress, St. Louis, Missouri, April 23-26.

[46] Section 701(22) and (26) of Pub. L. No. 95-87 (August 3, 1977), 30 USC 1291(22) and (26).

[47] This author is not arguing the merits or demerits of this consolidation, but rather pointing out a "political fact of life."

[48] Informal conferences under the federal Act are allowed for certain procedures, such as the permit application process and the release of performance bonds. See sections 513(b), 30 USC 1263(b) and section 519(g), 30 USC 1269(g) of Pub. L. No. 95-87 (August 3, 1977).

[49] Lord Heward, C.J., London County Council v. Less, (1939), 1 All E.R. 191, 194.

Seriously, money that would otherwise be spent in litigation could no doubt be put to a better use, such as for remedial measures. This would do more for the desired end result shared by all - which is successful and effective reclamation of surface-mined lands.

ENFORCEMENT OF FEDERAL SURFACE MINING ACT, PUBLIC LAW 95-87

```
┌──────────────┐      ┌──────────────┐      ┌──────────────┐
│ INITIAL      │      │              │      │ FEDERAL OR   │
│ REGULATORY   │─────▶│ INSPECTIONS  │◀─────│ STATE        │
│ PROGRAM      │      │              │      │ PROGRAM      │
└──────────────┘      └──────┬───────┘      └──────────────┘
                             │
                      ┌──────▼────────────┐
                      │ VIOLATION DETECTED │
                      └──────┬────────────┘
                             │
                      ┌──────▼────────┐
                      │   FINDINGS     │
                      └───────────────┘
```

```
┌─────────────────────┐   ┌─────────────────────┐   ┌─────────────────────┐
│ FINDING:  IMMINENT  │   │ FINDING:  NO IMMINENT│   │ FINDING:  PATTERN   │
│ DANGER TO PUBLIC    │   │ DANGER OR ENVIRON-   │   │ OF VIOLATIONS       │
│ HEALTH OR SAFETY OR │   │ MENTAL HARM          │   │                     │
│ IMMINENT ENVIRON-   │   │                      │   │                     │
│ MENTAL HARM         │   │                      │   │                     │
└──────────┬──────────┘   └──────────┬──────────┘   └──────────┬──────────┘
           │                         │                         │
     ┌─────▼──────┐           ┌──────▼──────┐           ┌───────▼──────────┐
     │ CESSATION  │           │ NOTICE OF   │           │ ORDER TO SUSPEND │
     │ ORDER      │           │ VIOLATION   │           │ OR REVOKE PERMIT │
     └────────────┘           └─────────────┘           └──────────────────┘
```

```
                    ┌──────────────────────────────┐
                    │ TEMPORARY RELIEF - OPTIONAL   │
                    └──────────────────────────────┘
┌──────────────────┐ ┌──────────────────────────────┐
│ FAILURE TO PERFORM│◀│ REMEDIAL MEASURES           │
│ UNDER NOTICE OF   │ └──────────────────────────────┘
│ VIOLATION - CESSA-│
│ TION ISSUED       │
└──────────────────┘

┌──────────────────┐ ┌──────────────────────────────┐
│ PENALTY MANDATORY │◀│ NOTIFICATION OF             │
│                   │ │ PROPOSED PENALTY (30 DAYS)   │
└──────────────────┘ └──────────────────────────────┘

┌──────────────────┐ ┌──────────────────────────────┐
│ HEARING NECESSARY │◀│ OPPORTUNITY FOR HEARING     │
│ TO CONTINUE CESSA-│ └──────────────────────────────┘
│ TION ORDER        │
└──────────────────┘ ┌──────────────────────────────┐
                     │ AGENCY DECISION              │
                     └──────────────────────────────┘
                     ┌──────────────────────────────┐
                     │ JUDICIAL REVIEW              │
                     └──────────────────────────────┘
```

APPENDIX A

THE FEDERAL SURFACE MINING AND CONTROL ACT OF 1977

Denis Binder*

INTRODUCTION

Dramatic increases in coal production are projected for the future. Although it is obviously impossible to fully predict future coal consumption, various scenarios for 1985 estimate consumption to range from 984.7 million tons to 1,186.8 million tons, as compared to an estimated 673 million tons in 1977.[1] Western production is expected to range between 380.5 million tons to 520.3 million tons, up sharply from an estimated 165.3 million tons in 1977.[2] Thus, much of the growth in production is expected to come from the West. With these increases in production envisioned, the impact of the recently enacted Federal Surface Mining and Control Act of 1977 will be substantial.

SURFACE MINING

There are three types of surface mining: area mining, contour mining and auger mining. Area mining occurs on relatively flat surfaces. Essentially, a series of parallel cuts are made, with the spoils matter from each cut being deposited in the preceding cut. Without reclamation, the surface looks like a giant washboard from the air.

Contour mining occurs in mountainous areas where coal seams run along the sides of hills. The overburden above a seam is removed until further cutting is economically impractical. The result can be viewed as a triangle cut out of a hill. From a distance, it looks like a road. Augers are used to get at any remaining coal that contour mining cannot economically reach. Augers are giant drills that can bore up to 20 feet back into a hill.

The problems of surface mining, both eastern[3] and western[4], have been extensively

*School of Law, Western New England College, 1215 Wilbraham Road, Springfield, MA 01119.

[1] Leasing Policy Development Office, Federal Coal Leasing and 1985 and 1980 Regional Coal Forecasts 5, Table 1 (1978).

[2] Id at 7, Table 2.

[3] See Binder, A Novel Approach to Reasonable Regulation of Strip Mining, 34 U. Pitt L. Rev. 339 (1973) and Reitze, Old King Coal and the Merry Rapists of Appalachia, 22 Case Western Res. L. Rev. 650 (1971). In general, see U.S. Dept. of the Interior, Surface Mining and Our Environment (1967).

[4] See Binder, Strip Mining, The West and The Nation, 12 Land & Water L. Rev. 1 (1977) and Imes & Wali, An Ecological-Legal Assessment of Mined Land Reclamation Laws, 53 N. Dak. L. Rev. 359 (1977). In general, see National Academy of Sciences, Rehabilitation Potential of Western Coal Lands (1974).

studied in recent years, and various legal measures adopted to ensure viable reclamation. The problems of eastern surface mining include acid mine drainage, suspended solids draining into waterways, erosion and sedimentation, landslides, high walls cutting off animal travel, and aesthetic damage. With proper mining and reclamation techniques, these problems can be minimized. These techniques include segregation of soil strata, prompt backfilling and reclamation, and various control methods to prevent acid mine drainage.

The high walls left by contour mining on steep slopes can cut off animal trails and cause landslides as well as erosion. However, use of the modified box cut technique will minimize the adverse consequences.[5]

WESTERN SURFACE MINING

While successful reclamation techniques have developed in the East, new methods must be developed in the West because of endemic differences between the regions. While the East is typically a wet, highly fertile area, the Western fields generally lie under semi-arid land. A fragile ecosystem has developed and gently nourished over centuries. Natural vegetation is so sparse that it may take 20 to 30 acres to sustain a cow. Natural precipitation levels are often low, and natural revegetation cannot be relied upon. Current attempts at revegetation incorporate four procedures to hasten sustainable revegetation on mine spoils: spoils segregation, surface manipulation of the graded and shaded spoils, addition of top soils, and seeding.[6]

Water resources are a critical factor in any development proposal for the West. Western water is poorly distributed, and frequently unavailable where needed. For example, of the five Upper Colorado River Basin states, only Wyoming has sufficient water to meet authorized, planned or projected energy development.[7] Nor are existing natural water supplies dependable, since natural streamflows fluctuate drastically from year to year.

On a micro level, development of the coal resources would radically change hydrologic patterns throughout the western coal regions. The water, be it surface, subsurface or ground, constitutes an integral flow system, developed and delicately balanced over thousands of years. A disruption, such as by a surface-mine, could radically affect the hydrologic balance of the area.

Some of the conspicuous hydrologic impacts that could occur away from the site of the surface mine include changes in volume of water flow, loss of groundwater, deterioration of water quality, channel changes caused by increases in sediment load, changes in runoff patterns, destruction of aquatic habitat and increases in endemic diseases among users of water that has been contaminated by mining.[8]

---

[5] Under this method, the operator makes his first cut well above the coal outcropping. He temporarily stacks the overburden on a prepared bench above the outcrop while he removes the coal from the cut. When this step is completed, he filis the cut with the original overburden. Then he makes another cut to the same slope further down the slope. The overburden from this cut is stacked on top of the first cut. When all the coal exposed by this cut has been removed, the overburden is returned to the tranch. The finished effect is a hillside with no overburden on the outslope.

[6] National Academy of Sciences, Rehabilitation Potential of Western Coal Lands 60 (1974).

[7] Denver Post, June 4, 1974 at p. 19, col. 1.

[8] National Academy of Sciences, supra n. 6 at 44.

INTRODUCTION TO THE ACT

After several years to study, and unsuccessful attempts at enacting a surface mining control statute, Congress and the President responded to social pressures and passed the Federal Surface Mining Control and Reclamation Act of 1977.[9] Compared with many of the environmental measures enacted by Congress, this statute is particularly well thought out and avoids many of the internal inconsistencies of the air and water acts. Instead, by looking at the past reclamation history of the States, the statute attempts to provide viable legislative solutions to practical problems. A delicate balance is sought between the recognized need to increase coal production while at the same time averting the past ravages of unreclaimed or inadequately reclaimed surface mining.

GENERAL FEATURES

The Act pertains to the mining of coal only;[10] it does not regulate the surface mining of other mineral resources. The Act covers existing as well as proposed mines. All existing surface and underground coal mines, except those producing not over 100,000 tons a year, must comply with the new standards within nine months of enactment.[11]

Other features stand out in the Act. First, a fund is established for the reclamation of abandoned mineral lands.[12] The fund is financed through a severance tax on coal of $0.35/ton on surface mined coal, and $.15/ton on underground coal, or 10% of the mine head value, whichever is less. A tax of $.10/ton, or 2%, whichever is less, is imposed on lignite.[13]

Secondly, unlike many regulatory enactments, these measures make specific provisions for Indian lands,[14] which are a major problem in the West due to the large deposits of coal on Indian reservations[15] and the complex jurisdictional problems of Indian lands.[16] The Act imposes minimum performance standards for surface mines on Indian lands.[17] In addition, the Secretary of Interior is directed to study the problems of surface mining on Indian lands and report back to Congress with proposed legislation to allow Indian tribes to assume full regulation over surface mining on Indian lands.[18]

[9] 30 U.S.C. § 1201-1328.

[10] The Act does maintain provision though under which the Secretary of Interior may designate federal lands as unsuitable for mining operations for minerals or materials other than coal. Essentially, this provision is dealing with the protection of residential uses. 30 U.S.C. §1281.

[11] 30 U.S.C. § 1252 (c).

[12] Id. at §§ 1231-1242.

[13] Id. at § 1323.

[14] See especially Id. at §1300.

[15] It is estimated that 7 to 13% of the nation's identified coal reserves are on Indian lands. Controller General of the United States, Indian Natural Resources - Part II: Coal, Oil and Gas. p. 2.

[16] See e.g., Oliphant v. Suquamish Indian Tribe, 46 Law Week 4210 (S. Ct. 1978), and Fisher v. District Court, 424 U.S. 382 (1976). The problem is exemplified by the decision of Region VII of the Environmental Protection Agency to deny a permit to Units III and IV of the Colstrip Power Plant because operation would conflict with the clean air designation of the Cheyenne Indian Reservation 30 miles away.

[17] 30 U.S.C. § 1300(c)(d).

[18] Id. at § 1300(a).

The Act also provides some financial aids[19] to alleviate the "boom-town syndrome,"[20] and includes some standards over peripheral development pressures.[21] The boom-town problem is particularly great since the ten sparsely populated Rocky Mountain states contain 95% of the nation's uranium, 90% of its oil shale, and 41% of its coal.[22] Coal especially has a great potential for rapid development. Adverse effects which must be countered include housing deficiencies, inadequacies in basic public services, such as police, fire, schools, recreational facilities, health care, and water and sewage lines, and high crime rates in addition to a radical disruption in the existing life style and culture.

Some states have already taken action to alleviate the strains caused by the boom town problem.[23] In addition, under the Federal Coal Leasing Amendments Act of 1975[24], Congress increased the percentage of lease payments paid to the states from 37.5% to 50%. These funds can be spent on a variety of public services as well as for schools or roads.[25] Finally, the Federal Land Policy and Management Act of 1976 provided for loans to states and communities up to their anticipated mineral royalties for any prospective ten-year period, which will likely amount to between $1.5-2 billion for the Rocky Mountain States.[26] Hopefully, the combined effects of these measures will provide impacted states and communities with sufficient funds and resources to solve the problem created by rapid energy development.

One of the most controversial items in the Act had to do with surface owner protection when severed mineral estates are involved. The Act only partially resolves the problem. When the United States is the owner of the mineral estate, but not the surface estate, the mineral estate cannot be leased out until written consent is obtained from the surface owner.[27] When the severed mineral estate is privately owned, the applicant has to show either written consent of the surface owner, express rights in the conveyance, or

---

[19] 30 U.S.C. § 1232(g)(a).

[20] The problem of Boomtowns is highlighted in Cummings & Mehr, Investments for Urban Infrastructure in Boomtowns, 17 Nat. Res. J. 223 (1977), and Little, Some Social Consequences of Boomtowns, 53 N. Dak. L. Rev. 401 (1977), and Federation of Rocky Mountain States, Resource City: Rocky Mountain (1974).

[21] 30 U.S.C. § 1241(28)(B).

[22] Comptroller General of the United States, Rocky Mountain Energy Resource Development; Status, Potential and Socioeconomic Issues, p. 4 (EMD-77-23, July 13, 1977).

[23] For example, Wyoming imposes a special coal severance tax to create a fund from which communities affected by coal production may obtain grants or loans to finance public water, sewer, highway, road or street projects. The tax will expire when $120 million has been collected for the fund. Wyo. Stat. § 39-277.1, .10 (Supp. 1975 & 1977).
North Dakota has imposed a privilege tax on coal conversion facilities. A percentage of the tax is returned to the county in which the facility is located. N.D. Cent. Code §§ 57-60-01 to 97 (Supp. 1977). In addition a coal severance tax is imposed with the proceeds allocated to coal impacted communities N.D. Cent. Code §§ 57-61-01 to 10, 57-62-01 to 05 (Supp. 1977).

[24] 30 U.S.C. § 181 et seq.

[25] Id. at § 191.

[26] Comptroller General of the United States, supra n. 22 at 69. These provisions are in addition to the numerous scattered existing federal programs, which dispensed $39.2 million to 78 energy affected counties in Colorado, the Dakotas, Montana, Utah and Wyoming in fiscal year 1975, and $183.7 million in federal mineral lease royalties and other indirect aid to these states, of which at least $20 million benefited the energy-affected counties Id. at 44.

[27] 30 U.S.C. § 1304-5.

approval under state law.[28]

The crux of the Act revolves around the establishment of primary performance standards with primary enforcement by the state. The Act continues the environmental practice of federal-state cooperation by delegating primary line enforcement powers to the state as long as they meet minimum federal standards.[29] Should the states fail to comply, federal programs would be implemented in the states. The state regulations and programs can be more stringent than the federal standards, thereby avoiding any Commerce Clause-Preemption problems.[30] The minimum federal standards[31] include a statutorily created permit system, a process for designating lands as unsuitable for surface coal mining, providing of sanctions, a state law providing for regulations in accordance with the requirements of the Act, and a process for coordinating the operating permit procedures with any other permit process applicable to the proposed operation. Finally, federal approval of a state program is contingent upon the state providing sufficient funding and staff to carry out its responsibilities,[32] thereby averting some of the past enforcement shortcomings.[33]

In addition, the states are able to enforce their rules on federal lands if they meet certain criteria.[34] So far the Secretary of Interior has adopted as applicable regulations for federal lands, the reclamation laws of Wyoming[35] and Montana,[36] and entered into cooperative reclamation agreements with Colorado, New Mexico, North Dakota and Utah.[37]

PERMIT, RECLAMATION PLAN AND BOND REQUIREMENTS

The Act perpetuated the now-standard permit application and bond posting system.

[28] Id. at § 1260. The problem of severed numeral estates is highlighted in Note, Kentucky's Experience with the Broad Form Deed, 63 Ky. L.J. 107 (1978). The general rule today is that a clause granting mineral rights will be construed in accordance with the intent of the parties at the time of the grant. See e.g. Reed v. Wylie, 554 S.W. 2d 169 (Tex. 1977). The question therefore revolves around whether or not the parties contemplated the use of surface mining techniques. The general answer is no absent specific evidence to the contrary. Id. However, Kentucky is different and poses an affirmitive presumption with respect to the grants and reservations in the old "broad-form" deeds. See Martin v. Kentucky Oak Mining Co. 429 S.W. 2d 395 (Ky. 1968).

[29] 30 U.S.C. § 1253. The effect, of course, is that the states will amend their statutes to meet the federal requirements. For a detailed examination of existing state statutes, illustrating the need for this type of federal action see Binder, Strip Mining, The West and The Nation, 12 Land & Water L. Rev. 1 (1977).

[30] 30 U.S.C. § 1255. There has been extensive litigation recently where state laws provide stricter standards than federal acts. For example, compare Ray v. Atlantic Richfield Co. 46 Law Week 4200 (S. Ct. 1978) with Askew v. American Waterways Operators, 411 U.S. 329 (1973).

[31] 30 U.S.C. § 1253.

[32] Id. at § 1253(a)(3).

[33] See e.g. Hager, North Dakota's Surface Mining and Reclamation Law - Will Our Wealth Make Us Poor? 50 N. Dak. L. Rev. 437, 441-43 (1974).

[34] 30 U.S.C. § 1273(c). In fiscal year 1977, 50.3 million tons were produced on federal lands, up 51% from 1966. U.S. Dept. of Interior, Annual Report on Coal: Fiscal Year 1977 51 (1977). Total prouuction from federal lands is expected to reach 122 million tons per year by 1980. Id at 58. Thus, the regulatory power being granted the states will be substantial.

[35] 30 C.F.R. § 211.76(1977).

[36] Id at § 211.76-1.

[37] Id. at § 211.77.

Permits are to last five years, and are renewable.[38] The five year period may be extended for a specified longer time if the applicant reasonably needs a specified longer time to obtain necessary financing for equipment and the opening of the operation.[39]

On the other hand, failure to commence surface mining operations in three years terminates the permit, unless the delays are caused by litigation precluding commencement, or by conditions beyond the control, and without the fault or negligence of the permittee.[40]

The permit application must include names and addresses of the owner and operator, a history of past permits held by the applicant or affiliated interests[41] sites, locations, types of mining,[42] and extensive environmental information, including detailed baseline studies, including an assessment of the probable hydrologic consequences of the operation, climatological factors (if requested by the agency), maps, cross sections, results of test borings or core samples. For lands which may be prime farmlands, a soil survey is required.[43]

Each applicant must include a reclamation plan with the permit application.[44] The reclamation plan must include the existing condition of the land, including its uses and capabilities, the proposed post-mining use, and detailed descriptions and engineering techniques proposed to achieve that goal. In disclosing the proposed use of the land, the applicant must include the relationship of such use to existing land use policies and plans, and the comments of any owner of the surface, or governmental agency which would have to approve the proposed land use. The plan must also include a detailed timetable, conform with land use plans and programs, steps taken to comply with applicable air and water regulations and health and safety standards, local physical environmental and climatological conditions, and a detailed description of the measures designed to protect existing water systems and rights.[45]

No permit can be approved unless the applicant can show that all requirements have been complied with, reclamation under the Act is achievable, the proposed operation has been designed to prevent material damage to hydrologic balance outside the permit area, the proposed area to be mined is outside an area designed as unsuitable for mining, and, in the West, that mining would not interrupt, discontinue or preclude farming on alluvial valley floors.[46]

In addition to the permit and reclamation plans, the operator must also post a performance bond, whose amount "shall be sufficient to assure the completion of the reclamation plant "if the agency has to carry it out, but not less than $10,000."[47]

---

[38] 30 U.S.C. § 1256.

[39] Id. at § 1256(b).

[40] Id. at § 1256(c).

[41] Id. at § 1257(b)(1)-(5).

[42] Id. at § 1257(b)(7)-(9).

[43] Id. §1257(b)(11)-(16).

[44] Id. at § 1257(d).

[45] See Id. at § 1258(a).

[46] Id. at § 1260(b).

[47] Id. at § 1259(a). Factors to be considered in determining the amount of the bond include the reclamation requirements of the approved permit, the probable difficulty of reclamation considering topography, site geology, hydrology and revegetation potential.

Liability under the bond shall be for the duration of the operation, and for a period commensurate with the revegetation requirements.[48]

FEDERAL STANDARDS

The federal act is to be administered by the newly created Office of Surface Mining, Reclamation and Enforcement. The minimal federal standards[49] call for detailed baseline studies,[50] detailed reclamation plans, the designation of lands as unsuitable for mining, detailed environmental performance standards and permit requirements.

Minimal general performance standards include maximization of the utilization and conservation of the coal being mined,[51] reclamation to previous or higher uses,[52] restoration to approximately the original contours,[53] backfilling,[54] stratification of the top-soil,[55] stabilization of waste piles,[56] minimization of disturbances to the prevailing hydrologic balance, including prevention of acid mine drainage, minimization of suspended solids, restoration of the recharge capacity of the mined area to the approximate pre-mining condition, and preservation of the essential hydrologic functions of alluvial valley floors.[57]

In addition, no new surface mines are allowed within 500' of an underground mine.[58] Restrictions are imposed upon the use of explosives.[59] Fire hazards must be eliminated from debris piles,[60] and landslides prevented.[61] Provisions are set forth with respect to roads. The construction, maintenance and post-mining conditions of access roads must be in such a way as to control or prevent erosion and siltation, pollution of water, damage to fish or wildlife or their habitat, or public or private property.[62] In addition, the operator must refrain from the construction of roads or other access ways up a stream bed or drainage channel or in such proximity to such channel so as to seriously alter the normal flow of water.[63]

In general, the land should be returned to the same shape and condition as before,

---

[48] Id. at § 1259(b).

[49] See Id. at §§ 1257(c) and 1265.

[50] The baseline studies include topographic, hydrologic, climatological and cross section studies, test-bore results, and soil surveys. Id. at § 1257(b)(11)-(16).

[51] Id. at § 1265(b)(1).

[52] Id. at §1265(b)(2).

[53] Id. at § 1265(b)(3). Exceptions exist, when approved in advance for industrial, commercial agricultural, residential or public facilities.

[54] Id. at § 1265(b)(6).

[55] Id. at § 1265(b)(6).

[56] Id. at § 1265(b)(4).

[57] Id. at § 1265(b)(10).

[58] Id. at § 1265(b)(12).

[59] Id. at § 1265(b)(15).

[60] Id. at §1265(b)(14).

[61] Id. at § 1265(b)(21).

[62] Id. at §1265(b)(17).

[63] Id. at § 1265(b)(18).

including prior uses and natural vegetation. A period of five years to measure the revegetation will be used, except in the West where a ten-year period is required.[64]

Subject to a few exceptions, the land must be restored to its approximately original contours.[65] Highwalls can be left only if the watershed is improved.[66] With respect to steep slopes (20° or more), no debris or other materials shall be placed on the downslope.[67] Complete backfillings are mandated, and again, the site must be restored to approximately its original contours.[68] Although highwalls, spoil piles and depressions must be eliminated, an exception is made for small depressions necessary to retain moisture.[69]

Several portective measures are included for farmland, water resources and alluvial valley floors. Prime farmland may be surface mined if the land can be restored to equivalent or greater yields.[70] Renewable resource lands may be deleted from the proposed mining operation where operations could result in a substantial loss or reduction of long-range productivity of water supply or food or fiber products, including aquifers and aquifer recharge areas.[71]

WATER RESOURCES

With respect to water resources, the permit application must include a study of the watershed and hydrologic consequences.[72] The reclamation plan must include protective measures for the rights of water owners and water systems quality, both on-site and off-site.[73] Mining practices must include the creation of permanent water impoundments, minimization of on-site and off-site disturbances to the prevailing hydrologic balance, avoidance of acid mine drainage and erosion, recharging the capacity of the mined area, and preservation of the essential hydrologic function of alluvial valley floors.[74] Mining is not permitted in western alluvial valley floors where the quality or quantity of water would be materially damaged.[75] In issuing a permit, the granting authority shall require

---

[64] Id. at § 1265(b)(20). The requirement for revetation is to establish "a diverse, effective and permanent vegetative cover of the same seasonal variety native" to the land and capable of self-regeneration and plant succession at least equal in extent to the area's natural vegetation. Id. at § 1365(b)(19).

[65] In addition to a specific exception tailored to the needs of existing Kemmerer Mine in Wyoming, see 30 U.S.C. § 1265(c)(2), the exceptions include, when approved in advance, industrial, commerical, agricultural residential or public facilities. Id. at § 1265(c)(3).

[66] Id. at § 1265(e)(1).

[67] Id. at § 1265(d)(1).

[68] Id. at § 1265(d)(2).

[69] Id. at § 1265(b)(3).

[70] Id. at § 1260(d)(1). See also, Id. at § 1265(b)(7).

[71] Id. at § 1262(a)(3)(c).

[72] Id. at § 1257(b)(11)-(12). The hydrologic consequences of energy development are detailed in Lobel & Lobel, The Rocky Road to Water for Energy , 52 N. Dak. L. Rev. 529 (1976).

[73] Id. at § § 1258(a)(5), (9), (13).

[74] Id. at § § 1265(b)(8), (10).

[75] Id. at § 1260(b)(5)(B). Alluvial valley floors form the lush, subirrigated hay meadows where winter feed is produced. They are defined in the Act as "unconsolidated stream laid deposits holding streams where water availability is sufficient for subirrigation or flood irrigation agricultural activities but does

that no damage be done to natural watercourses.[76] If the water supply of an owner of an interest in property is affected by surface mining, the operator must replace the affected water supply.[77] Finally, the Act does not affect existing water supplies.[78]

UNMINABLE LANDS

Lands to be designated as unsuitable for mining include those where reclamation is not technologically and economically feasible.[79] Thus, lands which cannot be reclaimed are not legally minable. Discretionary authority is imposed to bar mining on fragile or historic lands, where mining operations could result in significant damage to important historic, cultural, scientific, and esthetic values and natural systems.[80]

In this same discretionary category are renewable resource lands, where operations could result in a substantial loss of reduction of water supply, food or fiber products.[81] Also included within this category are areas where mining would be incompatible with existing land use plans.[82]

Also protected from mining are National Parks, National Wildlife Refuge Systems, the National Trails System, the Wilderness System, the Wild and Scenic River System, the National Recreation Areas[83] and the Custer National Forest.[84]

As to the national forests in general, mining operations are permitted only if the Secretary finds there are no significant recreational, timber, economic, or other values which may be incompatible with surface mining operations, and are incidental to an underground mine, or that the Secretary of Agriculture determine with respect to Western forest lands lacking significant forest cover, that surface mining is in compliance with the Multiple Use Act.[85]

REMEDIES

Remedies must include civil and criminal actions, bond forfeitures, suspensions, revocation and withholding of permits, and the issuance of cease and desist orders.[86] The

not include upland areas which are generally overlain by a thin veneer of colluvial deposits composed chiefly of debris from sheet erosion, deposits by unconcentrated runoff or slope wash, together with talus, other mass movement accumulation and windblown deposits." Id. at § 1291(1).

[76] Id. at § 1265(c)(4).

[77] Id. at § 1307(b).

[78] Id. at § 1307(a).

[79] Id. at § 1272(a)(2).

[80] Id. at § 1271(a)(3)(B).

[81] Id. at § 1272(a)(3)(C).

[82] Id. at § 1272(a)(3)(A).

[83] Id. at § 1272(b)(1). However, mining is permitted on the National Grasslands, which is unfortunate because there grasslands represent some of the last remaining areas of native prairie lands.

[84] Id. at § 1272(e)(2)(B).

[85] Id. at § 1272(e)(2).

[86] Id. at § 1253(a)(a).

Act provides for inspections and rights of entry.[87] It also provides, as is common with environmental statutes today,[88] for citizen's suits[89] and the award of attorney's fees.[90] The citizen's suit provision allows any person leaving an interest which may be adversely affected to seek equitable relief against government agencies to compel compliance with the Act, after exhausting administrative remedies.[91] A suit for damages can be brought by anyone injured by a violation of the Act in his person or property.[92]

If an imminent danger to health or public safety exists, immediate cessation can be imposed. Otherwise, the Act provides for a 30-day notice to abate.[93]

MISCELLANEOUS

Fears have been raised about excessive concentration of our coal and energy reserves in the hands of a few giant companies, especially the oil companies. These fears are excessive as to coal reserves.[94] A critical constraint on any oligopolistic or monopolistic trend is the large amount of coal reserves in the hands of the federal government. Should concentration become excessive, the government could either lease or otherwise develop these reserves to counteract the oligopolistic trends. In fact, one provision in the Federal Coal Leasing Amendments Act of 1975 requires the Justice Department to monitor the state of competition in the coal industry,[95] and also requires the Secretary of Interior to consult with the Attorney General regarding the effect on competition of all proposed leases.[96]

The combined effect of these leasing regulations and the enactment of the Surface Mining Control and Reclamation Act is to ensure that the nation's coal reserves are developed to maximize the public good which minimizes the adverse consequences.

[87] Id. at § 1267.

[88] See W. Rodgers, Jr., Environmental Law 75-89 (1977).

[89] 30 U.S.C. § 1270.

[90] U.S.C. §1270(d).

[91] Id. at § 1270(a).

[92] Id. at § 1270(f).

[93] Id. at § § 1271, 1240.

[94] The top four firms control 25% of the coal industry, the top eight firms 34%, and the top 20 firms 50% which figures are far below the generally recognized oligopoly criteria of the top 4 firms controlling 50% of the market, Oil firms control 14% of coal production, and only 14% of the reserves. See Comptroller General of the United States. The State of Competition in the Coal Industry i-iii (EMD-7822, Dec. 30, 1977).

[95] 30 U.S.C. § 208-2.

[96] Id. at § § 184(e)(i)(2).

SURFACE COAL MINING LAW AND
WILDLIFE IN THE WESTERN UNITED STATES

Robert E. Beck*

Since the surface mining in the western United States could have a substantial impact on wildlife and wildlife habitat, this paper explores the extent to which state laws in six western states deal with these aspects. These states are Colorado, Montana, North Dakota, South Dakota, Utah, and Wyoming. The data presented in this paper were gathered prior to any changes in state laws that may have occurred as a result of the federal Surface Mining Control and Reclamation Act of 1977.

STATUTORY AUTHORIZATION FOR WILDLIFE PROTECTION

All six states have enacted statutes specifically dealing with surface mining for coal. In addition they have statutes that do not specifically relate to coal but which also may give a basis for protection of wildlife and wildlife habitat during surface mining for coal. Both types are considered herein.

Surface Mining Statutes

Only three of the six state statutes specifically require consideration of wildlife at some point in the surface mining process. Thus Montana and South Dakota have provisions in their surface mining statutes that prohibit granting of mining permits for land areas where there would be a specified impact on wildlife or wildlife habitat. The Montana statute bans such permits for "unique" areas, a term defined to include those areas that have special value for their "biological productivity, the loss of which would jeopardize certain species of wildlife." (Rev. Codes of Mont., §50-1042(2)(a)) The South Dakota statute bans such permits where the land is unsuitable for reclamation and lists as a specific criterion for determining such unsuitability that "the biological productivity of the land is such that the loss would jeopardize certain rare species of wildlife indigenous to the area." (S.D. Comp. Laws, §45-6A-9.1(4) In both states it is necessary to have a mining permit before surface mining for coal begins.

Montana and Wyoming have provisions in their surface mining statutes that require consideration of wildlife or wildlife habitat in the reclamation process. The Montana statute requires land to be reclaimed so that vegetative cover will sustain "grazing pressure from a

*School of Law, Southern Illinois University, Carbondale, IL 62901.

quantity and mixture of wildlife and livestock at least comparable to that which the land could have sustained prior to the operation." (Rev. Codes of Mont., §50-1045(a)) The Wyoming statute sets a standard requiring reclamation to the "highest previous use of the affected lands, the surrounding terrain and natural vegetation, surface and subsurface flowing or stationary water bodies, wildlife and aquatic habitat and resources." (Wyo. Stat., §35-502.21(a)(1)) Wyoming also requires the applicant for a mining permit to include in his proposed reclamation plan which accompanies the permit application, procedures "to avoid .... endangering .... animal life .... wildlife and plant life in or adjacent to the permit area," (Wyo. Stat., §35-502.24(b)(xiii)) and in the application itself he is required to include a description of the land noting "its vegetative cover .... [and] indigenous wildlife." (Wyo. Stat., §35-502.24(a)(vii))

While only the Montana, South Dakota, and Wyoming statutes *require* consideration of wildlife in some aspects, the surface mining statutes in all six of the states contain language that can be construed as *authority for* considering or protecting wildlife and wildlife habitat at various stages of the surface mining process. In some of the statutes the authority is expressed through specific references to wildlife; in the other statutes it can only be implied from general language.

In Colorado, Montana, and Wyoming, the statutes specifically state as one purpose for their enactment the "protection" of wildlife while the North Dakota statute refers to the "enhancement" of wildlife. The South Dakota and Utah statutes do not refer to wildlife protection or enhancement as a purpose for their enactment, but since South Dakota has the protective requirements discussed above, wildlife protection is an obvious purpose of its statute.

The statutes in Colorado and North Dakota require that the applicant for a mining permit indicate in a proposed reclamation plan the area that is going to be reclaimed for wildlife purposes, although these statutes do not require that any portion be so reclaimed. The Colorado statute goes one step further in requiring the applicant to describe in the reclamation plan how the plan will rehabilitate the "natural vegetation, wildlife, water, air, and soil." (Colo. Rev. Stat., §34-32-112(3)) Furthermore, in Colorado once a portion of the area has been designated for reclamation for wildlife purposes, then the minimum requirements are those agreed upon by the operator and the supervising board.

Although the statutes in Colorado, North Dakota and South Dakota, either give authority to deny or require denial of a mining permit if the land is not reclaimable, they do so without express mention of wildlife in the statutory reclamation standards. However, the general statutory language is broad enough to include wildlife, particularly when related to the purposes for which the statutes were enacted. Furthermore, wildlife may benefit from the mere fact that reclamation is required in all six states and to be completed with "reasonable diligence."

Although the provisions just referred to relate to reclamation, an event that occurs as the last stage of the mining process, they authorize taking into account wildlife before mining begins since reclamation plans must be submitted with a mining permit application and in general mining cannot commence until a permit has been issued. Utah, however, does not require a permit; it requires only that a reclamation plan be approved in advance of mining, and it is the only one of the six states not to mention wildlife or wildlife habitat anywhere in its surface mining statute. Wildlife can be included within the stated general objectives of the Utah statute, however.

In addition to the purpose and reclamation provisions already discussed, several other relevant provisions exist in several of the statutes. Montana, South Dakota and Wyoming specifically protect land of "ecological" importance. Such areas could have an important relationship to wildlife also. Thus, in Montana if an area has such "ecological fragility" that once disturbed it could not return to its "ecological role in the reasonable foreseeable future" or if the area has such "ecological importance" that impact on it could "precipitate a systemwide reaction of unpredictable scope or dimensions" it qualifies. (Rev. Codes of Mont., §50-1042(2)(b) & (c)) The South Dakota and Wyoming provisions are similar.

Montana, in addition to a surface mining reclamation statute, also has a statute regulating the location of new surface mines. One aspect to be considered in determining whether a mining proposal involves a "new" mine or merely an expansion of an existing mine is "important differences in .... wildlife .... from an existing .... mine." (Rev. Codes of Mont., §50-1603(4))

Non-Coal Related Statutes

All six states have air quality, water pollution control, land use planning, and water resource allocation statutes either following federal mandates or setting forth more stringent requirements than federal laws mandate. Generally wildlife or wildlife habitat protection will fall within the scope of these laws. To the extent then that surface mining for coal would either affect air quality, introduce pollutants into the waters of the state, affect land use planning or necessitate water use or protection of water supplies, the development could be controlled for the benefit of wildlife. In addition several of the states have enacted comprehensive solid waste disposal statutes.

All six states have wildlife statutes that deal with protecting wildlife and wildlife habitat within the state, but which do not have any specified relationship to the laws relating to surface mining. Traditionally state wildlife statutes have dealt with game animals or fish. In recent years, however, there has been considerable movement to encompass nongame species. This has occurred in Colorado and Montana. Thus, the 1973 Colorado Nongame and Endangered Species Conservation Act stated that it is the policy of Colorado to "manage nongame wildlife for human enjoyment and welfare, for scientific purposes, and to insure their perpetuation as members of ecosystems . . . ." (Colo. Rev. Stat., §33-8-102) To the same intent is the 1973 Montana Nongame and Endangered Species Conservation Act.

The relationship between these wildlife statutes and the statutes specifically directed toward surface mining for coal is not clear; however, all of the wildlife statutes provide for setting aside various types of game management areas. It seems probable that surface mining will not be permitted in these areas; however, it would clarify the issue substantially if, when next amending their surface mining laws, the legislatures stated that surface mining will not be permitted in game management areas set aside pursuant to state law. Whatever the relationship is, however, there appears to be a general trend toward broader, not narrower, protection for wildlife and wildlife habitat.

IMPLEMENTATION

Having reviewed the basic statutory authority that exists for protecting wildlife and wildlife habitat from the impacts of surface mining for coal, it is now appropriate to consider how that authority is or has been implemented. In all six states the statutes designate a state agency or agencies as principally responsible for implementation of the surface mining statutes. Generally it is only one agency; however, this varies from state to state. On the other hand, in each of the six states a different agency, often in a different department even, is principally responsible for management and protection of wildlife.

The two principal tools for implementation are the power to promulgate rules and regulations and the authority to approve or deny mining permits and/or reclamation plans in advance of mining. These are effective because a variety of sanctions such as criminal and civil penalties, performance bond forfeiture, injunctive relief and denial of other permits are available to back them up, although not all of these sanctions exist in every state.

In Colorado, Montana, South Dakota, and Wyoming, the rules and regulations expand upon the consideration that wildlife and wildlife habitat protection is to receive in the implementation process. On the other hand, in North Dakota and Utah the rules and regulations do not refer to either wildlife or wildlife habitat. Three of the states that expand upon the consideration of wildlife and wildlife habitat also specify a role for their state wildlife management agency to play, but in none of the states is this specified role the full role that the wildlife management agency plays.

In Colorado, the rules and regulations require the submission of an exhibit with the mining permit application form that provides "wildlife information" as follows:

(a) A description of the significant wildlife resources on the affected land.
(b) Seasonal use of the area.
(c) The presence and estimated population of threatened or endangered species from either federal or state lists.
(d) A description of the general effect during and after the proposed operation on the existing wildlife in the area, including but not limited to temporary and permanent loss of food and habitat, interference with migratory routes, and the general effect on the wildlife from increased human activity, including noise.

The application shall be reviewed and commented upon by the State Division of Wildlife in a timely manner prior to the Board's consideration of the application. (Rules at 17-18).

In addition to this information required in the application process, the Colorado rules and regulations require that:

(a) All aspects of the mining and reclamation plan shall take into account the safety and protection of wildlife on the mine site, at processing sites and along all access roads to the minesite with special attention given to critical periods in the life cycle of those species which require special consideration (e.g., elk calving, migration routes, peregrine falcon nesting, grouse strutting grounds).
(b) If compatible with the subsequent beneficial use of the land, the proposed reclamation plan shall provide for protection, rehabilitation, or improvement of wildlife habitat.
(c) Habitat management and creation, if part of the reclamation plan, shall be directed toward encouraging the diversity of both game and nongame species. Operators are encouraged to contact the Colorado Division of Wildlife and/or federal agencies with wildlife responsibilities to see if any unique opportunities are available to enhance habitat and/or benefit wildlife which could be accomplished within the framework of the reclamation plan and costs. (Rules at 34-35)

Whereas the Colorado surface mining statute did not impose any duty on its supervising agency to consult the wildlife management agency, it did impose a duty on the wildlife agency to assist if requested to do so. "It is the duty of .... the division of wildlife .... to furnish the [supervising] board and its designees, as far as practicable, whatever data and technical assistance the board may request and deem necessary for the performance of total reclamation and enforcement duties." (Colo. Rev. Stat., §34-32-106(2)) The Colorado surface mining rules and regulations have provided a more definitive role for the wildlife management agency.

The Montana rules and regulations require that to obtain a surface mining permit, an operator must submit a mining and reclamation plan which includes a "Wildlife Survey." This survey must contain:

(i) A listing of the fish and wildlife species utilizing the permit area, including any species on the rare and endangered list [now officially called "endangered and threatened wildlife and plants" list] prepared by the U.S. Bureau of Sports Fisheries and Wildlife [now officially called "Fish and Wildlife Service"] (Threatened Wildlife of the United States).

(ii) Population density estimates of each species insofar as practicable. Wildlife includes, but is not limited to, birds, mammals, reptiles, amphibians.

(iii) Season or seasons of use by each species must be noted along with a discussion of winter concentration areas, fawning or calving areas, nesting or brooding areas in the area affected. (Mont. Adm. Code, R 26-2.10(10)-S10300(2)(c))

The Montana rules and regulations are supplemented by a five- page set "wildlife survey guidelines." One guideline under methods referring to "standard techniques" lists "communications with local residents, Fish and Game personnel, or any knowledgeable parties." (Guidelines at 3)

The South Dakota rules and regulations require that the reclamation plan include a "wildlife survey" which is defined as "a statement describing the dominant species of wildlife inhabiting the area of the affected land." (Rule 12:04:02:05) "Dominant species" is defined to mean "the species in a plant or animal community exerting the greatest degree of control upon other species. Dominance may be determined by relative size, numbers and permanence of the species." (Rule 12:04:01:02(2))

The Wyoming rules and regulations specify with reference to wildlife in the permit application process that:

(a) The operator shall submit a list of the indigenous vertebrate wildlife species by common and scientific names observed within one (1) mile of the proposed permit area.

(b) Special attention shall be paid to the possible presence of wildlife on or adjacent to the proposed permit area which are listed on the "Endangered Species List," of the Wyoming Game and Fish Department.

(c) If significant habitat or migration route disruption is possible or likely, the Wyoming Game and Fish Department shall be contacted in order to determine the types and numbers of wildlife likely to be disturbed or displaced. (Rules, Ch. II, §1)

Furthermore, the Wyoming rules and regulations restate the statutory policy of reclaiming all affected lands "to a use equal to or greater than the highest previous use." (Rules, Ch. II, §1(b)) They continue: "Previous uses of affected lands must be ranked on an individual basis according to the overall economic or social value to the community or area in which these lands are found." (Rules, Ch. II, §1(b)(3)) As to wildlife habitat they provide that "[o]perators are required to restore wildlife habitat, whenever possible, on affected land in a manner commensurate with or superior to habitat conditions which existed before the land became affected, unless the land is used for a recreational or agricultural purpose which precludes its use as 'wildlife habitat.' " (Rules, Ch. VI, §4) Thus, current Wyoming rules and regulations appear to interpret "highest" use to mean greatest economic return, since recreation and agriculture are given higher preference than "wildlife habitat."

All four states that expand on the consideration to be given wildlife do so in relation to the surface mining permit application process, primarily through requiring specific types of detail in information about wildlife. Although it appears that the information will be used in considering the adequacy of a proposed reclamation plan as well as for purposes of deciding whether or not to grant a mining permit, only two of the states, Colorado and Wyoming, specifically expand upon the consideration that wildlife is to get in the reclamation process.

In all six states a reclamation plan must receive the approval of the surface mining regulatory agency before surface mining can begin and in five of the six states, the operator generally must obtain a mining permit as well. Only in Utah is no permit required. In all six states the wildlife management agency has a role to play in the advance approval process, whether it pertains to assisting the person who is applying for a permit or providing data to the surface mining regulatory agency or evaluating the proposed reclamation plan and making comments thereon. This role differs from state to state. A brief look at practice and provisions in three of the states should be helpful.

In Montana even though the agency has its own staff wildlife specialist, it asks the wildlife management agency for a recommendation regarding a mining permit application and provides it with a copy of the environmental impact information that was compiled as a part of the application process. There is no Montana statutory provision that requires this interaction between the two agencies. In North Dakota, the surface mining regulatory agency is given sixty days in which to reject a permit application or it is deemed approved, but before it gives its approval, the statute requires it to consider the advice and technical assistance of, among others, the State Game and Fish Department. In Wyoming once the completed application is submitted by the prospective operator, the surface mining regulatory agency relays the material to the wildlife management agency for its comments. In addition to using the Wyoming wildlife management agency, the surface mining regulatory agency has the authority to "utilize qualified experts in the field of hydrology, soil science, plant or wildlife ecology, and other related fields to advise on mining reclamation practices." (Wyo. Stat., §35-502.62(a)(i))

Frequently wildlife agency comments and recommendations are put to use by rephrasing them and attaching them to permits as conditions that must be compiled with. However, regardless of the exact use to which the wildlife agency comments and recommendations are put, the net result is that the agencies have fairly substantial input into the permit application and reclamation plan approval process.

Once permits have been issued and reclamation plans approved, all six states provide for supervision by the surface mining regulatory agency once mining begins. Such supervision includes both inspections by the agency and submission of annual reports by the mine operators. However, even though protection of wildlife is at least a part purpose of the statutes in most of the states and otherwise recognized in most of the statutes and rules and regulations, it appears to get little if any consideration in the monitoring process.

Generally the wildlife management agencies have no role in this process even though the surface mining statutes appear broad enough to allow a role if such was desired by the surface mining regulatory agency. Certainly none of the statutes and none of the rules and regulations give the wildlife management agency any specific role to play, and only in Montana does the surface mining regulatory agency have a staff wildlife specialist. Wyoming is the only state to specifically provide that the state may recover the reasonable value of "fish, aquatic life or game or bird life" destroyed by a violator of the surface mining statute or any rules or regulations promulgated thereunder. (Wyo. Stat., §35-502.49(b))

Citizens who are concerned about wildlife and wildlife habitat protection can have some input into the surface mining regulatory process since all six of the state surface mining statutes seem to recognize such a role for state citizens to play. All of the statutes, except the one in South Dakota, specifically provide for publication of notice about the mining permit application process, and in South Dakota the rules and regulations require publication of notice "that the .... [regulatory agency] intends to give final consideration to a permit application." (Rule 12:04:03:02) In Colorado, North Dakota, and Wyoming the statutes go on to provide that "any person" may submit written objections, petitions, or the equivalent concerning the mining permit application. These could lead to public hearings. Other statutes contain references to "aggrieved person", without, however, defining the phrase. In addition to these provisions relating to citizen input into the mining permit application process, the statutes in Montana, North Dakota, and Utah specifically provide for citizen input into the enforcement process. In addition, the Wyoming statute seems to contemplate that citizens will notify the regulatory agency of violations, and the South Dakota rules and regulations provide for such citizen notice of violations to the agency by way of a "signed affidavit." (Rule 12:04:05:01)

None of the six state statutes provide for any specific input by the federal government into the implementation process. They do authorize variously the state agency to receive assistance from the federal government, to comply with federal laws, or to "cooperate with" the federal government. Only in Wyoming does the statute impose a duty on the director of the supervising agency to "advise, consult and cooperate with .... agencies of the .... federal government .... in furtherance of the purposes of this act." (Wyo. Stat., §35-502.9(a)(ii))

CONCLUDING REMARKS

All six states have enacted legislation of recent vintage regulating surface mining for coal. Consideration of wildlife is required to some extent in three of these states, Montana, South Dakota, and Wyoming. In addition, it is authorized expressly in Colorado and authorized by implication in North Dakota because of specific references in the North Dakota statute to wildlife. However in Utah consideration of wildlife is authorized only by implication from general language since there is no specific reference to wildlife in the Utah statute. Furthermore, except in North Dakota and Utah, the rules and regulations promulgated pursuant to these statutes by the supervising agencies expand upon the consideration that wildlife will get. Certainly in none of the six states can it be said that consideration of wildlife is the predominant factor despite what appears to be a growing trend to protect wildlife and wildlife habitat.

All six of the states appear to recognize some role for the state's wildlife management agency in the surface coal mining regulatory process; however, very little of that role has been formalized either in the statutes or in the rules and regulations. The formalization that does exist, as well as the informal input, seems to focus on the permit application and reclamation plan approval process. Thus the wildlife management agencies appear to have almost no input into the monitoring and enforcement processes. Whether the wildlife management agency roles should be further clarified or not, what should be clarified is whether or not game management areas established pursuant to state wildlife management statutes are to be subject to surface mining.

The surface coal mining regulatory statues have been changed substantially during the past several years, often during each legislative session. Thus before the supervising agencies could begin operating under one set of implementing rules and regulations, changes have been made in the enabling statutes. With the newness of these statutes and the rules and regulations promulgated thereunder and the frequent changes, there is no history or tradition of interpretation or practice. Furthermore, there will be more changes in the near future at least as a result of the 1977 federal surface mining act if not as a result of each states own experience.

ACKNOWLEDGMENT

The bulk of the data for this paper was collected as a result of the expenditure of funds from a grant provided by the U.S. Fish and Wildlife Service. Assisting in collecting this data were then (1975-1977) University of North Dakota law students: Greg Hennessy, Rick Johnson, Karen Klein, Dan Kohn, and Margaret Schrier. The author has updated the data with the assistance of Southern Illinois University law student Michael Sherman.

REFERENCES

Statutes

(1) Colo. Rev. Stats. 1973, tit. 24, art. 65; tit. 25, arts. 7 & 8; tit. 29, art. 20; tit. 33, art. 8; tit. 34, art. 32; and tit. 37.

(2) Rev. Codes of Mont. 1947, tit. 11, ch. 38; tit. 16, chs. 41 & 47; tit. 26, ch. 18; tit. 50, ch. 10, § §50-1034 through 50-1057; tit. 69, chs. 39, 40, & 48; tit. 81, ch. 27; and tit. 89.

(3) N.D. Cent. Code, tit. 11, ch. 33; tit. 20.1; tit. 23, chs. 23-25 & 23-29; tit. 32, ch. 32-40; tit. 38, chs. 38-14, 38-16, & 38-18; tit. 40, chs. 40-47 & 40-48; tit. 55, ch. 55-11; and tit. 61.

(4) S.D. Comp. Laws 1967, tit. 11; tit. 34, chs. 34A-1, 34A-2, 34A-6, & 34A-10; tit. 41; tit. 45, ch. 45-6A; and tit. 46.

(5) Utah Code Ann. 1953, tit. 10, ch. 9; tit. 17, ch. 27; tit. 23; tit. 26, ch. 24; tit. 40, ch. 8; and tit. 73.

(6) Wyo. Stats. 1957, tit. 9, ch. 14; tit. 23.1, chs. 1 through 6; tit. 35, ch. 9.1; tit. 41.

Rules and Regulations

(1) Colorado Mined Land Reclamation Board, Rules and Regulations (1977).

(2) Mont. Adm. Code, Reclamation, Sub-chapter 10 (1973).

(3) Reclamation Division, Montana Department of State Lands, Wildlife Survey Guidelines (undated).
(4) North Dakota Public Service Comm., Rules and Regulations for Reclamation of Strip-Mined Lands (undated).
(5) South Dakota Conservation Comm., Surface Mining Land Reclamation, art. 12:04 (undated).
(6) Utah Board of Oil, Gas, and Mining, Mined Land Reclamation General Rules and Regulations and Rules of Practice and Procedure (1975).
(7) Land Quality Division, Wyoming Department of Environmental Quality, Land Quality Rules and Regulations (1975).

Law Journals

(1) Comment, Strip-Mined Reclamation Requirements in Montana—A Critique, 32 Mont. L. Rev. 65 (1971).
(2) Hagen, North Dakota's Surface Mining and Reclamation Law—Will Our Wealth Make Us Poor?, 50 N.D.L. Rev. 437 (1974).
(3) Comment, South Dakota's Coal and the 1971 Surface Mining Land Reclamation Act, 21 S.D.L. Rev. 351 (1976).
(4) Comments, Wyoming Environmental Quality Act of 1973, Section III Land Quality: The Regulation of Surface Mining Reclamation in Wyoming, 9 Land & Water L. Rev. 65, 97 (1974).

COMPLIANCE WITH ENVIRONMENTAL ENFORCEMENT REGULATIONS AS AFFECTED BY HYDROLOGIC EXTREMES

M.M. Fogel, L.H. Hekman, Jr. and D.R. Davis*

INTRODUCTION

Energy utilization and environmental protection are two extremely critical issues confronting the United States today. The frightening realization that U.S. petroleum resources are both finite and rapidly being depleted has prompted an extensive search for alternative energy sources. Coal is one alternative currently being stressed as that best able to alleviate the problem in the short run. Large deposits of coal are located in the arid and semiarid western United States. The character of these reserves suggests that the majority will be extracted through surface mining techniques, with environmental disturbance being an unavoidable by-product.

Concurrent with the push for increased coal production, is a growing emphasis on environmental protection, as is evidenced by the Surface Mining Control and Reclamation Act of 1977. This Act directs the Department of the Interior to develop and enforce regulatory standards governing surface mining reclamation in a manner to "strike a balance between protection of the environment and agricultural productivity and the Nation's need for coal as an essential source of energy" (Section 102).

Key items in the proposed standards concern revegetation, erosion, groundwater recharge and the containment on site of mine-area runoff (Federal Register 1977). The effectiveness of reclamation efforts in these categories is dependent on two main classes of factors, i.e., the rehabilitation measures that are undertaken and the local climate, primarily precipitation. The first class is controllable, while the second is not. Precipitation is variable and the more arid the region, the greater will be this variability. Since the effectiveness of rehabilitation measures are dependent on the climatic variables (precipitation amount, intensity and distribution, temperature, etc.), all characteristically random, the actual effectiveness of specific reclamation efforts will itself be a random variable which will change over space and time.

The purpose of this paper is to examine the "horns of the stochastic dilemma" which face regulatory agencies and mining operators as well. Current regulations are interim ones which have been changed in the past and will no doubt be changed in the future. A realistic evaluation must consider the impacts of hydrologic variability on system responses. Regulatory enforcement standards should be developed which incorporate consideration for the inherent uncertainties in the natural hydrologic system. We realize that this is an exceedingly difficult task but the stakes are high. Such standards will help achieve an

*School of Renewable Natural Resources, Center for Quantitative Studies and Department of Hydrology and Water Resources, University Arizona, Tucson, AZ 85721.

optimal balance between the development of coal-based energy reserves and the protection of the surface-mined environment.

Mining operators, as well as the regulatory agencies, are being forced to make decisions now, decisions which are known in the literature as being made under uncertainty. This paper presents a brief overview of this class of problems and focuses on specific aspects of the interim regulations in light of the uncertainties in the system.

DECISION MAKING UNDER UNCERTAINTY

In addition to the uncertainty created by climatic variability there are other uncertainties that create additional dilemmas for mining companies who must reclaim mined land and for the regulators "who must protect society and the environment from adverse effects of such mining" (Section 102 of the Surface Mining Control and Reclamation Act of 1977). The following discussions summarizes the different types of uncertainties that are encountered and presents several basic approaches with which these uncertainties can be handled.

Types of Uncertainties

Intuitively, the random variation in factors which determine the effectiveness of reclamation efforts will affect both the mining companies' choice of reclamation activities and the manner in which the regulatory agency judges the effectiveness of these measures. However, although the mining operators and the regulatory agencies are generally aware of the uncertainties caused by the randomness in the system, these are not considered directly.

Uncertainties arise in three general areas:

(1) Natural uncertainty,
(2) Sample uncertainty, and
(3) Model uncertainty.

Natural uncertainty is a direct result of the random nature of climatic variables. Of particular importance to reclamation success are the hydrologic variables, chief of which is precipitation. Precipitation serves as the main input into the hydrologic system and is transformed directly or indirectly into many variables of interest, such as runoff volume, pollutants in runoff, soil moisture for revegetation, sediment, erosion, etc. Unfortunately, the uncertainties inherent in the climatic variables are carried across to these derivative products.

Sample uncertainty arises from two sources: data quality and data bias. Clearly, the poorer or more erroneous the data, the less certain one can be in describing the system which the data supposedly represents. Examples are inaccurate precipitation and soil moisture measurement. Data bias stems from a non-representative sample. No matter how accurate the data collected, if the total picture is not represented, incorrect inferences will be made regarding the system in question. Even under the best of conditions there is always some degree of sample uncertainty. Anyone who has been involved in the collection and use of hydrologic data can attest to some of these problems.

Model uncertainty refers to the relationships by which inputs are transformed into outputs. Models need not be explicit mathematical formulations, (such as equations transforming rainfall to runoff) but are often implicit conceptual relationships. For example, the legal requirement of topsoiling and associated potential penalty points are based on assumptions concerning the effect of topsoil on revegetation. In general, regulatory standards and mine company reclamation activities are based on the assumption that the achievement of certain conditions now, will result in a specific, desired set of conditions in the future. Obviously, these relational expressions, whether implicit or explicit, are less than perfect and subject to considerable uncertainty. The choice of the best model or relationship to use is also uncertain. Statistically several models might satisfactorily fit and explain the limited data available, but could render radically different future extrapolations.

Thus, mining operators and regulatory agencies have to deal with decisions under uncertain and imperfect knowledge. The obvious question is "how are uncertainties handled?" This is the subject of the following discussion.

Handling Uncertainty

There are three basic approaches to handling uncertainty, each of which seeks to reduce the uncertainties inherent in a given problem. These approaches can be labeled as: (1) overcompensating, (2) waiting for favorable circumstances, and (3) collecting additional data.

Overcompensation refers to the taking of action excessive to the general demands of a situation, thereby all but eliminating the possibility of failure. A mining company, for example, may overirrigate, fearing an inadvertant violation of the revegetation standards. This additional margin of safety can be very costly, however, even if sufficient water is available. Typically, costs rise at an increasing rate as one seeks to protect himself from increasingly rare occurrences. "Overkill" approaches may also be employed by regulatory agencies. In these cases, very conservative regulations may be promulgated in order to insure the complete achievement of objectives, one of which may well be the avoidance of criticism from the public and other agencies.

A second means for reducing the uncertainties associated with the outcomes of actions is the "do nothing until circumstances are more favorable" approach. Revegetation efforts may not be undertaken until there is evidence that the current year is unusually wet. Or, even more likely, a mining company might do nothing, waiting for further definition of regulatory requirements, the issuance of legal opinions, changes in political climate, etc., all of which may reduce the likelihood of incurring unnecessary costs. On the other side, a regulator may set liberal standards which carry out the intent of the law only if nature cooperates, e.g. a greater than average precipitation year is encountered.

The third approach to reducing uncertainty consists of actively collecting additional data. As with the other approaches, however, additional costs are involved. Both time and effort are required, with associated delays in the issuance of regulatory standards and/or the taking of actions to meet the established requirements. It is typically difficult to get additional data quickly when dealing with natural resource systems. For example, the need for additional site specific rainfall data may necessitate writing for x-number of future precipitation events and associated rain guage readings. The greater the natural uncertainty involved, the more time will be required for additional observation. This is reflected in the current regulation's specification of a five-year waiting period to judge the success of revegetation efforts in areas receiving over 26 inches of annual precipitation, while a ten-year observation period is declared for areas receiving less than 26 inches.

Due to the nature of their objectives, it is not particularly surprising that mining companies and surface mining regulatory agencies generally find themselves at loggerheads. In a very real sense they are antagonists with the mining companies seeking to satisfy their stockholders with dividends derived from healthy net returns and the regulatory agencies seeking to preserve or reestablish pre-mining environmental conditions. Complicating matters is the fact that the entire conflict takes place in an arenan in which outcomes and consequences of actions are not completely predictable due to natural, sample, and model uncertainty. In essence, each side takes a stance based on their goals and perceptions of associated risks. Nature then rolls the dice, thereby determining the level of success of failure experienced by each side.

It can be argued that actually two levels of conflict characterize the surface-mining–reclamation scene: (1) mining company versus regulatory agency, and (2) both mining company and regulatory agency versus nature. The Office of Surface Mining (OSM) is charged with maintaining a balance between environmental protection and the nation's need for coal as an energy source. This depicts what is considered to be in the public interest or for the public good, and describes a position roughly in the middle of the continuum between coal company goals and those of hard core environmentalists. An optimum balance can be achieved if mining companies and regulatory agencies cooperate in developing and adhering to regulations in a framework cognizant of the uncertainties involved. Neither foot dragging nor overcompensation are necessary, indeed each causes waste.

An obvious question at this point is "do methodologies exist which can aid the mining companies and regulatory agencies in making decisions in the face of the uncertainties involved?" The immediate answer to this question is yes. The nature versus man, man versus man conflict within an uncertain environment falls within the general class of problems covered by what is known as game theory. Game theory is a body of decision-making approaches which have been developed to aid in planning under uncertainty or imperfect knowledge (Agrawal and Heady 1972). Essentially, mining operators, regulatory agencies and nature are all playing games with each other, deadly serious games with tremendous stakes. Several "gaming" approaches appear suitable for adaptations to problems involving energy and the environment. These approaches differ from each other chiefly in terms of the criteria upon which decisions are made. The following section presents four applicable decision criteria.

Criteria for Making Decisions

In making a decision (choosing among alternatives and thereby solving a game), the decision-maker may wish to:
  (1) Consider the "worst" outcomes and select the most favorable of these, or
  (2) Choose an acceptable level of risk, and select that alternative that satisfies the risk requirement at least cost, or
  (3) Choose the alternative that leaves him with the smallest regret in case he makes a wrong decision, or
  (4) Select the alternative which maximizes the expected net benefits.

Each of these form objectives calls for a different method (or model) for solving the problems (games).

The first approach above involves determining the minimum gain or least favorable outcome associated with each possible action and then taking that action whose worst outcome is most favorable. This is a pessimistic criterion that selects the "best" of the "worst". This is the maximin criterion, since one maximizes the minimum gain. While one player selects this criterion, another may select the minimax outcome or the minimum of the maximum losses which he might encounter. This approach does not require quantification of uncertainties, but rather looks at only the worst possible outcome for each alternative. Maximin or minimax is best suited for the decision-maker who must be conservative because of his psychological make-up, capital position, or the stance of the regulatory authority. This approach yields the best guarantee of meeting the requirements of the law. However, the cost for this insurance against uncertainty is high. Excessive measures are often undertaken, especially in games against nature, since nature does not actively try to do its worst against the other game players.

The second approach to decision-making entails the specification of a level of uncertainty with which the decision-maker feels he can operate. The action strategy is then chosen which best meets his goals within the desired level of certainty. For example, a mining company may choose the least expensive alternative which will insure compliance with reclamation standards under 95% of all conceivable circumstances.

The minimum regret criterion entails the selection of that alternative that is least disappointing in the sense that it neither causes huge losses nor foregoes large gains. For example, a mining company may choose to irrigate in order to insure reestablishment of vegetation, having decided that a "do nothing" policy would result in severe non-compliance with reclamation standards. However, if it were subsequently determined that a recontouring scheme involving such water conservation practices as terracing, pitting and mulching would have resulted in sufficient water retnetion in the soil for the satisfactory establishment of vegetation, the company may greatly regret having put in the more costly irrigation system. Regret can arise from either overcompensation or non-attainment of objectives. The problem is to strike a balance between these two extremes. The fourth criterion or decision approach offers a means of achieving this balance.

The maximization of expected net benefit is the criterion recommended for decision-making when the probabilities associated with each possible outcome for a given alternative action are known (Benjamin and Cornell 1970). Using these probabilities, the average or expected value of these outcomes is determined for each alternative. The alternative is selected which generates the greatest expected net benefit. The activity chosen under this criterion will, on the average, or in the long run, yield the maximum benefits. A problem may arise in the short run, however. For example, even though average annual precipitation may be sufficient for successful vegetation establishment, there is no guarantee that the rainfall actually received will be adequate in terms of amount and/or timing. In this light, a successful criterion might well be a combination of expected value and minimax, a combination in which the actions taken are based on long-term expectations, but which also take into account the necessary provisions for avoiding specific extreme catastrophic occurrences.

The above are just a few of the criteria used in decision-making under risk and uncertainty. Other criteria exist, including combinations of the above, which are often tailored to specific needs. The scope of this paper does not allow more details on this topic. The main point to consider is that mining companies and regulatory agencies are in reality playing games with each other and with nature, the latter being not necessarily an innocent bystander. The mining companies are trying to maximize their returns while the regulatory agencies should "strike a balance between protection of the environment and agricultural productivity, and the nation's need for coal as an essential source of energy."

PERFORMANCE STANDARDS

This section discusses various aspects of the performance standards found in current interim regulations with respect to decision-making by either mining companies or the regulatory agency.

Revegetation

It is generally recognized that the most important limiting factor in successful revegetation of disturbed land surfaces in the western United States is moisture (National Academy of Sciences 1974). Also, it is generally agreed that in desert areas natural plant regeneration occurs only when two or more successive years with favorable amounts and distribution of precipitation occur. In drier areas of the West, such a situation may occur with a probability of only 10% or less. University of Arizona researchers have developed probabilistic models of both summer and winter precipitation which can be an important aid in planning revegetaion operations (Fogel et al. 1974, Duckstein et al. 1975). The vegetation of mined lands can be enhanced by practices such as mulching, pitting, replacement of productive soil, addition of fertilizer and soil amendments. However, all this may be for nought if precipitation, either natural or artificial, is not available. As mentioned earlier, to reduce the uncertainties in rainfall, mining companies have to resort to irrigation to establish and sustain plant growth. Since water requirements for this maintenance type of production is unknown (another uncertainty), the tendency will be to overirrigate in order to comply with the standards.

Mining companies and regulatory agencies both have a need to know what is the penalty for deviation from standards. In economic terms, what is the loss function of under-performance and overperformance? This type of information is needed in order to make optimal decisions in the game plans of the contestants, the mining companies and the regulatory agencies.

Sediment Control Measures

The regulation states that sedimentation ponds must be designed to contain the runoff from a 10-year, 24-hour precipitation event. In addition, if the embankment is over a given size, the pond must have a spillway that can handle the 100-year, 6-hour precipitation event. Despite the fact that the National Weather Service has published numbers for such events (U.S. Dept. of Commerce 1973), the runoff from these events are quite uncertain as the model transforming rainfall to runoff is not well known. What is more important is the implication that the economics are universal, the same everywhere. In hydrologic design, a return period should be selected because it represents a balance between the cost of the control structure and the losses that the structure prevents.

Such terminology as the 10-year, 24-hour or the 100-year, 6-hour precipitation event may be applicable to eastern U.S. where it is used in the context of a unique set of circum-stances. In the West, where conditions are much more variable, the 100-year runoff event, may be the result of a 6-8 inch precipiatation event lasting 12-24 hours, a 3-4 inch local thunderstorm lasting about an hour and falling on dry soil, or a 2-2½-inch storm falling in 30 minutes on wet soil. Obviously, a precipitation event with a given return period does not necessarily result in a runoff event with the same return period. The obvious point here is a great deal of hydrologic uncertainty in the system which must be considered in making optimal decisions.

DISCUSSION AND CONCLUSIONS

Not only are revegetation and sediment control subject to uncertainties, but similar conclusions can be drawn concerning the standards pertaining to groundwater with its recharge capacity and alluvial valley floors. There is no intent to unearth a can of worms, perhaps in this case a whole bucket, which may very well be of the expensive variety. On the other hand, no panacea is being offered to solve the uncertainty problems. We do believe, however, that a greater understanding of the uncertainty situation by the mining operators and the regulatory agencies will be of benefit to all.

We are suggesting that other sectors of our society have learned to live with uncertainty, to cope with it and to prosper. Mining companies have long lived with uncertainty in mineral exploration and should, therefore, be able to handle uncertainty.

Wild flora and fauna live with the uncertainty in their environment. It is recognized that forest fires, naturally or artificially induced, are at times beneficial to the forest ecosystem. Thus, those who are charged with preserving the environment must realize that the environment is subjected to the random components of nature, as they will surely find when they get into the problem of evaluating the effectiveness of reclamation on the basis of reference areas. Regulators, too, therefore should be able to handle uncertainty.

Our thesis is that statistical and probabilistic decision-making techniques are necessary in dealing with the effects of uncertainty in planning the restoration of strip-mined lands. The regulations appear to be moving in this direction as seen, for example, in the standards for measuring the success of revegetation. The interim regulations which state that the ground cover on the revegetated area shall not be considered equal if it is less than 90% of the reference area ground cover for any significant portion of the mined area can be viewed as a statistical test of a hypothesis. Another example found in the regulations is when the "probability of occurrence of the event which a violated standard is designed to prevent" is used as a means for determining extent of penalty.

In conclusion, three points bear repeating:

(1) A good deal of uncertainty exists in the rehabilitation of strip-mined lands from both the standpoint of the mining operator and the regulatory agency.
(2) Methods are available for handling uncertainty.
(3) Given reclamation efforts are mandatory, all parties, including the public will best be served by recognizing and incorporating uncertainties into the decision-making process.

REFERENCES

Agrawal, R.C. and E.O. Heady. 1972. Operations Research Methods for Agricultural Decisions. Iowa State Univ. Press, Ames, 303 p.

Benjamin, J.R. and C.A. Cornell. 1970. Probability, Statistics and Decision for Civil Engineers McGraw-Hill, NY, 684 p.

Duckstein, L., M.M. Fogel and D.R. Davis. 1975. Mountainous winter precipitation: a stochastic event-based approach. pp. 172-188, In Proc., AGU Symp. on Precipitation

Analysis for Hydrologic Modeling.

Federal Register. 1977. Surface mining reclamation and enforcement provisions. U.S. Dept. of Interior, Office of Surface Mining Reclamation and Enforcement. The Natl. Archives of the U.S., Vol. 42, No. 239, Tues. Dec. 13.

Fogel, M.M., L. Duckstein and J.L. Saunders. 1974. An event-based stochastic model of areal rainfall and runoff. pp. 247-261, U.S.D.A. Agr. Res. Serv. Misc. Pub. No. 1275.

National Academy of Sciences. 1974. Rehabilitation Potential of Western Coal Lands. Ballinger Pub. Co., Cambridge, MA, 198 p.

National Weather Service. 1973. Precipitation - Frequency Atlas of the Western United States. NOAA Atlas 2, U.S. Dept. of Commerce, Silver Springs, MD, 51 p.

PART III: MINING DEVELOPMENT AND ECONOMICS

Societal perceptions and costs of coal mining are the main emphasis of this part. An analysis of the economics of coal mining in a major coal-bearing region like the Northern Great Plains is presented together with the price structuring processes in the markets of the eastern and the western United States. The imperatives of including the reclamation costs, and the use of byproducts in coal mining are highlighted.

AN INVENTORY OF WESTERN
SURFACE-MINED LANDS: COAL, URANIUM, AND PHOSPHATE[1]

A. Kent Evans*, Edward W. Uhlemann* and Philip A. Eby**

The rapidly growing demand for surface extractable western energy resources in the United States has recently stimulated considerable research into the reclamation and rehabilitation of western surface-mined lands. As part of an attempt to develop an ecological synopsis of the past, present, and future of western energy development, the Western Energy and Land Use Team of the U.S. Fish and Wildlife Service contracted NALCO Environmental Sciences to inventory and present in atlas format, all lands with disturbance in excess of 10 acres that were surface-mined for coal, uranium, or phosphate prior to 1976 in 11 contiguous western states and North and South Dakota. The purpose of this atlas was to document the current status of western mined lands for these commodities, and to provide a broad range of potential sites suitable for historical research into natural vs. man-induced rehabilitation of western mined lands. This paper is presented as an introduction to the Atlas of Western Surface-Mined Lands: Coal, Uranium, and Phosphate. The atlas was completed in late 1977 and is available from the National Technical Information Service (NTIS-PB-287-846).

The completed atlas has provided a geographically comprehensive examination of ecological conditions of western surface-mined lands previously unavailable from any one source. Although other inventories of western mines, including extensive computerized inventories of all mineral deposits and mining sites, are currently in preparation by several federal agencies for a variety of purposes, data compiled in these sources are generally oriented toward mineral production and ecological information is sketchy or absent.

The primary objective of the inventory of western surface-mined lands was to assemble and consolidate those data relevant to the disturbance history and current conditions of lands surface mined for coal, uranium, and phosphate in the West. Individual tasks included locating and consolidating available information on all surface mines meeting the inventory criteria, supplementing this information with that from on-site visits to many of the mines, and indexing and presenting these data in a fashion that would allow a systematic review of surface-mined lands in all or portions of the study area. For each inventoried mine, information on ownership, size, age, mining and reclamation practices, spoil configurations,

[1] This research supported by U.S. Fish and Wildlife Service Contract No. 14-16-0009-77-004, Office of Biological Services.

* Hazleton Environmental Sciences, 1500 Frontage Road, Northbrook, IL 60062.
** Eby and Associates Ltd., 2525 Willow Street, Vancouver, British Columbia, Canada V5Z 3N8.

land uses, and current ecological conditions was compiled and summarized in tabular format. Evaluation of reclamation success was not an objective of the inventory, although reclamation histories were compiled and current conditions described for each mine site.

The basic approach of the surface mine inventory was to proceed from the general to the specific in identifying and describing the surface mines of the 13 western states. General information sources were initially screened including all federal agencies with mining jurisdiction. The Mineral Industry Locating System of the U.S. Bureau of Mines provided considerable location information on all commodities and the Energy Research and Development Agency (now Department of Energy) provided much information concerning uranium. Relatively complete information on phosphate mines was available through the U.S. Geological Survey. The second phase of the inventory involved visitation and file searching with various state personnel including state mine inspectors and state geologists. Most information on inactive and abandoned mines came either from state files, or orally from state personnel. The final phase of the inventory consisted of contacts with mine owners and operators, and visits to over 100 mines throughout the study area. Mine visits were concentrated on older abandoned mines, because on-site data were available for many active mines from an ongoing study of P. Packer and E. Noble of the U.S. Forest Service, and from other investigators.

Data from the various information sources were synthesized into an individual table entry in the atlas for each inventoried mine. The mine tables are ordered by region, state, and commodity; the regions include: Southwestern (Arizona, New Mexico), Northern Great Plains (Colorado, Montana, North Dakota, South Dakota, Wyoming), Intermountain (Idaho, Utah), and Far Western (California, Nevada, Oregon, Washington). Each table provides information for a particular mine concerning location, ownership, size, age, disturbance history, mining and reclamation methods, and pre-mining and current ecological conditions and land use. Spoil configuration, notable substrate characteristics, and vegetation composition and structure are qualitatively described for most mines. Data and information sources are listed for each mine. Accuracy and reliability of data in the tables varies considerably, depending upon the source.

A total of 231 mines, 72 operating and 159 inactive, were inventoried in the 13-state area encompassed by the scope of the atlas (Fig. 1). The number of inventoried coal, uranium, and phosphate mines totaled 129, 84, and 18, respectively. Respective estimated acreages of disturbance by coal, uranium, and phosphate mining were approximately 44,460 acres, 10,470 acres, and 6,160 acres for a total of 61,090 acres (Table 1). Of these, an estimated 16,160 acres have been treated in some reclamation attempt. These acreage values are estimates and do not represent the total mining disturbance because they do not include mines or exploratory diggings of less than 10 acres, or associated disturbances such as roads and processing facilities.

Both coal and uranium activity were concentrated in the Northern Great Plains Region, which contained the majority (82%) of mines and the greatest disturbed acreage. The Southwestern Region, with 10% of the inventoried mines, constituted a secondary concentration of coal and uranium mines. Phosphate mining was primarily confined to the Intermountain Region; phosphate constituted all mines for this region and 6% of the total mines inventoried. Less than 2% of inventoried mines occurred in the Far Western Region; one coal and two uranium mines were located in Washington, and one uranium mine was located in Oregon. No mines of sufficient size were recorded from California or Nevada.

The size and age distributions of inventoried mines were related to past and present commodity demand, depositional characteristics of the commodities, and mining technology. Older coal surface mines were generally small dozer pits in shallow deposits

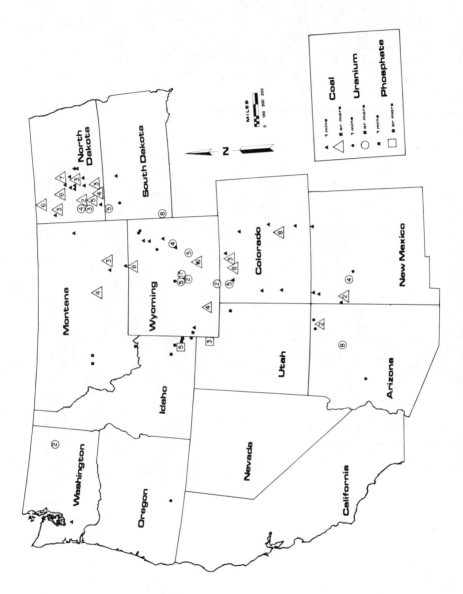

Fig. 1.   Distribution of coal, uranium, and phosphate surface mines exceeding 10 acres in size prior to 1976 in the 13 western states.

TABLE 1   Number of mines and estimated total and treated acreage (pits and spoils only), for all coal, uranium, and phosphate mines of 10 acres or greater inventoried in the 13 western states, organized by state and region.

State		Commodity	No. of Active Mines	No. of Inactive Mines	Estimated Treated Acreage	Estimated Total Mined Acreage
Arizona		Coal	2		100	2500
		Uranium		11		191
	Total		2	11	100	2691
New Mexico		Coal	5	1	2072	5681
		Uranium	3	2	80	2798
	Total		8	3	2152	8479
Colorado		Coal	10	16	3551	5890
		Uranium	1	4		160
	Total		11	20	3551	6050
Montana		Coal	7	3	2812	4876
		Phosphate		3		37
	Total		7	6	2812	4913
North Dakota		Coal	9	41	850	12817
		Uranium		7		205
	Total		9	48	850	13022
South Dakota		Coal		1		60
		Uranium		14		345
	Total		0	15	0	405
Wyoming		Coal	12	21	3622	10355
		Uranium	12	27	1148	6483
		Phosphate	1			700
	Total		25	48	4770	17538
Idaho		Phosphate	5	5	1392	4726
	Total		5	5	1392	4726
Utah		Phosphate	1	3	125	700
	Total		1	3	125	700
Oregon		Uranium	1			20
	Total		1	0	0	20
Washington		Coal	1		407	2280
		Uranium	2			270
	Total		3	0	407	2550
Southwestern Region		Coal	7	1	2172	8181
		Uranium	3	13	80	2989
	Total		10	14	2252	11170
Northern Great Plains Region		Coal	38	82	10835	33998
		Uranium	13	52	1148	7193
		Phosphate	1	3		737
	Total		52	137	11983	41928
Intermountain Region		Phosphate	6	8	1517	5426
	Total		6	8	1517	5426
Far Western Region		Coal	1		407	2280
		Uranium	3			290
	Total		4	0	407	2570
Total		Coal	46	83	13414	44459
		Uranium	19	65	1228	10472
		Phosphate	7	11	1517	6163
	Grand Total		72	159	16159	61094

or outcroppings, or small contour mines. More recent mined sites were large and had utilized area-stripping methods. The oldest coal mines in the West were located in North Dakota, where many mines exceeded 35 years of age and had usually been abandoned for several years. Many coal mines in the Northern Great Plains Region have operational histories encompassing several decades; often older spoils are orphaned and more recent spoils have been reclaimed within the same mine property. Reclamation of western coal mines prior to 1970 was very sporadic and primarily experimental. By the mid 1970's, the advent of reclamation requirements by most states and federal agencies had stimulated the initiation of complete reclamation programs for all western coal mines.

The majority of inventoried uranium mines, both in the Northern Great Plains and Southwestern regions, were small pit mines averaging 15 years in age. This is due to the erratic and limited distribution of uranium ore and to the past market demand for uranium which was concentrated in the late 1950's and early 1960's. Most uranium mines were abandoned by the mid 1960's but a recent increase in uranium demand has promoted the development of new mines and the reopening of old ones. Recent uranium mines are generally larger than older ones because mining of large-area, lower-grade ore deposits has become economically feasible. Reclamation of western uranium mines has not been as extensive as that of coal; by 1977 most reclamation was very recent and limited to the states of New Mexico and Wyoming. Although reclamation of current and future uranium operations will be required, the value of spoils as future millable ore has often been the cause for indefinite postponement of reclamation.

All phosphate mines inventoried in the Atlas were located in the Western Phosphate Field centered in Southeastern Idaho. Most phosphate surface mines were less than 20 years of age, and most were long contour or pit operations following ridges or mountainsides. Reclamation of spoil dumps at western phosphate mines, primarily under the guidance of the U.S. Geological Survey and the U.S. Forest Service, began in the late 1960's and was active on all mines by the mid 1970's. Reduction of extensive highwalls from the contour operations and backfilling of pits has generally been delayed, as with uranium, because of potential future value of lower-grade ores.

The number and acreage of western surface mines are given in Table 2 following Kuchler's Potential Natural Vegetation Types. The geographical distribution of mines and total acreage disturbed by mining is such that the greatest disturbance has been within the grassland ecosystems of the Northern Great Plains and the Sagebrush Steppe vegetation unit of the Northern Great Plains and Intermountain regions. Major grassland vegetation units disturbed by mining include the Wheatgrass-Needlegrass, Wheatgrass-Bluestem-Needlegrass, and Grama-Needlegrass-Wheatgrass units. Forested vegetation units with significant disturbance by mining are the Eastern Ponderosa Forest of the Northern Great Plains Region and the Douglas Fir Forest of the Northern Great Plains and Intermountain regions. The Juniper-Pinyon Woodland vegetation unit is a woodland ecosystem with significant disturbance, particularly in the Southwestern Region. Precipitation patterns and/or spoil characteristics in the above vegetation types, with the exception of the Douglas Fir Forest, are such that natural revegetation has taken place slowly and reclamation has often been difficult. Severe conditions for reestablishment of native plant communities in these vegetation types have often resulted from the sparse and/or erratic precipitation combined with the varied textural and sometimes toxic properties of the spoils.

The results of many reclamation procedures that have been practiced at numerous sites over wide-ranging ecological conditions across the west defy a detailed account in this paper. However, in general, most plant communities on reclaimed sites were ecologically unstable monocultures often comprised of nonnative species such as crested wheatgrass.

TABLE 2. Acreage of mined land by potential natural vegetation type within the 13 western states, organized by region.[a]

Each cell below is given as mines / acres. Commodity columns: C = Coal, U = Uranium, P = Phosphate.

Potential Natural Vegetation Types	SW C	SW U	NGP C	NGP U	NGP P	IM C	IM U	IM P	FW U	Total C	Total U	Total P	Grand Total
Juniper-Pinyon Woodland	8 / 7977	3 / 1366	8 / 1130	2 / 20	–	–	–	1 / 250	–	16 / 9107	5 / 1386	1 / 250	22 / 10743
Creosote Bush-Bursage	–	1 / 10	–	–	–	–	–	–	–	–	1 / 10	–	1 / 10
Great Basin Sagebrush	–	9 / 153	1 / 230	–	–	–	–	–	–	1 / 230	9 / 153	–	10 / 383
Blackbrush	–	1 / 17	–	–	–	–	–	–	–	–	1 / 17	–	1 / 17
Grama-Galleta Steppe	1 / 98	6 / 1442	–	–	–	–	–	–	–	1 / 98	6 / 1442	–	7 / 2140
Saltbush-Greasewood	1 / 105	–	3 / 616	–	–	–	–	–	–	4 / 721	–	–	4 / 721
Sagebrush Steppe	–	–	34 / 9015	29 / 3603	1 / 700	–	–	8 / 3876	1 / 10	34 / 9015	30 / 3613	9 / 4576	73 / 17204
Mountain Mahogany-Oak Scrub	–	–	3 / 2223	–	–	–	–	–	–	3 / 2223	–	–	3 / 2223
Grama-Buffalograss	–	–	3 / 52	–	–	–	–	–	–	3 / 52	–	–	3 / 52
Wheatgrass-Needlegrass-Shrub Steppe	–	–	1 / 315	1 / 125	–	–	–	–	–	1 / 315	1 / 125	–	2 / 440
Grama-Needlegrass-Wheatgrass	–	–	10 / 3428	10 / 2875	–	–	–	–	–	10 / 3428	10 / 2875	–	20 / 6303
Wheatgrass-Needlegrass	–	–	43 / 8482	13 / 310	–	–	–	–	–	43 / 8482	13 / 310	–	56 / 8792
Wheatgrass-Bluestem-Needlegrass	–	–	10 / 5252	–	–	–	–	–	–	10 / 5252	–	–	10 / 5252
Northern Floodplain Forest	–	–	1 / 15	–	–	–	–	–	–	1 / 15	–	–	1 / 15
Black Hills Pine Forest	–	–	–	10 / 260	–	–	–	–	–	–	10 / 260	–	10 / 260
Eastern Ponderosa Forest	–	–	8 / 3239	–	–	–	–	–	–	8 / 3239	–	–	8 / 3239
Douglas Fir Forest	–	–	–	3 / 37	–	–	9 / 1300	–	–	–	12 / 1337	–	12 / 1337
Cedar-Hemlock-Douglas Fir Forest	–	–	–	–	–	1 / 2280	–	–	–	1 / 2280	–	–	1 / 2280
Ponderosa Shrub Forest	–	–	–	–	–	–	–	–	1 / 10	–	1 / 10	–	1 / 10
Western Ponderosa Forest	–	–	–	–	–	–	–	–	2 / 270	–	2 / 270	–	2 / 270

Number of Mines/Estimated Acreage

[a] Mines occupying more than one type were counted in each type.
[b] C - Coal, U - Uranium, P - Phosphate.

Russian thistle and other drought-resistant weedy annuals were often important or dominant components on these reclaimed sites. At abandoned mined sites, although the vegetation was usually of lower cover and density than on adjacent reclaimed sites, the irregularity of topography and the resultant diversity of edaphic and moisture conditions generally resulted in a greater diversity of vegetation. A large number of native grass, forb, subshrub, shrub, and tree species were recorded on orphaned mined sites; species composition varied greatly with soil texture and moisture regime.

The Atlas of Western Surface Mining summarizes existing physiographic and ecological conditions for all coal, uranium, and phosphate mines greater than 10 acres mined prior to 1976 in the 13-state area. We anticipate that the baseline information in this atlas will serve as a useful tool for those ecologists who wish to continue to develop management schemes and reclamation methodologies for the rehabilitation of western mined lands. Of particular value to reclamation specialists should be the identification in the atlas of the native perennial species that readily colonize and stabilize untreated mine spoils in a given region during the process of natural restoration. The atlas is well suited to the selection of research sites for detailed investigations into the relative value of both orphaned and reclaimed mined lands for the reestablishment of viable ecological communities and compatible land uses. Finally, the atlas should also be of considerable use to the Office of Surface Mining Reclamation and Enforcement in determining the needs and priorities for utilization of the Abandoned Mine Reclamation Fund in the western United States.

CITIZEN PERCEPTIONS OF COAL-RELATED COMMUNITY GROWTH

Osbin L. Ervin*

INTRODUCTION

National Energy Plans call for the doubling of coal production by 1985, and coal industry executives are devising industry plans to meet that goal. Whether or not the 1985 target is desirable or attainable, it is clear that there will be a considerable increase in coal mining and conversion activity over the next decade, and this prospect poses a major challenge to planners and managers in local coal communities and to community-oriented researchers and policy analysts. The challenge to administrators and researchers is to provide analysis, plans, and skills for managing coal-related community growth, to the end of translating community growth into favorable local government fiscal conditions.

The rural nature of coal resource development makes it especially important that we give attention to local impacts and alternatives for local government action. Domestic coal reserves lie mainly in the mountains of Appalachia, the Illinois Basin, the high plains, and the Rocky Mountains. All of these areas are essentially rural with few major population centers. In such rural areas the impacts of new activities on the community are likely to be more severe than in urban areas, and the potential for dislocation and problems is furthered by a shortage of planning and management capacity in the governments of most rural communities.

Researchers are now beginning to devote some attention to coal-related community fiscal impacts and public management alternatives (Nellis 1974, Leistritz et al. 1975, HUD 1976). This is a very promising area of research, and one hopes that the effort will grow. However, there is a closely related and constraining public management parameter to which little research attention is being given - the opinions and preferences of the citizens of energy-impacted communities (for a recent and helpful study in this area, see Peele 1976).

Articulation between local citizens and officials often is not very well developed in energy-impacted communities. Both officials and citizens are in a new and unfamiliar situation. Citizens may not know what sorts of alternatives are available for official action, and officials may not have a very good understanding of citizen beliefs and expectations in the new situation. There is a tendency for local officials to assume that citizens are highly favorable toward any new job-creating development, and that they would respond negatively to public management strategies that might cause inconvenience for project developers. Given the economic development ethic of rural communities, this is an understandable assumption on the part of local officials. However, it may be a misconception in many cases, and in most cases local officials need a clearer reading of public beliefs if they

*Coal Extraction and Utilization Research Center, Southern Illinois University, Carbondale, IL 62901.

are to consider politically feasible policy and management alternatives (for a thorough discussion of opinion-policy linkages, see Luttbeg 1968).

Lynton Caldwell's (1970) argument for the importance of public perceptions of the natural environment is pertinent here. Caldwell has written:

"This knowledge is important to the process of environmental management chiefly as "feedback". Environmental administration is largely the management of men in relation to their environments, and therefore the behavioral tendencies of men and the beliefs that motivate them are of practical relevance to the administrative process. If men are to relate wisely to their environments, it is necessary that they perceive their environments accurately and realistically. In order to guide men's actions in relation to the environment, it would obviously help the administrator to understand the prevailing perceptions of environmental relationships." [p. 235]

So it is with regard to community fiscal and environmental impacts of coal-related projects; citizen perceptions are of practical relevance to public policymaking and administration.

This paper addresses this research need by reporting on citizen views in New Athens, Illinois following the announcement of plans to construct a coal gasification plant (the proposed "Coalcon" plant).

According to the Coalcon Plan, construction and operation of the gasification plant would proceed according to the schedule below:

1/78	6/79	6/82	1/86
	Employment: 1000	Employment 300	
Analysis	Pilot Plant	Operating	Comm.
Engineering	Construction	Feasibility	Plant
		Testing	Decision

Thus, construction would start in 1979, followed by the beginning of demonstration operations in 1982 and by full commerical operation in early 1986. This information had been widely disseminated in the New Athens area during the six months preceeding our survey.

The public opinion survey was part of a larger effort to establish a baseline and conceptual framework for future analysis of fiscal impacts and public management alternatives in the New Athens area. A major element of this conceptual framework was the view that local fiscal systems are composed of four interacting subsystems - the economy, land use, public revenues, and public service demands (Ervin 1978). Therefore the public opinion questionnaire focused largely on these matters, although related matters such as environmental pollution and general perceptions of local government were also included.

METHOD

A sample of two hundred persons was randomly selected using the New Athens telephone directory. A short questionnaire was then mailed to each of the persons selected. Ninety-six of the individuals responded, for a response rate of 48%. The data were then coded and key punched, and frequency distributions were computed using the Statistical Package for Social Science (Nie et al. 1975).

FINDINGS

Economy

As was expected, local citizens were highly optimistic about favorable economic impacts of the proposed plant. Eighty-four percent of the respondents felt that the economy of New Athens and the surrounding area would be improved by the plant. Regarding anticipated population increases, an overwhelming majority of respondents (77%) projected a population increase of under 1,000 persons to be associated with the plant, with about 43% believing the increase would be in the 500-1,000 range.

Citizen expectations of beneficial plant economic effects were expected because the local news media presented the plant as an important boon to the local economy, bringing new jobs and increased business. An earlier public presentation by Coalcon officials (held in the Village meeting hall) had also emphasized this aspect of the plant. Regarding population growth, available evidence and opinion indicate that commerical operation of the plant would bring a population increase of about 1,000 persons to the New Athens community. On this matter, as in the case of general economic effects, the citizenry seemed reasonably well informed.

Land Use and Environment

Respondents were asked several questions about land use and environmental issues. Included were items about surface mining and reclamation, water and air pollution, and environmental regulation.

New Athens citizens were favorably disposed toward surface mining, agreeing by a majority of about 2 to 1 that this method of coal extraction is necessary and acceptable. But, they also felt strongly that vigorous efforts should be made to reclaim stripped land and that the reclamation efforts of the past have been inadequate; over 90% asserted the importance of reclamation and 70% indicated that past efforts have been inadequate.

One need only visit the New Athens area to recognize that past land reclamation efforts have indeed been inadequate, as perceived by the respondents. Given this background, it is somewhat surprising (and perhaps reassuring to coal operators) that the public showed such strong support for the surface mining of coal. The message from the public regarding future reclamation, however, was quite clear: The record should be improved.

A majority of the respondents felt that significant increases in both water and air pollution would result from the plant. It is also important that over 25% of the respondents indicated that they "don't know", or do not have any opinion, about the plant's potential for air and water pollution. While citizens felt that the plant would bring a significant increase in environmental pollution, they indicated in response to other questions that they did not feel public health would be adversely affected. Again, however, a high percentage (28%) indicated that they "don't know".

Citizens are clearly correct in their perception that coal conversion processes are likely to have a deleterious effect on local air and water quality. There are various points in the mining and conversion process at which chemical pollutants may enter the environment. Preventive technologies may, of course, reduce the level of pollution emission at many of these points. Nonetheless, emissions are likely to remain significant over the foreseeable future.

Public Services and Revenues

The respondents felt that the Coalcon plant would bring service demands beyond the present capacity of local governments, and they felt that the company, NOT current residents of the village, should bear the financial burden of the expanded services; when asked if present services would be adequate, the response was "no" by a margin of 52 to 37%, and when asked specifically about maintenance of plant access roads, 84% indicated that the expense should be borne by Coalcon. However, citizens were not in such agreement about actual expectations of future tax burdens. By a margin of 53 to 46%, they indicated that they did not expect their taxes to increase as a result of the plant.

It is well known that manufacturing companies are sometimes given special property tax concessions in an effort to make the community more attractive to the company. Such concessions might have the effect of reducing the likelihood that public revenues will be available for new service demands. New Athens residents were asked if the Coalcon Company had been given tax breaks. By a very close margin of 54 to 46%, they said "no". When asked if they were for or against such tax breaks, half said they were opposed, 13% were in favor, and 35% indicated they they were unsure.

Several studies suggest that the net fiscal impact of new manufacturing plants may be negative in many cases, at least over the short-term (Garrison 1970). New Athens citizens appear to recognize this possibility, and they are firmly committed to the idea that the industry should play a major role in resolving local fiscal problems.

The Coalcon Company, our research indicates, would indeed receive favorable tax treatment at the hands of local government. The Illinois constitution allows counties of at least 200,000 population to separate property into various classes for tax purposes, and to assess each class at a different ratio of assessed to market value. It appears that there has been an agreement that would place Coalcon in a special class that would be assessed at the lowest ratio allowable by law. It is clear that citizens are not sympathetic to such arrangements.

General Perceptions of Community and Plant

Respondents were also asked a number of questions pertinent to their general perceptions of potential plant impacts and local government planning.

When asked about the magnitude of local government planning in preparation for the plant, those responding indicated by a margin of almost 2 to 1 that very little or no planning had occurred. Oddly, however, citizens also felt that their welfare vis-a-vis the coal conversion plant was being given adequate consideration by local governments. It also seemed important to inquire about citizen perception of the efficacy of local governments. When asked how much effect local government has on their day-to-day lives, respondents indicated by a ratio of almost 3 to 1 that they DO consider local governments efficacious.

Regarding general perceptions of plant impact, respondents indicated overwhelmingly that the plant would be a "good thing" and, further, that it is the "best thing that's happened to New Athens in years". However, when asked: "in general, how will the opening of the new plant effect your quality of life", only 5% of the respondents indicated that they expect an improvement in their individual lives. Another question was aimed at discovering citizen perceptions of the social/community awareness of Coalcon management. Of the 67% responding, 40% indicated the company would "insure that the plant does not have any bad effects on the community".

The assessment of the amount of community planning in preparation for the plant seems well-justified. Our research indicates that, with the exception of the school district, local governments had made little attempt to plan for future needs. Nonetheless, citizens seem to feel that local officials and plant executives would assure that community needs were met. Reports coming from coal communities do not justify this faith in local industrial and government leaders, and such a passive orientation is likely to contribute to future community problems. It is encouraging that respondents did view their local governments as meaningful and powerful community institutions, presumably capable of exerting some control over future events.

The highly optimistic assessment of general plant impact is consistent with earlier findings. The public generally felt that the plant would be an improvement to the community. However, the finding regarding individual "quality of life" indicates that citizens were unable to relate that improvement to their own day-to-day experiences. This may be due to inadequate information about relationships between community and plant. Of course, additional information might also have resulted in a different general assessment of plant impacts.

CONCLUSION

Our data indicate that at the time of the survey the opinion in New Athens was favorable toward both the coal gasification plant and the idea of an active planning and regulatory role for the local governments of the area. While perceptions of the plant were generally favorable, the public clearly indicated that the plant should pay its own way with respect to budgetary demands on the community and that more attention should be given to reclamation of stripped lands. The willingness of citizens to be supportive of vigorous local government action is encouraging. However, they did not show a knowledge about specific current local government behavior vis-a-vis the plant. This ambiguity, or lack of specificity, was also apparent in responses to the "quality of life" question; citizens suspected that the plant would be an asset to the community, but they were not able to see ways in which the plant might affect individual quality of life. This situation suggests that citizens had not received information adequate for relating abstract impressions with concrete events in the community.

The responses and the response rate in this survey suggests that local citizens are very interested in and concerned about coal-related community growth. If local governments, the news media, and coal companies provide the public with adequate information and if mechanisms for citizen input are developed, then citizens may be able to play a meaningful role in the community policymaking process.

Although this paper has reported some of the findings of a study of public opinion in one community in which coal-related growth was anticipated, it was felt that the information would be important to applied research on fiscal impacts and management alternatives. Future research on citizen preferences regarding specific local policy and management alternatives and on underlying attitudinal dimensions might be very fruitful.

ABSTRACT

The national emphasis on exploitation of coal resources means rapid growth for many small coal communities across the country. Effective local management of this growth will require knowledge of citizen perceptions and policy preferences regarding community impacts. Research reported here was conducted in a small Illinois community following the announcement of plans for construction of a major coal gasification plant in the community. The findings indicate that citizens were reasonably well-informed about economic, land use, and fiscal impacts and that they were positively oriented toward the idea of local government planning and management. However, there are ambiguities in citizen perceptions that deserve further research.

ACKNOWLEDGMENT

The author is indebted to Jane Langford and Glen Bogart (both former graduate students in Public Affairs) for their assistance in duta collection.

REFERENCES

Caldwell, L.K. 1970. Environment: A Challenge for Modern Society. The Natural History Press, NY, 292 p.

Ervin, O.L. 1978. Local fiscal effects of coal resource development: A framework for analysis and management. Policy Studies Journal 7:9-17.

Garrison, C.E. 1971. New industry in small towns: The impact on local government. National Tax Journal 24:493-500.

Leistritz, F.L., A.G. Leholm and T.A. Hertsgaard. 1975. Public sector implications of a coal gasification plant in western North Dakota. pp. 429-441, In Proc. of the Fort Union Coal Field Symp., Eastern Montana College, Billings.

Luttbeg, N.R. 1968. Models of Political Linkage. The Dorsey Press, NY, 469 p.

Nellis, L. 1974. What does energy development mean for Wyoming. Human Organization 33:229-238.

Nie, N.H., C.H. Hull, J.G. Jenkins, K. Steinbrenner and D.H. Bent. 1975. Statistical Package for the Social Sciences. McGraw-Hill, NY, 675 p.

Peele, E. 1976. Social effects of Energy Facilities. pp. 132-145, In W. Fulkerson (ed.), Energy Division Annual Progress Rpt., ORNL 5124, Oak Ridge Natl. Lab., Oak Ridge, TN.

U.S. Department of Housing and Urban Development. 1976. Rapid Growth from Energy Projects: Ideas for State and Local Action. Department of Housing and Urban Develop., Washington, DC, 59 p.

COMBINING SURFACE MINING AND RECLAMATION
TO MAXIMIZE THE SOCIAL PRODUCT OF A REGION

Webb M. Smathers, Jr.* and Alan Randall**

Coal mining has historically played a major role in the economy of the eastern Kentucky coalfields, and presently is the most important basic sector of the regional economy, in terms of income and employment generated (Sherafat 1978). Surface mining has been steadily increasing in importance since the 1950's and in 1975 accounted for 51% of the coal produced in the region.

This study focuses upon the watershed of the North Fork of the Kentucky River, an area of just less than 500,000 ha. Surface mining has occurred on 2.6% of the study region and 1.5% is currently in a disturbed state due to recent surface mining and/or reclamation activity (Randall et al. 1978).

The Study Region

The North Fork Watershed is contained wholly in the Central Appalachian coalfields. The area has rich coal deposits and some natural gas reserves. Elevations of ridges are typically 400 to 400 m above sea level while some approach 1,000 m in height in the southern most part of the area. The ridges slope downward sharply from 20 to 60 degrees toward the narrow valley floors. Within the many hollows are numerous small tributaries to the North Fork which usually have a seasonal low flow in the late, dry summer months. The slope of the North Fork and its tributaries in general vary from a fairly rapid slope of about 2.5 m km^{-1} to a slight slope in the lower portions.

The population of the North Fork is approximately 80,000 with most of the persons residing in small towns and rural areas. Hazard with a population of around 9,000 is the largest city. The socioeconomic characteristics of the North Fork are typical of Appalachia. There is a heavy dependence on government transfers, median family incomes are low, much of the housing is below national standards, and services and amenities in many cases do not meet national standards.

The Problem

Simply stated, the economic problem addressed in this paper is that while mining, particularly surface mining, generates many benefits to the regional economy, it also results

* Department of Agricultural Economics, University of Georgia, Athens, GA 30620.
** Department of Agricultural Economics, University of Kentucky, Lexington, KY 40506.

in substantial damages. Due to the physical nature of the surface mining process, disturbance of large amounts of geologic materials is inevitable, resulting in off-site damages from land slides, erosion, deterioration of water quality, ecosystem disturbance and aesthetic impairment. When one activity affects the quantity and/or quality of another activity, in a negative manner, the results are termed external diseconomies. Some level of external damage is highly probable under any set of mining and reclamation techniques. However, a central economic question is: what level of environmental protection, during and after surface mining is economically justified?

Reclamation (which we define, for the purposes of this study, as including all treatments to prevent environmental damage during and after mining) is a costly activity which, while most effectively undertaken as an integral part of the mining process, is performed for the purpose of minimizing the environmental damage accompanying mining, that is, producing a mix of environmental services and amenities beyond that which would occur in the absence of reclamation.

The primary problem in evaluating the benefits from reclamation is that the economic value of many of the benefits is not readily observable from market transactions. Reclamation benefits in the form of reduced damage to land and buildings and reduced costs of treatments to restore water quality, for example, can be valued from market observations. On the other hand, reduction in aesthetic damages, for example, is a public good (in the traditional economic meaning of that term) and is not priced in observable markets.

In a recent study Randall et al. (1978) estimated the benefits and costs of surface mine reclamation. Benefits from reclamation were defined as reductions in the economic costs of environmental damage. Five categories of damages were evaluated for the North Fork study region: (1) aesthetic, (2) water treatment, (3) flooding, (4) land and buildings, and (5) fish, wildlife and recreation. Values for categories of damage which involve a public good aspect were estimated using contingent valuation techniques. In categories where market determined prices were available those prices were used. The empirical estimates of damage are the most comprehensive available. However, data limitations resulted in an underestimate of the lower bounds of total costs of damage. The Randall et al. (1978) study estimated the environmental damage resulting from surface mining under the Kentucky regulations in force in 1976, as follows:

Categories of Cost of Damage	Hectares Disturbed
Aesthetic	770
Water Treatment	58
Flooding	122
Land and Buildings	834
Fish, Wildlife and Recreation	126
Total	1,910

That study also provided estimates of the costs of environmental damage from surface mining under a hypothetical "no reclamation" regime, and under a set of regulations similar to those which will be enforced under the federal Surface Mining Control and Reclamation Act of 1977.

Given the data base provided by Randall et al. (1978), this study attempts to determine the combination of surface mining and reclamation activities which, in the social sense, would provide the most efficient use of regional resources. In addition, the study

attempts to cast some light upon the relative efficiency of the Kentucky regulations as of
1976 and the Federal regulations which will be forthcoming.

Objectives

The major objective of this study is to determine the resource use which will maximize
the value of social product in the study region. To meet this objective, the research
technique must have three primary attributes: (1) it must use some kind of optimizing
algorithm; (2) it must be able to maximize the product of an economy producing both
private and public goods; and (3) its objective function must be specified in social (as
opposed to private) costs and benefits. Such a research technique will generate solutions
which internalize all external diseconomies resulting from mining and, thus, can be expected
to be quite different from those which would be generated by an unregulated surface mining
industry.

The significance of public goods (which include aesthetic benefits and water quality
as it affects swimming, boating and the biological requirements of sports fish species) is
that, once produced, they are available to all. The fish example is pedagogically useful
here. Water below a given qulaity level will not support a given fish species. However, water
which achieves a threshold level of quality will support fish in sufficiently large numbers
that their economic value to humans is limited only by congestion in the recreation fishery.
Thus, these public goods are either produced at some upper limit level or not produced at
all. Private goods, on the other hand, are produced in continuous functions which may often
be satisfactorily approximated as linear.

The requirements for an appropriate research technique were met by using a mixed
integer programming (M.I.P.) algorithm, with the objective function specified in social
benefits and costs. Recreational activities are specified as two level threshold (high, low)
zero-one integers, with dollar consumer surplus values. The surface mining and reclamation
sector are dollar valued, based on market prices as is the agricultural and silvicultural sector.

The objective function formulation of the model is:

(1) Maximize $\sum_{i=1}^{m} (a_i w_i - b_i x_i) + \sum_{j=1}^{n} c_j y_j + \sum_{t=1}^{r} d_t z_t$

where $a_i w_i$ is the mining sector

$b_i x_i$ is the reclamation sector

$c_j y_j$ is the agricultural and silvicultural sector

$d_t z_t$ is the environmental sector.

The system is subject to the familiar resource and non-negativity constraints in
addition to restricting integer variables to values of zero or one.

Mixed Integer Programming

Theoretically M.I.P. algorithms reduce a nonconvex region to a convex one and
permit global rather than local maximums to be obtained. Integer lattice points necessarily
result in a reduction of the feasible region which would be available to a mathematical
programming problem containing only continuously defined variables. Therefore, unless
a feasible integer lattice(s) also coincides with the continous frontier an optimal M.I.P.
objective function will be less than its continous analogue (Dantzig 1963, Dorfman
et al. 1958).

When threshold tolerances and/or public goods are involved, integer specification represents an organizational plan which can actually occur. It is not possible to have a fractional amount of the public good. If an amount less than one is permitted (continous case) then its provision is not possible.

Data Sources

Data sources used in construction of the regional M.I.P. model were adapted and modified from many sources. Since a complete representation of the model cannot be presented here, only major empirical sources will be briefly cited. The five categories of damage were derived from Randall et al. (1977). Objective function values of the recreational sector were derived using as a basis Gum and Martin (1975). Threshold levels of the recreational sector were modified from the National Academy of Sciences (1972). Studies by ICF, Inc. (1977), and Nephew and Spore (1976) were used as the basis for cost estimates of alternative mining and reclamation techniques.

Some Initial Results

The results reported below are optimal solutions to the problem of maximizing the social benefits from the use of the land and mineral resources in the study region. If it could be assumed that the output of the industrial, commercial, service and governmental sectors in the region was independent of the output from the use of the land and mineral resources, the optimal solutions reported below would be solutions which maximize regional social product.

Solutions are presented (Table 1) for three regulatory regimes: (1) the Kentucky regulations as of 1976, (2) the forthcoming federal regulations (insofar as they can be predicted from examination of the 1977 Act), and (3) a "no reclamation permitted" regime. While the third case is absurd (What government would actually ban reclamation?), it serves to illustrate the extent of the economic costs associated with mining in the absence of reclamation and hence the economic benefits from reclamation.

Surface mining and reclamation activities are classified by method: contour mining (CTR) or mountaintop removal (MTR); and by slope of land mined: 10, 20 and 30 degrees. In every solution, mining activities were carried out until the constraint on reserves available for mining in a given year was met. In our study region, at current coal prices, mining is a dominant economic activity.

Reclamation of contour mined sites to meet 1976 Kentucky standards involves terracing and sloping toward the highwall. Up to 40% of the overburden may be placed beyond the solid bench. Federal regulations will require back-to-contour reclamation. Both sets of regulations address many other important concerns, such as haul roads, runoff control, and revegetation. Typically, the Federal regulations are equally or more demanding than the Kentucky regulations.

The results suggest that social benefits from the land and mineral resources of the study region would decline about 13% if the federal regulations replaced the 1976 Kentucky regulations. While the federal regulations would reduce environmental damages and increase the productivity of regional waters for fishing and swimming, they would increase reclamation costs by a greater amount than the increase in benefits. This is a very tentative result, since Randall et al. (1978) report that their estimates of recreation benefits are underestimates in several respects.

Table 1 Summary of Results under Three Regulatory Regimes

Item	Integer Activity (yes, no)	Kentucky (1976)	Federal Act	No Reclamation Permitted
Optimal Integer Objective function value ($000,000)		77.557	67.519	42.804
Surface Mining:				
CTR/10° (ha.)	no	180	180	180
CTR/20° (ha.)	no	860	860	860
CTR/30° (ha.)	no	630	630	630
MTR/20° (ha.)	no	200	200	200
MTR/30° (ha.)	no	130	130	130
Deep Mining:				
Deep/(000 tons)	no	1,333.3	1,333.3	1,333.3
CTR or Deep (000 tons)	no	100.0	100.0	100.0
Surface Mine Reclamation*:				
CTR/10°/k(ha.)	no	180	0.0	0.0
CTR/10°/f(ha.)	no	0.0	180	0.0
CTR/20°/k(ha.)	no	860	0.0	0.0
CTR/20°/f(ha.)	no	0.0	860	0.0
CTR/30°/k(ha.)	no	630	0.0	0.0
CTR/30°/f(ha.)	no	0.0	630	0.0
MTR/20°/k(ha.)	no	200	0.0	0.0
MTR/20°/f(ha.)	no	0.0	200	0.0
MTR/30°/k(ha.)	no	130	0.0	0.0
MTR/30°/f(ha.)	no	0.0	130	0.0
Deep Mining Reclamation:				
Deep/(000 tons)	no	1,333.3	1,333.3	0.0
CTR or Deep/(000 tons)	no	100.0	100.0	0.0
Environmental Sector:				
Damages:				
Aesthetic ($000)	no	7,042.9	4,261.1	15,756.7
Water Treatment ($000)	no	358.7	196.6	1,421.2
Flooding ($000)	no	1,131.8	995.3	1,735.2
Land and Buildings ($000)	no	5,230.9	2,590.0	42,473.9
Downstream Fish and Recreation ($000)	no	496.8	243.5	1,627.0
Recreation:**				
Fishing B($000)	yes	0.0	2,348.2	0.0
Swimming B ($000)	yes	0.0	928.5	0.0
Boating B ($000)	yes	74.6	74.6	0.0
Camping B ($000)	yes	1,917.5	1,917.5	0.0
Agriculture and Silvaculture:				
Ag. Crops (ha.)	no	19,508.0	19,508.0	19,508.0
Ag. Pasture(ha.)	no	26,823.0	26,823.0	26,823.0
Clearcut Forestry (ha.)	no	500.0	500.0	500.0
Selective Forestry (ha.).	no	2,500.0	2,500.0	2,500.0

*k denotes reclamation to meet Kentucky standards; f denotes Federal standards.

**In no cases did the highest (i.e. A) quality recreation activities enter optimal programs.

The "no reclamation permitted" regime generates much lower net social benefits than the 1976 Kentucky regime. Reclamation costs are avoided, but environmental costs of substantially greater magnitude are suffered. While mining operators may save money if "no reclamation" was permissable, the net social benefits of land and mineral resource use are much lower in the total absence of reclamation. Initial calculations have indicated that in the absence of any regulatory constraints (positive or negative), net regional social benefits are maximized at a level of reclamation effort similar to that required by the 1976 Kentucky regulations.

The Direction of Future Research

The authors plan future research along the following lines: (1) analyses to determine the sensitivity of optimal programs to varying levels of coal prices and environmental benefits; (2) attempts will be made to define levels of reclamation effort intermediate between the 1976 Kentucky standards and the federal standards, in order to test the hypothesis that some intermediate level of reclamation effort might maximize social benefits; and (3) type II income multipliers, determined by Sherafat (1978), will be used to modify the objective function values for land and mineral using activities. This last modification will permit the determination of solutions to maximize regional social product without reliance on the assumption that the industrial, commercial, service and governmental sectors are independent of the land and mineral resource based sectors.

Conclusions

This application of an M.I.P. model with the objective function expressed in social benefits and costs has generated some interesting empirical results. In particular, it has demonstrated beyond doubt that "no reclamation" is not a reasonable alternative, if maximization of the social benefits of land and mineral resource use is the objective. Further, this application has shown that M.I.P. is a most promising tool for analysis of resource allocation in an economy with both public and private goods. While this is the first such application of which the authors are aware, many applications in environmental economics seem feasible and desirable.

REFERENCES

Dantzig, G. 1963. Linear Programming and Extensions. Princeton Univ. Press, NJ, 627 p.

Dorfman, R., P. Samuelson and R. Solow. 1958. Linear Programming and Economic Analysis. McGraw-Hill, NY, 525 p.

Gum, R. and W. Martin. 1975. problems and solutions in estimating the demand for and value of outdoor recreation. Amer. J. Agr. Econ. 57:558-566.

ICF, Inc. 1977. Energy and Economic Impacts of HR 13950 (Surface Mining Control and Reclamation Act of 1976). CEQ and USEPA, Washington.

National Academy of Sciences. 1972. Water Quality Criteria. EPA-R3-73-033. USEPA, Washington.

Nephew, E. and R. Spore. 1976. Costs of Coal Surface Mining and Reclamation in Appalachia. Oak Ridge Natl. Lab., TN.

Randall, A., O. Grunewald, A. Pagoulatos, R. Ausness and S. Johnson. 1978. Estimating Environmental Damages from Surface Mining of Coal in Appalachia: A Case Study. EPA-6002-78-003, USEPA, Cincinnati, OH.

Sherafat, N. 1978. The Impact of Coal Industry on Output, Income and Employment in Eastern Kentucky: An Input-Output Analysis. Ph.D. dissertation, Univ. Kentucky, Lexington.

ENERGY INDUSTRY USES OF
SOCIOECONOMIC IMPACT MANAGEMENT

William C. Metz *

As the production and use of coal expands during the remainder of this century, hundreds of small, rural communities situated in the country's coal regions will experience a by-product—socioeconomic impact. The construction and operation of coal mines, coal-fired power plants and gasification and liquefaction facilities produce both short and long-range socioeconomic impacts of varying intensity and focus. In some instances, a single energy project may impact one or more surrounding communities. More often however, multiple energy projects will impact the same communities, thus intensifying the socio-economic impacts.

NEW COAL—RELATED PROJECTS

In surveying the top 100 coal producers (2,000 smaller producers not included), the National Coal Association (1978) found that 190 new coal mines, both deep and surface, have been slated for start-up between now and 1985. The U.S. Government Accounting Office (1977) estimates approximately 438 to 825 new coal mines will be developed between years 1975 and 2000. Two hundred and sixty new coal-fired steam electric generating units are planned for completion between now and 1986 by National Coal Association (1978) estimates and an additional 400 new units are foreseen before the end of the century. Approximately a dozen commercial size coal gasification plants and liquefaction plants will be in operation by the year 2000. The actual number of coal-related energy projects will be heavily influenced by such variables as federal coal leasing policy, federal synthetic fuel subsidy or price support policy, federal project review approval schedule, state agency approval regulations and schedule, possible new environmental regulations, number and tenacity of project intervenors, new technology, industry finances, country's financial picture, rate of inflation, water availability, world and regional energy supply and demand and endangered species.

Capital costs, manpower requirements and project schedules can vary extensively with each coal-related project. Even for those projects of similar size and type, differences occur as a result of location, terrain, state regulations, union requirements, owner, project management, climate, project need, economics, local labor productivity and availability, and reporting policies. An estimation of coal-related average project sizes, costs, manpower needs, years to full production and expected project size ranges are presented in Table 1.

*Brookhaven National Laboratory, Building 475, Upton, NY 11973.

TABLE 1   Estimated Average Coal-Related Projects

Type	Average Size	Usual Project Size Range	Manpower Peak (Construction)	(Operation)	Cost (Millions)	Years To Full Production
Mine						
Surface-Western	4 MT/Y	1-20 MT/Y	225	200	$ 60	4
Surface-Eastern	.025 MT/Y	.0002 - .5 MT/Y	5	5	$ 0.25	1.5
Underground	2 MT/Y	1-3 MT/Y	250	650	$ 160	8
Power Plant	500 MW	20 - 1300 MW	1000	75	$ 500	6
Gasification	250 MMCF/D	11 - 360 MMCF/D	3000	700	$ 1300	6
Liquefaction	6000 T/D	100 - 6000 T/D	2500	500	$ 1500	6

ASSESSING POTENTIAL SOCIOECONOMIC IMPACT

In assessing the potential for socioeconomic impact on a project's surrounding communities, the project parameters and area's profile must be known. Project parameters include: the project timetable (date of construction initiation, peak, conclusion and operation); the manpower requirements (by quarter year and skill) and project cost (wages and salaries, local expenditures, total cost and tax payment). The area's profile includes: local labor availability; demographic characteristics; housing; education facilities; infrastructure capabilities and safety services; medical services; recreational facilities; commercial establishments; and fiscal situation. The project parameters are superimposed on the area profile and the number of project employees forecasted to relocate into the area in excess of the area's accommodation capacity is perceived as negative socioeconomic impact.

MITIGATING OR MANAGING SOCIOECONOMIC IMPACT

The company or companies proposing the coal-related energy project or projects have several options available in mitigating or managing potential adverse or unwanted socio-economic impacts. They could adjust the project construction parameters (e.g., lengthen the project schedule to reduce the construction manpower peak, fabricate components else-where, use workers for several tasks, select a more urban site for coal conversion projects where less socioeconomic impacts would conceivably occur and stagger multiple project and unit schedules), but each can be expensive. Adjustments to project operation parameters (e.g., retrain construction personnel into operations staff) are eaiser. On the other hand, the area's accommodation (housing, schools, sewer and water facilities, private and public services and recreation facilities) capacity could be changed and possibly at a greater cost/benefit ratio than that from the adjustment of the project parameters. One adjustment which involves neither the project parameters or area accommodations is the lowering of the number of in-migrants through company initiated car pooling or multiple transport of workers from their present residences in communities beyond a normal, daily commuting distance.

Industry, at an every increasing pace, is becoming involved in socioeconomic impact management. Costs can range from a few hours of a company's time to tens of millions of dollars. In a few instances, such as the Missouri Basin Power Project's (MBPP) Laramie River Station, a state siting council, Wyoming Industrial Siting Council, set forth a list of mitigating actions as a precondition to permit approval. The vast majority of mitigating actions are undertaken by companies on their own initiative. A community's quality-of-life can be adversely affected by inadquate sewer and water systems, insufficient and price-inflated housing, school overcrowding, overburdened government and medical services, lack of adequate police and fire protection, unsupportive recreational facilities, traffic congestion and social chaos. Regardless of the situation that existed in a community prior to a project or would be caused by the influx of project workers, industry has recognized that the above adverse community factors can result in increased construction and operational problems and costs. These varied and numerous problems and costs can be due to high turnover, recruitment costs, training costs, lowered productivity, accident increases, production inefficiency, absenteeism rise, higher equipment maintenance costs, walkouts, poor workmanship, a tarnished company reputation and finally, penalty and interest charges. The U.S. Environmental Protection Agency (1977) estimates that the Colorado-Ute Electric Association saved $100 million in construction costs as a result of the socioeconomic mitigating measures used at the Yampa Project in Craig, Colorado.

Responsibility for the management of project-caused socioeconomic impact is not specifically legislated, although management programs have been requested as permit application preconditions by a few state and federal agencies. Specific responsibilities for the planning and implementing of management measures have varied considerably from project to project due to industry philosophies, local government capabilities and the availability of state and federal programs. In some instances, many of the involved parties did not assume any of the responsibility.

SOCIOECONOMIC IMPACT MANAGEMENT ACTIONS

Coal-related energy industries can initiate a variety of long-term and short-term socioeconomic management actions parallel to their planning for new coal development projects. These socioeconomic impact management actions involve the following: (1) whole new community, (2) dramatic alteration of an existing community, (3) subdivision development, (4) temporary construction phase housing, (5) community services being upgraded, (6) community planning and (7) industry-community communication.

Whole New Community

The building of whole new communities in conjunction with new coal mines was a common occurrence as several thousand coal mine-related company towns were developed between 1850-1950. Few of these old company towns exist today.

The concept of a company, building a new town adjacent to its coal mine is being resurrected with a new twist: the company does not retain town ownership. Wright, Wyoming is being developed by the Atlantic Richfield Company (ARCO), at a cost of over $10 million, to accommodate more than its Black Thunder Coal Mine's 250 miners. The 735 acres are being master-planned for 2,200 families (an estimated 6,800 persons), with appropriate zoning and design restrictions to make it a first-class community. In time, the company will extricate itself from the town, recouping a part of its investment through land and housing sales with the remainder being written off to mine efficiency, worker productivity and lower turnover (Metz 1977).

Two other new towns have been proposed, but dropped as their corresponding projects were canceled. Kaiparowits, a new town planned for Kane County, Utah, was to be associated with the now canceled 3,000 MW electric power plant of that name. The other new town was to be associated with El Paso Natural Gas Company and Western Gasification Company coal gasification and coal mine complex proposed for the Navajo Reservation south of Farmington, New Mexico. The town would have housed the construction workers first, then after changes, the permanent personnel (AIF/EEI 1978).

Dramatic Alteration of an Existing Community

The Town of Colstrip, Montana is an example of a revamped community. In 1952, the Northern Pacific Railroad sold its old company town of Colstrip, which consisted of a few commercial structures and 62 residences housing approximately 100 people, to the Montana Power Company. In 1968 Western Energy Company, a wholly owned mining subsidiary of the Montana Power Company, undertook a plan to markedly revamp the town of Colstrip via company-sponsored planning, newly enacted zoning and building codes and a construction commitment of approximately $10 million. Over the next five years the company will extract itself from the "company town" with expectations of recouping $7 to $8 million. The difference is felt to be balanced off against low employee turnover, high productivity and a savings of $5/day travel allowances ($1,400/day to Western Energy Company) which a neighboring mine pays to each of its commuting miners (Metz 1977).

Subdivision Development

Industry initiated subdivision developments can be located within a community's corporate limits or sometimes up to 10 miles away from a community. The subdivision can accommodate a dozen families or several hundred families and can contain few amenities or a multitude of good quality-of-life features. The extent of industry's participation can be a gift of money or land, a loan, front-end financing, lot development, unit construction or subdivision management.

There are three categories of subdivisions: (1) mobile home park, (2) an adjustable mobile home to single-family development and (3) a single-family and/or multi-family development.

Mobile Home Park

Amax Coal Company is the sole developer of the Prospector Village, a mobile home community having the potential development capacity of 300 ± pads and 50 ± recreational vehicle (RV) spaces seven miles from Gillette, Wyoming at a cost of approximately $1.2 million (Metz 1977).

Eastern Associated Coal Corporation noticed that many of its young miners who could not yet afford a conventional house were having trouble finding suitable sites in Boone County, West Virginia for mobile homes. Therefore, the company committed several hundred thousand dollars for a 35-unit park and is developing plans for a second mobile home park (Metz 1977).

Peabody Coal Company has been involved in several mobile home parks, one in Kayenta, Arizona, situated on leased Indian land. Now Peabody is beginning construction of a 26 acre, 119 unit mobile home park adjacent to the existing 1969 one of 124 units in Kayenta, Arizona (Turk 1977).

In order to provide housing in a very rapid growth area for the peak construction work force of 1,250 workers at the 330 MW Wyodak Power Plant, the two partners, Pacific Power and Light Company (PP&L) and Black Hills Power and Light Company, invested over $3 million in the Foothills Mobile Home Park, two miles west of Gillette, Wyoming. There are 379 trailer spaces. Flexibility in accommodating an inexact number of relocaters was provided by allowing two recreation vehicles to locate on one mobile home site in specified areas for short periods of time. At some future time it is anticipated that the mobile home park will be sold off. The companies will then benefit from the park's mitigating quality during the construction period and a recouping of all or a portion of its investment through its sale (Blankenship 1978).

Adjustable Mobile Home to Single-Family Development

Four utilities are participating in the construction of the two 380 MW coal-fired units of the Craig Station with Colorado-Ute, the project manager, at an estimated cost of $700 million. Due to a potentially great socioeconomic impact on the small community of Craig, Colorado, it was agreed to build Shadow Mountain Village at a cost of approximately $5 million. It will accommodate some of the 1,700 construction workers expected at peak, 205 plant operations personnel and 160 coal miners. The village was constructed to accommodate 568 mobile homes with provisions in a few cases for two RVs to a mobile home space. On completion of the power plant, with the construction workers gone, the village will be sold to a developer who will build single-family homes on each pair of mobile home spaces. Presently, the village is operating under a temporary zoning ordinance which will revert to single-family residential (Hoving 1978).

At the MBPP's $1.4 billion Laramie River Station, it was felt that mitigation measures as of December 1976 had exceeded $19 million (Valeu 1977). By March 1977 however, with the project 45 days ahead of schedule, approximately $17 million had been saved just during construction (West 1977). In attempting to manage the growth in Wheatland, Wyoming and provide housing for its workers, Basin Electric Power Cooperative (project manager) budgeted approximately $8 million for a housing development. This money has gone going into a subdivision called Black Mountain which contains 550 temporary mobile home spaces which later will be converted into 275 single-family residences (Valeu 1978).

A Single-Family and/or Multi-Family Development

When the Energy Development Corporation, a wholly owned subsidiary of Iowa Public Service Company, drew up plans to open its Vanguard No. 1 Mine near Hanna, Wyoming in 1971, it found that the old company town was in poor condition and hardly conducive to the attraction of a stable work force. In keeping with the company's policy of having its supervisors and miners live close to the facility for convenience and efficiency, 10 acres of land were purchased in town and, under company direction, 52 homes were built at a cost of $1.5 million. Sale of the homes recouped $1 million. A loss of one-half million dollars was acceptable to the company in its housing venture in view of the lower incidence of manpower problems (Metz 1977).

ARCO is the backer of a housing subdivision in Gillette, Wyoming called Killarney. The plans call for a total of 63 single-family homes built by private builders on lots optioned from the company. In this manner, the heavy front-end financing of land purchase, streets, water and sewer lines and engineering is not placed on the small, local builder. The company breaks even on the investment via lot sales while stimulating area housing (Metz 1977).

Ideal Basic Industries, in partnership with Rocky Mountain Energy Company (RME), decided that housing was a necessity for its miners at the Stansbury Mine Project near Rock Springs, Wyoming. With an investment of $4.2 million, 119 housing units (45 single-family, the remainder being duplexes and townhouses) are being built in the Springland Addition subdivision. House size, mixture and type of living units were determined by researching family size, income ranges and life styles in the Rock Springs area (Metz 1977).

Indian Hills is a 260-unit condominium and townhouse development jointly funded by PP&L, Sun Oil Company, ARCO, Amax and Carter Mining Company (Exxon Corporation subsidiary). Each company is responsible for the guaranteed purchase or rental of a certain number of units and apartments within a given time frame. The project has had management problems, deciding who or what company was in charge and to whom does the builder answer. To compound these problems, the consortium hired a Houston, Texas developer who was unfamiliar with Wyoming weather, terrain, rapid growth problems and local labor, thus resulting in cost overruns, delays, escalation and occasional quality problems (Metz 1977).

At the Jim Bridger Power Plant in Rock Springs, Wyoming, PP&L management recognized a tight housing market problem due to area trona mine expansion and gas, oil, coal and uranium exploration increases. Approximately 500 acres of land west of Rock Springs was purchased from Upland Industries and in 1971, White Mountain Village was started. The development was to be based on the California concept of planned-unit-development (PUD), where front and side lawns are communal property and home exteriors and lawns are maintained by a Homeowners Association with strong protective convenants governing home owner activities. There was room for 180 single-family units in the $38,000-$53,000 range (plus monthly home owners association and recreational association fees) and the village was open to PP&L employees and non-employees. White Mountain Village will only have 150 single-family units due to a PUD acceptance problem, because home owners prefer control over their lawns without activity restrictions and monthly maintenance fees. Included within the PUD was a large amount of land, a community center and recreation facilities which are owned and operated by a Recreational Association. Presently, a large shopping center is under construction on a 30-acre portion of the PP&L land (Blankenship 1978).

A joint funding effort by seven coal companies (U.S. Steel, Consolidation Coal, Georgia-Pacific, Eastern Associated Coal, Armco Steel, Westmoreland Coal and Beckley Mining) and the United Mine Workers (UMW) is causing an expansion of housing in McDowell County, West Virginia. The Coalfield Housing Corporation, formed in September, 1976, is a nonprofit union and company coalition whose role is to identify suitable housing sites, obtain them and then bring together potential builders/developers and lenders from public and private agencies to initiate new housing developments. The type of housing needed at each site (single-family or multi-family, rental or private ownership) is determined by the Coalfield Housing Corporation (Metz 1977).

In 1976 over 1,000 new trailers were haphazardly located in Letcher County, Kentucky. Presently though, two large tracts of land are to be developed to relieve some of the housing pressure. Due to a combined effort by the Beth-Elkhorn Coal Company (conveyed 606+ acres valued at approximately $160,000 to a nonprofit sponsor for $2,000); Kentucky County Fiscal Court ($55,000 cash contribution), Kentucky Department of Transportation (access roads worth approximately $250,000) and the Appalachian Regional

Commission (contribution of $514,000) housing tracts are being readied. Private developers will purchase the developed lots (land with existing roads and sewer and water systems) in an open-bidding process and build and sell houses in accordance with the specifications established by the Kentucky Mountain Homes, Inc. (Metz 1977).

Two other projects which involve the ARC and coal company participation are the Big Stone Gap and Black Joe housing projects. The Big Stone Gap housing project will result in 305 new housing units in Wise County, Virginia. Westmoreland Coal Company provided a $100,000 interest-free loan to cover some critical engineering site improvement costs. The Black Joe housing project in Harlan County, Kentucky (160 units) involved the donation of a former coal company camp and land by the Eastover Mining Company to the project sponsor, Harlan County Homes, Inc. ARC is providing $60,000 (80 percent of the project's cost) (Metz 1977).

Temporary Construction Phase Housing

Temporary construction phase housing is often necessary at a coal-conversion facility project to accommodate the workers who would not be able to find acceptable, temporary housing or recreational vehicle (RV) hookups in nearby communities. This construction-worker-oriented housing usually takes the form of bachelor quarters and RV parks.

Colorado-Ute developed bachelor quarters with associated facilities at Craig Station at a cost of almost three-quarters of a million dollars. The bachelor quarters were composed of five modular units, 20 rooms to a unit and had two men to a room. A mess hall, recreation center and laundry facilities were located next to the bachelor quarters. Workers were charged a fixed fee for room and board. Temporary RV spaces were included in the Shadow Mountain Village moible home park, two to a mobile home space (Hoving 1978).

PP&L built bachelor quarters for its Jim Bridger and Wyodak workers with adjacent mess hall and indoor recreation facilities. At both plant sites, RV parks were built where workers could rent spaces with sewer, water and electricity hook-ups and use communal laundry, shower and recreational facilities. The RV park at Wyodak accommodated 400 units and when that proved insufficient, some RVs were placed temporarily on single mobile home spaces in the company built mobile home park. As demand for the bachelor quarters and RV parks diminishes, they will be torn out, having served their purpose (Blankenship 1978).

At the Laramie River Station, MBPP has built 200 bachelor apartments with associated dining and recreational facilities, along with a 300 parking space RV park (Zelinger 1977).

Montana Power and Western Energy invested almost $2 million in temporary trailer parks and bachelor quarters at Colstrip, Montana during the construction of Units 1 and 2 (West 1977).

Sierra Pacific Power Company has stated it will have bachelor quarters for 156 workers and 66 RV spaces available at its North Valmy Power Plant site. Mess hall, indoor recreational and shower facilities will accompany the construction work force living quarters (SPPCo 1977).

Community Services Being Upgraded

While many coal-related companies focus on the immediate worker need for housing, numerous other stress points sometimes go unnoticed. Influxes of hundreds of employees into small towns near energy developments may call for company efforts in regard to community service. These company efforts can heavily influence a community life style. There can be involvement in sewer and water systems, recreation, commercial sectors, education, medical and social services, child care and organizations, etc.

In conjunction with its Shadow Mountain Village plans, Colorado-Ute paid $915,000 to the City of Craig to improve its sewer and water systems sufficiently to accommodate the subdivision (Hoving 1978). The City of Gillette is having its waste water piped to the Wyodak Power Plant, where it is treated and used as cooling water makeup (Blankenship 1978). RME is assisting the Douglas municipality in securing sewer and water system funding from Wyoming state agencies. Mine-water from Kaiser Steel Corporation's Sunnyside Mine in Utah is used by the Town of Sunnyside (Metz 1977).

Within many of the company sponsored subdivisions, new towns and revamped communities recreational facilities are provided in abundance. Tens of millions of dollars in recreation centers, community centers, swimming pools, tennis courts, playgrounds, bicycle paths, baseball fields, open areas, "tot" parks and large sodded parks are being built for the relaxation and enjoyment of not only company workers, but entire communities. PP&L and Idaho Power built a park on the edge of the Jim Bridger Plant's large surge pond for the use of Rock Spring's citizens (Blankenship 1978). Arch Mineral Company loaned the use of men and strip mining equipment to the Town of Hanna to level school athletic fields (Metz 1977).

Companies (e.g., ARCO, Amax, MBPP, PP&L, RME) have also helped in the growth of commercial developments by incorporating them into new town and subdivision plans. Occasionally, more than land is sold to developers; sometimes the structures are built by the companies and rented (e.g., Western Energy). Many company personnel are active in local chambers of commerce (Metz 1977).

Colorado-Ute in Craig, ARCO in Wright, PP&L in Rock Springs, Western Energy in Colstrip and MBPP in Wheatland, to name a few companies, have deeded over land to school districts at no charge. Basin Electric has guaranteed $5 million in tax exempt bonds for a nonprofit organization which leases school facilities to the Platte County School District No. 1 (Valeu 1978). In older company coal towns like Hiawatha and Sunnyside, Utah, Marianna and Mather, Pennsylvania, school buildings were built by the company. Many companies have made commitments to the field of education by underwriting vocational programs and donating technical and visual materials and assistance. The Tennessee Valley Authority makes payments to impacted schools on the basis of project-related new students.

In the area of medical and social facilities and services, companies have individually and collectively committed themselves to doctor and nurse recruitment, clinic development, hospital expansion, gifts of ambulances and medical communication equipment, mental health programs, hospital donations and committee membership. The Southwest Industrial Association (SWIA), composed of Sweetwater County, Wyoming companies, has contributed $250,000 for clinics and doctor recruitment. In one instance, they paid for a doctor's recruiting visit, his moving expenses and guaranteed a $20,000 bank note which could be spent at the doctor's discretion (Zelinger 1977). Kerr-McGee Corporation contributed $1,000 in 1975 to Campbell County, Wyoming for nurse recruitment and $1,000 in 1976 for doctor recruitment (USGS 1977). A coal mining company in Hanna donated an ambulance to the town.

Besides showing concern for community youth through recreational facilities, some companies go further. ARCO, for example, underwrote an equestrian facility in Campbell County, Wyoming. Companies such as Kerr-McGee give contributions to area agencies:

$1,900 in 1976 to Gillette area Youth Emergency Service, Bicentennial Fund, Boy Scouts, etc. Others donate company time (USGS 1977).

Community Planning

It is in the energy companys' interest to have orderly community growth. Companies can encourage comprehensive planning, provide technical assistance and even fund a community planning effort.

TVA has a basic policy of encouraging the formation of local planning commissions in cities and counties affected by coal-fired power plants. "Encouragement" may take the form of funding contributions to pay part of staff costs, providing TVA staff planning assistance in drawing up necessary ordinances or preparing plans (AIF/EEI 1978).

The six coal companies who make up the Gillette Subcommittee of the Wyoming Mining Association paid the first year's salary ($16,000) of a city-county planner and assisted city officials in preparing a job description. SWIA has also contributed funds for a planning effort in Sweetwater County (Zelinger 1977).

Basin Electric granted $18,000 to the City of Wheatland to pay for the preparation of an application for federal funds and to establish a Department of Planning. One result was the enactment of stringent development codes within corporate limits. A later problem was the surrounding unzoned county land (West 1977).

Planners have been hired by companies involved in new town developments, the major revamping of existing towns and subdivisions. Many companies now have planners on their staffs to handle the constant involvement in community affairs and housing efforts.

Industry - Community Communications

Since the passage of the National Environmental Policy Act in 1969 and the past decade of growing environmental awareness by industry and communities, industry-community communication is more frequent. This is not to say that solutions to impacts are more frequent, for many times the communication solves nothing. But industry, partly as a result of increasing state and Federal permits and agency reviews, and occasionally on its own volition because of the perceived benefits of a prepared community, is sharing information on manpower requirements, schedules and potential impacts with project-adjacent communities.

Basin Electric, ANG Coal Gasification Company, Peoples Gas Company, Otter Tail Power Company and Montana-Dakota Utilities Company voluntarily organized an Inter-Industry Technical Assistance Team (ITAT) in early 1977 to monitor socioeconomic change and provide Mercer County, North Dakota citizens and public officials with technical assistance (Valeu 1978). In Sweetwater County, Wyoming, on authorization of the county and the Cities of Rock Springs and Green River, a "Priorities Board" was established. It was composed of county commissioners, mayors, school district representatives, industry representatives and two citizens at large. The purpose of the Board was to provide regular communication between local government and industry, analyze problems, recommend priorities and determine solutions (AIF/EEI 1978). In conjunction with the formation of the Priorities Board, 12 major companies involved in coal, electrical generation and trona mining formed the Southwest Wyoming Industrial Association (SWIA). It provides annual industry employment projections, limited legal, engineering and management services to the community and helps in front-end community financing efforts (AIF/EEI 1978). In Platte County, Wyoming in 1974, a 15-member Platte County Impact Alleviation Task Force was formed in response to MBPP pressure to function as a capability and impact information transfer point. The formation of a Wheatland Project Area Coordinating Council, funded by MBPP up to $10,000 per year, was a requirement of the Wyoming Industrial Siting Administration. Its function is to receive monthly reports from MBPP, review and evaluate monitoring reports and design and implement needed mitigating measures (Valeu 1978).

Colorado-Ute notified the City of Craig that it would be building a coal-fired power plant near that community in 10 years. During that 10-year interval, plans were drawn up by private developers and discussions held, but no actions were taken. Realizing this, the utility established a Front-End Funding Committee to bring city, county and company representatives together on a regular basis to discuss: (1) community needs, (2) methods of financing and (3) impact mitigation measures (Zelinger 1977).

CONCLUSION

The large financial investments which companies are making in coal-related projects and the magnitude of the consequences of project delay and/or worker problems are causing these companies to study and mitigate socioeconomic impacts. Schedule delays during the construction of large energy facilities can cost a company several hundred thousand dollars a day. Every new underground coal miner can cost a company approximately $25,000 for the first 90 days, all unproductive, for salary, benefits, training and recruitment. Every minute of downtime in a coal mine costs approximately $100 in a large stripping operation or a ton of coal at a working face in an underground mine.

During the remainder of the 20th Century, coal-related projects will be occurring with greater frequency, project impacts compounding project impacts on each community. Companies in recognition of the effects of adverse socioeconomic impacts on their projects are investing time and capital in socioeconomic impact management actions. This involvement fosters positive relations with project-adjacent communities, helps produce a worker and community acceptable quality-of-life, diminishes worker productivity problems and ultimately produces greater corporate profit. Some company impact management actions return all or part of the investment directly through sales or rentals, while all company actions produce indirect returns on the investment through worker productivity and project efficiency.

REFERENCES

Atomic Industrial Forum and Edison Electric Institute. 1978. Social Impact Assessment Monitoring and Management by the Electric Energy Industry: State-of-the Practice, Washington, DC.

Interviews by W.C. Metz with Richard Blankenship of PP&L, Casper, WY (January 26, 1978), Robert Hoving of Colorado-Ute, Montrose, CO (January 25, 1978) and Robert Valeu of Basin Electric, Bismarck, ND (February 8, 1978).

Metz, W.C. 1977. Residential aspects of coal development. AIP Annual Conf., Kansas City, MO.

Missouri Basin Power Project. 1975. Environmental Analysis for the Laramie River Station. Burns and MacDonnell, Kansas City, MO.

National Coal Association. 1978. Communication from Carl E. Bagge, President to The President of the United States. Doubling Coal Production and Use by 1985.

Sierra Pacific Power Company. 1977. North Valmy Station Environmental Report, Westinghouse Environmental Systems Department, Pittsburgh, PA.

Turk, R. 1977. New Mobile Home Park for Kayenta. Peabody Magazine, December, 5 p.

USEPA, Office of Research and Development, Energy, Minerals and Industry, Decision Ser., Energy/Environment II. 1977. Methodology for the Analysis of the Impacts of Electric Power Production in the West, pp. 275-281. GPO, Washington, DC.

USGAO. 1977. U.S. Coal Development - Promises, Uncertainties. GPO, Washington, DC.

USGS. 1977. Draft EIS, East Gillette Mine. GPO, Washington, DC.

West, S.A. 1977. Opportunities for Company-Community Cooperation in Mitigating Energy Facility Impacts. MIT, Cambridge, MA.

Zelinger, S.K. 1977. Energy Planning - The Rural Context. AIP Annual Conf., Kansas City, MO.

EXTERNALITY COSTS ASSOCIATED
WITH ENERGY RESOURCE DEVELOPMENT

Carl E. Ferguson, Jr., Ronald E. Bird and William O. Bearden*

"Ecology and environmental quality are of interest to all people. It appears that the quality of the environment is a generally populist movement, appealing to people regardless of political views, religious beliefs, ages, or income levels. Probably, pictures of Earth from space did more than anything else to convince people that the Earth is a tiny planet covered with a thin sheet of life-giving air and orbiting in hostile nothingness. If so, then this idea alone was worth the cost of all space exploration, because it may have saved mankind from extinction by irreversible pollution" (Davis and Blomstrom 1974).

Concern over the adequacy of nature's endowments and man's pollution goes back a long way. For example, in 1285, the city of London experienced air pollution problems from the burning of soft coal (Fisher and Peterson 1976). The natural environment even to Malthus was a concern because of increasingly scarce resources needed to sustain economic activity (Samuelson 1976). Stanley Jevons observed the physical limits of coal deposits in England and predicted the end of the industrial revolution as early as 1866. And most interestingly, though the environment may have originally been viewed as a source of extractive resources, John Stewart Mill (1865) emphasized its importance for the quality of life as evidenced by the "opportunity for experiencing solitude and natural beauty."

The issues surrounding environmental externalities are numerous and complex. Consequently, a number of suggested formats for dealing with questions of conservation and pollution have been developed. The structure developed by Fisher and Peterson (1976), and Fisher et al. (1972) provides a workable framework for evaluating externality costs and is followed in the present effort:

"The new view [of the environment] has two distinct focuses which, interestingly, parallel the traditional ones on extractive resources. One focus is on specific natural environments, which can be put to extractive *or* amenity uses and are akin to stocks of non-renewable resources that are consumed once and for all. The second is on pollution, a use of the assimilative capacity of the environment that is similar to sustainable yield exploitation of renewable resources--both are reversible, except in cases of extreme abuse, and both involve flows rather than stocks" (Fisher and Peterson 1976).

*College of Commerce and Business Administration, P.O. Box AK, The University of Alabama, Birmingham, AL 35486.

VALUATION OF AMENITIES

Empirical research to date regarding the benefits from environmental preservation has been limited.

"Earlier, the wilderness environment was large in relation to lands under cultivation. Under the circumstances it could have been argued that the reduction of wildlands represented a transformation of resources that were abundant, hence of small value at the margin, into goods and services of greater marginal value in a developing economy" (Krutilla and Fisher 1975).

Krutilla and Fisher (1975) have suggested that now the central issue involves the problem of ". . . providing both for the present and for future amenities associated with unspoiled natural environments for which the market frequently fails to make adequate provision."[1] Their concerns center around the natural environment whose use for extractive purposes precludes further use for non-extractive purposes which also give value and are irreversible. . .

". . . private market allocations are likely to preserve less than the socially optimal amount of natural environments. Moreover, the optimum amount is likely to be increasing over time—a particularly serious problem in view of the irreversibility of many environmental transformations" (Fisher et al. 1972).[2]

Further, Barnett and Mores (1963) suggest that the traditional concerns of conservation economics, the husbanding of natural resource stocks for the use of future generations, may now be outmoded by advances in technology.

Most authors would, however, agree with Harold Hotelling, a major contributor to the effort to quantify the value of environmental amenities, that

". . . the world's disappearing supplies of minerals, forests, and other exhaustible assets have led to demands for regulation of their exploitation. The feeling that these products are now too cheap for the good of future generations, that they are being selfishly exploited at too rapid a rate, and that in consequence of their excessive cheapness they are being produced and consumed wastefully has given rise to the conservation movement" (Solow 1974).

Surely, as Fisher et al. (1972) suggest, there are important economic issues related to the clear-cutting of a redwood forest or to the development of a hydroelectric project in the Grand Canyon.[3] They note that while there is a vast amount of literature dating back to the 1930s on the benefit-cost evaluation of water resource projects, economists have said little about environmental opportunity costs. Where reference is made to the despoilation of

---

[1] One might also remark that the "problem" might come into better focus if economists began to observe these unspoiled environments as commodities essential to the well-being of man and not simply as "amenities." Recognizing, of course, the term "amenities" is established jargon, it does imply a certain lack of "importance."

[2] For a comprehensive study of optimum depletion rates, see Dasgupta and Heal (1974) and Burt and Cummings (1970).

[3] This paper developed a model for the allocation of natural environments between preservation and development. It then applied the resulting model to the issue: should the Hell's Canyon of the Snake River, the deepest gorge of the North American continent, be reserved in its current state of wilderness for recreation and other activities or further developed as a hydroelectric facility?

natural environments, "extra-economic" considerations are given marginal attention.[4] Similarly, in texts on land economics, little mention is made of the economic issues involved in the allocation of wildlands and scenic resources. And cost estimates of land development frequently fail to include the opportunity returns foregone as a result of destroying natural areas.

Given that very little has been done in the past and that the time has come to begin to try to value these amenities, what alternatives are available? An ingenious way around the difficulty was proposed by Harold Hotelling in 1947, to the director of the National Park Service. The first published version of Hotelling's method is found in the seminal piece by Marion Clawson (1959), which has in turn stimulated substantial research on the economics of outdoor recreation:[5]

> "In principle, the method is very simple. It recognizes that even though there is no explicit charge for the use of the site, the user pays a price measured by his travel costs. The rate of use, say visitor days divided by population, is related to the cost of a visit for each of a number of suitably defined visitor origin zones. The resulting demand relationship may then be integrated to obtain a measure of value, consumers' surplus for the site. The advantage of this measure is that it is rooted in the theory of consumer demand. With it, the cost-benefit analysis need not impute an arbitrary value to a day of recreation" (Fisher and Peterson 1976).

However, given that some value can be established for the amenities, the analyst is still confronted by the conflicts associated with trade-offs in preserving the environment (see Edmunds 1977). While it would be reassuring to believe that the resulting cost-benefit analysis with dollar evaluation was an absolute measure, it is difficult not to recall Daniel H. Gray's (1972-73) warning that what often results is "a chain of rigorous reasoning beginning with a humble confession of unreal assumptions which then tend to be forgotten, once a logically or ideologically pleasing conclusion has been reached."

Therefore, it seems that a "quantitative" decision to conserve resides largely on the economist's ability to measure the amenities (often the intangible qualities) of the environment. Though at times easier to estimate when the alternative has the far-reaching effects associated with pollution, valuation remains a most frustrating issue in the drive to improve the management of our natural resources.

VALUATION OF ABSORBING RESOURCE

Pigou was the first economist to systematically treat pollution as an external phenomenon. Still it was not until the decade of the 1960s that pollution was widely recognized by economists and others as a serious threat to human well-being.

In 1966 Kenneth Boulding published a provocative paper that viewed the Earth as a spaceship, a closed vessel that can neither receive nor dispose of materials. Boulding's work is acknowledged as being suggestive in the very important study by Ayres and Kneese

---

[4] See, for example, Proposed Practices for Economic Analysis of River Basin Projects, report to the Interagency on Water Resources, prepared by the Subcommittee on Evaluation Standards (Washington 1958), p. 44; Krutilla and Eckstein (1958); McKean (1958); and Hufschmidt, Krutilla, and J. Margolis (Washington 1961). Cited in Fisher, Krutilla, and Cicchetti (1972), p. 605.

[5] For an informative review, see Knetsch and Davis (1966).

(1969) of pollution as a problem of materials balance.[6] Drawing on the physical concept of conservation of mass, residuals in the form of disposal (pollution) are depicted as a pervasive phenomenon and not the exceptional case earlier imagined (see Kneese et al. 1970).

Society appears ready to place higher prices on environmental amenities. Through this valuation process (revaluation if one is inclined to accent the idea that society originally placed a zero dollar value on the amenities), society will begin to quantify the concerns which often fall under the general industrial rubric of "social responsibility." It will not be an easy task (though estimating the "social costs" of the "externalities" of production may prove easier than estimating the benefit of a grant to the Public Broadcasting System or a minority hiring program). How then does one begin to "valuate" the social costs?

Kneese (1962, and Kneese and Bower 1968) appears to be the first economist after Pigou to treat externalities analytically and express serious concern about pollution. His major contributions to water quality management are: (1) an explicit use of the Pigovian externality framework which has provided an approach for further development and application by economists and (2) a recognition of the range of management alternatives. Thus, management must consider not only shutdown of waste generating production activity or end-of-pipe treatment of the waste, but also internal process change, recovery and recycle of residuals, public investment in centralized treatment, and flow augmentation (Kneese 1964).

But who owns the absorbing resource?

"Suppose property rights to the environment are assigned to the polluter, then its value to the damaged party (assume just one, to abstract from the problem of transaction cost)[7] will be measured by what he is willing to pay the polluter to refrain from polluting. If this amount is less than its value in waste disposal, the theorem tells us that waste disposal is the most efficient use of the environment.[8] But suppose property rights were assigned to the receiver. The value of the environment as a source of amenity services then would be measured by the minimum amount acceptable to permit its diversion to other use. Alternatively, for a given assignment of property rights, and a given pre-pollution starting point, the different measures correspond to the receiver's equivalent and compensating variations of consumer's surplus, respectively. One reason why these measures may differ is that the first is constrained by the receiver's income, the second is not. Where the pollution-competing use of the environment is by a producer, the income constraint vanishes and the two measures coincide" (Fisher and Peterson 1976).

Pollution is pervasive and remains an ever-increasing problem. However, some hope for explanation and control planning is provided by recent theoretical approaches.

Though partial equilibrium models have yielded useful insight into the sources and implications of pollution, recent efforts demonstrate the need for use of general equilibrium techniques. Two approaches can be observed. One strategy incorporates environmental externalities and a system of corrective taxes into the general competitive equilibrium model

---

[6] Credit for the idea of applying materials balance concepts to water disposal problems is given by Ayres and Kneese to a Ph.D. dissertation by F.A. Smith, The Economic Theory of Industrial Waste Production and Disposal (Northwestern University 1968).

[7] In reality the damaged party is society and society rarely can be said to be of a single mind.

[8] This is often to make an all or nothing decision. Probably, it should be framed in marginal terms with partial protection of the environment as an alternative.

(Tietenberg 1973, Maler 1974, Baumol and Oates 1975). A complementary approach extends the input-output framework to take account of the flow of materials between the economy and the environment (Cumberland 1966, Daly 1968, Isard 1969, Leontief 1970, Converse 1971, Victor 1972).

In order to apply or test these theories, dollar estimates of pollution damages and abatement costs are required. Though reliable damage estimates are not available, much of the ongoing research in the environmental area is devoted to developing respectable methodologies. The following discussion is representative of the current state of the art:

> "We know less about the step from ambient conditions to damaging effects, because pollution has many suspected effects that have not been identified, let alone quantified. We cannot know within an order of magnitude how many people sicken or die from pollution in general, so any number purporting to quantify the health effects of specific pollutants must be viewed with caution. Where a damaging effect has been identified, be it a reduction in crop yields or the stimulus of bronchitis cases, it is hard to determine which pollutants if any are to blame. Multicollinearity is the bug-a-boo of pollution damage estimation, with high correlations existing among the pollutants, climatological conditions, and socio-economic factors expected to cause the damages use multiple regression analysis to correlate deaths from various diseases with pollution variables, especially sulphur oxide and particulates (Lave and Seskin 1970, 1971). In their cross section regression of burrows in England and metropolitan areas in the United States, they control for numerous factors, but it is still possible that the pollution variables used are just proxies for the "real" causes of mortality. It appears, for instance, that sulphur dioxide is not as pernicious as results indicate (Lave and Seskin 1971, 1975). Reductions in sulphur dioxide levels in New York City have not changed mortality patterns there (Schimmel and Murawski 1975). And much of the daily variation in death rates may be due to weather conditions that happen to be correlated with pollution.[9] In Berlin, New Hampshire, significant reductions in both sulphur dioxide and particulates produced scant changes in respiratory disease and pulmonary function (Faris et al. 1973). Despite these problems, Lave and Seskin probably have demonstrated a statistically significant relationship between air pollution and human health, with the size of the effect and the relative importance of these pollutants yet to be determined" (Fisher and Peterson 1976).

As complex as the problem is, establishing the relationships between pollution and health effects is just the first step. Given that they are related, accurate costs cannot yet be determined until the degree/extent of the causal relationships involved are estimated. These estimates are not yet available. Ignoring psychic costs, Ridker and Henning (1967) compute the cost of the mortality and morbidity as the present value of lost earnings, plus the costs of premature burial, medical treatment, and absenteeism. However, an estimate must also be made of the percentage of burial, medical, and absentee costs experienced per unit of time that is directly attributable to pollution effects. At present, these estimates are not available. It should be clear by now that though the starting point may be evident, the problems to be addressed are formidable.

In the preceding examples, the authors dealt with estimating the costs when the

---

[9] Preliminary findings of R.W. Bechley, communicated in an oral conversation with Fisher and Peterson.

effects, though difficult to isolate, were easily measured. But consider on the other hand such amenities as recreation. Water pollution reduces recreational activities by closing lakes and streams to swimming, fishing, and boating as dissolved oxygen levels fall. In order to evaluate an abatement problem, the use of the improved water body is usually forecasted and values placed on that use. Boating, fishing, and swimming activities on other water bodies are regressed on variables for income, population densities, travel costs, user fees, and the location of substitute sites. Davidson et al. (1966) ran regressions on a survey of 1,352 households to forecast the number of recreational boaters, fishermen, and swimmers who would use the Delaware Estuary at various levels of water quality, measured by dissolved oxygen. They used arbitrary values of $1.00 to $5.00 per day of recreational activity to assess the value of estuary cleanup. While the Hotelling-Clawson method of valuation discussed earlier could eliminate the arbitrariness, it would be exceedingly difficult to apply over a wide area like the Delaware Estuary (Fisher and Peterson 1976).

Adding up pollution damages effect by effect would require substantial work, not to mention the necessity of making many assumptions. Results would probably be under-estimated, given that some effects cannot be quantified. The Barrett and Waddell study of air pollution in the United States is probably the best known attempt to examine damages by the Hotelling-Clawson method (Barrett and Waddell 1973, Waddell 1974). Easier survey methods are being currently researched. For example,

"To the extent that people perceive pollution damages and answer honestly, surveys and bidding games can be used to evaluate abatement programs. One's fear of answers biased by the method of inquiry is partially relieved by the results of an experiment by P. Bohm, who asked people in various ways what they would pay to see a special movie and found no statistically significant differences in their answers (Bohm 1972). Randall and Eastman evaluated air pollution abatement benefits in the Four-Corners region of the Southwest by showing tourists and residents pictures of pollution from the power plants there and determining the maximum bids for a given level of abatement (Randall et al. 1974). Davis (1964); Gardner et al. (1973); and Sinden (1974) used questionnaires and interview techniques to determine peoples' willingness to pay for hunting and other recreational experiences. These techniques seem crude, but they may be validated if many people use them and receive about the same answers" (Fisher and Peterson 1976).

To make matters worse, data problems are severe. Urban land values are difficult to impute. Estimation proceeds on the basis of property values, which include the value of improvements and are themselves scarce and unreliable. A sparse network of frequently malfunctioning pollution stations provides inadequate air quality data; consequently, many of the variables describing neighborhood characteristics must be fabricated. Problems of multicollinearity make it difficult to determine whether sulphur oxides, carbon monoxide, traffic noise, high crime levels, or other factors have depressed residential property values. And as suggested earlier, though significant correlations may result, there is no assurance that the independent variables are not in fact surrogates for the "real" determinants (see Straszheim 1974).

While most researchers have focused on measuring the benefits of specific abatement programs, Nordhaus and Tobin (1973) and their NBEER conferees have tried to measure the overall quality of life. Their measure of economic welfare (MEW) took into account urban disamenities as well as leisure time, nonmarket activities (e.g., housework), and nonproductive activities (e.g., commuting to work). National income and product figures are, of course, not meaningful indices of social welfare, and economic growth can also be deceptive. Olson (1975), Weinrobe (1973), and others (e.g., Moss 1973) have analyzed these problems and present ways to improve the figures or construct alternative measures. Most economists agree with Arthur N. Okun (1971) that other indices should be constructed and that basic income and product accounts should not be reevaluated.

CONCLUSION

Pollution and other environmental disruptions are getting worse. As the economy grows, the size of our "Spaceship Earth" remains constant. The marketplace does not seem to be able to adjust and allow polluters and society to "agree" on acceptable levels of pollution and rates of resource consumption.

"Given the potentially very useful analytical techniques ... to aid environmental decision-making, it is unfortunate that policies on pollution control are being set without substantial input from economists. The U.S. Government sets abatement standards, enforces them, and sometimes even prescribes the technology to be used, without attempting to equate marginal costs across pollution sources or provide incentives for technical progress. The blame for this lies partially with the Congress and executive agencies for ignoring economists, and partly with economists for recommending impractical policies and for not offering compromises. As one compromise, for example, the combined effluent standard and tax suggested by Baumol and others would be almost as efficient as the pure tax solution.... and would be politically more palatable. If we hope to influence environmental policy, we will have to work with politicians and with representatives of other disciplines. To state the point more positively, environmental problems appear to offer an opportunity for economists to engage in multi-disciplinary research that is theoretically respectable and of practical importance" (Fisher and Peterson 1976).

Man's actions in an ecological system involve social trade-offs. All things cannot be done at once. If time and resources are allocated to reduce air pollution, then less time and resources are available for the reduction of water pollution, improving education, and constructing recreational facilities. How much is society willing to give up to achieve a cleaner world? Will society give up the individual automobile and accept public transportation? Will society pay for the municipal sewer system and the new street and park cleaning labor forces?[10] Many increases in the standard of living mean a related rise in pollutants produced by the individual consumer. Further, as consumption increases, economic demand requires an increase in industrial production with its attendant pollution.

"The environment has been mostly an economic free good for a firm to use as needed. This reasoning especially applied to air and water, two of society's main areas of pollution. They have been considered part of a public common available to all persons. They have been an economic externality that business did not need to incorporate into its internal cost system. The steel maker could use oxygen from the air for his blast furnace without paying society a penny for it. Similarly, he could draw water

---

[10] Each of these questions involves costing out the environmental amenities which are "consumed" when these activities occur. Until this can be done, these questions cannot be adequately answered.

from the river and discharge his wastes into it without paying for this service. Society placed no economic value on these public commons. They were free goods. In this manner both the businessman and his customers avoided paying direct costs for degradation of the common. However, these costs were transferred to society as social costs. This was not a serious problem as long as the load on the common was light, but when it became heavy, society found itself with burdensome costs that it did not care to bear. Examples of these costs are fish kills, expenses of purifying water for drinking, and eye irritation from air pollutants" (Davis and Blomstrom 1974).

The economic system has allowed those who continue to degrade the environment an economic advantage over those who attempt to reduce degradation. It is an Alice-in-Wonderland situation in which socially undesirable acts are encouraged and socially desirable acts are penalized. However, as we have seen, there are economic incentives that can encourage pollution abatement. But who should bear these economic costs?

If industry wants to avoid government regulation and "interference" in their activities, the major polluting industries must begin to apply rigorous methods to value the environment which they "consume" in their industrial processes. In this way they will be defining their *own* cost structure, as they should, and continuing to manage their own affairs. These costs would be accepted as "true costs of production" and thus quite appropriately would go into the final price of the products paid by consumers.

REFERENCES

Anderson, R.J., and T.D. Crocker. 1971. Air pollution and residential property values. Urban Studies 8:171-180.

Ayres, R.U. and A.V. Kneese. 1969. Production, consumption, and externalities. Amer. Econ. Rev. 59:282-297.

Barnett, H. and C. Mores. 1963. Scarcity and Growth: The Economics of Natural Resource Availability. Johns Hopkins Press, Baltimore. MD, 288 p.

Barrett, L.B. and T.E. Waddell. 1973. The Cost of Air Pollution Damages. Pub. No. AP-85, U.S. EPA, NC.

Baumol, W.J. and W.E. Oates. 1975. The Theory of Environmental Policy. Prentice Hall, Englewood Cliffs, NJ., 272 p.

Bohm, P. 1972. Estimating demand for public goods: an experiment. Eur. Econ. Rev. 3:111-130.

Boulding, K.E. 1966. The economics of the coming spaceship earth. pp. 3-12, In H. Jarrett (ed.) Environmental Quality in a Growing Economy, The Johns Hopkins Press, Baltimore, MD.

Burt, O.R. and R. Cummings. 1970. Production and investment in natural resource industries. Am. Econ. Rev. 60:576-590.

Clawson, M. 1959. Methods of Measuring Demand for and Value of Outdoor Recreation. Reprint No. 10, Resources for the Future, Washington, DC.

Converse, A.O. 1971. On the extension of input-output analysis to account for environmental externalities. Am. Econ. Rev. 6:197-198.

Cumberland, J.H. 1966. A regional inter-industry model for analysis of development objectives. The Regional Science Association Papers 17:65-94.

Daly, H.E. 1968. On economics as a life science. J. Pol. Econ. 76:392-406.

Dasgupta, P. and G. Heal. 1974. The optimum depletion of exhaustible resources. Rev. Econ. Studies 41:3-28.

Davidson, P., F.G. Adams and J. Seneca. 1966. The social value of water recreational facilities resulting from an improved water quality: the Delaware Estuary. pp. 192-208, In A.V. Kneese and S.C. Smith (ed.) Water Research. The Johns Hopkins Press, Baltimore, MD.

Davis, K. and R.L. Blomstrom. 1974. Observations on ecology and business responsibility. Ariz. Bus. 21:19-26.

Davis, R.K. 1964. The value of big game hunting in a private forest. pp. 393-403 In Proc. of the 29th North American Wildlife and Natural Resources Conf., Wildlife Management Institue, Washington, DC.

Edmunds, S. 1977. Environmental impacts: conflicts and trade-offs. Calif. Mgmt. Rev. 19:5-11.

Faris, B.G., Jr., I.T.P. Higgins, N.W. Higgins and J.N. Peters. 1973. Sulphur oxides and suspected particulates. Archives of Envir. Health 27:179-182.

Fisher, Anthony C. and F.M. Peterson. 1976. The environment in economics: a survey. J. Econ. Lit. 14:1-33.

Fisher, A.C., J.V. Krutilla and C.J. Cicchetti. 1972. The economics of environmental preservation: a theoretical and empirical analysis. Am. Econ. Rev. 62:605-619.

Freeman, A.N. III. 1971. Air pollution and property values: a methodological comment. Rev. Econ. Stat. 53:415-416.

Gardner, N., N. Brown, Jr. and J. Hammack. 1973. Dynamic economic management of migatory water fowl. Rev. Econ. Stat. 55:73-82.

Gray, D. H. 1972-73. Commentary on let's go with the social audit. Bus. & Society Rev. Winter 1972-73:47.

Hufschmidt, M.N., J.V. Krutilla and J. Margolis. 1961. Standards and Criteria for Formulating and Evaluating Federal Water Resources Development: Report to the Bureau of the Budget. Government Printing Off., Washington, DC.

Isard, W. 1969. Some Notes on the Linkage of the Ecologic and Economic Systems. Mimeo.

Jevons, W.S. 1965 [1866]. The Coal Question, 2nd ed. Macmillan, London.

Kneese, A.V. 1964. The Economics of Regional Water Quality Management. Johns Hopkins Press, Baltimore, MD, 215 p.

Kneese, A.V. 1962. Water Pollution: Economic Aspects and Research Needs. Resources for the Future, Washington, DC.

Kneese, A.V. and B.T. Bower. 1968. Managing Water Quality: Economics, Technology, Institutions. Johns Hopkins Press, Baltimore, MD, 328 p.

Kneese, A.V., R.U. Ayres and R.C. D'Arge. 1970. Economics and the Environment: A Materials Balance Approach. Resources for the Future, Washington, DC, 120 p.

Krutilla, J.V. and O. Eckstein. 1958. Multiple Purpose River Development. Johns Hopkins Press, Baltimore, MD, 301 p.

Krutilla, J.V. and A.C. Fisher. 1975. The Economics of Natural Environments: Studies in the Valuation of Commodity and Amenity Resources. The Johns Hopkins Press, Baltimore, MD.

Lave, L.V. and E.P. Seskin. 1975. Acute relationships among daily mortality, air pollution, and climate. pp. 325-347, In E.S. Mills (ed.) Economic Analysis of Environmental Problems, Columbia University Press, NY.

Lave, L.V. and E.P. Seskin. 1970. Air pollution and human health. Science 169:723-733.

Lave, L.V. and E.P. Seskin. 1971. Health and air pollution. Swed. J. Econ. 73:76-95.

Leontief, W. 1970. Environmental reproductions and the economic structure: input-output approach. Rev. Econ. Stat. 52:262-271.

McKean, R.N. 1958. Efficiency in Government Through Systems Analysis. Wiley, NY, 336 p.

Maler, K.G. 1974. Environmental Economics. Johns Hopkins Press, Baltimore, MD.

Mill, J.S. 1961 [1865]. Principles of Political Economy. Augustus M. Kelley, NY, 1,013 p.

Moss, M. (ed.). 1973. The Measurement of Economic and Social Performance. Studies in Income and Wealth, Vol. 38, National Bureau of Economic Research, NY.

National Academy of Sciences-National Academy of Engineering. 1974. The Costs and Benefits of Automobile Emission Control. Air Quality and Emission Control, Vol. 4, Government Printing Off., Washington, DC.

Nordhaus, W.D. and J. Tobin. 1973. Is growth obsolete? pp. 129-133, In N. Moss (ed.) The Measurement of Economic and Social Performance. Studies in Income and Wealth, Vol. 38, National Bureau of Economic Analysis, NY.

Okun, A.N. 1971. Social welfare has no price tag. Survey of Current Business, Pt. II 51:129-133.

Olson, N. 1975. The lack of the measuring rod of money. Mimeo, Univ. Maryland, College Park.

Randall, A., B. Ives and C. Eastman. 1974. Bidding games for valuation of aesthetic environmental improvements. J. Envir. Econ. Mgmt. 1:132-149.

Ridker, R.G. 1967. Economic Costs of Air Pollution. Praeger, NY, 214 p.

Ridker, R.G. and J.A. Henning. 1967. The determinants of residential property values with special reference to air pollution. Rev. Econ. Sta. 49:246-257.

Samuelson, P.A. 1976. Economics, 10th ed. McGraw-Hill, NY, 886 p.

Schimmel, H.N. and T.J. Murawski. 1975. The relation of air pollution to mortality, New York City, 1963-1972. Mimeo., submitted to the New York State Dept. of Environ. Conservation.

Sinden, J.A. 1974. A utility approach to the valuation of recreational and aesthetic experiences. Am. J. Ag. Econ. 56:61-72.

Small, K.A. 1975. Air pollution and property values: a further comment. Rev. Econ. Stat. 57:105-107.

Solow, R. 1974. The economics of resources or the resources of economics. Am. Econ. Rev. 64:1-14.

Straszheim, M. 1974. Hedonic estimation of housing market prices: a further comment. Rev. Econ. Stat. 56:404-406.

Tietenberg, T.H. 1973. Specific taxes and pollution control: a general equilibrium analysis. Quar. J. Econ. 87:503-522.

Victor, T. 1972. Pollution: Economy and Environment. Alen and Unwin, London, 247 p.

Waddell, T.E. 1974. The Economic Damages of Air Pollution. Socio-Economic Environ. Studies Ser., EPA-600/5-74-012, Government Printing Off., Washington, DC.

Weinrobe, M. 1973. Accounting for pollution: pollution abatement and the national product. Land Econ. 49:115-121.

Wienand, K.F. 1973. Air pollution and property values: a study of the St. Louis area. J. Reg. Science. 13:91-95.

AN INTER–INDUSTRY
INPUT–OUTPUT ANALYSIS OF ENERGY INTENSIVITY

John Griffith and Dave Stibich*

Exigencies of the energy problem have forced us to consider price consequences of different anti-trust and regulatory policies. It is obvious that any policy-caused alterations in the price structure of the various energy sources will affect some industries more than others.

There are at least three concepts giving insight into the energy intensivity of different industries. The energy elasticity concepts, for example, give insight into the change in arrantity used relative to change in price.[1] As another example, the btu equivalent of each of the energy industrial production series has been compiled, allowing for duplication resulting from the same btu representation at more than one stage of output.[2] Finally, Input/Output studies provide insight into relative energy intensivity. Input/Output data indicate the components required for each sector's production, including the value of key raw materials obtained from other industries, labor compensation, profits, and taxes.[3]

By examining input-output tables using two energy use configurations, current account and capital account, we will try to give some insight into those particular industries most likely to be affected by price changes.

Breaking up "Big Oil" or otherwise altering price mechanisms in the energy-producing industries might work in either one of two ways: increased competition might increase the availability of oil and lower prices, or decreased production efficiency might raise prices. Lowered prices could cause a shift to oil out of other energy sources, tending also to lower their prices and increase their availability. Increased prices, on the other hand, would tend to cause other fuels (mainly coal at this stage of our technology) to gain at the expense of oil, of the industries contributing to oil production, and (in the short run) of energy-intensive industries. The fulfillment of these expectations, of course, would depend largely upon the operational effectiveness of the market mechanism.

In order to estimate how various industrial sectors might be affected financially by divestiture, a set of ordinal comparisons have been tabulated from the Department of Commerce input-output matrices using the industrial classifications listed in Table 1. The

*Resource Management Program, Eastern Illinois University, Charleston, IL 61920.

---

[1] Earnest R. Berndt and David O. Wood, "Technology, Prices and the Derived Demand for Energy," Review of Economics and Statistics 57 (August 1975): 264.

[2] Clayton, Gehman, "U.S. Energy Supplies and Uses," Federal Reserve Bulletin, December, 1973.

[3] Survey of Current Business, "The Input-Output Structure of the U.S. Economy: 1967," February, 1974. Volume 54, No. 2, pp. 24-56.

top eleven energy-intensive industries, ranked according to energy use on the basis of FEA data, are Nos. 27, 37, 38, 31, 35, 36, 24, 25, 14, 41 and 42.[4] Those qualifying as closely energy-related are Nos. 7, 8, 65 (by virtue of its contribution to both 8 and 31).

Next, those industries contributing at least 4-cent input per dollar of final demand were ranked according to their aggregate direct and indirect input to energy-intensive industries. These contributing industries were weighted to show that for any given input, the smaller the contributor, the greater the impact of a change in any energy-intensive industry's of a change in any energy-intensive industry's production level on the revenue, profits, and stock prices of the contributing industry.

Table 1. Input-Output Classifications. Source: The Input-Output Structure of the U.S. Economy: 1967, U.S. Dept. of Commerce.

1. Livestock and livestock products
2. Other agricultural products
3. Forestry and fishery products
4. Agricultural, forestry and fishery services
5. Iron and Ferroalloy ores mining
6. Nonferrous metal ores mining
7. Coal mining
8. Crude petroleum and natural gas
9. Stone and clay mining and quarrying
10. Chemical and fertilizer mineral mining
11. New construction
12. Maintenance and repair construction
13. Ordnance and accessories
14. Food and kindred products
15. Tobacco manufactures
16. Broad and narrow fabrics, year/thread mills
17. Miscellaneous textile goods and floor coverings
18. Apparel
19. Miscellaneous fabricated textile products
20. Lumber and wood products, except containers
21. Wooden containers
22. Household furniture
23. Other funiture and fixtures
24. Paper and allied products, except containers
25. Paperboard containers and boxes
26. Printing and publishing
27. Chemicals and selected chemical products
28. Plastics and synthetic materials
29. Drugs, cleaning and toilet preparations
30. Paints and allied products
31. Petroleum refining and related industries
32. Rubber and miscellaneous plastics products

---

33. Leather tanning and industrial leather products
34. Footwear and other leather products
35. Glass and glass products
36. Stone and clay products
37. Primary iron and steel manufacturing
38. Primary nonferrous metal manufacturing
39. Metal containers
40. Heating, plumbing and structural metal products
41. Stampings, screw machine products and bolts
42. Other fabricated metal products
43. Engines and turbines
44. Farm machinery and equipment
45. Construction, mining and oil field machinery
46. Materials handling machinery and equipment
47. Metalworking machinery and equipment
48. Special industry machinery and equipment
49. General industrial machinery and equipment
50. Machine shop products
51. Office, computing and accounting machines
52. Service industry machines
53. Electric industrial equipment and apparatus
54. Household appliances
55. Electric lighting and wiring equipment
56. Radio, television and communication equipment
57. Electronic components and accessories
58. Misc. electrical machinery, equip. and supplies
59. Motor vehicles and equipment
60. Aircraft and parts
61. Other transportation equipment
62. Scientific and controlling instruments
63. Optical, ophthalmic and photographic equipment
64. Miscellaneous manufacturing
65. Transportation and warehousing
66. Communcations; except radio and TV broadcast
67. Radio and TV broadcasting
68. Electric, gas, water, and sanitary services
69. Wholesale and retail trade
70. Finance and insurance
71. Real estate and rental
72. Hotels; personal and repair serv. except auto
73. Business services
74. Automobile repair and services
75. Amusements
76. Medical, educational serv./nonprofit organ.
77. Federal Government enterprises
78. State and local government enterprises
79a.Directly allocated imports
79b.Transferred imports
80. Business travel, entertainment and gifts

81. Office supplies
82. Scrap, used and secondhand goods

Then the same ranking procedure was followed, without weighting, for the aggregate direct and indirect receipt by different industries of input from energy intensive industries.

Table 2 integrates the results of those two steps, ranking industries by a composite score reflecting both their contribution to and receipt of input from energy-intensive industries. This ranking was done by adding each industry's input contribution percentile to that industry's input receipt percentile. (In many cases industries that contributed did not receive input from the energy-intensive industries.)

Table 2.   Composite Industry Ranking Accordint to
Input to Energy-Intensive Sector and Receipt
of Input from Energy-Intensive Sector.

Industry Code	Composite Score	Industry Code	Composite Score
9	136.8	63	61.6
25	129.8	64	61.2
38	127.7	60	60.0
28	127.4	29	59.6
1	118.8	16	58.4
24	106.2	11	58.0
5	100.5	13	56.8
39	98.4	50	56.4
37	97.4	17	55.2
40	95.2	23	54.8
41	93.5	62	52.0
82	91.9	32	50.4
42	90.3	83	48.8
8	88.8	35	47.1
52	88.7	27	45.5
59	87.1	20	44.0
81	85.5	22	43.9
54	83.8	51	42.3
43	82.2	75	40.7
58	80.6	33	39.0
44	79.0	73	38.4
45	77.4	19	35.8
46	75.8	24	34.2
49	74.2	31	33.8
62	72.6	18	32.6
26	70.9	56	29.4
55	67.6	6	24.4
53	66.0	12	21.7
47	64.4	10	21.2
57	63.2	2	17.9
48	62.8	34	14.5

Last, in Tables 3 and 4, the same procedures were followed for industries contributing input to and receiving input from the energy-related industries individually.

Although a detailed projection of possible changes in stock prices and/or borrowing costs is impracticable because of the many factors involved, these tables do serve to suggest some significant points. In Table 4, for example, of the ten industries that would seem to be most affected by any policy change by virtue of contributing to or receiving input from the

Table 3. Industry Ranking According to Input Contributed to Energy-Related Industries.

Energy-Related Industries	Contributing Industry	Score	Weighted Ranking
#65	12	.047	2
#65	31	.052	1
#65	69	.052	3
#65	80	.064	Unranked
#68	65	.046	4
#68	7	.049	3
#68	79	.156	1
#68	8	.098	2
#71	70	.056	
#8	12	.048	2
#8	71	.196	1
#8	80	.114	Unranked

Table 4. Industry Ranking According to Input Received from Energy-Related Industries.

Industry #65

Code	Score	Code	Score
81	.531	35	.058
78	.186	82	.056
36	.101	6	.056
25	.094	18	.056
15	.093	52	.056
31	.091	41	.055
30	.084	44	.053
37	.084	64	.052
39	.083	42	.051
24	.083	23	.051
5	.083	51	.050
28	.081	75	.049
27	.080	43	.048
38	.069	2	.046
1	.067	49	.046
17	.065	68	.046
40	.065	53	.046
11	.064	55	.046
61	.062	45	.045
22	.062	46	.044
32	.060	62	.044
29	.060	58	.044
13	.059	34	.043
19	.059	3	.042
59	.058	48	.041
54	.058	67	.041
33	.058		

Industry #8

Code	Score
31	.509
68	.098
8	.064

Industry #68

Code	Score	Code	Score
79	.150	9	.054
10	.085	5	.052
24	.071	38	.052
28	.075	35	.055
29	.068	26	.055
25	.065	37	.050
23	.064	6	.045
36	.059	31	.042
27	.059		

Industry #71

Code	Score	Code	Score
8	.196	4	.064
31	.138	70	.064
5	.118	9	.064
76	.114	54	.052
66	.105	7	.049
72	.095	25	.048
51	.081	75	.048
1	.079	5	.047
29	.078	3	.047
10	.078	6	.047
26	.077	57	.045
27	.075	63	.044
73	.072	55	.044
28	.072	24	.044
77	.070	62	.043
69	.070	60	.043
30	.067	52	.043
82	.064	58	.042
		78	.041

energy-intensive industries, four are themselves energy-intensive, Nos. 25, 38, 24 and 37. From Tables 3 and 4 it appears that Nos. 31, 12 and 69 contribute relatively greatly to No. 65, while that industry itself contributes substantially to Nos. 81, 78, 36 and 25, the last two of which are energy-intensive industries. Tables 3 and 4 also indicate those industries that would be most greatly affected by any changes in the energy-related industries. It is assumed that if a particular policy increased competition, the profits of Nos. 68 and 71 would benefit, whereas the opposite effect could come about if the policy created too much confusion, decreasing efficiency and thereby increasing prices. The effects on No. 8 are assumed to move roughly in the same direction as No. 68 and 71 because of the energy input into the production of electricity and the involvement of "Big" Oil in many phases of natural gas production and marketing. It is also assumed that higher oil prices and/or lower oil supply would benefit both energy-related industries No. 7 and 65 (the latter because of the increased need for coal transport). Coal mining is not entered in Tables 3 and 4 because there is only one industry (No. 71) to which coal contributes substantially and only one (No. 68) receiving substantial input from coal. Finally, the effects of increased competition in the oil industry itself are probably indeterminate. Paradoxically, the reduction of oil monopoly, while reducing oil profits, would tend to increase profits of associated industries.

These estimates of the effects of changing policies must be qualified in several ways. For example, No. 65 which includes railroad coal transport for hire, also includes a number of other activities that may not be so closely affected by the energy situation, such as public warehousing, air transportation, and passenger transportation. Furthermore, inputs to a consuming industry represent transactions on current account only: capital purchases are not shown as inputs but are aggregated elsewhere as gross private domestic investment. Unfortunately, oil extraction and coal mining equipment are contained within the same industry classification, No. 45. Although it may be impossible to tell how a particular policy might affect oil as compared with coal in regard to capital requirements, it is interesting to note that in 1972, petroleum capital expenditures were about 7 times those of coal and that the capital intensity of their operations appeared to be quite similar. A factor that might alleviate the effect of this current account constraint is the capability of many industries to increase production without increasing capital expenditure. This is especially the case now when many businesses operate at substantially less than capacity due to deficient but growing aggregate demand.

Energy use in the ten most energy-intensive (E-I) industries discussed ranged from a high of 4.25×10^{15} btu's to a low of 4.42×10^{14} btu's (1972 figures) for the Primary metals and the Fabricated Metal Products industries respectively. Sources of energy for these industries include coal, coke, electricity (purchased and self-generated), fuel oils, liquefied petroleum products, natural gas, steam (purchased and self-generated), and self-generated fuels.

The Energy Policy and Conservation Act of 1976 set final energy usage target decreases of 9% per unit output in the Primary Metals industry to 24% for the Fabricated Metal Products industry by January 1, 1980, based on 1972 figures. Also the FEA is emphasizing reduction in consumption of natural gas or petroleum and increasing the use of coal.

In order to comply with these standards, each of the E-I industries will need to make modifications on existing equipment or, in many cases, purchase new equipment. The degree of capital expenditures depends upon the type of conversion, which in turn is dependent on the availability and cost of alternate fuels.

The energy situation varies among energy-intensive industries, depending upon the fuel source mix. Those industries relying heavily on natural gas face more immediate problems, in the form of spot shortages and curtailments than those relying on other fuels. However, concern exists in all industries using large amounts of petroleum products which face possible future scarcity of these fuel sources.

Industry groups in which natural gas constitutes a substantial percentage of total fuel sources include:

(1) Food and Kindred Products. 60%
(2) Stone, Clay, and Glass Products 56%
(3) Fabricated Metal Products. 48%
(4) Petroleum Refining and Related Products 37%
(5) Paper and Allied Products. 35%
(6) Primary Metals 22%

Conversion from natural gas to alternate energy supplies by these six groupings is as follows:[5]

(1) Food and Kindred Products - fuel oils
(2) Stone, Clay, and Glass Products - fuel oil and liquefied petroleum gas
(3) Fabricated Metal Products - fuel oils
(4) Petroleum and Related Products - oil-fired systems
(5) Paper and Allied Products - fuel oils and self-generated fuels
(6) Primary Metals - fuel oil and electricity

Coal, our most abundant commerically available fossil fuel, is the least desirable energy alternative for natural gas in all energy-intensive industry groupings. In the present technological situation, coal is ill-suited for the following reasons:

(1) Capital costs of conversion
(2) Environmental protecting equipment costs
(3) Storage and transportation
(4) Thermal efficiency
(5) Temperature control
(6) Personnel requirements
(7) Impurities in final products

It is interesting to note that the effects on amounts and composition of capital goods expenditures will continue to have an increasing impact on E-I industries as conversions from cleaner burning fuels in limited supply (i.e., natural gas) to more abundant-polluting fuels are substituted (i.e., coal).

Five industries, viz., iron and steel, primary non-ferrious metals, chemicals, paper, petroleum refining, face increased business and financial risks via pollution control expenditures. They face these risks because they are the industries with the highest capital spending on pollution control in relation to total capital spending.

The iron and steel industry is most affected by pollution control expenditures. According to Chugh et al. empirical studies show a substantial percentage of firms tested in the iron and steel industry have experienced increased Beta (risk) coefficients.[6] These

---

[5] Ibid., pp. 3-6.

[6] Lai C. Chugh, Micheal Hanemann, S. Mahapatra, "Impact of Pollution Control Regulations on the Market Risk of Securities," Prepared for the Financial Management Association Meeting (1977-Montreal).

financial risks result from pollution abatement expenditures being generally considered non-productive and non-cash generating entries. This will typically decrease the profitability of the industry if costs cannot be passed on to the consumer. If external financing is required the debt/equity ratio will increase causing unfavorable financial leverage, bringing firms within the industry closer to debt capacity and increasing risk factors with resulting higher cost of borrowing.[7]

Examining the iron and steel industry, for the EPA, Temple, Barker and Sloane, Inc. estimate total capital requirements for an abatement equipment (stack and fugitive emission controls to 1980) at 3.3 billion with external financing of 2.1 billion. When all pollution control equipment (air and water) is in operation, requirements for energy will increase by 41,000 barrels of oil per day in the iron and steel industry.[8]

Adverse environmental effects can also result from pollution control. In the case of iron and steel industry, sources contend that in terms of energy expended per pound of dust removed from electric furnaces, extraction of the last traces of dust, requires 6×10^3 times the quantity of energy required to remove the first major amounts of pollutants. This in turn results in 15 additional pounds of pollutants being emitted at the power generating facility per pound of dust removed.[9]

The current account tables (2, 3, and 4) show inter-industry transactions in goods and services. Capital account (Table 5) shows relationships of transactions between producers and users of new capital goods. For purposes of this paper, Tables 2, 3, and 4 indicate industrial expenditures connected with increased output with given capital equipment, whereas Table 5 indicates the industrial reverberations associated with changes in production involving increased expenditures on plant and equipment.

Of the 10 energy-intensive (E-I) and five energy-related (E-R) industries, four industries (Nos. 38, 42, 65 and 71) are producers of new capital goods. Two of these are energy-intensive (Nos. 38 and 42) and two are energy-related (Nos. 65 and 71). All but one of the four industries under consideration (No. 38 of which total output is purchased by No. 66) sell significant amounts of their capital goods output to energy-intensive and energy-related industries. E-I producing industry No. 42 contributes 66 percent of its total output of capital goods to E-I industries in the following proportions: Nos. 24-10%, 27-34%, 37-22%. Fifteen percent of E-R industry No. 65 capital goods output is purchased by E-R No. 65-9% and E-R No. 68-6%. E-I producing industry No. 71 relies on itself for 97 percent of its capital goods production.

Table 5 illustrates transactions between energy-intensive and energy-related industries (vertical columns) in percentage of total dollar expenditures, and industries contributing new capital goods. For example, energy-related industry No. 7 purchases 23% of its total capital expenditures from industry No. 11 and 51% from industry No. 45.

In summary, E-I and E-R industries' contribution to other industries' capital goods is greater than E-I and E-R industries' expenditure on capital goods. That is, E-I industries (Nos. 38 and 42) and E-R industries (Nos. 65 and 71) which produce capital goods are dependent on the user E-I industries (Nos. 24, 27, 37) and E-R industries (Nos. 68 and 71) for purchases of their capital goods, more so than the E-I industries (Nos. 14, 24, 27, 31, 35, 36, 37, 38, 41, 42) and E-R industries (Nos. 7, 8, 65, 68, 71) are dependent on the E-I industries (Nos. 65 and 71) as suppliers of their capital goods.

[7] Marvin E. Ray, The Environmental Crisis and Corporate Debt Policy, (Lexington Books, Inc., 1973).

[8] Iron Age, February 20, 1978, p. 48.

[9] Iron Age, November 22, 1973, p. 31.

Table 5.   Capital Goods Expenditures by Energy-
Intensive and Energy-Related Industries.*
Source: <u>Survey of Current Business</u>, September
1975, pp. 10-14.

Contributing Industries

	11	45		
7	23%	51%		
8	11	45		
	79%	9%		
14	11	48		
	28%	23%		
24	11	48		
	22%	35%		
27	11	40	49	
	24%	21%	13%	
31	11			
	64%			
35	11	46	47	48
	30%	12%	15%	17%
36	11	48		
	27%	19%		
37	11	47		
	27%	21%		
38	11	47	49	
	34%	20%	13%	
41	11	46	47	
	20%	10%	43%	
42	11	47		
	25%	36%		
65	11	59	60	61
	14%	13%	27%	28%
68	11	53		
	66%	16%		
71	11			
	92%			

*In percentages of total capital expenditures,
amounts lower than 10% are not entered.

The numbers in the left-hand column are the E-I
and E-R Investing Industries.

We must examine both capital and current accounts to see which industries are most vulnerable to changes in energy costs. On current account, those industries most vulnerable to energy source price change seem to be Nos. 9, 25, 38, 28, 1, 24, 5. On capital account E-I and E-R expenditures on capital will not be greatly affected by energy price change. E-I (Nos. 42) and E-R (Nos. 65 and 71) industries are affected as capital goods contributors. Of these three, only one (No. 42) is high on the list of price vulnerability on both capital and current accounts.

REFERENCES

Industry Week. 1976. Antitrust, divestiture likely to heat up again. 1 November 1976, 19 p.

Berndt, E.R. and D.O. Wood. 1975. Technology, prices and the derived demand for energy. Review of Economics and Statistics 57:259-267.

Oil and Gas Journal. 1976. Divestiture again. 21 June 1976, 82 p.

Executive Office of the President, Office of Management and Budget. 1972. Standard Industrial Classification Manual. Washington, U.S. Government Printing Off.

Energy Users Report. 1977. FEA sets final industrial efficiency improvement targets. pp. 3-6, 9 June 1977.

Gitman, L. and D. McPeek. 1976. A forecast of capital demand and supply in the domestic petroleum industry, 1975-1985. Paper prepared for the Annual Meeting of the Financial Management Association, Montreal, 14-16 October, 1976.

Johnson, W.A. and R.E. Messick. 1977. The economic and financial implications of the dismemberment of U.S. oil companies. Journal of Energy and Development 2:110-122.

Kim, S. 1977. An inter-industry analysis of petroleum use in the United States: An input-output approach. Journal of Energy and Development 2:310-321.

Silverman, S. S. 1972. Tax consequences of spin-offs and shells. In Techniques in Corporate Reorganization. Presidents Publishing House, N Y.

U.S. Department of Commerce, Social and Economic Statistics Division. 1974. Definitions and Conventions of the 1967 Input-Output Study. Bur. of Economic Analysis, Inter-industry Economics Division (BE-51).

MARKET CHANGES FOR COAL OF THE EAST AND THE WEST

Thomas C. Campbell *

Historically, the east and west producing and consuming regions for coal have been much the same. The eastern and midwestern states of Illinois, Ohio, Pennsylvania, Indiana, West Virginia, and Kentucky are the largest consuming states. They, too, have been among the largest producers, with only slight changes in the order in which they ranked in both consumption and production. Even as late as 1975, these and the six additional states of Missouri, Tennessee, North Carolina, Michigan, Alabama, and Georgia consumed more than 70 percent of all of the coal that was shipped to electric utilities throughout the country (Coal Traffic Annual 1977). Only one of these states, Missouri, is west of the Mississippi River, and it is a short distance from the mines of Illinois and West Kentucky.

With both production and consumption areas being close to each other, the distances it had to be shipped seldom exceeded 200 miles. Coal is a heavy-weight commodity of relatively low value per unit of weight and is consumed as a fuel. Therefore, transport costs are a significant portion of the total price paid by the consumer. Thus, shipments have continued to be for relatively short distances. Eastern utilities have relied upon oil and those of the South and Southwest upon natural gas. But industrial states such as New York and New Jersey can no longer depend upon oil, nor can Texas, Louisiana, Georgia, or Flordia upon natural gas or oil. They, like states as far away as New England and the West Coast, must look to coal for increasing portions of their fuel for the generation of electric power. Michigan, Minnesota, and Missouri must rely more heavily upon coal than in the past and are looking to mines in the West, at least for supplemental supplies. In effect, coal is being marketed on a national rather than a regional basis. Consumption by states, as can be seen in Fig. 1, will be changing as this occurs. Yet, the changes are occurring at slower rates than was anticipated as late as 1974 and 1975.

INCREASING PRODUCTION

It is now widely accepted that production of bituminous coal in the U.S. will increase substantially, if not double, within the next one to two decades. Even if some of the forecasts of Project Independence Reports of 1974 are not met, the basic patterns of increases are realistic, despite the fact that the rates of increase in the early years of the forecast have not been met. Nevertheless, the Keystone Coal Industry Manual forecasts an additional 765 million tons in new coal capacity by 1986. This is based upon an industry-wide survey completed in January 1978. The expansion in capacity will require 391 new mines, with the largest number being in West Virginia and the greatest capacity increase in Wyoming

*Regional Research Institute, West Virginia University, Morgantown, WV 26506.

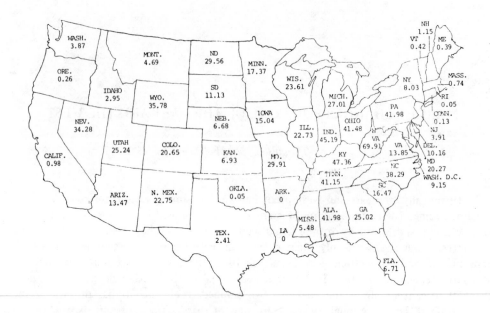

Fig. 1.   Consumption in U.S. by States.   Source: New York Times, February 19, 1978,
Section 4, p. 1.

(Coal Age 1978, p. 113). With changes of such great magnitude, problems of many kinds
have arisen and will have a significant impact on many industries and regions. Among these
are the increasingly long hauls from mines to power plants, as much as 1,000 to 1,500
miles. With the worldwide energy concerns of recent years, the higher transport costs relative
to mine prices and the correspondingly higher consumption of energy in the
transportation of coal, greater depth of analysis has become a matter of increasing
importance.

Major changes are virtually certain to occur with production increases in the existing
large coalfields, as well as in the fields from which only small tonnages have been mined
in the past. Some of the changes are evident at this time; others can be anticipated with a
high degree of certainty. Three distinct changes are occurring simultaneously, but the
rates of change differ. One is the conversion of natural gas and oil burning power plants
to coal. A second is the construction of new power plants that will burn coal. Third is
the dramatic production increases in the mines west of the Mississippi River, especially
in the Northern Great Plains states of Montana and Wyoming.

More than two-thirds of all coal mined in the country is consumed in the generation
of electric power, and the portion is becoming greater each year. While railroad consumption
and home heating virtually have been eliminated and other markets have been declining,
conversion of plants to coal is considered feasible. This can be seen in Table 1, with the
electric utilities using 477 million of the 634 million tons consumed in the domestic market
in 1977. Consumption in other markets and exports have declined or have been unstable
as that by the electric utilities continues to remain high and to increase at a steady pace.

TABLE 1. Bituminous and Lignite Consumption by Markets: 1975-1977. Source: Coal Age, 1978, p. 61.
(millions of tons)

	1975	1976	1977
Electric utilities	403	446	477
Coking coal	83	84	80
General deliveries	63	61	70
Retail deliveries	5	7	7
Total U.S.	554	598	634
Exports			
Canada and Mexico	17	17	17
Overseas	49	42	37
Total U.S. and exports	620	657	688

CHANGING TRANSPORTATION PATTERNS

The historical flow pattern of bituminous coal has been largely an east-west movement. This has been especially true with extensive consumption of oil by the East Coast electric utilities in the past two to three decades. By 1975 and beyond, increasingly large tonnages had begun, and will continue, to move eastward from many of the western mines. A study prepared by the Electric Power Research Institute forecasts that "western coal will be competitive in midwestern markets as far east as Cleveland in 1982 if coal demand between 1975 and 1982 increases 25 percent per year or more" (EPRI 1976, p. 180). Production did not increase at nearly the 25 percent rate in 1976 and 1977 and is unlikely to do so in the next two to three years, at least. However, marketing of western coal in the Midwest, as well as in the Southwest, is expanding each year at rates significantly exceeding the annual coal-production increases on a national scale. For example, more than 76 percent of the coal consumed in Minnesota in 1976 originated in the West. Nearly 26 percent of that used in Wisconsin and 28 percent in Illinois was from the same region (Bureau of Mines 1976). These are markets that have depended upon Midwest and Appalachian coal in the past. Yet, consumption of the western coal in these states is growing much more rapidly than is consumption in the same markets of coal from mines east of the Mississippi River. The longer-run possibilities, however, seem to indicate that the nation's energy needs will be so great, and alternative sources are so limited, that coal will have to be sold in virtually all markets.

Studies have been conducted in recent years that forecast the need for continued expansion of the electric power generating capacity throughout the country. A matter of considerable concern in this regard has been the location of new power plants relative to mines or mining regions. A report by the National Coal Policy Project released in February 1978 concluded that "coal-burning plants should be cited near energy users, rather than at remote mines" (Chemical Engineering 1978, p. 64). This is consistent with the views expressed in earlier studies and serves as further indication that coal will move to distant markets in greater tonnages in each of the next several years, at least. A report by the Congressional Research Service concluded that in the absence of new and rather significant changes in the technology of burning coal by the electric utility plants, eastern coal is unlikely to "penetrate much farther than 300 miles beyond its point of origin, but western coal, primarily because of its low-sulfur properties could penetrate markets as far away as 1,300 miles" (Congressional Record 1977).

TRANSPORTATION–CHANGES AND NEW MODES

New coal transport patterns have become evident, and this has given rise to possible new modes as well. As output of western mines increases and is shipped to markets in the Midwest, Southwest, and along the Pacific Coast, and Appalachian coal moves in larger quantities to New England, the South and East, the average distance the coal is traveling is growing. The average length of haul in 1969 was reported to be 225 miles (ICC 1974). By 1973, the average haul was 290 miles, and a 1976 study suggested that the averages by 1985 and beyond will be in the range of 460 to 670 miles (EPRI 1976, p. 15). As early as 1973, the Burlington Northern was hauling coal 525 miles on the average, with its longest haul being 1,430 miles (EPRI 1976, p. 15).

Another factor of significance in the distances coal is being transported to markets is the size and output of mines in different regions of the country. Those of the Appalachian fields are much smaller than those of the West, which are predominantly surface mines that operate on a large scale. Few mines in the Appalachian fields have ever produced more than 3 million tons of coal a year or more than 5 to 6 million tons in the Midwest (Coal Age 1976, p. 35).

These are among the factors that have led to concern about the capability of the existing transport modes to move the additional coal supplies as they are needed. This has been a critical factor in the West where coal was not a major traffic source until recently. Coal provides more traffic for both railways and waterways than does any other commodity. The significance of these large volumes become even greater when the concentration of the traffic on a few waterways, specifically the Ohio and Monongahela, and on such railways as Conrail, the Chessie System, the Norfolk and Western, and the Burlington Northern is considered. Although truck shipments are important in the East where the mines are small, they tend to be of short distances, frequently from mines to nearby power plants.

Expansion of production and long-distance shipments from the western mines are major reasons for the great interest in slurry pipelines. This interest has been concentrated in the West where the mines are large and the lengths of haul are great. Currently, the ability of mines to supply enough coal for large-capacity slurry lines appears to be less formidable than the capacity of power plants to cope with huge tonnages. As an indication of this, only five states consumed as much as 25 million tons of coal in 1976. Capacity of the proposed slurry pipelines ranges from 10 to 25 million tons per year. Few plants consumed more than 5 million tons and only two more than 6 million in 1976 (Coal Traffic Annual 1977). Nevertheless, with the combination of new and larger plants to be constructed and the conversion of existing plants from oil and natural gas to coal, plants will be large enough to consume tonnage much in excess of past records. Another factor in the slurry pipeline interest has been the limitation in competition from alternative carrier modes in the West. While the railroads do seem to have the ability to deal with considerably larger coal tonnages without exceeding the practical capacities of their lines, some shippers, at least, prefer an alternative and not having to depend solely upon the railroads.

It is from this background that interest in coal slurry pipelines has developed. Most of those under any degree of advanced consideration or planning are to be located in the West and to transport the coal to the South, Southwest, and West (see Fig. 2), regions that have not depended upon coal in the past. Slurry pipelines have been a matter of great public interest since 1974, at least, when a bill to grant the right of eminent domain was introduced in Congress (Campbell 1977). Similar legislation was introduced in each session since then, with a vote expected by both Houses of Congress in the spring or early summer of 1978. For some years in the future, pipelines are unlikely to operate because of the long period of time needed for further planning and construction. While plans have been progressing, as can be seen in Fig. 2, actual construction will not likely be underway until a federal eminent domain law is enacted and becomes effective. This or similar legislation is necessary in order to have long distance lines constructed (OTA 1978).

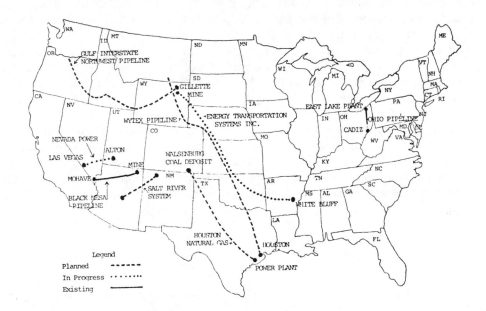

Fig. 2. Map of Slurry Pipelines. Source: Pipeline and Gas Journal, 1977, Vol. 204, p. 38.

INTEREST IN OPTIMAL MARKETS

Transportation is a great energy consumer, and the increasing distances and tonnages of coal shipments are becoming matters of some concern, at least to economic analysts. In 1975, transportation accounted for about 24 percent of the gross national energy consumption and more than half of the consumption of petroleum products (Department of Transportation 1977, p. 33). In addition, indirect energy used in transportation is much greater than is revealed from only superficial investigation. For example, a study based on 1971 data concluded that "the amount of fuel consumed indirectly by transportation equipment, services, and infrastructure is 47.5 percent as great as the energy consumed directly by vehicles" (Shoake 1977, p. 182). The transportation sector is the largest single consumer of energy in the country. Furthermore, there is a tendency for the indirect energy uses to continue rising even when direct uses are being held in check, if not reduced. Even though there are wide differences among the transport modes in terms of energy intensiveness, and rail, water, and pipelines are among the least energy intensive of the carriers, the huge volumes together with the long distances the coal must be shipped assure that the total energy consumed in hauling the coal inevitably will rise. This is one of the major factors which is inescapable as coal becomes increasingly important as the principal fuel for the electric utility industry.

Concern has been shown about the energy intensiveness of the principal transport modes of air, pipelines, railroads, trucks, and waterways. Only air is of little significance in coal transport analysis. At the present time, studies have offered only limited insight into specific shipments because, as Zandi and Gimm (1976, V. 5, p. 12) indicated, "energy consumption is not only a function of the transportation mode" but also depends upon such other factors as the topography of the territory served, density and regularity of shipment, and method of operation. The studies referred to by Zandi indicate that pipelines, railroads, and waterways are much less energy intensive than trucks and airlines. Differences among these studies, however, are not consistent for rail, water, and pipeline transport, at least not for shipping coal. In fact, the studies do not specify energy consumption by commodities, only by modes of transport. Nevertheless, this is a topic for further and more intensive up-to-date investigation and analysis, especially with regard to specific routes and volumes and regularity of shipments.

In addition, preliminary studies have been indicating optimal marketing patterns for coal. Any conclusions are unavoidably tentative at this time and can be expected to remain so until such time as more intensive research and critical analysis have been completed. An illustration of this analysis is represented by Fig. 3, an attempt to offer a preliminary model for three regional coal markets that cover the entire country (Campbell and Hwang 1978).

Fig. 3. Market Centers. Source: Campbell and Hwang, 1978.

This analysis takes into account the vast differences in the heat content and other factors which have an impact on the actual cost of the energy provided by the coal-consuming firm. High quality steam and coking coal are known to be among the Pennsylvania and West Virginia deposits. The heat content is highest in the Appalachian fields, with the Midwest fields being next and the lowest in the coal deposits of the West. Ash and sulfur content also vary. Generally speaking, eastern deposits are geologically older than those of the West. Also, much of the western and even the midwestern coal is near the surface and can be mined without having to depend upon deep mining methods. Typically, this enables the output per man-day to be much higher when surface mining is practiced than when underground is the only feasible method. For example, the average production per man-day in Montana was 127 tons in 1977. In West Virginia, the rate was slightly more than 8 tons per day for the same year. Output in Montana is from surface mines of seams of 100 feet thick, while that in West Virginia is from underground mines primarily with seams barely one-tenth as thick as those in Montana (Congressional Record 1977).

The mine prices per ton are higher in the Appalachian fields than in the Midwest, which are higher than at the mines of the West. The analysis leading to the boundaries of Fig. 3 did consider mine prices, transportation rates, and heat or btu content. When the curve of the market boundary is bent toward a market center, it signifies that the transport costs in that region become relatively more expensive as distances increase. The relatively high mine prices and transport rates in the East cause the market area to be smaller than the market area of the West. The boundaries will be modified as these factors change among and within the three regions. In addition, other factors that were not included in this model could also cause modifications in the boundary lines. The divisions as designated will help to minimize the distances the coal must be transported.

Another factor that is related to distances coal will be hauled is the tendency in recent years for mine prices to rise more rapidly than freight rates. This can be seen in Table 2,

TABLE 2. Comparison of f.o.b. Mine Realization and Railroad Rates of Bituminous Coal and Lignite in the U.S. Source: Coal Slurry Legislation, 1975, p. 267.

(selected years)

Year	Average Mine Prices	Average Rail Rates	Percent of Destination Value, Rail Rates
1965	$ 4.44	$3.13	41.3
1970	6.26	3.41	35.3
1971	7.07	3.70	34.4
1972	7.66	3.67	32.4
1973	8.53	3.71	30.3
1974	15.00	3.95	20.8
1975	20.00	4.23	17.5

as transport costs have declined from 35.3 percent of the destination value in 1970 to only 17.5 percent in 1975. With the price increases by 1977, this decline is even more pronounced.

The divisions among the regions would appear to minimize shipments across the borders from one region to another. Taken into account also are substantial increases in demand for coal in New England, the South, the Southwest, and the West, as well as in the Rocky Mountain and Northern Great Plains states. Also, as energy prices rise along with coal market expansion and growth, transport costs will inevitably rise tending, in the long run, to cause the major coalfields to become the primary sources of supply for their own natural market areas. This will tend to minimize energy consumption in the transportation of coal, the commodity that provides the greatest tonnages for both railways and waterways, and the cost to the consumers, as well.

This tendency will likely be reenforced by recent references to some slackening of production increases of coal in the West, as noted in 1977 and 1978. In addition to water problems that are of special significance in slurry pipeline transportation, and to the greater distances the coal must be transported, there are "intricacies of the permitting system necessary for opening" of mines in the West, and high state severance taxes (Congressional Record 1977). The combination of these and other possible factors could have a substantial impact on the rate and time new mines are opened in the West.

SUMMARY AND CONCLUSION

That coal production in the West will increase is almost certain, if not completely obvious to all. Much of the concern has been related to an over-emphasis on catastrophic rates of expansion. Viewing this matter in 1978, that does not seem to be necessary or even likely to occur. An orderly development of the industry and markets for the coal from all regions seems possible. Indeed, this appears to be what is actually happening. Markets are expanding, even to the point of becoming national in scope. Railroads such as the Burlington Northern and Union Pacific are major coal carriers along with Conrail, the Chessie System, and the Norfolk and Western. New modes, such as slurry and possibly other kinds of pipelines, and new patterns of traffic flow and combinations are emerging and will develop further. But the ability of coal, transportation, and electric utility industries to cope with the expansion and other aspects of the new emerging patterns seem to be matters of meeting new challenges rather than of concerns and apprehensions of a pessimistic nature.

The orderliness of these changes will permit time to deal with reclamation, water shortages, additional increases in transport capacity, and expansion of electric power generation capacity at the same time plants are being converted to use coal. At the same time, the nation is becoming increasingly sensitive to the larger volume of western coal needed to equal the heat content of each ton of eastern coal, the longer distances it must be hauled, the rising mine prices relative to transport costs, and the energy intensiveness of transportation in general. These are factors which, in the long-term, influence the tendency for each major coalfield to function as the primary source of supply for its own natural market. This can be done as bituminous coal becomes an industry that is truly national in scope and one that is meeting its broad responsibilities to those near the supply sources and to others who are consumers hundreds and even thousands of miles away.

REFERENCES

Campbell, T.C. 1977. Eminent domain: its origin, meaning, and relevance to coal slurry pipelines. Transportation J. 17:5-21.

Campbell, T.C. and M. Hwang. 1978. Market area analysis of three major coal markets. Paper presented before the Southern Regional Science Association Meetings, Richmond, VA, April 1978.

Chemical Engineering. 1978. Conclusion of National Coal Policy Project. 85:64.

Coal Age. 1976. The 50 biggest bituminous mines in 1975. 81:35-36.

Coal Age. 1978. Keystone forecasts 765 million tons of new coal capacity by 1987. 83:113.

Coal Slurry Legislation. 1975. House of Representatives. Hearings before the Committee on Interior and Insular Affairs on H.R. 1963, H.R. 2220, H.R. 2553 and H.R. 2986.

Coal Traffic Annual—1977 Edition.   Bituminous Coal Association, Washington, DC.

Congressional Record. 1977. Senate. Analyst Makes Study About Western Coal. V. 123, November 29, 1977.

Electric Power Research Institute (EPRI). 1976. Coal Transportation of the Existing Rail and Barge Network, 1985 and Beyond.

Interstate Commerce Commission (ICC). 1974. Investigation of Railroad Freight Rate Structure—Coal. 34 ICC 71.

New York Times. February 19, 1978. Section 4, p. 1.

Office of Technology Assessment (OTA). 1978. A Technology Assessment of Coal Slurry Piplines.

Pipeline and Gas Journal. February 1977. 204:38.

Shoake, D.B., A.S. Loebl and P.D. Patterson. 1977. Transportation Energy Conservation Book—Edition 2, Oak Ridge Natl. Lab., Oak Ridge, TN.

U.S. Bureau of Mines. 1977. Bituminous Coal and Lignite Distribution—Calendar Year 1976.

U.S. Department of Transportation. 1977. Transportation: Trends and Choices.

Zandi, I. and K.K. Gimm. 1976. Transportation of Solid Commodities Via Freight Pipline—Impact Assessment. Department of Transportation, Washington, DC.

WHAT CONSTITUTES THE PRICE OF
COAL IN THE NORTHERN GREAT PLAINS

*V.H. Wood**

To a large segment of the general public, the rapid increase of energy prices in the United States is puzzling, and in some circles, even suspect. For the past few years much attention has been given to a pending energy crisis, and the environmental and social consequences of energy production and consumption have spawned many legislative programs. The public has been promised a comprehensive energy policy on a federal level designed to give assurance of continuing supply and realistic price patterns, which has not yet been developed. The cost of all fuel has risen far above the inflationary trend of the times. In the midst of these warnings of impending problems, fuel surpluses suddenly appear to further perplex the energy consumers and payers of those rising costs. No wonder there is confusion, and questioning.

Coal in the Northern Great Plains states of North Dakota, Montana, Wyoming, and what constitutes the cost of mining that coal for shipment to the ultimate user is the subject of this paper. To the electrical utility and industrial buyer, the consumed cost expressed in units of electricity or heat is paramount and in addition to the mine price involves transportation, coal handling, boiler efficiency and ash disposal expense at the destination. These latter factors have increased over the past years at about the same rate as the general domestic inflation trend. The price of coal at the mine, however, has changed radically both in new cost components and rapid increases in existing cost components. This discussion is intended to recognize the relative importance of each segment in the total coal price at the mine so that a better understanding might be obtained by sympathetic observers and critics alike.

To reach this understanding, it is important to review some historic guidelines. From 1950 through 1969 the Consumer Price Index rose 52%. General domestic coal prices on the other hand remained about the same, largely due to efficiency gains. Mechanization which reduced mine employment from 416,000 to 125,000 persons and an increase in surface mining from 25% to about 40% of total production made possible an increase in the average productivity in the United States from about 7 tons to 19 tons per man-day. This was a period of rapid growth in total energy consumption but not in the coal sector. The annual domestic energy consumption increased by about 1.4 billion tons of coal equivalent over the period, while coal production itself fluctuated between 392 million and 561 million tons, for a net gain of only 44 million tons. It is interesting to note that while there were no regulations requiring reclamation after strip mining during this time, there were voluntary efforts by many operators.

About 1970 the public awakened to an energy consciousness never before

*V.H. Wood Associates, 1400 West 47th Street, Minneapolis, MN 55409.

experienced. One of the concerns was a general apprehension of increased coal use and the large scale mining necessary to meet the rapidly increasing needs in the face of the highly publicized dwindling domestic oil and natural gas reserves. Legislation was encouraged by many groups sensitive to the apparent environmental hazards and social consequences of the increased coal mining activity. Thus began the era of legislation, regulation, preoperational studies, environmental impact statements, permit applications and public hearings.

By 1977, the overall coal mining productivity had dropped to 15 tons per man-day inspite of a further increase in surface mining reaching 60% of domestic production and the average price of coal at the mine climbed dramatically to over $20 per ton. This was a 400% increase in price since 1969 while the Consumers Index rose only 65% during the same period. In view of these trends of decreasing productivity and rapidly rising costs, one might question the prudence of providing capital for the coal industry. The answer is simply that we have no other choice than to increase coal production if we are to meet our domestic energy requirements at least until new forms of energy reach their potential.

Assuming that the need is well established, let us review some of the steps necessary in starting a new coal mine. The development of a large mining operation today, requires that both buyer and seller assume a greater degree of risk for that mining operation. Much of the initial capital requirement of over $10 per annual ton of production must be committed before final operating permits are received. In fact, the design of the boiler to burn the coal must often be established before the mining of that coal is permitted. However, most coal users are familiar with the permit and regulatory process since the same general procedures are necessary for power plant siting, construction and operation.

The first step is to bid or negotiate for contiguous mineral and surface leases. This requirement is more complicated today since most of the easily available sites are controlled by existing mining interests and new leases are encumbered by uncertain federal leasing regulations. Mineral leases usually contain provisions for periodic renewal with renegotiation to update royalty levels while surface leases generally are designed to carry through the entire mining operation. In both cases there could be advanced royalty payments that encourage early production. Depending upon many factors, it is not unusual for the cost of securing the necessary leases to range from $10 million to $20 million for a new mining operation capable of supporting 5 million tons of annual production over a 20-year period.

Prior to seeking market acceptability, initial exploration and feasibility studies must be completed. This establishes a preliminary cost of mining and determines the probability of the reserve being competitive in the marketplace. The coal quality information also points out any unusual chemistry that would affect boiler design or encourage preparation or specific mining techniques. This step is basic and is one that has remained relatively unchanged over the years. Also during this period of time, the longer range environmental baseline studies would begin and the resulting data used when preparing the environmental impact statement.

Once it appears the coal is mineable and will be competitive, the baseline reviews should be completed. The baseline studies include geology, vegetation, soil, wildlife, archaeology, history, paleontology, air quality, hydrology, socioeconomic and overburden. The costs to obtain the data are significant and require engineering and technical talents throughout the entire process. These studies take up to 18 months to complete and form the data base for the environmental impact statement, which is then prepared and distributed for comment. By this time about 3 years have elapsed since the initial engineering and baseline work began. This first phase of preoperating development work can cost up to $5 million for a typical 5 million ton mine. In some instances, a substantial portion of this investment must be made before the coal production is committed, a risk supported solely by the operator. In the event a new off-site railroad extension is required, a separate environmental impact report must be prepared. It is interesting to note the current federal administrative proposals to streamline the required statements on the environmental effects of federal actions. Also there appears to be a growing concern in regulatory circles that while impact statements meet the current legal requirement there may be better methods of assessing the meaningful environmental consequences.

The second phase of development involves detailed exploration and engineering to establish the final mine design leading toward application for the environmental and mining permits. This work can take place concurrently with the baseline studies, while environmental permit application and issuance may require one year after the release of the impact statement.

The permits, approvals and possible public hearings required for a typical mine in the Northern Great Plains are as follows:

	Permits or Approvals	Possible Public Hearing
Prospecting	x	
Mining	x	x
Coal Conservation Act	x	
Air Quality - Constructing	x	x
Operating	x	x
Water Use	x	x
Discharge	x	
Impoundment	x	
Major Facility: Power	x	

During this period of seeking approvals and necessary permits, the final design of facilities is completed and mine construction must begin. By this time it would be normal for the operator to have reached an agreement with a coal buyer offering sufficient tonnage and sales price to warrant proceeding. The entire project to this point for the hypothetical 5 million ton mine described has required over 3 years of time, up to $20 million for lease acquisition and $5 million for pre-operational development work. Mine construction will cost from $40 million to $60 million for the initial equipment and facilities needed to produce and ship coal, depending on the type of operation desired. Construction requires about 3 years to complete with the first coal production begun about 6 years after the initial development work started. During the construction period additional development work continues, reaching a total cost up to $10 million by the time mining can begin. Even though a buyer and seller may have made commitments to each other early in the approval process, each permit application is a potential threat to the purchase arrangement. For this reason a close working relationship is necessary between the parties for continuous knowledge of activities and early awareness of developing problem areas.

The typical contract between buyer and seller must protect both parties for subsequent changes in regulation and yet provide incentive to the operator to improve mine productivity. New legislation or changes in interpretation of existing laws relative to environmental concerns or reclamation usually affect productivity adversely. One of the current problems in coal contract administration is the inability of the producer to recoup all cost increases from customers for new legislation. While it is relatively easy to determine the direct cost increase the more subtle changes in productivity that affect the unit cost of production are more difficult to detect and quantify. A more rigorous cost accounting of each component and its subsequent effect on efficiency is necessary if the price the operator receives for coal production is to keep pace with his costs as originally intended. Once a general agreement is reached between a buyer and seller regarding mine price, coal quality, quantity and term of shipment, a formal agreement can be prepared. Usually the mine price is divided into major components and each is treated separately for subsequent escalation purposes. Adjustments are made as frequently as necessary based upon actual cost changes when incurred for most items and changes in published price indexes in the case of components that do not easily lend themselves to normal accounting procedures. The major contractual components of a new mine are typically as follows:

Cost Component	Approximate Portion of Original Mine Price[1]	Method of Escalation	Frequency of Escalation
Direct Labor	15% to 25%	Changes in labor agreement	As Incurred
Material & Supply	20%	Price Indexes	3 to 6 months
Initial Capital[2]	40% to 50%	Actual Change of initial capital and interest rate	One time only

[1] Excluding production taxes and royalty

[2] Depreciation, income taxes and return

These items are the largest single cost factors, forming about 85% of the controllable expenses. The range shown for direct labor and initial capital reflects the type of mining equipment selected. For example, the higher labor cost for truck and shovel removal of overburden is countered by lower capital requirement as compared to a dragline operation having a reversed cost pattern. The effects of current reclamation and environmental regulations as they relate to the three major components are included. The remaining contractual components are usually recognized at times of change and include the following:

(1) Rates of payments made to or for the benefit of employees for pensions, retirements, old age benefits, unemployment insurance, social security taxes, premiums for workmen's compensation and other payments to or for the benefit of employees, to the extent that such payments are required by law or by employment contracts with employees.

(2) Rates of compensation paid to administrative, supervisory, technical and clerical employees regularly employed at the mine;

(3) Federal, state and local laws (excluding ad valorem or corporate income tax laws) that affect the cost of producing, selling and delivering coal.

(4) Insurance premiums paid in connection with the production, delivery and sale of coal.

(5) Explosives

(6) Electric Power

(7) Administrative and general expense at the mine and those prorated from general offices.

(8) Depreciation and return on equipment with a depreciable life less than the term of agreement.
(9) Royalty payments.

In addition to the foregoing it has become common practice to protect the sellers profit against devaluation of the dollar. This can be accomplished by using a published price index that is mutually felt to follow the inflationary trend.

In some cases a gross-inequity clause is used to provide relief for potential unknown cost changes. It is presumed that this affords umbrella protection for the operator. However, a gross inequity does not exist in the eyes of the regulatory accountants, if the cost overruns can be identified as a permissable cost escalation under general contract terms. It should also be recognized that such a method works for buyer and seller alike, and if the buyer fully exercises his rights, the incentive for the operator to improve efficiency could be eliminated unless other contractural terms are provided. In some circles, the gross inequity clause is losing favor as a protector of the sellers profit. Contracts can be written to give the seller full protection, and not curtail incentive, as long as he accepts the risk of the coal quality and of his ability to mine under existing laws.

The foregoing addressed the contractural components of the mine price, and does not give insight to the effects of new legislation. For example, the addition of labor and equipment to satisfy new regulations affect direct costs, productivity and in most cases incur additional administrative expenses as well. The normal equipment roster for reclaiming the land in this western area includes dozers, scrapers and various types of farming machinery. This equipment requires operators and the entire process administrated by qualified technical personnel.

Reclamation expense varies both between and within states, depending upon the varying character of the overburden. Generally the costs will range from about $3,000 to $7,000 per acre which includes:

(a) Recontouring the spoils and highwall
(b) Removing, storing and replacing topsoil
(c) Seedbed preparation and seeding

These costs recognize the individual state surface mine regulations. The requirements of the new federal surface mining law will result in some additional operating expense as well as the $0.35 per ton fee imposed on surface mined coal to reclaim abandoned mine sites.

While there are inherent productivity differences between coal mining in North Dakota, Montana and Wyoming that influence the cost of operation, perhaps the largest factors affecting sales price are royalties and state production taxes. These costs are beyond the direct control of mine operators but play a decisive role in the marketability of their coal production. Royalties range from a current low of about 15 cents per ton to as high as 8% of the sales price. New federal leases are slated to reach 12½% of the sales price.

State production taxes also vary from a low of $0.74 per ton in North Dakota to a high of 26% of the total sales price in Montana. Where the state taxes or royalties are levied as a percentage of the sales price, the effect of new legislation and resulting higher mining cost is further aggravated. This has become a controversial situation, for some feel that only the bare cost of extracting coal should be recognized for such purposes, without involving externally imposed factors. As subsequent cost increases are incurred the effect of percentage calculations will compound coal price increases beyond normal inflationary trends and artificially warp competitive positions. This should not have been the original intent of such a tax and royalty structure.

Although about one-half of the increase in western coal prices since 1970 has been associated with environmental and social legislation, the purpose of this discussion on costs is not to criticize the direction of these efforts. In today's industrial world we are all environmentally and socially sensitive to the adverse effects of failing to address these issues. It is only the degree of effort felt necessary to moderate or eliminate these effects that brings about conflict. The only cost component of interest to the general public is what appears on their energy bills. Accordingly, on an issue by issue basis many of the added requirements and their resulting higher cost would probably not pass the test of popular vote. Yet the mining industry has an obligation to be responsive to both the public and its stockholders throughout this time of changing attitudes and regulatory scrutiny. It will be with a thorough recognition of local and regional sentiment and responsible legislation in these matters that will encourage continued interest by financial backers to develop coal production. That production is caused by demand that grows on a relatively orderly basis with long lead times and consistent with economics, reliability of supply and adherence to the regulatory process. The Northern Great Plains will be ready to respond to those demands on an environmentally and socially acceptable basis.

ALLOCATING ELECTRICITY DELIVERY COSTS TO CUSTOMER TYPES

Donald E. Vaughn *

INTRODUCTION

In the mid-1960's when industrial electric customers were paying about 1 cent per KWH of electricity utilized and residential customers were charged about 2.7 cents per KWH (on the average), the trend was away from on-site generating facilities for large users and toward purchase of energy from a nearby electric generating company. Inflation and rate structure changes had altered this pattern by 1977. Industrial KWH rates had risen about 125% while residential rates had grown about 60%. Such costs for delivering electricity by the private electric companies have, of course, escalated primarily due to the doubling of market interest rates over the past 12 years (and imbedded interest costs will continue to rise until such factor closes on the market rates), the air and water pollution control equipment and heavy plant additions brought on stream (increasing plant carrying costs), and the tripling of coal and heating oil costs.

Rate-setting agencies spend considerable amounts of time on cost of service arguments. And yet, few easily applied computations have been designed in this area. Industrial customer and consumer advocate intervenors view such analysis performed by utility officers as being self-serving and unfair to one or the other groups. Rate making agencies often times strike a compromise. Record keeping on costs and assets committed by customer type are woefully inadequate but needed.

Applying a "fair and just" cost of service analysis is important if the electric utility industry is to best serve its customers at the lowest cost. Moreover, the U.S. Congress has recently mandated, among other things, that a hard look be taken at the cost of providing service by customer types (Dingell and Hill 1977). The conservation of energy in the nation is our number one priority in the short run. A high priority in the intermediate term, of course, is to develop additional supplies and sources of energy at economically reasonable prices. Wholesale abandonment of the private electric sector by large industrial and large commercial customers would assuredly lead to more rapidly rising costs for residential and other customers remaining with the private electric energy companies with less than optimum utilization of plant and fuels.

THE REGULATORY PROCESS

Throughout the history of regulation in the United States, rate review cases have been

*Department of Finance, College of Business and Administration, Southern Illinois University, Carbondale, IL 62901.

built around the concept that "rates must be just and reasonable and not unduly discriminatory" (Walters 1976). Such rates, of course, have done much to lead to the growth in electric consumption in the country by almost 8% per year from the beginning of the century until about 1973. Since that time, such growth rates have faltered. The U.S. Congress in 1976 required the administrator of the Federal Energy Administration to submit to Congress proposals to improve electric utility rate design which would "encourage energy conservation, minimize the need for new electrical generating capacity, and minimize cost of electric energy to consumers" (Treadway 1977). This program should, over the next few years, lead to more load management techniques to be applied by electric utility companies, time-of-day metering experiments such as those being conducted by Florida, Michigan, and other utilities, and greater usages of off-season power exchange with nearby electrics.

Over the past five years, state utility commissions have become increasingly caught up in almost yearly rate increase filings from most of their electric firms. Utility officials complain that the rate review process of filing, corporate submission of information supporting the need for additional revenues, public hearings and testimony by utility officials and consultants, counter proposal filings by intervenors (suppliers, customers, and public service staff), public hearings, revised information filings of both groups, a final round of public hearings, and a review process time for utility commissions to act, combine to involve a time period of up to almost one year. Many state commissions, therefore, act on such rate cases only a few days before such rate requests would otherwise become law. Such a long review process, it has been claimed by utility management, has led to declining returns on book equity to utility common stockholders, some downgrading of utility bond issues' ratings, and falling utility common stock prices generally over the 1967-1975 period. Automatic fuel adjustment clauses permitted in many of the states, of course, have reduced the severity of the crunch on adequate return to capital contributors, and in some cases have deferred for a time the need for an additional rate adjustment. Increasingly, regulators are beginning to view with suspicion facility expansion plans submitted by utility management (Cudahy 1976). The federal energy regulators have also developed some worthwhile and some misdirected rules and regulations for the industry over the past 20 years (Connole 1978). What is needed, is an overall national energy policy which is acceptable to suppliers, users, and regulators alike.

RATE DESIGN

Some writers have developed extensive lists of objectives that may be sought in rate design (Ferguson 1975, Galligan 1976). Such a list should certainly include: (1) revenues sufficient to cover costs; (2) revenues from each class of customers sufficient to cover costs associated with serving each class; (3) rates which encourage conservation of energy; (4) rates which encourage conservation of capital; and perhaps (5) rates which attract industry. Some of these objectives are at least partially mutually exclusive (e.g., No. 2 and No. 5). Let me show by description and example how the first two objectives may be met. I shall then consider the latter three goals.

Writers representing utility management and regulation have recently published articles suggesting that the total costs of the electric utility company should be grouped into about three or four categories (Grainger 1976, Ranniger 1977) which might logically include customer related expenses; energy costs; and facilities costs. These might then be apportioned on a logical basis to the customers in various customer classes. Such concepts, are well designed in the literature dealing with cost accounting, merchandise management accounting, and customer profitability analysis.

The next problem is to develop, or collect cost information adequate to make meaningful allocations. Finally, rates must be designed to fairly recapture such costs. Virtually all the cost and other utility operating information needed for such an analysis is available in the Federal Power Commission's Form 1, which is filed by more than 400 Class A, B, C, and D electric companies early each year. Each utility company, would need to collect enough information to compare average consumption of electricity, by customer class, to demand during peaking periods. This final ratio would be the basis for allocating the capital related costs to the various types of customers.

Let me now consider how such allocations may be made for the Upstate Electric Company as shown in Tables 1 through 5. Table 1 provides some basic data on four major classes of customers—residential, commercial, industrial, and municipal and REA—indicating number of customers, annual KWH sales, electric revenues, and yearly average KWH usage by customer type. Table 2 provides expense data for the electric division (expenses relating to gas operations are excluded). Customer related expenses include: customer account expense, sales expense, and administrative and general. Such expenses are allocated to customers using weights of 1, 2, 3 and 4, respectively, for the R, C, I, and other accounts inasmuch as the latter two groups consume vast amounts of energy and more time per account would be needed for their management than for the average residential account. Fuel related expenses includes power production costs, purchased power, system control, transmission, and distribution expense (with the latter associated only with residential, commercial, and industrial accounts). Apportionment should be on the basis of KWH of sales. Other costs, such as maintenance, depreciation, property taxes, income taxes, interest, preferred dividends, and return on common equity, are capacity related expenses and should more properly be allocated on the basis of average to peak load demand. Let us assume that cost studies of the Upstate Electric Company show the latter ratio to be 0.33 for residential; 0.28 for commerical; 0.77 for industrial; and 0.48 for municipal and REA customers. The average generation for the company compared to its peak generating capacity, is 0.48. Table 3 shows, then, that weights applied to each KWH of energy consumed by the four classes of customers should be 1.45x, 1.71x, 0.62x, and .89x, respectively. Table 4 then computes capacity related costs for the four customer types and finds them to be 2.12; 2.50; 0.91; and 1.30 cents per KWH of energy used. The three classes of costs, customer related, fuel related, and capacity related are combined in Table 5 with computations of monthly billings shown for a typical residential customer using 1,000 KWH of energy ($31.70); a commerical business using 10,000 KWH of energy ($329.40); a large industrial customer using 1,000,000 KWH of energy ($16,410); and a large municipal or REA customer using 1,000,000 KWH of energy ($19,813). In comparing the actual costs paid by each customer type, residential customers are paying only their fair share and commerical and industrial accounts are subsidizing the municipal and REA accounts. Such subsidy, of course, may be due to long-term contractual arrangements with such customers, a goodwill gesture intended to assure renewal of operating franchises, or less than satisfactory rate relief from FPC wholesale rate review cases.

Utility management, state utility commissions, and power agencies in Washington, DC. are beginning to take a harder look at the cost of services provided, compared to the rates assessed. There is wide variation, of course, in the approach to such expense allocations, assets assigned, and related data taken by the Federal Power Commission, the state utility commissions, and the operating utility companies. A great deal of work, with perhaps some trend toward uniformity, appears warranted.

Table 1.   Important Sales Data for the Upstate Electric Company.
           Source: FPC Form 1 on subject company.

Customer Type	Number of Customers	KWH Sales (Millions)	Revenues (Millions)	Yearly Average KWH	Average Charge Per KWH*
Residential	246,000	1,750	$ 58.1	7,114	3.32¢
Commercial	35,880	673	26.1	18,757	3.38
Industrial	2,450	2,798	53.5	1,142,040	1.91
Municipal and REA	800	1,510	21.9	1,887,500	1.45
Total	285,130	6,731	$159.6	NMD	2.37¢

*Including fuel adjustments.
Source: FPC Form 1 on subject company.

Table 2.   Expense Data on the Upstate Electric Company by Distribution Centers.
           Source: Expense data obtained from FPC Form 1 on subject company.

Item	Total (In Millions)	Method of Distribution
Customer Related Expenses		
Customer account expense	$ 3.1	Allocate to customers
Sales expense	1.9	using weights of 1, 2,
Administrative and general	7.6	3, and 4.
Total	$ 12.6	
Fuel Related Expenses		
Power production expenses	$ 43.0	Allocate on basis of KWH
Purchased power	1.3	of sales.
System control	0.2	
Transmission expense	1.5	
*Distribution expense	2.7	
Total	$ 48.7	
Capacity Related Expenses		
Maintenance	$ 16.1	Allocate to all accounts
Depreciation	17.8	on the basis of average
Property taxes	14.1	to peak load demand.
Income taxes	11.4	
Interest	16.6	
Preferred dividends	3.3	
Return on common	19.0	
Total	$ 98.3	
Total electric costs	$159.6	

*Prorated to residential, commercial and industrial accounts.
Source: Expense data obtained from FPC Form 1 on subject company.

Table 3.   Allocation of Capacity Related Costs to Customer Type for Upstate
           Electric Company.   Source: Distributed KWHs and capacity obtained
           from FPC Form 1 for subject firm.

Customer Type	Average to Peak Loads*	Ratio**	Weights	Method of Allocation
Residential	0.33	.48/.33	1.45x	Allocate $98.3 million to
Commercial	0.28	.48/.28	1.71x	6,731 million KWH on the
Industrial	0.77	.48/.77	0.62x	basis of average to capac-
Municipal & REA	0.54	.48/.54	0.89x	ity of company and average
				to peak load for each
				customer type.

*Based on company estimates.
**Monthly average generation = 612,900 MW; Capacity = 1,270,200 MW 612,900/1,270,200 = 0.48
Source: Distributed KWHs and capacity obtained from FPC Form 1 for subject firm.

Table 4. Distribution of Capacity Related Costs to Customer Types for Upstate
          Electric Co. Source: Tables 2 and 3.

Customer Type	Company Average Per KWH*	KWH Sales by Class	Weights (Table 3)	Total Col. 1x2x3	Capacity Cost Per KWH Consumed
Residential	$0.0146	1,750 M	1.45x	$37.05 M	2.12¢
Commercial	0.0146	673	1.71x	16.80	2.50¢
Industrial	0.0146	2,798	0.62x	25.33	0.91¢
Municipal & REA	0.0146	1,510	0.89x	19.62	1.30¢
Total				$98.80 M	

*$110.9 M/6,731 M KWH Sale = 0.0164 average.
Sources: Tables 2 and 3.

Table 5. Cost Justified Rate Schedule for Customers of Upstate Electric Company.

Customer Type	Monthly Charges			Typical Monthly Charges		
	Customer Related	Fuel (Per KWH)	Capacity (Per KWH)	1,000 KWH	10,000 KWH	1,000,000 KWH
Residential	$ 3.20	.0073	.0212	$31.70		
Commercial	6.40	.0073	.0250		$329.40	
Industrial	9.60	.0073	.0091			$16,409.60
Municipal/REA	12.80	*.0068	.0130			$19,812.80

*Excludes distribution expense.

Fuel and capital conservation rate design suggestions involve such approaches as
flattening rates, inverting the rates (Mann 1977), incremental costs rates (Francfort and
Philip 1977), improving load management (Sweet and Jones 1977), implementing meters
and time-of-day pricing (Bossert 1977, Malko and Stipanuk 1976, Nissle 1977), and lifeline
rates. Except for improved load management, with deferment of generating capacity
additions, many of these merely shift the cost to other customers. All have some merit and
benefit certain classes of customers while working to the disadvantage of other customers.

IMPLICATIONS

The price of fuel has increased by about 300% in the United States over the past
15 years. The delivered cost of electricity has increased by about 100% over this time
period. Such costs will continue to rise in the future, but hopefully at a lesser rate. Large
industrial customers and some large commerical accounts (office buildings or shopping
centers, perhaps) will be adding partially self-supporting solar energy systems. If private
electric utility rates charged to large industrial customers are much above those justified
by the economics of costs, some large customers will begin to install their own generating
systems. Large scale installations, of course, would lead to the need to spread the capital
related costs of the electric utilities (about 60% of total costs) to fewer remaining customers,
thus increasing the cost to residential and commercial accounts. Federal regulations in the
1960's, requiring electrics to switch to clean burning natural gas and fuel oil and away from
polluting coal (and thus supporting the position of the OPEC nations in their oil price
increases) with later switches back to coal because of the unfavorable balance of trade
problems, have cost the electric utility customers billions of dollars. Certainly Congress,
regulatory fuel agencies, suppliers, and customers must very soon consider the wisdom of

developing a national energy policy which will lead to adequate supplies of energy without overly escalating prices.

REFERENCES

Bossert, R.W. 1977. Defining time-of-use periods for electric rates. Public Utilities Fortnightly 95:19-24.

Connole, W.R. 1978. Energy—its use and abuse: 1957-1977. Public Utilities Fortnightly 96:11-15.

Cudahy, R.D. 1976. The role of the regulator in utility financing. Public Utilities Fortnightly 94:29-31.

Calligan, R.A. 1976. Rate design objectives and realities. Public Utilities Fortnightly 94:30-32.

Dingell, J.D. (Congressman) and R.L. Hill. 1977. A congressman speaks up on energy and utility legislation. Public Utilities Fortnightly 95:25-30.

Ferguson, J.S. 1975. Building blocks of rates-revisited. Public Utilities Fortnightly 93:38-43.

Francfort, A. and W. Philip. 1977. Lifeline and incremental cost residential electric rates. Public Utilities Fortnightly 95:15-20.

Galligan, R.A. 1976. Rate design objectives and realities. Public Utilities Fortnightly 1974:30-32.

Grainger, G.H. 1976. A practical approach to peak-load pricing. Public Utilities Fortnightly 94:19-23.

Hoffman, W.H., Jr. and D.E. Vaughn. 1963. Departmental and item profitability for retailers. The Journal of Accountancy 116:50-58.

Malko, J.R. and D. Stipanuk. 1976. Electric peak-load pricing: A Wisconsin framework. Public Utilities Fortnightly 94:33-36.

Mann, R. 1977. Rate structure alternatives for electricity. Public Utilities Fortnightly 95:29-34.

Nissle, H. 1977. The European experience with peak-load pricing. Public Utilities Fortnightly 95:13-18.

Ranniger, J.H. 1977. Electric rates—where we have been, where we are going. Public Utilities Fortnightly 95:29-33.

Smith, R. 1976. The developing direction of electric rate structures. Public Utilities Fortnightly 94:28-30.

Sweet, D.C. and D.E. Jones. 1977. Capital conservation in the electric utility industry. Bulletin of Business Research 52:1-3, 8.

Treadway, H. 1977. Congress and electric rate design. Public Utilities Fortnightly 95:11-14.

Walters, F.S. 1976. The great rate debate. Public Utilities Fortnightly 94:17-20.

BENEFITS AND COSTS OF LAND RECLAMATION
IN THE CENTRAL APPALACHIAN COALFIELDS

*Alan Randall, Angelos Pagoulatos and Orlen Grunewald**

The economic impacts of regulatory alternatives for the reclamation of surface mines have come under intense scrutiny in recent years. The costs to mine operators of achieving various degrees of mine reclamation in various types of mined environments and the expected impacts of proposed federal reclamation regulations on coal production, employment, and the interregional allocation of coal extraction effort and coal output have been studied.

In broad summary, recent studies have found that the impacts of proposed federal surface mine reclamation regulations will be noticeable, but perhaps not as substantial as some had expected. Nationwide, surface mine production would be reduced by about 5%, with a similar increase in underground mine production (Schlottman and Spore 1976, I.C.F. 1977). In Appalachia, the effects, both reducing surface mine output and increasing underground production, would be a little more pronounced (Schlottmand and Spore 1976, I.C.F. 1977). Nevertheless, the total decrease in Appalachian coal output and employment in coal mining was projected to be quite small, i.e. of the order ot 2% (Lin et al. 1975). These findings suggest that federal reclamation legislation, depending on the regulations eventually adopted for its implementation, is unlikely to be a major disruptive influence in the coal industry, or a significant impediment to the long-run national goal of increased utilization of coal.

None of the above mentioned studies address the benefits which accrue from surface mine reclamation under existing state regulations, or which could be expected to occur under Federal legislation. Here, we report the results of a study which is addressed specifically at estimation of the benefits from surface mine reclamation in a case study region of central Appalachia. Our estimates of the benefits or reclamation can then be compared with reclamation costs, as estimated by the researchers cited above.

The Study Region

The study area is the watershed of the North Fork of the Kentucky River, an area of about 4,100 sq. km. with a relatively impoverished population of about 80,000. The terrain is mountainous, with narrow valleys, and is typical of the central and southern Appalachian coalfields. The area has experienced both deep and surface mining for coal, and surface mining has expanded in recent years. In 1974, there were 157 active surface mines, which

*Department of Agricultural Economics, University of Kentucky, Lexington, KY 40506.

produced 11.2 million tons of coal (Bureau of Mines 1975). Permits for surface mining of 8,700 ha acres were active as of March 31, 1976. Coal mining is the major basic industry, far surpassing agriculture and forestry in the value of output.

The surface mining industry in the region has major environmental impacts. Mining typically takes place on slopes in excess of 20 degrees, and often greater than 25 degrees. The contour mining method is commonly used, and current state regulations (KRS Chapter 350) permit 40% of the overburden to be placed beyond the solid bench. While current regulations require that overburden be stabilized, the exposed seam and all acid-bearing and toxic materials be buried, the bench be revegetated, and runoff be collected in silt control structures, negative environmental impacts persist. Highwalls remain exposed, aesthetic impacts are significant, slides occur when spoil stabilization is adequate, streams suffer siltation, water quality is diminished by suspended sediment and polluted by various chemicals.

The Benefits of Reclamation

Environmental damage from surface mining creates external diseconomies and thus generates social costs. The benefits from reclamation are conceptualized in terms of the reduction of social costs of mining.

In ascribing economic values to the impacts of surface mining on environmental quality, resource quantity and quality changes due to mining are quantified in physical terms, and the net economic impacts of these changes on later uses of affected resources are determined. Then, a general model of the economic value of damage from surface mining, consistent with the later uses framework, is presented.

Symbolically, let $C(t_0)$ denote the present value of time t_0 of the sum of the net environmental costs accruing at all times $t(t=t_0, t_0+1, \ldots . T)$ as a result of surface mining in the study region in time period t_0. Then

$$C(t_0) = \sum_{t_0}^{T} P.V. \left[\sum_{1}^{J}\sum_{1}^{K} (Ct)_{jk}\right] \tag{1}$$

where

P.V.   =   present value, and

$C(Ct)jk$ =   the net loss in social benefits derived from resource using activity k due to the change j in resource quality which resulted from mining.

In any given time period, t, the net value of environmental impacts upon resource using activity k is

$$C(t)_{jk} = \int_{Q_j^o}^{Q_j^w} \pi_k' \, dQ_j \tag{2}$$

where

where

$$\pi_k' = \left[\sum_{1}^{n} P_n \frac{\partial Y_{kn}}{\partial Q_j} - \sum_{1}^{M} P_m \frac{\partial X_{km}}{\partial Q_j}\right] \tag{3}$$

and

π	=	the net value of resource using activity k (e.g. the profit from activity k if it is a market oriented production process; or the consumers' surplus arising from k, if it is a direct consumption activity).
$Q_j^o, \ldots Q_j^w$	=	a continuum of quality levels of the resource j from the no mining situation, Q_j^o to the level with mining, Q_j^w.
P_n	=	the price (or value, if unpriced) of commodity n which is produced in the resource using activity k.
Y_{kn}	=	the quantity of commodity n produced in the resource using activity k.
P_m	=	the price (or value) of input m which is used in the production of commodity n.
X_{km}	=	the quantity of input m used in the production of commodity n.

It is evident from equation (3) that resource quality changes occurring as a result of mining are hypothesized to affect the net benefits of resource using activity k both directly and indirectly, that is, having a direct effect through their influence on quantity of outputs being produced and an indirect effect through their influence on the quantities of inputs needed to produce each unit of output. These various effects may, as the case may be, take positive, negative or zero values.

ESTIMATION OF THE COSTS OF ENVIRONMENTAL DAMAGE

Five broad categories of environmental damage were identified, and their economic costs were incorporated in the general model: the costs of additional water treatment; recreational damages; damages from flooding; damage to land and buildings; and aesthetic damages. These categories of damage were carefully defined so as to be mutually exclusive and thus additive for the purpose of estimating total damage.

For each of these categories of damage, problems in economic valuation were handled in ways which seemed appropriate to peculiar needs of the particular case. Where feasible and appropriate, inputs and outputs were valued at their observed market prices. In other cases, alternative valuation techniques were used. Below, the methods of economic analysis used in this study to estimate the five identified categories of damage are outlined briefly. Substantial additional detail may be found in Randall et al. (1977).

WATER TREATMENT COSTS

The impact of mining activity on water quality in the region was determined using pooled time series and cross-sectional data obtained by monitoring at 38 locations in a sub-watershed in the study region. Monitoring data were provided by Appalachian Regional Commission (1975). A model consisting of 18 seemingly unrelated simultaneous equations was estimated by generalized least squares. Details of the analytical technique and the results obtained can be found in Randall et al. (1977).

The most significant variable in explaining water pollutant concentrations was consistently found to be surface mining activity in the immediate catchment above the monitoring site. From our estimated water quality equations and a model developed by

Smathers (1974), which relates required water treatments to water quality, stream temperature and rainfall, an estimate of the costs of water treatment due to the degradation of water as a result of surface mining was obtained. The total water treatment costs attributable to surface mining in the study region (including effects on water quality downstream) was found to be $125,000 annually (in 1976 dollars).

RECREATIONAL LOSSES

There are indications from scientific literature and the results of a personal interview survey conducted during this study (Randall et al. 1977), that surface mining has been associated with declining opportunities for hunting and fishing in the study region. However, due to the highly unsatisfactory recreational data base for the region, these losses remain unquantified. The annual replacement cost of the fish losses due to water quality changes was determined to be $65,300. Recreational losses due to degradation of water quality downstream in the main Kentucky River were estimated as follows. Expected recreational use was calculated using a model adapted from Appalachian Regional Commission (1969). Expected use was then compared with actual use as recorded by U.S. Army Corps of Engineers. After several appropriate adjustments were made (Randall et al. 1977), downstream recreation losses due to surface mining in the study region were calculated to be $211,500 annually. Thus, total quantified losses were $277,000 annually. Since several major sources of recreational loss remain unquantified, this figure represents a substantial underestimate.

FLOODING

Using data describing the relationship between surface mining and peak stream flows (Curtis 1972) and a U.S. Army Corps of Engineers' study of flood damge in the study region (1962) updated to 1976 economic conditions, annual flood damages in the region and downstream attributable to surface mining in the study region, were estimated to be $269,000.

DAMAGE TO LAND BUILDINGS

Surface mining causes on-site and off-site damage to land and buildings. However, reclaimed surface mined land is valued in the market more highly than unmined land (typically steep hillsides carrying a cover of scrub timber) in the study region. Considering all the possible effects, the net value of damage to land and buildings resulting from surface mining in the study region was estimated, using survey data, to be $1,837,000 annually.

AESTHETIC DAMAGE

The value of aesthetic damages from surface mining was determined using a modified and improved version of the bidding game technique developed by Randall et al. (1974) and replicated by Brookshire et al. (1976). The survey instrument, used with a random sample of 1% of the households in the region, provided three different bidding games and one nonmonetary preference scale. The results using all four test items were remarkably consistent (Randall et al. 1977). Under existing regulations, annual aesthetic damage in the study region was valued at $1,048,000 (Regional Willingness to Pay for abatement) or $56,487 (Total Consumer Payment). In calculating TCP, the bidding game results are applied not only to regional residents (as in the case of RWP), but to all citizens who use coal produced in the region.

It must be emphasized that TCP and RWP are not alternative estimates of the same quantity, but are estimates of two fundamentally different quantities. RWP estimates the total amount that residents of the study region would be willing to pay to obtain relief from the aesthetic environmental damage visited upon them by the surface mining industry. Thus, it (1) provides a willingness to pay (i.e. smaller) measure of the consumers' surplus of environmental improvements and (2) ignores use, option and preservation values which visitors and other nonresidents may place on the mountain environment. TCP estimates the social costs of the total aesthetic environmental damage caused by the industry, assuming that all users of coal produced in the region either *would be willing, or should be expected*, to pay at the same rate as regional residents to reduce the external costs of the industry.

Total costs of environmental damage due to surface mining in the study region under existing regulations as currently enforced is shown in Table 1. The present value of the environmental costs of mining one acre of land in the study region were calculated to be $18,190 (TCP) and $772 (RWP). The present value of the environmental costs of mining one ton of coal are $8.30 (TCP) and $0.36 (RWP).

TABLE 1 Total Annual Environmental Costs of Surface Mining in the Study Region (1976).

Category of Costs	TCP	RWP
	$ Millions	$ Millions
Aesthetic	56.487	1.048
Water Treatment	0.125	0.125
Recreatinal	0.277	0.277
Flooding	0.269	0.269
Land and Buildings	1.837	1.837
Total	58.995	3.556

BENEFITS FROM RECLAMATION

The economic value of environmental damage from surface mining was then calculated assuming no regulations, and regulations which would be enforced assuming passage into law of the federal reclamation bill as introduced to the 1977 congress. By subtraction, the environmental benefits of reclamation under existing state regulations and the proposed federal regulations were calculated.

BENEFITS AND COSTS OF RECLAMATION

The benefits of reclamation as determined in this study were compared with the costs of reclamation as estimated by I.C.F., Inc. (Table 2).

TABLE 2 Benefits and Costs of Reclamation of Surface Coal Mines in the Study Region. Per Ton of Coal Mined (1976).

Regulations	Benefits ($)		Costs ($)
	TCP	RWP	
Existing State	10.42	1.38	0.82
Proposed Federal (incremental costs & benefits)	3.30	0.16	1.72
Residual Environmental Costs (assuming Federal regulations)	5.00	0.20	----

The benefits of existing regulations, whether estimated as TCP or RWP exceed the costs to mining operators of reclamation. The benefits (measured by TCP) of reclamation required under proposed federal regulations exceed the costs. However, RWP is less than the costs of reclamation. For the federal bill, both benefits and costs are calculated as incremental, given existing state regulations. In all cases, the governmental costs of operating regulatory programs have not been considered.

It should be noted (Table 2), that, even assuming that proposed federal regulations are enacted and enforced, some positive residual social environmental costs of surface mining remain. That is, given current mining and reclamation technology, surface mining in the mountainous environment generates some irreversible environmental costs.

REFERENCES

Appalachian Regional Commission. 1967. Mine Drainage Pollution and Recreation in Appalachia (prepared by Robert R. Nathan and Associates, Inc.), 114 p.

Appalachian Regional Commission. 1975. Surface mine pollution abatement and land use impact investigation. Rpt. ARC-71-66-T2, 279 p.

Brookshire, D., B. Ives and W. Schultze. 1976. The valuation of aesthetic preferences. J. Environment Economic Manag. 3:325-346.

Curtis, W.R. 1972. Strip mining increases flood potential of mountain watersheds. pp. 357-360, In Proc. of National Symp. on Watersheds in Transition, American Water Resource Assoc. and Colorado State Univ., Ft. Collins, CO, June 19-22.

I.C.F., Inc. 1977. Draft Final Report: Energy and Economic Impacts of H.R. 13950, Submitted to U.S.E.P.A. and Council on Environmental Quality, February, 248 p.

Lin, W.W., R.L. Spore and E.A. Nephew. 1975. Land reclamation and strip-mined coal production in Appalachia. Paper presented at the American Agricultural Economics Assoc. Annual Meeting, Columbus, OH.

Randall, A., B. Ives, C. Eastman. 1974. Bidding games for valuation of aesthetic environmental improvements. Journal of Environmental Economics and Management 1:132-149, 1974.

Randall, A., R. Ausness, O. Grunewald, S. Johnson and A. Pagoulatos. 1977. Draft Final Report: Estimating Environmental Damages from the Surface Mining of Coal in Appalachia: A Case Study. Submitted to U.S.E.P.A., 131 p.

Schlottmann, A. and R.L. Spore. 1976. Economic impacts of surface mine reclamation. Land Economics 52:265-277.

Smathers, W.M., Jr. 1974. The economic impact of surface mining on water quality, unpublished Thesis, Univ. Kentucky, Lexington, 61 p.

U.S. Army Corps of Engineers. 1976. Kentucky Rivers and Tributaries. U.S. Army Engineer District, Lousiville, KY, 219 p.

U.S. Bureau of Mines. 1975. Coal-Bituminous and Lignite in 1974. Mineral Industry Surveys, Washington, DC, 60 p.

MARKET POTENTIAL OF
ABATEMENT GYPSUM PRODUCTION IN THE U.S.

Angelos Pagoulatos,* David Debertin,* Milton Shuffett* and Jim Ransom**

The electrical utility industry in the U.S. faces difficult problems and decisions in implementing the Clean Air Act of 1967 as amended in 1970 with respect to SO_2 emissions. U.S. Department of the Interior has projected that net electrical generation by fossil-fired power plants will increase from 1,310 billion kwh in 1971 to 1,950 kwh in 1980. The EPA recently projected that flue gas desulfurization (FGD) control systems will be installed on 90,000 MW or about 25% of total estimated coal-fired utility generation capacity by 1980. That would result in an annual production of 131,000,000 tons of throwaway sludge if the limestone slurry process were used. Disposal costs for the limestone slurry process are high, and the process is wasteful of large quantities of sulfur, a vital economic resource. To the extent that these emissions can be economically recovered and abatement gypsum marketed, society would be the net beneficiary.

THE MARKET FOR GYPSUM

It is important to evaluate abatement gypsum FGD systems under U.S. conditions. The product has immediate uses which are alternatives to throwaway systems. Sulfur can be stockpiled for future needs. In the U.S., a demonstration gypsum-producing FGD system on a coal-fired facility is being operated by Gulf Power and Light in cooperation with EPA. Samples of gypsum have been used successfully in wallboard manufacture. Hence, we assume that abatement gypsum can be substituted for gypsum in the wallboard and cement industries.

While gypsum reserves are extensive both in the world and the U.S., with the exception of one producing area in southwest Virginia, no economic reserves are located in the southeastern portion of the U.S. Transportation costs are a large proportion of the value of the product (Appleyard 1975).

Gypsum use in the U.S. is estimated at 15 to 20 million tons annually, of which about one-third is imported. Seventy-three percent of all gypsum goes into calcined materials, cement uses 20% and 7% goes into agricultural uses. Despite the close dependence on the construction industry, gypsum demand does not have a significant seasonal pattern. Gypsum markets represent a potential to use large quantities of abatement product rather than resorting to conventional throwaway systems. In addition, gypsum may be stockpiled for later use with minimal environmental problems.

* Department of Agricultural Economics, University of Kentucky, Lexington, KY 40546.
** Tennessee Valley Authority, Muscle Shoals, AL 35660.

In terms of value of product sold, the industry is highly integrated from mining through calcining and sale of manufactured products. However, wallboard permits are sold to independent building supply dealers or building contractors. Increasingly by-product gypsum from fertilizer manufacturing operations is replacing gypsum for agricultural uses.

The industry is highly concentrated. From 1947 to 1972, the leading four firms accounted for approximately 80% or more of value of industry shipments in every year. The eight-firm ratio has consistently been above 90% and the costs of entry are suspected to be very high.

Consumption of gypsum has been growing at a 2% per year rate through 1976, despite large yearly fluctuations. Based on the projections of the Bureau of Mines (1975), consumption is expected to reach 20.6 million tons in 1978 of which 14.6 million tons will be used in calcining plants, 4.1 million tons in cement use, and 1.4 million in agriculture.

COSTS AND SUPPLY OF ABATEMENT GYPSUM

The study is based on the premise that all utilities (currently out of compliance) comply by 1978 by choosing one of the following alternatives: (1) scrub by limestone slurry process, (2) scrub by gypsum-producing process, (3) use low sulfur fuel (clean fuel), and (4) use combinations of one or two with alternative three.

Estimates were developed from the Emission Control Development staff of TVA. The supply of abatement gypsum was determined on a plant-by-plant basis for 1978. The analysis is based on projections of fuel use and other operating characteristics as reported by the utilities themselves.

The limestone oxidation to gypsum process was used for comparing gypsum production costs with the scrub limestone throwaway process. The cost model calculated cost of scrubbing on a boiler-by-boiler basis and then sums to a plant level. The appropriate air quality regulation (SIP) for the plant was determined and translated into the allowable SO_2 admission. The clean air act as amended allows states and air quality regions to establish implementation regulations and standards to meet local needs. Substantial variation exists between districts as to standards and how they are to be applied. Regulations may apply at each specific boiler, or they may apply at a stack or plant level. When regulations apply at the boiler level, each boiler out of compliance must scrub. When regulations apply at the stack or plant level, only a sufficient number of boilers must scrub to bring total SO_2 emissions into compliance with the point source standard.

The next stop was to determine if the plant would be in or out of compliance in 1978 if operated as projected. Emissions were calculated based on the projected quantity of fuel to be burned in each boiler and its sulfur content. If calculated SO_2 emissions exceeded calculated allowable SO_2 emissions by 10% or more, the plant (or boiler) was determined to be out of compliance for purposes of this study. Costs were calculated. Industry costs were summarized and the supply of abatement gypsum determined. The study considered all fossil-fired utilities in the U.S. A total of 800 plants with 3,382 boilers having a total capacity of 411,404 megawatts will be in operation in 1978.

A total of 187 plants will be out of compliance in 1978. These plants would have to remove a total of 4,440,180 tons of sulfur to meet compliance regulations. This is over twice the quantity of sulfur that was imported into the U.S. in 1974 and equal to 38% of domestically mined sulfur in 1974. If this amount of sulfur were to be abated in the conventional limestone slurry FGD systems, a total of 25,393,504 tons of calcium solids would be made and have to be ponded in the first year. Total investment would be 6.89 billion dollars if all sulfur were to be abated by the limestone slurry system.

MARKETING POTENTIAL OF ABATEMENT GYPSUM

To determine the market potential for abatement gypsum, consumption was projected at each demand point, and the delivered price of crude gypsum was calculated at each demand point. To caluclate the delivered cost of crude gypsum, the current rail rate for gypsum was escalated by 15% to reflect estimated 1978 rates. Rates were calculated by use of a computer program to select appropriate tariff and to calculate miles from each supply point to each demand point. Rate-per-ton mile was multiplied by miles to each point to obtain transportation cost which was added to f.o.b. price at supply points. This assured that the lowest delivered cost of gypsum to each demand point was calculated. A detailed description of the mixed integer linear programming formulation can be found in Ransom (1977) and Pagoulatos et al. (1978).

The market analysis was limited to the industry east of the Rocky Mountains after it was determined that only three plants were out of compliance in the western states. These three plants are located in Nevada and Wyoming, and because of their location, would have limited opportunity to market abatement gypsum. In the study area an estimated 15,043,301 tons of gypsum will be used in 1978 by the wallboard and cement industries at 187 demand points. The total cost to market that crude gypsum under the study assumptions will amount to 124.4 million dollars. Approximately 58% of the total cost is for transportation. Calcining plants are located either at domestic mine sites or at deep-water ports to utilize imported gypsum; therefore, the major portion of transportation costs is borne by the cement industry.

Fifty-five demand points are calcining plants. These plants are estimated to use 11,855,910 tons of gypsum in 1978. Estimated consumption per plant ranges from a low of 58,260 to a high of over 500,000 tons. Average consumption per plant is estimated at 215,562 tons. Delivered cost to calcining plants is based on estimated domestic variable mining costs of 3 dollars per ton and 2 dollars per ton for imported gypsum. Imported gypsum (mainly from Canada) is transported to coastal calcining plants at rates ranging from 3 dollars to 5 dollars per ton. All interior calcining plants but three are located at or near mine sites. In these cases a flat 1 dollar per ton is assumed to cover costs of moving the material from mine to plant. Rail rates are calculated from company-owned mines to calcining plants for the plants located away from mine sites.

Imports are estimated at over 5.9 million tons (in the study area) in 1978. Under the study assumptions, 66 demand points will use imported crude gypsum. Forty-three are cement plants which use an estimated 1,164,378 tons. This gypsum is imported to the calcining plant and then shipped to the cement plant. Rail rates are calculated in each point. Twenty-three calcining plants will directly use 4,777,320 tons of imported gypsum.

One hundred and thirty-two demand points are cement plants. The cement industry is projected to use a total of 3,187,391 tons gypsum in 1978. This is based on each plant in the industry operating at 85% of rated capacity and each plant using a finished cement containing 5% gypsum. Use per plant ranges from a low of 2,550 tons to a high of 65,875 tons. Average use per plant will amount to 24,147 tons. Delivered prices are based on a conservative average f.o.b. price of 6 dollars per ton from nearest supply points. Rail transportation is assumed in each case, and minimum delivered cost of crude gypsum is calculated to each cement demand point. Delivered costs range from a low of $12.43 per ton to a high of $21.18. The majority of tonnage used will have a delivered cost of between 15 dollars and 18 dollars per ton. This tonnage was supplied by small abatement producers that could supply requirements of cement plants located near the utility. Fifteen of the 30 utilities in the final solution actually were calculated to have lower cost gypsum production than for the limestone slurry throwaway product. An additional seven plants had an incremental cost of less than 1 dollar per ton of gypsum. The average annual production at these steam plants was 65,377 tons.

When average savings per ton to the gypsum using industry were calculated to be only 86 cents per ton, these economies using abatement gypsum by the existing industry are questionable. However. the steam plants could pass additional savings to the gypsum using industry to compensate for added costs to use abatement produce in lieu of crude gypsum. For example, if these costs amounted to 2 dollars per ton, 27 steam plants would continue to produce. At a 3 dollar-per-ton price reduction, 24 plants would continue to produce and market abatement gypsum to the cement industry. The analysis indicates that 74% of imported material used by the cement industry would be replaced. The results of the analysis are summarized in Tables 1 and 2.

TABLE 1   Summary of Steam Plants Calculated to Produce and Market
Abatement Gypsum and Net Revenue Per Plant

FPC Number	State	Tons Gypsum Produced	Incremental Cost/Ton ($)	Net Revenue ($)
1385000100	DE	11,288	-12.66	199,063
5250001000	VA	38,520	- 5.56	396,425
2345000200	FL	28,677	- 3.56	320,266
2770000700	IA	56,278	- 2.95	488,383
3945000600	MD	89,101	- 2.37	511,865
5430000250	TX	65,887	- 1.44	337,968
5440000100	OK	55,371	- 1.15	294,934
3080000400	MS	106,933	- 0.92	912,828
0805002700	ME	43,895	- 0.90	183,935
4050001150	NH	72,128	- 0.32	194,889
4740000100	FL	96,176	- 0.31	874,427
2920000500	MI	14,520	- 0.28	84,715
4480000075	SC	92,238	- 0.23	809,931
3080000150	MS	85,829	- 0.23	543,275
5235000100	NJ	6,679	- 0.03	42,814
4045000800	IN	69,132	0.06	427,859
4785000575	TX	73,647	0.16	331,036
5420000400	PA	15,749	0.29	167,451
1415000150	KY	101,706	0.57	388,260
3590000200	NY	20,977	0.57	146,367
2605000150	MI	58,079	0.59	327,902
0720000900	NC	76,788	0.68	393,633
3795000350	PA	158,716	0.92	342,920
5250001400	VA	150,519	1.01	328,600
0785000500	IL	170,139	1.60	569,098
2260000100	IN	134,105	2.00	101,735
3085000350	MS	131,672	2.02	205,045
0700000550	NY	164,582	2.46	492,155
4820000700	MI	50,070	3.00	46,109
3840000500	PA	159,690	3.02	612,098

TABLE 2 Summary of Results of Analysis in Eastern U.S.

Number of plants out of compliance (total)	187
Lowest-cost strategy	
Clean fuel, number of plants	71
Limestone slurry process, number of plants	86
Gypsum production and marketing, number of plants	30
Total gypsum produced (tons)	2,399,081
Average production per steam plant (tons)	79,970
Smallest gypsum supplier (tons)	6,679
Largest gypsum supplier (tons)	170,981
Total gypsum sold (tons)	2,228,100
Total gypsum stockpiled Itons)	170,981
Number plant stockpile part of production	5
Wallboard plants served	1
Cement plants served	92
Sold to wallboard plants (tons)	95,307
Sold to cement plants (tons)	2,132,793
Total net revenue to utilities ($)	11,075,970
Total savings to gypsum industry ($)	1,922,731
Savings to gypsum industry (% of total cost)	1.5
Average savings per ton of gypsum purchased ($)	0.86
Total first-year compliance cost for 113 plants using the limestone slurry process ($)	2,037,721,214
Reduction by marketing gypsum ($)	11,075,970
Cost reduction (%)	0.5
Required sulfur removal (tons)	4,109,000
Sulfur removed by gypsum process (%)	8.7
Tons imported gypsum displaced	855,992
Tons domestic gypsum displaced	1,372,108
1978 calcining market served with abatement gypsum (%)	0.8
1978 cement market served with abatement by gypsum (%)	67.0

CONCLUSIONS

Gypsum is a low-value product used in substantial quantities by wallboard manufacturing plants. The cost of SO_2 removal by the gypsum-producing process is higher than it is for the limestone slurry throwaway process. The only exceptions were some new small plants in terms of SO_2 removal have a cost advantage to produce gypsum. This works to the disadvantage of the gypsum process to supply the existing wallboard industry. The analysis was based on conservative estimates of gypsum mining costs, but in all other respects the analysis was based on premises favorable to abatement gypsum.

Production and marketing of abatement gypsum to the cement industry appears to offer an opportunity for steam plants with low annual volumes of sulfur removal to lower cost of compliance. By the same token, there appears to be little opportunity to lower compliance cost by marketing abatement gypsum to the existing wallboard products industry. The gypsum-producing alternative appears to offer only a limited potential to solve the larger problems of sulfur conservation and disposal of calcium solids. However, in terms of a total program of by-product marketing, the gypsum-product alternative may fill a specific role in that it appears to meet the needs of small plants when other by-products may be better suited to large plants. If that proves to be the case, the gypsum process would appear to be of more total importance than the analysis indicates.

REFERENCES

Appleyard, F. 1975. Construction Materials-Gypsum and Anhydrite. Pub. in Industrial Minerals and Rocks, American Institute of Mining Metalurigcal and Petroleum Engineers, NY.

Ransom, J. 1977. Feasibility of gypsum production and marketing as an alternative SO_2 emission control strategy for fossil-fired power plants. Ph.D. dissertation, Dept. Agr. Econ., Univ. Kentucky, Lexington.

Pagoulatos, A. D. Debertin, M. Shuffett and J. Ransom. 1978. Alternative strategies in marketing of abatement gypsum from fossil-fired power plants. Research Rpt. 28, College of Agr., Univ. Kentucky, Lexington.

U.S. Bureau of Mines. 1975. Gypsum mines and calcining plants. Washington, DC.

ECONOMICS OF REUSE OF POWER PLANT ASH

Oscar E. Manz *

NATURE OF POWER PLANT ASH

Power plant coal ash is composed largely of compounds of silica, alumina, iron and lime, together with smaller quantities of magnesia, titanium, potassium, phosphorus, sulfur and alkali compounds. The silica, alumina and titanium oxide are derived from sand, clay, shale and slate; the iron oxide is derived mainly from iron pyrites; and the lime and magnesia from their corresponding carbonates and sulfates. These ash-forming constituents consist of (1) "inherent" or "intrinsic" impurities that are present in an intimate mixture with the coal substance and are derived either from the original vegetable material or from external sources by sedimentation or precipitation during the process of accumulation of coal-forming vegetation; (2) impurities deposited either during the laying down of the coal bed or, subsequently, which occur in the form of partings, veins and nodules of clay, shale, pyrite and calcite; and (3) impurities that become mechanically mixed with the coal in the process of mining, such as fragments of roof and floor. The ash as determined usually weighs less than the inorganic matter from which it is produced. This is due to loss of volatile constituents and other changes during the burning. Shale and clay lose their water of hydration, the carbonates are decomposed giving off carbon dioxide, and the iron pyrite is changed to ferric oxide giving off sulfur dioxide, either to the atmosphere or to the free calcium oxide that has been formed from the carbonate. In coals containing calcium carbonate, a large proportion of the sulfur may be retained in the ash as calcium sulfate.

The ash content of coals varies over a wide range. This variation occurs not only in coal from different parts of the world or from different seams in the same region but also in coal from different parts of the same mine.

Coals may be classified into two groups based on the nature of their ash constituents. One is the bituminous-type ash and the other is the lignite-type ash. The term "lignite-type" ash is defined as an ash having more calcium oxide, CaO, plus magnesium oxide, MgO, than ferric oxide, Fe_2O_3. By contrast, the "bituminous-type" ash will have more ferric oxide, Fe_2O_3, than calcium oxide, CaO, plus magnesium oxide, MgO (Morrison 1972).

NEW SOURCES OF ASH

"Ash is expected to become increasingly important to electric utilities operating coal burning steam generating stations, to both deep and surface mine coal producers, and to

*Coal By-Products Utilization Institute, University of North Dakota, Grand Forks, ND 58202.

all coal producing states. A recent survey by the National Coal Association in 1977 indicates the demand for coal by utilities will rise by 400 million tons a year by 1985. The study lists 259 new coal-fired plants that are to be on stream by 1986 requiring an additional 430 million tons of coal yearly above current needs. In 1976, utilities burned 446 million tons. Location-wise, the report shows a strong shift toward building these new units in the southwest. One-fourth or 59 of the stations are planned for the Arkansas, Texas, Oklahoma, Louisiana area while another 36 are to be located in Arizona, Colorado, Montana, Nevada, New Mexico, Utah, and Wyoming (see Table 1). The projected plants are, of course, being sited to take advantage of the rapidly developing western coalfields.

Table 1. New Coal-Fired Plants by Region. Source: National Coal Association 1977.

Region (and States)	New Coal-fired Units Planned for 1977-86	
	Units	Megawatts
New England (CN,ME,MA,NH,RI,VT)	1	600
Middle Atlantic (NY,PA,NJ)	7	5,500
East North Central (IL,IN,MI,OH,WI)	50	22,124
West North Central (IA,KS,MN,MO,NE,ND, SD)	40	18,727
South Atlantic (DE,DC,FL,GA,MD,NC,SC,VA,WV)	31	18,444
East South Central (AL,KY,MS,TN)	30	14,940
West South Central (AR,LA,OK,TX)	59	32,398
Mountain (AZ,CO,MN,NV,MN,UT,WY)	36	13,952
Pacific (CA,OR,WA)	5	2,630
Total U.S.	259	129,315

When fully operational the new stations will have a dramatic effect on ash availability, pushing the annual nationwide tonnage beyond 100 million tons. It will mean these areas will have commerical amounts of these versatile construction materials available to them for the first time at locations which will minimize transportation costs" (Ash at Work 1977).

USES OF POWER PLANT ASH

As indicated in Table 2, the most economical use of large tonnages of fly ash is for highway construction such as structural fill, soil stabilization, portland cement concrete, mineral filler, etc. Other important uses include land fill, agricultural applications and manufacture of light weight aggregate. The coarser bottom ashes also serve as aggregates. The reuse of power plant fly ash and bottom ash is a serious problem since only about 20% is utilized. Mine mouth power plants have the advantage of disposal of ash in decoaled mine seams. However, an increasing number of power plants are hauling coal tremendous distances and therefore have an added incentive to find economical uses for the ash.

PROMOTION OF UTILIZATION OF ASH

Many organizations are promoting the use of power plant ashes, including the National Ash Association, American Society for Testing Materials, Federal Highway Administration, Transportation Research Board, U.S. Army Corps. of Engineers, Bureau of Reclamation, State Departments of Transportation and many university research organizations.

Table 2.   Ash Collection & Utilization 1976.   Source: National Ash Association and Edison Electric Institute 1977.

	Fly Ash Tons x 10^6	Bottom Ash Tons x 10^6	Boiler Slag (if separated from Bottom Ash Tons x 10^6
1. Total Ash Collected	42.8	14.3	4.8
2. Ash Utilized	5.7	4.5	2.2
3. Utilization Percentage			
A. Commercial Utilization			
a. Used in Type 1-P cement- ASTM 595-71 or mixed with raw material before forming cement clinker.	9	2	2
b. Partial replacement of cement in concrete or concrete products.	16	---	---
c. Lightweight aggregate.	2	2	---
d. Stabilization and roads.	4	15	10
e. Fill for roads, reclamation & ecology dikes, etc.	26	---	---
f. Filler in asphalt mix	4	---	---
g. Ice Control	---	10	5
h. Blast grit and roofing granules.	---	---	55
i. Miscellaneous	9	20	14
B. Ash removed from plant sites at no cost to utility.	5	23	8
C. Ash utilized from disposal sites after disposal costs.	25	28	6
	100	100	100

Four major ash conferences will be held here and abroad during the next 12 months and worldwide participation is expected (Ash at Work, No. 1, 1978).

The Federal Highway Administration has been supporting research studies involving the use of power plant ash in highway construction and recently published a very comprehensive manual titled "Fly Ash: A Highway Construction Material."

The American Society for Testing Materials has several committees working on specifications and methods of tests involving the use of power plant ash in cement, concrete soil stabilization, bituminous products and other related materials.

The Transportation Research Board is a clearing house for publication of research reports concerning all phases of transportation.

Several state departments of transportation as well as many university organizations are conducting studies involving the use of power plant ash.

COAL BY-PRODUCTS UTILIZATION INSTITUTE

Until recently there were limited quantities of lignite and subbituminous ash available. At the University of North Dakota the Coal-By-Products Utilization Institute under the direction of Oscar E. Manz is investigating the utilization of these western ashes. The Institute is well equipped to both test and do research involving concrete aggregates, concrete, masonry products, asphaltic mixtures, cement, fly ash, soil and ceramic products. Recently the Institute was awarded an EPA research grant for two years to investigate the environmental effects of disposal of high alkaline fly ash power plant sludge in a decoaled mine seam at Center, North Dakota. The adjacent mine mouth power plant will be the first lignite fired power plant to use fly ash rather than lime or limestone as the SO_2 medium.

CONCLUSIONS

With the surge of coal-fired power plants being built, there will be tremendous quantities of power plant ash available over larger portions of the country. Therefore, the utilization should increase considerably both in total tonnage as well as percentage. The widespread availability of power plant ash will make it an economical natural resource.

REFERENCES

Ash at Work. 1977. Ash importance to increase in coming months. Natl. Ash Assoc. 6:1.
Ash at Work. 1978. Four major ash conferences are scheduled. Natl. Ash Assoc. 1:1-3.
Morrison, R.E. 1972. Characteristics of power plant ash. Construction specification Institute, Huntington, WV, 10 p.

PART IV: PRINCIPLES AND PRACTICES OF RECLAMATION

Because of its length and general importance, Part IV has been divided into six sections. Having passed the stage of skepticism and debate, the enunciation of sound principles and implementation of proper reclamation practices are the basic requirements of achieving the targeted goals of coal production. The constraints imposed on coal resource development in the absence of adequate reclamation practices are tremendous. The designated sections within this part deal with the imperative of reclamation in its most applicative sense—the design and management criteria , the geological and ecological processes involved, and feasible strategies based on the judicious use of amendments and proper selection of species.

RECLAMATION—OUR LEGACY TO THE FUTURE

Gerald D. Harwood*

"Men make their own history, but they do not make it just as they please: they do not make it under circumstances chosen by themselves, but under circumstances directly encountered, given and transmitted from the past." [Marx, circa 1894]

INTRODUCTION

In recent history, man has taken pride in his ability to shape the environment, and to some extent, the future. For nearly two centuries, science and technology have given us confidence in the belief that virtually nothing is beyond our eventual grasp, if only we are given sufficient time to accomplish it. We have drastically reduced the threat of many infectious diseases which plagued mankind for centuries. It is now possible to instantly communicate with or rapidly travel to virtually any part of the world. Living in space and travel to other planets has become a reality. But in this century, the luster of our confidence has dimmed; gradually, mankind has emerged from the naivete of childhood to be confronted with the cold reality of new limitations and responsibilities.

The nations of the world have become increasingly aware of the finite character of mineral and energy resources and of the inherent inequities in their geographic distribution. Improved communications and growing literacy are rapidly spreading this awareness to all of the earth's peoples. Ever increased demands are being made upon the earth's resources in the hope of improving the quality of life through the elevation of living styles and standards; these demands come from developing and developed nations alike.

Many of the social, political and economic problems that face all nations, individually and collectively, have two common denominators: the unchecked growth of human population and the facts that our planet has a finite surface area and a finite supply of non-renewable natural resources. In both of these areas, we seem to be on a collision course with ecological disaster. We have the knowledge to deal effectively with both problems, but the necessary social and political wisdom to take meaningful action has and continues to elude us. The problem of human population control, while now technologically feasible, presents us with a plethora of sociological and moral dilemmas. Fortunately, many of our food, mineral and energy resources are renewable and can adequately provide for a large (but at some point limited) population; however, fossil fuels and undisturbed lands are both in finite supply.

Precisely how and when our non-renewable resources should be exploited and by whom are questions that will undoubtedly concern us for the foreseeable future. Should all

*School of Renewable Natural Resources, University of Arizona, Tucson, AZ 85721.

of our available known non-renewable resources be developed and consumed as rapidly as economic conditions permit? Should decisions to reclaim or not to reclaim mined lands be made strictly upon a cost-benefit basis? Some propose that these issues should be rapidly decided on the basis of relatively short-term needs and cost-benefits, while dismissing most other considerations as being merely "emotional" and therefore somehow unworthy of serious consideration. But the meanings of such everyday terms can be complex and, in this context, they have not yet been fully defined. The relative importance of economic costs versus aesthetic and emotional costs differs considerably with the context: Precisely whose needs are being considered? What are the bases for these needs? What kinds of costs are being considered? Are costs which cannot be described in monetary terms worthy of consideration? Are considerations that might be labeled as "emotional" by some valid and should they have equal weight with economic considerations? We should resolve these questions and formulate workable policies based upon the answers we find before irreversible damage is done to our non-renewable aesthetic resources.

Murdy (1975) has noted that it is important for each of us to appreciate the degree to which our individual and collective actions can affect the future. There seems little question that the exhaustion of useable energy resources will have highly tangible effects upon the lives of our children and their descendants unless alternative energy sources can be developed. It is likely that the eventual exhaustion of useable petroleum reserves will be unavoidable. Even if we learn to temper wasteful use of petroleum, it will be needed in ever increasing quantities for intensive agricultural production required to feed the rapidly growing world population. As Marx and Engels (1968) observed, we can only shape our own future within the limitations we inherit from the past. Accordingly, the decisions we make now concerning disposition and care of the earth's remaining non-renewable natural resources will have a direct bearing on the options available to future generations for all time.

THE IMPORTANCE OF RECLAMATION

While we work toward the development of alternative energy technologies, the utilization of world coal reserves will rapidly increase. In the western United States, there are massive deposits of this resource. Much of it lies under land of great scenic beauty and environmentalists are endeavoring to protect such areas from the disruptive effects of strip mining. The damage that would be produced by strip mining in many areas would be virtually irreparable (Anon. 1975). But given the facts of an ever-growing world population, the pending depletion of petroleum reserves and increasing world political pressure for equitable distribution of our planet's resources and wealth, it seems ultimately to be a question of when, rather than whether, most of these reserves will eventually be mined. Exactly how they will be mined and utilized is still to be decided.

Also yet to be answered are questions which concern reclamation of the land after it has been mined: When is reclamation necessary? How extensive should reclamation efforts be? When should the term land "reclamation" imply "restoration" of the land to its original pre-mining condition and use? There is not yet universal agreement among those in the mining industry and in those agencies that control it that reclamation is necessary at all. Some argue that the mined land should be left to naturally occurring reclamation processes, and to the question of aesthetics they respond that within half a century or so the abandoned mines will be regarded as sites of historical interest.

In many instances, there are obvious ecological and/or economic reasons for reclamation of mined land. If the land is needed for agriculture or if erosion or flooding will endanger adjacent lands of economic value, few will question the need for reclamation, even at great expense. If the land is adjacent to an inhabited area, a national park or other land of appreciable interest to the public, again there is little debate on the need for reclamation. But what of land that is remote from public view or land of marginal economic value - is the expense of reclamation justified in these cases? How important is the restoration of what remains of our "natural" environment for non-economic reasons that are usually voiced only by environmentalists? How can significant expenditures for protective mining procedures and/or restoration of economically intangible environmental qualities be justified to those who do not perceive their aesthetic value and may not derive direct economic benefit from them? At the present time, those who would protect the environment are pressed for answers based upon "hard" data that cannot be dismissed as "emotional" by their detractors. Although public emotion has proven to be a powerful economic and political force, these issues cannot be permanently resolved until data can be provided that can be understood by all concerned, and which can serve as a rational basis for policymaking.

SYSTEMS OF ENVIRONMENTAL THOUGHT

A traditional approach to resolving dilemmas is to consider past courses of human action. In our present situation, however, there is no real precedent: at no other time in history has human population been so numerically out of balance with nature or possessed capabilities of comparable magnitude for the permanent alteration or destruction of the earth's natural environment. Nonetheless, some insight can be gained from an examination of the past relationship between human activity and environmental philosophy as to what may be our eventual course of action.

Moos and Brownstein (1977) have briefly reviewed the history of systems of environmental thought. They found that philosophical methods have evolved with the passage of time. In ancient times, hypotheses embodied astrological and mystical elements, while modern work utilizes scientific methods including empirical classification, hypothesis formation, the examination and testing of data, and the drawing of generalized conclusions. While modern theorists may employ statistics and computers, the basic intent of analysis over the centuries has been to define and understand environments and the systems that operate within them, not to create or place value judgements upon them. In the interest of elucidating likely patterns of human response to environmental situations the findings of Moos and Brownstein are briefly considered here.

Determinism

Environmental determinism was espoused by both the Greeks and Romans of classical times, by Arab scholars during the Middle Ages and was still dominant in thinking during the early part of the twentieth century. Essentially, environmental determinism is a theory that defines man in a position of helplessness before the forces of nature. Not only does nature limit man's endeavors, but it causes his actions. In this context, social institutions are man's response to environmental conditions and free will exists only as an illusion. For example, the social structure of the horsemen of the steppe region was based upon the suitability of the land for grazing. Food and materials for crafts were essentially limited to by-products of the herd. The continual need for new forage forced a nomadic lifestyle which obviated the need for permanent structures and property value; land was valued only for its grass cover and once this was depleted, the herdsmen moved on. Moos and Brownstein note that the theory of environmental determinism came under increasing attack in the early part of the twentieth century; its critics argued that the concept could not explain social and political change in the context of a constant environment nor could the value of an environment be conceptualized without reference to the particular level of culture that inhabited it. For example, coal and oil would be of comparatively little value to non-technological societies.

Possibilism

Early in this century, possibilism was proposed as an alternative to determinism. Possibilism allows the dimension of the limited exercise of free will within a deterministic context. Febvre (1925) stated the thesis of possibilism: "There are no necessities, but everywhere possibilities; and man as a master of the possibilities is the judge of their use." Opportunities provided by environment delimit possibilities, but man has the option of selecting what will be done. Moos and Brownstein emphasize that: ". . . . possibilism never claimed that man could do whatever he pleased with regard to nature. On the contrary, the options of human action are always limited." They cite Brunhes (1920): "The penalty exacted for acting contrary to physical facts is all the more cruel as man's victory over them is great and glorious. . . . When man succeeds in building dikes to hold back the waters. . . . the risks he runs are proportional to the fruitfulness of his efforts. An invasion of the sea or an abnormal flooding. . . . is destructive to the very extent that the natural forces were victoriously tamed." The determinist and possibilist approaches to the relationship between environment and the stagnation or decline of a civilization differ: determinism might argue that a limited supply of natural resources was the cause, while possibilism would place the blame upon the failure of man's institutions. Several years of philosophical debate over the two systems unearthed some inconsistencies. For example, the two systems could not be differentiated when they were called upon to explain a technological response to an environmental situation. Either system could offer an explanation: determinism argues that the response would be dictated by the environment while possibilism would attribute the response to an example of human alteration of the environment in order to achieve a desired goal. Due to this and other problems, improved systems of environmental thought were sought.

Probabilism, Pragmatism and Neodeterminism

After World War II, Spate (1952) proposed a theory named probabilism which resolved some of the problems that existed between the systems of environmental causality and free will. Essentially, Spate proposed that some possibilities were more likely than others, depending upon environmental factors. Decision-making in this context can utilize statistical and mathematical models to predict the likely outcomes of alternative environmental policies. However, such models must be able to allow for the unpredictability of many environmental variables such as rainfall.

Moos and Brownstein note that few environmental theorists now espouse probabilism; instead, most of those who seek an alternative to determinism and possibilism can be labeled as pragmatists who state that they "... do not know whether the universe is organized according to determinism or free will .... [nor].... do they know how to find out." Rather than postponing research until such philosophical questions can be resolved, pragmatists will accept a working hypothesis of a qualified determinism to the effect that "....natural and human processes of sufficient regularity do exist."

There are situations in which a probable alternative is virtually certain; it can be argued that environment does determine action. This alternative is accommodated by Meggers (1954), who developed an environmental theory called neodeterminism. Moos and Brownstein conceptualize her thesis as arguing that: "....environment limits what man can do; it does not ordain what he will do within those limits." Thus, Meggers' theory accounts for the unequal development of parallel societies which exist under environmentally similar circumstances and limitations.

With respect to the present dilemma concerning our current energy and mineral needs and pressures to develop our non-renewable resources versus the value of the natural environment, its protection and reclamation, a strict application of determinism would seem to suggest that we must and will develop natural resources to the limits of our perceived need or ability or until altered environmental conditions place new limitations upon such activities. Possibly, such restrictions would take the form of depletion of the available resources or public reaction to severe disruption of environmental quality. Possibilism suggests that we have the latitude of choice to exercise our options or to choose between alternatives provided by our situation; it does not provide a license for the disregard of environmental consequences to our actions. Common to each of the systems is the premise that those actions we do take are limited by environmental factors and circumstance. It seems reasonable to conclude that, given our present circumstances, we will eventually develop all of our available resources unless compelling environmental limitations are perceived by us or imposed upon us. Further, at least to the extent that we affect the environment, whatever course we follow will directly limit the options available to subsequent generations.

MAN'S NEED FOR ENVIRONMENTAL QUALITY

There are many who argue that the urgency of our energy needs and economic factors should outweigh all other considerations with respect to what lands shall be mined and the stringency of reclamation and environmental quality regulations. This persuasion tends to view all other arguments by those who propose stringent reclamation and even withdrawal of some lands from exploration and mining as being based in "emotion" and therefore of questionable validity. However, with respect to the relative validity of concerns considered to be "emotional," such as the need for virgin wilderness areas, preservation of endangered species, etc. as bases for argument, this debate cannot be resolved at this point in history as all of the evidence is not in. At this time we neither understand the importance, nor know the full extent, of man's need for undisturbed land and other aesthetic entities. Perhaps, it will never be defined with the same quantitative precision that is possible in the physical and economic sciences. Criak (1968) has observed that the science of psychology has only recently begun to consider the effects of the physical world. The fact that we must deal with psychological environmental variables in an imprecise manner does not, however, negate their reality nor their importance. The fact that mining in many areas will result in permanent, non-restorable destruction of the land's surface value suggests that caution should be exercised and that irrevocable decisions should not be made until more facts have been gathered.

Arthur et al. (1976) note that the high value we have traditionally placed upon our public forests has been well documented by the activities of poets, painters, photographers and attorneys, but only recently have aesthetics become a primary concern in public land management. While only a few years ago it was considered bad form to discuss such intangible qualities as aesthetics and natural beauty in the context of natural resource management, it is now permissible and even mandatory to consider the visual landscape as a concrete resource in its own right (Litton 1970). Considerable research into the measurement of scenic beauty has been funded (see Arthur and Boster 1976).

Rene Dubos (1972) has expressed the belief that while man is a creature with the capacity to adapt to a variety of environmentally and biologically stressful situations, his mental creativity will diminish if he cannot periodically withdraw from the stresses of crowding and technology. "The quality of the environment obviously influences the well-being of the body, but its most important effects are probably on the productions of the mind." Dubos believes that the conditions which allow us to fulfill our need for privacy, empty space and independence, needs which are essential for the preservation and enlargement of the peculiarly human qualities of life, will become scarce long before we become critically short of food, energy and raw materials. He foresees a time when privacy and freedom will come to be regarded as antisocial luxuries.

Stainbrook (1975) reminds us that although our evolved human bodies are interdependent biological systems that are part of the natural universe, our science and technology strive toward the denaturalization of man and the rest of nature. Western man views nature as an opponent to be conquered and controlled, while Eastern societies have tended to collaborate with nature. Our technology and its pressures have made it both possible and mandatory for us to live out of synchronization with the rhythms of nature and our bodies. Stainbrook believes that these and other stressful aspects of our lives lead to fatigue, inefficiency and possibly other subtle maladaptive effects; to counter these, he urges: ".... a general consistent concern about the meaning and functions of the natural environment for reasons other than a romantic agony over the loss of natural man and of natural nature." Further, he suggests that: "Our basic task in assessing what man should do with nature is perhaps not so much a problem to be solved as a value to be established - not so much a discovery as a decision."

Stainbrook provides two examples of how the natural environment is essential to our mental health. The open space, aesthetic beauty and freedom from crowds and noise provided by natural settings all combine to provide us with opportunities to enjoy a very basic form of human gratification, the nature of which might be described as the sort of feeling one experiences while lying in the sun on a beach. This function can be partially fulfilled by parks and recreational areas which might be constructed in reclaimed mining areas, but the undisturbed natural environment fulfills yet another basic human need which is related to our concepts of permanency and change. Continual change and impermanence of virtually all things physical and social characterize our contemporary society. The psychological cost of this phenomenon is particularly visible in our children, but adults are also affected. Contact with a natural, undisturbed environment can fulfill an inner need to feel that at least some things endure.

It is likely that additional psychological and social functions of undisturbed land will be found. Until now, we have enjoyed an abundance of wilderness and we may have derived benefits from it of a nature and to an extent not yet understood. Should some of these benefits prove to be essential for individual or collective well-being, the irreparable destruction of a significant quantity of a resource vital to man's mental health, only in the interest of relatively short-term energy or economic benefit to a single generation would be more than a regrettable act in the eyes of posterity; it would represent a direct reduction of the earth's habitability for mankind.

OUR RESPONSIBILITY TO THE FUTURE

Glen Seaborg (1972) has noted that the development of human civilization has roughly paralleled our ability to control energy, whether provided by animals, coal or the atom. With respect to time, the rate of growth has been exponential in form. Until the 18th century, muscle, wind and water provided most of our energy; then, the invention of the steam engine began our development of fossil fuels. Seaborg believes that the steam engine signified much more than the beginning of the Industrial Revolution; it was a turning point in human history. Virtually overnight, mankind was released from a subsistence level existence to turn in large numbers toward intellectual development. Transportation, construction, food production and distribution were all affected. In the century that followed, energy and food consumption surpassed the total of all previous history. Significant modification of the environment became possible.

This pattern of exponential growth is important in the context of our own legacy from the past. Whether or not ancient civilizations such as those of the Egyptians or Romans contemplated their impact upon our present culture matters little, as their numbers were small and they did not have the technological capacity that we now do to massively disrupt the earth's surface or to irrevocably deplete its resources. The world which we inherited from our ancestors was relatively intact, and we have accordingly benefited greatly. But today, environmental planning is no longer optional. We are now dealing with issues which can have irreversible effects; accordingly, our responsibility to future generations cannot be neglected. Lands damaged by mining or other processes must be reclaimed to the extent that is possible. A major problem we must face is that of quantifying our relative responsibilities to those who live in the present and those who will live in the future. It seems important to note in this context that our perception of time tends to differ with respect to contemplation of past and future; it is somehow more difficult for us to conceive of our grandchildren living their lives a century from now than it is to contemplate our grandparents living a century ago. We speak comfortably of events that occurred 2,000 years in the past, and we acknowledge their impact upon our individual lives and our civilization; and yet our attitudes toward utilization of the earth's finite resources seem to reflect a disregard of any future more than a decade or two away.

It would be more than imprudent to rapidly dispose of questions concerning non-renewable resources in a manner that will provide only marginal short-term benefits to a few, whether now living or yet to be born. We are faced with the incontrovertible fact that once the resources are gone and/or the lands have been despoiled, we may very likely still be faced with our original needs, but find that they have been intensified by the fact that the resources with which time was purchased in the past no longer exist. Our position (or that of our descendants) will be even less enviable if time has been purchased by methods which have poisoned the earth or otherwise reduced its habitability or quality. At such time in the future, whether it be a few years, a century, or a millenium away, the absolute magnitude and justification of our twentieth century "need" may be seriously questioned. Those born first in time have the dual advantage of having first choice of the available resources and immunity from direct influence or intervention in their actions by those who follow. For example, we are now powerless to protect the Wooly Mammoth which was hunted to extinction by early North Americans.

Murdy (1975) observes that: ".... modern man now stands at a crossroad. Continued geometric growth in human numbers, consumption of resources and pollution of environments will propel mankind down a road of diminished options. . . a point will be reached where the only alternative to extinction will be the regimented ant-heap." Murdy views this as a process of evolutionary retrogression in which higher emergent values are destroyed on behalf of the fundamental value of biological survival. He believes that: ".... our greatest danger is not that the human species will become extinct, ... but that the cultural values which make us human will become extinct." The legacy of natural resources and environmental quality that we leave to the future will be one measure of the quality of our cultural values. It is essential that our best collective wisdom go into the making of decisions in these matters so that our actions will neither disrupt the homeostatic processes that balance nature nor decrease the quality of life for future generations.

REFERENCES

Anon. 1975. Irreversible and irretrievable commitments of resources if federal coal is leased. pp. 7-1–7-5, In Final Environmental Impact Statement: Proposed Coal Leasing Program, U.S.D.I., 1975, Superintendent of Documents, Stock No. 024-011-00062-3.

Arthur, L.M. and R.S. Boster. 1976. Measuring Scenic Beauty: A selected Annotated Bibliography. U.S.D.A. For. Serv. Gen. Tech. Rpt. RM-25, Rocky Mt. For. & Range Expt. Sta., Ft. Collins, CO.

Arthur, L.M., T.C. Daniel and R.S. Boster. 1976. Scenic assessment: An overview. Landscape Planning 4:109-129.

Brunhes, J. 1920. Human Geography. Rand McNally, Chicago.

Burton, R.L., Jr. 1970. Landscape and aesthetic quality. pp. 91-104, In R. Revelle and H.H. Landsberg (eds.), America's Changing Environment, Houghton Mifflin Co., Boston, MA.

Craik, K.H. The comprehension of the everyday environment. J. Amer. Inst. of Planners 34(1):24-37. [Cited in Burton 1970].

Dubos, R. 1972. Adaptation to the environment and man's future. pp. 60-78, In J.D. Roslansky (ed.), The Control of the Environment. Fleet Academic Editions, Inc., NY.

Febvre, L. 1925. A Geographical Introduction to History. Alfred A. Knopf, NY. 236 p. [Cited in Moos and Brownstein 1977].

Litton, R.B., Jr. 1970. Landscape and aesthetic quality. pp. 91-94, In R. Revelle and H.H. Landsberg (eds.), America's Changing Environment, Boston: Houghton Misslin Co.

Marx, K. and F. Engels. 1968. Selected Works. Intl. Pub., NY, 97 p. [Cited in Moos and Brownstein 1977].

Meggers, B. 1954. Environmental limitations on the development of culture. Anthropologist 56:801-824 [Cited in Moos and Brownstein 1977].

Moos, R. and R. Brownstein. 1977. Environment and Utopia: A Synthesis, Plenum Press, NY, 248 p.

Murdy, W. 1975. Anthropocentrism: A modern version.   Science 187:1168-1172.

Seaborg, G.T. 1972. The control of energy. pp. 92-112, In J.D. Roslansky (ed.), The Control of Environment, Fleet Academic Editions, Inc., NY.

Spate, O.H.K. 1952. Toynbee and Huntington: A Study in Determinism. Geographical Journal 118:406-428 [Cited in Moos and Brownstein 1977].

Stainbrook, E. 1975. Mental health and the environment: Do we need nature? pp. 186-202, In R.A. Rybout (ed.), Environmental Quality and Society, Ohio State Univ. Press, Columbus.

INCORPORATING ORPHANED MINE
SPOIL RECLAMATION INTO THE MINING PLAN

*James B. Gulliford**

INTRODUCTION

The increasing demand for energy in the United States coupled with decreasing supplies of oil and natural gas continues to put pressure on the coal industry to increase coal production and promote maximum utilization of all coal resources. These trends, plus a desire by the State of Iowa to become more energy self-sufficient, stimulated the Iowa Legislature to appropriate $3,000,000 in 1974 to Iowa State University's Energy and Mineral Resources Research Institute for a three-year study of the coal potential of Iowa. The primary goals of this study were to investigate the washability of Iowa coals and to examine coal mining and restoration economics in an agricultural environment. Secondary goals included a multidisciplinary environmental analysis of surface mining covering the physical, biological and social sciences.

In fulfilling these goals two major projects were undertaken. A 70-ton per hour coal preparation plant was designed and built on the Iowa State University campus employing heavy media separation and concentration tables to remove sulfur and ash. Continued coal preparation research is examining fine coal processing and recovery and chemical coal processing for sulfur removal.

As a part of the coal mining and restoration research, a steeply sloped, 40-acre pasture site of low agricultural productivity was chosen for Iowa Coal Project Demonstration Mine No. 1. During mining, 110,000 tons of coal were removed, impact on the surrounding environment was kept at a minimum and the site was restored to a series of level benched terraces suitable for intensive row crop production. Continuing experiments on this site will determine the effectiveness of the restoration with respect to environmental protection and agricultural productivity. As a part of this operation a unique project was initiated to develop a reclamation program for an abandoned surface mine site adjacent to the primary Demonstration Mine experiment.

HISTORY

Surface mining in Iowa parallels the Des Moines River in the south-central portion of the state. Strippable coal reserves typically occur in small 50-200 acre pods the size and

*Energy and Mineral Resources Research Institute, Iowa State University, 318 Spedding Hall, Ames, IA 50011.

nature of which were determined by a combination of depositional history and recent pre-Pleistocene and Pennsylvanian Age erosion. Past surface mining of these deposits followed a pattern of mining from natural drainages, where overburden was thinnest, deeper into hillsides until overburden depth became too great for economic feasibility. These practices have left more than 11,000 acres of orphaned mine spoils in Iowa which are agriculturally unproductive and pollute the watersheds.

As the economics of surface mining changes, these abandoned sites are becoming economically attractive for additional mining. Many of the present Iowa mines border abandoned spoils and future mine development can be expected to follow this pattern. It is possible when mining adjacent to old spoils to reclaim these spoils as a part of the mining operation while decreasing the cost of mining. This was the purpose of the reclamation experiment of the Iowa Coal Project conducted in conjunction with the primary experiment of mining and restoration.

Mining terminated on the Archie Childers property in the spring of 1975 leaving 28 acres of unreclaimed mine spoils and seven acres of unmined land. The topography of the site (Fig. 1) was typical of abandoned mine spoils featuring three impoundments, steep spoil banks, gullied slopes and considerable areas with pyritic, acid-producing shales exposed. The mined land was left with no productive value and little vegetative cover to prevent erosion and acid mine drainage runoff. The unmined area was isolated from the farmer's remaining land and littered with abandoned mining equipment making it also relatively useless. Overburden on the unmined acres averaged 20 feet of loess and glacial till, 10 feet of sand and 10 feet of black pyritic shale overlying four feet of coal.

RATIONALE FOR THE ABANDONED MINE LAND RECLAMATION PLAN

In developing the mining plan that included the reclamation of the mine spoils, three interrelated criteria were considered. These were the recovery of a small pocket of coal (31,000 tons) that was probably too small to be economically attractive to a mining firm; the reclamation of 28 acres of abandoned mine spoils, restoring the land to some level of productivity, and accomplishing the operation in an economically acceptable manner. The first two are criteria that relate to the proper utilization of natural resources and the preservation of land productivity and the third, the prospect of economic gain from reclaiming abandoned mine spoils, offers hope that projects of this nature could be incorporated into mining plans that have abandoned mine spoils adjacent to proposed new mining properties.

To be economical, the reclamation plan for the project was designed to require a minimum of rehandling of overburden materials. This was accomplished by a final reclamation plan that featured the filling of all impoundments and surrounding gullies and leaving a depression where the coal would be removed during mining (Fig. 1). Pre-mining exploratory drilling also determined that there were sufficient volumes of topsoil and clay over the remaining seven unmined acres to cover the entire site with at least two feet of non-toxic materials, and the reclamation plan called for maximum slopes of 4:1 to prevent excessive runoff and erosion from the reclaimed surface.

The final topographic configuration and topsoiling provisions of this proposed plan were not consistent with the existing state requirements or the present federal surface mining law with respect to the acres to be mined. However, because the post-mining topography was not inconsistent with the surrounding area and because the expected site productivity greatly exceeded the pre-mining productivity, the state mine inspector waived the state's topsoiling and topographic requirements in favor of the proposed reclamation plan.

Original Topography

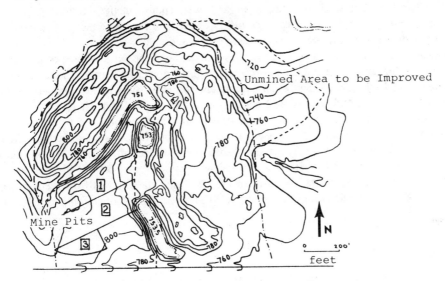

Reclamation Plan

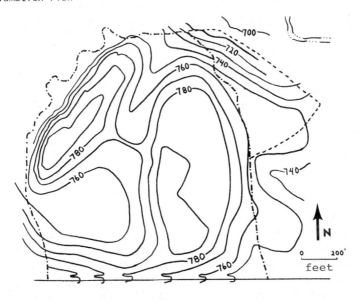

Fig. 1. Original Topography and Reclamation Plan

MINING AND RECLAMATION

Prior to mining, bulldozers leveled the spoil piles on the property to be reclaimed preparing it to be topsoiled. When mining began, 85,000 cubic yards of clay and topsoil from pit 1 (Fig. 1) were spread by scrapers over the eastern portion of the site to a minimum depth of two feet. The sand and shale from pit 1 were spoiled in five unmined acres in the northeast corner of the site to improve the utility of the land for the farmer and to eliminate the need to double-haul this material as mining progressed.

During coal removal from pit 1, the topsoil and clay from pit 2 were spread over the northern portion of the site and the improved area in the northeast corner. The sand of pit 2 was layered and mixed with clay as an experiment to determine whether the permeability of the reclaimed soil could be improved. Shale from pit 2 was spoiled in pit 1.

Topsoil and clay from pit 3 were spread over pit 1 and the northwest portion of the site and the sand and shale were spoiled in pit 2. Reclamation was completed by dozing down the highwalls around pit 3 and the southern impoundment. Nearly 31,000 tons of coal had been mined and the site was covered with at least two feet of clay or topsoil.

Work at the site terminated November 17, 1977 and the site was frost seeded in the spring of 1978 with a mixture of crown vetch, bromegrass, birdsfoot trefoil and red clover.

MINING ECONOMICS

The economics of this mining and reclamation experiment were very important because the project was only subsidized by the $10,000 reclamation bond of the original miner held by the mine inspector of the State of Iowa. It was necessary for the sale of coal to offset the cost of reclamation. The economic summary of the experiment is shown in Table 1.

TABLE 1 Summary of Iowa Coal Project Reclamation Project Economics

	Costs	Income
Coal Sales		$ 636,628.62
30,960.755 raw tons		
$1.16/MMBTU		
11,305 BTU/lb. (cleaned)		
78.4% recovery (cleaned)		
Reclamation Bond		10,000.00
Total Income		$ 646,628.62
Earthmoving	$ 328,029.71	
labor, equipment and maintenance		
Coal Removal @ $2.85/ton	88,238.15	
Transportation @ $5.10/ton	157,899.85	
Royalty @ $0.50/ton	15,480.40	
Coal Preparation @ $1.63/clean ton	39,565.37	
OSM Reclamation Tax @ $0.35/ton on 4,126 tons	1,444.10	
Total Costs	$ 630,657.58	
Net Income to Iowa Coal Project		$ 15,971.04

Nearly 31,000 tons of raw coal were mined and transported to the coal preparation plant at Iowa State University for cleaning and consumption in the University's physical plant. Costs of coal removal, transportation and royalty were paid on a "raw ton" basis. During cleaning, 78.4% of the coal was recovered and the heating value was increased to an average of 11,305 btu/lb. The cost of cleaning was $1.63/clean ton (operational cost, capital cost not included) and the cleaned coal was sold for $1.16/MMbtu netting $636,628.62. Following October 1, 1977, 4,126 tons of coal were mined and $1,444.10 ($0.35/ton) was paid as required for the Coal Production and Reclamation Fee of the Office of Surface Mining.

Earth-moving accounted for more than 50% of the mining and reclamation costs and can be broken down approximately as follows: 61% equipment rental; 14% labor; 10% contractor overhead; 8% fuel and lubricants; and 7% maintenance, insurance, taxes and miscellaneous expenses.

The economic benefit to the project that was gained by reclaiming the surrounding acres can be shown by examining the volume of overburden that was spoiled in the five acres of improved land and the volume of topsoil and clay that covered the 28 reclaimed acres. More than 230,000 cubic yards of material were disposed of in this manner eliminating the necessity of hauling it back to the mined acres to rebuild the original contour. At $0.55/cubic yard (approximate cost to transport unconsolidated material by scraper over the course of Iowa Coal Project mining operations), the savings to the project exceeded $125,000. The project would have failed economically if it would have had to rebuild the mined acres to satisfy PL 95-87 requirements.

DISCUSSION

The Iowa Coal Project mine spoil reclamation experiment has shown that it is possible to incorporate orphaned mine spoil reclamation into the mining operation. In this operation, 28 acres of orphaned mine spoils were reclaimed potentially to pastureland productivity, five acres of unmined land were improved and five of seven unmined acres were mined and reclaimed recovering nearly 31,000 tons of coal. Considering all of these benefits to the land owner, the miner was also able to operate profitably.

It is important, however, to realize the fragile nature of the site and the need for proper management to maintain it. With only two feet of topsoil covering acid-producing shales, permanent vegetation will be necessary to prevent erosion and the generation of acid "hot spots".

Reclaiming orphaned mine spoils as a part of a mining operation is also contingent upon common ownership of the land to be mined and reclaimed and the availability of the necessary volume of nontoxic overburden to topsoil leveled mine spoils.

Mining and reclamation plans of this nature have become potentially more feasible following the passage of the federal Surface Mining Control and Reclamation Act. The Office of Surface Mining Abandoned Mine Lands Reclamation Fund provides financial support for the reclamation of orphaned mine spoils, and when the economics of this type of operation are not completely positive, application by the landowner for partial federal funding may provide the necessary money to make the operation feasible. Mining plans that include orphaned mine spoil reclamation can in this manner enhance the value of federal reclamation funds by reclaiming more acreage than otherwise possible.

REFERENCES

Grieve, R.A., H. Chu and R.W. Fisher. 1976. Iowa Coal Project preliminary coal beneficiation cost study progress report. Energy & Mineral Resources Research Institute, Iowa State University, Ames, Iowa, 15 p.

Sendlein, L.V.A., C.E. Anderson and J.B. Gulliford. 1977. Land restoration: the Iowa experiment. pp. 283-297, Fifth Symp. on Surface Mining and Reclamation, NCA/BCR Coal Conf. and Expo IV, Louisville, KY.

A PLANNING AND DECISION MODEL FOR
THE AESTHETICS OF SURFACE-MINE RECLAMATION

Nicholas T. Dines*, Robert Mallary** and Charles R. Yuill***

INTRODUCTION

It need hardly be emphasized that the visual quality of reclamation is bound to affect not only the perceived quality of the reclaimed site itself, but must also inevitably either degrade, sustain, or possibly even improve the scenic character of the surrounding environment in which the site is located. Moreover, it should also be stressed that it is the visual quality of reclamation that most forceably impacts the consciousness of the general public, providing thereby the principal basis for its evaluation of the reclamation performance as a whole. For unlike the environmental and ecological components of reclamation, whose success can be measured precisely by the absence of slides, slumping, erosion, and so forth, the fact of beauty or ugliness is there for all to see, a symbol of neglect or stewardship on the part of those responsible for the planning and implementation of the reclamation (Cole 1976).

Although the importance of the aesthetic component is widely acknowledged within the surface mine industry and within the agencies of government responsible for regulating and improving the quality of reclamation, there is as yet no clear conceptual framework wherein aesthetic requirements can be effectively planned, nor are there clear standards and criteria for assessing aesthetic quality either at the planning stage or after the reclamation has been carried out. Unlike the requirements pertaining to environmental protection and pollution abatement, and unlike the ongoing improvements in the engineering and technological aspects of the concurrent extraction/reclamation process, prior research has been only peripheral in respect to land use, land use improvement, and reclamation aesthetics.

In an effort to make up for this serious deficiency in reclamation research and planning, a multidisciplinary faculty group at the University of Massachusetts in Amherst, in collaboration with the firm of Skelly and Loy in Harrisburg, Pennsylvania, is developing a computer-based approach to this neglected area of reclamation planning, an approach that, along with its other innovative features, stresses the importance of compelling site-specific requirements as they relate to the immediate surroundings and to macro-scale planning considerations on both a local and regional level. In proposing and adhering to its perception

*   Landscape Architecture and Environmental Design, University of Massachusetts, Amherst, MA 01003.
** Surface Mine Research Group, Institute for Man and Environment; also Center for Cybergraphic Systems, University of Massachusetts, Amherst, MA 01003.
*** Skelly and Loy, Harrisburg, PA, 17101.

of what comprises an authentic systems-theoretic approach to the problem, this joint research team," with its abundance of both theoretical and practical, field-oriented resources," is currently in the process of developing a multidisciplinary research format for:

(1) Identifying, describing, and classifying both current and potential approaches to reclamation;

(2) Relating reclamation aesthetics to the environmental, engineering/technological, legal/regulatory, and other requirements of reclamation and reclamation planning;

(3) Relating reclamation aesthetics to the professional disciplines of environmental design, landscape planning, and other fields of applied design that may also be relevant;

(4) Relating reclamation aesthetics to art theory, experimental aesthetics, and to fundamental principles of visual design and composition;

(5) Designing a computer-based planning "protocol" (i.e., a formal systematic procedure) for generating effective reclamation plans within a logical organizational and managerial framework.

This systems-oriented research, and the model that provides it with a structure and a direction, are based on the concept of a three-stage planning process described here (Fig. 1). But since it is basic to this systems-oriented approach that literally all of the significant factors influencing the character and quality of reclamation be considered as interdependent variables, it is essential that these factors be identified and described.

FACTORS INFLUENCING THE AESTHETIC QUALITY OF RECLAMATION

If considered in extremely broad terms, it could be argued logically that both the existence of reclamation along with the character and quality of its performance are the products of a cluster of social, economic, political, cultural, and even religious forces and attitudes which are quite general and elusive in character. But fortunately, the scope of our concern is much more manageable in that it is restricted exclusively to those factors that either: (1) are already subject to explicit and detailed consideration at the planning stage of reclamation (which refer primarily to environmental and engineering/technological considerations); (2) are presently considered to a certain extent but have the potential of being handled much more effectively than is now the case (primarily site after-use and land use planning considerations); or (3) are presently being dealt with inadequately or hardly at all, even though they can and should be fully assimilated into the planning process (here the reference is to the overly neglected area of aesthetics). Since all of them are important, they are singled out and briefly discussed under the headings that follow.

The Environmental Component

The aesthetic design of a reclaimed site as expressed in its topography and vegetative scheme must be in accord with stringent environmental and ecological requirements, particularly as regards resistance to erosion, sedimentation, and other potential instabilities. Hills, slopes, terraces, and contours can be designed so as to be beautiful in a visual and sculptural sense while at the same time be resistant to erosive forces (Coates 1973). Indeed, under certain circumstances it is possible to make the resculptured and revegetated landform *more* resistant to erosion than the original topography. Using the meters for physical design and sculptural form.

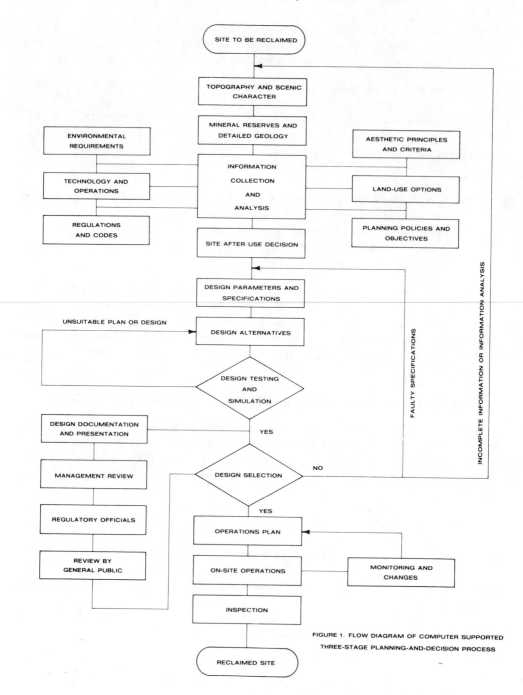

FIGURE 1. FLOW DIAGRAM OF COMPUTER SUPPORTED THREE-STAGE PLANNING-AND-DECISION PROCESS

The Technological Component

The topographic design of a reclaimed site must at least be in the realm of the feasible, given the mounting costs of earthmoving operations and the inherent limitations of existing equipment as tools for shaping and "sculpturing" landforms. In a sense, the various configurations of equipment as they work in different geologic and topographical environments, can be thought of as representing a variety of sculpting tools, each having explicit and well-defined constraints and potentialities in the gross and refined sculpting of proposed reclamation design (SEAM 1977). The combination of equipment capabilities and earth mechanics results in effective extraction and backfilling strategies necessary to execute any visual objective.

The Legal/Regulatory Component

A proposed reclamation plan must be in accord with state and federal laws and codes and with the constantly changing patterns of regulations and guidelines based on these codes. Particularly important to the aesthetic component in reclamation is the policy of "reclamation to approximate original contour and condition" as interpreted in different states and regions and applied to widely varying topographic environments and conditions. The policy is interpreted one way in the context of mountaintop-removal and head-of-hollow fill and another way when applied to the flat or gently rolling landscapes of Ohio, Illinois, and Indiana. But in all cases it is a decisive factor in its influence on the character and quality of aesthetics, a factor that is generally more conducive to restriction than to the creative freedom of an imaginative, enterprising designer.

The Land Use and Planning Component

Above all, the aesthetics of reclamation design is influenced by the after-use of the site, which may be consistent with restoring it to its original contour if it is also to be returned to its prior use, but which is likely to require a quite different topography and design if another application is chosen. It should also be noted that the aesthetic component of reclamation as influenced by the after-use of the site can also be used by government planning agencies to implement long-term policies for conserving the nation's heritage of natural beauty and of sustaining (and occasionally even *improving*) the visual quality of the environment.

The Aesthetic Component

Emphasizing aesthetics as the sole, or even the principal objective of a reclamation program risks an undesirable regression to the early naive stage of reclamation when it amounted to little more than a cosmetic cover-up of the worst effects of the completely unregulated surface mining process. A vast improvement ensued when, as the next stage in the progress of reclamation as a form of "environmentalism," aesthetics was combined with environmental imperatives in the form of terracing and other topographic configurations that were simultaneously resistant to erosion, adaptable to a variety of after-use applications, and could also be varied aesthetically in pleasing ways (Mallary and Carlozzi 1976). Nevertheless, while sounding a cautionary note against a regression to mere cosmetics, and while stressing that aesthetics is likely to be most expressive when artfully fused with land use and function, it should also be mentioned that an attractively designed site, in giving expression to fundamental and possibly ageless principles of design and composition, can be perceived as beautiful in and of itself and in this sense be in accord with at least one of the criteria defining an authentic work of art.

In sum, from the standpoint of a comprehensive systems approach, the aesthetic potential of reclamation is conceived as having a dual, complementary aspect: on one hand it must be subservient to the intergrated objectives of the reclamation program as a whole; on the other it should be conceded, as art involving drainage, topography, trees, shrubs, groundcovers, and other landscape features as its medium, a quasi-autonomous status as an uplifting "end value" in its own right.

A THREE—STAGE PLANNING—AND—DECISION MODEL

Having defined the major factor involved in planning for high-quality reclamation and reclamation aesthetics, it is now possible to show how they are incorporated into the planning process as a three-stage planning-and-decision cycle.

The First Stage

Information relevant to the site and its reclamation is identified, collected, evaluated, and analyzed. From this emerges a set of constraints, criteria, and standards that serve as guidelines and specifications for those involved in the actual design of the landforms and landscapes.

The Second Stage

Design alternatives are explored, and the most promising are improved and developed through an ongoing computer simulation-and-testing process that evaluates them against the topographic, environmental, economic, and other criteria discussed above and specified in the form of an agenda. Crucial to this second design-production stage of the three-stage process is an interactive computer graphic system that makes it possible to produce literally hundreds of designs and variations and to see them instantly, in accurate one- two, or three-point perspective, and from any chosen viewing angle or distance. The designs are also seen in a variety of styles, including color renderings, whose culminative effect is to provide a more vivid and conception of the landforms and landscape features.

The Third Stage

The designs are reviewed by those responsible for selection and decision-making. In this stage the contribution of the computer is to present designs clearly and realistically and to document them with backup information and statistics. The selected design is then translated into computer-generated working drawings and specifications for on-site use during the actual extraction/reclamation operations. At this stage the computer can also be used to generate striking high-information displays in the form of graphics and 3-D relief models for presentations to the public (see Section 102 (i) of the Surface Mine Control and Reclamation Act of 1977 for statements mandating public participation in the reclamation process). And as an additional benefit and service at this third stage, the computer-graphic system can generate drawings and color renderings to be used in papers, articles, publicity releases, lectures, symposia and other media events and activities that inform the public about surface mining and reclamation and that help to improve the public image of this essential energy industry.

THE FLOW OF INFORMATION THROUGH THE THREE STAGES OF THE MODEL

The three-stage process summarized above is now described somewhat more dynamically and in detail using the flow diagram (Fig. 1). The overall direction of the information flow is, of course, from the top down and includes several decision nodes and feedback loops that complicate the smooth course of this uni-directional flow.

Information Collection, Analysis and Organization

At the top of the flow diagram is the site to be surface-mined and reclaimed with the support of an efficient computer-supported planning-and-decision process of the sort described here. Immediately beneath this box are two others, the first labeled *topographic and scenic character*, to indicate the basic class of information pertaining directly to aesthetics, while the second—*detailed geology*—refers to both surface and subsurface data relevant to economic and operational constraints and to the entire planning, extraction, and reclamation cycle as a profitable energy producing enterprise. These and six other broad classes of information feed into *information collection and analysis process*, out of which emerges a *land use decision* (or a number of land use possibilities) followed by a set of *design specifications* reflecting and supporting the land use decision along with all of the other interdependent requirements, constraints and objectives that make up the entire reclamation program. Taken together, the sum total of information and information processes represented in this top portion of the flow diagram is "distilled" into these specifications, which can be thought of as information output from stage one and input for stage two.

The Manipulation and Refinement of Information

On the basis of these specifications and guidelines, and drawing upon the increasingly sophisticated technology of interactive computer graphics and computer-aided design, the designers and planners assigned to the project prepare plans for reclamation (or alternative sets of designs) for initial simulation and testing at the decision node shown as the first diamond-shaped box in Fig. 1. Based on the increasingly sophisticated techniques of computer-based mathematical modeling and simulation, the designs are tested for such features as resistance to erosion and sedimentation, full utilization of all of the overburden, operation economies and feasibility, and for a number of aesthetic requirements of scenic character and visibility from crucial viewing points and angles (Mallary and Ferraro 1977). When one or more of the designs have passed these tests, they become output from one stage and input for the stage that follows.

The Display and Presentation of Information

The four boxes shown on the lower left of Fig. 1 represent sub-stages of the decision process, which not only vary considerably in the real-world of surface mining and reclamation, but may soon be undergoing a period of drastic change given the trend towards public participation in reclamation matters, presumably at this stage of the planning process. But for the present, this set of boxes is intended to suggest the complexities of the decision-making process within the operating companies and government regulatory agencies and between these two groups. Representing this crucial phase of the planning cycle is a second diamond-shaped box, or decision node, at which a design is either accepted or is returned via one of the feedback loops to an earlier, middle phase of the planning-and-decision process, or rejected outright in favor of a virtual fresh start (note the feedback arrow leading all the way to the top of the flow diagram).

Later Stages of the Reclamation Process

Later stages of the total extraction/reclamation cycle are depicted in Fig. 1 to stress the continuity of information flow through and beyond the planning phase using computer processing and products at every step. In particular, computer graphics in various forms, and other computer-based information generated during the planning-and-decision process, are made available to the on-site work force as contour maps, sections, diagrams perspective renderings, 3-D relief models, and other visually-oriented materials.

CONCLUDING COMMENTS

This planning model, by virtue of its very abstractness and generality, has the limitations inherent in any model which is extremely complex, variegated, and undergoing rapid change and development. Nevertheless, we submit that the underlying concept is both sound and useful when it is applied to stress the connection between aesthetics and the other requirements of reclamation, the need to involve professional planners and designers in the planning, the aesthetics of reclamation, and the enormous potential of computer graphics and other computer capabilities for improving the aesthetic quality of reclamation and the efficiency of the planning-and-decision process.

REFERENCES

Cole, N.F. 1976. Visual Design Resources for Surface-Mine Reclamation. Institute for Man and Envrionment, Univ. Massachusetts, Amherst.

Coates, W.E. 1973. Landscape architectural approach to surface mining reclamation. pp. 26-42, In Research and Applied Technology Symp., National Coal Association Washington, D C.

Mallary, R. and C.A. Carlozzi. 1976. The Aesthetics of Surface-Mine Reclamation: An On-site Survey in Appalachia 1975-76. Amherst, Mass: ARSTECNICA: Center for Art and Technology and Institute for Man and Environment, Univ. Massachusetts, Amherst.

Mallary, R. and M. Ferraro. 1977. ECOSITE: A Program for Computer - Aided Landform Design. A Proceedings ACM/S166RAPH, N Y.

SEAM. 1977. MOSAIC/PHOTOMONTAGE: A System for Displaying a Proposed Modification Before its Impact on the Environment. SEAM: U.S. Forest Serv., Intermountain Forest and Range Expt. Sta., Ogden, UT.

SURFACE COAL MINE RECLAMATION AND MUNICIPAL SOLID WASTE DISPOSAL: A SYMBIOTIC RELATIONSHIP

*W. David Carrier, III**

INTRODUCTION

It is well known that U.S. energy policy now emphasizes an increasing reliance on coal. The reasons for this new policy are also well known: the price of foreign oil and gas has increased enormously, thereby affecting the U.S. balance of payments; imports of oil and gas have continued to rise despite conservation efforts; nuclear power has lost popularity; and, most important of all, coal is very abundant in the U.S.

Much of the increased coal production will come from the western coalfields, primarily from strip mines. Western coal is in demand by the utilities because of its low sulfur content. Due to air quality requirements, it has become economical to transport western coal long distances for consumption in high population centers. Most of the coal is transported by train, although slurry pipelines have been proposed and may be competitive under certain circumstances.

In an effort to reduce the environmental impact of the increased strip mining activities, as well as to clean up some old problem areas, the U.S. Government recently passed the Surface Mining Control and Reclamation Act of 1977 (P.L. 95-87, 1977). This act, together with other related federal, state, and local laws, imposes strict regulations on the reclamation of strip mines. Most mine planners are finding that, in order to meet these new reclamation standards, it is cheaper to restore the land on a continuous basis, as an integral part of mining, rather than as a separate operation. As a result, haulback systems are being designed in which the strip mine is continuously filled in behind as the mine advances. A fleet of haulers simply moves the overburden from the highwall to the back of the hole. A covering of stockpiled topsoil is then added, and the surface revegetated. The mine proper consists of a hole of very limited extent, which progresses in a pattern around the property. This type of system, as will be discussed here, lends itself very well to landfill disposal of solid municipal waste.

While all of these things have been happening in the coal industry, municipalities across the nation have been faced with the ever-growing problem of proper disposal of solid waste. The municipalities have also been confronted with a plethora of laws and regulations, the latest being the Resource Conversation and Recovery Act of 1976 (P.L. 94-580, 1976). Municipalities are finding that their options for disposal are becoming more and more constrained: incineration of trash is no longer economical because of air quality

*Woodward-Clyde Consultants, Three Embarcadero Center, Suite 700, San Francisco, CA 94111.

standards, open dumps will no longer be permitted, and refuse derived fuel has not been shown to be practical for general application. The main emphasis now is on recovery of as much recyclable material as possible, such as aluminum cans, and disposal of the remainder in a sanitary landfill. Even so, finding an acceptable landfill site is becoming more and more difficult.

As the in-town sites are filled up or closed, new sites have to be found which are farther out of town. These new sites are more expensive because of the increased haul distance, inflation in real estate, and increased cost for construction and operation of the fill in accordance with present standards.

One solution to the problem of finding an appropriate sanitary landfill site is to put the solid municipal waste into an active coal strip mine. The waste would be transported in the otherwise empty railroad cars of a unit train on its return leg to the strip mine. There, the waste would be incorporated into the reclamation operations as a sanitary landfill. In addition, the methane generated in the landfill would be tapped as a source of energy. This concept not only solves the municipality's dilemma of finding a disposal site at less cost, it also provides more revenue for the utility, the railroad, and the strip mine owner.

In the following sections, the key elements of such a system are discussed in more detail. These are (1) Processing and Recovery Center, (2) Unit Train, (3) Unloading Facility, (4) Strip Mine, (5) Methane Recovery. The overall System Economics is also discussed.

For illustrative purposes, a hypothetical model has been established. The assumptions made in this model regarding population of the municipality, distance from strip mine to power plant, etc., are summarized (Table 1).

Although it is beyond the scope of the present paper, it should be noted that there would be enormous legal and political problems associated with this system. In fact, the institutional barriers would probably outweigh the technical and economic factors. The mine, railroad, utility, and municipality would all have to be brought together in a mutually agreeable arrangement, in addition to local, state, and federal regulatory agencies that would have to be satisfied.

TABLE 1   Assumptions Used in Hypothetical Model

Population of Municipalilty	3 million people
Total Solid Municipal Waste	2.19 million tons/year
Resource Recovery	20 percent
Net Solid Municipal Waste to be Disposed	1.75 million tons/year
Coal Consumed by Power Plant	5.8 million tons/year
Distance from Strip Mine to Power Plant	1000 miles
Distance from Power Plant to Recovery Center	50 miles

PROCESSING AND RECOVERY CENTER

As indicated in Table 1, the processing and recovery center is assumed to serve a metropolitan population of three million people. Typically, this number of people would generate approximately 2.2 million tons of trash per year, or about 6,000 tons per day (Skilling 1977, EPRI 1977). The size of the center necessary to handle this much waste is considerably greater than any similar facility presently in operation, and is estimated to cost at least $100 million.

A processing and recovery center typically utilizes a complex system of hammermills, shredders, trommels, classifiers, air-knives, magnetic and eddy current separators, etc., to reduce the average particle size of the trash and to remove valuable by-products. In the hypothetical model, the roughly $100 million capital cost of the processing and recovery center, plus operating costs, are not considered marginal costs to the system. This is because portions, if not all, of the processing function are already being performed in large municipalities, and the recovery function should at least pay for itself.

In the model, it has been assumed that the recovery function will remove approximately 20% of the waste by weight. The remaining 80% of the waste will consist primarily of organic material, which, because it has been shredded, will have a bulk density of 2 to 9 pounds pcf (NCRR 1977). To facilitate handling, storage, and transportation, it will be necessary to densify this waste. It is conservatively estimated that to produce softball-sized particles with a bulk density of approximately 15 pcf will cost $0.50 per ton.

In addition, there will be extra costs associated with the bulk handling system for loading the railroad cars. In some respects, this system would resemble the coal loading system at the strip mine: car-positioner, hoppers, chutes, etc. It is estimated that the solid waste loading system would add roughly $2 million to the cost of the processing and recovery center.

UNIT TRAIN

A typical unit train consists of approximately 100 railroad cars. Each car has a capacity of 4,000 cu. ft., either 100 tons of coal at 50 pcf, or 30 tons of trash at 15 pcf. In the hypothetical model, it has been presumed that the power plant is located 1,000 miles from the strip mine and that it takes five days for a unit train to make a roundtrip. A two-unit power plant, at 800 MW per unit, would consume approximately 5.8 million tons of coal per year. The total number of unit trains, N, required to supply this power plant is given by

$$N = \frac{Qt}{365 \, qc}$$

where
Q = coal consumption (tons/year)
t = round trip time (days)
q = capacity of each car (tons)
c = number of cars per train

In this example, N = 8 unit trains.

Usually, the coal cars are owned by the utility and the locomotives are owned and operated by the railroad. This is because the railroad is legally prevented from entering into long-term contracts and therefore the utility assumes the investment risk in the railroad cars. Under this arrangement, the typical rate for transport of coal is approximately 1 cent per ton per mile, or in this example, $10 per ton. No typical rate exists for the transport of trash in the empty cars on the return leg to the mine, and this would obviously have to be negotiated with the railroad. However, an estimate can be made of the marginal costs, as follows.

In the hypothetical model it has been assumed that the power plant and recovery center are 50 miles apart. After delivering the coal to the power plant, each unit train would then be required to make a side trip totaling 100 miles to pick up the municipal waste before returning to the strip mine. This side trip will increase the total round trip time by approximately 10 hours, including four hours for loading the waste.

To maintain the delivery rate of coal to the power plant and trash to the mine, it would be necessary to increase the number of cars on each unit train. By rearranging Eqn. (1) above, it can be shown that eight more cars per train are required, or a total of 64 more cars. At $30,000 per car, this results in an additional capital investment of $1.9 million.

The additional operating expenses include labor for the side trip to the recovery center, extra maintenance for the locomotive and caboose, extra maintenance for the sideline and mainline tracks, extra fuel for the side trip, and extra fuel for the increased load back to the mine. There are many uncertainties in this calculation, but based on figures reported by Egge (1976), these additional operating expenses are estimated to total approximately $1.22 per ton of waste.

UNLOADING FACILITY

The unit train, carrying solid municipal waste, would terminate at the coal-loading facility near the strip mine. As the railroad cars are emptied of waste, almost simultaneously they would be refilled with coal for the return trip. Thus, only one car-positioner would be used for both operations and virtually no turnaround time would be lost. The waste unloading system would be compatible with the coal unloading system at the power plant: either bottom dump or rotating cars could be used, as necessary. The waste would fall into a reclaim pit and would then be raised by conveyor into a large bin for temporary storage. The same haulers that carry coal to the unit train would collect waste from the bin for return to the strip mine. It is estimated that the solid waste unloading system would involve an additional capital investment of roughly $2 million.

STRIP MINE

The strip mine is presumed to be located in one of the western states. Although not critical to the system, the arid climate and gently rolling topography in this area of the country makes the design simpler.

The strip mine is assumed to utilize a haulback system for simultaneous excavation and fill. A fleet of haulers, operating in a continuous cycle, would move the overburden from the highwall to the back of the hole. Another fleet of haulers would transport the coal from the mine to the loading facility at the railroad.

After unloading the coal at the railroad, each hauler would pause at a waste bin and receive a load of municipal waste. On the return trip to the mine, the hauler would divert to the back of the hole to unload the waste in the fill area, then continue on to the highwall to complete its cycle. In the fill area, the waste would be graded and covered with soil automatically as part of the haulback operation. This procedure would meet the requirements for a sanitary landfill.

As an extra benefit, the bulk provided by the waste permits a greater range of options for reclamation of the strip mine. In this model, the volume of waste put into the hole would be approximately equal to the volume of coal removed. Thus, the waste makes it possible to restore the surface of the land considerably closer to original elevation.

The transport of waste to the strip mine and its incorporation into the fill would be an extremely simple operation, less complicated than building, say, a zoned earth dam. Because of the scale of the operation, and its long-term nature, it would also be very efficient. It is estimated that the marginal cost would be less than $0.25 per ton of waste.

METHANE RECOVERY

It is well known that as organic matter, such as municipal waste, decomposes under oxygen-depleted (anaerobic) conditions, methane gas is generated. Methane poses a hazard to buildings constructed on or near landfills. Unless properly vented, the gas can accumulate beneath a building and explode causing death and destruction. Considerable research and engineering has been devoted to this problem and construction procedures have been developed to safely collect and disperse methane.

As the supply of natural gas in the U.S. has dwindled, and the price has increased, landfill gas is now thought of more as a resource rather than as a hazard. At least two landfills are presently being tapped for methane gas, Palos Verdes (Reserve Synthetic Fuels 1977) and Mountain View (Blanchet 1977), both in California. Other methane recovery projects are in various stages of planning.

The economics of methane recovery is dependent upon how and where the gas is to be used. Besides methane, landfill gas contains water vapor, carbon dioxide, hydrogen sulfide, oxygen, and nitrogen. Depending on desired heating value and purity, some or all of these gases must be removed. This treatment process is expensive. In addition, the quantity of gas produced is not large compared to a natural gas field. Thus, it is not economical to construct a pipeline of any significant length. The gas must either be consumed locally, or transported in an existing pipeline. Both of the projects mentioned above inject the treated gas directly into nearby natural gas pipelines.

The solid waste in the hypothetical model would yield nearly 4 trillion btu per year, or more than 20 times the quantity presently being produced at Mountain View. Obviously, there would be economies of scale which would lower the cost of treatment. Methane recovery at the strip mine would be at least a $9 million per year operation, which is significant in its own right. Needless to say, methane recovery would not be attempted unless it could pay for itself.

SYSTEM ECONOMICS

With the background of key elements of the proposed solid waste system as discussed above, the various component costs can now be combined to produce a marginal cost for the entire system. The marginal capital cost has been calculated to be $0.40 per ton of waste, based on a 20-year design life and an interest rate of 10%. Note that this does not include the roughly $100 million for the processing and recovery center. This is not considered a marginal cost for the reasons discussed earlier. Similarly, the capital cost for methane recovery is also excluded. The marginal operating cost is calculated to be $1.97 per ton. The total marginal cost is calculated as the sum of the marginal capital cost plus the marginal operating cost. This amounts to $2.37 per ton.

Having calculated the total marginal cost for the hypothetical model that has been used throughout this paper, it is a straightforward exercise to generalize the results. This is

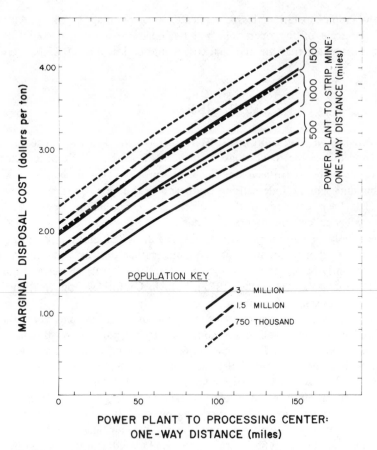

Fig. 1   Marginal disposal cost of unit train/strip mine system

shown in Fig. 1, which demonstrates the effect of varying the following parameters:

> population of municipality: 750 thousand to 3 million
> distance from power plant to strip mine: 500 to 1,500 miles
> distance from power plant to processing center; 0 to 150 miles

Figure 1 is intended to cover a broad spectrum of actual conditions. As would be expected, the marginal cost increases as the population decreases or the distances increase. The minimum disposal cost varies from $1.33 to $2.29 per ton and the maximum from $3.08 to $4.32 per ton.

CONCLUSIONS

A municipal waste disposal system has been described which utilizes a coal unit train for transportation and an active coal strip mine as a sanitary landfill. Ancillary benefits include resource recovery at the front-end of the system and methane recovery at the back-end. In addition, the bulk provided by the waste permits a greater range of options for reclamation of the strip mine.

A hypothetical model has been examined in which the population of the municipality is three million, the distance from the processing and recovery center to the power plant is 50 miles, and the distance from the power plant to the strip mine is 1,000 miles. The total marginal cost for disposal in this hypothetical model was calculated to be $2.37 per ton.

This system is not a panacea; it will not solve the solid waste disposal problem for all cities. However, for many cities, it appears to be a very attractive alternative which should be seriously considered.

REFERENCES

Blanchet, M.J. et al. 1977. Treatment and Utilization of Landfill Gas, Mountain View Project Feasibility Study. M.J. Blanchet et al., Pacific Gas and Electric Co., for the U.S. Environmental Protection Agency, Report SW-583, 1977.

EPRI. 1977. Municipal Solid Waste - Problem or Opportunity? pp. 6-13, In Electric Power Research Institute Journal, November, 1977.

Egge, K.A. 1976. Rail Transportation to the Pacific: An Economic Overview of Costs, Karl A. Egge, Consultant, Professional Lease Management, Inc., presented at a seminar on Coal's Future on the Pacific Coast, San Francisco, April 21-23, 1976.

NCRR. 1977. New Orleans Resource Recovery Facility - Implementation Study Equipment, Economics, Environment, National Center for Resource Recovery, Inc., September 1977.

P.L. 95-87. 1977. Surface Mining Control and Reclamation Act of 1977, Public Law 95-87, August 3, 1977.

P.L. 94-580. 1976. Resource Conservation and Recovery Act of 1976, Public Law 95-580, October 21, 1976.

RSF. 1977. Sanitary Landfill Methane Recovery Program. Reserve Synthetic Fuels, Inc., (company brochure), January 1977.

Skilling, K. 1977. Solid Wastes Program and the Resource Conservation and Recovery Act of 1976, The Bureau of National Affairs, Inc., Environment *Reporter*, Monograph No. 6, October 7, 1977.

PLANNING FOR REGRADING AND
RECLAMATION OF STRIP MINE SPOILS

*William O. Rasmussen, John L. Thames and Peter F. Ffolliott**

A method has been developed which shows promise in planning the recontouring of strip mine spoils. This reclamation planning method assists in the design of a post-mine landscape which is in dynamic equilibrium with the local environment and compatible with the surrounding area and potential land uses (Rasmussen et al. 1978). Elevation, slope, aspect, surface drainage network, solar radiation loading, plant requirements, aesthetics, potential erosion, and water yield are used in the analysis of possible land configurations. The method attempts to achieve a favorable balance of these factors with a minimal amount of earth movement and/or cost to the mining company. Spatial maps of topics such as topographic elevation, slope, aspect and erosion potential, as well as contour plots of any of the original, intermediate, and final surfaces are produced by associated computer programs. Cut and fill volumes are computed and displayed using graphic techniques. Three-dimensional perspective views of the surface of the spoils are produced which show the original and modified forms. The technique is being tested on several coal mines located in the southwestern United States.

STRIP MINING ACTIVITIES

Several activities accompany the extraction of coal from a strip mine operation. First, the resources of the area are analyzed to determine suitability of the site for mining. If the area is considered suitable, an extraction process is designed, followed by the coal removal operation and casting of waste. The resultant spoil banks must be recontoured and reclaimed in the third and final phase of the total operation. This paper addresses several components of each phase of the total operation.

An attempt is made to show how feedback of elevation information from the final surface configuration may be used in the design of the coal extraction procedure relating particularly to spoil bank shapes and locations. Once the final surface configuration is determined, the intermediate piling of material in the spoil banks may be conducted in a manner which may save money and resources in the overall operation.

GRAPHIC PRESENTATION OF THE RESOURCE SITUATION

In the current study, the potential mine area was gridded and drilled for a delineation

*School of Renewable Natural Resources, University of Arizona, Tucson, AZ 85721.

of the coal body. From the drill hole data showing the depths of intersection with the several coal seams and their thicknesses, maps were produced showing spatial variations in these thicknesses. The variations in thickness of the overburden and interburden were also represented using a graphic form of data presentation. Knowledge of the spatial variations in the overburden, interburden and coal seams thickness is useful in the design of the coal recovery operation.

To facilitate manipulation of the spatial data topics, the area is divided into an array of rectangular cells. Each cell represents a specific location on the mine area. This would provide a result similar to drawing a uniform grid on a topographic map of the area. Once the area of a cell has been selected, all data topics are produced with cells of equal size. Generally the value of a data topic associated with a given cell is the average or predominate value of that parameter within the cell.

Several computer programs have been developed for displaying and manipulating the spatial data arrays. The display format is similar to that used by SYMAP (Dougenik and Sheehan 1975) which was used in the interpolation of the data to form the filled spatial data arrays. The name of the local program used for display is SLMATH. This program produces printer maps of the spatial data arrays. The technique used for the data presentation is to assign symbols to each of the intervals into which the range of the resource variable has been divided. The darkness of the symbol or the greyness that a collection of the symbols appears to have is the characteristic used to show variations in the data. Those data intervals with the lowest numeric values are represented by a symbol which has a very light grey shade. The data with highest values are represented by very dark symbols.

The volume of material of a given thickness at any cell location is computed as the product of that thickness by the area of one cell. Spatial interpolation from the drill hole locations to all other locations or cells in the mine area allows for approximate computations of the volume of material in each stratum and its spatial variation.

3-D PERSPECTIVE PLOTS, CONTOUR PLOTS
AND CROSS SECTIONS OF THE RESOURCE

In addition to printer maps representing thickness of the various layers, other graphic techniques may be used to represent numeric data fields for greater comprehension of resources and waste. Three-dimensional perspective plots (Rens 1971) of any of the layers may be produced where the elevation of the surface is indicative of the layer thickness or numeric value of some other type of parameter. This is analogous to the darkness or greyness of the symbols used to represent numeric values on the printer map. Another technique for data presentation often used to depict elevation and thickness data is that of contour plots. In the case of the thickness data, the contour lines represent lines of equal thickness.

Cross sections of the data arrays may be presented using printer symbol graphs or line drawings from a computer plotter. With respect to the plotter, the cross-sectional thickness of several layers may be plotted on the same figure or they may be plotted individually.

SPOILS SURFACE CONFIGURATION

The surface elevation of the spoils may be calculated from: the width of each cut; the elevation of the original surface; the spatial variations in thickness of the coal; the spoil swell factor; the waste casting pattern; and the angle of repose of waste material.

The surface configuration of the spoil bank is usually not a simple transformation of the original surface; it is often the result of continual variations in several parameters, such as overburden thickness, throughout the operation of the mine. Therefore spoil banks vary in width and height. In the event a mine involves a multiple seam situation, the probability of variations in the surface of the spoils is increased.

The surface configuration of the spoils may be computed through the routine development of the mine simulated with the use of computer software (Gibson and Lehman 1977). The characteristics of the spoils surface may be determined from a questioning of the mine engineer regarding the characteristics of the equipment to be used, the nature of the coal setting, and the production schedule.

DEVELOPMENT OF ELEVATION AND OTHER DATA ARRAYS

Two elevation maps of the mine area are used for input to the computer: a map of the original elevation of the land before the coal extraction operation was begun; and a map of the existing spoils surface after the material has been deposited from the dragline and, in some instances, lightly bladed. The original surface topography of the mine area is represented on contour maps. The elevation map of the study area is placed on a point line digitizer and converted into a set of data triplets representing the elevations and map coordinates of points at various locations on the map. These data triplets are used by the computer program, SYMAP (Dougenik and Sheehan 1975), to calculate interpolated values for all locations in a uniform spatial data array representing the study area. Each cell in the data array represents a specific location on the area. The assemblage of all cells comprises the entire study area. The final product of the interpolation process is a spatial data array composed of average elevation values for each cell location on the study area.

A similar operation is performed on the spoils surface elevation data to generate a data array representing the average spoils elevation at each cell location on the area.

Using either of the elevation data arrays, slope and aspect for each cell location is computed. These values approximate those which would be measured in the field. The slope value is calculated for each cell location by mathematically positioning a plane over a given cell so that the sum of the squares of the deviations between the elevations of the plane and the elevations of the four nearest surrounding cells is minimal. Slope and aspect values of the plane are assigned to the central cell. The procedure is repeated for each cell of the elevation data array. The resultant data arrays of slope and aspect for each of the two elevation data arrays are stored in the computer for use later in the analysis.

DATA BASE

Elevation, slope, aspect and other information relevant to the area are loaded into a data base. The data base may be thought of as a three-dimensional cube of data cells. Each horizontal plane is the spatial data for a given topic of information, such as the original elevation. The two previously mentioned elevation data arrays and the four generated data arrays for slope and aspect represent six topics of information and, thus, occupy six layers in the data base. Data are actually stored with each cell location being a record in the computer. Values for all data topics associated with the given location are on each record. This scheme of storing data allows for rapid updating and editing of the data.

FINAL SURFACE CONFIGURATION

The general nature of the resultant recontoured surface of the land is arrived at after several considerations. First, the final surface must tie into the existing surrounding undisturbed surface so that regional hydrologic drainages are not affected by the modification of the surface over the mine area. Secondly, the elevation of the land must also tie into the surrounding terrain. Both of these requirements place boundary conditions at the edges of the mine area on the recontoured surface.

Variations of the surface at interior points within the mine boundary may be done to achieve effects needed or desired for the reclaimed land which may not be general for the surrounding country. The surface may be modified in order to have a predominant exposure which is largely southern, northern or some direction in between. Exposure of the land is an indication of the amount of solar radiation loading which the land will receive. If the land is to be revegetated, the species of vegetation may be better suited for an environment having a particular radiation loading. Therefore, the surface exposure may be modified to accommodate this vegetation type or types.

A final surface configuration may be sketched to show the locations of ridges and channels along with boundary conditions which must be met. The computer system will handle adjustments in the spoils elevations to relax to a surface with these characteristics as nearly as possible. Elevations will be modified slightly to make adjustments for the actual volume of material.

Another means of obtaining a final configuration for the recontoured surface is to fit it into the existing topography by trend surface techniques. The original topographic surface is known at the perimeter of the mine and its surrounding area. From this information, a surface can be developed which will fit into the general trend of the area; that is, the rolling nature of the land will be continued over the mine site. The trend surface solution to the surface over the mine will closely approximate the surface as it existed prior to mining operations. Based on the trend surface solution of the final surface, elevations of ridges and other features may be adjusted to account for the material extracted and the expansion of the material due to blasting and manipulation. The trend surface gives, as in the case of the sketched surface, a final surface configuration to be used as a goal. The computer program may then distribute the known volume of material to fit this surface as closely as the operator of the computer system desires.

EROSION POTENTIAL

The selected recontoured surface of the mine spoils needs to be rated for its potential sediment production. This rating allows various surface configurations to be assessed relative to each other for potential erosion problems. A computer program, SOIL, has been developed to predict the potential soil loss for each cell on the study area. This program computes not only the total amount of material which may be lost by the entire area but also the amount lost from each cell. Those cell locations which have high values for potential soil loss are locations where intervention may be needed to help minimize the erosion problem. Special types of vegetation, water conveyances or reduction of the slopes will result in a lowering of the erosion potential for cells in specific locations. The erosion potential for the area is computed using a modified version of the Universal Soil Loss Equation.

Surface elevation adjustments are used to handle modifications of slope and aspect values at specific locations on the mine area. In the event that slopes in some part of the mine area are too high, the relative elevation differences are changed to reduce the slopes between the cells in the area. To maintain a balance of mass for the area where the slopes are being modified, the elevations of all cells are considered relative to some reference plane, and either raised or lowered to take into account any mass difference resulting from an adjustment in the magnitude of the slopes in the area.

For planning purposes, the runoff efficiency of the mine area is assumed fixed. Variations in the surface elevations and drainage networks do not consider a variable runoff efficiency. In reality this is not what may be expected; however, it is the condition used for the current level of analysis.

CUT AND FILL

From knowledge of the final recontoured surface elevation data array and the existing spoils elevation data array, the amount of material either cut or filled at each cell location is computed by subtracting one from the other, cell by cell. This difference data array shows the volume of material which needs to be moved to or from each cell. This data array is divided into two new arrays; one is the cut material and the other the fill material. Volumes of the material to be cut or filled are known at each cell location as the product of the area of a cell multiplied by the elevation change.

By examining the cut and fill volume maps, ways in which to move the material can be determined in order to keep the hauling distance minimal. One procedure to compute an approximation to the haulage distances involves the computation of centers of mass for individual cut and fill volumes. Volumes of cut or fill material are then assumed to be located at the center of mass of the material. From a knowledge of the distances between centers of mass and the volumes of cut or fill, values are computed for the haulage distance. These values do not take into account the road network and general operation of the cut-fill activity. As a result they are lower than might be expected to occur.

FEEDBACK

Knowing the final recontoured surface configuration, the design of the mine operation may be adjusted to locate the spoil banks in a manner which will assist in the minimization of the haulage or movement distance of the material in the recontouring phase. Such feedback of information from the planned final phase of the operation to the intermediate phase has the potential for saving money and resources. Conceivably, the locations of the spoil banks would require only slight modification to reflect significant changes in the time required to move the resultant waste material to the final surface configuration. The necessary road network for final material movement may also be designed into the location and shape of the mine spoils.

Design of the mine operation should then take into account both the coal resources and their distribution as well as the final recontoured surface configuration. The physical operation of the coal extraction should be conducted in such a manner as to minimize energy costs in the removal of the coal and at the same time to minimize the requirements of energy for the redistribution of material from the spoil banks in the final phase of operation.

SUMMARY

The methodology presented allows for the determination of the quantity and setting of the coal resource. This assists in the analysis of the situation to determine if a strip mine operation would be suitable.

Once the area has been rated suitable for coal extraction by strip mining, several computer tools are available to assist in the selection of the best casting distribution of waste so that both the extraction of coal and recontouring of the spoils require minimum amounts of energy. The final surface configuration of the mine spoils results from considerations of vegetation types to be used in reclamation and their requirements in terms of solar radiation, slope, and other parameters. The final surface configuration may also take into account water harvesting. Impoundments may be designed in the final surface to collect water and hold it. In all cases, the erosion potential of the final surface configuration is ascertained to allow modification to be made if severe conditions are found to occur within a selected topography.

Computer programs allow the operator to sketch the location of ridges and stream channels for the final surface topography. The computer programs then relax elevations from the spoil banks configuration to the sketched configuration, taking into account a balance of mass in the elevation changes of the spoil banks. A final surface configuration may also be produced using trend surface techniques. The computer program also relaxes from the spoils elevation toward this goal maintaining a balance of mass. Other constraints may be imposed on the redistribution of material from the spoil banks to the final recontoured surface.

Feedback of elevation data from the final surface configuration may assist in the design of the coal extraction procedure such that the resulting spoil banks will be located and shaped so as to minimize earth movement in the redistribution of material for the final surface.

Various aspects of the total resource withdrawal and reclamation effort are addreseed by a collection of interrelated computer programs which assist in the selection of an extraction scheme which meets the numerous constraints placed on various components of the overall process. Additional components are being added as their need becomes apparent.

REFERENCES

Dougenik, J.A. and D.E. Sheehan. 1975. SYMAP User's Reference Manual. Laboratory for Computer Graphics and Spatial Analysis, Harvard Univ., Cambridge, MA, 178 p.

Gibson, D.F. and T.E. Lehman. 1977. Productivity improvement of surface coal mining operations. pp. 19-26, In Proc. AIIE 1977 Spring Annual Conf., Dallas, TX.

Rasmussen, W.O., P.F. Ffolliott, T.R. Verma and J.L. Thames. 1978. Environmental analysis for land use planning in an arid zone. In Proc. of the Intl. Symp. on Arid Zone Research and Develop., Jodhpur, India (in press).

Rens, F.J. 1971. SYMVU Manual. Laboratory for Computer Graphics and Spatial Analysis, Harvard Univ., Cambridge, MA, 60 p.

THE NEED FOR COMPREHENSIVE
AQUATIC IMPACT ANALYSES: THE NORTH CENTRAL
UNITED STATES--MISSISSIPPI RIVER TRACE METAL CASE STUDY

David P. Bernard*

INTRODUCTION

Just as there exists no widely accepted method for projecting energy supply and demand for periods of 10 to 25 years (Basile 1977), there is no standard approach for analyzing long-term alternative national energy futures. During the past five years or so, the federal Energy Research and Development Administration (ERDA), now the DOE, has increasingly relied upon a "regional studies" approach for evaluating various strategies for fulfilling future national energy demands. Currently this approach is being used at each of six national laboratories to identify and evaluate possible future energy options. The regional studies approach involves disaggregating the country into several multistate regions, each with its own unique patterns of energy supply and demand, land and resource availability, environmental factors, and so forth. Each of the national laboratories is charged with conducting an independent study of one such region according to the terms of reference for the specific project. Although this particular method of carrying out a national assessment may be suitable for some disciplines, in conducting a thorough evaluation of all the ecological impacts which could result from relatively large projects--such as shifting the nation to a coal-based energy system--attention needs to be given to potential ecological effects of transfrontier pollution, a problem which may be not only of national interest but of international concern as well (see OECD 1974).

Since both air and water flow freely through most parts of the country, pollutants released within a specified study area are not likely to remain within the boundaries of that region. In addition, since freshwater ecosystems commonly span large geographic areas, activities that take place within a specific portion of the watershed may affect not only nearby aquatic communities, but distant ones as well. For these reasons the environmental effects of proposed activities should be investigated no less thoroughly for downstream and leeward ecosystems beyond the study area than they are for ecosystems inside the circumscribed boundaries.

The National Coal Utilization Assessment (NCUA) is an example of a nation-wide study that uses the regional studies approach. In this investigation, initiated in 1977 by ERDA, Argonne National Laboratory (ANL) was chosen to identify possible environmental, health, and socioeconomic impacts which could result from increased coal mining and use in the North Central region (Fig. 1) during the next half century. The siting pattern

*Division of Environmental Impact Studies, Argonne National Laboratory, 9700 South Cass Avenue, Argonne, IL 60439.

developed by ANL (1977) for electrical power plants and synfuel facilities is shown in Fig. 1 along with the predicted air-quality impact areas.

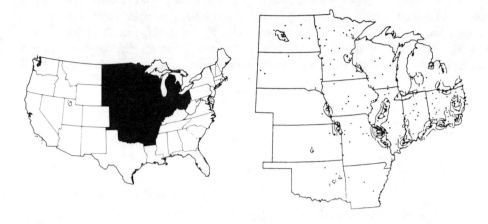

Fig. 1.   North Central study region and predicted A.D. 2020 pattern for electrical power plants (points) and resulting air quality impact areas (isopleths). (From ANL, 1977).

As part of the ANL assessment, an investigation was undertaken to analyze potential impacts which could occur to aquatic ecosystems as a result of trace metals released through increased coal use for electrical generation in the 14-state study region. An attempt was made to identify potential impacts to aquatic ecosystems both internal and external to the study region. The results are presented here to demonstrate that pollutants generated by activities within a prescribed study region do not always remain within that region, and to illustrate the initial steps of an aquatic impact analysis in which systems inside and outside the assigned study region were considered as part of a regional studies project.

RELEASE OF TRACE METALS USED TO GENERATE ELECTRICITY

Although trace metals in coal are usually each present at low concentrations (<50 ppm), enormous quantities of coal contain as an aggregate substantial metal masses. It has been estimated that by the year A.D. 2020, 800 million tons of coal could be required annually in the North Central states to generate 50% of the required electrical energy, assuming that coal is increasingly chosen as a substitute for nuclear fuel for electrical generation facilities (ANL 1977). Use of this much coal will liberate significant quantities of trace metals, thereby creating a potential ecosystem contamination problem.

Although the term "heavy metal" appears commonly in both popular writings and scientific literature, it is difficult to find a precise definition. The term trace metal is used here in place of "heavy metal" and is defined as a metal normally found in aquatic systems at less than 1.0 mg/1 (after Hem 1970). The eight metals chosen for study are: cadmium (Cd), chromium (Cr), copper (Cu), lead (Pb), manganese (Mn), mercury (Hg), nickel (Ni), and zinc (Zn). The selection was made based upon the concentrations of these metals in coal, their rates of release from coal power plants, their toxicities to aquatic organisms, their potentials for aquatic bioaccumulation, and their residence times in natural waters.

MASS–BALANCE FOR SELECTED TRACE METALS

Trace metals can enter aquatic systems from coal-fired power plants via three main routes: (1) leaching from terrestrial ash and boiler sludge waste-disposal sites and coal storage piles, (2) atmospheric fallout as wet (rainfall) and dry (particulate) deposition of materials discharged from the power plant stacks, and (3) direct discharge into fresh or marine waters of effluents from waste water treatment facilities at the plants (Fig. 2). To

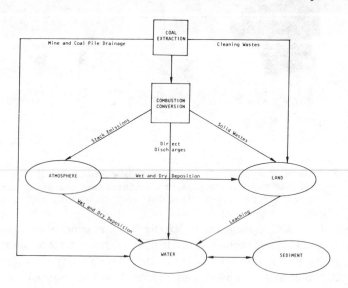

Fig. 2. Movement of trace metals into fresh and marine
waters from two stages of the coal-fired cycle.

investigate the relative importance of each of these pathways in dispensing metals to streams, lakes, and ponds, loadings were caluclated for wet and dry atmospheric deposition as well as for leaching from solid waste disposal sites. Data concerning the contribution of metals from direct discharges from coal combustion/conversion facilities were obtained from the Water Quality Modeling Group of the Energy and Environmental Systems Division at ANL. Although leaching from disposal basins containing coal-cleaning solid wastes probably contributes a significant quantity of metals to groundwaters and, hence, possibly to fresh-water environments, the contribution from this source is not considered here, for this study is concerned only with the release of metals from coal used for electrical generation purposes.

The amount of each metal in the incoming coal and its predicted release from combustion/ conversion facilities are presented in Table 1. These annual values reflect a projected A.D. 2020 use of coal of 800×10^6 tons of coal having an assumed elemental composition equal to the mean values of 101 U.S. coals given by Ruch et al. (1974). These values are in reasonable agreement (except for Zn, which is higher in U.S. estimates) with world mean coal concentrations (Bertine and Goldberg 1971). Partition factors describe the segregation of individual metals released during coal burning into various effluent channels draining the combustion by-products from the reaction chamber. They are taken from Klein et al. (1975) and represent traditional coal combustion techniques. Recent studies (USEPA 1977, Vogel et al. 1975) suggest that fluidized bed combustion (FBC) offers a significant potential for reducing atmospheric trace-metal emissions when compared with conventional

TABLE 1   Mass Balance of Selected Trace Metals for Proposed A.D. 2020 Use of Coal
in the North Central United States for Electrical Generation

| Metal | Mean Concentration of Selected Trace Metals in United States Coal[a] (ppm) | Partition Factors[b] | | Annual Flows (10^3kg/yr) | | | |
		Slag Mean Ash	Outlet Ash Inlet Ash	Coal[c]	Slag[d]	Collected Fly Ash[e]	Atmospheric Discharge[f]
Cd	2.5	0.25	6.4	1800	130	1620	50
Cr	13.8	0.91	3.0	10000	2550	7350	100
Cu	15.2	0.26	1.4[g]	11000	800	10150	50
Pb	34.8	0.14	8.1	25200	990	23230	920
Mn	49.4	0.94	1.44	35800	9420	26200	180
Hg	0.2	0.025	-	145	1	3	141[h]
Ni	21.1	0.57	-	15300	2440	-	-
Zn	272.3	0.14	4.0	197600	7740	186290	3570

[a]From Ruch *et al.* (1974).

[b]From Klein *et al.* (1975). Ratio of concentration of element (×) in slag to its concentration in an undifferentiated ash; ratio of concentration of element (×) in fly ash at the electrostatic precipitator outlet to (×) in the fly ash entering the precipitator.

[c]Calculated using average U. S. coal elemental concentrations (Column 2), multiplied by a total coal consumption of 800×10^6 tons.

[d]Assumes that 28% of the total ash leaving the boiler leaves as slag and 72% exists as fly ash; the element flow in slag is (flow in coal) × (0.28) × (partition factor, slag/mean ash).

[e]Calcualted by subtracking the combined flows of metal (×) in slag and atmospheric discharge from the flow in coal.

[f]Assumes electrostatic precipitators working at 99.53% efficiency (data of Klein *et al.* 1975); this yields ratio of outlet fly ash to inlet fly ash of 0.0047; atmospheric discharge is (flow to precipitator) × (0.0047) × (partition factor, outlet ash/inlet ash).

[g]Calculated from data in Kaakinen *et al.* (1975).

[h]Assumed that 97% of the mercury entering with the coal exists in gaseous form (Anderson and Smith, 1977).

combustion, but because detailed metal partition factors are not yet available for FBC, coal gasification, or coal liquefaction processes, the release of trace metals from these facilities cannot be accurately estimated.

As seen in Table 1, most metals entering the electrical generation facility with the coal leave as solid waste (slag plus collected fly ash), the major exception being Hg, almost all (<95%) of which is discharged into the atmosphere as a gas (Anderson and Smith 1977). A substantial fraction of the entering trace elements accumulate on the fly ash, and are subsequently removed by pollution control devices such as electrostatic precipitators. The predicted flow of trace metals into the atmosphere ranges from a high of over 3×10^6 kg/yr for Zn to a low of 0.05×10^6 kg/yr for both Cd and Cu. It is predicted that the annual flow of metals in solid wastes will range from a low for Hg of 4000 kg/yr to a high of $\sim$ 194 million kg/yr for Zn. For most metals, the major path from the incoming coal to the waste disposal pit is through the electrostatic precipitator, leaving as collected fly ash.

Annual aquatic loadings for the three main pathways are presented in Table 2. To calculate the atmospheric metal loading, several assumptions (see Table 2) were made resulting in the estimate that approximately 10% of the amount of each metal annually discharged into the atmosphere enters North Central freshwater systems. Consequently, the annual atmospheric contribution of metals is predicted to range from a high of over 300,000 kg of Zn to a low of 5,000 kg for both Cd and Cu.

To calculate the amount of solid waste leaching it was assumed that only 0.5% of the metals entering solid-waste disposal pits each year will leach out through time. This figure reflects a general pollution control efficacy of 99.5% in controlling the leaching of metals from solid-waste disposal pits, and is considered to yield an estimate of the minimum quantity of metals which could be expected to leach from these storage pits through time. This value is considerably lower than the 5% leaching figure used in a recent study in which

TABLE 2   Projected Annual Aquatic Trace Metal Loadings Compared
to Existing Mississippi River Trace Metal Fluxes

| Metal | Aquatic Loadings (10^3kg/yr) | | | | Mississippi River Annual Flux[d] (10^3kg/yr) | Increase in Annual Flux from Increased Coal Use (%) |
	Atmospheric[a] Contribution	Solid Waste[b] Leaching	Direct[c] Discharge	Total		
Cd	5.0	8.8	0.7	14.5	450	3.2
Cr	10.0	49.5	8.9	68.4	20300	0.3
Cu	5.0	54.8	28.0	87.8	13100	0.7
Pb	92.0	121.4	2.8	216.2	13100	1.6
Mn	18.0	178.1	5004.1	5200.2	471700	1.1
Hg	14.1	0.02	3.0	17.1	–	–
Ni	–	–	464.4	–	16900	–
Zn	357.0	970.2	3171.6	4498.8	57700	7.8

[a]Assumes: 1) No net export of atmospherically discharged metals from airshed,
            2) Partition factor for wet deposition/dry deposition = 0.3,
            3) Watershed retains 75% of the wetfall metals and 95% of metal dryfall.

[b]Calculated using following equation:

$$L_x = (S_x + A_x) \times 0.005$$

Where L_x = total amount of metal x leached annually from all refuse basins

S_x = amount of metal x in slag (Table 1)

A_x = amount of metal x in collected fly ash (Table 1)

0.005 = leaching constant (see text).

[c]These data were obtained from the Water Quality Modeling section of the Energy and Environmental Systems Division of Argonne National Laboratory; includes discharges from waste water treatment facilities at both coal mines and coal-fired electrical generation plants and is based upon New Source Performance Standards regulations.

[d]From Turekian *et al.* (1976).

it was reported that "95% removal was chosen to illustrate compliance with even the most rigid proposed standards for each element" (Holland et al. 1975). As seen in Table 2, Zn is predicted to be leached in the greatest quantity from solid waste disposal pits, and Hg the least.

Unfortunately in the direct discharge data, metals contributed by drainage from coal mines are not separated from those released with treated boiler and cooling tower blow-downs and process effluents; in general the data reflect maximum emissions allowed by the New Source Performance Standards for both mining and electrical generation sites. Manganese, Zn, and to a lesser extent Ni, are the metals projected as being released in the greatest quantity through direct discharges into nearby waters (Table 2). In large part, Mn, Zn and Ni are contributed by mining activities, although combustion and conversion activities also release them. Of the metals contributed mainly by coal use, Cu appears to be the one which will be released in the greatest quantity, while Cr, Hg and Pb discharges are all predicted to be higher than those of Cd.

PATTERN OF EXPECTED TRACE METAL IMPACTS TO AQUATIC ECOSYSTEMS

Given these expected amounts of trace metals entering into aquatic systems, the next important question is, how will these metals be distributed, geographically, throughout the study region? Although in the mass balance analysis the entire study area was treated as a homogeneous region, the actual ecological impacts to aquatic biota would be correlated with the particular geographical siting pattern of coal-fired electrical generation activities. Figure 1 shows the predicted 2020 A.D. siting pattern and the areas where air-quality impacts are projected to result. It appears that aquatic impacts will not be evenly distributed throughout the North Central region, but rather concentrated along major rivers, such as the Illinois, Ohio, Missouri, and Mississippi (Fig. 1). Since these watercourses are good transportation corridors and provide adequate supplies of cooling and process waters, their banks are preferred locations where plants are most likely to be sited.

Impacts to aquatic ecosystems resulting from increasing the trace metal concentration in certain sections of running waters will be influenced by the nature of the biological community, annual flow regimes, chemistry of the receiving waters, and existing pollution stresses, in addition to the siting pattern. In areas where industrial activity will be dense, along the Illinois and Ohio Rivers for example, impacts to aquatic ecosystems may be particularly severe. These river systems have already undergone heavy industrialization, which has resulted in a reduced species diversity of organisms and additions of trace metals may begin to affect species that have thus far exhibited tolerance to existing levels of aquatic pollution.

Since soils can act as filters for certain substances accumulating, for example, Pb and Hg, in the upper part of the soil profile (Heinrichs and Mayer 1977), regional differences in soil characteristics may affect the transfer of metals from the atmosphere or solid-waste disposal basins into aquatic systems. This filtration capacity is important to aquatic ecosystems for, in one sense, it "shields" them from increased metal fluxes from atmospheric sources. However, acid precipitation (which is likely to accompany increased coal use) can increase the mobility of many elements in the soil, thereby decreasing the capacity for filtration (Norton 1977). A decrease in filtration capacity can, as a result, be expected to increase the flux of trace metals to the groundwater and aquatic systems. It has been suggested (Norton 1977) that the impacts due to decreased ion removal as a result of acid precipitation may be significant on a time scale of 10 to 100 years, viz. similar to the time period of increased coal usage. We can therefore expect increased leaching of metals into aquatic systems to occur during the projected period of coal use.

As metal fluxes to aquatic systems increase due to leaching, the amount of metals exported downstream may also rise. If one assumes that the entire annual aquatic load of a given metal, as calculated in the preceding mass balance, escapes from the study area and is exported downstream through the Mississippi River to the Gulf of Mexico, it allows a quantitative comparison to be made between the present flux of this metal and the hypothetical amount to be contributed to it from increased coal use. The amount of Cr, Cu, Mn, Pb, Cd and Zn predicted to be contributed from coal mines and electrical generation facilities represents less than 10% of the current fluxes for each of these metals (Table 2). Preliminary values for Hg and Ni were calculated, and these estimates suggest these metals, too, would be released in quantities of less than 10% of existing Mississippi River fluxes.

While the input of trace metals is expected to affect aquatic ecosystems locally in major rivers, it will apparently not cause marked changes in the annual metal flux from the Mississippi River into the Gulf of Mexico. The reader should, however, recall that the data presented are for electrical generation activities only and do not include releases from industrial activities which consume electricity. Further, the assumptions concerning the leaching of metals from solid-waste disposal pits (the largest contributing source) yield minimal estimates, so it is not unlikely that higher fluxes will be observed. Increasing electrical generation will probably also be paralled by increasing industrialization, much of it along the same watercourses. Thus, the two, electrical generation and industrialization, are, from an ecosystem perspective, coupled and the impacts additive or perhaps multiplicative.

SUMMARY AND RECOMMENDATIONS

The regional studies approach now being used to conduct analyses of alternative national energy futures is not wholly adequate for conducting environmental impact assessments for large projects because the effects of pollutants displaced from the assigned study areas are not fully investigated. It is suggested that in projects using a regional studies approach, the responsibility for assessing trans-study-area impacts should be assigned to the team in whose area the pollutants originate, for its members are already familiar with the sources, magnitudes, and types of pollutants which will result from the proposed activities. This recommendation should apply equally well to projects in which transnational pollution problems may develop.

Trace metals are predicted to enter North Central freshwaters from increased coal use for electrical generation during the next half-century via three main pathways, listed in descending order of importance for most metals: solid waste leaching, atmospheric contribution, and direct discharge. In addition to the numerous localized impacts which are expected to affect aquatic ecosystems in the North Central study area from the release of trace metals, it is expected that other, more distant communities outside the study area may be affected as well. However, it appears that metals released from accelerated coal use in the North Central states for electricity generation will not be contributed at a rate which would cause marked changes in the annual flux of metals from the Mississippi River into the Gulf of Mexico.

While a certain proportion of metals introduced into Midwestern waters will become bound in the sediment, this removal must be considered temporary, for metals are continually remobilized through physical, chemical, biological or human activities, and hence the sediments are not a static sink for trace metals deposited in North Central rivers and streams. As time progresses, the flux of metals to aquatic systems from leaching may increase due to acid precipiation and other causes, thereby promoting the export of metals to downstream ecosystems.

REFERENCES

Anderson, W.L. and K.E. Smith. 1977. Dynamics of mercury at coal-fired power plant and adjacent cooling lake. Environ. Sci. Technol. 11:75-80.

Argonne National Laboratory. 1977. An Integrated Assessment of Increased Coal Use in the Midwest: Impacts and Constraints. Vol. 1 and 2. Regional Studies Program. ANL/AA-11 (draft).

Basile, P.S. (ed.). 1977. Energy Supply-Demand Integrations to the Year 2000. MIT Press, Cambridge, MA, 706 p.

Bertine, K.K. and E.D. Goldberg. 1971. Fossil fuel combustion and the major sedimentary cycle. Science 173:233-235.

Heinrichs, H. and R. Mayer. 1977. Distribution and cycling of major and trace elements in two central European forest ecosystems. J. Environ. Qual. 6:406-407.

Hem, J.D. 1970. Study and interpretation of the chemical characteristics of natural water. 2nd ed. Geol. Survey Water-Supply Paper 1473. U.S. Government Printing Off., Washington, DC., 36 p.

Holland, W.F., K.A. Wilde, J.L. Parr, P.S. Lowell and R.F. Pohler. 1975. The Environmental Effects of Trace Elements in the Pond Disposal of Ash and Flue Gas Desulfurization Sludge. Electric Power Research Institute, Palo Alto, 49 p. + Appendices.

Kaakinen, J.W., R.M. Jorden, M.H. Lawasani and R.E. West. 1975. Trace element behavior in coal-fired power plant. Environ. Sci. Technol. 9:862-869.

Klein, D.A., W. Andren and N.W. Bolton. 1975. Trace element discharges from coal combusion for power production. Water, Air, Soil Pollut. 5:71-77.

Lunt, R.R., C.B. Copper, S.L. Johnson, J.E. Oberholtzer, G.R. Schimke and W.I. Watson. 1977. An Evaluation of the Disposal of Flue Gas Desulfurization Wastes in Mines and the Ocean: Initial Assessment. U.S. Environmental Protection Agency, Off. of Research and Develop., EPA-600/7-77-051, 307 p.

Natusch, D.F.S., J.R. Wallace and C.A. Evans. 1974. Toxic trace elements: preferential concentration in respirable particles. Science 183:202.

Norton, S.A. 1977. Changes in chemical processes in soils caused by acid precipitation. Water, Air, Soil Pollut. 7:389-400.

Organization for Economic Cooperation and Development. 1974. Problems in Transfrontier Pollution. OECD, Paris, France, 316 p.

Ruch, R.R., H.J. Gluskoter and N.F. Shimp. 1974. Occurrence and Distribution of potentially volatile trace elements in coal: A final report. Environ. Geol. Notes 72, Ill. State Geol. Survey, Urbana, IL, 96 p.

Trefry, J.H. and B.J. Presley. 1976. Heavy metal transport from the Mississippi River to the Gulf of Mexico. pp. 39-76, In H.L. Windom and R.A. Duce (eds.), Marine Pollutant Transfer, Lexington Books, Lexington, MA.

U.S. Environmental Protection Agency. 1977. The U.S. Environmental Protection Agency's Fluidized-Bed Combustion Program, 1976. Off. of Research and Develop., EPA-600/7-77-012, 55 p.

Vogel, G.J., W.M. Swift, J.C. Montagna, J.F. Lenc and A.A. Jenke. 1975. Application of pressurized, fluidized-bed combustion to reduction of atmospheric pollution. Institute of Fuel Symp. Series No. 1: Fluidized Combustion, Paper D-3, 11 p.

DETERMINATION OF APPROPRIATE SITES
FOR COAL MINING OPERATIONS: THE ROLE
OF ENDANGERED PLANTS AND CRITICAL HABITATS

K. T. Killingbeck and E.J. Crompton *

Landform and vegetation changes associated with strip mining operations have increased dramatically in direct response to the recent realization that the demand for energy is outdistancing the supply. As of 1971, over 1.47 million ha of land in the U.S. had been disturbed by all types of surface mining operations (Paone et al. 1974). Almost 70,000 ha were disturbed in surface coal mining operations in Illinois in the same time period (Haynes and Klimstra 1975) and nationally, more than 30,000 ha yr^{-1} were altered by surface mining of fossil fuels in 1971 alone (Paone et al. 1974). If the mandate for energy self-sufficiency in this country is followed as planned, U.S. coal may be surface mined at a rate of 844 million mT yr^{-1} altering over 64,000 ha of land annually (GAO 1977) by the year 2000. The magnitude of this landscape modification necessitates land management practices designed to insure the integrity of land after mining and to reduce the possibility of permanently eliminating irreplaceable elements of the earth's flora and fauna.

During recent times of rapid, large-scale energy acquisition, an international awareness of the plight of rare and endangered plant species has emerged. It is becoming increasingly evident that all species, no matter how seemingly insignificant, play vital roles in the main-tenance and stability of ecosystems. Although even two decades ago most persons believed that the irreversible loss of a plant species was merely aesthetically displeasing, present day considerations, suggest that such a loss is of pragmatic importance (Simmons et al. 1976, Smith 1976, Woodwell 1977). Extinction of any plant species is both ecologically and economically unacceptable, and an intolerable alternative to judicuous land management.

To successfully preserve plant populations that are threatened with extinction, the ecosystems in which these species are found need to be protected. It is not possible to sustain a plant species in nature without first assuring the protection of its habitat. Ecosystems maintaining populations of threatened or endangered plants have been termed "critical habitats" by the U.S. Fish and Wildlife Service (1975a). It is the future of these habitats that is of utmost concern in relation to mine site determination because as Smith (1976) notes, "destruction of habitat is the most important indirect cause of extinction today."

Legislators charged with the responsibility to develop laws regulating coal mining

*Project SAFARI, University of North Dakota, Grand Forks, ND 58202. Present Address of K. T. Killingbeck: Division of Biology, Ackert Hall, Kansas State University, Manhattan, KS 66506. Present Address of E.J. Crompton: 6700 Cabot Drive, Nashville, TN 37209.

operations and protecting critical habitats must consider the fact that both coal reserves and endangered species are non-renewable resources that are presently essential to man's well-being. The conservation and prudent management of both of these resources should proceed so as to maximize the benefits of both the protection of critical habitats and surface mining of coal deposits are not mutually exclusive processes and should not be considered as such. To do so would certainly jeopardize the existence of one or the other.

The purpose of this paper is to establish a means by which the surface mining of coal deposits can be carried out without the concomitant destruction of endangered plant populations. In this attempt, a discussion of the strong and weak provisions in a portion of the existing legislation at the state and federal levels dealing specifically with surface mining and/or endangered plants will be pursued. Recommendations suggesting ways in which states can manage lands so as to protect threatened or endangered plant species while also utilizing coal resources, will follow.

In 1973, the United States Endangered Species Act became law. The stated purpose of this law is to protect endangered or threatened species of plants or animals and the ecosystems in which they live. An endangered species, in the Act, is "any species which is in danger of extinction throughout all or a significant portion of its range" excluding certain members of the class Insecta considered to be harmful pests. A threatened species is "any species which is likely to become an endangered species within the foreseeable future throughout all or a significant portion of its range".

Five criteria were established to determine whether a given species is entitled to protection under the law. Any species can be considered to be endangered or threatened in the event that any or all of the following occur:

(1) The present or threatened destruction, modification, or curtailment of its habitat or range;
(2) Over-utilization for commercial, sporting, scientific, or educational purposes;
(3) Disease or predation;
(4) The inadequacy of existing regulatory mechanisms; or
(5) Other natural or manmade factors affecting its continued existence.

The Secretary of the Interior ultimately decides which species are to be included for protection under this law.

Diligent enforcement of the Endangered Species Act will protect endangered plants from direct or indirect destruction by projects administered and funded by federal agencies. The law prohibits any act which will destroy or modify critical habitats so as to further decimate an endangered or threatened species. The Act also prohibits citizens of the United States or persons subject to jurisdiction by the United States from possessing, importing, selling, delivering, or transporting any species which have been determined to be endangered or threatened.

Although the aforementioned provisions of the Endangered Species Act have helped enormously to protect endangered species, there are two major shortcomings in the law with respect to strip mining operations. First, no protection is afforded to locally rare, threatened or endangered plants which are economically and/or ecologically important. Many plant species may be extremely rare in one region of the country yet abundant in other regions. If this is the case, a given species may not be included on the federally accepted list of threatened or endangered species even though it may be considered to be rare or even endangered in certain states (Fig. 1). For example, only three plant species occurring in North Dakota were included by the Fish and Wildlife Service in their proposed

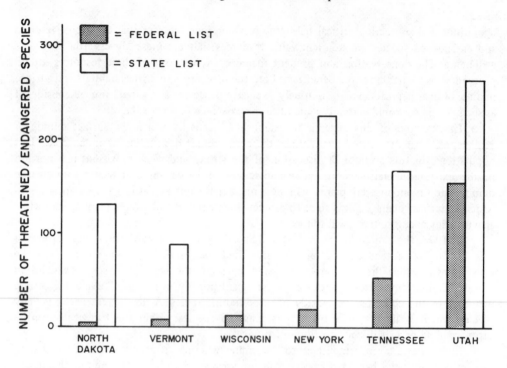

Fig. 1. Numbers of threatened and/or endangered plant species appearing on state and federal lists for six states. Species on the federal list for each state are from the U.S. Fish and Wildlife Service (1975b). Species on the state lists are from the following: ND, Barker et al. unpub. ms.; VT and NY, Countryman 1977; WI, Read 1976; TN, Wofford et al. unpub. ms.; UT, Welsh et al. 1975.

list of threatened or endangered plant species (U.S. Fish and Wildlife Service 1975b). The most recent listing of vascular plant species considered to be rare or unique in North Dakota, however, includes 130 species (Barker et al. unpublished). The U.S. Fish and Wildlife Service initially proposed that 13 plant species found in Wisconsin be included as endangered or threatened species yet the Wisconsin Department of Natural Resources recognizes 226 plant species as threatened or endangered in that state (Read 1976). The 1973 federal law therefore affords no protection to plant species that have been determined to be only regionally rare, threatened, or endangered.

Second, the Endangered Species Act provides little protection from destruction or disturbance of cirtical habitats by the private sector. Only federal agencies (or projects funded with federal monies) are prohibited from altering the immediate environment of endangered species (End. Sp. Act of 1973, see Sec. 7). Critical habitats found on lands not owned or administered by the U.S. government are open to possible destruction or modification without subsequent penalty of law. Private mining operations are not bound to the protection of endangered species or their habitats by federal law. The restrictions applicable under the law to private mining operations merely forbid the possession, sale, or transportation of protected plant species.

Since the passage of the federal Endangered Species Act of 1973, several states including Nebraska, Minnesota (Mohlenbrock 1977) and Michigan have acted independently to formulate legislation to safeguard plant species within their boundaries. Such an example is Michigan's Endangered Species Act of 1974. This law complements the federal law and alleviates at least one of its shortcomings. Specifically, the Michigan Act furnishes protection to plant species not appearing on the federal endangered or threatened species list but that have been deemed to be endangered or threatened within the state's borders. As recently as

July 1977, 17 plant species appeared on the state listing of endangered or threatened plants and 196 others were being considered for inclusion on the list (Taylor 1977). To maintain its usefulness, the state list is to be reviewed and amended every two years.

Another positive feature of Michigan's Endangered Species Act is that it enables the director of the Department of Natural Resources to purchase lands containing critical habitats if funds are available. This type of acquisition can allow for the continued survival of a given species while research pertaining to the environmental requirements of that species continues. However, since funds for projects of this kind are always at a premium, many threatened species may never benefit from this provision.

Although this type of state legislation is certainly a step in the right direction, it is not entirely adequate because it does not provide for the protection and maintenance of critical habitats other than those parcels purchased outright. It, as does the federal law, restricts its regulatory power to the prohibition of the selling and transportation of protected plant species. This in itself cannot insure the long-term survival of any species.

The third piece of legislation to be considered here is the recently enacted United States Surface Mining Control and Reclamation Act of 1977. This Act was established to "protect society and the environment from the adverse effects of surface coal mining operations" and contains regulations which are intended to serve that purpose. The intent of the Act was to issue baseline regulatory mechanisms which can then be adopted and expanded by those states involved with surface mining. Congress recognized the fact that since surface mining presents unique problems to each state, the major governing responsibility for the control of mining operations should rest with the states rather than the federal government.

Guidelines established in this 1977 mining act pay particular attention to the successful reclamation of lands disturbed by mining operations. These post-mining laws should be instrumental in reinstating native vegetation to mined sites, yet in many instances, fragile ecosystems containing endangered plant species may not become reestablished after mining operations have ceased even if diligent reclamation efforts are pursued. Certain precautions have been outlined in the Act to help prevent this possible situation, but the wording of this legislation is vague and does not actually refer to either endangered plants or critical habitats.

Section 522 of the Surface Mining Control and Reclamation Act provides for the inclusion of certain land areas to be listed as unsuitable for surface coal mining. Each state is responsible for recommendation of lands that it deems unsuitable for disturbance by mining. The recommendations must be based on information pertaining to standards listed in Section 522. Lands meeting one or more of the five standards may be officially declared unsuitable for mining subsequent to the submission of a petition for such status. The two standards that may potentially affect critical habitats indicate that areas may be declared unsuitable for strip mining of coal if the mining will:

"(a) Be incompatible with existing state or local land use plans or programs; or
(b) Affect fragile or historic lands in which such operations could result in significant damage to important historic, cultural, scientific, and esthetic values and natural systems".

From these two standards we can assume that if a particular state has no land use legislation protecting its own critical habitats, those habitats will not be declared unsuitable for mining unless they qualify to be included under standard (b) as listed above. The terminology in (b) is sufficiently inexact to warrant further clarification. The terms "fragile or historic lands" and "natural ecosystems" may or may not include endangered or threatened plants growing in critical habitats. Since it is unclear as to whether critical habitats can be declared unsuitable for mining under this act, the burden for protection again seems to lie with the individual states.

Several states have now passed bills pertaining to strip mining which are more rigorous and detailed than the federal Surface Mining Control and Reclamation Act of 1977. By design, the state laws tend to be more explicit than the federal legislation and include rules and regulations that may not be pertinent to other states with markedly different topography and vegetation. In 1977, Mississippi enacted the Surface Mining and Reclamation Law. This law calls for the identification of ecologically sensitive natural areas and their subsequent protection. These lands can be declared unsuitable for mining and thus be effectively classified as off-limits to mining operations. This type of state legislation sets the framework for the needed preservation of endangered species and critical habitats. Modification of such laws to include the term "critical habitats" in addition to "ecologically sensitive natural areas" (or other similar terminology in other state laws) would then establish a means by which all critical habitats on *or* off federal lands could be sustained.

From the above discussion, it seems clear that many endangered species and their critical habitats have no official protection from the disruptive effects of mining operations. To circumvent this situation we recommend that the following six guidelines for pre-mining legislation be adopted by all states having stripable coal deposits. States already having laws governing mining operations would be encouraged to amend their original legislation if it does not give adequate protection to endangered and threatened plant species.

RECOMMENDED GUIDELINES FOR PRE-MINING LEGISLATION

(a) **A survey and inventory of endangered and threatened plant species within the state shall be conducted.**

The resulting information will be used to compile an official list of plant species considered to be threatened or endangered in the state. The list should additionally include all species found in the state that appear on the federal threatened and endangered species list. Presently, at least 47 states already have one or more lists of rare, unique, threatened, or endangered plant taxa (Lawyer 1977). In North Dakota, the Regional Environmental Assessment Program has been instrumental in initiating the acquisition of inventories of endangered species.

(b) **Location of the critical habitats for each plant species on the above list shall be determined.**

Any habitat capable of the long-term support of populations of any plant species considered to be threatened or endangered should be declared a critical habitat. The geographical locations of these critical habitats should be documented for all lands within the state. When possible, information of this type should be stored in computer networks to allow for easy access and retrieval.

(c) **Areas designated as being unsuitable for surface mining because of the occurrence of critical habitats will be identified.**

Petitions requesting the inclusion of specific critical habitats as areas unsuitable for surface mining should be submitted to the designated regulatory authority in the state. Upon review of the petition, the lands in question can be declared unsuitable for mining operations if the regulatory agency concurs that the lands actually are critical habitats. Mining permits will not be granted for these lands except as provided for in (e).

(d) **Areas designated as being suitable for surface mining with respect to occurrence of critical habitats will be identified.**

Mining permits can be granted for areas which do not contain critical habitats. These areas will be considered suitable for surface mining and permits for mining these areas can be granted by the designated state regulatory agency. In the event that mining permits are requested for land areas which have not as yet been designated as suitable or unsuitable for surface mining, on-site investigations to determine the status of the land will be carried out before permits can be granted or denied.

(e) **Conflicts as to whether lands should be declared unsuitable or suitable for mining will be resolved by use of a priority ranking system.**

In any given state, coal reserves sufficient to meet current demands and not overlaid by lands containing critical habitats should be available for mining. However, circumstances may arise to preclude successful mining in areas designated suitable for mining (i.e. all such areas were previously stripped of their coal, mineral rights are not available for lease, other considerations such as the presence of historic or archeological sites prevent mining in the area). If such a conflict should occur, a priority ranking system based on 100 points for the coal resource and 100 points for the plant resource will be established. A sample of a hypothetical priority scoring system for a given land area is provided in Tables 1 and 2 (format followed as in Tans 1974).

After *all* areas in question have been rated, the total scores for both coal and plant resources will be compared. Those areas with high PRS score:CRS score ratios may remain unsuitable for mining while those with high CRS score: PRS score ratios may be declared suitable for mining upon recommendation by the state regulatory agency in charge.

(f) **If, as provided for in (e), surface mining is to be established on lands previously considered to be unsuitable for mining, efforts must be made to collect and transport all endangered/threatened plants from the site before mining operations begin.**

The plants could then be transplanted into a similar habitat nearby or taken to a suitable botanical garden. This procedure has been practiced with some degree of success by the North Carolina Botanical Garden's rescue team at Chapel Hill (Ayensu 1976) but is definitely an undesirable alternative to the maintenance of the original habitat.

Taken collectively, the six measures outlined above could provide the basic format needed by individual states to conserve their remaining endangered plant species through the rational placement of mining operations in areas other than designated critical habitats. With almost 10% of the vascular flora in the U.S. being endangered, threatened, or extinct (Jenkins and Ayensu 1975) and over 5% of the flora in all temperate regions combined being threatened (Raven 1976), the time has come to protect our natural diversity of plants. Legislative protection can be a step in the right direction, but ultimately, more sophisticated means of energy acquisition must be developed so as to eliminate large scale land disturbances which are presently the by-product of our efforts to obtain energy through surface mining operations.

Table 1   Hypothetical Coal Resource Scale (CRS). The scale
           is not intended to be applied to any particular
           state but merely indicates the types of data that
           may be useful in this type of system.   Scores are
           not restricted to multiples of five and can range
           anywhere from zero to 20.

                                                              Score

1c. Coal seam thickness:
       a. thicker than 30 m   20
       b. 21 to 30 m   15
       c. 11 to 20 m   10
       d. 0 to 10 m   5

2c. Overburden thickness:
       a. 0 to 5 m   20
       b. 6 to 10 m   15
       c. 11 to 20 m   10
       d. thicker than 21 m   5

3c. Total area available for mining:
       a. more than 150 ha   20
       b. 51 to 150 ha   15
       c. 11 to 50 ha   10
       d. 0 to 10 ha   5

4c. Access to existing roads, railways, or
    coal-fired generating or gasification plants:
       a. near three of the above   20
       b. near a generating or gasification plant   15
       c. near a railway   10
       d. near existing roads   5

5c. Quality of the coal to be mined:
       a. high BTU rating (>19,000 BTU kg^{-1}) +
          low sulfur content (<1%)   20
       b. moderate BTU rating (15-19,000 BTU kg^{-1}) +
          moderate sulfur content (1-3%)   10
       c. low BTU rating (<15,000 BTU kg^{-1}) +
          high sulfur content (>3%)   0
                                                        _____

                               Maximum Total   = 100

Table 2   Hypothetical Plant Resource Scale (PRS).   The scale
          is not intended to be applied to any particular
          state but merely indicates the types of data that
          may be useful in this type of system.   Scores are
          not restricted to multiples of five and can range
          anywhere from zero to 20.

                                                              Score
1p. Number of endangered/threatened plant species:
        a. more than 4 species   20
        b. 3 species   15
        c. 2 species   10
        d. 1 species   5

2p. Relative abundance of the critical habitat type:
        a. area constitutes the last known critical
           habitat for one or more species   20
        b. area constitutes one of the 2-5 known
           sites of occurrence of this critical
           habitat   15
        c. area constitutes one of the 6-10 known
           sites of occurrence of this critical
           habitat   10
        d. area constitutes one of the more than
           10 known sites of occurrence of this
           critical habitat   5

3p. Total area of the critical habitat and the
    surrounding buffer zone:
        a. critical habitat large enough to maintain
           its integrity + large buffer zone preventing
           encroachment of disturbance   20
        b. critical habitat large + minimal or no
           buffer zone   15
        c. critical habitat small + adequate buffer
           zone   10
        d. critical habitat small + minimal or no
           buffer zone   5

4p. Quality of the critical habitat:
        a. pristine condition with little or no
           previous disturbance   20
        b. only minor amounts of previous disturbance   15
        c. moderate previous disturbance   10
        d. major previous disturbance which may
           totally disrupt this critical habitat   5

5p. Degree of threat to the critical habitat from
    future disturbance other than surface mining:
        a. destruction not likely to occur   20
        b. threat of destruction is moderate   10
        c. destruction will take place even if mining
           operations are excluded   0
                                              _____

                              Maximum Total   = 100

ACKNOWLEDGMENT

Funds for this study were provided, in part, by a grant from the North Dakota Regional Environmental Assessment Program to Dr. M.K. Wali.

ABSTRACT

The recent intensification of coal development and the subsequent disturbance of the land by surface mining operations in the United States have been accompanied by concern for endangered species of plants and, more importantly, their critical habitats. Both coal reserves and critical habitats are non-renewable resources which require prudent management. In 1973, the Endangered Species Act established guidelines for the protection of plant species found to be threatened or endangered throughout their range. However, no protection is afforded to locally rare, unique, or threatened plants which are economically and/or ecologically important. Since surface mining operations are disruptive by nature, rare plants and their habitats may be eliminated if mining sites are not judiciously located. To circumvent this situation, we are recommending six guidelines for establishing pre-mining legislation at the state level. Included in these guidelines is a priority ranking system designed to resolve conflicts as to whether specific lands should be declared suitable or unsuitable for mining. The above guidelines for pre-mining legislation will support already established post-mining laws and will enable the rational placement of mining operations in areas other than designated critical habitats.

REFERENCES

Ayensu, E. 1976. International cooperation among conservation-oriented botanical gardens and institutions. pp. 259-269, In J. Simmons, R. Beyer, P. Brandham, G. Lucas and V. Parry (eds.), Conservation of Threatened Plants, Plenum Press, NY, 336 p.

Barker, W., G. Larson and R. Williams. Rare and unique plants of North Dakota, Dept. of Botany, North Dakota State Univ., Fargo, (unpublished manuscript).

Countryman, W. 1977. The northeastern United States. pp. 30-35, In G. Prance and T. Elias (eds.), Extinction Is Forever, New York Botanical Garden, NY, 437 p.

Endangered Species Act of 1973. Public Law 93-205, 93rd Congress, S. 1983, December 28, 1973. 87 Stat. 884-903, 16 U.S.C., 21 p.

Haynes, R. and W. Klimstra. 1975. Illinois Lands Surface Mined for Coal. Illinois Institute for Environmental Quality, Southern Illinois University, Carbondale, 201 p.

Jenkins, D. and E. Ayensu. 1975. One-tenth of our plant species may not survive. Smithsonian 5:92-96.

Lawyer, J. 1977. Guide to U.S. state lists of rare and endangered plant taxa. New York Botanical Garden, NY. (draft ms.).

Michigan Endangered Species Act of 1974. Michigan Compiled Laws Annotated, Secs. 299.221-299.230.

Mississippi Surface Mining and Reclamation Law. Mississippi Code Annotated, Secs. 53-7-1 - 53-7-75.

Mohlenbrock, R. 1977. The midwestern United States. pp. 41-44, In G. Prance and T. Elias (eds.), Extinction is Forever, New York Botanical Garden, NY, 437 p.

Paone, J., J. Morning and L. Giorgetti. 1974. Land Utilization and Reclamation in the Mining Industry, 1930-1971. U.S. Dept. Interior, Bureau of Mines Circular 8642, Washington, DC, 61 p.

Raven, P. 1976. Ethics and attitudes. pp. 155-179, In J. Simmons, R. Beyer, P. Brandham, G. Lucas and V. Parry (eds.), Conservation of Threatened Plants, Plenum Press, NY, 336 p.

Read, R. 1976. Endangered and Threatened Vascular Plants in Wisconsin, Department of Nat. Res. Tech. Bull. No. 92, Madison, 58 p.

Simmons, J., R. Beyer, P. Brandham, G. Lucas and V. Parry (eds.). 1976. Conservation of Threatened Plants, Plenum Press, NY, 336 p.

Smith, R.L. 1976. Ecological genesis of endangered species: the philosophy of preservation. Ann. Rev. Ecol. Syst. 7:33-55.

Surface Mining Control and Reclamation Act of 1977. Public Law 95-87, 95th Congress, H.R. 2, August 3, 1977. 91 Stat. 445-532, 16 U.S.C., 88 p.

Tans, W. 1974. Priority ranking of biotic natural areas.   Mich Bot. 13:31-39.

Taylor, S. 1977. States implementation of Endangered Species Act of 1973, P.L. 93-205. Report to U.S. Senate Subcommittee on Environment and Public Works, July 22, Washington, DC.

U.S. Fish and Wildlife Service. 1975a. Endangered and threatened species; notice on critical habitat areas. Federal Register, April 22, 40(78):17743-17827.

U.S. Fish and Wildlife Service. 1975b. Threatened or endangered fauna or flora; review of status of vascular plants and determination of "critical habitat". Federal Register, July 1, 40(127):27823-27924.

United States General Accounting Office. 1977. U.S. Coal Development - Promises, Uncertainties. EMD-77-43, Washington, DC, 452 p.

Welsh, S., N. Attwood and J. Reveal. 1975. Endangered, threatened, extinct, endemic, and rare or restricted Utah vascular plants.   Great Basin Natur. 35:327-376.

Wofford, B., R. Kral, A. Evans, H. DeSelm and J. Collins. Tennessee Committee for Rare Plants.   Botany Dept., Univ. Tennessee, Knoxville (unpublished manuscript).

Woodwell, G. 1977. The challenge of endangered species. pp. 5-10, In G. Prance and T. Elias (eds.), Extinction Is Forever, New York Botanical Garden, NY, 437 p.

ESTIMATING REVEGETATION POTENTIALS
OF LAND SURFACE MINED FOR COAL IN THE WEST

Paul E. Packer, Chester E. Jensen, Edward L. Noble and John A. Marshall*

INTRODUCTION

An emerging problem in the interior West is the adverse effect on environmental quality of spoils left in the wake of surface mining for coal. Needed are criteria and guides for predicting revegetation potentials on various kinds of surface-mined land. Equally important is the need to define and prescribe revegetation treatments and post-treatment management measures for such land.

Passage and implementation of the Surface Mining Control and Reclamation Act (Public Law 95-87) and attendant regulations have placed a new emphasis on revegetation of spoil materials from coal surface mines in North Dakota, Montana, Wyoming, Colorado, Utah, New Mexico, and Arizona. Although most coal surface mines within the interior West are applying revegetation practices, requirements of the new Federal Reclamation Act in this regard will, in most cases, necessitate a reassessment and evaluation of techniques and methodologies employed in present revegetation activities. Currently, many research activities are under way to determine the best "mix" of cultural practices and plant species needed to satisfactorily revegetate disturbed land. However, in the interior West not enough time has elapsed since either surface mine revegetation research or application began to assure that any particular combination of revegetation methods will be successful in the long run. Consequently both mining applicants and administrators granting approval to mine have been put into a position where they only guess as to whether the required reclamation standards can be met.

In view of this uncertainty concerning the probability for successfully revegetating western surface coal mines, an investigation, financed jointly by the Environmental Protection Agency, U.S. Fish and Wildlife Service, and the Forest Service's Surface Environment and Mining (SEAM) program, was begun in 1976 to identify criteria for measuring the success of revegetation efforts, to evaluate past and ongoing revegetation efforts conducted at most of the major surface coal mines in the interior West, and to develop a capability for predicting the probable degree of revegetation success to be expected on coal lands that are surface-mined in the future. That investigation and its results are the subject of this paper.

*Intermountain Forest and Range Experiment Station, Forest Service, U.S. Department of Agriculture, Ogden, UT 84401.

INVESTIGATIVE METHODS

Investigative methods used were predicated on the assumption that, unless some other revegetation objective is defined, the primary goal of revegetation on surface-mined coal in the interior West is to establish a productive and protective cover of durable plants, consisting predominantly of needed species adapted to and characteristic of these areas or other similar areas before mining. It was further assumed that differences in the degree of success of revegetation efforts to date on surface-mined coal lands of the West should be related to variations in natural climatic components, changes in site-specific physical and biological characteristics, and differences in the revegetation methods.

The degree to which plant cover is established, either in natural or revegetated stands, can be measured and evaluated in a number of ways. One of the most important measures of success in plant cover establishment is the capability of the vegetation to produce aboveground biomass for forage or some other useful purpose. Another is the capability of the vegetation to produce ground cover for protection of the soil against the erosive forces of raindrops and surface runoff. Accordingly, the degree of success of vegetation reestablishment was measured in terms of total weight of aboveground biomass and total percent density of ground cover (plant basal area and accumulated litter).

During the growing seasons of 1976 and 1977, data were obtained from 28 revegetated major coal surface mines located throughout the surface-minable coal areas of the West. These data provide information about important climatic features, physical and biological characteristics of each site, treatment measures employed to effect revegetation, the age of each revegetated area, and amounts of forage and ground cover density developed by both native and introduced types of vegetation. Similar information, except for vegetation age, was also obtained from unmined areas near each mine. These unmined areas had evidently been long undisturbed and were characterized by predominantly native vegetation.

Information about general climatic features was obtained from tabulations of State climatic data and consisted of total annual precipitation, growing season precipitation, and length of the frost-free growing season.

Data concerned with site-specific physical and biological factors were obtained from systematically distributed transects on each of the unmined and mined study areas. Measurements included the aspects, slope steepness, and elevation of each transect. Soil samples from the unmined areas and spoil samples from the mined and revegetated areas were obtained to a depth of eight inches belowground and were analyzed for texture, conductivity, nitrate-nitrogen, phosphorus, potassium, sodium, calcium, magnesium, acidity (pH), production quality, sodium absorption ratio, and saturation percentage.

Along each study transect, mil-acre plots were located randomly for use in determining species composition, aboveground biomass or forage production, and plant cover density. All current growth of perennial plants within these plots was clipped to a height of one-half inch aboveground, bagged by species, ovendried for 24 hours, and weighed.

The age of each revegetated area, expressed as number of years since it was planted, as well as information concerning the treatments applied during and subsequent to its establishment, were obtained through consultation with reclamation personnel employed at each of the mines. These treatments included tillage, seeding methods, topsoiling, fertilizing, supplemental irrigation, mulching, and time of seeding.

All of the data obtained from 176 sets of transects on the 28 mines comprised the information base available for analyses. While these data are the best known to the authors, it is important to appreciate their limitations and to utilize the associated analytical results with a suitably precautionary attitude.

First, there are only 36 mines in the entire area covered by this study wherein revegetation has even been attempted. The kinds of revegetation efforts, insofar as specific treatments or combinations of treatments are concerned, differ between mines and even between years on the same mine, in many cases. For example, whereas seeds of native species may be broadcast in the fall on the spoils of one mine, seeds of introduced species may be drilled into the spoils of another mine in the spring. In each case, the combinations of other treatments, such as topsoiling, tilling, mulching, or fertilizing might be substantially different. Of the very large number of possible treatment combinations, relatively few exist on the 28 mines, and the comparative revegetation success of those that do exist is confounded by mine-to-mine differences in climatic and growing media environment. Further, "treatments" cannot be considered to be standardized. For example, the depth and quality of topsoil (when added) are almost certain to differ between mines. Fertilizer composition and rates and times of application are largely unknown. Also unknown are rates of seed application, depths of drilled seed, the quality of seed, the mix of species seeded, the depth of tillage, the kinds and amounts of mulch applied, and supplemental irrigation amounts and frequencies. Consider, too, that about half of the revegetation efforts are 2 years old or less, so that on the mines involved, seeded plants have not had time to respond fully to the growing environment and revegetation treatments. Also, consider that revegetation success is strongly affected by the particular amount and timing of precipitation during the year or period of years involved in the revegetation effort.

With this drastic disarray of analytical amenities, the results of this investigation and the information developed therefrom should be regarded as interim only.

DATA AND INFORMATION ANALYSES

Six series of analyses were made. These analyses followed multiple regression strategies for estimating forage production and plant cover densities as functions of climatic environment components, growing medium characteristics, and revegetation treatment alternatives. The simple linear effects of independent variables on forage production and cover density were screened statistically in all additive model combinations as a means of isolating the stronger variables for use in synthesizing final models.

Forage Production Model for Unmined Areas

Eighty-three of the 176 transects sampled during this investigation were located on unmined and otherwise long undisturbed areas adjacent to each of the 28 mines studied. For these areas, annual precipitation and growing season each added significantly (Pr ≤ 0.005) to the regression for forage production. Soil potassium content, while not adding significantly to the overall regression based on precipitation and growing season alone, did display unusual strength in the short to medium length growing season and medium to high precipitation range and, so, was retained in the model. Strong interactions, not likely to be well represented by the simple linear additive effects initially screened, were expected to exist among these variables. Accordingly, attention was focused on the interactive effects of these three variables on forage production. Forage production was expected to increase upward concavely with increasing precipitation, to reach a peak somewhere within the broad range of growing season lengths encountered, and to increase with increasing amount of potassium in the soil. The interactive effects of these variables were modeled under the constraints of expectation, following Jensen and Homeyer (1970, 1971) and Jensen (1973, 1976). This model was fitted by least squares to data from the 83 unmined transects. The effects of precipitation, growing season, and soil potassium on forage production, as expressed by this model, are shown in Fig. 1. (See appendix, Equation 1).

Estimates of forage production made from the equation of this model for selected values representative of the ranges of precipitation, growing season, and soil potassium encountered are presented in Table 1.

The least amount of forage, less than 100 pounds per acre, was produced on sites characterized by approximately 5 inches annual precipitation and a long growing season

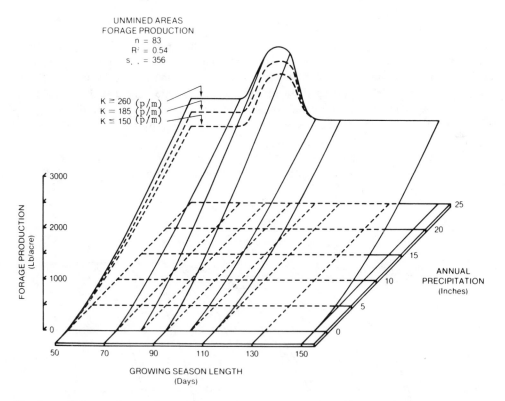

Fig. 1.   Effects of annual precipitation, growing season length, and soil potassium content on forage production of unmined sites on surface mineable coal lands.

Table 1. Effects of annual precipitation, growing season length, and soil potassium content on forage production of unmined sites on surface mineable coal lands (lbs/acre).

NO POTASSIUM				200 PARTS/MILLION POTASSIUM				400 PARTS/MILLION POTASSIUM			
DAYS OF GROWING SEASON	INCHES PRECIPITATION			DAYS OF GROWING SEASON	INCHES PRECIPITATION			DAYS OF GROWING SEASON	INCHES PRECIPITATION		
	5	15	25		5	15	25		5	15	25
50	155.	725.	1485.	50	198.	927.	1897.	50	211.	984.	2015.
85	333.	1313.	2487.	85	388.	1531.	2899.	85	404.	1593.	3017.
120	90.	644.	1608.	120	90.	644.	1608.	120	90.	644.	1608.

of 120 days or more, irrespective of the potassium content of the soil. The greatest amount of forage, more than 3,000 pounds per acre, was produced on sites characterized by about 25 inches of annual precipitation, an intermediate growing season of about 85 days, and a high level of approximately 400 parts per million of potassium in the soil. This model provides a basis for estimating forage production on unmined areas. Such forage production estimates can be considered to comprise a minimum requirement or standard against which the success of revegetation on mined areas can be measured.

Plant Cover Density Model for Unmined Areas

Procedures for modeling the density of plant cover on unmined areas were similar to those used to model forage production. Screening of linear effects again revealed that annual precipitation and growing season were strong variables (Pr <0.025) and that potassium showed strength at short-to-medium length growing seasons and medium-to-high precipitation. Interactive models involving these variables were generated and fitted to data from the 83 transects located on unmined areas. Relations of annual precipitation, growing season, and soil potassium to plant cover density are illustrated by the response surfaces in Fig. 2 (See appendix, Equation 2).

Whereas there is no theoretical limit to the weight of forage produced on the study areas, the top limit of plant cover density is 100 percent. Accordingly, plant cover density

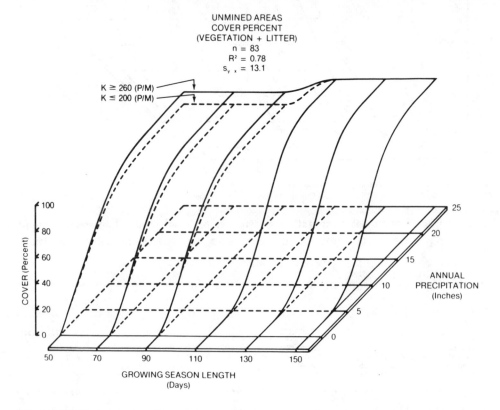

Fig. 2.   Effects of annual precipitation, growing season length, and soil potassium content on vegetative cover density of unmined sites on surface mineable coal lands.

Table 2. Effects of annual precipitation, growing season length, and soil potassium content
on vegetative cover density of unmined sties on surface mineable coal lands
(percent).

NO POTASSIUM			200 PARTS/MILLION POTASSIUM			400 PARTS/MILLION POTASSIUM		
DAYS OF GROWING SEASON	INCHES PRECIPITATION		DAYS OF GROWING SEASON	INCHES PRECIPITATION		DAYS OF GROWING SEASON	INCHES PRECIPITATION	
	5 15 25			5 15 25			5 15 25	
50	34.	76.	78.	50	34.	76.	78.	50	37.	85.	87.
85	34.	76.	78.	85	34.	76.	78.	85	37.	85.	87.
120	1.	83.	98.	120	1.	83.	98.	120	1.	83.	98.

approached 100 percent as annual precipitation increased. Plant cover density also increased
as the growing season became longer than about 90 days and as the soil potassium content
increased. The equation represented by this model was used to estimate plant cover
densities for selected values of annual precipitation, growing season length, and soil
potassium content. These estimated plant cover densities are shown in Table 2.

The lowest density, only 1 percent, occurs on areas where the annual precipiation
is about 5 inches and the length of the growing season is more than 110 days, irrespective
of the soil potassium content. Although the highest plant cover density, about 98 percent,
occurs on areas where the annual precipitation is about 25 inches and the growing season
is longer than 110 days, again irrespective of the amount of potassium in the soil, it will be
noted that the effect of potassium changes with precipitation at short and intermediate
lengths of growing season.

This model provides a basis for estimating plant cover density on unmined areas. These
estimates, like those from the previous model, can also be considered to comprise minimum
requirements or standards against which the degree of revegetation success on mined areas
can be measured.

Forage Production Model for Mined Areas

Two models were developed to estimate forage production to be expected from
revegetation of surface-mined areas. One of these models was generated to estimate the
amount of forage produced on revegetated areas dominated by native plant species. The
other model was developed to provide similar estimates where revegetated plants consist
principally of introduced species.

The age of revegetated plants, the climatic components of annual precipitation and
growing season, and the potassium content of spoils (fitted in that order) each added
significantly (Pr ≤ 0.10) to the regression for forage production from both native and
introduced vegetation. Attention was then focused on interactive relations between forage
production and the first three variables: age, annual precipitation, and growing season.
Forage production was expected to be convex upward over age, reaching a maximum level
at some point in time; to be concave upward over precipitation; and to reach a peak somewhere within the broad range of growing season lengths encountered. The interactive effects
of these variables were modeled under the constraints of expectation and refitted separately
by least squares to the data from 44 transects with predominantly native species and to the
data from 33 transects with introduced species. This interactive portion of the model for
forage production from native plant species is illustrated by the response surfaces in
Fig. 3 (See appendix, Equation 3).

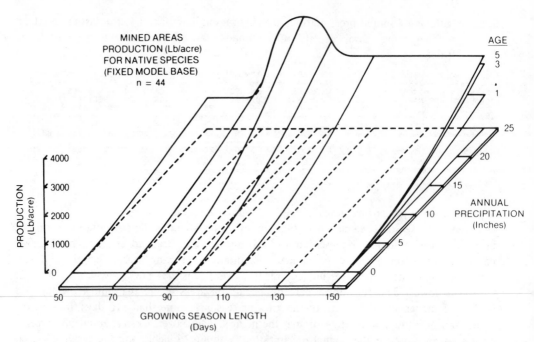

Fig. 3.   Effects of annual precipitation, growing season length, and age of planting on
forage production of mined and revegetated sites on coal surface mines.

The amount of forage produced by revegetated native plant cover increased at an increasing rate as the annual precipitation varied from about 5 to 25 inches. The amount of forage produced also increased, but at a decreasing rate, to an age of about 5 years. While some increases in forage production might occur as revegetation stands become older than 5 years, the shape of regression curves for stands older than 5 years suggests that such increases are likely to be rather inconsequential. The amount of forage produced also increased to a peak at an intermediate growing season length of approximately 85 days. Quite possibly, areas with shorter and longer growing seasons did not possess optimum temperature conditions for maximum forage production.

A comparable model for estimating forage production on revegetated areas comprised mainly of introduced plant species is identical in shape to the model for native plant species. These refitted models were adopted as fixed prediction bases, residuals from which were expressed as linear additive effects of potassium, sodium, pH, and the revegetation treatment variables: tilling, seeding method, topsoiling, fertilizing, supplemental irrigation, mulching, and time of seeding. The sum of the interactive fixed base and linear residual effects constitutes the estimate of total forage production. This two-step fitting procedure prevented erosion of the scale of the well-expressed interaction by subsequent fitting of the less well-defined simple effects of the remaining variables. Interactions of the revegetation treatment variables were not modeled because the data for these treatments are too limited to prevent proper evaluation of all of the interaction effects. There is no question that these revegetation treatments exert interactive effects on forage production which are not evaluated here. Before these effects can be evaluated, however, additional data are needed on more areas than were available for this investigation.

Selected values of annual precipitation and growing season length were utilized in the equation for the interactive model shown in Fig. 3, together with the additive effects of

Table 3. Effects of climatic factors, spoil properties, and revegetation treatments on production of forage from predominantly native species (lbs/acre).

Block 1 — PR 5, GS 85, K 200, NA 150, PH 6

TIL	SM	TPS	FER	IRR	MUL	ST	PROD/ACRE
							0
X							0
	X						190
		X					0
			X				218
				X			0
					X		0
						X	184
X	X						203
X		X					0
X			X				231
X				X			0
X					X		0
X						X	197
	X	X					107
	X		X				559
	X			X			225
	X				X		12
	X					X	524
		X	X				135
		X		X			0
		X			X		0
		X				X	101
			X	X			253
			X		X		40
			X			X	552
				X	X		0
				X		X	219
					X	X	6
X	X	X					120
X	X		X				572
X	X			X			238
X	X				X		26
X	X					X	538
X		X	X				148
X		X		X			0
X		X			X		0
X		X				X	114
X			X	X			266
X			X		X		54
X			X			X	566
X				X	X		0
X				X		X	232
X					X	X	19
	X	X	X				475
	X	X		X			142
	X	X			X		0
	X	X				X	441
	X		X	X			593

Block 2 — PR 15, GS 85, K 200, NA 150, PH 6

TIL	SM	TPS	FER	IRR	MUL	ST	PROD/ACRE
							1247
X							1260
	X						1587
		X					1164
			X				1615
				X			1282
					X		1069
						X	1581
X	X						1601
X		X					1177
X			X				1629
X				X			1295
X					X		1082
X						X	1595
	X	X					1504
	X		X				1956
	X			X			1622
	X				X		1410
	X					X	1322
		X	X				1532
		X		X			1198
		X			X		986
		X				X	1498
			X	X			1650
			X		X		1438
			X			X	1950
				X	X		1104
				X		X	1616
					X	X	1404
X	X	X					1518
X	X		X				1969
X	X			X			1636
X	X				X		1423
X	X					X	1935
X		X	X				1546
X		X		X			1212
X		X			X		999
X		X				X	1511
X			X	X			1664
X			X		X		1451
X			X			X	1963
X				X	X		1117
X				X		X	1629
X					X	X	1417
	X	X	X				1873
	X	X		X			1539
	X	X			X		1327
	X	X				X	1839
	X		X	X			1991

Block 3 — PR 25, GS 85, K 200, NA 150, PH 6

TIL	SM	TPS	FER	IRR	MUL	ST	PROD/ACRE
							3382
X							3395
	X						3723
		X					3299
			X				3751
				X			3417
					X		3204
						X	3717
X	X						3736
X		X					3312
X			X				3764
X				X			3430
X					X		3218
X						X	3730
	X	X					3640
	X		X				4091
	X			X			3758
	X				X		3545
	X					X	4057
		X	X				3668
		X		X			3334
		X			X		3121
		X				X	3634
			X	X			3786
			X		X		3573
			X			X	4085
				X	X		3239
				X		X	3752
					X	X	3539
X	X	X					3653
X	X		X				4105
X	X			X			3771
X	X				X		3559
X	X					X	4071
X		X	X				3681
X		X		X			3347
X		X			X		3135
X		X				X	3647
X			X	X			3799
X			X		X		3586
X			X			X	4099
X				X	X		3253
X				X		X	3765
X					X	X	3552
	X	X	X				4008
	X	X		X			3675
	X	X			X		3462
	X	X				X	3974
	X		X	X			4126

selected values of soil potassium, sodium, and pH content and the additive effects of the seven revegetation treatments--all to estimate the expected amounts of forage produced at 5 years of age on surface-mined areas revegetated with predominantly native species. A sample portion of the forage production tables developed from these estimates is shown in Table 3.

Information in this 729-page table is divided into three blocks, each of which represents a different level of annual precipitation (PR). In order from left to right, these levels are 5 inches, 15 inches, and 25 inches. On this particular page of the table, all of the remaining variables are similar for each of the three blocks. The growing season length (GS) is 85 days. The soil potassium content (K) is 200 parts per million. The soil sodium content (NA) is 150 parts per million and the soil pH is 6. Each of the three blocks comprising the table consists of eight columns, seven of which are occupied by the seven revegetation treatments. The last column in each block consists of the dry weight of forage produced under the combination of revegetation treatments indicated by the letter X. Tillage of the soil (TIL), consisting of ripping, disking, or plowing prior to seeding, is indicated by an X. A blank indicates that the soil was not tilled. Drilling as a seeding method (SM) is indicated by an X, whereas broadcast seeding is represented by a blank. Addition of topsoil prior to seeding (TPS) is indicated by an X; a blank shows that topsoil was not added. An X indicates that fertilizer (FER) was added; a blank indicates that it was not. Supplemental irrigation (IRR) is indicated by an X and no irrigation is represented by a blank. Mulching (MUL) is indicated by an X, and lack of mulching is represented by a blank. Fall seeding is shown by an X, whereas a blank represents spring seeding.

The forage production values in Table 3 can be compared with the appropriate production values for unmined areas summarized in Table 1. Production values from mined and revegetated areas equal to or greater than the comparable values from unmined areas denote successful revegetation at 5 years of age in relation to the ecological production potentials on similar undisturbed areas.

Similar tabular summaries of estimated amounts of forage produced were generated from the interactive and additive components of the model for forage production by introduced species. The amounts of forage produced on revegetated areas by introduced species are estimated to be 12.53 percent higher than those produced by native species. This is not surprising if one stops to realize that introduced plant species have generally received substantially more agronomic attention as a source of range forage improvement in the West than have native species.

Plant Cover Density Model for Mined Areas

Procedures for modeling the density of plant cover on mined areas were similar to those used to model forage production. Two interactive models, one for revegetated areas characterized predominantly by native species and the other for areas dominated by introduced species, were generated, relating annual precipitation, age of vegetation, and growing season to plant cover density. These interactive relations for mined areas revegetated with native species are illustrated by the response surfaces shown in Fig. 4 (See appendix, Equation 4).

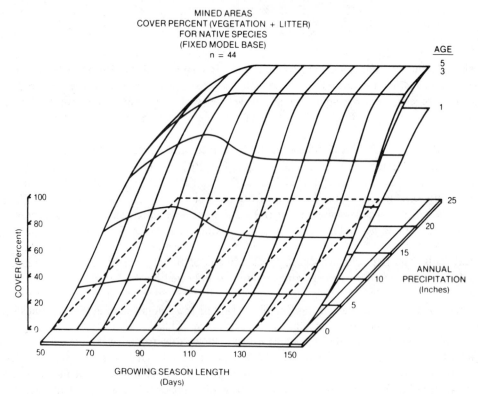

Fig. 4.   Effects of annual precipitation, growing season length, and age of planting on vegetative cover density of mined and revegetated sites on coal surface mines.

Plant cover density increased with increasing amounts of annual precipitation and with increasing age of vegetation to about 5 years. It was also greatest at an intermediate growing season length of about 85 days. Selected values of annual precipitation and growing season length were utilized in the equation for this interactive model, together with the additive effects of selected values of soil potassium, sodium, and pH content and the additive effects of the revegetation treatment--all to estimate the plant cover densities expected at 5 years of age on surface-mined areas revegetated with predominantly native species.

A sample portion of the plant cover density tables developed from these estimates is shown in Table 4.

Table 4. Effects of climatic factors, spoil properties, and revegetation treatments on density of plant cover developed from predominantly native species (percent).

Constant parameters per block: GS = 85, K = 200, NA = 150, PH = 6. Three cover columns correspond to PR = 5, 15, and 25.

TIL	SM	TPS	FER	IRR	MUL	ST	% Cover (PR 5)	% Cover (PR 15)	% Cover (PR 25)
X							18	87	100
	X						14	84	100
		X					16	86	100
			X				24	94	100
				X			29	99	100
					X		19	88	100
						X	33	100	100
X	X						12	82	100
X		X					12	82	100
X			X				20	90	100
X				X			25	95	100
X					X		15	84	100
X						X	29	99	100
	X	X					8	78	96
	X		X				22	92	100
	X			X			27	97	100
	X				X		17	86	100
	X					X	31	100	100
		X	X				11	80	98
		X		X			35	100	100
		X			X		25	94	100
		X				X	39	100	100
			X	X			18	88	100
			X		X		30	99	100
			X			X	44	100	100
				X	X		24	93	100
				X		X	34	100	100
					X	X	13	82	100
X	X	X					28	97	100
X	X		X				18	88	100
X	X			X			23	93	100
X	X				X		13	82	100
X	X					X	27	97	100
X		X	X				7	76	94
X		X		X			31	100	100
X		X			X		21	90	100
X		X				X	35	100	100
X			X	X			15	84	100
X			X		X		26	95	100
X			X			X	40	100	100
X				X	X		20	89	100
X				X		X	30	99	100
X					X	X	9	79	96
	X	X	X				24	93	94
	X	X		X			33	100	100
	X	X			X		23	92	100
	X	X				X	37	100	100
	X		X	X			17	86	100
	X		X		X		28	97	100

The plant cover density values in this table can be compared with the appropriate density values for unmined areas summarized in Table 2. Plant cover density values from mined and revegetated areas equal to or greater than the comparable values from unmined areas denote successful revegetation at 5 years of age in relation to the ecological potential for plant cover density development on comparable undisturbed areas.

Similar tabular summaries of estimated plant cover densities were generated from the interactive and additive components of the plant cover density model for introduced species. The plant cover densities developed on revegetated areas by native species are about 6.46 percent higher than the densities developed by introduced species. In contrast to the superiority of introduced species for producing forage, native species appear able to provide somewhat better protective ground cover. Thus, both kinds of vegetation have an important role in determining the productive and protective characteristics of revegetated coal mine spoils in the western United States.

DISCUSSION

The primary objectives of this investigation were to develop capabilities for predicting the degree of revegetation success to be expected under a wide variety of climatic conditions, soil and spoil properties, and revegetation treatments, utilizing site-specific revegetation data and information from most of the major coal surface mines in the interior West. This investigation shows that practical criteria for measuring revegetation success, namely, the amount of forage produced and the density of plant cover developed, are affected significantly by at least two major climatic factors that are not readily susceptible to alteration; by three properties of spoil materials that are subject to limited modification through management; by seven revegetation treatments, each of which provides at least two management choices; and by the age of the vegetation. These characteristics account for about one-half to three-fourths of the variances in forage production and plant cover density.

Lest the reader be quick to discount as unimpressive these amounts of accountable variance, they are, in fact, surprisingly large in view of the necessary exclusion from the investigation of other site factors that probably exert important effects on the amount of forage produced and the density of plant cover developed. Information about some of these other factors, such as depths of tillage and planting, kinds and amounts of fertilizer applied, amounts and frequencies of irrigation water used, and kinds and amounts of mulch applied, are simply not existent on any uniformly recorded basis from mine-to-mine or from year-to-year. Further, with limited data due to limited revegetation efforts, the short time period in which revegetation has been under way on western coal spoils, and the wide differences in treatments and their application by different operators--all superimposed on different climatic and soil characteristics--substantial confounding occurs between effects of the variables considered. Accordingly, the estimates developed in this investigation should be used with highly cautious optimism. Caution is warranted because of the necessary exclusion of some important factors and the confounding caused by limited information about some of the included factors. Conversely, optimism is warranted because the information from this investigation is the best available. The information reflects results of revegetation efforts on most of the major western coal mines. Finally, as mining progresses over the next 5 to 10 years, a much greater reservoir of data and information about revegetation potentials and limitations will be developed. This new knowledge can and should be used to revise, refine, and improve the kinds of relations developed by this investigation.

REFERENCES

Jensen, C.E. 1973. Matchacurve-3: multiple-component and multidimensional mathematical models for natural resource studies. USDA For. Serv. Res. Pap. INT-146, Intermt. For. and Range Expt. Sta., Ogden, Utah., 42 p.

Jensen, C.E. 1976. Matchacurve-4: segmented mathematical descriptors for asymmetric curve forms. U.S.D.A. For. Serv. Res. Pap. INT-182, Intermt. For. and Range Expt. Sta., Ogden, Utah, 16 p.

Jensen, C.E. and J.W. Homeyer. 1970. Matchacurve-1 for algebraic transforms to describe sigmoid- or bell-shaped curves. U.S.D.A. For. Serv., Intermt. For. and Range Expt. Sta., Ogden, Utah, 22 p.

Jensen, C.E. and J.W. Homeyer. 1971. Matchacurve-2 for algebraic transforms to describe curves of class X^n. U.S.D.A. For. Serv. Res. Pap. INT-106, Intermt. For. and Range Expt. Sta., Ogden, Utah, 39 p.

APPENDIX

EQUATIONS AND SUPPLEMENTAL TABLES FOR USE IN ESTIMATING FORAGE PRODUCTION AND PLANT COVER DENSITY

The figures and partial tables presented in this paper are useful as an aid in understanding the relations described by the models for predicting forage production and plant cover density. They are not particularly effective, however, as a tool for generating such predictions. The equations for the interactive portions of these models and the associated lists of the additive components, both of which are needed to predict useful values of forage production and plant cover density, follow. Statistics pertinent to each prediction model follow the equations and associated lists (Table 5).

1. Unmined areas: forage production (lbs/acre, dry wt.), cover density (percent) = f (annual precipitation, growing season, potassium).

    a. Forage production model equation.   (Equation 1)

$$\widehat{\text{Production}} = \left\{ \frac{YP1}{(25)^n} \, (PR)^N \right\} * 0.94584$$

$$N = 1.8 - 0.56 * e^{-\left| \frac{\frac{(180-GS)}{106} - 1}{0.3} \right|^{3.8}}$$

If $GS \le 87$

$$YP1 = YPFL + 560 * e^{-\left| \frac{\frac{K}{450} - 1}{0.6} \right|^{18}}$$

$$YPFL = 1570 + 1060 * e^{-\left| \frac{\frac{GS}{86.6} - 1}{0.12} \right|^{4}}$$

If $GS > 87$

$$YP2 = 1700 + (YP1 - 1700) * e^{-\left| \frac{\frac{(180-GS)}{93.4} - 1}{0.09} \right|^{3}}$$

LIMITS

$\quad 5 \le PR \le 25$ $\qquad$ PR = annual precipitation, inches
$\quad 50 \le GS \le 180$ $\qquad$ GS = growing seasons, days
$\quad 0 \le K \le 450$ $\qquad$ K = potassium, p/m

b.   Plant cover density model equation.   (Equation 2)

$$\widehat{Cover} = YP * \left\{ \frac{e^{-\left|\frac{\frac{PR}{25} - 1}{(1-I)}\right|^5} - e^{-\left|\frac{1}{(1-I)}\right|^5}}{1 - e^{-\left|\frac{1}{(1-I)}\right|^5}} \right\} * 0.97917$$

$$YP = YPFL + YPAD$$

$$YPFL = 80 + 20 * e^{-\left|\frac{\frac{GS}{180} - 1}{0.46}\right|^{15}}$$

$$YPAD = \left\{ 9 * e^{-\left|\frac{\frac{K}{400} - 1}{0.43}\right|^{15}} \right\} * \left\{ 1 - e^{-\left|\frac{\frac{GS}{180} - 1}{0.46}\right|^{15}} \right\}$$

$$YP = YPFL + YPAD$$

$$I = 0.14 + 0.285 * e^{-\left|\frac{\frac{GS}{180} - 1}{0.46}\right|^{15}}$$

LIMITS

$5 \le PR \le 25$	PR = annual precipitation, inches
$50 \le GS \le 180$	GS = growing season, days
$0 \le K \le 450$	K = potassium, p/m

2. Mined areas: forage production (lbs/acre, dry wt.), cover density (percent) = f_1 (annual precipitation, growing season, age of planting) + f_2 (soil, potassium, sodium, pH, and 7 revegetation treatments).

    a.   Forage production model.

        (1) Interactive component equation.   (Equation 3)

$$\hat{Production} = 0.0061896 * YPPR * YPGS * (PR)^{1.6} * \begin{vmatrix} \text{Spp.} \\ 1.04368 \ \text{(native)} \\ 1.17448 \ \text{(introduced)} \end{vmatrix}$$

$$YPPR = e^{-\left|\frac{\frac{AGE}{7} - 1}{0.9}\right|^{4.6}}$$

If GS ≤ 85

$$YPGS = 940 + 2510 * e^{-\left|\frac{\frac{GS}{85} - 1}{0.16}\right|^{4}}$$

If GS > 85

$$YPGS = 2250 + 1200 * e^{-\left|\frac{\frac{GS}{85} - 1}{0.12}\right|^{4}}$$

LIMITS

    $5 \leq PR \leq 25$ PR = annual precipitation, inches
   $50 \leq GS \leq 180$ GS = growing season, days
    $0 \leq AGE \leq 7$ AGE = age of planting, years

        (2) Additive component list.

Component	Additive forage production (lbs/acre)	
	Native	Introduced
Soil potassium (K)	[1]+5.4	[1]+4.1
Soil sodium (Na)	[1]-0.1	[1]-1.4
Soil pH	[2]+117.9	[2]+143.4
Tillage (TIL)	+13.0	-308.0
Seeding method (SM)		
broadcast	0	0
drilled	+341.0	-783.0
Topsoil (TPS)	-83.0	+99.0
Fertilizer (FER)	+369.0	+430.0
Irrigation (IRR)	+35.0	+418.0
Mulching (MUL)	-178.0	+160.0
Seeding time (ST)		
spring	0	0
fall	+335.0	-78.0
Intercept	[3]-2216.0	[3]-1181.0

[1] Multiply these production values by parts per million of soil component (potassium or sodium).
[2] Multiply these production values by pH units of soil acidity.
[3] These intercept values must be added.

b. Plant cover density model.

   (1) Interactive component equation.   (Equation 4)

$$\widehat{Cover} = YP * \left\{ \frac{e^{-\left|\frac{\frac{PR}{26}-1}{1-I}\right|^{N}} - e^{-\left|\frac{1}{1-I}\right|^{N}}}{1 - e^{-\left|\frac{1}{1-I}\right|^{N}}} \right\} * \left.\begin{matrix} 0.95387 & (\text{native}) \\ 0.89595 & (\text{introduced}) \end{matrix}\right\} \quad \text{Spp.}$$

Where

$$N = 1 + NYP * (1.1397 * e^{-\left|\frac{\frac{AGE}{10}-1}{0.88}\right|^{5.8}} - 0.1397)$$

$$NYP = 1.8 + e^{-\left|\frac{\frac{(180-GS)}{180}-1}{0.52}\right|^{15}}$$

$$I = 0.38 + (IYP/10) * AGE$$

$$IYP = 0.29 * e^{-\left|\frac{\frac{GS}{180}-1}{0.5105}\right|^{12}} - 0.2$$

$$YP = YPGS * \left\{ \frac{e^{-\left|\frac{\frac{(AGE+1)}{10}-1}{(1-IGS)}\right|^{10}} - e^{-\left|\frac{1}{(1-IGS)}\right|^{10}}}{1 - e^{-\left|\frac{1}{(1-IGS)}\right|^{10}}} \right\}$$

$$YPGS = 100 * e^{-\left|\frac{\frac{GS}{180}-1}{0.78}\right|^{8}}$$

$$IGS = 0.1 + 0.23 * e^{-\left|\frac{\frac{(180-GS)}{180}-1}{0.36}\right|^{6.5}}$$

LIMITS

$5 \le PR \le 25$ PR = annual precipitation, inches
$50 \le GS \le 180$ GS = growing season, days
$0 \le AGE \le 10$ AGE = age of planting, years

(2) Additive component list.

Component	Additive plant cover density (percent)	
	Native	Introduced
Soil potassium (K)	[1]0.0892	[1]0.0205
Soil sodium (Na)	[1]-0.0186	[1]0.0093
Soil pH	[2]-4.2	[2]+7.6
Tillage (TIL)	-3.9	-10.0
Seeding method (SM)		
broadcast	0	0
drilled	-1.8	+1.0
Topsoil (TPS)	+6.0	+0.4
Fertilizer (FER)	+11.2	+30.9
Irrigation (IRR)	+0.6	+15.0
Mulching (MUL)	+15.2	+4.8
Seeding time (ST)		
spring	0	0
fall	-5.6	+19.0
Intercept	[3]+12.9	[3]-74.3

[1]Multiply these density (percent) values by parts per million of soil component (potassium or sodium).
[2]Multiply these density values by pH units of soil acidity.
[3]These intercept values must be added.

3. Statistics pertinent to each model (Table 5).

Table 5.   Statistics pertinent to each model.

Prediction Model	Statistic		
	Number of transects (n)	Coefficient of determination (R^2)	Standard error of estimate ($S_{y.x}$)
Forage production on unmined areas	83	0.545	356 lbs/acre
Plant cover density on unmined areas	83	.785	13.1 percent
Forage production on mined and revegetated areas			
native vegetation	44	.685	380 lbs/acre
introduced vegetation	33	.735	547 lbs/acre
Plant cover density on mined and revegetated areas			
native vegetation	44	.666	17.5 percent
introduced vegetation	33	.615	19.2 percent

COMPUTERIZED RECLAMATION PLANNING SYSTEM
FOR NORTHERN GREAT PLAINS SURFACE COAL MINES

*M. Douglas Scott**

INTRODUCTION

During the last decade much surface mining for coal has developed in the Northern Great Plains of the U.S. - a region covering 63 counties in Montana, Wyoming, South Dakota, and North Dakota (U.S. Dept. of the Interior 1975:vii). In response to this rapid growth in mining activity and the possible adverse environmental conditions that might result, a multitude of reclamation-related research projects has been initiated by scientists in colleges, state and federal government, and industry. The research covers all of the major environmental divisions - climatic, edaphic, hydrologic, biologic, and socioeconomic, and is published in various books, symposia, scientific journals, leaflets, Agricultural Experiment Station bulletins, and Government Printing Office mimeographs (Honkala 1974, Bituminous Coal Research, Inc. 1975, Boyd and Schilinger 1977, University of Arizona 1977).

The desired final recipients (and hopefully, users) of all the information generated by research projects is the mine reclamation manager and his staff. Since the size of the total reclamation management staff at a large surface coal mine generally ranges only from one to five persons, it is obvious that these people cannot obtain and digest, much less evaluate and integrate, all of the reclamation information available to them. This is especially so considering that they must spend most of their time supervising and evaluating applied reclamation in the field, as well as obtaining the necessary legal permits and performing environmental impact studies.

The answer to this "technology transfer" problem lies in the development of a computerized reclamation planning system, the need for which was described several years ago (Wali 1975). This paper outlines the development at Montana State University of such a system, called CLAIM, which will summarize the relevant reclamation data, and encourage the reclamation manager to quickly analyze the options available to him before he makes a final reclamation plan.

CHARACTERISTICS AND LIMITATIONS OF SYSTEM

The current system is limited to the environmental conditions of only the Northern Great Plains Coal Province. It may be used for either of the region's two main surface mining techniques - dragline type strip mines, and shovel and truck area mines.

*Institute of Applied Research, Montana State University, Bozeman, MT 59717.

It must be emphasized that this is a system for planning the most efficient reclamation goals and techniques, and not an environmental impact monitoring or control system. It is assumed that required environmental impact studies have been performed, and that mining of the area is deemed feasible by the company and regulatory agencies.

This system is "goal oriented," in that all reclamation plans should be directed toward a final land use goal (National Academy of Sciences 1974, Dick and Thirgood 1975). On the basis of logic and new Federal reclamation laws which, happily, are nearly the same in this instance, five major land use goals are identified in the system. These are: (1) cropland (including grain and hayland); (2) native vegetation (primarily native range, but can include riparian and upland woodlands); (3) wildlife habitat (for both game and nongame species); (4) outdoor recreation (primarily water-oriented); (5) intensive human use (including the construction of foundations for homes, businesses, and roads). A sixth, optional goal, which may be entered by the user, is also allowed by the system.

The primary inputs to the reclamation system are "critical operations and environmental data" (see Appendix for a current list of these data). The data items were selected on the basis of literature surveys and field experience, and are deemed to be *absolutely essential* in determining if the area, after mining, can be reclaimed to one of the major land uses. The proof of "absolutely essential" data is based on two criteria: (a) much research throughout the Northern Great Plains has shown the parameter(s) to be definitely harmful or helpful in establishing a final land use; (b) research has been done whereby the quantity or quality of the parameter(s) has been modified, and a definite, repeatable response on the part of the land use material (such as vegetation) has been observed. A good example of this type of datum is soil salinity. Highly saline (electrical conductivity of greater than 16 mmhos per cm) spoils are known to be very limiting to plant growth. By burying these materials under nontoxic soil materials, this inhibitor of plant survival can be eliminated.

The critical data listed in the Appendix were gleaned from an extensive literature survey, but primarily came from major review papers. Some of the more comprehensive sources used were: (a) climatology - George (1971), Skidmore and Woodruff (1968), Woodruff and Siddoway (1965), and Woodruff et al. (1977); (b) soils-overburden - Anonymous (1977), Cook et al. (1974), Hodder (1975), Omodt et al. (1975), Power et al. (1976), and Sandoval et al. (1973); (c) Hydrology - Hardaway et al. (1977), USDI Geological Survey (1974), Van Voast (1974), Van Voast and Hedges (1975), and Van Voast et al. (1977); (d) biological factors - Dollhopf and Majerus (1975), Donovan et al. (1976), May et al. (1971), National Academy of Sciences (1974), Packer (1974), and U.S. Department of Agriculture (1975); (e) socioeconomic factors - LaFevers and Imhoff (1977), National Academy of Sciences (1974), and Williams (1975). Most of the operations-related critical data are based on the author's experience in the mining industry, and are his responsibility alone. The critical data list is subject to modification as new research results become available.

For reclamation planning purposes, it is necessary that the critical data be collected from reasonably homogeneous tracts of land. This means that each pre-mining planning unit be fairly uniform with respect to topography, soils, and vegetation (e.g., the plan for a small alluvial valley would be different from an upland range site). The planning units may well coincide with the 6-month to 1-year mining plan, and may be from 40 to 100 acres in size.

SYSTEM OUTPUT

The reclamation system is designed to be operated on a privately owned minicomputer, or a larger time-shared machine, with output displayed on a cathode ray tube terminal and a high speed line printer. The major output features are as follows:

Feasibility Ranking Unit

Within the system, each critical environmental parameter is broken down into logical categories - usually based on literature sources. Each category can then be ranked by a simple numerical system according to generally how feasible it would be to return a parcel of land with that environmental condition back to one of the main land uses. The reclamation manager may insert his own rank values in the system, or he may rely on the default ranking values already programmed (see Table 1 for an example of the ranking

TABLE 1 Sample Feasibility Ranking System

	Value Observed	Cropl.	Native Veg.	Wildl.	Recr.	Int. Use	Other
A.	Average Total Annual Precip. (in.)						
	1.　 5 - 10	1	1	1	1	1	-
	2.　10.1 - 15	1	2	2	2	2	-
X	3.　15.1 - 20	3	3	2	2	1	-
	4.　20.1 - 25	3	3	2	2	1	-
B.	Topsoil Sodium Adsorption Ratio (meq/L)						
	1.　.1 - 4.9	3	3	3	3	3	-
	2.　5.0 - 9.9	2	2	2	2	2	-
	3.　10.0 - 14.9	1	1	2	1	2	-
X	4.　15.0 +	0	2	2	2	1	-
	Total Value Observed	3	5	4	4	2	-
	Average Value Observed	1.5	2.5	2.0	2.0	1	-

system). The 5 ranking numbers are based on *relative* expectations of success, given a certain environmental condition. They are: 0 - no expectation of success - such as growing grain crops on 30° slopes; 1 - negative expectation of success - such as growing crops on 11° slopes; 2 - neutral expectation of success - such as growing crops on 5° slopes; 3 - positive expectation of success - growing crops on flat land; 4 - must achieve that goal (required by reclamation laws) - such as the pre-mining presence of "prime agricultural lands."

The feasibility system is designed to sum and average the ranking values for the appropriate categories observed for all of the critical environmental parameters in the Appendix. For the two hypothetical environmental conditions and rankings in Table 1, native vegetation (average value 2.5) is the most feasible land use option. This is followed by wildlife and recreation, then cropland, and lastly, intensive human use.

There are two main assumptions in the feasibility system. One is that all of the environmental parameters are of equal importance to the reclamation effort. This is not always true, but data showing the exact importance of each parameter are lacking. The second assumption is that, generally, the most feasible reclamation option is the pre-mining land use; but, the spoil is a resource, and almost any land use can be developed (within legal constraints) if enough effort and money is spent.

Basic Methods and Cost Unit

The most environmentally feasible reclamation option may not always be the most economical, so a second feature of the reclamation system is to produce a set of preferred methods, and costs of each, for each of the five land use options. The preferred methods are related to the given set of environmental conditions by a detailed set of programmed assumptions which, in turn, are based on proven field techniques reported in the literature. Two examples of these assumptions would be: (1) final graded slopes greater than 6° - cropland not established; (2) SAR value of surface soil greater than 16, and a more suitable soil material available - bury the high SAR soil.

Table 2 shows a comparison of the reclamation methods and costs for three land use options. Costs are based on data by Luft and Schaefer (1977), Morey and Draffin (1977), and Smith (1976), as well as author's personal experience and interviews with mining personnel.

TABLE 2   Comparison of Methods and Costs for Three Reclamation Options (Dragline Mine)

	Ave. Costs Per Acre ($)		
Reclamation Method	Wildlife[1]	Cropland A[2]	Cropland B[3]
Rehandle Spoil 20%	-	-	$ 4,356.00
Grade Spoil	$ 656.25	$ 837.97	837.97
Strip and Replace 1.5 ft. Topsoil	2,178.00	2,904.00	2,904.00
Stabilize Topsoil Pile	47.57	63.43	63.43
Rip 3 ft. Centers	337.50	450.00	450.00
Chisel Plow	10.50	10.50	10.50
Disc and Harrow	3.75	3.75	3.75
Drill Seed	2.80	3.75	3.75
Buy Seed	40.00	40.00	40.00
Drill Fertilizer	.75	1.00	1.00
Buy Fertilizer	16.00	6.80	6.80
Hydromulch, Seed, Fertilizer	100.00	-	-
Hay Mulching	22.50	30.00	30.00
Purchase Hay Mulch	28.12	37.50	37.50
Buy, Apply Herbicide	2.75	2.75	2.75
Snow Fence	8.25	8.25	8.25
Animal Fencing	40.00	40.00	40.00
TOTAL	$ 3,496.74	$ 4,439.70	$ 8,795.70
15% Administration	524.21	665.96	1,319.36
GRAND TOTAL/ACRE	$ 4,018.95	$ 5,105.66	$10,115.06

[1] Final slopes of $19°$ (25%), $11.5°$ (50%), and $1°$ (25%)
[2] Final slopes of $5.7°$ (50%), $1°$ (50%)
[3] Same conditions as cropland A, but a toxic spoil layer has to be buried by re-handle.

From Table 2 it is apparent that spoil and topsoil handling are the major reclamation costs, and that land uses which minimize these factors, such as wildlife management, are more economical to create. When a special problem arises from a toxic spoil layer that has to be rehandled (Table 2 - "Cropland B"), the reclamation cost escalates markedly.

The grading costs in Table 2 include default values for a standard "wildlife mix" and "cropland mix" of final slopes. However, the CLAIM system contains a major grading subroutine that allows the manager to insert data pertaining to his mine, and he can then receive output telling what his projected grading costs would be for a variety of final slope conditions. Figure 1 is one example of these outputs.

FUTURE SYSTEM DEVELOPMENTS

In the future, this system will make use of a digitizing tablet, which will allow the reclamation manager to sketch his desired final topography on a map so that it blends in with nearby undisturbed land features, and he will receive as output an estimate of the total volume of spoil and total grading cost for achieving that landform.

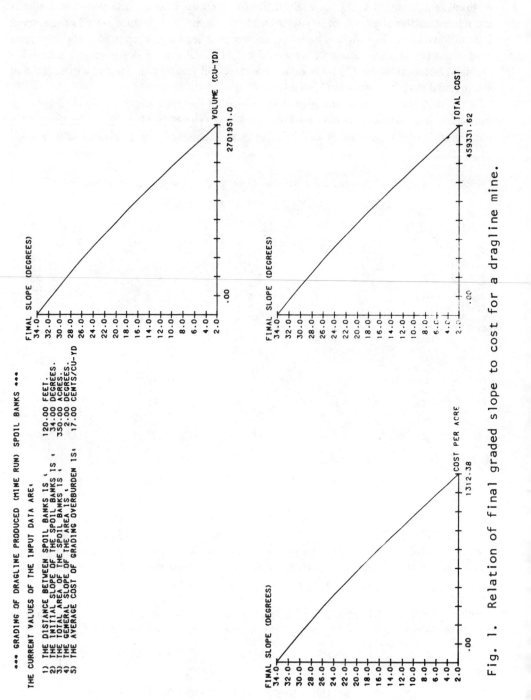

Fig. l.   Relation of final graded slope to cost for a dragline mine.

The system is being designed to interface with a mine planning system developed at Montana State University (Gibson et al. 1977, 1979). The reclamation system will analyze the mine plan output (particularly the spoil handling techniques), and will determine if the mine is reclaimable for a desired land use option. If not, a new mine plan is requested. Likewise, if a certain reclamation option is so expensive that it makes the total venture uneconomical, the mine plan system will be able to request a new reclamation option.

ACKNOWLEDGMENTS

Funds and computing facilities for this project were provided through a cooperative agreement between the Montana State University Institute of Applied Research and the U.S. Forest Service Intermountain Forest and Range Experiment Station, Surface Environment and Mining (SEAM) program. Mr. Steve Eastman did the initial programming for this project.

REFERENCES

Anonymous. 1977. North Dakota progress report on research on reclamation of strip-mined lands - update 1977. U.S.D.A. Agric. Res. Ser. and N. Dakota Agric. Expt. Sta., Mandan, ND., 26 p.

Bituminous Coal Research, Inc. (Compiler). 1975. Reclamation of Coal-Mined Land. A bibliography with abstracts. National Coal Assoc. Bituminous Coal Research, Inc., Monroeville, PA, 188 p.

Boyd, C. and L. Schillinger (Compilers). 1977. Energy research information system. Old West Regional Commission, Billings, MT, 2(4):98.

Cook, C.W., R.M. Hyde and P.L. Sims. 1974. Revegetation guidelines for surface mined areas. Range Sci. Ser. 16, Colorado State Univ., Ft. Collins, 73 p.

Dick, J.H. and J.V. Thirgood. 1975. Development of land reclamation in British Columbia. pp. 65-78, In M.K. Wali (ed.), Practices and Problems of Land Reclamation in Western North America, Univ. North Dakota Press, Grand Forks.

Dollhopf, D.J. and M.E. Majerus. 1975. Strip mine reclamation research located at Decker Coal Company, Decker, MT, Montana State Univ., Animal and Range Sci. Dept., 42 p.

Donovan, R.P., R.M. Felder, and H.H. Rogers. 1976. Vegetative stabilization of mineral waste heaps. U.S. Environmental Protection Agency, Off. Research and Develop., 306 p.

George, E.J. 1971. Effect of tree windbreaks and slat barriers on wind velocity and crop yields. U.S. Dept. Agric. Production Res. Rpt. 121, 23 p.

Gibson, D.F., E. Mooney and G.A. Sattoriva. 1977. A minicomputer system for planning surface mining operations. pp. 211-219, In Proc. Systems Engineering Conf. Kansas City.

Gibson, D.F., T.E. Lehman and E.L. Mooney. 1979. Interactive computerized planning of surface coal mining operations. In M.K. Wali (ed.), Ecology and Coal Resource Development, Pergamon Press, NY. (this volume).

Hardaway, J.E., D.B. Kimball, S.F. Lindsay, J. Schmidt and L. Erickson. 1977. Subirrigated alluvial valley floors. pp. 61-135, In Natl. Coal Assoc./Bituminous Coal Res., Inc. 5th Symp. Surface Mining and Reclamation, Louisville, KY.

Hodder, R.L. 1975. Montana reclamation problems and remedial techniques. pp. 90-106, In M.K.Wali (ed.), Practices and Problems of Land Reclamation in Western North America, Univ. North Dakota Press, Grand Forks.

Honkala, R.A. (Compiler). 1974. Surface mining and mined land reclamation. A selected bibliography. The Old West Regional Commission, Washington, DC., 154 p.

LaFevers, J.R. and E.A. Imhoff. 1977. Land use planning in surface mine areas. pp. 311-317, In Natl. Coal Assoc./Bituminous Coal Res., Inc., 5th Symp. Surface Mining and Reclamation, Louisville, KY.

Luft, L.D. and J. Schaefer. 1977. Custom rates for farm work in Montana. Coop. Ext. Service Circular 242, Montana State Univ., Bozeman, 8 p.

May, M., R. Lang, L. Lujan, P. Jacoby and W. Thompson. 1971. Reclamation of strip mine spoil banks in Wyoming, Univ. Wyoming Agric. Expt. Sta. Res. J. 51, 32 p.

Morey, P. and C.W. Draffin. 1977. Surface coal mine evaluation and equipment selection. pp. 136-175, In Natl. Coal Assoc./Bituminous Coal Res. Inc., 5th Symp. Surface Mining and Reclamation, Louisville, KY.

National Academy of Sciences. 1974. Rehabilitation Potential of Western Coal Lands. J.B. Lippincott, Cambridge, MA, 198 p.

Omodt, H.W., F.W. Schroer and D.D. Patterson. 1975. The properties of important agricultural soils as criteria for mined land reclamation. Agric. Expt. Sta. Bull. 492, North Dakota State Univ., Fargo, 52 p.

Packer, P.E. 1974. Rehabilitation potentials and limitations of surface mined land in the Northern Great Plains. U.S.D.A. Forest Service Gen. Tech. Rpt. INT-14, 44 p.

Power, J.F., R.E. Ries, and F.M. Sandoval. 1976. Use of soil materials on spoil - effects of thickness and quality. Farm Research 34(1):23-24.

Sandoval, F.M., J.J. Bond, J.F. Power and W.O. Willis. 1973. Lignite mine spoils in the Northern Great Plains - characteristics and potential for reclamation. pp. 1-24, In M.K. Wali (ed.), Some Environmental Aspects of Strip Mining in North Dakota. Educ. Ser. 5, N.D. Geol. Surv., Grand Forks.

Skidmore, E.L. and N.P. Woodruff. 1968. Wind erosion forces in the United States and their use in predicting soil loss. U.S. Dept. Agric., Agric. Res. Serv. Agric. Handb. 346, 42 p.

Smith, C.M. 1976. Fertilizer guide. Grass-legume nonirrigated. Montana State Univ., Coop. Ext. Serv. Fert. Guide AG 55.610:03, 2 p.

University of Arizona (Compiler). 1977. SEAMALERT. Current surface mined reclamation literature alerting service. Univ. of Arizona Off. of Arid Lands Studies, Tucson, Arizona, 11:88.

U.S. Department of Agriculture. 1975. Guide to rehabilitating surface mined land in the west. U.S.D.A. Forest Service Intermountain Forest and Range Expt. Sta. Ogden, Utah, 13 chapters.

U.S. Department of the Interior Geological Survey. 1974. Shallow groundwater in selected areas in the Fort Union Coal region. Open-file Rpt. 74-48, Helena, MT, 72 p. + Appen.

U.S. Department of the Interior. 1975. Water for energy in the Northern Great Plains area with emphasis on the Yellowstone River Basin. Water for Energy Management Team, 7 Chapters (Mimeo).

Van Voast, W.A. 1974. Hydrologic effects of strip coal mining in southeastern Montana - emphasis: one year of mining near Decker. State of Montana Bur. Mines and Geology Bull. 93, 24 p.

Van Voast, W.A. and R.B. Hedges. 1975. Hydrogeologic aspects of existing and proposed strip coal mines near Decker, southeastern Montana. State of Montana Bur. Mines and Geology Bull. 97, 31 p.

Van Voast, W.A., R.B. Hedges and J.J. McDermott. 1977. Hydrogeologic conditions and projections related to mining near Colstrip, southeastern Montana. State of Montana Bur. Mines and Geology Bull. 102, 43 p.

Wali, M.K. 1975. The problem of land reclamation viewed in a systems context. pp. 1-17, In M.K. Wali (ed.), Practices and Problems of Land Reclamation in Western North America. Univ. North Dakota Press, Grand Forks.

Williams, A.S. 1975. Anticipated effects of major coal development on public services, costs, and revenues in six selected counties. Montana State Univ. Agric. Expt. Sta. Res. Rpt. 82, 143 p.

Woodruff, N.P. and F.H. Siddoway. 1965. A wind erosion equation. Proc. Soil Sci. Soc. Amer. 29:602-608.

Woodruff, N.P., L. Lyles, F.H. Siddoway and D.W. Fryrear. 1977. How to control wind erosion. U.S. Dept. Agric. Res. Serv. Agric. Infor. Bull. 34, 23 p.

APPENDIX

Critical Data Inputs

I. Operations Data

    A. Average slope of 10 random points

    B. Stage in mining sequence (opening cut, etc.)

    C. Dragline mine description

        1. Area of spoil banks

        2. Distance between spoil peaks

        3. Height of spoil banks

        4. Initial slope of spoil banks

        5. Average slope of mining surface

        6. Average cost of grading spoil

        7. Final slopes desired

    D. Shovel and truck mine description

        1. Cubic yds. of rehandle

        2. Cost per cubic yd. for rehandle

        3. Highwall heights

        4. Highwall lengths

        5. Highwall angles

        6. Final slopes desired

        7. Final benches desired

        8. Total acres of spoil

        9. Cost per cubic yd. to grade spoil

II. Environmental Data

    A. Climatology

        1. Average total annual precipitation

    2. Average annual wind velocity
    3. Average annual evapotranspiration

B. Topsoil and Subsoil (Separately)

    1. Thickness
    2. Percent organic matter
    3. Texture
    4. Structure
    5. Bulk density
    6. Salinity
    7. Sodium adsorption ratio
    8. Available nitrogen
    9. Available phosphorus

C. Overburden (for each distinct unit)

    1. Number of boulders after mining
    2. Thickness
    3. Texture
    4. Bulk density
    5. Salinity
    6. Sodium Adsorption ratio
    7. Available nitrogen
    8. Available phosphorus

D. Surface water hydrology

    1. Type (perennial stream, lake, etc.)
    2. Amount available for appropriation
    3. Index of dissection (miles of stream/acre)
    4. Index of meander
    5. Salinity
    6. Sodium adsorption ratio

E. Groundwater hydrology

    1. Depth of highest water table
    2. Amount available for appropriation
    3. Salinity
    4. Sodium adsorption ratio
    5. Presence of alluvial valley floor

F. Vegetation

    1. Broad community types

G. Wildlife

    1. Broad wildlife types

H. Socio-Economics

    1. Presence of historic or archaeologic sites
    2. Primary present land use
    3. Secondary present land use
    4. Future land use desire - surface owner
    5. Future land use desire - communities
    6. Future land use desire - govt. agencies

THE DIVERSIFIED RECLAMATION PROGRAM AT SOUTHWESTERN ILLINOIS COAL CORPORATION

Robert W. Holloway *

Coal mining, particularly surface mining and the new land reclamation techniques, are becoming an integral part of the coal mining process. Surface mining is no newcomer to the gently-rolling counties of southern Illinois approximately 112 km southeast of St. Louis where Southwestern Illinois Coal Corporation (hereafter referred as Southwestern) operates two surface mines, The Captain Mine and the Streamline Mine. In fact, although coal mining is better known for its historical and social perspectives in the eastern Appalachian states, coal actually has had a very colorful and interesting history in Southern Illinois.

The first surface mine in the U.S. opened up approximately 256 km northeast of Southwestern's mines in 1866. Since that time the solid, relatively level seams of Herrin 6 and Harrisburg No. 5 coal, predominant in Illinois, have been stripped in ever increasing quantities with larger ever-more efficient machinery. In total, approximately 85,020 ha of Illinois land have been surface-mined in the past 112 years. Compared to residential expansion, highway corridors and other developments, that really is not much when one considers that of the 40,486 ha of Illinois farmland that are lost annually to different types of development, only 5% are lost temporarily because of surface mining. But, unlike Appalachia, where many mines are relatively small, Illinois has only 45 surface mines, all of them large, with an average annual permit of about 142 ha, and production averaging over one million tons per mine. Only recently, surface mining has contributed significantly to local and regional concerns about appropriate land use and maintaining a balanced mix between energy and agriculture production. Early surface mining methods, which consisted only of cut and fill techniques, resulted in a vast rolling moonscape of sometimes barren but always rather unproductive, deeply sloped land. Fifty years ago, when coal was less than $2.00 a ton, virtually no one thought about the social costs of reclaiming the land to its former productive use. But after World War I, Illinois coal production peaked, and when it became increasingly clear that Old King Coal was going to be a major source of fuel in the unforeseeable future, surface mining increased in acreage and surface mining equipment increased in size. New electric generating stations were being constructed up and down the Mississippi, Ohio, Illinois and Missouri Rivers at a rate commensurate with the American's growing thirst for electric power in the U.S. Strippable coal reserves became more in demand and the ratio between surface and deep mining became considerably closer to one another. People complained about the damage caused by strip mining, but no one was ready to legislate reclamation programs because of the resulting rural electrification programs and the relative invisibility and localized impact of mining. It was in response to this growing

*Southwestern Illinois Coal Corporation, 500 North Broadway, St. Louis, MO 63102.

electrical demand that Southwestern was formed in 1935. Purchasing a number of small properties around Cutler, Willisville, Percy and Steelville, in Randolph and Perry counties, Illinois, Southwestern began producing over 1,000,000 tons of coal per year in the vast No. 6 Seam approximately 12 m below the surface, with what was then a huge stripping machine - about 25 cubic yards.

The land in this part of Illinois is much less productive than that found in the central and northern part of the State. What Mother Nature provided in the form of virtually endless energy reservoir through the lower reaches of the Pennsylvanian System, the geologic structure in which the coal is found, she denied as great a bounty on the surface of the earth in the form of potential agricultural productivity. In addition to the coal in the Pennsylvanian System, the bedrock is overlain by shale, sandstone and limestone. The bedrock was covered by Illinoian period glaciers which left vast glacial till deposits, a mixture of clay, silt, sand, gravel and boulders. Till deposit varies in thickness from area to area, but is about 17 m thick. After the glacial ice period, a long period of weathering and soil formation on the Illinoian till plane ensued. The latter glacial period, the Wisconsonian, did not penetrate southward far enough to deposit till in Perry County; thus, the characteristics of the more productive farm fields of central and northern Illinois are not found as far south as Perry and Randolph counties. The loess which covered much of the Illinoian tilled plane and the soil that developed in it was blown from the floodplains from the swollen Mississippi and Missouri riverbeds. The loess is about a meter thick in level areas around the coal mine areas. A loamy zone occurs between the loess and the underlying glacial till throughout much of Perry and Randolph counties. This material is sandier than the loess and lacks many of the characteristics of the richer till and buried soil formed by it. This loamy material is approximately a meter and very high in clay content.

There are three major soil associations in Perry and Randolph counties, but only the relatively scarce Cisne-Hoyleton series has a dark surface color and a thick loess cover of up to 1 m or more with virtually no slope. Generally speaking, the slope in the areas of the mines is not more than 7-10% and the coal seam runs parallel to the surface virtually throughout the entire area. Still the principal characteristic of all of the soil associations in which mining takes place is that they have a very clayey subsoil layer. These soils absorb water slowly and rain tends to collect in depressions. This clay hardpan is impervious to water and is sticky and plastic when wet and very, very hard when dry. Root growth is thus restricted on unfertilized soils. Water movement from subsoils below is similarly restricted, where mineral content is higher than the surface, or "A" horizon.

For years, the farmers in these southern Illinois counties of Randolph, Perry and Williamson have tried to rattle, shake and poke through this hardpan realizing that mixing it up would provide much more freedom for root growth and considerably more potential for allowing these minerals below the clay to be better integrated, and thus more usable. These methods were almost never successful and consequently row crop productivity has never matched the other parts of the state which benefited from the Wisconsonian till and an absence of the claypan so close to the surface.

The first owners of Southwestern studied the geology of the soil as well as the coal and were socially conscientious enough to be aware that the potentially barren spoils could provide little use to anyone if not properly managed. A health 5-foot mantel of limestone has been the principal reason why there is so little acid mine drainage in the old surface mine spoils today and that water, a major resource in Southern Illinois, can be returned as a significant recreational and wildlife asset in the lakes formed by the final cut of the mining process. Southwestern began an aggressive tree planning program, one of the state's first real reclamation programs soon after their mining operations began in the late 1930's. The result today is a considerable and impressive stand of hardwood trees on land that was mined over 40 years ago. As mining methods became even more efficient, reclamation methods concentrated on trees and grazing land. The social conscience of the public and the price of coal simply did not demand as extensive a reclamation job as we find today. What with the price of coal never exceeding $4.00 a ton, it would seem hard to justify an expenditure to reclaim the land to equal its former productivity especially in southern Illinois. Illinois' first real reclamation law was in 1962, requiring that the tops of spoil banks be dozed off to maintain slope stability, and that ground cover be established. Southwestern's response had aesthetically been made decades earlier, but the more level grade was used to restore grazing acreage in the area.

Southwestern began Galum Creek Farms in 1961. Having now been in the area for over 25 years, a considerable amount of land had been put together for the coal reserve and it seemed natural that this land resource be fulfilled to this higher use. This, combined with the now maturing trees previously planted on the graded mine land, formed the gensis for what is today perhaps the most diversified comprehensive reclamation and coal development program in the Midwest.

In 1965 Southwestern began operation of its Marion Model 6360, destined to remain the world's largest stripping shovel. This towering earthmover, a mini-glacier in itself, can move 180 cubic yards of dirt with each bucket-full and was designed to simultaneously mine the No. 6 and No. 5 coal to depths of more than 30 m. In this coal bed, which is perhaps the most continuous flat strippable reserve east of the Mississippi River, this machine continues to dominate the horizon and new, exciting reclamation methods follow in its wake.

Southwestern today is the fourth largest coal producer in Illinois. Southwestern's original mine, now called the Streamline Mine, is the second oldest operating mine in Illinois. Interestingly enough, the Streamline Mine which is utilizing a 65 cubic yard shovel, combined with crosspit bucket wheel excavator, is now mining in the same land which was mined during the second decade of the mine's operation in the 1940's and 50's. Having mined the Herrin No. 6 coal during the early years of the operation the larger equipment is going back through and mining the No. 5 coal which lies anywhere from 4 to 14 m deeper than the No. 6. The neighboring Captain Mine, with the famed 6360 shovel, has recently added another dragline machine to boost production. Both mines now have an evolution of reclamation that spans four decades and three distinct state regulatory programs. In 1968 and 1971, the 1962 state law was strengthened to require additional contouring, but it was not until 1975 that the Illinois General Assembly passed the law requiring the segregation, storage and replacement of all topsoil in the mining and reclamation process. The law further mandates that once the topsoil is replaced on the graded land, it had to be relatively rock free; no rocks can be larger than 4 inches in the top 18 inches of soil where they could be churned up by farm equipment. This law is relatively similar to the provisions of PL-95-87, the federal Surface Mining Reclamation and Enforcement Act of 1977, which requires companies not only to segregate the topsoil and return them rock-free, but to segregate each horizon, re-stratify them, and demonstrate the resulting reclamation can return the area to its former productivity.

An aerial view of the mining operations distinctly shows the evolutionary pattern of the pre-law reclamation efforts of tree planting and aerial seeding on ungraded land to today's federal and state mandate to return all agricultural land to original or higher productivity. In the process of studying this evolution, some interesting facts concerning the soil should again be noted. The pre-law land mined in the 30's, 40's and 50's now has a healthy selection of pines and hardwoods. Recent studies by the Forestry School of

Southern Illinois University have shown a remarkable growth of these trees when planted in surface mine spoils rather than in virgin till. The clay hardpan, as mentioned previously, prohibits the root system from reaching down into the lower horizons, and is mixed with the subsoil and dispersed in the mining process to form a soil with a richer content. These trees have been studied and measured in a very comprehensive 30-year analysis by Southern Illinois University. They have found that the trees in the pre-mined spoil had a startling 29% better growth rate than trees planted the same time on virgin land. This potential raises some exciting possibilities and questions with regard to developing agricultural productivity on mined land to a higher state than could be possible prior to the mining process. Can the reclamation process create a superior soil? Will segregating horizons produce the same potential productivity in a cost-efficient manner?

Two of the most exciting things happening at Southwestern which could help answer these questions are the university research being done on test plots on the reclaimed land adjacent to the current coal mining pit, and the introduction into southern Illinois of a brand new breed of surface mine reclamation equipment which foregoes the traditional methods of scraping, stockpiling and haulback to achieve the reclamation process. The University of Illinois, in a five-year experiment involving several mines in Illinois, is experimenting with different types of topsoil found in the area along with different thicknesses of A, B and C horizons. They are studying the effects of irrigation, the dispersal of the clay hardpan, and different reclamation methods. The end result will be a true and distinct catalog of the most successful reclamation techniques and capabilities on the areas soils. It's a very exciting venture and one which will undeniably assist coal companies and the state regulatory agencies in determining the best reclamation procedures available for their particular area. It is no secret that the coal companies all over the Midwest are nervous about the prime farmland provisions of PL-95-87. There is simply no way that we can say unequivocally that this land can be returned to its former productivity within a certain amount of time. However, we are, as an industry, committed through research to discover the bottom line in reclamation, what is really feasible within the given soil structure and topography of the area in which the coal is mined. The author would be happy to correspond with those interested regarding the annual results of this five-year reclamation research because I know it will have positive impact on the procedural methods by which coal companies all over the Midwest comply with the mandate of the new surface mine law.

The second program is quite possibly the most exciting and innovative approach to reclamation ever undertaken by any coal company in the midwest. Recently I traveled to West Germany where I visited a number of area surface mining operations which utilized bucket wheel excavators and conveyor systems to transport the topsoil around the mined side of the pit to effect contemporaneous reclamation. In mere minutes after the soil had been removed from the highwall, it was deposited on the mined side of the pit waiting to be graded to its original contour by stackers and bulldozers. Southwestern has recently installed a similar system at the Captain Mine, the first of its kind in the U.S. and we believe it will result in the best reclamation in the area, and more importantly, achieve the ambitious goal of returning mined land to its former productivity within five years and thus respond to the intent of the federal surface mine law. In West Germany it was quite evident that the rowcrop capabilities on the mined side of the pit are equal, and sometimes superior to that of the virgin till. The plant roots have better access to the overall mineral content of the soil, the soil is synthesized to achieve a higher degree of organic matter and oxygen and the handling involved in redepositing the soil makes the land less dense. The system is by no means perfected yet, but our company is confident enough in the potential capabilities of mining with conventional draglines and shovels and reclaiming with wheel excavators and belt systems that two more similar systems will be installed in Illinois.

In 1971, St. Louis based Arch Mineral Corporation, purchased Southwestern and took over operation of the Captain and Streamline Mines and the farm. Renaming the farm subsidiary Arch Farms, this operation today raises approximately 2,000 head of cattle which roam free on the range all year long. Unlike conventionally run farms in Illinois and other states in the Midwest which have a variety of barns and out-buildings, the mined land on which the cattle roam comprises several thousand acres and management techniques for the cattle have become an interesting combination of western range land and midwestern management and marketing. Arch Farm has also developed a progressive swine operation which boasts 500 prime hogs. The diet for the hog is comprised of a formula of grain developed especially for the Arch Farm operation. The farm, though, is really the agricultural laboratory by which we can maintain equipment and personnel to return the mined land into productive farmland. In 1977 Arch Farms planted the first commerical crops ever grown on Southwestern's reclaimed land. The current goal through the mining process and synthesizing of this soil is to become so advanced in reclamation techniques that the coal mining can take place and the land returned to productive row-crop land in one year. It is an extraordinary proposition. Ultimately, when the farming techniques have been perfected to a point where a large continuous acreage can be reclaimed, it is Arch's goal to prove that this synthesized soil, reclaimed in the absence of the clay hardpan, will provide some of the best row crops that these counties of southern Illinois have ever seen.

Along with the other agricultural programs one of the newest and busiest ventures has turned into a real "honey" of a program. Close to four tons of honey will be produced this year from bees which are maintained on the mined property. The mined land, originally seeded in hay grasses and legumes grows a fine crop of clover which keeps Arch's bees humming with activity. This sweet harvest is expected to increase each year and has become a real source of local pride for the farming subsidiary. Just as importantly, this has helped farm programs to be implemented into a well-received visible complement to the mining.

There are so many aspects of coal mining that are not directly related to the actual mining process, that Arch feels strongly about the importance of maintaining a healthy relationship with the local communities. Many mines in the area keep the public off their land, and Southwestern, starting back in the early days of the mining activities, has opened up this land to the public for recreational use. The many trees and hundreds of acres of scenic lakes resulting from the mining process, have become an impressive and much needed addition to the recreation base of southern Illinois. Lakes, picnic areas, fishing, boating, horseback riding, hunting, camping, skeet and trap shooting, archery, golf and motorcycle trails are now an integral part of Arch's farm and reclamation programs. The limestone mantel between the coal has kept the water in the final cuts of the mined land at such a high quality that channel catfish, blue gill, and large-mouthed bass and crappie are stocked in abundance in the areas numerous lakes. The final touch is the nearby, Scuttle Inn, restaurant and lounge, established in 1972. This award-winning restaurant serves meals not only to the area miners, but also serves as a local gathering point and fine local eating place. Adjacent is the Southwestern's pro shop which serves one of the longest and most difficult nine-hole golf courses in Southern Illinois. It should be emphasized that all of these programs are not meant to be exploitive of the vast land holdings of the coal company. We believe it makes sense to not only utilize the land that has been mined along with the land to be mined as a competitive business, but also to allow the local area people to make the most of this land. The public mandate and the intent of the industry must combine its energies to prove that coal mining, particularly surface mining, can produce a valuable and needed resource without alienating the local community and without discouraging alternative land uses on the mined land.

It is no secret that surface mining's less than sterling past has suffered from poor community relations because the cost of land reclamation was never able to be justified on the customer's monthly electric bill prior to the environmentally conscious 1970's. The Southwestern coal reserve, along with the land currently in mining and land that has been previously mined comprises a total of 28,000 acres. By anyone's account this is a large area of land and a diversified program such as this makes good sense for the proper utilization of this much land. In the state, which is not only the largest agricultural exporter of any state in the nation and which boasts agricultural productivity and efficiency far in excess of most other areas of the world, but also has the largest bituminous coal reserve of any state, coal mining and farming will have to work hand in hand to achieve the dual goals of the double harvest of coal and farm products.

With all of the potential success that these investments and programs represent, there are other issues and challenges which lie ahead. The return to row crop mandate being effected by federal and state regulations is turning surface mining into a vast land clearing operation. Local and state officials must realize that reclaimed land is most valuable when a wide variety of land uses are available. We should be careful that agricultural production does not become a preoccupation with reclamation legislation; that trees, water and recreational facilities are not forgotten in our effort to return this land to its highest possible use. Another important social challenge is to return some of the mined land to private ownership once the reclamation process has matured to the point that the land is stable, not susceptible to subsidence and easily accessible from public roads. In Illinois the surface must be purchased along with the coal reserve and the only way that the mined and reclaimed land can be returned to the private landowner will be to assure that the reclamation process is so complete that a landowner will not think it to be wholly inferior with other available farmland in the area. To do this, the companies will have to remove those ingrained ideas that surface-mined land is generally unusable as it has occasionally been in the past. Arch believes that all of this is possible, given our ability to effect these new reclamation techniques, within five years.

These policies and programs are all part of some hard thinking combined with an idealism--a goal. There is no doubt in our minds whatsoever that a diversified reclamation program such as we have at Southwestern is the only way in which coal companies will be given the public mandate to continue to operate in the future. It will be expensive and risky, but the engineering challenges involved are enormous. There is no diminishing the fact that the coal industry has, through technology and legislation, matured to a point now where it can truly operate as a good neighbor, is an important part of the local community' environment and is a contributing factor to positive social and economic stability. Coal is as new as it is old and the industry must accept that if it is to recapture its markets that were lost to oil and gas, to regain its dominance as a viable, but acceptable, energy source, then it must become aware of its responsibilities to the compelling and persistent public demand that it do so with complete regard to the surrounding environment. A diversified reclamation program is what Arch feels will prove coal's worthiness to this challenge.

CONVENTIONAL WISDOM IN 1975 AND THE REAL WORLD IN 1978 IN SURFACE MINE LAND RECLAMATION AT THE NAVAJO MINE

Sterling Grogan, Chase L. Caldwell, Orlando J. Estrada and William Skeet*

The Navajo Mine, operated by Utah International, Inc., is a coal strip mine located in northwestern New Mexico on the Navajo Indian Reservation. It supplies approximately 7 million tons per year of subbituminous coal to the Four Corners electric generating station. Mine operations require a labor force of nearly 500 persons, most of whom are Navajo Indians.

The mine leasehold of 31,400 acres is located at an altitude of 1,700 m on the Colorado Plateau. It is a cold desert in the shortgrass grassland ecosystem. The most common perennial vegetation includes the grasses alkali sacaton, sand dropseed, and Indian ricegrass, and the saltbush plants of the genus *Atriplex*. The climate is mild and dry with moderate winds, low humidity and over 300 days of sun each year. Annual precipitation averages about 15 cm per year, most of which comes as rain in the late summer.

The geology of the mine area consists of a succession of sandstone, shale, coal and conglomerate, deposited originally as marine, brackish, and fresh water sediments ranging in age from Triassic to recent.

Mining operations begin with the removal of a material we euphemistically refer to as "topsoil". This material is primarily aeolian sand and possesses few characteristics of what is commonly called topsoil. This material is removed using self-loading scrapers and once removed is usally placed directly on graded mine spoil. In some cases it may be stockpiled. Topsoil removal is followed by the drilling and blasting of the overburden and then removal of the overburden by walking draglines of the 50 cubic yard class. The uncovered coal seam is drilled and blasted and the coal is removed and hauled out either to intermediate railroad stockpiles or directly to the coal crushing and blending facility prior to delivery to the mine mouth power plant. Grading of the spoil piles is the next step in the process; HD 41 and D-9 dozers grade the spoil piles to the required configuration.

Our mining and reclamation activities are governed by the New Mexico Coal Surface-mining Commission permit we received in 1974. That permit, which includes the mine plan Utah International Inc. submitted in 1973, constitutes the "conventional wisdom of 1975," the year in which large scale revegetation began. The purpose of this presentation is to compare that conventional wisdom with what we have learned during three years of field experience with the implementation of the plan.

Reclamation at Navajo Mine can be divided into three major areas:

(1) Land preparation, which includes topsoiling, grading, and minesoil analysis and mapping;

*Utah International Inc., Navajo Mine, P.O. Box 155, Fruitland, NM 87146.

(2) Revegetation, which includes seed bed preparation, seeding, mulching, and irrigation; and

(3) Results, which include range and revegetation surveys and research.

Land Preparation

In 1975, the conventional wisdom of topsoiling was basically that replacing the "suitable" surface material would probably result in better plant growth. Tests have shown us that our "topsoil", though an adequate growth medium, is highly erodable and has low water holding capacity. Revegetation results on topsoiled areas have been variable thus far.

Topsoiled areas have been improved by discing the topsoil into graded mine soil to break up the interface between the sandy topsoil and the clayey mine soil. This reduces erosion and increases water holding capacity. Now we are developing a justification, based upon empirical data, to reduce the area of minesoils to be topsoiled. If we can get adequate plant growth on unamended minesoils, energy and expense in topsoiling can be saved. While in some cases topsoiled areas show improved species diversity, the poor water-holding characteristics of the soil have resulted in added moisture stress in some instances.

In 1973, an intensive mine soil analysis and mapping program was begun at Navajo. Twelve distinct groups of spoils were identified and mapped based on standard agronomic diagnostic criteria. Through continued analysis and observation of vegetative response, the original 12 groups of soils were reduced to three. Soil color, and texture (measured by feel), were highly correlated with salinity, infiltration and permeability. Therefore, our minesoils classification system, which is still being refined through cooperative work under the Forest Services's SEAM Program, has been simplified to identify only those specific diagnostic properties that appear to be directly related to the most growth-limiting factor: effective moisture. On this basis, topsoil applications and seeding and irrigation rates are determined.

The restoration of mined lands to the "approximate original contour" is as controversial a topic today as it was in 1975. At that time we were confident that a slope of three horizontal to one vertical was an adequate minimum, and this standard was adopted as a permit requirement. Now, however, it has become clear that a three to one slope on unconsolidated mine soils is too steep for safe and efficient operation of the farm machinery used for revegetation. Most important of all, soil moisture characteristics are so much better on less steep slopes that substantially improved plant growth and virtually no significant erosion is evident. Our forthcoming proposal to the regulatory authority on surface configuration to meet requirements in the Surface Mining Act of 1977 will specify slopes that will be less steep than five to one in most cases.

Revegetation

Seed bed preparation, accomplished with an offset disc, was originally limited to overly compacted minesoils. Those areas which were not heavily compacted were not treated. Observations of plant response show that discing of all areas has proved beneficial.

When seeding began on a large scale, conventional wisdom told us to use a variety of equipment. In addition to a Rangeland drill, a broadcaster and a conventional agricultural hoe drill were used. Immediately the hoe drill fell apart, high winds blew broadcast seed away, and the broadcaster was extremely difficult to calibrate. Today we use, with much success, the Rangeland drill for large seed and a modified agricultural hoe drill which simply drops the light seed on the ground surface and covers the seed by a chain drag pulled behind. Some seed that is too trashy to run through a drill is hand-seeded.

Field tests on more than 30 species of native and introduced plants conducted between 1972 and 1975 led to the selection of twelve species for the revegetation program. Seven were native to the immediate mine area: *Atriplex canescens, A. confertifolia, Chrysothamnus nauseosis, Epherdra nevadensis, Oryzopsis hymenoides, Sporobolus airoides,* and *S. cryptandrus.*

All of these native species have proven successful over the past three years, but under the irrigation regime uneven germination of *Atriplex confertifolia, Chrysothamnus* and *Ephedra* was observed. Since then, *Hilaria jamesii,* an excellent native grass, for which seed has only recently become available in quantity, has been added to the list.

In addition to native species, our 1975 seed mix included five introduced species: *Agropyron smithii, A. desertorum, Bouteloua gracilis, Elymus junceus,* and *Festuca arundinaceae.*

None of these introduced species have been as consistently successful as the native plants, so introduced species were deleted from the seeding program. A large part of current research now is concentrated on the selection and breeding of various *Atriplex* shrubs and some grasses that demonstrate particular adaptability of climatic and edaphic conditions. This long-term research is under the direction of Dr. Howard Stutz of Brigham Young University.

Our 1974 permit requires mulching of all revegetated areas. Barley straw mulch is used, applied with a machine designed to chop and blow out the straw at a uniform rate, The mulching rate is about 1 ton per acre. Mulch has been found to be of limited value in many areas, and much of it is blown away by strong spring winds. Research in New Mexico has shown that some unmulched areas have germination rates as high as mulched areas. Although mulch is required in all cases by new federal regulations, our results show that it should not be a nationwide requirement.

In arid regions of the Southwest, early research showed that to get uniform stands of vegetation in a short period of time, supplemental irrigation is required. Large scale revegetation using irrigation had never been done in northwest New Mexico, so there were many unanswered questions concerning application rates, scheduling, and the proper system for application. Several research projects between 1972 and 1974 led to the basic procedures begun in 1975.

Three inch aluminum laterals, which are systemically moved by hand across each revegetation plot, are used. The irrigation season coincides roughly with the natural cycle of precipitation. Over the past three years, the biggest improvement has been in reducing water application through better scheduling and improved efficiency without adversely affecting seed germination. The initial application rate was about 12 to 15 inches net during the first season. This has now been reduced to about 6 inches net the first season, while final spring irrigation in the year following seeding remains at about 2 inches net. This year, because of unusually good winter precipitation, we elected to irrigate only a portion of the revegetated area that would normally have been irrigated this spring. No areas are irrigated after the second growing season.

Results

Although our 1974 State permit specifies that an annual survey of the undisturbed native range is required for the determination of standards of reclamation performance, experience in the annual collection of an enormous amount of range survey data led us to reevaluate this concept. We began in 1977 to consider alternatives to the annual survey that would describe range conditions at a point in time rather than trends over a period of time.

Obviously, new federal regulations requiring reference areas as standards of performance have channeled our thinking toward the establishment of reference areas that will accurately reflect the unique range environment that exists at Navajo Mine. The most difficult problem is that all of the available land on and adjoining our leasehold has been severely overgrazed and mismanaged for more than 30 years. Therefore, the selection and long-term maintenance of suitable reference areas will be extremely difficult.

Research has been and continues to be one of the most important aspects of our overall reclamation program. We have found over the past four years that reclamation of strip-mined lands is far from an exact science and only through experience and research will the problems be solved. Through continuing research at the mine, the conventional wisdom of 1975 has developed into our standard operating procedures of 1978. Problems in soil amendments, irrigation systems, plant genetics, and basic plant, soil and water relationships have been investigated. Although not all the answers are known, the results are encouraging.

The problems and solutions we have discussed up until now have been of a technical nature and certainly describe the bulk of the work at Navajo Mine. However, as environmentalists at a coal strip mine, we are required to wear hats other than those of the ecologist, soil scientist, or environmental engineer. Traditionally, mining has not been among the most environmentally aware industries. Over the years of working at Navajo Mine, we of the environmental staff have learned some hard lessons. The most important has been that the successful completion of any phase of a reclamation program requires close cooperation with the engineering and operations personnel of the mine. We have found that only by thoroughly understanding all aspects of mine operations, and by using good salesmanship of a well-planned, environmentally sound program, can the goal of good reclamation be achieved. And then, once the program is accepted, day to day contact with mine operating personnel is a must. We need their assistance in solving problems with scheduling of equipment and people, engineering, and maintenance. The real world of environmental work at a mine poses numerous problems for which the average researcher or environmentalist is not formally trained. But the education comes quickly.

We feel strongly that it is the obligation of an environmental staff to identify not only what is required by law but also the most economical approach to reclamation in terms of wise energy use and capital investment. As economics change, our programs must adjust accordingly. We must consider national energy objectives and make whatever changes are required to meet them. At the same time, we hope that requirements of various regulatory authorities are considered in light of those same objectives.

At the Navajo Mine, the long-term goal is the reclamation of all disturbed lands to provide for livestock grazing by the Navajo people. The conventional wisdom today is that by 1985, our first 540 acres of revegetated mine land will be ready for return to its approved post-mining land use: grazing. Judging by the changes we have already made to accommodate the real world, the question we face now is: What will the real world look like in 1985? How will today's conventional wisdom, as expressed by regulatory requirements, have to change to accommodate the real world?

THE ESTABLISHMENT AND MAINTENANCE OF
VEGETATION ON MINESOILS IN THE EASTERN UNITED STATES

*William T. Plass**

About 40 years ago, a southern Indiana surface mine operator planted fruit trees on land he had disturbed while mining coal. This may be the first documented attempt to revegetate areas after surface mining disturbance. Since then thousands of acres have been disturbed in the Interior and Appalachian coal provinces of the eastern United States. Reclamation, which was once a voluntary activity by conscientious mine operators, is now mandatory and vigorously regulated by state and federal laws. It is an integral part of the mining plan and commands increasing attention by company executives.

Years of research and experience produced today's complex reclamation technology. Techniques utilizing the fundamentals of forestry and agronomy dominated early reclamation efforts. Later, expertise from related disciplines developed more reliable revegetation techniques. Now a broad array of scientific disciplines is required to meet the demand for better environmental protection. This trend will continue as the search for more reliable and efficient techniques continues.

Future demand for coal assures surface mining of a place as an important mining method. New mining technology will permit recovery of a higher percentage of the nation's reserves by surface mining. Improved processing and utilization techniques will permit the use of coals once environmentally undesirable or uneconomical. More stringent environmental laws and regulations will be enforced on the surface mining industry. Intensive reclamation will be encouraged when it is recognized that the productivity of minesoils on selected sites can equal or exceed that of pre-mining soils. Demands for forest and agricultural products will stimulate interest in integrated management plans for land holdings having more productive minesoils. These factors indicate challenges and opportunities in future reclamation.

This discussion of reclamation practices in the eastern U.S. summarizes current technology. Where appropriate, historical references are used to illustrate the development of specific technology. Future trends in reclamation technology will also be identified.

MINING AND RECLAMATION PLANNING

The new Federal surface mining law requires detailed planning of many mining and reclamation activities. Technology to accomplish this exists and is in use by the more

*Northeastern Forest Experiment Station, Forestry Sciences Laboratory, P.O. Box 152, Princeton, WV 24740.

progressive mining companies. Research and experience will improve the existing methods and provide more efficient and reliable procedures.

Basic to all mining and reclamation are the chemical and physical characteristics of the coal, the rock strata above the coal seam, and the soil on the land surface. All are important if the mine operator is to achieve acceptable environmental protection and future economic benefits from the disturbed land.

The quantity and quality of the coal establishes the economic base for determining whether mining is feasible. The cost of mining now includes all costs relating to permit application, mining, reclamation, environmental controls, and the maintenance of vegetation until the bond is released.

The overburden, or rock strata above the coal seam, is a resource we must learn to use. Knowledge of the chemical and physical properties of the overburden is used in planning mining and reclamation. Mining activities relating to overburden movement and placement depend on the nature and properties of the rock above the coal. Proper handling of the overburden may reduce reclamation costs, simplify treatments required for environmental protection, and expand future land use options.

Overburden sampling may be required. Intensity of sampling, sampling methods, and parameters required are site-specific. Characteristics that relate to potential environmental problems are often emphasized, but factors affecting plant growth are also important. An understanding of potential acidity may be useful for predicting conditions that will limit the establishment and growth of plants. The concentration of toxic metallic ions such as aluminum, manganese, and iron, and the availability of macro- and micro-nutrients are important (Berg 1966, Barnhisel and Massey 1969).

Variation in the chemical and physical properties of rock strata is well known to the geologist and petrologist. Its importance to reclamation was demonstrated by research showing that potential acidity was related to rock type, and that plant-available phosphorus varied among rock strata (May and Berg 1967, Berg and May 1969). A research team has developed a practical method, termed acid-base accounting, for overburden analysis (Sobek et al. 1976). Research at the University of South Carolina shows the relationship between paleoenvironments and the type of pyrite in rock strata (Caruccio and Ferm 1974).

Future overburden analysis will be refined to provide practical and reliable methods to prevent environmental problems and provide more favorable materials for plant growth. In regions with thin and infertile soils, overburden analysis may justify substitution of selected rock strata for topsoil.

Practical post-mining land uses are selected after considering site characteristics, overburden analysis, and landowner preference. These decisions establish the reclamation objectives; mining and reclamation options are then considered to achieve them. Consideration must be given to state and federal laws and regulations that specify acceptable reclamation practices and the qualifications for release of performance bonds.

MINING AND RECLAMATION

The interrelationship between mining and reclamation is clearly established. It is increasingly difficult to classify specific activities as either mining or reclamation.

Site preparation requires removal and disposal of vegetation on the area to be disturbed. If the soil will be used as a top dressing for vegetation, it should be removed and either redistributed or stored. Overburden removal proceeds in a systematic manner. Efficient practical methods based on information developed during the planning phase are used to minimize environmental problems, create a surface configuration compatible with the post-mining use, and provide a growth medium suitable for the intended vegetation.

Regrading is required in area mining to meet environmental requirements and to achieve the land use objectives. Less regrading is done in mountainous terrain as present mining methods permit systematic placement of the overburden. Appropriate configurations are created as mining progresses and little regrading is necessary. Systematic placement of the overburden minimizes the need to bury large rocks or potentially toxic material. Regrading is used to establish surface configurations appropriate for the intended land use, drainage channels for surface runoff, and erosion control structures. Surface configurations incorporating features that minimize the negative aesthetic impact of surface mining are receiving more consideration. A computer program to design acceptable land forms for specific sites has been developed (Mallary 1977).

Topsoiling is an important reclamation option where topsoil is more productive than minesoil. Where topsoils are thin and infertile, selected overburden materials or a mixture of soil and overburden rock may be used instead. Topsoiling is intended to improve the physical, chemical, and biological properties of minesoil; its effectiveness depends on the methods used for handling and storage. Topsoiling is a more complex operation than is commonly believed; it should be considered one of several options to maintain or increase minesoil productivity. Standardized methods of comparing productivities of soils and minesoils are needed so that decisions can be made about the need for topsoiling. Changes in the chemical, physical, and biological properties of important soil types during removal and storage need to be documented, and methods used to apply topsoil need investigation.

Amendments are applied to modify conditions that limit plant establishment or to improve growth and productivity. The need for acid-neutralizing treatments decreases as methods of moving and placing overburden improve. Lime is the most widely used material for neutralizing acid minesoil. Established laboratory procedures determine the rates of application. Conventional application equipment is used on flat or moderate slopes; specially designed throwers permit efficient treatment of steep slopes. The surface configuration and physical properties determine when discs and rippers can be used to incorporate lime into the rooting zone. Steep slopes and rocky minesoils may make it impossible to mix lime with the minesoil.

Alkaline fly ash is used to a limited extent to neutralize acid soil. Large quantities per acre are often required, as its neutralizing potential is low. This material may add varying quantities of micro- and macro-nutrients (Plass and Capp 1974). Large quantities can modify the texture of the minesoil and increase infiltration rates.

Quick-developing grass and legume covers are required on all surface mining disturbance. The establishment of herbaceous covers usually requires the application of fertilizer. It is widely accepted that fresh minesoils are deficient in nitrogen; insufficient phosphorus is common (Cummins et al. 1965, Plass and Vogel 1973); and potassium is often adequate for the establishment of a cover crop but inadequate for acceptable productivity of some agricultural crops. Other plant nutrients may be required on some minesoils or for intensive cropping. Some of the established methods of soil analysis are useful when appropriate fertilization plans are required for agricultural crops.

The selection of plant materials depends on site characteristics and land use objectives. Research and experience have identified a large number of grasses. legumes, forbs, trees, and shrubs adapted to mined land reclamation in the eastern United States (Plass 1977a). Species compatability will receive more consideration now that it is required to establish and maintain a vegetative cover of acceptable density and composition for at least 5 years. For example, species composition may affect the establishment and maintenance of legumes.

Also, tree and shrub survival and growth may be determined by the composition of companion herbaceous covers (Vogel 1973).

Annual grasses are used as initial cover crops for erosion control and modification of the microclimate. Selection of season-adapted species permits establishment of a cover crop at any time during the growing season (Vogel 1974, Jones et al. 1975). On some sites cereal crops can be harvested before the permanent vegetation is established. Perennials are sown with the annual cover crop or after it matures.

The emphasis on herbaceous vegetation caused a decline in tree and shrub planting. Other contributing factors were increases in labor costs and a scarcity of trained tree planters. Species recommendations for minesoils are similar to those for soils. Native species are recommended but exotics are useful for some management plans. Planting arrangement and spacing depend on the site and management objectives. Mixtures that include nitrogen-fixing trees and shrubs as nurse crops for interplanted species are recommended (Plass 1977b).

Experimental results in West Virginia and Alabama indicate that some species of trees and shrubs can be successfully seeded directly on minesoils (Plass 1976). Seeds are applied with a hydroseeder or helicopter. Continued testing of the most promising species may result in specific recommendations for the central Appalachians.

Mulches and soil stabilizers are used to aid vegetation establishment and reduce erosion. Straw, hay, and wood fiber are the most commonly used mulches. Shredded hardwood bark and other agricultural residues have limited or local use. Rates of application depend on the material, degree of slope, aspect, and physical characteristics of the minesoil.

Chemical soil stabilizers in liquid or powder form are used on selected sites with wood fiber or as chemical tacks for hay or straw. These materials form a permeable film on the soil surface, bind the soil particles together, and glue the seed in place until it germinates.

MAINTENANCE AND MANAGEMENT

Federal law requires an operator to establish and maintain an acceptable vegetative cover for 5 years. An acceptable cover on minesoils must equal or exceed the density and productivity of a similar vegetative cover growing on soils adjacent to the disturbance. Previously, many state laws permitted bond release 2 years after the application of vegetation treatments that resulted in a vegetative cover that met specific standards.

Present regulations encourage the use of mining and reclamation practices that quickly establish an acceptable vegetative cover. This can be achieved on most sites at reasonable cost with existing reclamation technology. Revegetation cost may be higher and the time required to establish an acceptable cover may be longer on difficult sites.

Evidence from areas revegetated under existing state laws indicates that adequate initial treatment can establish and maintain a vegetative cover for several growing seasons, but vegetation density may decline over a period of time. This often results from initial treatment and site characteristics. Maintenance treatments which include seed, fertilizer, or other amendments, individually or in combination, may be required to maintain productivity or ground cover density. Specific maintenance requirements are determined by site characteristics and land use objectives.

When trees and shrubs are established with an herbaceous cover, a gradual decline in the grass and legume density is desirable: initial growth of trees is reduced by competition from herbaceous cover. As the size of trees increases, the effect of competition is reduced and tree growth will increase. Maintenance treatments can be minimal on areas designated for forest management after acceptable stocking and distribution are achieved.

A management schedule should be an integral part of revegetation plans for sites developed for agricultural, horticultural, forage, or pasture crops. Research and demonstrations show that selected minesoils can be as productive as soils (Armiger 1976); management systems should be similar. Existing technology can be used to develop realistic management plans.

Minesoils with moderate to low natural productivity may have marginal potential for intensive management. More success may be expected when a managed minesoil is integrated with an established agricultural enterprise. Yields from unmanaged forest plantations indicate that many minesoils have a good potential for wood products (Plass and Burton 1967, Lyle et al. 1976). Important considerations for managed forest plantations are the selection of suitable species and planting arrangements that recognize the space requirements for acceptable growth. Thinning and improvement cuts may be necessary to maintain growth. Documentation of yields of various commodities under different management systems may provide a greater incentive for intensive management of minesoils. This largely undeveloped land resource has a good potential for providing needed food and fiber.

SUMMARY

As the era of federal regulation of surface mining begins, reclamation technology in the eastern United States provides guidelines for revegetating all current and future mining disturbance. Accomplishment of this goal depends on many economic and technological variables. A continuing problem is the inadequate system for technology transfer between our research organizations and practicing reclamationists. Results from expanding research are not reaching the field. Attempts are being made to assemble existing data and to identify current research projects. The increased number and quality of informal and formal meetings devoted to mined land reclamation have been useful. This is progress, but a more imaginative approach must be developed to supply those responsible for reclamation with the assistance they need to achieve acceptable reclamation on all lands.

Formal and informal research and demonstrations have contributed and will contribute to improvements in reclamation technology. The complexity of present-day reclamation and the interaction between all its facets confirm the value of multidisciplinary research programs. These can be achieved by an expansion of cooperative research between existing research groups. Selective development of a cooperative group would permit the most efficient use of the expertise and facilities available to research a priority problem. Research groups from academic institutions and government research agencies should join with industry, regulatory agencies, environmental organizations, and private consulting firms to develop comprehensive research projects. Input from these groups will identify relevant problems, develop appropriate research programs, and permit practical application of the results. Participation of groups with divergent backgrounds will stimulate interest in research and provide opportunities for dissemination of research results.

Past accomplishments in reclamation have been impressive, but the opportunities for the future are challenging. The Federal law recognizes the productivity of minesoils and the need to develop them for specific land use. Development of minesoil productivity deserves equal emphasis with environmental considerations in mining and reclamation.

ABSTRACT

Surface mine reclamation in the eastern U.S. has achieved a high degree of success. The methods in use today were developed through years of research and experience. Basic to present day technology is the concept that reclamation planning begins when the decision is made to open a new mine. If this concept is accepted, reclamation activities may be classified under the following categories: planning for mining and reclamation; mining and reclamation; and maintenance and management. The methodology for some categories is not well developed. These will require more research. This is a review of reclamation practices in the eastern United States and factors contributing to the development of present day technology, and an assessment of future trends in reclamation.

REFERENCES

Armiger, W.H., J.N. Jones and L. Bennett. 1976. Revegetation of land disturbed by strip mining of coal in Appalachia. U.S. Dept. Agric., ARS-NE-71, Beltsville, MD, 38 p.

Barnhisel, R.I. and H.F. Massey. 1969. Chemical, mineralogical, and physical properties of eastern Kentucky acid forming coal spoil materials. Soil Sci. 108:367-372.

Berg, W.A. 1966. Plant-toxic chemicals in acid spoils. pp. 91-94, In Proc. Coal Mine Spoil Reclamation Symp., Pennsylvania State Univ.

Berg, W.A. and R.F. May. 1969. Acidity and plant available phosphorus in strata overlying coal seams. Min. Congr. J. 55:31-34.

Caruccio, F.T. and J.C. Ferm. 1974. Paleoenvironment--prediction of acid mine drainage problems. pp. 5-10, In Fifth Symp. Coal Mine Drainage Res., Natl. Coal Assoc., Washington, DC.

Cummins, D.G., W.T. Plass and C.E. Gentry. 1965. Chemical and physical properties of spoil banks in eastern Kentucky Coalfields. U.S. Dept. Agric. Forest Service Research Paper CS-17, 12 p.

Jones, J.N., Jr., W.H. Armiger and O.L. Bennett. 1975. A two-step system for revegetation of strip mine spoils. J. Environ. Qual. 4:233-235.

Lyle, E.S., D.J. Janes, D.R. Hicks and D.H. Weingartner. 1976. Some vegetation and soil characteristics of coal surface mine spoils in Alabama. pp. 140-152, In Fourth Symp. on Surface Mining and Reclamation, Natl. Coal Assoc., Washington, DC.

Mallary, R. 1977. Ecosite: An application of computer graphics to the design of land forms for surface mine reclamation. pp. 32-36, In Fifth Symp. Surf. Min. and Reclam., Natl. Coal Assoc., Washington, DC.

May, R.F. and W.A. Berg. 1967. Overburden and bank acidity--eastern Kentucky strip mines. Coal Age 71:74-75.

Plass, W.T. 1977a. Seeding and planting to achieve land management objectives. pp. (1) 102-116, In Douglas M. Considine (ed.), Energy Technol. Handb., McGraw-Hill, NY.

Plass, W.T. 1977b. Growth and survival of hardwoods and pine interplanted with alder. U.S. Dept. Agric. Forest Service Research Paper NE-376.

Plass, W.T. 1976. Direct seeding of trees and shrubs on surface-mined land in West Virginia. pp. 32-42, In Keith Utz (ed.), Proc. Conf. For. Disturbed Surf. Areas, U.S. Dept. Agric. Forest Service.

Plass, W.T. and J.D. Burton. 1967. Pulpwood production potential on strip-mined land in the South. J. Soil and Water Conserv. 22:235-238.

Plass, W.T. and J.P. Capp. 1974. Physical and chemical characteristics of surface mine spoil treated with fly ash. J. Soil and Water Conserv. 29:119-121.

Plass, W.T. and W.G. Vogel. 1973. Chemical properties and particle-size distribution of 39 surface mine spoils in southern West Virginia.   U.S. Dept. Agric., Forest Service Research Paper NE-276, 8 p.

Sobek, A.A., R.M. Smith, W.A. Schuller and J.R. Freeman. 1976. Overburden properties influence minesoils.   pp. 153-159, In Fourth Symp. on Surf. Min. and Reclam., Louisville, KY, Natl. Coal Assoc., Washington, DC.

Vogel, W.G. 1973. The effect of herbaceous vegetation on survival and growth of trees planted on coal mine spoils.   pp. 197-207, In Proc. Res. and Appl. Technol. Symp. on Mined Land Reclam., Bitum. Coal Res., Inc., Monroeville, PA.

Vogel, W.G. 1974. All-season seeding of herbaceous vegetation for cover on Appalachian strip mine spoils.   pp. 175-188, In Second Symp. on Surf. Min. and Reclam., Natl. Coal Assoc., Washington, DC.

RECLAMATION & MINE PLANNING
AT THE FORDING RIVER OPERATIONS

J.L. Popowich*

INTRODUCTION

Fording Coal Limited operates the Fording River coal mine located in southeastern British Columbia, Canada. The mine site is within the medial range of the southern Canadian Rocky Mountains approximately 136 km north of the United States-Canadian border and 6 to 11 km west of the British Columbia-Alberta provincial borders.

The Fording River operations produce an average of 3 million mT of cleaned metallurgical coal per annum primarily for export to Japan. Mining operations commenced in 1972 and are carried out on a three eight-hour shift, seven days per week basis. The operations employ both truck-shovel and dragline mining techniques in multiple seam pits. Shovels are in the 15-cubic yard range with trucks in the 120-ton to 170-ton size. The dragline is in the 60 cubic yard range. Total material moved annually is approximately 25 million bank cubic yards of waste and 4 million mT of raw coal.

Coal mining in mountainous terrain poses unique problems for reclamation and ultimate land use. This paper considers some of the problems and solutions of spoiling in a narrow mountainous valley and the related problems in preparation of spoils for reclamation.

BIOGEOCLIMATIC DESCRIPTION

Fording operations lie within the continental temperate climatic zone. Annual precipitation averages 85 cm of which half occurs during the growing season. Temperature extremes are -40°C in winter and to 35°C in summer.

The area is described as the Englemann Spruce Sub Alpine zone with mining operations occurring from 1,600 to 2,500 m above sea level. Vegetation cover on the valley bottom and lower slopes is mainly forest with dominant coniferous species being engleman spruce, lodgepole pine and minor amounts of balsam fir and western larch. Grass-shrub communities exist on south and southeast aspects.

The high elevation grassland is classed as high winter range for elk and sheep. Elk and moose population inhabit the valley bottom. Black bear abound in the area and are often seen feeding on reclaimed areas.

Land use in the Fording Valley prior to mining was primarily forestry, hunting, fishing and other outdoor recreational activities. Ultimate land use objectives are consistent

*Fording Coal Limited, Box 100, Elkford, B.C. VOB 1HO, Canada.

with prior land uses. The long range reclamation program objective is the restoration of the disturbed land to previously existing resource capability. This includes resloping of spoils in a manner that will blend the restored land form with the natural undisturbed adjacent land-surface.

GEOLOGY AND MINE LAYOUT

Metallurgical and thermal coal seams occur in the lower 600 m of the 1,300 m Kootenay formation on both sides of the Fording River Valley. Figures 1 and 2 show the existing mine layout and geological sections. The major structural features are two sub-

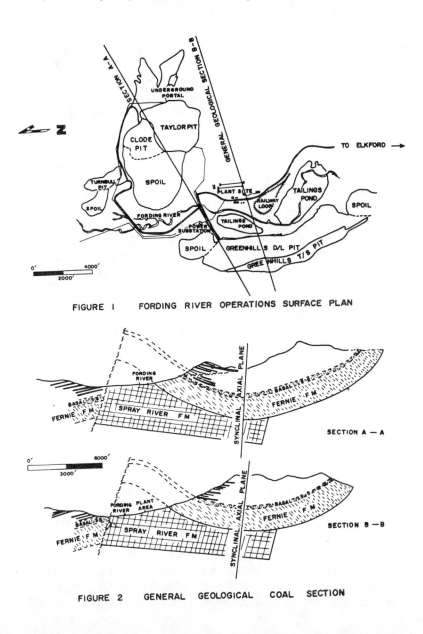

FIGURE 1   FORDING RIVER OPERATIONS SURFACE PLAN

FIGURE 2   GENERAL GEOLOGICAL COAL SECTION

parallel synclines, one on each side of the valley running north-south and a regional fault along the west side of the Fording River.

Truck-shovel operations exist on the eastern side of the valley in Clode and Turnbull pits. Dragline mining with truck-shovel prestrip exists on the western side of the valley. Both operations create massive quantities of waste which will require extensive site preparation for reclamation purposes.

WASTE SPOILING CONSIDERATIONS

Multi-seam coal mining operations in mountainous terrain create more waste volume per unit of surface area as compared to single seam operations. The narrow steep Fording River valley and lateral and vertical extent of the coal formations in the area result in problems of fitting large spoil volumes into non-resource areas available. It is necessary that all economic open pit reserves are recovered prior to being covered by millions of yards of waste material. Figure 3 shows the relative surface area available for waste dumps at the Fording River operations. In addition to resource area considerations other factors involved are the Fording River meander belt, local drainage requirements, wildlife corridors, haulroad and powerline right-of-ways, plant-site location, tailings ponds and the need to minimize total land disturbance.

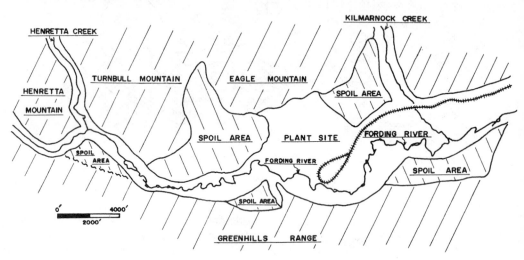

FIGURE 3   PROPERTY PLAN SHOWING COAL RESOURCE AREAS &
              POTENTIAL SPOIL AREA

It is essential that spoil volumes in any given area be maximized. This is achieved by optimizing the slopes at which spoils may be resloped while allowing for adequate reclamation. Current guidelines require that a slope of 26 degrees (biological angle of repose) be used. Some doubt remains as to this being the most suitable economic reslope angle when natural areas in the Fording valley support growth on slopes well in excess of 30 degrees. There are obvious benefits if adequate reclamation can be achieved on slope angles in excess of 26 degrees. These include a reduction in the total land area disturbance, a reduction in material movement required during the resloping stage of reclamation, a reduction in mining costs as haul distances are reduced by increasing spoil capacity of a given area and a reduction in revegetation materials as the net reclaimed surface area is decreased.

These benefits increase as the total height of spoil dumps increase. Current spoils at the Fording operations can exceed 300 m in height. However, final slope angles must provide for safety of operations during resloping and revegetation, efficient revegetation techniques, adequate drainage control and land surfaces consistent with final land use objectives.

SPOIL CONSTRUCTION

Spoil dump construction at the Fording River operations is of two types - formed and free dumps (Fig. 4). Formed spoils are defined as the deposition of waste materials in layers or lifts starting from the valley floor and extending up the valley sides. Height of lift is dependent on the operating parameters and normally does not exceed 66 m. Free dumps consist of the deposition of materials from a specific elevation and in one lift only. Dumps of this type can exceed 330 m in height.

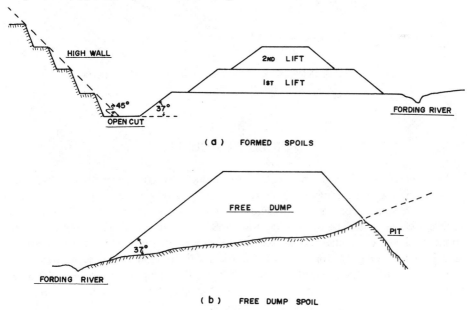

FIGURE 4   SPOIL   DUMP   CONSTRUCTION

The free-dump method is used primarily for higher elevation truck-shovel pits with formed dumps associated with the valley floor dragline and truck-shovel mining. Mining costs show free-dump construction to be more economic. However problems of spoil stability, safety of operations during dumping and reclamation requirements limit the extent of free-dumping. These problems are overcome by maximizing the free dump portion followed by wrap-around dumping. Wrap-around dumps (Fig. 5) are constructed at vertical intervals of up to 66 m depending on the overall dump height and access to the mining area.

The wrap-around method reduces overall costs of reclamation of high spoils. Rehandling of materials during resloping is reduced as waste material is hauled into place as compared to high cost dozing over long slope distances.

RESLOPING TECHNIQUES

The normal angle of repose of spoil materials is 37 degrees. Resloping to a suitable angle is achieved by crawler dozers working from the wrap-around dumps. Terraces (small benches) of approximately 7 m width are constructed as half the wrap-around interval as shown in Fig. 5. These terraces will provide access for revegetation purposes as well as provide for drainage and erosion control. The terraces will also provide for wildlife migration.

Field research has shown the 66 m wrap-around dump interval to be the most practical. Dozer productivity is at an optimum and operator safety is insured.

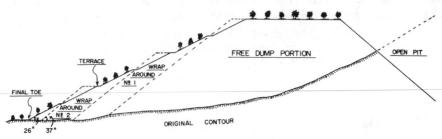

FIGURE 5. IDEALIZED FREE DUMP SPOIL CONSTRUCTION & FINAL RESLOPING
SPOIL COMPOSITION

SPOIL COMPOSITION

Waste materials consist of fragments of sandstone, carbonaceous mudstone, silt stone, shales and some glacial till ranging from dust-size particles to boulders several cubic yards in size. Normal free-dump construction by end dumping form the crest results in a segregation of particle sizes as materials roll or slide down the face of the spoil. The more competent sandstone boulders accumulate at the toe of the spoil with the less competent materials remaining on the upper portion of the spoil. The accummulation of the segregated coarse rock at the base provides an excellent drainage layer. Resloping of the spoil results in the finer crest materials being spread over the face of the spoil covering the coarse competent rock. The fine materials degrade quickly providing an adequate growth medium for revegetation. Fording reclamation plans are designed to utilize as much of the *in-situ* spoil materials as possible for growth media. Research work on material suitability began prior to mining operations. Numerous test plots are being studied to aid in the selection of proper vegetation species related to material types, altitude and maintenance requirements. Large volumes of topsoil and peat have been recovered from spoil areas prior to dumping. This material is in reserve in case of unsuitable waste rock.

EROSION CONTROL

Resloping using crawler dozers results in a major down-dip drainage pattern in the finer surface materials. Minor cross-dip patterns are created by the crawler grouser marks. Heavy precipitation or spring runoff result in gullying down the face of the spoil. Terraces reduce this type of erosion. Equipment operating in parallel or adjacent terraces can move harrows across the face of the resloped spoil creating a major cross-dip drainage pattern. This pattern will also assist in holding vegetation materials on the spoils during initial reclamation work.

Terraces can also be sloped across the spoil to carry runoff away from the face to reduce gullying. Cross-dams in the terrace can be constructed to prevent major erosion along the terrace. The use of coarse rock drains from terrace to terrace at intervals along the resloped face is being considered as a method of controlling drainage and erosion.

Experience at Fording has shown that inadequate surface drainage can result in localized failures of the fine surface materials thus the need for proper drainage.

SUMMARY

Current spoiling plans at the Fording River operations utilize 26 degree reslope angles. Research work is underway to determine if angles can be increased to maximize spoil volumes in a given area and minimize total land disturbance.

Economics of dozer resloping vary with the lift interval and the push distance involved. Costs are $1,000 per plan acre for less than 100 foot lift intervals increasing to $5,000 per plan acre for 200 foot lift intervals. Experience at Fording has shown the optimum vertical interval for lift development is 200 feet. However, parameters of spoil development may change due to site-specific conditions such as relation of pit area to spoil location, use of larger equipment for resloping and balance of suitable materials for growth medium.

The large volumes of spoils to be handled and reclamation requirements at the Fording River operations require that reclamation planning be integral with all stages of mine planning and mine development.

ACKNOWLEDGMENTS

The author expresses his appreciation to the staff of the Fording Mine Engineering and Environmental Services departments for their work on which this paper is based. The support of the management of the Fording River Operations is gratefully acknowledged.

RECLAMATION AND COAL EXPLORATION
PEACE RIVER COAL BLOCK—BRITISH COLUMBIA—CANADA

*D. Murray Galbraith**

Exploration for coal, and potential coal development in the Peace River area of British Columbia, presents an opportunity to the Province, and a challenge to the Ministry of Mines and Petroleum Resources. The Peace River Coal Block which extends along the Hart Mountain Range for 192 km had, until 1970, experienced little exploration. A few hunting camps, and limited forestry access was the extent of human habitation. Increased demand and rising price for metallurgical coal resulted in exploration activity in B.C. increasing from a value of $2.1 million in 1973 to $9.8 million in 1976. This increased pace is continuing into 1978 partially due to the fact that applications for new coal licenses are being actively considered in significant numbers for the first time since 1972.

The Reclamation Section responded to the challenge in three ways: first, a booklet of guidelines was finalized; second field crews were sent to the area in 1977; and third, a contract was let for an inventory of surface disturbance through the use of air photos. The object of this paper is to discuss the effectiveness, and the relationship of these three elements in the obtaining of compliance with the environmental sections of the mining legislation.

The legislation which regulates the industry is included in the "Coal Act" and "Coal Mines Regulation Act". The former is oriented to title and the latter to conduct of work. To comply with the latter a company must submit annually a report of work and a reclamation program both before the season starts and after it ends. It is currently a requirement that other resource agencies approve these programs.

With respect to the booklet "Guidelines for Coal and Mineral Exploration in B.C." it required 1½ years to write, from first assembly of notes and (research) material to receipt from the printers. Chapters in the booklet deal with legislation and administration, planning principles, revegetation techniques and work guidelines. Two printings of 2,000 copies each have been made to date. This booklet is a valuable aid in the obtaining of better environmental performance, not only specifically for the protective measures which it outlines, but also because it shows the companies how their work and reclamation plans should be documented, which form this is to be done on, who receives them in the administration, and how this is related to the legislation. Further work is being done oriented to reclamation techniques and sensitivities of more specific application to the Peace River Coal Block.

Two field crews were stationed in the Peace River area in the summer of 1977, all contract personnel. One studied vegetation, zonation, and natural and cultured revegetation, to analyze the parameters which determined plant growth and survival. These include

*Department of Mines and Petroleum Resources, Parliament Buildings, Mineral Resource Branch, Victoria, British Columbia, V8V 1X4, Canada.

elevation (which ranged from 1,300 to 2,600), aspect, soil and moisture condition, seed mix, schedule and technique, site preparation, fertilizer application and maintenance. The function of the second crew was primarily to advise the companies on environmental protective measures. Under ordinary circumstances the reclamation inspection task is difficult, requiring a professional knowledge of industry, the environment, legislation and amateur capability in psychology. The 1977 experience suggested that the inspection function required the services of permanent staff, and a technician is now in the field in light of this.

The inventory of surface disturbance through the use of air photos was completed in two months time. It cost $10,800 and covered 543 sq. km. Mosaics were prepared at a scale of 1:10,000 from a variety of private and government sources including both color, and black and white. One hundred twenty-nine of the 212 licenses showed exploration disturbance and although in 1977 there were 721 licenses in all, we feel that we covered about 3/4 of the work with the budget available. Estimated disturbance totaled 400 ha or an average of 3.2 ha per worked license. Non-coal work (gas, oil, seismic and forestry) amounted to ½ ha per license. A digitized planimeter was used which considerably reduced time required to estimate areas.

The air photo mosaics proved to be useful for a variety of purposes in addition to the ability to estimate disturbances for bonding: (1) as road maps; (2) as an indexing method for referencing specific disturbances for discussion; (3) as a means of dating the time of disturbance for revegetation analysis; (4) for documentation of the environment as a basis for obtaining approvals from other agencies; (5) As a format upon which reclamation measures can be documented in discussions with the company.

There were, however, disadvantages: (1) they were found in mountainous terrain to be less useful than large scale single photos, because of the heavy distortion caused by change in elevation. Large areas at higher elevation were lost. Because of the slow and expensive procedure entailed orthophotos were not considered; (2) The cost of making mosaics, and the time involved is significant in the inventory process.

We feel there is a simple way to maintain the advantages of scale in the work, and avoid the disadvantages of mosaics. By having the original negatives taken at a scale of 1:25,000 and having prints blown up to 1:10,000 with boundaries added. An individual desk size print would then cover 20 licenses which is satisfactory for both field and office work. After completion of the 1978 field season reporting of reclamation, work will be done on this format. By using a photographic enlargement rather than a blueprint from a diapositive of a mosaic, detail is considerably improved.

The 1:10,000 enlargement will in future also provide the reclamation technician on the ground with a format upon which to notate outstanding reclamation for discussions with the company. Defining 'Outstanding Reclamation' is important in documenting approval of reclamation satisfactorily performed and in the release of bonding. In order to encourage a positive attitude on the part of the company, it is desirable to be able to demonstrate that the Ministry reduces bonding liability where good work has been done. Establishing the status of work, reclamation and bonding is best done on a license-by-license basis. A status sheet can be easily and simply maintained for each license when used in conjunction with the 1:10,000 air photo. It thereby becomes possible to make measurements and comparisons of work done and reclamation achieved on a given license, or project, or group of projects on other than a subjective basis. Change in ownership, when it occurs, is also a situation which is improved if statistical means are at hand to help define reclamation responsibility.

An aspect which we had hoped to have better in hand at this time, was the processing of information and statistics which are required in the regulatory procedure. Three factors however have delayed this: first, the integration of aerial photography into current procedures must be allowed to be completed to satisfaction; second, the uses and applications of other Ministry sections require coordination with reclamation for best efficiency; and third, data processing should acknowledge current status of bonding and this is best organized on a license basis, which is not yet done.

The Geology Section has already organized its data processing system on a license basis, and we could in fact contribute to the effectiveness of their efforts through out ability to document surface work. This must be done in the future.

If Peace River Coal Block Development is considered as a whole, funding provided to Mines Reclamation by the ELUC ministers may be viewed as recognizing that continual effort is required oriented to finding a 'better way to do it'. This entails a slightly different process than the major data-oriented exercises which typified the ecological assessments of the mid-seventies. It is now realized that the success of the search for the constructive alternative is predicated on the ability to rapidly appreciate the nature of the proposed work, and to provide judgment from the government side where the legislation is not being satisfactorily served. This imposes a ponderous administrative load, but is entirely necessary. It is this task which is most often forgotten in the undertaking of environmental programs. Fortunately this was not the case in the Peace River Coal Block, and findings developed here will be applied not only on site but in the rest of the Province.

RECLAMATION, RESEARCH AND DEVELOPMENT IN MOUNTAINOUS REGIONS

Louis J. Cherene *

In 1968, Kaiser Resources Ltd. announced its intention to develop extensive coal deposits in the southeastern corner of British Columbia. In the summer of 1969, a Reclamation Department was established by Kaiser Resources Ltd. to determine the feasibility of reclamation and investigate the equipment, vegetative material and procedures necessary for a full scale reclamation program. In the spring of 1970 the Reclamation Department became fully operational with the hiring of two full-time personnel charged with the development of a viable revegetation program for the whole property. Two years later, in 1972, the Environmental Services Department was formed, comprised today of 10 full-time scientific and technical specialists. This department handles all matters of environmental nature.

The Kaiser Resources Ltd. property is located in the southeast corner of British Columbia. The title to some 110,000 acres of coal bearing land previously held by Crows Nest Industries was acquired by Kaiser Resources Ltd. in February 1969. The acreage acquired by Kaiser consists of two separate tracts of land, the larger being in the Crows Nest Field and the second is a portion of the Elk River Coalfield.

The overburden on both coalfields is composed mainly of sandstone and carbonaceous shale with some conglomerate and calcareous shales. The pH of this material ranges from 4.2 to 7.8. The coal itself is a low volatile bituminous type with a low sulphur content of 0.3-0.4%. The vegetation of this area is comprised of three different Biogeo-climatic Zones: (a) the Interior Douglas fir zone from the valley bottom to 5,000 feet; (b) the Englemann spruce-Alpine fir zone at elevations from 4,500 to 7,000 feet; and (c) the Alpine zone at elevations above 6,500 feet.

Steep topography and generally rugged terrain have broken these biogeoclimatic zones into generally localized areas which blend into one another. Also, fires and past industrial activities have left a variety of successional stages throughout. Southern aspects tend to be composed of grasslands and shrubs whereas the more northerly slopes tend toward a conifer overstory.

To understand the reclamation problems on this site a brief description of the mining methods will help. The coal and overburden are moved using shovel and truck. After blasting, the overburden is moved by truck beyond the pit limits for spoiling. Mining starts at the highest point of the pit and the spoil is dumped in a terraced, wrap-around formation on the inactive side of the mountain. As the pit is lowered the dump terraces are also successively lowered at vertical intervals of 100 feet.

The downstream water values from the open-pit mines have been protected with two

*Kaiser Resources Ltd., 1500 West Georgia, Vancouver, B.C., Canada V6GU68.

sedimentation dams. The exploration areas are each served by a main 4-wheel drive access road. From this main road a series of secondary roads are constructed to trace the coal seam or to adit and drillsites.

Kaiser Resources Ltd.'s stated policy has been to rehabilitate all industrially disturbed lands under company control caused both by present and past industrial activity. To achieve this objective the reclamation program has two basic aims: (1) to reestablish watershed values on disturbed lands as soon as possible after the cessation of industrial activity; and (2) to accomplish this watershed restoration in a way that is compatible with a potential prime surface use of the land.

When the Reclamation Department became fully operational in the spring of 1970, it was fortunate that the property had several dormant mine sites where reclamation could begin field scale trials instead of having to wait for areas to become dormant and limit its research to small test plots.

These larger areas have proved more informative over the period of operation than a series of smaller test plots. Because of the urgency of the program and the limited information available on revegetating mined lands the field scale approach was employed as opposed to a long-term research program. All the problems created by slope, aspect, and diverse spoil material were present on the one site. Prior to mining disturbance the main use of these coal bearing lands was recreation and forestry. The lower elevations have been heavily logged in earlier years and now support stands of second growth. The whole site is extensively used by ungulates for summer and winter range. The rivers support excellent fish communities.

The reclamation program in early years was based on the potential prime surface land use as designated by the Canada Land Inventory Land Capability Analysis. Experience, however, has shown that rather than attempt to replace, for example, a high yield forest with similar material, best results would be obtained by starting a natural succession at the primary level of grasses and shrubs. In this way, the vegetation provides not only initial cover but also replaces the summer and winter range alienated by coal mining and exploration activities.

As a measure of the success of this program in attaining this, a survey conducted by the Department of Fish and Wildlife during the summer of 1974 showed that ungulates were using earlier reclaimed sites rather heavily for forage during both winter and summer. This survey is being continued in 1978 and certain findings are altering the pattern of the reclamation program. One being that game do not like to browse too far from cover; this means that larger sites will have clumps of trees planted as cover to encourage the animals to move over the whole site rather than feeding on the perimeter.

The research program undertaken by Kaiser Resources has been an ongoing project since the inception of the Reclamation Department and covers every facet of concern. The first concern was to find which vegetation would survive on reclaimed sites and what techniques should best be used for their establishment. The grasses used were the available agricultural species. Initially test plots were established at different elevations and then field scale trials were accomplished, the results of which were used to modify grass mixtures on an annual basis. The present vegetation assessment program which is undertaken every fall on all reclaimed sites, includes a statistical analysis of slope, aspect, soil type, species growth and production. These results have provided a broader base of knowledge from which to plan future revegetation.

A study has been initiated in the methods of stratification of native shrub and tree seed. Some success has been achieved to date, but research into this field is long-term and will be continued into the future. A direct sowing of native shrub seeds was included in the

1975 seeding program and also on areas sown in previous years. This will be monitored on an annual basis.

Fertilizer trials are being set up to determine the quality and quantity of necessary for optimum growth. These results may also determine criteria for deciding when an area has become self-sufficient and thus fully reclaimed. A herbarium is being built up of all the species of vegetation on the property.

Slope stability and erosion control are of vital importance on the large dumps left by open-pit mining. At this time a decision has been made to implement the theoretical proposals in the field and the results will be evaluated over the coming year until final criteria have been evolved for the dumps at this elevation. On smaller sites such as encountered in the exploration areas, techniques such as benching steep cut slopes and the use of a woodchipping machine for surface stabilization and vegetation protection are being used and evaluated.

Aside from major research concerns already mentioned, other experimental work is also continuing. This has been concerned with both the immediate and long-term needs of the program and as such is quite diverse in nature. In the greenhouse and nurseries most of the research effort has gone into developing appropriate fertilizer schedules for various species grown, producing high-elevation deciduous stocks for the planting program and in general, working toward more efficient means of production through the use of artificial lighting, purified water, CO_2 enhancement and modified heating and ventilation systems.

In the field program, experiments with the hydroseeder have included the use of chemical binders for steep slopes, the use of pulp fiber instead of peat moss as a mulch, applying bentonite as a soil conditioner and using the seed of native species in order to obtain a more diverse vegetative cover. Planting trials have concentrated on using and monitoring the success of both native and introduced species. Some work with various planting techniques has been done and at one point fertilizer tablets were tried as a means of ensuring a nutrient supply to newly planted seedlings.

Experiments with fertilizing have been few, the main concern of those done being to do with the amounts of fertilizer to be used and the post-maintenance periods for which fertilization is necessary. The mixture of the agronomic species used, has been modified annually. Aside from this, some work has been done with seeding different individual species and with using native seed collected on the property. Other research work has included the use of jute netting on steep slopes, the collection and identification of native vegetation and the use of snow-fencing as a windbreak to aid in establishing seed on lagoons.

The goal of all research ultimately will be to produce a practical program that will outline for any area on the property the necessary procedures for successful reclamation. Details on the Kaiser Resources reclamation programs within the prescribed guidelines of the Province of British Columbia may be requested from the author.

RECLAMATION PROBLEMS AND PRACTICES IN EASTERN CANADA

Edward M. Watkin*

INTRODUCTION

Eastern Canada, comprised of the provinces of Ontario, Quebec, New Brunswick, Nova Scotia, Prince Edward Island and Newfoundland and Labrador encompasses approximately 3.07 million km^2 (Fig. 1). Geologically, three major areas are dominant; the Canadian Shield, the St. Lawrence Platform and the Appalachian Orogen (Fig. 2).

The Shield region, comprised of rocks of Precambrian age exposed or covered only with overburden, has many resources and has been Canada's leading source of metals. It produces many industrial minerals, and because of its size and the many areas in which geology is favorable, it has a great potential for the discovery of additional economic mineral deposits. Forest products are derived from many parts of the Shield and its numerous rivers provide a major source of hydroelectric power.

The St. Lawrence Platform flanks the southern part of the Shield from Lake Huron to Quebec City, except for a small area of the Shield called the Frontenac Axis. The surface of the Platform southwest of the Axis is known as the Great Lakes Lowland and that to the northeast as the St. Lawrence Lowland. Both areas are underlain by limestone, dolomite, sandstone and shale. Apart from the agricultural importance of the Platform, it is a large producer of aggregate for the intensively settled areas of the region. Only a few metalliferous occurrences have been found.

The Appalachian Orogen, which is the northeastern extension of a much longer belt in the United States, includes the part of Quebec lying south of the St. Lawrence River and east of a line between Lake Champlain and Quebec City, and all of New Brunswick, Nova Scotia, Prince Edward Island, and the island of Newfoundland.

The Appalachian Orogen now yields about 9 percent of the Canadian production of minerals (Lang 1972), including fuels. Important industrial minerals are asbestos, associated with basic rocks in the Eastern Townships of Quebec and gypsum, barite and salt produced in Nova Scotia. Some gypsum is also mined in New Brunswick. From Newfoundland comes most of Canada's production of fluorite. Coal deposits occur in Nova Scotia and New Brunswick. Copper, zinc, lead, gold and silver are produced, mainly from central Gaspe and central Newfoundland.

Constant reference is made to the "harsh" winters experienced in Canada, and the effect that this has on plant growth. In fact, snow cover ameliorates the effect of low temperature on survival of vegetation. The greatest effect of low temperature is the

*Crop Science Department-Noranda Mines Ltd., University of Guelph, Guelph, Ontario, Canada.

Fig. 1 - Provincial boundaries and major agricultural and forest regions within Eastern Canada.

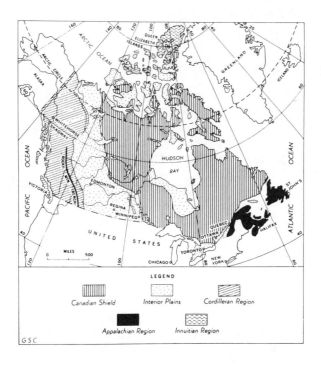

Fig. 2 - Distribution of major geological regions in Eastern Canada.

451

limitation it imposes on the choice of species for use in land reclamation programs.

Climatic conditions contrast sharply between the southernmost and more northerly areas of the eastern Ontario/western Quebec border (Table 1):

Table 1. Comparison of Several Climatic Parameters between Southwestern Ontario (Windsor) and Northeastern Ontario/Northwestern Quebec (Kirkland Lake - Val d' Or)*.

	S.W. Ontario	N.E. Ontario N.W. Quebec
Mean daily temperature (F)		
January	26	2
April	46	34
July	72	63
October	53	41
Mean annual frost-free period (days)	165	90
Mean annual length growing season (days)	220	160
Mean annual growing degree days	4200	2200
Mean May/September precipitation (mm)	356	406
Mean annual snowfall (mm)	813	2972

* Compiled from several sources, and does not represent exact meteorological station data.

In eastern Quebec and the four maritime provinces summer rainfall varies between 40 and 60 cm. The severest growing conditions are in the northernmost regions of Quebec and Labrador, where the growing season ($\pm$ 1,000 growing degree days) starts in mid-June and ends in September. In the south, by contrast, the growing season (2,600 growing degree days) extends from mid-April to late October. Throughout eastern Canada, no severe climatic conditions exist which greatly restrict plant establishment and growth. Extended periods of summer drought (30-40 days) can occur, but these are relatively minor when compared to the distribution patterns of precipitation in the western regions of North America. The most difficult climatic factor affecting reclamation through plant establishment is the decrease in length of growing season as one moves from the southern to the northern regions of eastern Canada. Such difficulties are, perhaps, self-imposed. Emphasis on the use of legumes, as opposed to grasses, is responsible for this situation. The legumes selected for use in eastern Canada as reclamation species are slower to establish than most grasses and require the longest possible growing season if adequate vegetative cover is to be established in the seeding year.

NATURE AND EXTENT OF PRACTICES AND PROBLEMS

Several factors are responsible for the amount and varied form of disturbed land that is found in eastern Canada. As already indicated, hard rock mining dominates the northern regions. Some of the minerals being recovered on a commercial basis are copper, lead, zinc, gold, silver, nickel, uranium, iron, asbestos, gypsum and coal. Processing of bauxite ore is important in Quebec.

By virtue of population concentration in a 1,120-km corridor from Quebec City in the east to Windsor in the west, the demand by industrial, commercial and residential interests for energy and mineral aggregates is high, and this is reflected in well-developed systems for the transmission of oil, gas, electricity and for the production of aggregates. The above interests have also been the cause of much disturbed and eroded lakeshores along Lake Huron, Lake Erie, Lake Ontario and the St. Lawrence River.

Disturbed land has resulted from the disposal of milling wastes, construction of oil, gas and electric transmission lines, highway construction, residential development and heavy industrial activity such as steel and fertilizer plants. Equally important, but insidious in nature, is the erosion and resulting stream sedimentation arising from a large and sophisticated agricultural industry. Obviously many of the activities are common to other areas of North America, but their effect in eastern Canada is often accentuated by the distances involved, as for example an electric power transmission line in northern Ontario approximately 33 m wide and 1,400 km long. In such circumstances, reclamation of disturbed land arising from construction represents a major undertaking. Similar problems of distance apply to oil, gas and highway systems. Hard rock mining activity is, by comparison to similar activities in the western United States, Africa and Australia, small in terms of milling wastes disposed. For example, the average iron property handles between 10,000 and 15,000 tons per day; uranium, 5,000 tons/day; gold, 700 tons/day compared to Bougainville Copper in the Pacific, where a 200,000 tons-per-day open pit feeds a 90,000 tons/day concentrator. However, Ontario and western Quebec represent one of the richest mining areas in the world, and what is lacking in individual mine size is compensated by the fact that the number of significant and active mining operations greatly exceeds 100.

Precise data on the extent of land directly disturbed by the above-mentioned spectrum of activities is not available. Only disturbance due to hard rock mining operations has been surveyed in detail (Murray 1978). Some 21,939 ha, or 216.5 sq. km, are listed by Murray as having been disturbed by overburden, waste rock or tailings deposition. Sixty-eight percent of the total disturbed area occurs within Ontario and Quebec. Assessment of disturbed areas was undertaken using LANDSAT-1 and LANDSAT-2 satellite imagery. Certain limitations of this technique were recognized, but the data obtained provided a relatively acceptable assessment of the extent of disturbed areas larger than ten hectares, when surveyed in 1974 (Table 2).

SPECIFIC PROBLEM AREAS

Three major problem areas where reclamation is urgently required may be identified in Eastern Canada. They are sulphide-containing mine wastes which can produce acid tailings seepage, highly alkaline asbestos tailings and shoreline erosion on the Great Lakes. Acid tailings seepage (ATS) occurs throughout the northern portion of Eastern Canada from northwestern Ontario to Newfoundland. The problem of asbestos tailings is confined to the Eastern Townships of Quebec, while shoreline erosion problems occur along the shores of Lake Huron, Lake St. Clair, Lake Erie and Lake Ontario. ATS and shoreline erosion have received considerable attention in the past five years. They will be discussed in some detail. Reclamation of asbestos tailings has received only marginal attention and will not be considered further.

TABLE 2 Total and Reclaimed Areas (Hectares) of Land Disturbed by Hard Rock Mining* in Eastern Canada

Commodity	Ontario Total	Reclaimed	Quebec Total	Reclaimed	New Brunswick Total	Reclaimed	Nova Scotia Total	Reclaimed	Newfoundland Total	Reclaimed	All Provinces Total	Reclaimed
Asbestos	77	2	1,863	197					217		2,157	199
Base metal (Cu,Pb,Zn,Ni)	2,596	279	2,034	62	614	18	39	26	257		5,540	385
Gold/Silver	2,714	265	778	238							3,492	503
Iron Ore	2,465	259	1,686	62					1,451	19	5,602	340
Uranium	512	33									512	33
Molybdenum			119								119	
Barite							49				49	
Titanium			49								49	
Coal					4,291	1,663	128	15			4,419	1,678
	8,364	838	6,529	559	4,905	1,681	216	41	1,925	19	21,939	3,138

* - Strictly speaking, coal is not considered a form of hard rock mining, but convenience prevails.

The problem of ATS has been chosen as an example of a reclamation problem because of its similarity with acid mine drainage that occurs predominantly in the eastern and midwestern coalfields of the United States. There are, however, several very important differences between the acidity problems in the two countries. Shoreline erosion on the Great Lakes has few equals elsewhere in terms of size and concentration of an erosion problem; it is also a problem where the combined expertise of the agronomist and the engineer is desperately needed, but is sadly lacking.

Reclamation of Tailings Containing Iron Sulphides

Acid tailings seepage was not identified in Ontario until the mid-1960's (Hawley 1972). Subsequently the problem was recognized at other base metal mining areas in Quebec, New Brunswick and Newfoundland. The seepage of acid solutions from tailings deposits is of greater concern than acid drainage from underground mines, which typifies coalfields in the eastern and mid-western United States. Acidity values of seepage water in eastern Canada can be 10 to 15-fold those reported for acid mine drainage in the eastern United States (Caruccio - personal communication).

In 1974, following initial reclamation attempts, Noranda Mines Limited (Horne Division) initiated a joint research program with the University of Guelph to devise reclamation methods for tailings areas containing iron sulphides that fell within their jurisdiction in northwestern Quebec. The project had several objectives: Establishing vegetation on the acid wastes (pH range 1.5 - 3.0) in order to minimize seepage by evapo-transpiration and increase the aesthetic appearance of tailings areas; evaluating the effect of vegetation established on fresh tailings (pH 9-10) in reducing the degree of oxidation of iron sulphides; characterization of tailings composition in order to predict the degree of difficulty likely to be encountered in revegetating oxidized and non-oxidized (fresh) tailings and future tailings from as yet non-mined ore bodies containing iron sulphides.

Several methods of amending acid tailings were evaluated through growth room and on-site studies. Amendments included agricultural limestone, rock phosphate, anhydrous ammonia, fly ash - (Table 3), precipitator dusts from the cement and phosphate fertilizer manufacturing industries and a number of other chemicals. Because of variation of unknown causes, both between and within tailings deposits, the efficacy of the above amendments was very variable. However, it is now possible to make specific recommendations on the use of agricultural limestone in large-scale reclamation projects. None of the other amendments have proven practical for one or more reasons of efficacy, consistency, or cost.

TABLE 3   pH of Waite Amulet Tailings Treated with Anhydrous Ammonia, Fly Ash and
Agricultural Limestone x Rock Phosphate

(pH at 50-ft. intervals from outside baseline to centre of tailings dam –
approximately 180 days after treatment)

			0	50	100	150	200	250	300	350	400	450	500
Anhydrous ammonia	0	lbs/acre	2.3	2.7	2.4	2.4	2.8	3.3	2.6	2.5	2.6	2.8	3.0
	500	"	2.2	2.4	2.5	3.2	3.3	3.6	2.7	2.7	2.6	3.0	2.6
	1000	"	2.3	6.9	2.4	3.1	2.8	3.2	3.0	2.5	2.8	2.6	2.8
	1500	"	2.2	2.9	2.4	2.6	3.2	3.5	3.1	3.1	3.2	3.6	2.8
	2000	"	2.3	2.4	2.3	2.6	2.8	3.4	3.5	2.9	3.1	2.8	2.7
Fly ash	0	tons/acre	2.2	4.0	4.0	2.5	2.6	2.8	-	-	-	-	-
A/S*	250	"	6.7	7.1	5.6	3.4	3.5	3.4	-	-	-	-	-
A/S	500	"	4.6	7.6	6.8	5.0	4.7	2.6	-	-	-	-	-
Raw	250	"	6.2	6.6	6.8	6.4	6.5	6.5	-	-	-	-	-
Raw	500	"	6.3	7.1	5.5	3.7	4.3	4.0	-	-	-	-	-
Agricultural limestone	25	tons/acre	2.4	2.3	2.5	2.7	2.5	2.6	5.1	5.6	4.3	5.9	3.8
	50	"	2.6	6.2	2.5	2.4	2.8	2.7	5.0	2.8	3.9	5.0	5.3
Agricultural limestone/	10/5	"	2.6	2.7	2.5	2.4	2.6	2.6	4.4	3.7	2.7	3.4	3.2
rock phosphate	10/10	"	2.7	2.5	2.3	2.3	2.8	2.7	2.8	3.6	2.6	3.5	6.1

* - A/S = aero separated fly ash.

A standard form of bioassay test has been developed to determine the agricultural limestone requirements necessary for sustained plant growth to occur on a tailings area. Such a technique has taken preference over chemical analysis. The latter, following a two-year investigation, has proven unsuitable as a method for developing a reliable field reclamation program. Using the above technique approximately 200 acres were assessed in 1977. The assessment revealed widespread differences within and between sites in agricultural limestone requirements over a range of 10 to 70 tons per acre, and also showed areas where overburden should be considered. In 1978, reclamation of the 200 acres was begun utilizing treatments that permit seeding directly into the acid wastes.

The use of vegetation and/or chemical treatments to prevent the oxidation of iron sulphides in newly deposited tailings is still uncertain. Nevertheless, laboratory and growth room studies have provided sufficient indication that such an approach is worthy of further investigation.

Although traditional analytical methods commonly used in mineralogical and soil chemistry analysis have so far failed to distinguish between tailings known to have a high, medium or low vegetation potential, a recent study has indicated that the morphology of the iron sulphides in the tailings being investigated varies very distinctly both between and within tailings sites. (Caruccio, personal communication). The significance of such variation is presently being assessed.

Control of Shoreline Erosion on the Great Lakes

Storm action superimposed upon record and near-record high water levels during the fall of 1972 and spring of 1973 caused extensive damage to Great Lakes shorelines and connecting channels by flooding and erosion. Environment Canada (a federal department) and the Ontario Ministry of Natural Resources subsequently entered into an agreement to survey the nature and extent of these damages and to make preliminary recommendations related to shoreline management and planning. Acquisition of data on which these recommendations were made commenced in the spring of 1973 and was completed in the summer of 1974. Much of what follows is a brief summary of the technical report of the survey (Canada - Ontario Great Lakes Shore Damage Survey, 1975).

Shoreline damage due to erosion and inundation is most severe when lake levels are high. Changes in lake levels result when the amount of water supplied to the lake is less than the amount of water leaving the lake. The Great Lakes are an effective naturally-regulated water system because of their immense storage capacity and restricted outflow capacity. Variations in Great Lakes levels and outflows are small compared to most major North American river systems. The maximum range of annual levels on the Great Lakes is 1 to 2 m depending on the lake, which is small when compared to the 7 meter tidal variations every 12 hours at Quebec City. The maximum outflow of any of the Great Lakes is only 2 to 3 times the minimum outflow. This is in marked contrast to the 30 to 1 ratio of maximum to minimum flow for the Mississippi River.

Erosion and inundation are natural processes which occur, to a varying extent, on most shorelines. The high water levels that occurred in 1972/73 and the storm periods that accompanied these high levels are, similarly, natural phenomena. It is probable that the high water levels of 1973 will be exceeded sometime in the future, and subsequent shore damage inevitable.

Some of the quantitative conclusions which evolved from the acquired data were as follows:

1) Great Lakes shore damage due to erosion and inundation amounted to more than $19 million (Table 4) during the period of survey and, combined with $9 million in lost land value due to erosion (Table 5), resulted in total costs in excess of $28 million. Contributing to this total in some measure was a lack of understanding of suitable methods of shoreline protection, resulting in increased costs and decreased effectiveness.

2) Future shore damage through erosion and inundation is inevitable as evidenced by more than $19 million in immediate potential damage attributed to the unpredictable nature of the phenomena acting upon the shorelines.

TABLE 4   Shore Damage on the Great Lakes, 1972 - 1973

Lake	Shoreline length (km)	Total damage $ millions	Total damage $ per km	Immediate potential damage $ millions	Immediate potential damage $ per km
Lake Huron	969	2.5	2,551	0.5	545
Lake St. Clair	93	4.2	45,326	2.5	26,287
Lake Erie	635	4.8	7,506	1.3	2,086
Lake Ontario	1,062	3.2	3,052	0.6	585
Total	2,759	14.7		4.9	

TABLE 5 Great Lakes Erosion and Accretion, 1972 - 1973 (in m^3)

	Erosion	Accretion	Net Erosion
Lake Huron	961,828	298,006	663,822
Lake St. Clair	150,352	53,853	96,499
Lake Erie	18,441,128	960,375	17,480,753
Lake Ontario	2,403,511	704,525	1,698,986
Total	21,956,819	2,016,759	19,940,060

3) The survey demonstrated regional variance in the extent of property damage and intensity of shore erosion. An example of the variance in shore damage was found on Lake Huron, with average damages of $20,447/km in Lambton County to $327/km in Bruce County. Shore erosion varied from 5.62 m^3/m/m/yr in Lambton County to a negligible amount in Bruce County. These data are useful in establishing areas with hazard land characteristics. The degree of shore damage and the intensity of shore erosion or inundation are not necessarily in direct proportion. A great deal of shore damage may be attributed to the effects of storms and subsequent wave action. An example is the Regional Municipality of Peel where shore damage was relatively high at $36,193/km while the shoreline was not subject to heavy erosion or inundation relative to other areas on the Great Lakes.

4) The total value of Great Lakes riparian property in the study area was $1.3 billion, with an average value of $364/m of shoreline. The estimated cost of long-term protection for the entire shoreline is $1.02 billion or $287/m. This cost estimate was based on reinforced concrete protection for the entire shoreline at 1973 prices. Amortized over 20 years at 7 percent, the benefit cost ratio is .669, which suggests that structural protection of the real erodible shoreline is not economically sound. This is supported by the fact that 54% of the total hazard-land shoreline is worth less than the cost of long-term shore protection based on present economic trends.

In reviewing the consequences of shoreline erosion the report discussed what strategies or alternatives are available to mitigate the effects. It states that a strategy is needed for effective management and planning within Great Lakes coastal areas. Long-term shore protection is a structural approach in dealing with shoreline damage, although it may be difficult to justify economically and environmentally. This becomes obvious upon comparison of land values with estimates of long-term shore protection. For example, in one area of shoreline the value of the land was about $25 million while the estimated cost of long-term protection was $64 million. Environmental problems could result through interference with the natural shore processes and subsequent effects to areas adjacent to the protected shoreline. Water level regulation to reduce the occurrence of high lake levels is another technological solution, but excavation, and the construction of regulatory works would be costly. Other possibilities are shoreline planning and management methods such as public acquisition, shoreline setback requirements and easements. It would seem reasonable to regulate development to ensure public safety. There are clear and stringent regulations for the design of buildings to protect their inhabitants, but there is no comparable concern reflected in municipal by-laws which ensures that a person's home is not built on a floodplain or too close to the edge of an eroding bluff. So while the electrical wiring in a house must meet rigid safety standards, the building itself may be washed away during a storm.

In describing methods of controlling shore erosion the report lays heavy emphasis on engineering solutions such as groynes, jetties, breakwaters, dykes, revetments, Maccaferri Gabions and other structures. It is disappointing to note the lack of emphasis on vegetative techniques as a means of controlling or aiding in shoreline stabilization. Obviously vegetation cannot be used in place of many man-made structures to reduce erosion caused by wave action. Its role, though, in preventing subsequent or further erosion of a breached shoreline is generally underestimated. Of great importance is the fact that vegetative stabilization is usually within the financial resources of an individual property owner, where construction solutions are often prohibitive. As Haras (personal communication) has pointed out, there is no stereotyped method of shore protection which might be applied to all sections of shoreline, or even to all locations within any one section. If it were possible to develop such a method which would provide adequate protection to any locality under all conditions, shore protection would present few difficulties. But the problem is not that simple, and many types must be considered in the light of local conditions and the results to be achieved. Each of the different types have their own advantages, disadvantages and limitations and these attributes generally dictate the method and degree of protection to be employed.

Recently a descriptive manual (Great Lakes Basin Commission, 1977) has been prepared for shoreline property owners along the Great Lakes with 1) a comprehensive review of shoreline erosion problems, 2) an explanation of why these problems occur, 3) guidelines to help individual property owners identify their particular problems, and 4) some suggestions of how the property owner may remedy some of these problems. The solutions emphasize vegetation establishment and management and its role in shoreline stabilization. The role of vegetation in retarding shoreline erosion on the Great Lakes has also been discussed in detail by Haras et al. (1977).

It was pointed out that while vegetation can accomplish a great deal in the way of slope stabilization, there are limits to its use which must be realized from the beginning. In almost all cases, vegetation will not control wave action. It may decrease the rate at which the beach or bluff is eroded during a storm, but it cannot stop wave action. Some form of shore protection measures, or lower lake levels will be required to reduce wave action. Because of this, shoreline management requires a comprehensive review of a property section prior to attempting an erosion control program. In this regard the shoreline property owner is urged to consider the use of vegetation to complement his shore protection efforts. Several levels of vegetation management may be used depending on the need of a given situation. These are as follows.

Minimal Management

This applies to shoreland areas which presently have good vegetative cover along the backshore or bluff, or have a stable beach. For example:

a)   Bluffs which have good vegetative cover should be maintained, and any bare patches along these bluffs should be planted with an appropriate plant material.

b)   Shoreland areas which have a good natural beach to serve as a buffer where wave action is dissipated, but whose bluffs are too high [greater than 10 m (30 ft)] and too steep [greater than 1:1.5 (33°)] to support vegetation without regrading, should at least be planted at the toe and on top of the bluff.

c)   All sand dunes and wetland areas are susceptible to damage from just minimal human disturbances, so it is important to maintain or reestablish the vegetation which these areas support. This maintenance will, in turn, preserve the important ecosystems associated with both sand dunes and wetlands.

Heavy Management

This applies to areas with stable shorelines but poor vegetative cover. It also includes those areas with gentler slopes [less than 1:1.5 (33°)] and those areas with successful man-made shoreline protection. Under these conditions, intensive planting and management of vegetation is both possible and strongly encouraged. For example:

a)   Shoreland areas with good natural beaches for bluff toe protection and backshore or bluff areas with gradual slopes [less than 1:1.5 (33°)] should be planted in order to protect against surface erosion. Surface runoff should be controlled during this planting effort.

b)   Shoreland areas with successful, structural protection against wave action (groynes, breakwaters, or revetments) should be supplemented by establishing vegetation on the adjacent backshore or bluff areas. In those areas where the slopes are too steep [greater than 1:1.5 (33°)] but not too high [less than 10 m (30 ft)], regrading to gentler slopes may be desirable.

Special Management

This applies to areas which presently have little or no natural beach, steep slopes, groundwater seepage problems, and poor vegetation. To adequately deal with these problems, a combination of structural, drainage and vegetation controls is required. These may include structural toe protection, regrading of the slope, internal drainage of the bluff, and intensive planting on the slope face. This is the most effective method of dealing with the entire problem of shoreline erosion, but it is also the most expensive. These costs should be investigated thoroughly before such a project is undertaken.

CONCLUSIONS

During the past decade of environmental awareness, the reclamation of drastically disturbed lands has developed as a major field of endeavor. Yet despite the obvious and critical role of crops in land reclamation procedures, the involvement of the crop scientist has remained marginal as far as eastern Canada is concerned. Reclamation research and practical implementation, where undertaken, has been by personnel from other disciplines such as engineering, forestry, ecology and soil science. This lack of involvement, or interest by the crop scientist is an enigma, particularly when consideration is given to the type and amount of crop knowledge required to successfully accomplish land reclamation programs.

The input of engineers, landscape architects, soil scientists, and ecologists is of necessary and vital importance in the overall design and implementation of operations which result in drastically disturbed land areas, if environmental effects are to be minimized. Almost invariably, though, the endput of any reclamation scheme is the establishment of a vegetative cover for practical use as a crop, or for reducing polluting effects of erosion or toxic drainage or for aesthetic reasons, either alone or in combination. To this end, the knowledge and training of the crop scientist in soil and tissue analysis, crop selection and adaptation, methods of seeding, fertilizer usage and awareness of amelioration techniques such as limestone, sewage sludge and compost applications, is probably unique.

Three reasons are suggested as a partial explanation for that type of situation, two generally applicable to both countries, the third more applicable to Canada than to the United States:

1) The concept held by many non-agriculturalists that crop establishment and maintenance is a simple procedure and, as such, presents no problems in the overall design and implementation of a land reclamation program.

2) That the transference of knowledge applicable to agricultural soils, to atypical soils (e.g. subsoils) or non-soils (e.g. mine wastes) is often entirely subjective. In some instances commonly accepted agricultural concepts do not apply; soil pH has long been considered a reasonable parameter for indicating the presence or absence of nutritional problems in agricultural soils. For acid mine tailings, it is now known that initial pH determinations have little relevance as indicators of potential crop establishment and persistence (Watkin, unpublished data).

3) The lack of government funding for research on crop growth problems on drastically disturbed land. This is a reflection of the attitude outlined above (1). In eastern Canada, nearly all of the studies on vegetation of drastically disturbed lands have been undertaken by private industry. Although this work has been successful on an individual site basis, the practical nature of the studies has not enabled any worthwhile common understanding of the various problems to be achieved. Each new reclamation project has, at the present time, to develop its own waste amelioration and cropping practice techniques.

REFERENCES

Environment Canada, Ontario Ministry of Natural Resources. 1975. Canada-Ontario Great Lakes Shore Damage Surv. Tech. Rpt., 97 p.

Great Lakes Basin Commission. 1977. The role of vegetation in shoreline management. A guide for Great Lakes shoreline property owners, 32 p.

Haras, W.S., E.M. Watkin and T.S. Dai. 1977. The role of vegetation in retarding shoreline erosion on the Canadian Great Lakes Shoreline. Vegetation Workshop, U.S.D.A. Soil Conservation Service and Great Lakes Basin Commission, Ann Arbor, MI.

Hawley, J.R. 1972. The problem of acid mine drainage in the Province of Ontario. Mining Industrial Wastes Branch, Ministry of the Environment, Toronto, Ontario, Canada, 338 p.

Lang, A.M. 1970. Prospecting in Canada. Econ. Geol. Rpt. No. 7, Geol. Surv. Canada, Dept. of Energy, Mines and Resources, Ottawa, 4th Ed., 308 p.

Murray, D.R. 1977. Pit Slope Manual, Supplement 10-1 - Reclamation by vegetation: Vol. 2 - Mine waste inventory by Satellite Imagery; CANMET (Canada Center for Mineral and Energy Technology, formerly Mines Branch, Energy, Mines and Resources Canada), CANMET REPORT 77-58, 216 p.

SOME ALTERNATIVE APPROACHES
TO THE ESTABLISHMENT OF VEGETATION
ON MINED LAND AND ON CHEMICAL WASTE MATERIALS

*R. Neil Humphries**

INTRODUCTION

It has been estimated by Wallwork (1976) that 24,142 ha of derelict land in England originate from mineral workings and may account for over 50% of the listed derelict land. Of these, the spoil heaps contribute 13,118 ha, the excavations 8,717 ha and the remainder is quarry plant. The distribution of this dereliction is concentrated in several regions of the British Isles for geological, geographical and historical reasons (Wallwork 1974). In some localities, like Cornwall, mineral workings are almost the sole source of despoiled land. Sands and gravels are the largest mineral extractive industry producing over 105.6×10^6 mT of aggregates in 1972 from land deposits (Harris et al. 1974). Excavations for this resource probably cover more than 20,000 ha of land but only 9% is likely to become derelict. Far more dereliction is likely from the extraction of coal and limestone (Table 1) though the most despoiling workings are considered to be those of china clay and igneous rock.

The history of reclaiming the legacy of mineral workings is described by Oxenham (1966), Barr (1969) and Wallwork (1974). Between 1968 and 1974, the rate of derelict land clearance was estimated to be 12% per year. This was concentrated in areas of aesthetic merit, areas of high agricultural production, in areas adjacent to urban development and in those regions where regional grants were available. This trend is likely to continue. Current

TABLE 1   The Potential Dereliction Associated with the Extraction of Six Mineral Resources

Resource	Extraction area, ha	Potential dereliction after extraction, ha	% dereliction of extraction area
Sands and Gravels	20156	1712	8.5
Coal	8925	3985	44.6
Limestone	5451	2598	47.7
Chalk	2132	376	17.6
China Clay	1749	1224	70.0
Igneous Rock	1347	809	60.0

Data adapted from Wallwork, 1976

*Department of Applied Biology, University of Cambridge, Pembroke Street, Cambridge, England CB2 3DX.

workings are often reclaimed by the operators under agreement with the planning agencies. Where sufficient material, from the quarry (waste, overburden) or from other nearby sources (P.F.A., coal shales, refuse) is available, satisfactory re-contouring is possible. Outstanding examples of overburden in filled sites are the ironstone and opencast coal workings which have been restored to agriculture, forestry and recreation. Since 1952 over 24,000 ha have been worked for coal and restored to agriculture alone (Davies et al. 1975). In many pits and quarries insufficient materials are available locally and the overburden has already been tipped outside the workings. The establishment of vegetation on these tipped materials, other wastes and on the exposed mineral surfaces are for purposes other than agriculture, i.e. pollution control, landscape, recreation, wildlife, brushwood etc.

THE CONVENTIONAL APPROACH

In Britain, agricultural grasses and legumes are invariably used to establish vegetation on derelict and mined land materials for agricultural and non-agricultural purposes. They are the most favored source of seed because: (1) there is a wide choice of grass and legume species (and their varieties) available which span the range of soil, climatic and biological conditions encountered in the UK, (2) seed is available throughout the year from merchants, (3) seed is much cheaper than non-agricultural alternatives, (4) seed quality is guaranteed (i.e. seed is cleaned and germination certificates are authentic), (5) most agricultural species germinate rapidly (few have dormancy though several contain a proportion of "hard seed"), (6) their early growth is rapid and often they compete in closed swards better than non-agricultural varieties and species, (7) many are long lived perennials, (8) a lot is known about their response to management (burning, cutting etc.) and other stresses (drought, trampling) thus enabling effective after-care plans to be devised well in advance, (9) the legume species are capable of fixing nitrogen and the bacterial-inoculum is available, (10) some of the species have additional merits for example, *Melilotus alba* (white sweet clover) has been used to remove boron from pulverized fuel ash, and (11) most of the species of grasses and legumes used are a component of the British flora.

The choice of species and sowing rates are generally based on agricultural criteria of climate, soils and stocking rates (Blaser et al. 1952, Spedding and Diekmahns 1972). The species recommended for the restoration of opencast coal sites to agricultural grassland are given in Table 2. The temporary leys, hay or pasture, are used for up to five years before permanent pasture is reestablished to ensure the restoration of soil fertility and structure. The alternative mixtures are recommended for site variation in altitude, soil texture, drainage and grazing regime. Similar mixtures have been used on thinly soiled colliery shales (Univ. Newcastle 1971) and directly on burnt colliery shale (Coates 1964). Agricultural techniques are used to prepare the site and ameliorate the "spoil" materials to agricultural standards (Oxenham 1968, Hackett 1977), where access is limited hydroseeding is usually employed (Brooker 1974).

In the latter case, seed bed preparation, pH correction and fertilizer applications are not carried out to agricultural specifications. Some adjustment should be made to the agricultural mixtures by incorporating species like *Agrostis tenuis* and *Festuca rubra* which are more tolerant of extremes in soil pH, higher levels of toxic elements and low levels of mineral nutrients. In the absence of seed bed preparation, seed rates up to 150 kg ha^{-1} have been used to offset the reduced establishment rate.

Seed mixtures containing more than five different species are preferred by most practitioners and contractors for non-agricultural situations as an insurance policy and because species like *Lolium multiflorum* which germinate rapidly, yet have short persistence,

TABLE 2   Forage and Hay Species Recommended for the Restoration of
Open-cast Coal Sites to Agriculture by the Ministry of
Agriculture, Fisheries and Food

Species ≠		Grassland type	
Latin binomial	Common name	Temporary (the first 1-4 years)	Permanent
Lolium multiflorum	Italian ryegrass	+	+*
Lolium perenne	Ryegrass	+	+*
Phleum pratense	Timothy	+	+
Dactylis glomerata	Cocksfoot		+
Festuca arundinacea	Tall fescue		+
Festuca pratensis	Meadow fescue		+
Agrostis tenuis	Common bent		+*
Poa trivialis	Rough-stalked-meadow grass		+*
Trifolium pratense	Broad red clover/Late flowering red clover	+	+
Trifolium hybridum	Alsike clover	+	+*
Trifolium repens	Large white clover/wild white clover	+	+*
Plantago lanceolata	Ribwort plantain		+*

* Components used for poor upland sites intended for sheep grazing.

≠ The mixtures may contain different cultivars

can be used as nurse crops and soil stabilizers. Despite such measures, several schemes have failed to provide an adequate ground cover. The most common explanation being the inclement weather during the establishment period, low standard of work by the contractor, failure to use the appropriate specification to deal with the extreme site conditions, the materials being phytotoxic, and a failure to implement subsequent aftercare treatments where the system is not self-maintaining.

ALTERNATIVE APPROACHES

Owing to the overall success and availability of agriculturally bred species, there has been little initiative in Britain to research into and develop alternative specifications. The notable exception is the work on vegetating non-ferrous metal mine spoils using indigenous tolerant varieties of grass (Smith and Bradshaw 1972).

Substitution of Species

The most obvious alternative is the substitution by non-agricultural species for agricultural ones. The use of ecotypes (Turesson 1922) found growing on the spoil material is of particular interest. The ecological significance of ecotypes has been discussed in detail for metal mine spoils by Antonovics et al. (1971) and for serpentine soils by Proctor and Woodell (1975). To use them on a practical scale, a breeding program has to be initiated. This has enabled seed of heavy metal tolerant *Festuca rubra* and *Agrostis tenuis* populations to become commercially available (Humphreys and Bradshaw 1977). Successful substitution of species has been made in a number of landscaping schemes. With the increase in the cost of maintaining roadside grassland areas, some local authorities have experimented with species having more prostrate growth forms, slower growth rates and those less dependent on fertilizer application. They have achieved this by increasing the clover content in the seed mixtures and there are examples where only white clover has been used to vegetate roadside embankments. The number of mowings needed to maintain a short vegetation have been markedly reduced, although some management is still required to control the invasion and growth of the taller ruderal species. In a scheme to revegetate old colliery (coal mine waste) tips in Stoke-on-Trent for 'urban green-space', some areas were successfully seeded with commercially obtained *Achillea millefolium, Vicia sativa, Poterium sanguisorba* and *Cichorium intybus* as well as seed cleanings (mainly *Holcus lanatus*) (Tandy 1975, Land Use Consultants 1976). A very successful scheme is one undertaken by the Ministry of Transport on a steep chalk cutting near Rochester, Kent. The grass-legume mixture included seven dicotyledon species but only *Poterium sanguisorba, Dacus carota, Circhorium intybus* and the legume *Onobrychis viciifolia* established (Wright, unpublished). The success of these species is attributed to their tap roots penetrating deep into cracks in the chalk for moisture and anchorage and the plants' low mineral nutrient requirements. The difference in their phenology provides a welcome relief in color and texture in the landscape from the typical green-brown monotony of a grass sward. Ecologically, it is the appropriate solution because it has been completely maintenance free and the open structure of the vegetation has allowed the invasion of many chalk grassland species.

Interest by some researchers has been shown in the reestablishment of semi-natural grasslands on former agricultural soils. T.C.E. Wells at Monks Wood (Institute of Terrestrial Ecology) has been investigating this possibility for chalk grassland species (Monks Wood Research Station Report 1973). From hand collected, screened, cleaned and tested seed, he is now confident that a chalk grassland of faithful structure can be established on calcium carbonate rich soils (Wells, personal communication). With natural seed, problems do arise. It is difficult to buy or collect large quantities of seed of adequate viability, many species have dormancy mechanisms which have to be broken (Grubb 1976) and mechanized collection requires that unwanted species have to be removed. In the case of semi-natural chalk grasslands some management like burning, mowing or grazing will be necessary to maintain the structure. One source of seed would be the utilization of mowings from floristically rich areas (parkland, road verges, hay meadows, nature reserves etc.). We have found that fresh mowings from a chalk-heath grassland described by Grubb et al. (1969), which are normally tipped, can be used to establish several components of the flora (Table 3). From the material taken in a 10 m^2 cut during October enough seed was available to establish 1 m^2 of vegetation. At present the mowings are taken once or twice a year, depending on the location, as a management trial to reestablish the herbaceous flora following scrub invasion (Green 1972). To include seed of all the species, mowings would have to be taken at other times too. However, valuable seed material is available in the mowings and it could be profitably used somewhere. A similar approach has been suggested (Brent-Jones, personal communication) for the establishment of *Calluna vulgaris* heath on disturbed land by taking mowings after seed set and laying them on the soil surface during the winter.

Table 3. The Species Established from Chalk-Heath Mowings.

Species Established from Mowings

Trifolium repens, Poterium sanguisorba, Galium saxatile, Galium verum, Leontodon sp., *Calluna vulgaris, Erica cinerea, Veronica officinalis, Teucrium scorodonia, Thymus drucei, Plantago lanceolata, Plantago media, Agrostis stolonifera, Agrostis tenuis, Dactylis glomerata, Holcus lanatus*

Some of the Listed Species not Established

Polygala vulgaris, Lotus corniculatus, Ulex europaeus, Filipendula hexapetala, Potentilla erecta, Rubus spp., *Epilobium angustifolium, Achillea millefolium, Cirsium arvense, Betonica officinalis, Glechoma hederacea, Rumex acetosella, Anthoxanthum odoratum, Sieglingia decumbens*

The Use of Alternative Seed Sources and Propagules

Chippindale and Milton (1934) demonstrated that in many soils there is a large number of seeds in the top 2.5 cm. The numbers decrease with depth (some species are only represented in the upper horizons) and the species may differ in the number of years they remain viable (Brenchley and Warrington 1930, Roberts 1968). On topsoiled areas the cover by volunteer plants, where seeding has been delayed, bear witness to this. Topsoiling has been advocated by some people to reestablish a natural vegetation cover but it will be too unpredictable in most cases (seed numbers, viability etc.) and sufficient quantities are unlikely to be available. It could be used as a technique to provide the species of interest in specific but small areas (Wathern 1976). The more promising situation arises when a deep litter layer is associated with the vegetation. Litter collected from beneath *Calluna vulgaris* heath contains large quantities of seed and this can be used as a cheap and convenient to handle seed source (Wathern 1976).

Some species of plants will regenerate from plant parts and/or spread vegetatively by bulbs, rhizomes, stolons, tillers etc. Many weeds of arable soils are perennial dictyledons (Fryer and Evans 1970) and these survive by being able to regenerate following mechanical injury from ploughing, discing etc. Very little experimental work has been reported on the establishment of native British species from fragments or turf.

Preliminary experiments under controlled environmental conditions demonstrated that several grassland species found growing on waste lime tips were capable of rapid regeneration from fragments in a potting compost (Table 4). In a field experiment (Humphries 1977a) weathered lime waste material was removed to a depth of 15 cm, tipped, mixed and then spread to two final depths of 2.5 cm or 5 cm after compaction, over newly exposed waste. A further preparation method was superimposed over half the plots which entailed the incorporation of top material into the unweathered waste. Three vegetation treatments were used; a high yield and low yield agricultural seed mixture, and a treatment containing plant fragments only. Agricultural levels of fertilizer were applied to the seeded areas each year, but only in the first season to the plant fragment treatment. The results after three seasons are summarized in Table 5. The aboveground standing crop and

Table 4.   The Regeneration of a Number of Grassland Species from Shoot and Root Fragments.

Species Regenerating from 'Shoot' Fragments

Trifolium pratense, Trifolium repens, Cardus nutans?, Chrysanthemum leucanthemum, Hieracium pilosella, Hieracium vulgatum, Leontodon taraxacoides?, Taraxacum officinale, Prunella vulgaris, Plantago lanceolata, Agrostis stolonifera, Festuca ovina, Festuca rubra

Species Regenerating from 'Root' Fragments

Heracleum sphondylium?, Achillea millefolium, Carlina vulgaris?, Centaurea nigra?, Tussilago farfara

Species Failed to Regenerate

Cerastium vulgatum, Linum catharticum, Lotus corniculatus, Leontodon hispidus, Senecio jacobaea, Campanula glomerata, Gentianella amarella, Thymus drucei, Carex flacca, Arrhenatherum elatius, Briza media, Dactulis glomerata, Lolium perenne, Poa annua, Rhinanthus minor

TABLE 5   The Performance of Vegetation Established from Different Propagules on Lime Waste Materials

Vegetation technique	kg/ha*	SE	% ground cover
seeded high yield mixture	3332	758.0	80
seeded low yield mixture	656	140.8	41
plant fragments	1012	438.8	63
Method of preparation			
weathered and unweathered mixed 1:1	1576	483.2	84
weathered layer over unweathered	1980	627.6	65
Amount of material used			
weathered waste 25m^3/ha	1008	248.4	53
weathered waste 50m^3/ha	2628	728.8	66

* dry matter of standing crop

percentage ground cover using the plant fragment technique proves to be as good as sowing the weathered wastes with a low yield agricultural seed mixture. The effect of the method of preparation was inconclusive but the depth of material used is important. In a further experiment it was demonstrated that the higher rate of waste application favored the establishment of plants from seed and fragments present in the lime waste (Table 6).

TABLE 6   Species Establishing from Plant Fragments and Seed Contained
in Weathered Lime Wastes

Species established	Lime waste application rate	
	$25m^3$/ha	$50m^3$/ha
Viola sp.	1	0
Cerastium vulgatum	1	2
Linium catharticum	0	78
Trifolium pratense	0	4
Trifolium repens	1	0
Heracleum sphondylium	0	1
Chrysanthemum leucanthemum	2	32
Hieracium vulgatum	1	8
Leontodon hispidus	4	15
Taraxacum officinale	0	1
Tussilago farfara	0	6
Campanula glomerta	1	0
Euphrasia officinale	22	40
Plantago lanceolata	35	245
Agrostis stolonifera	1	0
Briza media	2	1
Total number of individuals/$7500cm^2$	105	501

Four other species established from wind blown seeds

Similar experiments were carried out on a quarry floor and waste materials to re-establish components from a local and species-rich turf (identified by Shimwell (1968) as *Helictotricho-Caricetum flaccae typicum* association. An area of grassland was stripped as a complete turf, cut into 5 cm diameter cores which were then randomly planted into experimental plots (the treatments were a factorial of soil and peat additions at three levels in all combinations). The mean number of surviving turf units in the entire experiment after one season was 25.4/2 m^2 (SE 3.30) out of 37.4 (SE 1.90) planted. The species present over the seasons are given in Table 7. The range of species established using small pieces of turf is most encouraging. Despite the unfavorable weather conditions during 1975 and 1976, several species grew rapidly, particularly on plots amended with a peat-soil treatment. All plots were fertilized each year at a relatively low rate. The mean area of the plots covered by turf increased from 4% to 10% during the trial and the final mean diameter of each turf was 8.4 cm (SE 0.26).

A Successional Approach

On difficult but not phytoxic substrates, greater success might be achieved if the vegetation components were established in more than one operation. Jones et al. (1975) have demonstrated that a superior end product is achieved when a "two step approach" is used to establish small grain legume species on surface mine spoils in West Virginia. The legume crop was introduced into a pioneer cereal prior to which had been sprayed with herbicide. There are numerous techniques to promote the establishment of oversown species into existing vegetation, even where the cover is complete, which include burning, cultivation and chemical treatment (Wathern 1976). The purpose of using pioneer vegetation is to ameliorate the edaphic conditions (by surface stabilization, accumulation of plant

Table 7.   The Reestablishment of Plants from Species Rich Turf Fragments on a Quarry Floor.

Species Present at Start and in Third Season

Helianthemum chamaecistus, Geranium sangiunium, Hippocrepis comosa, Lotus corniculatus, Trifolium repens, Poterium sanguisorba, Potentilla tabernaemontani, Chrysanthemum leucanthemum, Cirsium acaulon, Hieracium pilosella, Leontodon hispidus, Thymus drucei, Allium oleraceum, Dactylis glomerata, Festuca ovina

Species Present at Start but not After Second Season

Fragaria vesca, Leontodon taraxacoides

Species Present at Start but not After One Season

Arabis hirsuta, Cardamine hirsuta, Erophila verna, Koeleria cristata

Species Present at Start and After Third Season, but Absent in Second

Sedum acre, Linum catharticum

Species Invading Soil Between Turfs After Three Seasons

Cerastium vulgatum, Epilobium angustifolium, Aethusa cynapium, Senecio vulgaris

litter, aid the formation of 'soil' structure etc.) and to provide a more hospitable micro-climate. This enables the successful establishment of the more sensitive species. The approach may consist of several phases in order to achieve a specific type of plant community. On most sites and materials, the process of amelioration of edaphic conditions has to be aided by one or more techniques (fertilizer applications, irrigation, grazing, etc.)

The serial (and seral) introduction has worked well on a coarse crushed limestone spoil tip (93% $CaCO_3$, < 20% < 2 mm particle size fraction) where *Festuca rubra* was the only only species to persist on the material. Experiments on site had demonstrated that water stress and mineral nutrient deficiencies limited the establishment and persistence of agricultural species like *Trifolium repens* (Table 8).

To introduce *T. repens* onto the spoil tip, the edaphic conditions have to be ameliorated. The effect of modest levels of NPK fertilizer applied each spring for three years to the *Festuca rubra* sward increased the amount of organic matter in the spoil (Humphries 1977b). Sowing   *T. repens* into these plots was more successful, 148 individuals/m^2 persisted. However annual phosphatic fertilizer application is necessary to achieve sufficient growth to meet the landscape objectives and to promote nitrogen accumulation in the soil. In the light of this experience, I would recommend the use of less sensitive legumes like *Lotus*

Table 8. The Effect of Irrigation and Fertilizer Application on the Persistence of *Trifolium repens* on a Limestone Spoil Tip.

	Numbers of individuals*/m^2
Control	0
NPK fertilizer	48
Irrigation	4
NPK fertilizer + irrigation	105

*Number of seeds sown 296/m^2

corniculatus and *Medicago lupulina* from the start to aid soil development. Though to achieve the desired landscape objective, *T. repens* almost certainly would have to be introduced in time.

An alternative approach currently being investigated is the inclusion of all the 'seral' components in the succession from the start. This is possible when the components of the later stages are slow growing or/and have seed dormancy. Scrub and woodland establishment from seed offers this opportunity. A herbaceous ground cover, if carefully chosen, will act as a nurse crop in which the woody species eventually grow and dominate. Initial experiments indicate that annual legumes like *Medicago lupulina* and *Lotus corniculatus* are ideal cover crops. It appears there is a considerable potential to engineer succession in this manner for a range of woody species. Where possible, nitrogen fixing plants should be included as they are very important in the rate and direction of seral development in temperate climates. Recently Dancer et al. (1977) have not only shown the importance of leguminous species and nitrogen accumulation in the nature of natural succession on kaolin mining wastes, but also point out that they are likely to be the most successful species on materials deficient in mineral nitrogen.

DISCUSSION

From the outline case histories it is clear there are alternative ways of establishing plants on mined land and chemical wastes. An acceptable case could be made for their use if they were demonstrated to have practical and not just academic advantages over the current methodology. Among the criteria on which judgement might be made by a practitioner would be a superior performance on difficult sites and materials, a more convenient method and a more appropriate ecological or landscape solution. However much more research and development is needed before fair comparisons can be made.

Ecological Aspects

Most ecological research in Britain has concentrated on the establishment and persistence of grass-legume mixtures. Most emphasis has been given to toxic elements and their effects and to various aspects of mineral nutrition (Goodman and Bray 1975). Although much more work could be done especially on mineral nutrition, there is a real need to alter the emphasis. For instance, little is known about the population biology (Harper 1977) of many of the plants currently used, besides those that might have a potential. This is important when considering the long-term persistence of the vegetation cover established and the management of the post-establishment phase. The absence of suitable agriculturally bred plant material for the arid and semiarid areas of North America and Australia has given rise to a much broader approach to revegetation (see various contributions to this Congress). In Britain the changes most likely to find acceptance will be the direct substitution of commercially available grasses, legumes and some dicotyledon herb species for the traditional hay-forage species. For their use to be successful more expertise will be required in the field to judge their suitability for each site. It has been suggested that on the more difficult sites, a seed mixture containing stress tolerant species will be most successful. On a limestone spoil tip, the following species were sown: *Lolium perenne, Poa pratensis, Cynosurus cristatus, Dactylis glomerata, Trifolium repens, T. campestre, T. pratense* and *Festuca rubra* but only the last species survived without the application of NPK fertilizer. Clearly without a regular application of fertilizer, the use of this conventional multi-species seed mixture hardly seems justified. The use of a single species is fine on a homogenic material but on heterogenic materials a species mixture should be used. For example the embankments and cuttings along Britains's Motorways pass through many types of subsoils and topsoils, the relaid material on the surface prior to sowing is extremely variable. The species mixture recommended by the Department of Transport is *Lolium perenne, Festuca rubra, Poa pratensis, Cynosurus cristatus* and *Trifolium repens* but it has rarely established faithfully. The initial loss of species is accounted for by the physical conditions at time of sowing (angle of slope, aspect, texture, compaction, available mineral nutrients (especially nitrogen), available moisture and the weather at sowing) and later on biotic factors of competition and pests. The surviving species are those most suited to the prevailing conditions. It is not practical in most schemes to detect the variation or treat each portion separately, so a mixture of species which has the necessary ecological amplitude (Rorison 1969) to span the conditions should be used.

Agricultural species fall into a narrow band of ecological amplitude and it may be necessary to widen this by incorporating other species. Where possible, the local ecotype populations should be included but unfortunately plant material is unavailable on the scale required. The expense of a breeding program has been justified only where agricultural and commercial alternatives persistently fail. However, the harvesting of 'wild' populations is a possibility.

The use of existing vegetation on a site should be seriously considered whether a spoil tip is being remodeled or a new development is taking place on virgin land. Providing the species will regenerate from fragments, there is no reason why the vegetation cannot be conserved and re-used, as has become customary for topsoils. The methods outlined could also be employed in the conservation of the same species, but much more work on the biology of possible species and the means to promote establishment from fragments is needed. There are several horticultural techniques which could be adopted to ensure success.

The use of a successional approach may not find favor because of the multiple treatment phases, and because seral engineering is too novel. As costs rise these will become more attractive. Their adoption should not add to the overall costs where a post-establishment management program of aftercare would normally be budgeted for. To many, the idea of a successional approach is one of 'laissez-faire'. This is too slow and erratic for practical purposes. Direct intervention is necessary, for example propagules of new species must be supplied as it is unlikely that each site will be surrounded by all the desired species and all will have a dispersal mechanism which facilitates their invasion (Harper 1977). It is essential to introduce and establish those species that play an important role in directing the successional development. The role of leguminous plants has already been mentioned but little is known about the precise conditions (microclimatic, edaphic) required for the successful establishment of many plant species, particularly on mined land materials. The latter point is important and one which is often overlooked. The establishment of vegetation on mined land materials is equivalent to primary colonization and the subsequent directional changes to succession (Wali and Freeman 1973), and not a process of secondary succession. If more attention was given to this fact in the design of revegetation schemes, undoubtedly more success would be achieved, particularly in conjunction with the successional approaches described.

Practical Issues

In the development of new reclamation techniques the practical aspects are often neglected resulting in unforseen problems when they are applied on a field scale, especially the unsuitable nature of conventional mechanized equipment. All proposed alternatives should be tried using contractors and their equipment before they are recommended (by the researcher) or specified (by the customer).

Many schemes have performed badly because sowing has been done at an unfavorable time of year. For germination, the requirements for moisture and temperature must be met. These conditions occur during two periods in most areas of Britain when precipitation exceeds evaporation and the mean air temperature is above $5°C$ (Fig. 1). For seedling growth, moisture and temperature requirements have to be met, this generally occurs between the points indicated in Fig. 1. The survival of a spring sowing is dependent on sufficient seedling growth being attained for it to withstand drought and in a late season sowing sufficient growth must be attained for winter hardiness, particularly for legume survival (Spedding and Diekmahns 1972). Sowing in the spring cannot be recommended for all the locations owing to the likely occurance of drought during seedling establishment. A late summer sowing is preferred but in many schemes spring seeding is specified to coincide with completion of earthworks etc. In this case a temporary cover could be adopted as suggested by Jones et al. (1975). It is fortunate that the optimum time for earthworks and soil movement is during the summer period (Fig. 1) and this should be complemented by an autumn revegetation program. In Britain the year to year variation in the weather pattern is considerable and this must be taken into account. Ideally as much flexibility as possible should be incorporated into the specification. The germination and establishment of agricultural and turf-grass bred species is more predictable than non-agricultural ones. The use of alternative species may impose further restrictions on seeding times (their biology, availability of seed etc.) and demand more technical expertise to ensure success in the field. Current developments in soil conditioners and hydroseeding mulches are such that establishment on a range of materials and in a wider range of weather conditions will be possible. This will be of benefit to both conventional and unconventional specifications.

The simpler the operation is, the more fool-proof it will be in practice; where complex procedures or different approaches are adopted, the education of the contractor is essential. Failures of some schemes can be blamed on the quality of the contract work. This is why guarantees are required by the customer. There is a major problem area in the definition of failures; who is liable, and precisely, what the cause was. In adopting the alternatives suggested it will be even harder to determine these, hence, the contractor is likely to raise his quotation or not tender. If a more flexible contract is given, this would allow the

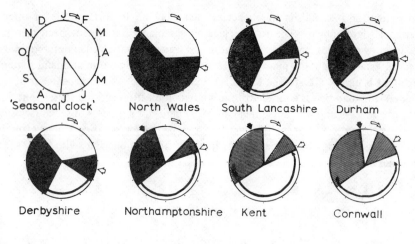

key:

optimum sowing time   when PT<R & T°C>5

optimum period for soil movement

𝒟   growing season starts
▲   "   "   ends

fig.1   Optimal Periods for the Establishment of Vegetation from Seed.

adapted from Smith, 1976

contractor to put in a more competitive tender. To ensure customer satisfaction a longer period of aftercare by the contractor might be included in the contract, normally they are responsible for 12 to 24 months. The costs would be higher but the management of the post-establishment phase should be budgeted for in any case. This would be acceptable to most contractors of repute (Visser, personal communication).

The cost difference in using the alternatives is likely to be small and insignificant when the costs of earthmoving, acquisition of land etc. are taken into account (Wallwork 1974, Davies et al. 1975). If topsoiling or earthmoving is made unnecessary the alternative will be even more attractive.

In non-agricultural and non-recreation end-use developments, little financial return is likely though the land value may increase (Wallwork 1974). Vegetation will still be a necessity and the scheme should be considered in the terms of the potential of the site and materials available. Only then will a satisfactory end product be achieved; perhaps, it is on this basis that the financing of revegetation should be argued and not relative cheapness. However, there are numerous arguments that could be leveled against this and several unfortunate consequences may arise.

Relevance to Industry

Many of the more difficult site and substrate problems should not occur in mineral workings of the future. This will be achieved through developments taking place in industrial technology and by adequate advanced planning and design for reclamation. For example there should be few instances of slopes being too steep for mechanical preparation of the seed bed.

At first sight there would seem to be little point in developing the alternatives suggested other than for specialized cases. The development of new reclamation techniques are more likely to take place outside Britain. However there will be a need for a non-agricultural specification when a mineral development extends or enlarges into an area defined as having 'wildlife and/or landscape merit'. There, standard grass-legume mixtures will be unacceptable and native species will have to be used. It is also likely that some companies will have to undertake the *restoration* of existing ecosystems to win the right to mine some deposits. Then some 'alternative approach' will have to be adopted.

In the past, many quarry operators have accepted almost any type and standard of vegetation cover established for non-agricultural purposes by a contractor, so long as it was initially green. Now the larger companies employ or contract professional landscape and 'reclamation' advisors. The standard expected by industry has thus increased with its greater awareness of the technical possibilities for a given site. Landscape and land management schemes are now being drawn up in advance of mineral extraction, planning 10 to 30 years ahead is not uncommon. Therefore there is more time to allow vegetation systems to develop and achieve desirable results. In this sense, industry is becoming the landscape engineers and managers of the future. The techniques outlined will be useful tools in their landscape technician's armoury.

ACKNOWLEDGMENTS

I am extremely grateful to Mr. Brent-Jones (Opencast Executive, National Coal Board), Mr. T.C.E. Wells (Monks Wood Experimental Station, Institute of Terrestrial Ecology), Mr. W. Visser (Comtec U.K. Ltd.) for their helpful comments and to Mr. T.W. J. Wright (Wye College, University of London) for the use of his observations. I wish to thank those who assisted with the work presented in this paper, in particular the Officers of Derbyshire and Kent County Councils, Staff of Imperial Chemical Industries Ltd., and D. Harvey of the Nature Conservancy Council (South East Region, Lewes). Financial support for the various projects has come from Derbyshire County Council, Kent County Council, Natural Environment Research Council, Science Research Council and Imperial Chemical Industries Ltd.   Mrs. B. Leonard and Mrs. S. Humphries are thanked for preparing the manuscript.

REFERENCES

Antonovics, J., A.D. Bradshaw and R.G Turner. 1971. Heavy metal tolerance in plants. Adv. Ecol. Res. 7:1-85.

Barr, J. 1969. Derelict Britain. Penguin, Middlesex, 240 p.

Blaser, R.E., W.H. Skrdla and T.H. Taylor. 1952. Ecological and physiological factors in compounding forage seed mixtures. Adv. Agron. 4:179-219.

Brenchley, W.E. and K. Warrington. 1930. The weed seed population of arable soil. II Influence of crop, soil and method of cultivation upon the relative abundance of viable seeds. J. Ecol. 21:103-127.

Brooker, R. 1974. Hydraulic seeding techniques: an appraisal. Techniques No. 21. Landscape Design 108:30-32.

Chippindale, H.G. and W.E.J. Milton. 1934. On the viable seeds present in the soil beneath pastures. J. Ecol. 22:508-531.

Coates, U.A. 1964. Experiments in grassland establishment on colliery shale, Bickershaw Reservoir Site. Lancs. C.C. County Planning Deparment, Preston, 21 p.

Dancer, W.S., J.F. Handley and A.D. Bradshaw. 1977. Nitrogen accumulation in kaolin mining wastes in Cornwall. I. Natural communities. Plant and Soil 48:153-167.

Davies, I.V., C. Brook and R.T. Arguile. 1975. Opencast coal mining: working, restoration and reclamation. pp. 313-322, In M.H. Jones (ed.) Minerals and the Environment. Inst. of Mining and Metallurgy, London.

Fryer, J.D. and S.A. Evans (eds.). 1970. Weed Control Handbook, Volume I: Principles. Blackwell, Oxford, 494 p.

Goodman, G.T. and S.A. Bray. 1975. Ecological Aspects of the Reclamation of Derelict Land. Geoabstracts, Norwich, 351 p.

Green, B.H. 1972. The relevance of seral eutrophication and plant competition to the management of successional communities. Biol. Conserv. 4:378-384.

Grubb, P.J. 1976. A theoretical background to the conservation of ecologically distinct groups of annuals and biennials in the chalk grassland ecosystem Biol. Conserv. 10:53-76.

Grubb, P.J., H.E. Green and R.C.J. Merrifield. 1969. The ecology of chalk heath. J. Ecol. 57:175-212.

Hackett, B. 1977. Landscape Reclamation Practice. IPC Science and Technology Press, Guilford, 235 p.

Harper, J.L. 1977. Population Biology of Plants. Academic Press, London, 892 p.

Harris, P.M., R.C. Thurrell, R.A. Healing and A.A. Archer. 1974. Aggregates in Britain. Proc. R. Soc. Lond. A. 339:329-353.

Humphreys, M.O. and A.D. Bradshaw. 1977. Heavy Metal toxicities. pp. 95-105, In M.J. Wright (ed.) Plant Adaption to Mineral Stress in Problem Soils. Cornell Univ. Agri. Expt. Sta., NY.

Humphries, R.N. 1977a. The establishment of vegetation on lime wastes, Dove Holes, Derbyshire. Res. Rept. 2, Univ. Cambridge, 30 p.

Humphries, R.N. 1977b. The development of vegetation in limestone quarries. Quarry Management and Products. 4:43-47.

Jones, J.N., W.H. Armiger and O.L. Bennett. 1975. A two-step system for revegetation of surface mine spoils. J. Environ. Qual. 4:233-235.

Land Use Consultants. 1976. Central Forest Park Reclamation Project Stoke-on-Trent. Land Use Consultants Ltd. London, 18 p.

Monks Wood Experimental Research Station. 1973. Report for 1972 to 1973. Natural Environment Research Council, London, 103. p.

Oxenham, J.R. 1966. Reclaiming Derelict Land. Faber and Faber, London, 204 p.

Proctor, J. and S.R.J. Woodell. 1975. The ecology of serpentine soils. Adv. Ecol. Res. 9:255-366.

Roberts, H.A. 1968. The changing population of viable weed seeds in an arable soil. Weed Research 8:253-256.

Rorison, I.H. 1969. Ecological inferences from laboratory experiments on mineral nutrition. pp. 155-175, In I.H. Rorison (ed.) Ecological Aspects of the Mineral Nutrition of Plants. British Ecological Society Symp. 9, Blackwell, Oxford.

Shimwell, D.W. 1968. The vegetation of the Derbyshire Dales. A report to the Nature Conservancy Council, Bakewell, 72 p.

Smith, L.P. 1976. The Agricultural Climate of England and Wales. M.A.F.F. Technical Bulletin 35. H.M.S.O., London, 147 p.

Smith, R.A.H. and A.D. Bradshaw. 1972. Stabilization of toxic mine wastes by the use of tolerant plant populations.   Trans. Instn. Min. Metall. 81A:230-237.

Spedding, C.R.W. and E.C. Diekmahns (eds.). 1972. Grasses and Legumes in British Agriculture. Commonwealth Agr. Bur. Oxford, 511 p.

Tandy, C.R.V. 1975. Reclamation of derelict land at Stoke-on-Trent. pp. 421-427, In M.J. Chadwick and G.T. Goodman (eds.), The Ecology of Resource Degradation and Renewal. British Ecological Society Symp. 15. Blackwell, Oxford.

Turesson, G. 1922. The genotypical response of the plant.   Hereditas 3:211-350.

University of Newcastle. 1971. Landscape Reclamation, IPC Science and Technology Press, Guildford, 135 p.

Wali, M.K. and P.G. Freeman. 1973. Ecology of some mined areas in North Dakota. pp. 25-47, In M.K. Wali (ed.) Some Environmental Aspects of Strip mining in North Dakota. Educ. Ser. 5, North Dakota Geol. Surv., Grand Forks.

Wallwork, K.L. 1974. Derelict Land. David and Charles, Newton Abbot., 333 p.

Wallwork, K.L. 1976. Mineral working dereliction in England. pp. 1-14, In (unedited) Proc. Conf. Land Reclamation, Thurrock, England (In press).

Wathern, P. 1976. The ecology of development sites.   Ph.D. Thesis, Univ. Sheffield.

RECLAMATION AFTER STRIP MINING
A VITAL MEANS IN LONG-TERM DEVELOPMENT
PLANNING IN THE RHENISH LIGNITE DISTRICT, GERMANY

*Hans Weise**

In order to cover its energy requirements, West Germany has to rely on imports to a great extent. Prime energy resources found within its boundaries are hard coal, which is mined exclusively (and expensively) in underground operations, and lignite, which lends itself to surface mining. There are some producing gas and oil wells; however, they contribute little to prime energy consumption. Lignite, more than 90% from the Rhenish district, contributes 30% in public power generating station production, adding up to more than 100 mT annually.

These brief comments highlight the situation of West Germany: The exploitation of native resources is imperative in order to decrease Germany's dependency on imported oil and nuclear fuels. They also explain why decades ago, problems concerning the protection of the environment or reclamation had to be faced and solved in a manner acceptable to those affected as well as to the mining industry.

The concentration of lignite or brown coal deposits in the vicinity of Cologne and Duesseldorf aggravated the ecological problem considerably. It is not widely known that by far the largest portion to be mined after 1955 is covered by one of the most fertile agricultural loess soils found in Europe. Since it occurs abundantly - up to 60 feet thick - the opportunity is there to use loess not only in reclamation on a "one square yard per one square yard" basis, but to improve areas where poorer soil qualities prevail, such as the southern part of the mining district.

The primarily agricultural structure of the lignite district accounts for the many villages with populations ranging from 300 to 3,000. The rural character of the landscape, however, should not be misleading. Cologne, an ever-growing center for rail and road traffic only 24 km away, is surrounded by many excellent highways and railroad tracks that cannot be abandoned.

Resettlement of villages, reclamation of farm and forest lands, relocation of roads, tracks and rivers - this would have been the "normal" task of the surface miner. But what he actually achieved went far beyond.

Reconstruction of the landscape as it looked prior to mining was not even attempted. The goal was the creation of a new and natural scenery where healthy natural conditions existed that would attract recreation-seeking city dwellers. In addition, the new villages offer considerably improved living conditions with modern layouts adaptable to increasing car traffic.

First, let me deviate a bit into an explanation of the mining and reclamation technique

*North American Mining Consultants Inc., 7501 East Marin Drive, Englewood, CO 80110.

without losing sight of the profitability aspect, and then explain the legal basis for surface mining in the State of Northrhine Westphalia.

The depth of the massive deposit and the value of the land it occupies require unique mining and reclamation technique.

The overburden masses excavated by bucketwheel excavators are dumped either inside the mine or on outside-dumps by stackers. By increasing the capacity of the excavator, suitable conveyors and stackers had to be developed. As the brown coal seam occurs in geological formations within several groundwater levels, it is also necessary to keep the deep opencast mines completely free of groundwater. A series of wells was dug in order to lower the groundwater level. Some wells are deeper than the base of the coal seam.

In comparison to last year's production of 120 million tons of brown coal, the pumping of 1.2 billion m^3 of water - ten times the coal quantity produced - looks rather impressive.

Not only does the bucketwheel excavator-conveyor-spreader technique produce 120 million tons of lignite in the Rhenish district, it also permits the *selective mining and dumping* of more than 500 million tons of overburden material, such as, clay, gravel, sand, or fertile topsoil.

The excavator carefully cuts layer after layer which the spreader deposits on the spoil-bank. Gravel, for instance, may be dumped on the base of the spoilbank to permit proper drainage, and clay may be hidden in the core of the spoilbank. Understandably, this selective mining method facilitates reclamation tremendously. The fertilie soils, classified on the excavator high wall, will be dumped on top of the spoilbank in whatever thickness the purpose requires.

Fertile loess, an aeolic deposit with high calcium content and the ability to stay moist even through long dry spells, abounds in the lignite area.

It is quite evident that this over rich deposit of fertile soil can be put to better use. Here also, the opencast mining method is a great aid in equalizing the distribution of loess in a far thinner layer of three to six feet, which is fully sufficient for agricultural use.

The Rheinische Braunkohlenwerke AG (Rheinbraun) goes so far as to transport loess via its own railway system approximately 32 km further south, where it is used to create farmland in locations where prior to mining only forest land prevailed, and it is here where the so-called slurry method is widely applied.

Loess is mixed in a ratio of one-to-one (1:1) with water and pumped through a pipe-line system onto the spoilbank which was previously graded 1.5% towards the south. The loess slurry is retained between dams of dry loess, confining rectangular ponds of about two to four acres each. It takes approximately two to six months, depending on weather conditions, until one of these "polders" can be cultivated by the farmer. Cultivation is rather difficult in the initial stage. However, it results in extremely valuable farmland, three to five years after the loess has completely dried out.

Using the slurry method the thickness of the loess is only about three feet. Intensive research by the Department of Agriculture of the University of Bonn has proved its fertility.

Five years of intermediate farming follow the initial agricultural reclamation. During this period the humus content is raised to 1.5% through cultivation of certain plants and the use of fertilizers. Erosion sensitivity of the freshly resettled loess soil determines the gradient of the farm areas covered by loess, and should not exceed 1.5%. This hardly notice-able gradient gives the impression of monotonous plains. However, by establishing different levels in the form of forest covered slopes, this situation can be remedied.

Additional measures to further improve the soil are undertaken by the mining industry on a *voluntary* basis and include fertilizing and intermediate farming. This is in the mining industry's own interest in order to avoid remunerations to make up for decreased values and to attain higher values for the real estate properties.

The company's own forest department is in a position to reforest within a very short time with the aid of company-developed planting equipment. These plantations raise the soil moisture and the temperature of the air.

The raw spoilbank is covered with a three to five meter thick layer of so-called *forest gravel* in order to facilitate the immediate planting of valuable trees and to *avoid* the planting of pioneer trees. Forest gravel consists of a mixture of sand, gravel, boulders and loess, so the soil is physically and chemically suitable for the growing of all types of trees. The correct mixture can be artifically achieved by deploying two excavators, one in loess, one in gravel, and joining their output on one spoilbank conveyor.

The removed overburden volume determines the surface character of the reclaimed areas. A *surplus* causes a piling up of high dumps, a deficit leaves pits. Problems will undoubtedly arise when landscaping is involved. Yet, this situation offers attractive opportunities to create a variety of landscape features, provided this is genuinely pursued.

Resettlement of villages and relocation of surface installations require much advance planning. A recently published article in a reputable New York Daily mentioned "several months" in an attempt to assess the gravity of this problem. In reality planning starts many years prior to resettlement, sometimes as long as ten years in advance, as in the case of the newly developed Hambach mine. This is six years longer than it used to be only a decade ago and, apart from other things, an example of the growing interest the affected citizen takes in his environment and its long-term preservation, respectively reconstruction.

At this point may I be permitted to linger a moment with the legal aspects of surface mining, particularly in the Rhenish district.

Mining in Germany is regulated by a mining law enacted in the late 19th century. Naturally, this law has been modified and amended as new minerals became valuable and new priorities were set. Lignite, in particular, was affected when after World War II the need became evident to expand into extensively cultivated farmland. In 1952 a special Brown Coal Mining Law was enacted in Northrhine Westphalia.

Based on the Brown Coal Mining Law of 1952, a Committee, called the "Braunkohlenausschuss" was formed, consisting of 27 members representing the Federal Government, the individual states (Laender), the various communities and the industry. The brown coal industry is represented by only three members. The Committee's function is to determine the areas in which brown coal may be mined and to decide on the relocation of populated areas. Furthermore, it is the Committee's task to generally outline agricultural areas and forests, taking into consideration the conservation measures with regard to monuments, nature, and landscape. The reclamation method applied to the various areas is also laid down in the appropriate law. All resolutions passed by the Committee are binding for all parties. The resolutions are then presented to the government of Northrhine Westphalia who, after careful consideration, will grant the right of eminent domain; confined, however, to the exact planning area discussed in the Brown Coal Committee.

The law states that the Brown Coal Committee must be in agreement or, in other words, come to a unanimous decision. This was always achieved in the past, but sometimes took years of deliberation - a sign of the good will and the skill of the mining company.

In the event an agreement cannot be reached, the matter is then brought before the Governor who will render his decision. As a astute politician, he undoubtedly would refer the matter back to the Brown Coal Committee to continue their negotiations until the desired agreement is reached.

Prior to 1952 the State of Northrhine Westphalia already recognized the need to control the development of urban sprawl, industrial concentration, highway construction, and the preservation of recreational facilities by establishing a land planning commission. By entrusting the chairman of the land planning commission with the chairmanship of the Brown Coal Committee, the link was forged which made the mining industry an essential tool in achieving long-term goals for a growing population. Resettlement can be used as an example.

To date 21,000 persons have been resettled and by 1990 approximately another 15,000 will follow, making a total of 36,000 people and thus equaling the average population of a medium-sized county seat. When resettling people, it must be ensured that conditions in their new surroundings enable them to make a good living and where they will not have the feeling of losing contact with their former social surroundings.

It can be stated today that resettling generally brought about a considerable improvement of living conditions. From the narrow streets of the old villages, where poorly lit houses prevailed and small estates were interwoven into one another; from the noise and dust of through-roads, the inhabitants moved into modern communities with a more open building layout. In the new location the village character was carefully preserved or even improved by the creation of new civic centers with church, village hall and business centers. Special attention was given to public parks.

It is a fact that resettlement represents a considerable improvement of the communities' structures, not only materially, but in human terms as well. Since resettlement in the area offers good opportunities to thoroughly improve the community structure, the opencast mining industry in their demand for very large areas, may widen these advantages to include specific features and scenic landscape improvements.

West of the growing city of Cologne, there were virtually no lakes for recreational purposes. Today more than 40 lakes beautifully landscaped and uninterrupted by public roads, invite city dwellers. Particularly the areas south of the brown coal district, where mining originated, became a charming scenery of forests and lakes after exploitation of the shallower seams. The water areas are of special importance since they enhance the scenic variety.

The total water area of 1,450 acres is divided into lakes, ponds and pools, noted for their high natural stock of fish which is being further improved by adding young fish. Appropriate planting on shores and banks, combined with a selected variety of matching plants, gave the water areas such a natural character that they cannot be distinguished from ordinary lakes any longer.

The manmade recreation area of the southern Ville, encompassing an area of more than 6,000 acres, today attracts more than 20,000 visitors on weekends from the urban area of Cologne. A grid of hiking paths was prepared and some lakes offer swimming and water sports.

In conclusion it can be stated that lignite mining in West Germany is a perfect example of what can be gained through cooperation of population, government agencies and the mining industry. The fact that more than 2,000 acres of former mining land were taken over by the state forest administration and, without any major changes, declared a state park, speaks for itself.

RECLAMATION PROBLEMS IN THE
UPPER SILESIA MINING DISTRICT, POLAND

Stanislaw C. Mularz *

INTRODUCTION

The Upper Silesia Mining District (USM-District), because of coal resources and actual output, is one of the largest mine districts in Europe comprising an area of about 5,500 km^2. It constitutes more than 80% of about 4,500 km^2 in the territory of Poland. The remaining part lies in Czechoslovakia (Ostrava - Carvina District). Estimated reserves of the USM-District located at a depth to 1,000 m are estimated at about 85 billion tons while reserves located to 1,200 m are about 100 billion tons. Actually, about 30% of the USM-District area and about 25% of its resources are developed as a mine region where the stage of development is different in individual parts of the district. The main regions of mining are located in the northern and western part of the USM-District, where one may find about 90% of all active mines (Fig. 1). Besides coal, zinc and lead are also found in the District. A great concentration of exploitative industry, coal processing (cokeries, thermal-electric power stations), and steel industry, causes a negative impact on the natural environment. Complex changes lead to a partial or even total degradation of the environment. It should also be pointed out, that these degradation processes are active for a long time. Coal exploitation over the past 200 years, has been in an unsystematic way, at times even wastefully, manged. These long-term destructive processes have caused serious disturbances and sometimes some irreversible changes in the environment. For example, a greater part of the area is dominated by a so-called "anthropogenic morphology" where, because of a lack of maps, it is impossible to reconstruct the original configuration of the surface. More than half of the total river system of this district now collects poisonous sewage and is biologically lifeless. Underground waters show pollution in the hydrogeological system and all water-bearing horizons. Soils in large areas are completely destroyed and a continuous increase of so-called "postindustrial wastelands" is observed. The air pollution is often many times greater than the admissible standards of concentration; particularly dangerous is the great concentration of sulphur dioxide.

Changes in the biosphere are also negative on human living conditions of this district. It is worth noting that the region of the USM-District is characterized by a high population density and a great degree of urbanization. The mean density of population here is greater than 2,200 persons/km^2; the maximum exceeds 4,500 persons/km^2.

*University of Mining and Metallurgy, Al. Mickiewicza 30, 30-059 Krakow, Poland.

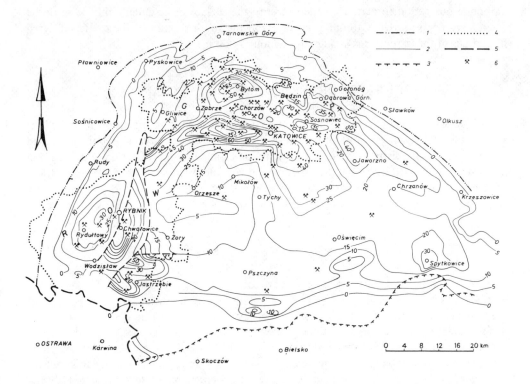

Fig. 1.   Map of dislocation of coal mines in the USM-District/after J. Kuchcinski/: 1 -
border of productive Carboniferous, 2 - isolines of the total thickness of coal
beds in meters to 1,000 m, 3 - border of Carpathians flysch, 4 - border of
industrial regions, 5 - State border, 6 - coal mines.

OUTLINE OF GEOLOGICAL CONDITIONS OF THE USM—DISTRICT

Geologically, the USM-District is a large synclinorium filled up with sediments of the
upper Carboniferous system with Namurian and Westfalian stratigraphic levels. The complex
of the productive Carboniferous system formations consist of a set of alternating layers
of shales and sandstones with coal beds. The thickness of coal beds is about 2,400 m in the
eastern part of the district and up to 6,000 m in the western part. The productive layers
are on the lower Carboniferous formations as sandstones and shales in the western part
and limestones in the east of the basin. The cover of the coal series is made up of deposits
of Permian and Triassic systems, Tertiary and Quaternary period, but the cover is not
uniform over the whole area. The Permian period formations (clays, limestone, sandstones)
and Triassic systems (dolomites, limestones, marls and clays) occur mainly on the northern
and eastern part of the synclinorium. Deposits of the Tertiary period, mainly miocene clays,
cover the central and southern part of the basin. Deposits of the Quaternary period, mainly
sands and Pleistocene clays occur almost in the whole area. The total thickness of the
formations creating the Carboniferous period cap-rock is 800 m in the southern part of the
district, being gradually reduced in the northern direction. In some regions the

Carboniferous period formations come out onto the surface or lie under a thin cover of the Quaternary deposits. The Carboniferous layers in the south sink under the overlaped flysch formations of the Carpathians at a depth of about 1,000 m.

THE RANGE OF THE ENVIRONMENTAL CHANGES

The scale of the changes in the natural environment are not uniform over the whole area of the USM-District. Most unfavorable changes are taking place in the northern and western part of the district, where the intenstiy and long duration of action of degradation processes and its influence on the environment are the greatest. With coal exploitation, changes of the geological environment (lithosphere), the water environment (hydrosphere), and the natural environment (biosphere) are directly or indirectly connected.

Changes in the Lithosphere

The modifications of the geological environment take place first through excavations by the exploitation of coal or gangues[†]. The equilibrium of the rockmass is unbalanced and the primary structure of individual geological layers is destroyed in the region over the deposit creating surface deformations. They can be continuous or discontinuous. Discontinuous deformations, like depression craters, slits, troughes etc., occur by a shallow exploitation and may be in tens of meters. This kind of deformation has usually an impulsive character and therefore is particularly dangerous. Depression craters registered during the last years in the western part of the district have a volume of over 50,000 m^3. Continuous deformations are the result of the imbalance of the rockmass over the excavation. Rock cracks and their gravitational dislocation tend to be in the direction of exploited space. Cracks and looseness of the rockmass are the greatest in the zone located directly over the excavation and gradually grows smaller in the direction of the terrain surface. It should be noted, that the size and character of runoff and continuous deformation depend mainly on the lithological formation of the overlying layers as well as on the depth and system of exploitation. Both types of deformation connected with the mining activity are processes that change the primary morphology of the terrain. In extreme cases, these processes may create the inversion of the land surface. The surface deformations from mining exploitation in the USM-District are about 100,000 ha by settlements of about 30 m; so the post-exploitation surface deformations here are an essential factor of topography, and with the cooperation of natural denudation processes in many regions cause a total change of the primary morphology of the terrain.

The anthropogenic morphology of the District is also evident from dumps and heaps of scrap materials. There are first of all dumps of gangues coming from drifting and flotation. A lot of dumps are also created from scrap materials coming from the coal and metallurgical processing (ashes, smoke dusts, slags etc.). In the USM-District, there exist more than 300 dumps with a volume of about 250 million m^3. The greater part, 95% are low ones averaging a height of up to 30 m, the remaining 5% are high dumps reaching 100 m. A separate group of superficially anthropogenic forms are the embankments for the railway. Because of the compact network of roads and railway lines in some regions of the

[†] gangues - undesirable ore

District, these forms dominate the scenery. Great changes in the geological environment also occur when sand is excavated for the needs of coal mining (backfilling of excavations). These excavations occupy an area of more than 10,000 ha, and the area increases by about 1 ha daily. The total land area disturbed by strip mining is about 300 million m^2. In 1975, the whole production of the USM-District from the beginning of the exploitation, was 5 billion tons of coal and about 1 billion tons of gangues, with surface deformations of about 1.5 billion m^3.

Changes in the Hydrosphere

The changes of the underground and surface waters on the USM-District are closely connected with the mining-industrial activity. Changes in the underground water are a result of geomechanic transformations of the exploited rockmass. Mining excavations may be treated as a function of the drainage system. Dehydration of the soil material is hastened by exploitation. Gaps and cracks and the loosening of overlying, as well as in many cases the interruption of continuity of the insulation layers hastens the infiltration, circulation and mixing of waters in the individual levels. Such being the case, deep waters may also be polluted by waters coming from the higher levels or polluted gutters on the surface.

In regions where the level of the underground water is located over an impermeable layer, excessive hydration takes place during the surface deformation. If the terrain surface settles below the local level of underground waters, the terrain may be flooded and marshy grounds, fens, or even larger water basins without outflow may occur. So the harmful influence of mining on the water environment occurs from drainage of the rockmass on one hand, and from excessive hydration and the flood of terrain on the other. It should be noted that the surface deformations change the run of the river net, watersheds and reception area. It has a direct influence on the size and dynamics of the erosion and accumulation processes in rivers.

Regional changes in water conditions take place in the USM-District as a result of the great concentration of mines and extensive exploitation. Often irreversible disturbances in the natural circulation of water and pollution of underground and surface waters are the result. Large deficits of water, in spite of apparent excesses in some regions, occur in the mining regions. The deficit of water increases because the rain-waters are not utilized. Great areas are built up by industrialization and urbanization, so the infiltration of rain-waters are diminished to about 30% over the whole area. Yearly, about 200 million m^3 of water are lost from this district. This fact has an essential influence on the regional water balance because the set-back of infiltration of rain-waters increases the process of rockmass drainage. It means that at deep water levels, with salinity of underground waters proportional to the mine depth, waters with a greater mineralization should be drained. On 1 ton of exploited coal, 4 m^3 of saline waters are pumped from the mines. At the existing stage of mineralization, about 100 kg of salt occur for each ton of exploited coal. The groundwaters in rivers are therefore extensively polluted by saline waters.

Changes in the Biosphere

Conversion and degradation of the biosphere are conditioned first of all by the state of soil, degradation and change of water environment, and atmospheric pollution. In the USM-District, the biosphere was hard hit by industrial and urban processes taking place during the past decades. The majority of the original ecological environments have been destroyed or changed. Large portions of rivers are biologically dead. The range of spatial conversions of biosphere in the USM-District is difficult to determine because there are no data concerning the output stage. The original flora on large areas have been completely destroyed or unfavorably changed, a result of many factors, the most decisive being the intensive fall of forests, particularly in the first period of industrialization, mechanical waste and degradation of soil cover, and atmospheric pollution and pollution of waters.

The forests, once covering about 70% of area of the district, have been reduced to about 20%. There are even areas several hundred km^2 without forests. The vegetation, and particularly forests, are an important factor of the ecological balance as well as for creation of human conditions. Mechanical waste of soil cover, its pollution with industrial refuses, advanced degradation processes caused by excessive drainage or flooding of terrain, and accumulation of harmful substances from the atmosphere have a direct or indirect influence on devastation or degeneration of the vegetation. On terrains under the direct influence of exploitation, the area of drained soils is greater than 50% and flood on about 10% of the area. This means that about 2,500 km^2 of drained areas and about 500 km^2 of terrains are excessively watered. Particularly favorable factors for biological life are atmospheric gas and dust pollution. It should be noted that long-term effects and great concentrations of toxic substances in the atmosphere can destroy even the very resistant trees. The mean sedimentation of dusts in great industralized parts of the district is about 500 tons/km^2 yearly, and with a norm of 250 tons/km^2 yearly, the permitted values are doubled. Extreme values of pollution are greater than 1,600 tons/km^2 yearly creating conditions of great impendence for some regions of the district. The problem of atmospheric degradation on the area of the USM-District may be illustrated by the results of studies made by utliization of the satellite data of the LANDSAT-System. The above mentioned investigations were made by the author in EROS Data Center, Sioux Falls, South Dakota. A computer compatible tape (CCT) with satellite images of the USM-District were taken by the Landsat system on 2 November, 1973. The visualization, processing, and interpretation of the image were made by the analyzing computer set - IMAGE - 100. The basic digital MSS tape of the Upper Silesia Mining District study area was arrived at after processing five sets of interpretative materials, those being:

(1) Standard unenhanced images;
(2) Stretched images;
(3) Stretched color composites;
(4) Stretched ratio images, and
(5) Color-stretched ratio composites.

The northeastern fragment of the Landsat-scene, comprising the area of the Polish part of the district, was used for special studies. This fragment was divided into 16 subscenes (Fig. 2), used in the detailed sociological analysis. The main object of interpretation was the problem of air pollution by industrial smokes in the regional scale, particularly the determination of the relative concentration, range, and propagation methods of these pollutions by given meterological conditions.

Using the tests stated, the most profitable materials for such sociological studies are: stretched color composite made from MSS-band 4, 5, 7 and images MSS band 4 and MSS - band 5. A good quality of interpretation is also possible on stretched ratio images: MSS 4/7 and MSS 5/7. In the stretched-color composite the effluents are visible as very distinct blue strips which after some distance resemble characteristic plumes. These strips contrast with the surroundings and simultaneously mask the surface. In viewing the whole image one may

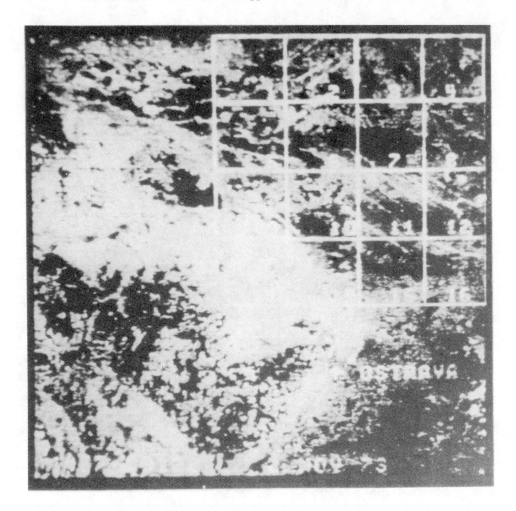

Fig. 2.   Satellite image Landsat MSS - band 5 with subscenes.

distinguish only areas of heavy concentrations; however, in the scale of individual subscenes it is possible to locate about 50 sources of smoke emission visible as bright points of differentiated dimension (Fig. 3). The character and range of smoke emission was dependent on the weather conditions with the structure of propagation directions being differentiated and specific. In the range of the Polish part of the district, the direction of propagation of air pollution is similar to the southeast wind direction. In the region of Ostrava in Czechoslovakia the initial direction of smoke propagation is northeast i.e. perpendicular to the wind direction. Further downward the smoke joins in a homogeneous wide stream, which meanders over Poland, finally going to the northwest. This way of pollution in industrial areas is called the "channeling effect", caused in this case by the valley of the Odra river. The range of emitted air pollution was from 70 to 80 km downward from the emission sources when the wind speed was 4-7 m/sec. The concentration of pollution 40-50 km from the emission source was about 30-40% aerosol, a value of pollution greater than the admissible standards. The range of harmful atmospheric air pollution is several tens of kilometers, enveloping an area of around 10,000 km^2. The knowledge of these facts is

Fig. 3.   Stretched-ratio image MSS 5/7 - subscene No. 11.

useful for planning of regional preventive reclamation practices, e.g. by design of protection forest strips around the upper Silesia agglomeration.

The sociologic interpretation of satellite images should initially be an art of regional studies, and then, by decreasing the area of investigation and magnifying the preciseness of recognition, separation of the so-called critical areas may be possible. Detailed, complex investigations of these areas were also made using classical methods. This way is conditioned by the synthetic character of the data carrier in the form of a satellite image. It should be noted that the presented scheme is an inverse of the classical method used in natural science, where the regional image is made on the base fragmentary information of a local range.

PREVENTIVE MEASURES AND RECLAMATION

The sociological problems connected with the USM-District has two aspects:

(1) Preventive measures for limitation or reduction of harmful processes, leading to unprofitable degradations of the natural environment,

(2) Reclamation activity, the object of which is the reinstatement of usable function of areas disturbed by mining and other concurrent industries.

The main objective of preventive measures is mine surface protection. The problem of surface protection is particularly important for new areas undergoing present mine development and for regions where the exploitation is geared towards regaining considerable coal reserves which were locked up in protection pillars. For example, about 28% of the coal obtained came from protection pillars in 1960 and in 1970, the proportion increased to 42% (Skawina 1976) (Fig. 4). Exploitation in protection pillars, particularly under large towns

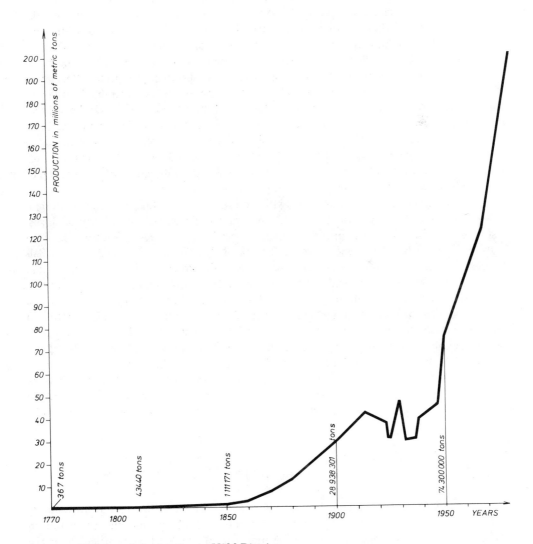

Fig. 4.   Total coal production in USM-District.

should be conducted under controlled circumstances. A detailed and accurate prognosis of the range and character of the surface deformation is necessary, and proper protective measures which counteract the harmful effects of exploitation of the environment should be assured. Complex preventive activities in the area of surface protection are also undertaken for newly developing parts of the district. These are based on the principle of minimizing geomechanic conversions, disturbance in the water environment and devastation in the biosphere. The protective activity also concerns structures located on the surface such as houses and industrial buildings, roads, railways, bridges, etc. One of the basic problems is the movement of very salted water into surficial waterways. Therefore, wherever it is possible and economically feasible, a closed industrial water circulation system is used with excess water being cleaned and diverted into rivers. In spite of great costs connected with this method, the cleaning of industrial water is unsatisfactory at present; however, the situation is slowly being improved. The reduction in subsidence is obtained through backfilling which reduces the need for the transport and storage of gangues. Detailed prognosis of subsidence allows for sensible development of the surface; for example, for localization of refuse dumps in regions where maximum subsidence is expected. Regulation of surface water conditions is necessary to protect against soil degradation. In order to diminish harmful effects of terrain drainage, the use of waterproof shields may be utilized. In Poland, the reclamation of mining areas is treated as a component of the mining activity. The principle of proper reclamation is a total restoration of desolated areas in the range of their utilization. The reclamative manipulations performed on the USM-District over 10 years are intensive and on a large scale. These involve the cultivation and restoration of wastelands and are partly or totally excluded from utilization.

In the USM-District, reclamation with forests for recreation needs is preferred. The reclamation of dumps, will solve such important problems as the stability of slopes, restoration of soil, and returning the dumps to aesthetically pleasing sites which blend with the surrounding landscape. About 5,000 ha of dumps were reclaimed in the USM-District, special reclamation for recreational needs is the Provincial Park for Culture and Rest in Chorzow. This park, with an area of about 600 ha, was built in the center of a most devastated region. Additional parks of this kind are being built in other parts of the District, as "green islands" in the most impacted regions. Along with this operation, a great undertaking of creating forest protective zones around the USM-District will occur. Simultaneously an intensive reconstruction of flora in the existing forests will be attempted; this should reduce the degradation caused by air pollution. This may be achieved after complex renovation of soils polluted by gases and industrial dust. Until now such work has been performed on about 30,000 ha of conifers (about 20% of the anticipated total). It is estimated that these protective reclamation activities will bring the expected results in the USM-District in 10 to 20 years.

CONCLUSIONS

In the USM-District, a complex unfavorable degradation of the natural environment has been observed. It is caused by a great concentration of mining and other industries. In the presence of a significant increase of excavation after World War II and particularly in the last 20 years, the range and intensity of degradation processes are growing. The so-called "capacity of environment" on a region has been disrupted on an unprecedented scale and demands reclamative and preventive measures and limiting the negative effects of the mining industry. Principally, the wasteland of dumps should be brought under cultivation, degraded soil should be reconstructed, the water economics of the region ordered, existing flora rebuilt and protective forest strips around the most important urban - industrial regions should be achieved. A governmental and technologic organizational base for this large activity was prepared in the range of environmental protection in the USM-District.

ACKNOWLEGMENTS

I wish to express my appreciation to Dr. Robert G. Reeves, EROS Data Center, and Dr. Charles L. Pillmore, U.S. Geological Survey for allowing me to utilize satellite data of the Landsat System as well as for the discussion on many problems involved with image processing and interpretation.

ABSTRACT

The Upper Silesia Coal Mining District is the largest coal mining area in central Europe. Coal in the Upper Silesia area has been mined since the 18th century in many mines, mostly underground.

This paper analyzes the main reclamation problems related to ground subsidence, changes of the groundwater conditions, drainage or flooding, and waste dump formation. The various environmental criteria, specific to heavily populated and industrialized areas are discussed. Finally, remote sensing studies, using the Landsat satellite data together with computer processing to identify and classify some environmental factors, are presented. The ability to monitor the progress of mining and reclamation activities is necessary for regional planning and control of environmental quality in mining districts.

REFERENCES

Mularz, S.C. 1977. [Interpretation of LANDSAT satellite images by inventory works of geographical environment conditions - in Polish].   Proc. VIIIth Polish Photo-interpretation Conf.

Skawina, T. 1977. [State and development prospects of post-industrial lands in Poland - in Polish]. Protection of Mine Areas 42:62-64.

Zumda, S. 1973. [Anthropogenetic changes in the natural environment of the Upper Silesian conurbation - in Polish].   Polish Scientific Publishers, Warsaw - Cracow, 211 p.

OPENCAST MINING AND RECLAMATION IN SOUTH AFRICA

J.J.J.P. van Wyk*

INTRODUCTION

This paper deals briefly with mining in South Africa. The economic importance of the natural resources are indicated and mining methods for the most important resources such as gold, diamonds, chrome, coal and iron are reviewed. Damage of the environment due to mining activities and the resulting pollution problems are discussed.

The ecological implications of strip mining for coal is dealt with in some detail, and the methods and techniques employed to restore environmental damage are discussed. Reference is also made to the revegetation of gold mine tailings dumps and slimes dams, and a new reclamation technique is introduced.

SOUTH AFRICA'S NATURAL RESOURCES

Very few countries in the world have the mineral resources that South Africa is endowed with. For its size of just under 6,500 sq km (0.8% of the land surface of the earth), its mineral wealth is virtually unsurpassed. South Africa has the largest known deposits of gold, platinum, chrome, manganese, vanadium and fluorspar in the world. Deposits of antimony, asbestos, coal, copper, diamonds, phosphates, titanium, uranium, zinc and vermiculite are also very well represented. Mineral exports account for about two-thirds of the country's total export income, and is estimated at †R5,000 million for 1977. Mining and minerals contribute approximately 15% to the gross domestic product. South Africa could therefore justly be called a mining country. A large percentage of its population of about 25 million, as well as many citizens of several neighboring countries, earn their living or benefit in some way from the mining activites. Mining, initially very primitive, started soon after the discovery of diamonds in 1866. More sophisticated mining operations followed after the discovery of gold in the Eastern Transvaal in 1974, and of the large gold fields of the Witwatersrand (Johannesburg area) in 1885-1886.

Gold Mining

Gold is by far the most important mineral and contributes more than 50% of the

*Department of Botany, Potchefstroom University, Republic of South Africa.

† 1 Rand = $1.15 (11-29-1978).

mineral revenue. Gold production amounted to 78.2% of the total production of non-communist countries during 1971. The second largest producer (Canada) supplied 7.1% during the same period.

The gold mines are deep and gold is extracted as deep as 3,500 m (11,500 ft). Extremely large quantities of waste and ore are therefore brought to the surface. The biggest gold mine processes 5 million mT of ore per annum and the richest mine (West Driefontein) produces 78,000 kg (2.4 million ounces) of gold a year. With an average of 15 grams of gold per mT of ore, the amount of material excavated is very large. These dumps cause serious pollution dangers and ecological problems. Figure 1 is a typical example of gold mine dumps in the Transvaal.

Fig. 1.   An unreclaimed gold slime dam. Note pollution of streams center left.

Diamond Mining

7.5 million carats of diamonds were produced in 1973, the majority from open cast mines such as Kimberley, Finch and Cullinan. The big Kimberley hole is an abandoned working where 22.6 million mT were excavated and 14,504,566 carats were recovered. This is the biggest man-made hole in the world, 400 m deep and 1.6 km in perimeter. It could accommodate three Empire State buildings on top of one another. Large areas are covered with waste material from this and other mines. The recently discovered Finch pipe is at least 1,300 m in diameter and will be one of the biggest opencast diamond mines in South Africa. The search for alluvial diamonds damaged the surface of thousands of hectares in the past. Digging still continues, but fortunately on a smaller scale, utilizing sophisticated methods.

Iron Mining

Iron ore is mainly obtained by means of open cast mining. The Iron and Steel Corporation of South Africa operates two opencast mines. The annual output of the Sishen mine (Fig. 2) is 78 million tons and that of Thabazimbi (Fig. 3), 12 million tons. These mines directly affect approximately 4,000 ha.

Fig. 2.   Open cast iron ore mine at Sishen.

Fig. 3.   Open cast iron ore mine in mountainous area at Thabazimbi.

Coal Mining

No commerically viable deposits of oil and gas have been discovered in South Africa to date, and the main energy source is coal. The deposits occur mainly in the Transvaal and Natal, and may be found from 20 to 300 m deep. Seams are from 1 to 8 m thick and the quality is generally low to medium grade. Reserves of high grade coal were recently discovered in the northeastern Transvaal. The extent of this deposit is not yet fully known.

Until 1970 no coal was extracted by means of stripping. Since only 66% of the reserves can be extracted by subsurface mining and due to the ever increasing price of crude oil and labor as well as the fact that a large percentage of coal is of medium quality, strip mining of certain deposits became necessary. Since 1971, strip mining is practiced on deposits which occur up to 60 m below the surface (Fig. 4). There are currently 68 deep coal mines and about 22 open mines in operation. The current annual output of coal is approximately 71 million tons.

Fig. 4.   Coal strip mine where seams are 30-40 meters deep.

MINING AND THE ENVIRONMENT

The development of South Africa's natural resources of 51 different minerals, of which 19 are considered to be of strategic value, causes serious disturbances of the environment (Atmore 1972). The most obvious are the slimes dams and tailings dumps from the gold mines of the Witwatersrand, the Western Transvaal and Orange Free State. The dumps are in continuous contact with rain water and air and the finely ground siliceous and pyritic material of the slimes oxidize, weather and leach, to pollute the water of the tributaries of the Vaal River. This water is strongly acid and contains a large percentage of minerals in solution. The clouds of dust originating from dry dumps on windy days enter towns and dwellings and often contain a higher silica concentration than that encountered underground in the mines (Grange 1973, Kitto 1965). The ecological disturbance of the surface by coal mines is less obvious but has a similar effect on streams and rivers in Eastern Transvaal and Northern Natal. This is due to the oxidation of large quantities of iron pyrites brought to the surface. Sulphur dioxide and hydrogen sulfide fumes from burning refuse dumps cause serious corrosion and pollution problems in some areas.

In Sasolburg where the biggest petrol from coal installation (Sasol) is located, 3 million tons of coal are used annually. Smoke, fumes and unpleasant odors contribute to air pollution. Sasol recently switched over to modern extraction techniques to cut down an air pollution. More than 50 tons of sulphur, which were previously vented, are currently reclaimed daily by means of the improved techniques.

The main categories of ecological disturbance associated with the South African mines are:

(1) The influence on the surface topography;
(2) Water pollution, due to oxidation and leaching;
(3) Air pollution due to dust, fumes and solid particles;
(4) Lowering of the water table or reentry of polluted water from old shafts into the reverine systems;
(5) The effects on the environment of strip and opencast mining;
(6) Communications, transport and supply demands.

South Africa, as many other countries, is aware of and concerned about the influence of the mining activities on nature in general, and in particular on the eocsystems which are directly affected.

All mining and prospecting activities must conform with the mining laws of 1956, 1964 and 1967 (Van der Spuy 1975). The Minister of Mines has an advisory committee on the environment which advises him on environmental matters. Several government departments such as Agricultural Technical Services, Department of Planning and the Environment, The Chamber of Mines, the South African Agricultural Society and the Department of Mines are represented on this committee. A special committee of the Chamber of Mines was set up in 1974 to produce a code of conduct for strip mining (Chamber of Mines 1976). This code has with a few reservations, already been accepted by the Minister of Mines. The code will probably serve as the basis for all future legislation pertaining to strip mining.

The existing legislation stipulates that a thorough ecological impact study must be conducted to the satisfaction of the authorities before any mining activities can start. This includes proposed restoration programs to be implemented during operation and after shutdown. The pollution effects on water, air and the environment must be fully indicated and approved before any activity may begin.

RECLAMATION

Reclamation of the disturbed areas will be discussed with reference to coal strip mines and gold mines only.

Reclamation at Coal Strip Mines

The two biggest strip mines, Optimum and Arnot are located on the Eastern Transvaal

Highveld. The natural vegetation of the area is grassland and is mainly used for crop production or grazing.

Four coal seams occur in this region, the depth varies due to topographic changes, but they generally occur from the surface down to 60 m. The seams are of medium quality, on the average 1-2 m thick, with relatively thin layers of rock separating them from one another (Rankin et al. 1972).

The strip mine technique is based on the U.S. system. The overburden of the box cut is placed on undisturbed adjacent land. After extraction of coal, the overburden of the next cut is dumped in the previous cut. This process continues for each successive cut, causing a fairly uneven and rough terrain with the last cut left open, as is illustrated in Figures 4 and 5. At Optimum, top- and subsoil of the overburden is not separated and is

Fig. 5.   Strip mine open-cut converted into a dam.

dumped in mixed form. At Arnot (Phillips 1977) topsoil is removed first and dumped on top of the overburden of the second last cut. The shifted overburden is finally spread by mechanical means to match the natural topography as closely as possible (Fig. 6), and as far as is economically feasible. At Optimum a 10 cm layer of topsoil is spread over the surface after landscaping, while at Arnot this is done during the mining operation.

These mines have a fairly good extraction ratio of 3:1 (three m^3 of overburden for one ton of coal) but a fairly low income of only R3.00 to R4.00 per ton. It is therefore remarkable that up to R6,000 per ha is spent to restore the damage on land with an actual agricultural value of less than R600 per ha. At Optimum roughly 300 ha have been mined while 170 ha have already been fairly satisfactorily restored. The same ratio is maintained at Arnot, i.e. roughly 50% of the stripped area.

Pioneering reclamation work was done at Optimum and the experimental trials conducted in 1971 were mainly pilot studies. Mounds were somewhat flattened, no topsoil was applied and *Ehrharta calcina* (a native grass) and *Cortaderia argentea* (pampas grass) were planted with some success.

Fig. 6.   Restored land two years after strip mining.

A mixture of grass seed was sown on the flat surfaces which were fertilized with calmafas and 2:3:2. The seed mixture consisted of *Cynodon dactylon, Eragrostis curvula, Ehrharta calcina, Pennisetum* spp., *Festuca* spp., *Lolium* spp., *Paspalum* spp., *Chloris* spp. and others.

Several hardy shrubs and small trees were also planted. The trees, however, mainly *Pinus* spp. such as *P. patula, P. teadia, P. engelmanii* and *P. radiata* took off well as is shown in Fig. 7, but seem to be poorly adapted. Further experimentation is needed to select suitable tree species.

The grass cover seems to do well as can be seen in Fig. 6. Basal cover is satisfactory and several native species, mainly pioneers from the vicinity, are abundant in the treated areas today.

It is, however, too soon to judge the reclamation efforts as a long-term solution. It is already clear that maintenance must continue and that grazing might have to be incorporated in the maintenance program. It is envisaged that a minimum maintenance period of five years might be needed.

The reclamation program at Arnot had severe setbacks due to drought since it was initiated in 1973. There, major findings are in line with the experience at Optimum and according to Phillips (1977) several valuable lessons have been learned. Research is still an integral part of the reclamation program.

The initial reclamation success, although at a fairly high cost, obtained by the first two strip mines in South Africa is certainly encouraging and will in all probability serve as guidelines for future legislation concerning strip mines. It is realized that more experience will be gained in time and that future reclamation programs might be superior to those currently employed.

These two mines each currently extract about 40,000 tons of coal per month. Large areas will thus still be strip-mined and have to be restored in the future.

Since strip mining is relatively new in South Africa, and since gold mining has been

Fig. 7.   Reclaimed land at Optimum coal mine with the introduction of pines in fore-
ground and only a grass cover in the background.

the backbone of the South African economy for more than a century, as well as the fact
that gold mining activities damaged more surface area than all the other mining operations
combined, attention will briefly be given to the revegetation efforts at gold mine dumps.

Reclamation of Gold Mine Dumps

Reclamation problems encountered at gold mine dumps is adequately covered by
Groves (1974), James (1966) and in numerous other internal reports of the various mining
companies and the Chamber of Mines.

Although it was realized as early as 1932 that something must be done to stabilize
and cover the slimes dams and tailings dumps to prevent serious air and water pollution it
was not until 1963 that enough information was available to start with the revegetation of
the slimes dams. A vegetation unit was set up by the Chamber of Mines and operates today
with an annual budget of approximately R1 million.

According to Clausen (1973), more than 22 km^2 of the total of 72 km^2 dumps on the
Reef alone have been rehabilitated successfully as is shown in Fig. 8. Holtz (1962) outlines
the main reasons for stabilizing slimes dumps as to eliminate the dust problem to prevent
pollution of watercourses and to change the general unsightly appearance. There are a
number of serious problems which cause difficulty in successful permanent establishment of
vegetation. The most important are:

(1) The deficiency of plant nutrients;
(2) Physical nature of the milled rock, consisting of 75% silt and clay;
(3) Low pH (3-5) near the surface due to oxidation of pyrites;
(4) Steep angles of slope (27 to 57 degrees); and
(5) Extremely dry conditions due to the chemical and physical nature of the soil.

Fig. 8.   Successful gold mine dump reclamation.

After many trials it was decided to change the condition of the surface layers to enable the more tolerant South African species to be grown. After extended mist spray irrigation, lime and fertilizer treatments are applied.

Windbreaks are made with culms of *Phragmites australis*. They are handplanted in small paddocks depending on the slope and the nature of the soil (See Fig. 9). Seeding and mulching is then carried out. A large variety of species is used such as:

Seed

Agrostis tenuis	"New Zealand Brown Top"
Bromus catharticus	"Rescue Grass"
Chloris gayana	"Rhodes Grass"
Dactylus glomeratus	"Cocksfoot"
Eragrostis curvula	"Weeping Love Grass"
Holcus lanatus	"Yorkshire Fog"
Poa pratensis	"Kentucky Blue"
Festuca elatior	"Fescue Type 31"
Phalaris tuberosa	"Canary Grass"
Trifolium Sp.	"Clovers" - 2 varieties
Cynodon dactylon	"Queek"
Paspalum dilatatum	
Cenchrus ciliaris	"Buffels Grass"
Lolium perenne	"Perennial Rye"
Atriplex semibaccata	"Creeping Saltbush"
Medicago sativa	"Lucerne"
Acacia melanoxylon	"Blackwood" tree
Acacia baileyana	"Silver Wattle" tree
Acacia mearnsii	"Green Wattle"
Gleditsia triacanthos	

Fig. 9.   Wind breaks are put in on gold mine dumps before seeding and mulching.

Plants

Cynodon plectostachyum	"Star Grass"
Cortaderia sellowiana	"Pampas Grass"
Kochia brevifolia	"Australia Blue Bush"
Pennisetum macrorum	"Hippo Grass"
Carpobrotus edulis	"Sour Fig"

In the Reef area more than 4,000 ha (1/3 of the total) have been planted with grass up to the end of 1977. After reclamation at least 10,000 ha will become available for use by humans or by wildlife.

Reclaimed areas are maintained by spreading fertilizer with a helicopter when necessary. This is continued for up to five years when indigenous vegetation has become sufficiently established to take over.

Reclamation of sand dumps and tailings is omitted in this review.

THE ALL–IN–ONE TECHNIQUE

Reclamation of disturbed areas is achieved by means of various methods and techniques, depending on aims, objectives, cost and local circumstances. Techniques such as wood gabions, synthetic mats, surface covering etc. all have certain advantages but also some disadvantages. The All-in-One technique was developed to eliminate most of the disadvantages of the existing techniques, to combine some of the advantages of promising techniques and to incorporate several new ideas. The All-in-One technique was originally developed to reclaim disturbed areas in road reserves, such as cuts and fills, where it was highly successful, and later adapted to other purposes such as the reclamation of mine dumps, dongas and sand dunes.

This technique, as the name implies, involves a single treatment through which soil stabilization, seeding and fertilizing is achieved, and maintenance is minimized.

The essential feature of the technique is a soil stabilizing structure constructed of plant material such as saw mill refuse, wood chips, hay or other plant material which might be available. The material is compressed to bricklike blocks with suitable dimensions e.g. 60x20x10 cm and glued together. The material may also be contained in suitable netting cylinders with acceptable dimensions. The seed and fertilizer are mixed with the contents of the structures. These structures are staggered over the disturbed area covering 30-50% of the surface (the actual percentage cover being governed by the steepness of the slope). They are then secured in place and partially covered with topsoil, or with a good quality subsoil. They prevent surface erosion by creating numerous draining points, which eliminate excess surface runoff and also act as barriers to prevent loss of topsoil.

The seed is treated with various germination inhibitors to ensure germination over a long period of time. Successive germination of seed for an extended period is extremely important in unstable climatic conditions where a large percentage of the seedlings are normally lost due to unexpected drought, high temperatures, etc.

Seed is pelleted in a mixture of paper pulp and topsoil. Fertilizer is also included to ensure a suitable growing medium during the initial period until the seedlings have become established.

The seed mixture is adapted for different climatic regions and normally also includes pioneers, seed from the immediate locality, as well as seed of specific ecotypes of *Eragrostis curvula* adapted to the particular environmental conditions. Eighty-three ecotypes of *E. curvula* are currently cultivated for seed.

The applied fertilizer mix is also adapted to the particular soil requirements and provided in pellet form. A percentage of the pellets are treated with a plastic coating to ensure slow release of nutrients.

The notable advantages of this technique are:

(1) A single treatment;
(2) Effective soil stabilization;
(3) Ensured germination over a long time;
(4) Slow release of nutrients;
(5) Biodegradable structures;
(6) Improved soil moisture conditions;
(7) Competitive in price;
(8) Simple to apply.

Ecological Seed Producers (Pty) Limited are the manufacturers of this product and are in a position to supply it worldwide for trials and evaluation.

Results achieved in road reserves in South Africa are very satisfactory and large problem areas have already successfully been reclaimed where all other techniques have failed (Fig. 10).

Experiments on mine dumps are very promising but too recent for final evaluation.

REFERENCES

Atmore, M.G. 1972. Mining and the environment. Optima 22:141-147.

Fig. 10. Revegetation by means of the All-in-One technique.

Chamber of Mines. 1976. Code of conduct for reclamation at strip mines.

Clausen, H.T. 1973. Ecological aspects of slimes dam construction. J.S. Afr. Inst. Min. Met. 74:178-183.

Grange, G.H. 1973. The control of dust from mine dumps. J.S. Afr. Inst. Min. Met. 74:67-73.

Groves, J.E. 1974. Reclamation of mining degraded land. S. Afr. J. Sci. 70:296-299.

Holtz, P. 1962. Gold mine waste dumps get a face lift. Can. Min. J. 83:74-76.

James, A.L. 1966. Stabilizing mine dumps with vegetaiton. Endeavour 25:154-157.

Kitto, P.H. 1965. Surveys of dust from mine dumps. Rpt. No. 71/65. Chamber of Mines. (Internal Rpt.).

Phillips, J. 1977. Surface rehabilitation opencast mining progress report, Arnot collery. (Internal Rpt.).

Rankin, D., K.B. McQuillin and P.D. Dickson. 1972. The planning of, and initial operations at the Arnot collery opencast strip mine. Anglo American, Internal Rpt. T5A2.

Van der Spuy (ed.). 1975. South Africa 1975: Official yearbook of Republic of South Africa, S. Afr. Dept. Information, Pretoria.

AN OVERVIEW OF REVEGETATION AND RECLAMATION OF MINE SPOILS IN JAPAN

Hiroshi Usui*

INTRODUCTION

Rapid economic progress of Japan is said to be quite mysterious. It seems to parallel the rapid progress of metal production. Japan needs natural resources. Since our country is totally dependent upon the import of oil, it was quite a shocking event when the oil prices quadrupled in 1973. During that time, many copper mines were closed due to economic reasons. Behind the rapid prosperity of Japan, damages to the environment - air, water and soil contamination have been most serious. Revegetation problems in mine areas can be said to be one of the legacies of rapid exploitation.

COAL MINE AREA

Coal mine area in Japan geologically belongs mostly to the Tertiary period. Figure 1 shows the location of coal and non-ferrous mines in Japan and is based on information issued by the Geological Survey of Japan in 1973 and Japan Mining Industry in 1975. Figures 2 and 3 show the production of copper and raw materials between 1958 to 1974. The coal is of lignite type but is not being mined presently. However, past coal mining activity is evident from pyramid-like waste piles found in our coal mining area. It consists of stones produced by digging out of drift or of galleries, of sandstones and shale inserted between coal beds. Annually an area of about 20 ha to a height of about 50 m were produced. This waste pile not only needs a wide area of land, but also poses potential hazards. For example, its toxic material caused killing of fish in the watercourses. When it rained heavily, massive discharge of the waste pile resulted in the death of 70 persons at Sasebo Coal Mine in 1955. Hitherto, more than 1,000 of these piles have been produced and these occupy a total area of about 3,000 ha in Kyushu District; 1,800 ha are in Fukuoka Prefecture. Revegetation studies of the waste pile began in 1948 (Sato 1961) and show:

(1) The middle of the waste pile is very sterile, composed mainly of coarse gravel with scarce fine particles. Soil reaction of the pile varies from strong acidity to strong alkalinity. Most of them are unsuitable for vegetation. It was shown that the strong alkalinity of these soils are caused by excessive amounts of exchange-

*Agricultural Faculty of Utsunomiya University, 320 Utsunomiya, Japan.

Fig. 1 **Location Map of Coal and Non-ferrous Mine in Japan**

able or free state sodium. For revegetation therefore, it is necessary to correct soil reaction. Using CaSO₄ was effective.

(2) Vertically, on southern slopes of the waste pile, the temperatures of the soil up to 50 cm are very high.

(3) Plant succession on the waste pile progresses slowly from the initial stage of *Digitaria adscendens* community to *Miscanthus sinensis* stage. Later it becomes a secondary forest of red pine (*Pinus densiflora*) or black pine (*Pinus thunbergii*). Plant growth was not noted on strongly acid (pH below 3.0) or strongly alkaline (above 8.0) soils. But for these two exceptions of the pH range, vegetation developed in most cases. For suitable species for plantation, the following were used: *Alnus sieboldiana, Alnus hirsuta, Acacia* spp. and *Amorpha fruticosa* etc. Ten years later, it was recognized that *Robinia pseudo-acacia, Lespedeza bicolor* and *Amorpha fruticosa* easily formed the secondary forest. Herb species, *Setaria viridis* and *Digitaria adscendens* were used in most cases and weeping lovegrass (*Eragrostis curvula*) showed good growth and germination. In some places,

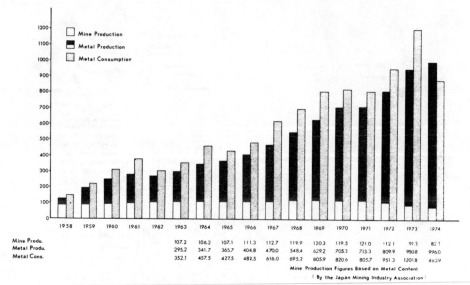

Fig. 2   Production and Consumption of Copper from 1958 to 1974

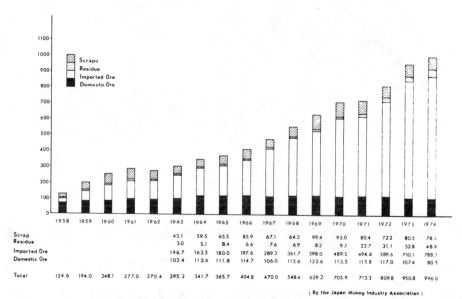

Fig. 3   Metal Production by Raw Material from 1958 to 1974

Kummerovia striata and *Solidago canadensis* were also used. Pine species, *Quercus acutissima* and *Elaeagnus umbellata* were not suitable because of their slow growth in the initial stages.

A couple of decades have passed since the revegetation was carried out in the coal mine area in Kyushu. After this, most of the coal mines were closed and remaining waste piles were removed and sites were used for housing.

LEAF ANALYSIS FOR REVEGETATION

Recently in Japan, there seems to be a great tendency for the use of exclusive import-ed grasses for all revegetation practices. Among these, miracle grass (*Festuca elatior* var. *arundinacea*) and weeping lovegrass (*Eragrostis curvula*) are the most popular. These seeds are imported from the U.S. and are widely used in Japan not only for erosion control on mountain regions, but also along the roadsides. Before World War II, it was customary to use *Zoisia japonica* or *Miscanthus sinensis*. After the War, the use of imported grasses was found more reliable, easy and cheap. However, recent trends favor the use of nature plants from the standpoint of nature conservation. Most studies of plant communities in Japan have continued since 1930 and vigorously pursued in the last two decades; those of the present author, are mostly of species composition, naming and classification. However, the study of climax natural vegetation has not contributed much to the revegetation problems since we do not know the germination properties, seed storage, growth process etc. of natural plants. In 1974, I had the opportunity to survey the evergreen broadleaved forest vegetation on the Chiba experimental forest of Tokyo University. I also conducted leaf analysis of many species. Using this analysis, one can obtain knowledge of plant nutrition, soil and stand condition, as well as the productivity of the area. Analyzed samples were divided into four groups - tree, shrub, herb and fern groups (Table 1). Most of the samples were collected in the same stand. Some of the main results are given below:

(1) **Potassium-Calcium Relations:** Most of the species are in the range of 2% potassium and 1.5% calcium. Some species however, showed a higher concentration of both. Comparatively, high percentages of calcium were found in *Rubus buergeri*, *Ardisia japonica*, *Hedera rhomber*, *Eurya japonica*, *Daphniphyllum teijsmanii*, *Dendropanax trifidus*, especially *Fiscus erecta*. These species are constant in ever-green broadleaved forest in Japan. *Alpinia japonica*, *Diplazium subsinuatum* showed a high percentage of potassium (Fig. 4).

(2) **Magnesium-Calcium Relations:** Percent Mg is extremely low when compared with potassium and calcium. All of the plants showed less than 0.8%. Magnesium content is higher in the fern group than in any others.

(3) **Potassium differences in each group:** For potassium:herb >fern >shrub >tree; for calcium:shrub >herb >tree >fern; Magnesium fern >shrub >herb >tree.

(4) **Potassium and calcium ratios:** Tree group - 0.8, shrub - 1.04, herb - 2.40, fern - 3.04. These data show that each tree group showed higher percentage of calcium than potassium, and shrubs were nearly the same. On the contrary, herb and fern groups showed much higher percent of potassium than calcium.

(5) Species showing very low total cations values (K+Ca+Mg) were *Dicranopteris dichotoma* - 1.05%, *Gleichenia japonica* - 1.05%, *Illicium religiosum* - 1.50%, *Rumohra aristata* - 1.64%, *Pleioblastus simmonii* - 1.74% and *Miscanthus sinensis* - 2.16%. The first two species are dominant on the poorest granite soils in Setonaikai-District where growth of red pine is also very poor. The stand of *Abies firma* which grows on dry and nutrient-poor sites has *Illicium religiosum* as its characteristic species. *Pleioblastus simonii* also indicates very low total cation values. *Pleioblastus* and *Sasa* are small bamboos covering very wide areas, almost over the entire area of Japan. Species of *Sasa* (*S. kurilensis*, *S. paniculata*, *S. purpurascens* and *S. nipponica*) are the most important dominants in the beach forest of Japan. The low calcium demands of *Sasa* and *Pleioblastus* (Table 1) explain the reason why the two species cover such wide areas in Japan.

Table 1. Result of Leaf Analysis in Chiba Tokyo University Forest.

No.	K %	Ca %	Mg %	K+Ca+Mg %	K/Ca	P %	SiO %
Tree group							
1 Cryptomeria japonica	0.88	0.83	0.20	1.91	1.06	0.18	0.04
2 Chamaecyparis obtusa	0.46	0.84	0.23	1.53	0.55	0.11	-
3 Abies firma	0.89	0.84	0.14	1.87	1.06	0.09	0.25
4 Cyclobalanopsis glauca	0.64	0.70	0.23	1.57	0.91	0.13	-
5 Cyclobalanopsis salicina	0.62	0.82	0.18	1.62	0.76	0.08	-
6 Cyclobalanopsis acuta	0.50	0.60	0.31	1.41	0.83	0.07	1.58
7 Shiia sieboldii	0.57	0.82	0.33	1.72	0.70	0.07	1.67
8 Machilus thunbergii	0.98	0.70	0.23	1.91	1.40	0.11	1.22
9 Pasania edulis	0.79	1.15	0.15	2.09	0.69	0.05	1.47
average	(0.70)	(0.81)	(0.22)	(1.74)	-	(0.10)	-
Shrub group							
10 Actinodaphne lancifolia	1.20	0.46	0.66	2.32	2.61	0.12	0.38
11 Mallotus japonicus	1.02	1.76	0.42	3.20	0.58	0.09	1.54
12 Daphniphyllum teijsmannii	0.62	1.86	0.65	3.13	0.33	0.06	0.16
13 Prunus spinulosa	1.44	1.12	0.55	3.11	1.29	0.09	C.24
14 Pittosporum tobira	1.64	2.46	0.31	4.41	0.67	0.12	0.17
15 Ficus erecta	2.58	3.16	0.74	6.48	0.82	0.11	4.78
16 Eurya japonica	1.18	0.85	0.46	2.49	1.39	0.08	-
17 Illicium religiosum	0.81	0.36	0.33	1.50	2.25	0.09	-
18 Dendropanax trifidus	1.82	1.58	0.41	3.81	1.15	0.13	0.07
19 Cleyera japonica	0.91	0.91	0.38	2.20	1.00	0.07	0.10
20 Maesa japonica	1.74	0.88	0.56	3.18	1.96	0.10	-
21 Ardisia crenata	1.46	0.51	0.16	2.13	2.86	0.08	-
22 Damnacanthus indicus	0.92	1.28	0.42	2.62	0.72	0.08	0.21
23 Aucuba japonica	1.16	1.23	0.39	2.78	0.94	0.10	-
24 Myrsine seguinii	0.99	1.06	0.39	2.44	0.93	0.06	3.16
25 Cephalotaxus harringtonia	2.50	0.72	0.33	3.55	3.47	0.17	0.86
26 Viburnum dilatatum	0.54	1.36	0.52	2.42	0.40	0.08	0.38
average	(1.33)	(1.27)	(0.45)	(3.05)	-	(0.10)	-
Herb group							
27 Hedera rhomber	1.62	2.23	0.45	4.30	0.73	0.18	0.35
28 Ardisia japonica	2.04	1.92	0.21	4.17	1.06	0.09	0.10
29 Trachelospermum asiaticum	1.80	1.42	0.32	3.54	1.27	0.08	5.69
30 Ophiopogon japonicus	2.12	1.12	0.22	3.46	1.89	0.14	0.27
31 Asarum kooyanum	4.06	0.88	0.39	5.33	4.61	0.07	0.38
32 Carex morrowii	1.94	0.16	0.15	2.25	12.13	0.05	-
33 Carex multifolia	1.94	0.34	0.16	2.44	5.76	0.03	8.26
34 Alpinia japonica	4.70	0.42	0.32	5.44	11.19	0.14	1.68
35 Piper kadzura	3.95	1.29	0.42	5.66	3.06	0.12	5.95
36 Rubus buergeri	1.70	1.00	0.62	3.32	1.70	0.06	0.56
average	(2.59)	(1.08)	(0.33)	(3.99)	-	(0.10)	-
Filicales group							
37 Rumohra pseudo-ariatata	0.72	0.90	0.73	2.35	0.80	0.08	0.50
38 Rumohra ariatata	0.68	0.39	0.57	1.64	1.74	0.09	0.35
39 Diplazium subsinuatum	2.90	0.74	0.43	4.07	3.92	0.08	12.25
40 Leptogramma mollissima	1.86	0.72	0.62	3.20	2.58	0.10	10.89
41 Woodwardia orientalis	1.90	0.56	0.57	3.03	3.39	0.12	8.19
42 Dryopteris varis	1.14	0.78	0.46	2.38	1.46	0.09	0.78
43 Cyclosorus acuminatus	1.17	0.91	0.69	2.77	1.29	0.17	9.57
44 Dryopteris erythrosora	1.64	0.53	0.69	2.86	2.09	0.12	0.16
45 Plagiogyria japonica	1.90	0.12	0.43	2.45	15.83	0.13	4.51
46 Pteris cretica	2.35	0.38	0.27	3.00	6.18	0.11	11.44
47 Plagiogyria adnata	2.20	0.28	0.41	2.89	7.86	0.13	-
48 Rumohra standishii	2.25	0.52	0.53	3.30	4.33	0.22	-
average	(1.73)	(0.57)	(0.53)	(2.83)	-	(0.12)	-
others in forest edge							
49 Pleioblastus simonii	1.27	0.32	0.15	1.74	3.97	0.17	7.12
50 Miscanthus sinensis	1.64	0.39	0.15	2.16	4.21	0.17	4.22
51 Gleichenia japonica	1.36	0.02	0.14	1.05	68.00	0.09	2.27
52 Dicranopteris linearis	0.89	0.02	0.14	1.05	44.50	0.06	3.75

These acid forest soils, show low cation content caused by severe rainfall, and the rhizomes of these species can easily extend their territories in these deep volcanic soils.

APPLICATION OF LEAF ANALYSIS IN REVEGETATION

Through my studies at the Chiba experimental forest, I realized the applicability of leaf analysis in revegetation. Meishin and Toumei Highways were constructed 15 and 10 years ago, respectively. Both of the highway slopes were covered in the beginning exclusively by weeping lovegrass and miracle grass. This vegetation still survives and covered about one-third of the highway area in 1977. Although both these grasses usually disappear within five years on contaminated soils such as Ashio Copper Mine, they seem to survive much longer on non-contaminated soils probably due to mowing every year. Approximately one-third of the highway slope area has been replaced by *Pueraria lobata*, which is a typical

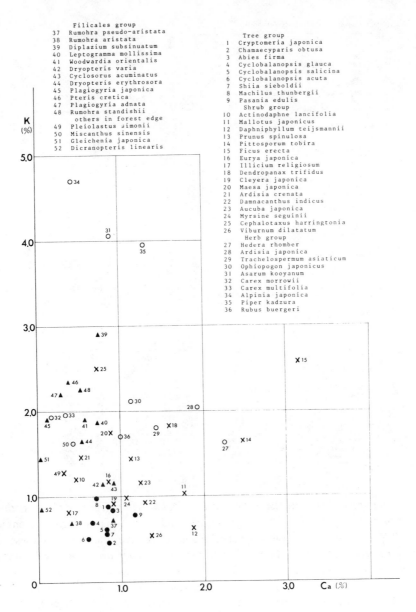

Fig. 4. K-Ca Relation in Chiba experimental Forest in the University of Tokyo. Sampled species were collected under Chamaecyparis obtusa Plantation.

dominant of mantle-community in Japan. Remaining one-third of the area is occupied by *Miscanthus sinensis* which is also a typical dominant of the grassland of Japan. The latter species cannot be maintained on long-term basis without mowing or burning every year. During our vegetation survey, we also found young trees of red pine and black pine. If succession proceeds at the present rate, it will soon become pine-dominated. Leaf analysis of the highway vegetation is given in Table 2. Many members of *Leguminosae* were found during our survey (Table 2). Because of its fast growing and vigorous runners, *Puerraria lobata* invades easily into other vegetation, a fact not appreciated by foresters. There are also

Table 2. Leaf Analysis of Highway Vegetation.

No.		K %	Ca %	Mg %	K+Ca+Mg %	K/Ca	N %
1	Pinus densiflora	0.84	0.28	0.12	1.24	3.00	-
2	Pinus thunbergii	0.19	0.77	0.13	1.09	0.25	0.60
3	" "	0.72	0.45	0.13	1.30	1.60	0.95
4	Robinia pseudo-acacia	3.09	0.91	0.18	4.18	3.40	4.52
5	" "	3.07	0.94	0.17	4.18	3.27	4.22
6	Pueraria lobata	0.87	3.04	0.46	4.37	0.29	2.86
7	" "	3.80	1.30	0.52	5.62	2.92	4.07
8	Lespedeza cuneata	1.18	1.55	0.28	3.01	0.76	3.31
9	" "	1.63	1.33	0.21	3.17	1.23	2.71
10	Lespedeza buergeri	2.15	1.24	0.22	3.61	1.73	2.79
11	Lespedeza thunbergii	0.80	1.66	0.18	2.64	0.48	2.43
12	Lespedeza bicolor	1.03	0.76	0.08	1.87	1.36	2.36
13	" "	0.89	1.44	0.16	2.49	0.62	3.24
14	" "	0.48	1.24	0.24	1.96	0.39	2.18
15	Amphicarpaea edgeworthii	2.36	2.97	0.89	6.22	0.79	2.53
16	Wisteria floribunda	1.03	1.64	0.17	2.84	0.63	3.06
17	Sophora flavescens	1.12	1.80	0.21	3.13	0.62	3.41
18	Aster ageratoides var.ovatus	3.84	1.64	0.25	5.73	2.34	0.40
19	Aster scaber	4.09	2.18	0.58	6.85	1.88	2.71
20	Xanthium strumarium	3.17	2.38	0.45	6.00	1.33	4.22
21	Solidago altissima	3.25	1.15	0.26	4.66	2.83	1.51
22	" "	2.15	1.31	0.26	3.72	1.64	2.59
23	Rhus javanica	1.92	2.62	0.33	4.87	0.69	1.61
24	" "	1.93	3.06	0.51	5.45	0.64	1.28
25	" "	1.67	2.27	0.28	4.22	0.74	1.33
26	Dendropanax trifidus	3.56	1.39	0.29	5.24	2.56	1.68
27	Clethra barbinervis	2.19	1.45	0.32	3.96	1.51	1.10
28	Daphyniphyllum macropodium	0.76	2.81	0.51	4.08	0.27	1.15
29	Eurya japonica	0.88	0.88	0.27	2.03	1.00	0.53
30	" "	0.80	0.67	0.22	1.69	1.19	1.10
31	Weigela coraeensis	1.48	0.94	0.35	2.77	1.57	0.35
32	" "	1.92	1.21	0.22	3.35	1.59	0.31
33	Miscanthus sinensis	1.37	0.36	0.16	1.89	3.81	1.05
34	" "	0.57	0.32	0.03	0.92	1.78	0.40
35	Eragrostis curvula	0.55	0.16	0.03	0.74	3.44	0.80
36	" "	0.38	0.11	0.05	0.54	3.45	0.50
37	Festuca arundinacea	1.14	0.34	0.31	1.79	3.35	0.65
39	Dicranopteris dichotoma	1.37	0.13	0.12	1.62	10.54	0.73
40	Gleichenia japonica	1.10	0.40	0.16	1.66	2.75	1.35
41	" "	1.52	0.11	0.15	1.78	13.82	1.41
42	Sphenomeris chusana	2.34	0.36	0.16	2.86	6.50	0.73
43	" "	2.48	0.33	0.15	2.96	7.52	0.90
44	Dryopteris erythrosora	2.20	0.86	0.71	3.77	2.56	-
45	Dryopteris nipponensis	1.18	0.45	0.62	2.25	2.62	1.10
46	Osumunda japonica	1.20	0.41	0.48	2.09	2.93	1.41
47	Cyclosorus acuminatus	1.41	0.94	0.50	2.85	1.50	1.71
48	Cyrtomium falcatum	3.57	1.15	0.07	4.79	3.10	1.26

Robinia pseudo-acacia, Lespedeza cuneata, L. bicolor, Amphicarpaea edgeworthy and *Wisteria floribunda* belonging to Leguminosae and indicating a high percentage of nitrogen. The presence of root nodulated species appears to favor the growth of these species on these otherwise poor soils. Members of Compositae, *Aster ageratoides* var. *ovatus, A. scaber, Xanthium strumarium* and *Solidago altissima* show high total cation values. These plants are considered to play a dominant role in succession. Low content of total cations and calcium appear to be characteristic of the fern group *Dicranopteris dichotoma* and *Gleichenia japonica. Rhus javanica* often appears in the initial stages of succession and has predominantly high total cation values. The latter is a rapid growth tree and is expected to play a major role for revegetation. Most predominantly, weeping lovegrass shows the lowest total cation value followed closely by species like *Sasa* (Table 2). Weeping lovegrass is a plant of the desert in South Africa, where excessive species occur generally in climax vegetation. This points to the need for needed research in the selection of species for revegetation.

CONCLUSION

Flora of Japan includes more than 5,000 species, but suitable species for revegetation are considered to be few. Although species differ in their nutrient requirements, a comparison of the total cation values, potassium-calcium ratios and nitrogen content will be extremely useful for selecting species in revegetation. Whereas the use of natural vegetation in reclamation is necessary, it must be pointed out that in the initial stages, erosion control must be of prime importance and must be considered first so that weeping lovegrass and miracle grass could be used for the first few years. And, as pointed out by Caplice and Shikaze (1970-1971): "Permanent cover of vegetation will maintain itself indenfinitely without further attention or artificial aid such as irrigation. Such permanence is only achieved by selecting species or grasses that will grow, spread and reproduce under the poor soil conditions encountered with tailings areas".

REFERENCES

Caplice, D.P. and K. Shikaze. 1970-71. Waste Control Problems in the Mining Industry, Ontario Water Resources Commission, Ministry of the Environment, Ontario.
Sato, K. 1961. Studies on Afforestation on the Waste Pile in the Kyushu Coal Mine District, Ariake-Shobo, Tokyo.

RECLAMATION AND USE OF
COAL—MINED ECOSYSTEM IN INDIA: A REVIEW

R.K. Gupta*

INTRODUCTION

Coal is the most important source of commerical energy in India. It contributed 20% of the total energy supply during 1960-61, and is projected to contribute 27.8% during 1980-81. A study of the rural fuel consumption (1960-61) revealed that only 5% of the energy needs of rural people were met by commercial fuels and the rest by noncommercial fuels such as cowdung, firewood and vegetable waste. The Committee on Energy Survey of India has estimated a 43% increase in energy generation from non-commercial fuels by 1980-81 while the rest of the requirements are to be met by commercial fuels. These estimates are based on an annual growth rate of 6% in annual income and 8.5% in industrial production. Among the commercial sources of energy, coal stands out prominently since other alternate sources of energy are not expected to contribute significantly to the energy balance before the end of the century.

EXTENT OF THE PROBLEM

Principal coalfields in India are in the eastern and central states like Bihar, West Bengal and Madhya Pradesh. Outside, there is only one coalfield in Singereni on Godavari Valley of Andhra Pradesh. Ninety-eight percent of the coal mines in India are of lower Gondwana age and the remainder are Tertiary. Total reserves of coal in India are estimated at 123,000 mT, the quality is poor since it is high in ash and low in Calorific value. Of a total reserve of 5,800 mT of coking coal, down to 618 mT in Jharia coalfield, only about 1,800 mT would become available for industrial use.

Extraction of coal, either by underground mining or opencast mining, leaves a considerable barren area. In the underground mining, there is subsidence of overburden and collection of spoilage on the surface while in opencast mining, overburden is dumped away from the pit mouth or within the quarried area without consideration for its reclamation. Sometimes, these spoils are steep, unstable and prone to erosion. The mine bottoms may be exposed rocks. The pits are full of water and adjoining slopes are most or partially water-logged. No exact estimates of the total area for reclamation are available.

*Central Soil & Water Conservation, Research and Training Institute, Dehra Dun, 248 195, India.

However, Coal India Ltd. plans to increase coal production substantially during subsequent plan periods.

It is desirable to reclaim the coal-mined spoils in order to prevent environmental degradation, pollution control of groundwater, to check surface erosion and make mined area productive for grazing/fuel plantations. Presently, there is no concern amongst the mine owners, primarily because of the reduction in immediate profits. Recently, a Committee to study the ecological impact of coal mining in India has been constituted which has yet to submit its report. There are no existing laws on mining operations in relation to land improvement and environmental degradation. Moreover, absence of a sound technology for rehabilitation is yet another factor.

PRESENT MINING PRACTICES VIS-A-VIS RECLAMATION

In order to mine coal, overburden over the seams has to be removed so as to expose the coal-bearing strata. The overburden has a distinct natural formation where the top plant-bearing strata and the subsoil are above the parent material. While this overburden is removed and dumped, the sequence of soil strata is upset; the top fertile soil goes down. Some of the layers of soil in the overburden may even be toxic. The subsoil layers and the rocky portion are not suitable for plant growth. These are characterized by low fertility status and organic matter, low moisture retention capacity, too poor or too good aeration, coarse texture and susceptibility to erosion with rains. The present mining laws do not make it obligatory to grade the overburden while some mine-owners do grade the spoils. The landscape undergoes drastic change during the course of mining.

APPROACH TO RECLAMATION

Reclamation of coal mine spoils could serve the twin objectives of both protection (from erosion and environmental conservation for recreation) and production (for forestry, agriculture, forage and fish husbandry). Before reclamation, appraisal of the existing conditions such as climate-including rainfall (time, intensity, drought spells), temperature (maximum, minimum and their duration) and other features like frost, wind and humidity, are important. Topography such as slope (length and degree) aspect, altitude and drainage are some of the important features in addition to soil (texture, structure, depth, pH, etc.). The intensity of biotic factors such as pressure of grazing, fire, illicit removal of trees and grasses, should be studied. The facilities created for mining such as fencing, pump house, pipelines, etc. are needed to be retained in the area for reclamation. It would reduce the cost and with irrigation, improve growing condition for plants.

OVERBURDEN ANALYSIS AND CLASSIFICATION

This would help in providing good guidelines for dumping spoils and preparing a ground for planting. It is desirable that the overburden of coal seam is analyzed before commencing the mining operation. On the basis of the analysis of overburden, the mined area can be classified as follows (Table 1):

Table 1. Classification on mined area using overburden analysis [Adapted from Knabe (1964a)].

Class	Symbol	Usability Group	Example
I	Ag	Good for agriculture	Topsoil intact, overburden undisturbed.
II	Ls	Good for landscaping and recreation use	Mines close to habitations, towns, colonies, etc. with exposed rocks and soil in pockets.
III	F	Good for Forestry	Partially disturbed or undisturbed overburden, coarse texture, cultivation.
IV	UF	Unfit for any productive use	Very coarse overburden or rocks, toxic to plant growth.
V	V	Fisheries	When the area is covered with water like the pit.

GRADING OF SPOILS

In strip mining operations, grading is reported to compact the soils thus reducing plant growth (Knabe 1964b) while some trees have been reported, to give better growth on graded soils (Anon. 1963). Steep and long slopes should be avoided. The best way to decide about usefulness or otherwise of grading could be determined by future land use. Whereever compaction is too much, it could be removed by loosening the soils' upper crust.

Table 2. Grading for different land uses and class of spoils. [Adapted from Knabe (1964b)].

Class	Land Use	Grading
I	Ag	Yes, in level benches.
II	Ls	Yes, to a limited extent.
III	F	May not be necessary - except to operations require grading, benches in multiples of 2m may be desirable.
IV	UF	Not necessary.
V	Fl	Not necessary.

SELECTION OF PLANTING MATERIAL

No ecological survey of the vegetation has so far been conducted for the mine spoils. According to Champion and Seth (1968), the forest types from the coal area are classified as Tropical Dry Deciduous and Tropical Moist Deciduous types. However, observations showed the existence of a number of other plants (*Eragrostis coarctata, Croton sparsiflorus, Sativa* sp., *Blumea lacera*, etc.). Since no reclamation work from afforestation viewpoint has ever been attempted, much of the information available is from temperate regions. Some of the species recommended are given below (Table 3):

Table 3. Recommended species for reclamation.

Plant Species	Method of Planting	Time of Planting	Area Suitability
Acacia auriculaeformis	Seedlings	July	Hardy for semi-arid regions.
Cassia siamea	Seedlings	July	Fast growing for semiarid regions.
Albizzia lebbek	Seedlings	July	Leguminous tree for semi-arid regions.
Dalbergia sissoo	Stump cuttings, seedlings	July	Fast growing for sub-humid and semiarid region.
Prosopis juliflora	Seeds, seedlings	July	Fast growing for poor areas with rainfall below 45-70 cm.
Terminalia arjuna	Seedlings	July	Moist places in semiarid zone.
Syzygium cumini	Seedlings	July	Sub-humid areas.
Pongamia pinnata	Seedlings	July	Semiarid areas.
Madhuca latifolia	Seedlings	July	Semiarid areas; slow growing.
Alstonia scholaris	Seedlings	July	Semiarid areas; fast growing.
Pterocarpus marsupium	Seedlings	July	Semiarid areas; slow growing.
Cleistanthus collinus	Seedlings	July	Semiarid regions.

Shrubs for Semiarid Regions

Vitex negundo	Self-sprouting	July
Ipomoea carnea	Self-sprouting	July
Tephrosia candida	Seeds	July
Sesbania aegyptiaca	Seeds	July

Grasses

Pennisetum pedicellatum	Seeds	July
P. purpureum	Seeds	July
Cenchrus ciliaris	Seeds	July
Chrysopogon fulvus	Seeds	July

PLANTING TECHNIQUES

Soil Working

For subsidence areas around open-pit mines with undisturbed soil, the flat lands are worked with pits of 50 cm^3 while on disturbed soils center of the pit is manured in the form of a core where planting is done. On slopes, trench and ridge type of soil working is adopted to conserve moisture, reduce length of slope and consequent erosion and to provide a seed bed for planting and sowing. These trenches are spaced 3-5 m apart along the slopes and could be laid on contour either in a continuous form or on a staggered pattern. For water-logged areas near the pit mouth, mound planting is recommended. The height of the mound will depend on the inundation expected during the rainy season. Soil working is done before the monsoon rains. Species like *Terminalia arjuna, Syzygium cumini, Lagerstroemia speciosa* and *Barringtonia acutangula* are suitable for such locations.

Planting and Sowing

Planting material for species such as *Acacia auriculaeformis, Albizzia lebbek* and *Dendrocalamus strictus* are raised in polythene bags, 15 cm long and 15 cm diameter, while species like *Dalbergia sissoo, Terminalia arjuna, Alstonia scholaris, Pterocarpus marsupium, Cassia siamea, C. fistula, Prosopis juliflora* and *Madhuca latifolia* are raised in a nursery. The grasses can be sown or by planting tussocks separated from existing clumps. Hydro-seeding and hydro-mulching methods adopted in other parts have not so far been tried here. However, grasses would provide a quick cover and protect the ground from erosion due to rain. The ideal time for planting is the onset of monsoon. Shrubs such as *Vitex* and *Ipomoea* could be planted through cuttings between trees. Weedings may be needed on sites where planting has been on undisturbed overburden while hoeing proves helpful. Soil working is desirable around the plants to improve aeration and infiltration. Where too much rill formation is observed on exposed overburden, a grass mulch is recommended. Since water and pumping facilities are available near the open-pit mines, these could be utilized to establish and improve plant growth during dry spells through irrigation. Protection of the area is required against cattle, human and fire influences. The fencing could be done by digging a trench or barbed wire with angle iron post (Choudhary 1957). Creation of fire lines is the standard fire protection method.

Habitations, townships, main roads and underground mined areas would be the ideal locations for recreational plantations. Considering the topography, outlying the rocks, pot holes, drainage etc. and the climate, a landscape plan will have to be made. Aesthetically unpleasing sites will have to be screened out, depressions converted into ponds and lakes, gentle slopes into lawns, spoil heaps into rockeries. Some of the ornamental trees, shrubs and climbers which could be raised are recorded as below:

Ornamental Trees

Evergreen:	*Polyalthia longifolia, Grevillea robusta, Saraca indica, Thuja orientalis.*
Deciduous:	*Delonix regia, Jacaranda ovalifolia, Cassia fistula, C. siamea, C. nodosa, C. javanica, Butea monosperma.*

Timber trees: *Terminalia tomentosa, T. chebula, Lagerstroemia speciosa, Albizzia lebbek, Tectona grandis.*

Shrubs: *Ixora coccinea, Musaenda frondosa, Euphorbia poinsetiana, Hibiscus* sp., *Hamelia patens, Caesalpinia pulcherrima.*

Climbers: *Bougainvillea, Bignonia venusta, Viseria chinensis, Almanda* sp.

REFERENCES

Anonymous. 1963. An appraisal of coal strip mining. Tennessee Valley Authority, Knoxville, Tennessee, Feb., 1963.

Champion, H.G. and S.K. Seth. 1968. A Revised Survey of the Forest Types of India. Delhi, 404 p.

Choudhary, K.N. 1967. Afforestation technique for laterite zone. Directorate of Forest, Govt. of W. Bengal, Calcutta, 61 p.

Knabe, W. 1964a. Methods and results of strip mining reclamation in Germany. Ohio J. Sci. 64:75-105.

Knabe, W. 1964b. A visiting scientist's observation and recommendations concerning strip mine reclamation in Ohio. Ohio J. Sci. 64:132-157.

SPOIL–HEAP REVEGETATION AT OPEN–CUT COAL MINES IN THE BOWEN BASIN OF QUEENSLAND, AUSTRALIA

*M.J. Russell**

INTRODUCTION

The process of open-cut coal mining in the Bowen Basin of Queensland by Utah Development Co., has been described by Collins (1976). The coal seams are overlain by Upper Permian Blackwater sediments of the Bowen Basin sequence. This contributes most of the spoils of the four presently operating mines which, from the south, are Blackwater, Saraji, Peak Downs and Goonyella. These four lie along a north-south axis some 240 km long.

The Blackwater sediments consist of coarse to fine clastics, with widespread interbeds of volcanic ash, and finally of coal measures mainly of carbonaceous mudstone, minor sandstone, and many thick seams of coal. The group ranges generally from 360 to 600 m thick but is up to 2,000 m thick at the northern end (Dickins and Malone 1973).

The resultant spoils are alkaline (pH 7.2 to 9.15), have high total soluble salts (conductivity 0.14 to 2.25 m siemens cm^{-1}) with very high levels of calcium, sodium, magnesium, carbonates and chlorides. Some metal cations such as zinc, copper and manganese are at low levels, and have reduced availability to plants due to high pH. Phosphate and nitrate are both at levels marginal for normal plant growth.

Particle size ranges from clay through sand to boulders. The exposed shales and mudstones weather rapidly to clay and silt. This results in severe crusting at the surface as reported elsewhere by Plass (1974) and Verma and Thames (1975) due to high intensity rainfall, or to vehicular compaction during spoil working. Such crusts severely reduce water penetration (Berg 1975). Chemical deflocculation is expected to vary with the proportion of divalent to monovalent alkaline earth cations, and with the clay types involved.

The parallel heaps of spoil are dumped by draglines at the angle of repose (35-37° here) and are thus subject to severe erosion. For rehabilitation this spoil must be reshaped to gentler slopes suited to maintenance of permanent use for grazing. The major costs involved in rehabilitation are those for reshaping and the maximum allowable slope is thus important. It also determines the shape and extent of the final topographic unit which must be formed from the spoil heaps between adjacent ramps from the highwall to the haul road (Fig. 1). New topographic units are formed with ponds and drainage channels. High intensity rainfall is common and for stability of drainage channels stoloniferous grasses are needed in distinction to the ordinary grasses used over most of the area; trials are proceeding.

*Darling Downs Institute of Advanced Education, Toowoomba, Australia.

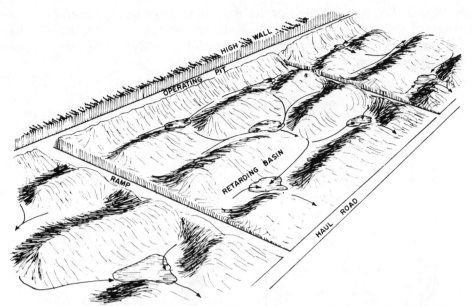

Fig. 1 Schematic Diagram of Landform After Reshaping of Spoil Heaps.

The experimental work involved in revegetating these spoils using pasture species has been described by Coaldrake and Russell (1978). Since the mines lie between latitudes 22.5° to 24.5°S, tropical and subtropical species are used that are known to tolerate the highly variable, summer-dominant rainfall.

The initial recommendation was to aerially seed the spoils with: Buffel grass (*Cenchrus ciliaris* cv. Biloela) 5 kg ha[-1]; Rhodes grass (*Chloris gayana* cv. Pioneer) 3 kg ha[-1]; Green panic grass (*Panicum maximum* var. *trichoglume* cv. Petrie) 3 kg ha[-1]. The legume is Siratro (*Macroptilium atropurpureum*) 1/2 kg ha[-1] inoculated with *Rhizobium* inoculum of approved strain e.g. CB 756 and pelletted. The fertilizer used is superphosphate 400 kg ha[-1] with Nitram 100 kg ha[-1]. These perennial species are deep rooted and usually take more than one year to establish fully (Weston et al. 1975). Coaldrake and Russell (1978) have discussed the importance of continued nitrogen supply to pastures on these spoils which commence with less than 10 ppm of available nitrate and show clear responses to added nitrogen fertilizer.

On non-intensive pastures there is clearly an economic advantage in replacing continued use of fertilizer nitrogen with a leguminous nitrogen supply which is as permanent and stable as the pasture itself (Henzell 1968). However, it is general experience that productive herbaceous legumes are not persistent in this environment (Russell and Coaldrake 1970, Anon. 1975). Work with legumes on these spoils has concentrated mainly on two tropical species, siratro and leucaena or hoakoale (*Leucaena leucocephala*), but legumes in the tropical genus *Stylosanthes* were investigated at Goonyella, and winter medics (*Medicago* spp.) were tried at Blackwater. Only siratro has been successful up to date.

Initial plot work showed hand seeding of pasture seed onto the surface to be adequate for establishment and, in consequence, company seeding of larger areas was done by aircraft. Latterly, as severe crusting has been encountered at Goonyella and Saraji, other methods of seeding have been investigated. Mulching with a surface layer of stony material resistant to weathering has been shown to ameliorate spoil crusts (Fairbourn 1974, Plass

1974, Berg 1975); this has relevance on these spoil heaps where shattered rock and carbonaceous shale are often intermixed on the surface. The procedures described have resulted in largely stable pastures but the process of complete development of normal pasture takes up to three years (Fig. 2).

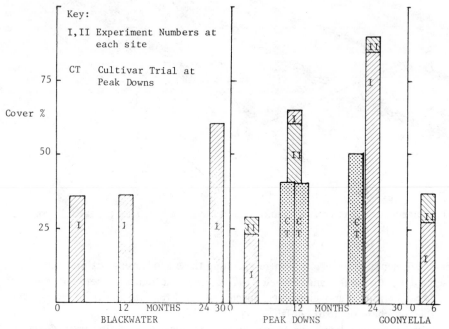

Fig. 2 Development of Revegetative Cover with Time at Three Mine Sites in the Bowen Basin

THE EXPERIMENTAL PROGRAM

Spoil heaps, initially at 35 to 37°, were spread by bulldozers and scrapers to a lesser angle. Experiments and trials were established either on leveled spoil surfaces or on these new slopes. Later work continued on the topographic units laying between ramps (described hereafter as watershed units) prepared as part of the revegetation program of each mine. These are described in the results.

The operating company now routinely monitors the shaped spoils of watershed units for pH and total soluble salts (TSS). Tests are made on 1:5 soil-water paste from samples taken at the surface and 5 cm depth at 50 m or 100 m grid points. pH and conductivity are read on these solutions using appropriate electrodes.

Soil Chemistry

Table 1 shows a summary of chemical analyses on spoil from the four mines.
The range of fertility at all four mines is essentially similar. But the range of nutrient supply or chemical condition in spoil at a single mine may vary widely.

TABLE 1 Spoil Chemical Analyses at Four Mine Sites in the Bowen Basin

Chemical Data	Blackwater	Saraji	Peak Downs	Goonyella
Phosphate (Bicarb.) ppm	2.5-9.0	1.0-16.0	8.5-12.0	3.7- 5.6
Organic carbon %C	0.9-2.1	0.8- 3.6	0.23-0.38	0.5- 1.0
Nitrate ppm N	2.3-9.0	n.a.	3.6-9.4	3.4-13.1
pH	7.3-8.4	6.0- 9.2	7.2-8.6	7.0- 8.8
SLT* mmho (m siemens) cm^{-1}	0.2-0.7	0.02-5.2	0.5-2.2	0.2-2.0
Cl ppm	340- 992	1000+	1920-5000	450-1000+
Na ppm	1670-1870	1000+	2550-3250	820-2350
K ppm	160- 270	231- 278	200- 180	100- 155
Ca ppm	1620-6000+	300- 486	799- 800	560- 860
Mg ppm	1290-2260	604-1000+	1150-1450	700-1220
Fe ppm	3.6- 39	19-39	3.0-4.5	4.2-30
Cu ppm	0.2-3.7	1.1-2.8	0.45-0.75	1.1-1.45
Mn ppm	1.2-8.0	4-8	0.5-1.5	3.7-5.2
Zn ppm	0.3-5.5	1.4-10.2	1.0-2.2	2.7-3.0

n.a. – not available
*   – Total Soluble Salts

The effect of vegetative cover on pH and TSS was investigated using paired samples, the first from beneath a cover of sown grass and the second from adjacent bare spoil. Samples were taken from three depths at seven sites. Results for TSS showed that, despite differences between sites, there was a highly significant reduction in TSS from 0.8 m siemens cm^{-1} under bare spoil to 0.49 under grass. An apparent drop in pH under grass from 8.04 to 7.82 was not significant.

Legumes

A few seedlings of *Leucaena* succeeded in early trials, but the species failed thereafter. Three species of *Stylosanthes* were tested in two experiments at Goonyella. Established plants did not persist. *Medicago littoralis* and *M. truncatula* both failed in a year of suitable winter rainfall at Blackwater.

Siratro has been planted at all mine sites in experiments and in main plantings. Initial establishment is slow and experimental results at Blackwater were not encouraging. However, in the main plantings, particularly where surface crusting was lessened by stones and coal shale fragments, establishment of siratro was much better and within three years large plants with very deep roots (> 3 m) were forming an important proportion of the cover. This pattern was repeated at Peak Downs but results have been less satisfactory at Goonyella.

An experiment to evaluate grass cultivars at Peak Downs included siratro sown at 5 kg ha^{-1} of seed with different rates of superphosphate and ammonium nitrate. Emergence counts 34 days after planting showed a mean of 3.3 siratro plants m^{-2} with no significant differences between effects of grass cultivars. There was a significant negative correlation (r^2= -0.79) between numbers of grass seedlings of all cultivars and numbers of siratro seedlings. The high fertilizer rate significantly depressed numbers of siratro plants.

Seeding Methods

In initial plot work, seed was distributed by hand onto spoil whose crust had recently been broken by a tined implement e.g. grader tines or peg toothed harrows. As a result it was recommended that broadscale seeding and fertilizing be done by aerial broadcasting onto spoils which had recently had the crust broken. Results of aerial seeding were good at Blackwater and Peak Downs but problems with crusting were encountered at Goonyella and, latterly, more severely at Saraji.

At Goonyella trials with a tractor-mounted seed and fertilizer drill produced a much denser establishment. But after one year heavy competition between plants appeared to restrict development of these pastures compared with sparser, aerially-sown, adjacent areas. A decrease of seeding rates for mechanical seeding seems to be indicated.

At Saraji, a year later, aerial seeding onto freshly tined spoils was a total failure due to reestablishment of a serious crust by the germinating rain. A tractor-mounted drill gave better emergence nearby, but dry weather in early summer and the crusting seriously reduced establishment. However, adjacent areas mulched with coarse reject or with sandy soil and aerially sown had good though patchy emergence and establishment under identical environmental conditions. The soil mulching was particularly satisfactory.

In December 1975, a rate of seeding experiment was planted at Saraji mine. Buffel, green panic and Rhodes grass were planted at 1, 2, 3, 8 and 16 kg of seed per hectare at two rates of superphosphate (100 kg ha^{-1}, 400 kg ha^{-1}) and with siratro at two seed rates (0.5 kg ha^{-1}, 2.0 kg ha^{-1}).

Results in terms of seedling numbers are shown for the effects of seeding rate on the grasses in Fig. 3.

Numbers of grass seedlings were linearly related to seeding rate. Buffel had significantly higher numbers than green panic which, in turn, had significantly higher numbers than Rhodes grass. The high level of superphosphate gave significantly greater seedling numbers than did the low level. Siratro was a failure.

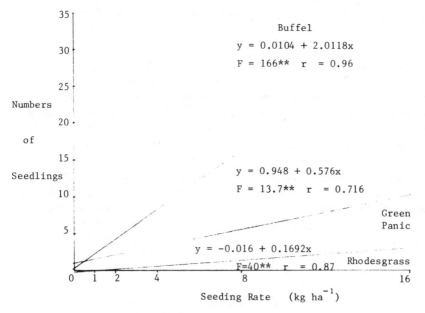

Fig. 3 Saraji Rates of Sowing Experiment
   Relationship between Seeding Rate and Numbers of Seedlings for Three Grasses

Slope Effects

The form of the topographic units referred to in the introduction is shown in Fig. 1. The slope to which the spoil is finally graded in these topographic units has varied from 10% (6°) to 20% (11°). To test the effect of slope on revegetation, samples have been taken of gradient, vegetative cover and erosion along transects from the bottom to the top of slopes. More than 20 transects at two mines failed to give any clear relationships. Spoil heterogeneity appears to mask other effects but it can be said that slopes greater than 18% are generally poorly vegetated.

Trials have been planted at Peak Downs mine in the drainage channels below ponds in two topographic units. The following grasses have been planted by hand using cuttings: Rhodes grass (*Chloris gayana* CPI 12799), Pangola grass (*Digitaria decumbens*), African Star grass (*Cynodon plectostachyus*), Para grass (*Brachiaria mutica*). African star grass has been the outstanding colonizer whereas Pangola has made limited growth.

DISCUSSION

Some 800 ha of reclaimed spoils have now been revegetated at Blackwater, Goonyella and Peak Downs mines. These spoils and those of Saraji mine are derived from similar geological material and therefore have, in general, rather similar chemical and physical properties. Variation is greater in adjacent areas on the small scale than it is between mines.

It is clear that the grasses selected previously for this environment (Coaldrake and Russell 1978) develop, in up to three years, to stable vegetative cover of about 60% which is summer active but winter dormant. Previous screening by pasture research groups referred to above suggested few herbaceous legumes of any potential other than siratro. In these experiments three other genera of legumes were evaluated but none were satisfactory. Siratro has found its place in spoil rehabilitation at Blackwater and Peak Downs but there are still problems to resolve at Goonyella and Saraji, especially where high clay content dominates at the surface. The negative correlation between siratro numbers and grass numbers in the Peak Downs experiment clearly suggests that competition between grass and legume is important, especially in the first year after seeding. This is probably due to competition for water but it is not proven.

Failure of pasture plantings to establish has been definitely associated wtih surface crusting and this has occurred particularly at Goonyella and Saraji mines. Where spoil consists of mud-stones and shales, as in the sites described in this paper, these weather rapidly to form a loose, clayey material (Kohnke 1950, Rai, et al. 1974) but with all particle sizes from coarse sand through silt represented (Doubleday 1974). This results in rapid re-sorting of particles at the surface under the influence of rain and wind, and of vehicles, particularly those with rubber tires (Doubleday 1974). A crust is formed which may be very hard (Plass 1974). Its physical nature is indicated by the lack of response to addition of calcium sulphate which was thoroughly investigated at Peak Downs and Goonyella (Coaldrake and Russell 1978). High levels of calcium prevail in these spoils (Table 1).

Such a crust must be expected to reform with the first rain after it has been broken; this has been found to be the case so that even mechanical seeding is not much more successful than broadcasting and aerial seeding. Fairbourn (1974) has reported amelioration of surface crusting if a surface layer of stoney material resistant to weathering is present, and Plass (1974) has shown similar affects. A mulch effect is used in hydroseeding techniques on coal mine spoils, and organic mulches are used in some revegetation on sand dunes after heavy mineral extraction (Barr and Golinski 1969). But high cost is a factor to be considered.

At Saraji coarse rejects and sandy topsoil produced marked improvement in establishment on seriously crusting spoil and a crust did not reform beneath these materials. The superiority of the topsoil may be due partly to microorganisms improving chemical and physical conditions for the plants; coarse reject acts simply as a sterile mulch.

In the context of crusting, the results of the seeding rates experiment are interesting. It has been the experience in previous experiments (Coaldrake and Russell 1978), and in this study, that the proportion of seedlings emerging (and also the proportion of those seedlings establishing), is a very small fraction of the seed sown. Seedlings emerge beside stones, in small hollows filled with sand, and in other discontinuities in the crust. Although these sites are very limited in number it is apparently necessary for there to be a seed on site for it to emerge there if given the opportunity. The linear response in seedling numbers to increasing seed rate up to 16 kg ha^{-1} (more than 700 buffel seeds per square meter) indicates that very large numbers of seeds are necessary to occupy sufficient of these sites to give a reasonable stand density. Since the cost of seed is perhaps 1% of total rehabilitation costs, the use of heavy seeding rates is financially justified.

ACKNOWLEDGMENTS

This work was done on the mines of Utah Development Co. by the author as a consultant to that company. He wishes to gratefully acknowledge facilities offered by U.D.C. and in particular by its environmental coordinators A.G. Collins and R. Kelly. The author is most grateful to Mr. J.E. Coaldrake, the initiator of this revegetation program, for his assistance and encouragement and for reading this paper.

SUMMARY

Agronomic experiments sponsored by Utah Development Co. at four open-cut coal mining sites in the Bowen Basin of central Queensland have led to a prescription for successful establishment of pastures on reshaped spoil heaps. Summer growing pastures based on sub-tropical species take up to three years to mature to a stable system suitable for continuous use by beef cattle. Superphosphate, nitram and heavy seeding rates for three grasses and one legume are the basis of the prescription. There are problems in some areas with surface crusting. Machinery costs for reshaping spoil heaps are the major part of the total cost.

REFERENCES

Anonymous. 1975. C.S.I.R.O. Tropical Agronomy Divisional Report 1974-75, C.S.I.R.O., Melbourne.

Barr, D.A. and K.D. Golinski. 1969. Marran grass, mulch and bitumen - a successful trial. J. Soil. Conserv. Serv. N.S.W. 25:251-257.

Berg, W.A. 1975. Use of soil laboratory analyses in vegetation of mined lands. Mining Cong. J. 61:32-35.

Coaldrake, J.E. and M.J. Russell. 1978. Rehabilitation with pasture after open-cut mining at three sites in the Bowen Coal Basin of Queensland. Reclamation Review 1:1-7.

Collins, A.G. 1976. Reclamation of open-cut spoil piles. Aust. Mining 68(7):17-19.

Dickins, J.M. and E.J. Malone. 1973. Geology of the Bowen Basin, Queensland. Bull. Bur. Min. Res. 130.

— Doubleday, G.P. 1974. The reclamation of land after coal mining. Outlook on Agric. 8(3):156-162.

Fairbourn, M.L. 1974. Effect of coal mulch on crop yields. Agron. J. 66:785-789.

Henzell, E.F. 1968. Sources of nitrogen for Queensland pastures. Trop. Grassl. 2:1-17.

— Kohnke, H. 1950. The reclamation of coal mine spoils. Adv. Agron. 2:317-349.

Plass, W.T. 1974. Revegetating surface-mined land. Mining Congr. J. 60:53-59.

— Rai, D., P.J. Wierenga and W.L. Gould. 1974. Chemical and physical properties of core samples from a coal-bearing formation in San Juan County, New Mexico. New Mexico State Univ., Agr. Expt. Sta. Res. Rpt. 287.

Russell, M.J. and J.E. Coaldrake. 1970. Performance of eight tropical legumes and lucerne and of four tropical grasses on semiarid brigalow land in Central Queensland. Trop. Grassl. 4:111-120.

— Verma, T.R. and J.L. Thames. 1975. Rehabilitation of land disturbed by surface mining coal in Arizona. J. Soil & Water Cons. 30:129-131.

Weston, E.J., C.N. Nason and R.D.H. Armstrong. 1975. Resources study in the Condamine-Maranoa Basin of Southern Queensland. Qld. J. Agric. Anim. Sci. 32(2):1-192.

ENVIRONMENTAL ASSESSMENT OF COAL MINING PROPOSALS IN AUSTRALIA: RECLAMATION AND REHABILITATION

W.J. Atkinson and H. Cooley *

INTRODUCTION

The environmental legislative framework established by the Australian Commonwealth Government in relation to development proposals is identified at present chiefly in terms of the *Environment Protection (Impact of Proposals) Act*. This legislation was introduced in December 1974 and the Administrative Procedures made under the Act came into force in June 1975.

The object of the Act can be put simply as an endeavor to ensure that those responsible for developing proposals which in any way involve the Commonwealth Government and those responsible for taking decisions on those proposals, think about and take into account environmental factors. The purpose of the legislation is no more than that. It does not give those responsible for the environment a right to stop developments that are likely to have adverse environmental effects. Nor does it give environmental considerations a veto power over decision-making.

The Act provides for the use of environmental impact statement technique in relation to environmentally significant proposed actions of the Commonwealth, including those involving decisions by the Commonwealth. It facilitates examination of the proposals and the release of impact statements for public review and provides for the conduct of public inquiries where directed by the Minister.

The environmental impact statement technique enables all aspects of a proposed action and its feasible alternatives to be objectively examined and impacts documented in a form suitable for consideration by all interested parties relative to all decision-making parameters, including community objectives. The impact statement is the public document which exposes this part of the planning process to the public who then respond appropriately.

In the context of mining developments, environmental assessment of proposals involves the examination of environmental impacts of the proposed mining project and its alternatives, and assesses these relative to the available planning options. The impact of the proposal on physical features of land surface is examined in relation to various land use alternatives available and the reclamation and rehabilitation program to minimize adverse impacts on the preferred land use is formulated. When it is possible to develop land use and mining planning concurrently, the preferred land use option can be selected with a view to

*Office of Environment Protection, Lombard House, 1 Allara Street, P.O. Box 1890, Canberra City, A.C.T. , Australia 2601.

minimizing the adverse impacts of the mining proposal or to utilize aspects of the mining proposal to benefit the land use option.

In development of a proposal, the decision-making process is considered to generally involve a series of decisions leading to the implementation of a proposal. In this hierarchy of decisions, one can be identified as the critical "approval" decision. An environmental impact statement, to be effectively used, must be prepared and considered before this decision is taken.

Environmental Assessment Procedures

The basic guidelines required for the management of environmental resources by industry are those which set down a framework within which the environmental consequences of operational practice and development proposals can be assessed. In areas of Commonwealth responsibility, the Administrative Procedures under the *Environment Protection (Impact of Proposals) Act* provide these guidelines.

These Procedures form the administrative basis for the environmental assessment of all types of proposed actions coming before the government for decision. The Procedures set down guidelines in relation to consideration of proposed actions which are environmentally significant. Steps in this process include:

- identification of an action Minister or Authority, (the Minister or Authority responsible for the critical "approval" decision);
- designation of a proponent in relation to the proposed action;
- provision of initial information to enable a determination to be made as to whether the preparation and submission of an environmental impact statement is required to achieve the object of the Act;
- making of this determination;
- setting of guidelines for environmental impact statement and preparation of the statement by the proponent:
- release of the draft impact statement for public review;
- revision of the draft statement, taking into account public comment received;
- direction and conduct of a public environmental inquiry;
- submission of the final impact statement to the Commonwealth Minister responsible for environmental matters;
- assessment of the final impact statement;
- provision of resulting comments and recommended actions by this Minister to the action Minister in relation to the environmental implications of the proposed action.

An important element of this environmental assessment procedure is the requirement for public review. The Environment Protection Administrative Procedures require that, as a matter of course, whenever an impact statement has been drafted on a proposed action, the statement be subjected to public review. Only in a situation in which the Commonwealth Minister responsible for environmental matters has agreed, can an impact statement be excluded from this review process.

Proponents are expected to consult with sections of the community which are directly affected by the proposal during the early planning stage which would coincide with the preparation of the draft environmental impact statement. The draft statement is advertised and released for public review for a specified minimum time period and members of the public are invited to comment on any aspects of the proposal. The substance of public comment must be incorporated as appropriate in the final document. If the Minister considers that substantial conflict has not been resolved, he may direct that a public inquiry be held under the Act.

Impact statements have been required for only a small proportion of the total number of proposed actions which have been considered under the Act to date. Since June 1975, about 10,000 proposed actions have been considered and environmental impact statements have been directed on about 50 of these. The proposals reviewed have comprised a wide range of developments including buildings, land development, communication facilities, mining and transportation projects.

In the case of many environmentally significant proposed actions, an environmental impact statement has not been directed on the grounds that the object of the Act has been achieved by other means.

The coverage of the *Environment Protection (Impact of Proposals) Act* is not limited to proposals being developed by the Commonwealth Government. It extends to the projects of industry where these require Commonwealth approval to proceed. In the case of the mining industry such approvals may be required where the minerals are to be exported and are thus subject to the *Customs (Prohibited Exports) Regulations*, or where the company involved requires exchange control approval for the import of foreign capital for development of the mining operation. This aspect raises important considerations in respect to cooperation with state governments in this area.

At present the Commonwealth *Environment Protection (Impact of Proposals) Act 1974* is the only legislation in Australia which is specifically concerned with environmental impact assessment. Detailed discussions are being carried out with the states aimed at reaching agreement on the best way for state and Commonwealth governments to achieve environment protection. Cooperative arrangements are being formulated in this regard.

Assessment of Coal Mining Proposals

As many coal mining projects in Australia have been developed to produce coal for export and, as a number of these have required the import of foreign capital for their development, they fall within the scope of the *Environment Protection (Impact of Proposals) Act*. Environmental impact statements have been prepared in relation to a number of these.

Impact statements prepared in relation to coal mining proposals have been composed of the following:

- examination of the need for the proposal;
- comprehensive description of the social and physical environment to be affected;
- detailed description of the proposed mining plan and feasible alternatives to it;
- identification of all potential environmental impacts;
- formulation of measures proposed to minimize the adverse impacts both during and after the mining activity; and
- selection of the preferred mining plan.

Measures proposed for the immediate protection of the physical environment have included control of air and water emissions, prevention of soil erosion, control of noise levels, visual screening of mining areas and control of access and transportation. Long-term impacts are generally assessed and treated in the context of post-mining land use planned for the area. Minimization of these impacts after cessation of mining operations is largely dependent on the reclamation and rehabilitation program carried out.

Reclamation and Rehabilitation

The disturbance of the land surface caused by mining operations is a major environmental impact and the proposed methods of land rehabilitation and reclamation are important means of minimizing these impacts both in the short and long-term. Consequently the assessment of these impacts and formulation of reclamation and rehabilitation proposals are of particular importance.

For the purpose of this paper, reclamation is defined as earth-moving and reshaping operations carried out of the disturbed land surface, overburden material and mining spoil.

Rehabilitation refers to activities carried out to return the reshaped land surface to an acceptable post-mining land use. During planning of the mining proposal, basic requirements for reclamation and rehabilitation must be identified and a works program incorporated in the mining plan.

The eventual land use of the area is, through necessity, a major factor in determining methods of reclamation and rehabilitation of disturbed areas. Proposals considered on impact statements to date have involved three post-mining land use categories. These are:

. native areas, for incorporation in natural wilderness, National park or Nature reserve areas;
. agricultural land, for grazing or crop production; and
. urban or associated developments, for establishment of urban areas, roadways or recreation facilities.

In most instances selection of planned land use has taken place independently and prior to planning of the mining operation. Where the mining land has been in an area of wilderness, it has been generally required, as a condition of approval of the project, that the land be returned to a condition as close as possible to that existing before mining operations commenced. However, where the land has been previously developed for agriculture and is required to be returned to such, there is some flexibility in the choice of reclamation and rehabilitation measures. Where the proposed operation is located adjacent to urban areas, the same flexibility does not exist and land is usually reshaped to contours suitable for any planned extension of the urban area.

While each of these planned land use categories place special requirements on methods of reclamation and rehabilitation, a number of basic requirements apply in all instances. Stabilization of the disturbed areas to minimize soil erosion and aesthetic amelioration are critical initial requirements.

As complete disturbance of the land surface occurs in open-cut coal mining operations, such operations disrupt water drainage patterns and as new flow patterns become established, the area is highly susceptible to erosion. Before revegetation, the reclaimed areas must be contoured to a gradient which minimizes erosion and encourages establishment of plants.

Maximum slope is dictated by the susceptibility to erosion. If slopes are too steep, soil erosion can occur and seeds of young plants will be washed away before vegetation can become established. Also, high runoff rates preclude significant infiltration to the detriment of plant growth.

As specific slopes depend on the situation and the land use intended, it is not possible to stipulate standard slopes which are suitable for plant growth and erosion control. It is generally accepted however that 35° angle of repose of spoil heaps is too steep for this purpose. Slopes in the range 5° to 15° have been selected in projects examined, depending on the relevant local considerations. The selection of minimum slopes is also important as extensive level areas create drainage problems and can result in large areas of shallow water pondage during wet conditions which preclude the planned land use. The method of land shaping is also an important aspect. Light grading on the contour minimizes soil erosion susceptibility. Tracked equipment in preference to rubber tyred machinery reduces surface compaction and provides ideal seed deposition locations.

Another factor in contour patterns in rehabilitation is aesthetic consideration which requires that unattractive features need to be removed or disguised. In relation to coal mining the most obvious features remaining after close of operations are the spoil heaps. These can be leveled or contoured to some extent, though it is usually impossible to restore the area to its original topography due to the swell factor of the disturbed rock. The shaping of spoil heaps and their revegetation are important factors in the amelioration of aesthetic damage to the area. Further special requirements for reclamation and rehabilitation apply for each planned land use category.

Native Areas

Areas which were covered with undisturbed native vegetation prior to mining are generally restored as closely as possible to their pre-mining state. Return of an area to its original condition requires particular attention to be paid to reclamation and rehabilitation methods. The area must be returned as near as possible to its pre-mining contours and as a minimum requirement, should blend in with adjacent unmined areas. Drainage lines should be reformed and care taken to avoid creating large bodies of water or poorly drained areas where these did not exist previously.

Revegetation is the major step in rehabilitation of these areas. The revegetation program, aimed at reestablishing the native vegetation, must be based on a pre-mining vegetation survey. Plant communities should be identified, their locations mapped, their composition recorded and if possible their distribution correlated with land characteristics. The revegetation program would then be based on this pre-mining survey. If topsoil has been removed prior to mining and stockpiled, and is returned after reshaping, establishment of vegetation is facilitated. Where topsoil has not been stockpiled, it may be necessary to bring it into the area. As "native" topsoil comprises a storage medium for seeds and root material of plants naturally occurring in the area, revegetation will be assisted by its use. If topsoil is brought into the area it should be obtained from other areas with similar vegetative characteristics. Similarly, care should be taken with the location of topsoil replacement; placing topsoil derived from a low-lying swamp area onto the top of a hill is of little use.

When topsoil is brought into the area or relocated within it, it is advisable to ensure that soil composition is adequate to support the proposed vegetation. Physical and chemical properties of the soil should be examined in the light of the requirements of plant species native to the area. Requirements for native plants will be different from those for pasture establishment.

Initial plantings are usually of quick growing species which will provide stabilizing cover of the land surface until a permanent cover can be established. Generally short lived exotic grasses or cereal crops are used to ensure that the nonnative species are phased out in later stages of revegetation.

Various techniques are available to assist rapid establishment of temporary cover crops. Care should be exercised in the use of fertilizers. Although these may be necessary to obtain rapid initial growth of a cover crop, prolonged fertilizer use may create soil nutrient conditions not suited to the reestablishment of native species. High fertilizer rates can also result in leaching of nutrients from the area and their retention in adjacent wetlands may change these communities.

In cases where an area had been developed before mining, restoration to its "natural" (pre-disturbance) state is not practical unless the mined area is large or adjoins an area of uncleared native land. If the area is small or isolated, re-colonization by original species of fauna is not likely to occur even if the original vegetation has been reestablished. That is not to say that there is no point in replanting native vegetation; this may be preferable on aesthetic or other grounds.

Agricultural Use

In Australia, many of the coal mining projects so far considered under the *Environment Protection (Impact of Proposals) Act* have considered deposits in areas previously used for grazing. In these projects the reestablishment of vegetation is generally not difficult. It is important, however, to consider the original productivity of the land and to return it to or above this level. Except for the emphasis on providing a medium suited to the establishment of plant species for grazing or cropping, comments made in relation to reshaping and topsoil replacement on natural areas also apply to agricultural areas.

When developing a reclaimed area for pasture use the selection of the grass and other species to be used warrants careful consideration, particularly in the light of pre-mining productivity and water supply location. Where water supplies have been disrupted by mining, planning of their relocation with regard to irrigation and stock watering are an integral part of the rehabilitation plan. Replanting of trees and shrubs for shade and windbreaks should also be included.

Development Areas

Planning of reclamation and rehabilitation of areas to be used for urban or other associated purposes is dependent on specific land use and details of the individual project. This option has not often been taken in Australia, and where it has, the introduction of a new activity has required detailed planning and environmental studies. Where some form of independent planning has taken place prior to mining, such as planning of urban development on the site, the rehabilitation plan has been drawn up accordingly.

Monitoring

Regardless of the final land use, it is considered necessary to establish long-term monitoring programs to ascertain the success or otherwise of rehabilitation measures. Revegetation in particular must be monitored to ensure that after its initial establishment, it progresses successfully through seasonal changes. Native species must be tested for their capability of reaching maturity and propagating a second generation. Revegetated pastures must be shown to be capable of carrying the same number of stock as were carried prior to mining. In the early stages it will be necessary to monitor soil conditions in order to predict nutrient deficiencies which may occur before there is any detectable damage to the plant community.

When the soil has stabilized, productivity will have to be examined. Vegetative cover and density values derived from predetermined consistent survey quadrants are very good measures of soil stability. These should be monitored over a number of years and in all seasons until it also has stabilized.

CONCLUSION

Since the introduction of the Commonwealth *Environment Protection (Impact of Proposals) Act*, the preparation and examination of environmental impact statements have been carried out for a number of Australian coal mining proposals.

A significant and extensive environmental impact of these proposals, particularly in open-cut operations, is the disturbance caused to the land surface. The environmental impact statement technique has enabled these impacts to be identified and assessed in relation to the proposed post-mining land use. Land reclamation and rehabilitation are the principal measures to minimize these impacts in the medium to short-term and these can be formulated to reform the land surface in accordance with the land use planning requirements. While detailed measures adopted are often specific to a particular mining project, general guidelines can be set down in relation to various land use categories.

The identification of impacts of mining proposals on land surface and the integration of a planned reclamation and rehabilitation program into the proposal at the time of the environmental assessment, allows the mining proponent to minimize these impacts and the decision-maker to consider them in the context of post-mining land use planning.

STRIP MINE RECLAMATION IN USSR, WEST GERMANY AND USA

Richard L. Hodder*

This is a brief report on an interesting reclamation inspection trip to the Soviet Union and West Germany in July, 1977. The visit was made possible through an agreement between the USSR and the USA signed on May 23, 1972, which provided for the exchange of technical information in the field of environmental protection. About 135 subject areas are covered by this agreement, and in 1977 a new project was initiated entitled Reclamation and Revegetation of Surface-Mined or Otherwise Disturbed Land. I was one of a team of five from the U.S. comprising the first working exchange group. Our inspection trip was extensive and included the following types of mining and reclamation: oil shale, coal, manganese, sand and gravel, and fire clay. Also included were salt marsh reclamation, sand dune stabilization and steep mountainside cultivation techniques. We covered western USSR from the Baltic in the north to the Black Sea in the south by flying between lengthy stops and by autovan for considerable distances of cross country travel.

Our first mine site inspection was located out of Tallin, Estonia in northern country at a latitude equivalent to Anchorage, Alaska. Production here is limited to timber and livestock. We saw extensive tree plantings on spoils accummulated at the Yarve oil shale mine during the last 15 or more years. Some of the tree plantings here were already 6 to 8 m high. Although many species of deciduous and coniferous species were responding well, scotch pine (*Pinus sylvestris*) was the most common species, a favored reclamation tree species in much of the USSR. Both hand (about 60%) and machine (40%) planting methods were used. Fertilizers are applied at the time of planting. Manure and peat were sometimes used as soil amendments and some remains of these materials were still discernable. Topsoil was not used on tree planting sites. It was explained that topsoil is neither necessary nor beneficial for most timber production. The soil at this location was gravelly with broken limestone and shale particles with fines in between. The water table at this site was exceedingly high and major depressions were filled with water supposedly of quality that supported wildlife and waterfowl. Spoils were reshaped from level to gradually undulating.

In Leningrad, we visited Leningrad ("Giproshakht") Institute which is one of the oldest (50 years) in the USSR. One of the Institute's primary missions is to solve problems associated with opencast strip mining. The area of their interest is north Russia extending to the Ukraine and east into Siberia. There is a staff of 1,100; 900 are headquartered in Leningrad. Recultivation began in 1960 in the Moscow Basin. Lands mined long ago pose difficult reclamation problems because of toxic materials at the surface. In reclamation, these lands are covered to 2 m by three layers: (1) the lowest is a sandy layer to retard capillary movement, (2) a loam layer, and (3) a humic layer near the surface. It is an expensive process but production may exceed that of the original soil. Where possible, soil

*Montana Agricultural Experiment Station, Montana State University, Bozeman, MT 59717.

material from new mines is used to cover old spoils. The present environmental law requires that the land be made no less productive than it was before mining. Reclamation costs are estimated to be as much as 60% of the cost of mining. This description however, was not exactly in line with what we observed, partially because we did not view many old spoils of such consequence.

The term "reclamation" in Europe is replaced by the word "recultivation" as agricultural production is almost exclusively the designated purpose. This became very clear as we approached the more cultivatable areas of the USSR. In Donetsk, a major environmental problem is the reclamation of numerous huge pyramids of spoils and coal slack from underground mining towering between the city buildings. There are about 23 mines at a depth of 300 m under the city. Some of the spoil is now compacted into the mine tunnels as coal is removed to prevent land subsidence. The product of the mines is coking coal, most of which is shipped to the Dombass industrial area. Natural gas is used in most homes and furnaces. We were told that about 300 million rubles (ca. 420 million dollars) had been spent in the Donetsk area for protection of air, land, and water. It was also expected that an additional 300 million rubles would be spent by 1980 to clean rivers of the area. Spoil piles in the Donetsk area are not suited for agriculture, and noncommercial timber species of trees are planted on them. About 20 deciduous tree species are used; the most commonly observed was yellow acacia. Many small fruit trees were also planted on these prominent spoil piles. We observed only one towering pile that was completely revegetated. The problem is staggering and there are many more steep piles to renovate; it is of course impractical to move them or to level them out to any extent as part of the reclamation process.

The new city of Donetsk was in many ways a marvelous example of predictive planning. Some phases of the 1980 Olympics will be held in Donetsk and the city is busily preparing for this event. There are many attractive buildings and monuments, but the most impressive feature was the quality of the city planning such as the design of the wide streets lined with rows of trees 33 to 66 m wide and walking paths under the trees. Numerous flower gardens containing countless roses, begonias, and other beautiful flowers bordered these paths. These attractive park-like thoroughfares although heavily used were a delight to experience within a busy industrial city.

Our next major stop was Drouzjkovka, about 200 km from Donetsk. Here we visited a fire-clay (Kaolinite) mine. Bucket-wheel excavators were used to move the massive amounts of overburden. These excavators can handle as much as 80,000 cubic m of material per day in conjunction with conveyor belt systems. Several draglines were used. Strip mining was initiated in 1961, and the recultivation process started in 1967. Fifty ha were reclaimed the first year, and 256 ha have been reclaimed since 1970. Where depressions occur as a result of subsidence, they are filled with red clay loam and covered with a layer of chernozem topsoil. Thirty to 35 ha of land are disturbed each year and approximately 40 ha are recultivated each year. The overburden thickness is about 30-35 m. Approximately 30-40 m of fire clay are removed. There are some toxic problem areas involving an alkali material which are identified in advance by drilling. It was stated that in the upper soil layers a sodium percentage of up to 4% is acceptable. The water table here is about 30 m deep. Rainfall is about 1.5 to 2 m per year.

In reclaiming the disturbed land, when using bucket wheel excavators and conveyors, it is possible to remove any given layer of soil or overburden and replace it in the pit in the same relative position from which it came; however, this is seldom done where there is an abundance of loess material to place beneath the topsoil. We were told that the upper layers of the reclaimed land consist of about 15 m of sand, then 2 to 3 m of red loam, topped by

60-70 cm of chernozem topsoil. Then a typical but not standard rotation of vegetation is planted as follows: an annual cereal grain for 1 year, a perennial grass for 2 years, winter wheat for 2 years, then alfalfa. This sequence varied at different locations and in different Republics. Roughly 1,500 workers are employed at this mine. They work 7 hours a day, 41 hours per week. The mine is expected to operate for another 33 years; however, the mineral deposit could last for about another 100 years. The fire clay is used mostly in the Ukraine, with some going to other parts of the USSR. This material is in great demand in the USSR, and extremely large quantities of fire clay are consumed.

An interesting innovation was observed concerning a dragline bucket that was working occassionally in mucky wet clay material which clung to the interior of the bucket. To facilitate dumping, a hinged bucket liner was built into it, anchored to the upper rear lip of the bucket. The inner liner was steel consisting of two plates hinged together. One plate covered the bottom and the other covered the rear. When the bucket was held vertically in dumping position, the plates slid out hanging straight from the top lip of the rear of the bucket, thus dumping the sticky load quickly by sloughing it off the shaking plates.

Traveling to Ordzjonikidze, we noticed very little contour farming or summer fallowing but much emphasis on shelterbelts to prevent wind erosion. Ordzjonikidze is the location of the largest manganese mine in the world. It was first mined underground starting in 1888 but surface mining began in 1952. Also, in the town are three large ore concentration plants. Recent mechanization has improved mine production per man by seventeen times. Mining disturbs 300 ha per year and 200 ha are reclaimed but their goal is to reclaim the same amount of surface area as is disturbed annually. The ore bed occupies 7,000 ha, and mining is projected to continue for 2,000 years. Thickness of the ore bed is 0.5-3 m. Waste materials from the concentration processes are stored for future more efficient processing. These dumps are covered with soil and farmed on level areas and trees planted on steep slopes. The estimated cost of reclamation is 4,000-4,500 rubles/ha.

I noticed that the Russian system of handling dusty mine road maintenance was unique. On several occassions I saw stacks of reinforced concrete pads with hook loops on the edges. These slabs were used for surfacing graded roadbeds. They were approximately 15-20 cm thick, reinforced with rerod or prestressed and were interlocking although I did not get details of the interlocking system. At an experiment station nearby, we saw plantings of orchards, berries, field crops, and medicinal plants. Of major interest were experiments with various amounts of chernozem topsoil and fertilizer to determine optimum amounts for crop production.

In general, reclamation research in Russia substantiates much of our work here. Although regulations may call for one or two m of topsoil in some locations, we were shown timber plantings and orchards of apple and cherry where alternate rows of trees were planted in raw spoils or in deep trenches filled with topsoil. Opened excavations showed that after 15 years of study, tree conformation, size and fruit production were not improved by the use of topsoil on these species. Alfalfa demonstrated its ability to produce four cuttings per year over the long-term on raw spoils without topsoil.

The advantages of topsoil became very apparent when considering grass and grass-legume forage production. The grains, too, demonstrated that from 30 to 60 cm of topsoil was necessary to produce crops equal to pre-disturbance production. It was agreed that where there is a wealth of loess material and topsoil available, all should be salvaged and used.

Previous to the availability of chemical fertilizers, it was explained that alfalfa was used for several seasons to build up soil fertility and then grain crops were grown until production dropped off. At this point, the alfalfa-grain cycle was repeated. With chemical fertilizers, the alfalfa can be eliminated.

Complete research institutes and experiment stations for reclamation experimental work were located entirely on or near reclaimed areas. Much of the work done was extremely impressive as were the fine facilities.

At Tbilisi, we met with Dr. G.A. Davidovich, Head of the Georgian Research Institute of Pedology. The staff consists of 280 specialists who study soil problems of the entire Republic. In addition to recultivation and erosion, saline soils in East Georgia and boggy soils of West Georgia are major problems of special concern. More than 50% of the Republic has erosion problems partly because only 10-13% of the country is flat. Soils are brought from problem areas to the Institute and placed in numerous elaborate lysimeters for detailed study. Two large (15,000 ha and 18,000 ha) "natural" drainages are also studied intensively.

We drove to Chiatura, a mining town located in a steep walled canyon, to review reclamation at another manganese mine. Here hilltop mining predominated and employed complicated cablecar transportation. Reclamation purposes varied from housing sites to parks to football fields because of the confinement of the canyon below. On steep slopes, only trees are planted. A favorite tree for this purpose is black locust (*Robina pseudoacacia*) native to the U.S. At another but flatter area, four years of croppings with grasses and alfalfa were required to prepare soil for the production of grapes. Nearby was an experiment station where optimum depths of topsoil and fertilizer were being determined.

At tropical Sochi on the Black Sea, Dr. V.V. Vorontsov, Director of the Research Institute of Mountain Gardening and Floriculture, discussed problems of slope utilization in agriculture and environmental protection. This, also, is one of the oldest institutes in the USSR, established in 1894. Flower production, erosion control, land amelioration, and environmental protection are investigated here. Older cropping systems caused excessive erosion, but sloping terraces with controlled drainage systems developed by the Institute effectively reduced erosion. The system used is called "vertical planting". Terraces about 4 m wide are used. They are now trying to put more of the steep slopes not formerly cultivated into orchards, thus reserving the flat lands for farming of truck crops. The Institute has a staff of more than 1,000 with 86 scientists, or a ratio of scientists to workers of about 1:12.

Following our stay in Russia, we were guests of the Rhinebraun Company of West Germany (The Federal Republic of Germany) near Cologne. This company operates the largest producing coal mine in the world and produces 30-40% of the coal mined in Germany. Production was 118 million mT last year. It is also probably the most efficient and technologically advanced in terms of both mining and reclamation techniques. Bucket-wheel excavators and conveyor belts are used to remove coal and handle overburden. The largest excavator moves 240,000 m^3 per day.

The coal seam, up to 100 m thick, is 100 to 600 m below the surface. It is expected that the deepest pit will be 480 m (1,575 ft) and mining will continue for 50-60 years. Power stations are within sight of the mines. All have electrostatic precipitators and little emission from them was observed. Ash is buried in the mine pit. Wells around the mine lower the water table by 600 m. The ratio of water removed per ton of coal is 11:1. Three million tons of water are pumped per day and, although of good quality compared to common depth groundwater, only 20% is used. Of this, some is distributed to relocated farms and hamlets, but by far the largest part is sold to the city of Cologne at a considerable profit.

There are many environmental concerns. Rivers, railroads, and highways have to be re-routed. Rivers must be lined to prevent excessive leakage. Entire hamlets and villages are eliminated and rebuilt. Prior approval by about 73 offices or agencies is required before acceptance of a mining plan. After approval, one agency administers execution of the mining plan. Attempts are made to return the land to its former contour and to create cropping and forest patterns that are aesthetically pleasing from both ground and air. Lakes built for water control provide fishing and planted forests, hunting, and other recreational activities for nearby inhabitants. Of about 17,000 ha in the area affected by mining, 12,000 ha have been reclaimed and 5,000 are in active opencast mines. Approximately 20,000 people were resettled during the period between 1945 and 1976. An equivalent number will be relocated in the proposed mining areas of Hambach I and Hambach II presently being approved.

I recognized some major differences in reclamation procedures, conditions, and equipment between Russia, Germany, and certainly the United States, but similarities between the three countries were very apparent, too. Perhaps the most obvious observation concerns the long-term experience and results that each of the European countries has acquired over the years and the outstanding determination exerted to make reclamation in these respective countries a productive and profitable effort. The cooperation between engineering extraction and rehabilitation aspects of mining were conspicuous and over-powering from the conception of a mining plan through to reclamation completion. The tremendous reclamation research effort, the institutions' experiment stations, and other facilities dedicated to reclamation work were certainly impressive. Many reputed scientists have been assigned to reclamation, recultivation, and rehabilitation objectives.

While in Russia, several instances of uneven subsidence were observed and discussed. In Germany, subsidence was observed, but in the latter case one might call it inconsequential settling. In comparing techniques to determine the cause of the difference, I recall that the spoils stacker booms in Russia were stationary and so created long series of conical piles which were not leveled but deeply inundated with better soil materials, loess, and topsoil. In constrast, in Germany the stacker booms were in constant motion, thus creating extensive areas of slightly undulating spoils as a base for topsoiling procedures. I believe that the stacker operation was the probable cause for differences in subsidence patterns.

Also, topsoiling techniques varied drastically, the USSR using more normal procedures while innovative slurry systems were in use in Germany. Topsoil was hauled by train to a mixing station where topsoil and water were mixed to form a slurry. This process segregated, by settling, the coarse rocky material from the finer topsoil. It also provided much moisture and weight to accelerate the subsidence process. One diked compartment was being filled with topsoil while another would be prepared for filling. The drying of these leveled compartments is apparently quite rapid, depending somewhat on temperature and precipitation and texture. As soon as cracks appear and the soil surface is sufficiently dense to support a farm tractor, cultivation begins followed by seeding and the production of a new crop on the reclaimed surface. Although dike construction requires the use of scrapers to haul and place topsoil, the slurry topsoiling system requires only two men to relocate and operate the slurry pipeline, an extremely economical arrangement. Subsidence under this system seems negligible.

My major disappointment of the mine rehabilitation exchange review was the lack of concern or effort applied to the trace element and inhibitory material placement in the spoils restructure. Because of a ubiquitous and very high water table, surface water has been polluted for so long in much of Russia and Germany that protection of the nonpotable groundwater has received low priority, in direct contrast to our assessment in Montana where groundwater quality is all important. This aspect of reclamation has been of particular concern to me.

The USSR - USA reclamation exchange program has a productive future, I am sure. The USSR is extremely interested in some of our approaches to reclamation in Montana, especially in our surface manipulation innovative work, in our unique selective placement of identified overburden, protection of groundwater systems, and new reclamation machinery design and development. On the other hand, we have much to gain in years of time by tapping their abundant data supply pertaining to long-term results of more standard approaches to disturbed land rehabilitation.

GENERAL REMARKS ON RECLAMATION IN THE USSR

Don Calhoun*

This brief report will include an explanation of the Soviet-American scientific exchange agreement, a description of the areas we toured, and the impressions of Russian reclamation we gained.

In discussing this Soviet-American scientific exchange agreement, I would like to cover 5 different points:

(1) What has happened to date
(2) Current plans
(3) Problems that exist
(4) Challenges
(5) Opportunities

In May 1972, a cooperative agreement was signed by President Nixon and Premier Breshnev which provided for the exchange of scientific information between the U.S. and USSR. There are currently about 135 subject areas covered by the agreement; the project I work with is titled "Reclamation and Revegetation of Disturbed Land."

During the last 2 years, we have hosted two different groups of Russian visitors, totaling 7 scientists. We have shown them mining and reclamation areas in Kentucky, West Virginia, Pennsylvania, North Dakota, Montana, Wyoming, Colorado, and Alaska. The types of operations visited included coal, oil shale, iron, and the Alaska pipeline.

I want to especially acknowledge the interest, cooperation, and assistance provided by the many coal companies and power plants, U.S. Steel, Alaska Pipeline, several universities, National Coal Association, and various governmental agencies which have been involved. They have all been just great to work with on this project. Another group of Russian scientists was to visit the U.S. at the present time, and participate in this Congress, however, their travels have been postponed until July of this year.

One important prospective aspect of this program involves the exchange of junior scientists who would be assigned to host research stations. The objective would be to spend up to two months doing actual research on reclamation problems. We feel this could be the most productive part of the entire program, and we will keep pressing for this to take place. However, a large obstacle in this type of exchange is the language barrier. Incidentally, I feel that this illustrates a significant defect in our educational system. Not many of our scientists are multilingual, and the importance of knowing other languages should be stressed in our schools.

*Bureau of Land Management, U.S. Department of the Interior, Denver Service Center, Denver, CO 80225.

Some of the problems that exist in the exchange program are as follows:

(1) The language barrier is significant. It seems that there are many Russians who know English, but very few Americans who know Russian. Their language is a difficult one. Three years of intensive study are probably required in order to converse in Russian. Many words and phrases cannot be translated.

(2) The matter of *trust* in Russian is an interesting point to consider. If you were a Russian citizen, whom would you trust? Aside from your family, would you trust a school teacher, a political leader, a party boss, a government worker, or someone from a foreign country?

   At any rate, there are significant problems involved in developing mutual trust between exchange scientists in a program such as this.

(3) *Mutual understanding* is another difficult problem; the key appears to be the interpreter who must have some knowledge of the scientific specialty to correctly interpret the information. Mr. Carter recently learned the importance of a good interpreter while in Poland.

(4) There are some basic differences in the *customs* of the two countries which can lead to problems. However, a good interpreter will usually take care of these.

(5) *Translation of publications* is a major problem for us, because this work is quite difficult, expensive, (up to 10 cents per word), time consuming, and few people are able to do it.

   Relative to the matter of translation of scientific publications, I would like to point out that last summer, while in Russia, we were given some 43 reclamation oriented publications. Translation of these is being done at Montana State University at Bozeman. It is our intent to have the publications printed in English and distributed widely within the U.S. If you would like to have your name added to the mailing list, contact me or Mr. Richard L. Hodder at Montana State University.

(6) The *closure* of certain areas to foreigners is a problem at times.

(7) There is also a problem of getting (practicing) scientists involved in the exchange program, as opposed to administrators and politicians.

Opportunities that exist in this exchange program are many. A few that I am aware of and that seem important are:

(1) Research into soils and topsoil requirements, revegetation techniques, toxic materials, and engineering and mining techniques.
(2) Plant materials
(3) Equipment - mining and reclamation
(4) Junior scientist exchange
(5) Land use planning and zoning
(6) Technology transfer
(7) Mining methods
(8) Reclamation techniques
(9) Water treatment
(10) Air and water pollution control

The Russians have developed a system to classify disturbed lands. This system is currently being evaluated to determine if it might fit our needs. At the very least, it will provide us with some worthwhile information, perhaps useful to the Office of Surface Mining.

While on this trip we spent 2 days in England, 16 days in Russia, and 4 days in West Germany. This was the first group of this type to visit the Soviet Union and more than likely, we were shown their best areas in terms of reclamation.

The primary Soviet objective in reclaiming mined lands is to return these lands to agricultural production. Some of their most important mineral deposits are located in the same areas as their best agricultural lands and they cannot afford to lose the land to poor reclamation. Reclamation concepts of cold or dry mined areas were not told to us. The Soviet Union is roughly twice the size of the U.S. Of that land area, only about 10% is fertile arable land, and only about 1 % of their land possesses these qualities with enough precipitation to grow crops without irrigation. The population of Russia is about 290 million.

These statistics indicate why food production is a critical issue in all land planning.

The purpose of our trip was to see agriculturally reclaimed areas and to identify opportunities for more detailed study, plant materials exchanges and information exchange.

The areas we visited included:

Moscow
Tallinn, Estonia
Leningrad

Donetsk   )
Zaporozhye   )   Ukraine
Ordzhonikidze   )

Tbilisi   )
Sukhumi   )   Georgia
Sochi   )

We were shown the following types of mining and reclamation:

Oil shale
Fire clay
Sand and gravel
Coal
Manganese
Sand dunes

We were also shown some State Farms and some steep slope areas that were transformed into agricultural producing lands.

The Soviet people who are ultimately responsible for the reclamation of mining areas are all mining engineers. Soils specialists, hydrologist, agronomists, etc. are used as advisors. I feel the concept has a lot of merit, and maybe U.S. mining engineers could take a lesson from this approach.

I was very impressed with the quality of their research work and with the capability of the scientists with whom we came in contact. Their system of technology transfer seems quite effective. The Russian people seem to be quite serious about everything, but it seems that they are especially serious about their reclamation work.

They realize that productive land is a precious commodity and must be preserved for now and the future. They seem fully committed to the principle that good quality reclamation work must follow mining or else mining will not occur.

The Soviets recognized that disturbance of land from mining is a global problem and that the area of land disturbance is enormous. One estimate is that 6 to 8 million ha (15-20 million acres) of land have been disturbed by mining.

The Russian visitors to the U.S. that I have escorted over the last 2 years seem completely baffled over the fact that our primary objective in reclaiming land can be something other than to produce food. They also seem puzzled that our future land uses after mined land reclamation are so non-specific. I feel very strongly that post-mining land use should be one of the first statements made in a mining and reclamation plan and one of the most important decisions to be made in these documents.

If I were asked to summarize my impression of Russia it would be this:

It is a very large country; blessed with a multitude of resources; with tremendous varieties in everything; the people are warm, friendly, courteous, curious, intelligent, and serious; their food supply is a serious problem, as well as the distribution of it; and their system of government imposes total and absolute control over every conceivable aspect of life. As Winston Churchill wrote in 1939: "Russia is a riddle, wrapped in a mystery, inside an enigma."

All of those involved in this program feel that it is worthwhile, productive, and most desirable to continue. And as far as we are able to determine, the Soviets feel the same. It is my sincere hope that international politics do not force this program to be canceled.

One sidelight to all this that deserves mention, involves the situation that the U.S. Government has an active scientific exchange program with the Soviet Union which is certainly desirable. However, I am not aware of a similar type program with some of our friends such as Canada, Australia, or West Germany where the exchange is equally important and might be more productive.